Learning SQL Server 2008 Reporting Services

A step-by-step guide to getting the most of Microsoft SQL Server Reporting Services 2008

Jayaram Krishnaswamy

[PACKT] PUBLISHING

BIRMINGHAM - MUMBAI

Learning SQL Server 2008 Reporting Services

First published: March 2009

Production Reference: 1160309

Published by Packt Publishing Ltd.
32 Lincoln Road
Olton
Birmingham, B27 6PA, UK.

ISBN 978-1-847196-18-7

`www.packtpub.com`

Cover Image by Vinayak Chittar (`vinayak.chittar@gmail.com`)

Credits

Author

Jayaram Krishnaswamy

Reviewers

Atif Shehzad

Marc Delisle

Senior Acquisition Editor

Douglas Paterson

Development Editor

Swapna V. Verlekar

Technical Editor

Bhupali Khule

Production Editorial Manager

Abhijeet Deobhakta

Editorial Team Leader

Akshara Aware

Project Manager

Lata Basantani

Project Coordinator

Neelkanth Mehta

Indexer

Monica Ajmera

Proofreader

Angie Butcher

Production Coordinator

Rajni R. Thorat

Cover Work

Rajni R. Thorat

About the Author

Jayaram Krishnaswamy studied at the Indian Institute of Science in Bangalore and Madras University, India and also taught at the Indian Institute of Technology in Madras. He went to Japan on the Japanese Ministry of Education Research scholarship to complete his PhD in Electrical Engineering from Nagoya University. He was a Post Doctoral Fellow at Sydney University in Australia, a Government of India Senior Scientific Officer at the Indian Institute of Science in Bangalore and Indian Institute of Technology at Kanpur, a Visiting Scientist at the Eindhoven Institute of Technology in Netherlands, a Visiting Professor of Physics at the Federal University in Brazil, an Associate Research Scientist at the government laboratory in Sao Jose dos Campos in Sao Paulo, Brazil, a visiting scientist at the National Research Council in Ottawa, Canada before coming to USA in 1985. He has also taught and worked at the Colorado State University in Fort Collins and North Carolina State University in Raleigh, North Carolina. He worked with Northrop Grumman Corporation on a number of projects related to high energy electron accelerators / free electron lasers. These projects were undertaken at the Brookhaven National Laboratory in Long Island and in the Physics Department at Princeton University. He has over 80 publications refereed and non-refereed publications and 8 issued patents. He is fluent in Japanese and Portuguese and lives in Plainsboro, New Jersey, USA.

He has been working in the IT related fields since 1997. He was once a Microsoft Certified Trainer in Networking and a Siebel developer. He has worked with several IT related companies, such as the Butler International in their Siebel practice; several other IBM sub contractors and smaller companies. Presently he is active in writing technical articles in the IT field to many online sites such as `CodeProject`, `APSFree.com`, `DevShed.com`, `DevArticles.com`, `OfficeUsers.org`, `ASPAlliance.com`, `ITToolbox.com`, `databasedev.co.uk`, `cimaware.com`, and many others. During 2006-2007 he wrote more than 200 articles mostly related to database and web related technologies covering Microsoft, Oracle, Sybase, ColdFusion, Sun, and other vendor products.

Acknowledgement

First and foremost, I thank Dr. Douglas Paterson for asking me to write this book and the encouragement throughout the duration of this writing. His guidance regarding the book format during the initial stages was most helpful as it provided me a template. I am most indebted to Packt Publishing for giving me this second assignment without which this book would not have been possible.

I would like to thank the reviewers who reviewed the book regarding technical content. I thank Atif Shehzad for his valuable time in reviewing the book. His suggestions and his insight and experience in the management aspects of SQL Server have added refinement to the book that I would have sorely missed. I am most grateful for this. I would like to thank Marc Delisle for the meticulous way in which he has gone through the book. His suggestions and recommendations have greatly improved the readability of the book that my original writing would have been lacking. As the book is replete with hands-on exercises, the reviewer's job is not easy as it calls upon him to check the accuracy of the various steps that a reader has to take. The reviewers have greatly contributed to making this writing error free and the flow smoother. For this, I am most obliged.

For coordinating and distributing the authoring tasks, I sincerely thank the Project Coordinator Neelkanth Mehta. I also thank his timely and periodic reminders that helped me to adhere to the schedule. For her technical editing of the several chapters of the book, I would like to thank the Development Editor Swapna V. Verlekar. I would like to thank Bhupali Khule, the Technical Editor and Rajni Thorat, the Production Coordinator who went through the final versions and for their suggestions to "fill the gaps" with missing elements. Finally I thank the many other fine folks at Packt who must have helped in bringing out this book.

I would like to thank my parents who would have very much shared my joy. I thank the whole hearted support of my brothers, sisters and the Subbagiri family. This book would have not been possible without the support and encouragement of my wife, Michiko Fukumoto; my son Krishna who kept the pressure up (who asked me every time he telephoned how much of the book I need to write more) and his wife Jannet, and I am most grateful.

Last but not the least, I would like to thank the members of the MSDN forum who have educated me on various aspects of SQL Server in general and Reporting Services in particular. I could not have written this book without belonging to this knowledgeable body. Finally, I sincerely thank Microsoft Corporation and SAP (Crystal Reports) for copies of the evaluation software used in the preparation of this book.

About the Reviewers

Atif Shehzad is a passionate DBA, serving in Pakistan Revenue Automation Limited a subsidiary of Federal Board of Revenue. He is the author of several SQL Server articles on `www.mssqltips.com`. He is an active member of several online SQL Server communities. Also he writes his SQL Server blog at `DBDigger.blogspot.com`. His main areas of interest are SQL Server BI, SQL Server Databases optimization and security.

Atif earned his BS (computer science) degree from International Islamic University Islamabad. He started his career in National Database and Registration Authority of Pakistan in 2004 as a System Engineer. Later, he joined Netsolace a known IT solution provider for franchise world, as a Software Quality Assurance Coordinator.

I would like to thank my family for the time they provided me to go on with review process of this book.

Marc Delisle is a member of the MySQL Developers Guild, which regroups community developers, because of his involvement with phpMyAdmin. He started to contribute to this popular MySQL web interface in December 1998, when he made the first multi-language version. He has been actively involved with this software project since May 2001 as a developer and project administrator.

Marc has worked since 1980 at Cegep de Sherbrooke, Québec, Canada, as an application programmer and network manager. He has also been teaching networking, security and PHP/MySQL application development. Marc lives in Sherbrooke with his wife and they enjoy spending time with their four children.

Marc authored the first ever Packt Publishing book, Mastering phpMyAdmin for Effective MySQL Management, and its revised editions. He also wrote Creating your MySQL Database: Practical Design Tips and Techniques, again with Packt Publishing.

I would like to thank the fine team at Packt for the support in reviewing this book.

Table of Contents

Preface

Microsoft SQL Server 2008 Reporting Services is far richer than its predecessors and provides a solid foundation for cutting edge business solutions. It is a one stop complete solution for business of any size. The departure of the architectural details from its immediate predecessor provides the motivation for writing a book. In my case, it is more than this. The idea to write in a style that helps make learning a pleasure and not drudgery was the overriding factor in writing this book. I come from a background in research, education, and instruction spanning more than 25 years. I have observed at first hand how the learning side reacts to instructions. I have taken some of these ideas into my online articles. The feedback I have received, and have been receiving was one of the driving forces. The book was completed soon after the RTM release, the differences between the RTM and the final version are minimal.

I have been through the gamut of reporting software from both Microsoft and others for several years. From the time when Visual Basic did not have proper reporting support (it was still bundled with Crystal Reports) to this day, I have seen and worked with all the various reporting software that Microsoft has produced as well as those from others. I have been involved in reporting activities both for profit and non-profit organizations. Over the years, the art of reporting has evolved in leaps and bounds (compare the charting support provided by MS Chart Control to what we see in MS SQL Reporting Services today). But the advent of internet and web-based reporting has changed the reporting landscape drastically and there is still more to come when the mobile platform begins its reign. I believe there will be yet another opportunity to write another book.

This book is replete with hands-on exercises. You begin your learning activity in Chapter 1 and finish it in the last appendix after going through 50 or more exercises. I believe this will give you a full flavor of what this product is about. If you have not been exposed to SQL Server you will still be able to understand the complete mechanics of how reports are generated and how they can be used. The book has assumed that you have Windows XP OS with copies of SQL Server 2008 Enterprise Edition, Visual Studio 2008 with SP1, Crystal Reports 2008 from SAP (all three are evaluation copies) and access to a copy of `Northwind` database (you can download from the link provided in Chapter 1).

The book is structured in such a way that you start learning and building what you learned. You get the best out of the book if you follow the chapters as they are laid out. If you are already experienced in an earlier version you may jump to what interests you. Every chapter has a little background information, information that has been distilled from Microsoft documentation. Each chapter is complete in itself and each hands-on gives you a complete picture of the task. Obviously it is not possible to address the myriad of variations that are possible with the software but most of the common ones have been addressed. The book does not deal with SharePoint support in integrating reporting services. This has been deliberate to keep the book size reasonable and make learning a lot easier.

Microsoft has strived hard and is striving harder to ramp up productivity (write less code) by advocating the idea of RAD (Rapid Application Development), what I call Microsoft Wizardry. The idea that anyone can generate a report even if he/she is not well versed in the intricacies involved is a great motivator. The major emphasis of this book is on this very idea, knowing the wizards. In doing so, coding has been kept to a minimum, but is not absent. The coding that is provided is enough to build upon, as there are many references provided in the last appendix. In fact one does not have to go very far, Microsoft has excellent documentation, the last word on anything you need to know. You can go beyond and invade its forums to learn even more, as I have done myself. Microsoft and Crystal Reports have an established relationship spanning many versions and Crystal Reports is a great technology. For this reason a chapter on Crystal Reports has been added to the book.

The reviewers have done a painstaking job of going through my writing. For any errors or omissions in the book, I am entirely responsible. I am confident that the book will be most useful for those who want to learn and become productive within a very short time. I will, of course, be looking forward to hearing from my readers who would like to share their learning experience.

What this book covers

Chapter 1 Provides background information on what reporting activity is about and lists major reporting software vendors. This chapter should not be skipped as the hands-on guides you to install the necessary infrastructure to work with the rest of the book—Installing SQL Server 2008, Configuring the Report Server, and getting a copy of the sample database.

Chapter 2 Provides architectural background and describes various components of Reporting Services. The chapter also deals with every tool at your disposal in working with Reporting Services such as Report Server, Report Manager, and Model Designer.

Chapter 3 describes about the ReportViewer control and the hands-on deals with both the Windows and web-based reports using this important tool. Report authoring, report modification, and publishing the report to the intranet server are detailed in the hands-on exercises.

Chapter 4 Visual Studio 2008 provides great support for authoring reports that are deployed to the report server, an integral part of SQL Server 2008. The option of creating reports deployable to Report Server using BIDS is also described. The various project types that are available for Reporting Services including the Report Model Project are illustrated by the hands-on exercises.

Chapter 5 This chapter is all about Report Manager, the frontend for the Report Server backend. The full interaction between the Windows operating system, the Report Server, and the Report Manager is amply illustrated with a large number of hands-on exercises. You also get a full dose of the security aspects, the scheduling, and delivery aspects of reporting.

Chapter 6 This chapter is all about Report Builder, a great standalone tool for authoring and deploying reports from a variety of vendor database products. After a complete illustrated introduction to the user interface, the hands-on exercises show how to author reports using the wizards as well as starting from scratch.

Chapter 7 This chapter deals with different kinds of reports that can be authored using the Report Builder. The hands-on exercises guide you to author free form reports, matrix reports, parameterized reports and drill through reports. Ad hoc report authoring as well as reports based on Report Models and XML data are also included in the hands-on.

Chapter 8 The programming interfaces to Reporting Services are discussed in this chapter. The hands-on exercises show the practical aspects of using URL Access, Reporting Web Services API, the Windows Management Instrumentation and the Reporting Services utilities.

Chapter 9 In this chapter you will be looking at Crystal Reports 2008 in Visual Studio 2008. You will be working with hands-on in importing a Crystal Report designed in Crystal Reports 2008 as well as generating Crystal Reports in Visual Studio 2008's IDE.

Chapter 10 In this chapter the process of programmatically creating a SQL Server Reporting Services tabular report is described. You will be creating a very simple report using the code provided. The approach is to introduce the programming by creating the three parts of a report: connection, dataset, and layout.

Appendix A This appendix deals with Queries and Datasets used in Report Generation. The differences between SQL Queries, MDX queries and Semantic queries are described.

Appendix B In this Appendix converting Reports with extensions RDL to RDLC as well as reports with extension RDLC to RDL are discussed. In the hands-on you will convert a RDLC to a RDL.

Appendix C Reporting Services command line utilities are described. In the hands-on exercise you will be practicing with the `rs.exe` utility.

Appendix D Numerous links to blogs download sites, open source reporting software, and white papers are listed.

What you need for this book

You need the following:

- Windows XP Professional Operating system software on a computer that meets the requirements specified in Chapter 1.
- SQL Server 2008 Enterprise Edition (evaluation copy will do).
- Visual Studio 2008 Standard Edition with SP1.
- Access to Northwind database (alternatives are described in Chapter 1). In lieu of this sample any other relational database such as Pubs or Adventure works can be substituted.
- IIS 5.1 Internet Information Services (should be available on Windows XP professional).
- Crystal Reports 2008 (evaluation edition will be OK).
- Note: Links to download sites are provided in the book. Links have been verified as of this writing.

Who is this book for

This book is for anyone who is new to SQL Server 2008 Reporting Services and needs to create and deploy reports. The book is suitable for auto didacts, computer programming trainers, report developers, data analysts, and report server database administrators.

You will need to know the basic concepts of SQL Server, but not necessarily be very familiar with SQL Server 2008.

Conventions

In this book, you will find a number of styles of text that distinguish between different kinds of information. Here are some examples of these styles, and an explanation of their meaning.

Code words in text are shown as follows: "An expression on the other hand represents a calculated value `[discount=cost*0.01] discount` using constants and functions using various operators".

A block of code will be set as follows:

```
    Imports CrystalDecisions.CrystalReports.Engine
    Imports CrystalDecisions.Shared
    Imports System.Data
    Imports System.Data.OleDb
Public Class Form1
```

New terms and **important words** are introduced in a bold-type font. Words that you see on the screen, in menus or dialog boxes for example, appear in our text like this: "Choose **[City]** in the drop-down list, check both the checkboxes and click on the **OK** button.".

> Warnings or important notes appear in a box like this.

> Tips and tricks appear like this.

Reader feedback

Feedback from our readers is always welcome. Let us know what you think about this book, what you liked or may have disliked. Reader feedback is important for us to develop titles that you really get the most out of.

To send us general feedback, simply drop an email to `feedback@packtpub.com`, making sure to mention the book title in the subject of your message.

If there is a book that you need and would like to see us publish, please send us a note in the **SUGGEST A TITLE** form on `www.packtpub.com` or email `suggest@packtpub.com`.

If there is a topic that you have expertise in and you are interested in either writing or contributing to a book, see our author guide on `www.packtpub.com/authors`.

Customer support

Now that you are the proud owner of a Packt book, we have a number of things to help you to get the most from your purchase.

Errata

Although we have taken every care to ensure the accuracy of our contents, mistakes do happen. If you find a mistake in one of our books—maybe a mistake in text or code—we would be grateful if you would report this to us. By doing this you can save other readers from frustration, and help to improve subsequent versions of this book. If you find any errata, report them by visiting `http://www.packtpub.com/support`, selecting your book, clicking on the **let us know** link, and entering the details of your errata. Once your errata are verified, your submission will be accepted and the errata are added to the list of existing errata. The existing errata can be viewed by selecting your title from `http://www.packtpub.com/support`.

Piracy

Piracy of copyright material on the Internet is an ongoing problem across all media. At Packt, we take the protection of our copyright and licenses very seriously. If you come across any illegal copies of our works in any form on the Internet, please provide the location address or website name immediately so we can pursue a remedy.

Please contact us at `copyright@packtpub.com` with a link to the suspected pirated material.

We appreciate your help in protecting our authors, and our ability to bring you valuable content.

Questions

You can contact us at `questions@packtpub.com` if you are having a problem with some aspect of the book, and we will do our best to address it.

Or

You may also directly contact the author, `jkrishnaswamy@comcast.net`.

1

Overview of SQL Server Reporting Services 2008

In this chapter, an overview of **enterprise reporting** in the IT area is presented together with a list of major **Business Intelligence** (**BI**) players. The major highlights of the Microsoft SQL Server Reporting Services 2008 are also described followed by the how-to topics: SQL Server 2008 and Reporting Services installation, verifying the installations, installing the database used in the book, and configuring Reporting Services.

Overview of enterprise reporting

You may have gems hidden in your corporate archives, but unless your BI suite brings them out, polishes them, and presents them to the interested parties, they are of no use. In the present day information-centric world we live in, the success of an enterprise depends enormously on how its information is generated, handled, and disseminated. Reporting software, therefore, should manage, execute, render, schedule, and deliver reports in a timely manner. It is no wonder that enterprise reporting occupies an important position in the dissemination of information and that a major portion of IT activity is in the reporting sector.

Reports are generated and consumed by many different IT professionals as well as non-IT users. Report developers, decision makers, power users, and end users consume reports in many formats on many different kinds of platforms. Reports may be parked on web servers in intranet sites for web access, or turned into board-room quality, hard-copies for distribution. Interactive reports are extensively used in enterprises from just look ups to making business decisions and forecasting. It should come as no surprise if this percolates to the small footprint, handheld devices such as **Smartphones** (`http://www.iec.org/newsletter/june06_2/analyst_1.html`) and **Mids** (`http://www.intel.com/products/mid/index.htm?iid=prod+prod_MIDs`).

Another development in enterprise reporting is to move part of the reporting from the hands of developers, who are expensive, to middle level managers, decision makers, and end users. This is not only to reduce cost but also to improve productivity. After all, it is the decision makers who know a lot more about the value hidden in their day-to-day data and archives. Also the decision makers and those who are intimately involved with the business are keenly aware of regulatory compliances that need to be strictly observed. Due to this perception, **ad-hoc reporting** has gained a lot of ground.

Distribution and security of reports are other equally important aspects of business reporting. **Web based** reporting has replaced the need for hard copy reports even in many sensitive areas, so much so that one can always request a printed format or digital format of a report. For enterprises, this has translated to hosting their reports on Report Servers. To satisfy this need, most of the major players have provided this functionality in their software.

Actuate's Business Intelligence and Reporting Tools (`http://www.actuate.com/products/business-intelligence.asp`), Business Objects' Crystal Reports (`http://www.businessobjects.com/product/catalog/crystalreports/`), IBM's Cognos 8 Business Intelligence (`http://www.cognos.com/products/cognos8businessintelligence/reporting.html`), and Oracle's Business Intelligence Publisher (`http://www.oracle.com/appserver/business-intelligence/bi-publisher.html`) which works with PeopleSoft Reporting and Analytics, Hyperion Planning, JD Edwards's EnterpriseOne Suite are some of the major players with whom Microsoft competes within enterprise reporting. It may also be noted that companies supported by the Open Source Eclipse foundation's reporting related project BIRT (`http://www.informationweek.com/news/business_intelligence/showArticle.jhtml?articleID=170102475`) such as Pentaho and JasperSoft have joined this fray as well.

Microsoft SQL Server Reporting Services 2008, SSRS 2008 for short is the latest reporting software from Microsoft. SSRS 2008 is a dedicated server-based, one-stop platform that handles reporting related activities to deliver focused information where needed in a timely and flexible manner. Microsoft has also integrated SSRS 2008 with Office 2007 and the SharePoint Server. In addition to this, there are Microsoft Partners (`http://www.microsoft.com/sql/technologies/reporting/partners/softwareapps.mspx`) such as Dundas, Proclarity, Data Dynamics, and SoftArtisans, to mention a few who are providing reporting support for non-Microsoft applications, either to work with Microsoft Reporting Services, or with the .NET Framework. While high end products like Cognos, Crystal Reports, and others may require support of a database product and an ETL tool to generate intelligent reports, SSRS together with SSIS (Microsoft SQL Server Integration Services) and the data engine, provides an integrated solution at what is believed to be a reasonable cost.

Some highlights of SQL Server Reporting Services 2008

SSRS has gone through many changes from the time it made its debut with SQL Server 2000. In the latest version, SSRS 2008, the architecture has changed from its 2005 version. It has gone from an Internet Information Services based server to an independent Reporting Server Web Service. It installs as a windows service similar to the Database Engine and the Analysis Services. In SSRS 2008, in addition to the changes in Report Server architecture discussed later, there are several other documented changes worth noting. These are described in the following sections.

Scalability

Related to scalability is the memory management issue addressed to reduce the OutOfMemory exceptions that may occur during report execution. The memory is self-managed dynamically, but can also be set manually (`http://msdn.microsoft.com/en-us/library/ms178067.aspx`). The file system is leveraged to adjust for memory pressure. The details are outside the scope of this book and interested readers should look up John Gallardo's Weblog (`http://blogs.msdn.com/jgalla/archive/2008/03/11/more-on-ssrs-2008-memory-management.aspx`).

New Tablix design feature

The Tablix feature leverages the best of both worlds of Table and Matrix and includes the List control. This adds enormously to design time flexibility. The Tablix feature retains the flexibility of table design and makes it possible to generate a side-by-side line up of crosstab sections, which is not possible with the matrix.

Enhancement to Report Design

On October 17, 2008 Microsoft SQL Server 2008 Report Builder 2.0 was released as part of the SQL Server 2008 Feature pack. This has a full featured design surface for designing all elements of RDL (Report Definition Language). Usability enhancement features such as Zoom and Snap are also new. The Report Builder 2.0 tool has the familiar look and feel of Office 12 products with the "Office button" and the "ribbon" creating a familiar environment for business users. Report Builder 2.0 supports the full capabilities of SQL Server Reporting Services, which includes flexible data layout, data visualization, and richly formatted text capabilities. Report Builder 2.0 uses a rich assortment of wizards and can directly edit reports on the Report Server as well as utilize shared data sources with a graphic query designer for SQL Server Data Sources.

Data visualization

Dundas Visualization Charts replace the Microsoft chart design of the previous versions. Dundas Gauge control is another new feature of this version.

Installing SQL Server 2008

In this section, installation of SQL Server 2008, the hardware and software requirements, and the specifics of the installation details used for this book are described.

Version of SQL Server 2008 to be installed

An evaluation version of the SQL Server 2008 Enterprise Edition is installed for the purposes of working with this book. It may be noted that there are several editions of SQL Servers with varying capabilities available. For details of versions and the features they support follow this link: `http://msdn.microsoft.com/en-us/library/cc645993.aspx`.

Hardware requirements

In this book we will be using the SQL Server 2008 Enterprise Evaluation Edition (32Bit). The requirements have been extracted from the `http://msdn.microsoft.com/en-us/library/ms143506.aspx#EE32` site for the SQL Server 2008 32-bit Enterprise Edition for Windows XP Professional SP2 Computer OS. Here are the requirements:

1. Processor: Pentium III compatible processor with 1.0 GHZ or faster with a recommended speed of 2.0 GHZ.
2. Hard disk space requirements:

Service\Resource	Disk Space
Database Engine, data files, replication, and Full-Text Search	280MB
Analysis Services and data files	90MB
Reporting Services and Report Manager	120MB
Integration Services	850MB
Books on Online and SQL Server Compact Books Online	240MB

3. Memory: Minimum 512 MB RAM. Recommended is 2.048 GB or more.
4. Drive: A CD or DVD Drive for disc-based installations.
5. Display: High resolution VBA 1024 x 768 pixels for SQL Server Graphic tools.
6. Others: Microsoft mouse or compatible pointing device.

System and software requirements

The following are the system and software requirements:

1. Operating System:

   SQL Server 2008 can be installed on all versions (in 32Bit and 64-Bit) of Windows Vista, Windows Server 2008, Windows Server 2003 (SP2 and Enterprise Edition SP2) and Windows XP Professional SP2.

2. Software:

   Microsoft Windows Installer 4.5 or later

   Microsoft Data Access Components (MDAC) 2.8SP1 or later

   Standalone named and default instances support the following network protocols:

   - Shared Memory
   - Names pipes
   - TCP/IP
   - VIA

   Microsoft Internet Explorer 6.1 or later

3. Framework (all installed during SQL Server 2008 install):

   .NET Framework 3.5

   SQL Server Native Client

   SQL Server Setup support files

> System Configuration Checker will check and the required items will be flagged if they are not present.

Hardware and software used for working with the book

The following are the hardware and software details of the Toshiba Laptop Computer used in the preparation of this book:

- Operating system: Microsoft Windows XP Media Center Edition Version 2002 SP3
- Hardware: Intel Pentium® 3.00 GHZ, 1 GB of RAM
- Disk Capacity: 180 GB
- Internet Explorer: Version 7.0
- Drives: DVD Read/Write

Hands-on exercise 1.1: Installing a named instance of SQL Server 2008

The exercises like these will help you to install the SQL Server 2008, review the installed items, install an example database to use with this book, and configure the SQL Server Reporting Services.

While installation of both named and default instances of SQL Server 2008 are possible, installation of a named instance is described for the examples used in this book. A named instance would be required if there is already a default instance of SQLServer 2008 (only one default of any version is allowed), or a default instance of another version (for example SQL Server 2000 or SQL Server 2005) is already present. If this is the only SQL Server (any version) on the computer then a default instance can be a good choice as well.

Getting ready

The following are some of the verifications you have to make before starting an installation:

1. Make sure that your setup satisfies the Hardware and System/Software requirements discussed earlier.
2. Make sure that there are no previous installations of SQL Server 2008 (CTP's). Read note after the conclusion of *Hands-on exercise 1.1*.

3. If you are installing on a machine with Visual Studio 2008 already installed, make sure you have installed Visual Studio SP1.
4. The SQL Server and the components will run as windows services and you should have windows accounts configured to run services. These could be Domain User Account, Local User Account, Local Service Account, Network Service Account and Local System Account. In this example the local user account with administrator's privilege is used. For details see: `http://msdn.microsoft.com/en-us/library/ms143504.aspx`.
5. Download the SQL Server 2008 RTM Enterprise Edition from the following link (requires registration): `http://msdn.microsoft.com/en-us/evalcenter/bb851668.aspx`. The downloaded image, `SQLFULL_ENU.ISO`, is an archive file. It is best opened with the WinRAR program. It can be downloaded from the WinRAR web site: `http://www.download.com/WinRAR/3000-2250_4-10007677.html`. The following screenshot shows the contents of this archive. Extract the contents to a folder.

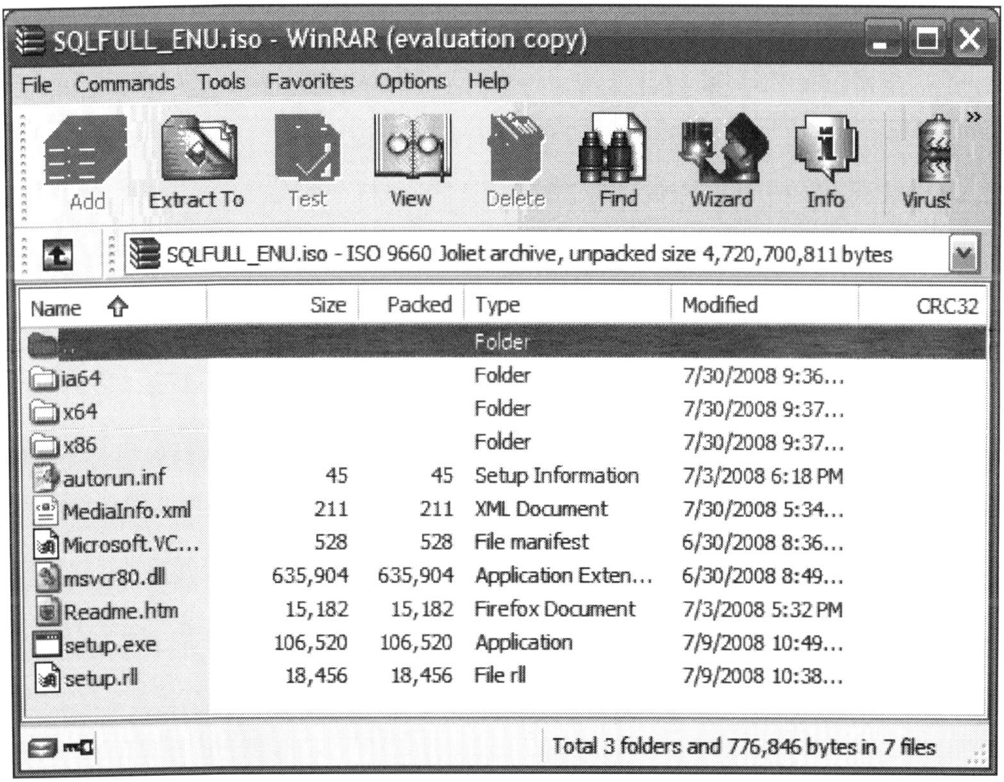

Follow the steps

1. Click on **setup.exe** in the folder.

   This brings up the **Microsoft SQL Server 2008 Setup** window as shown:

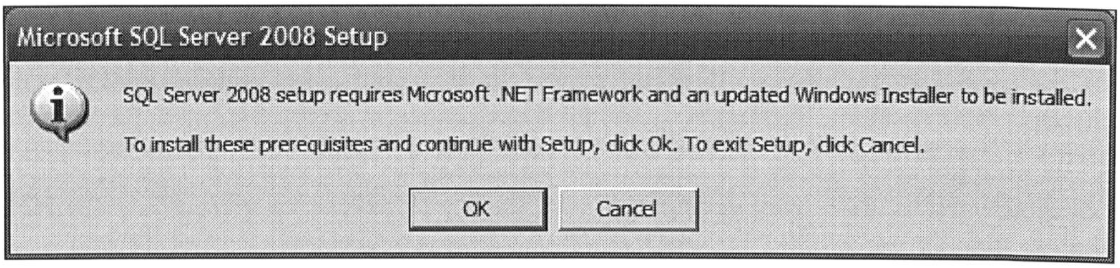

2. Click on the **OK** button.

   The Microsoft .NET Framework 3.5 SP1 setup window comes up and after some 30 minutes you will be asked to reboot.

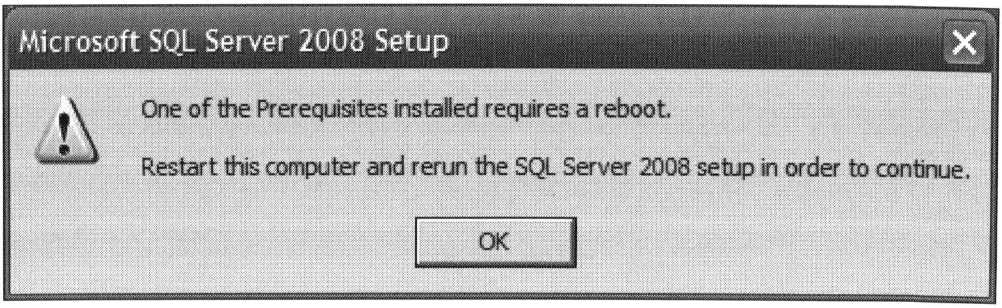

3. Click again on **setup.exe** after rebooting the computer.

   The setup program extracts files from the ISO and the SQL Server 2008 starting display comes up followed by the **SQL Server Installation Center** window as shown:

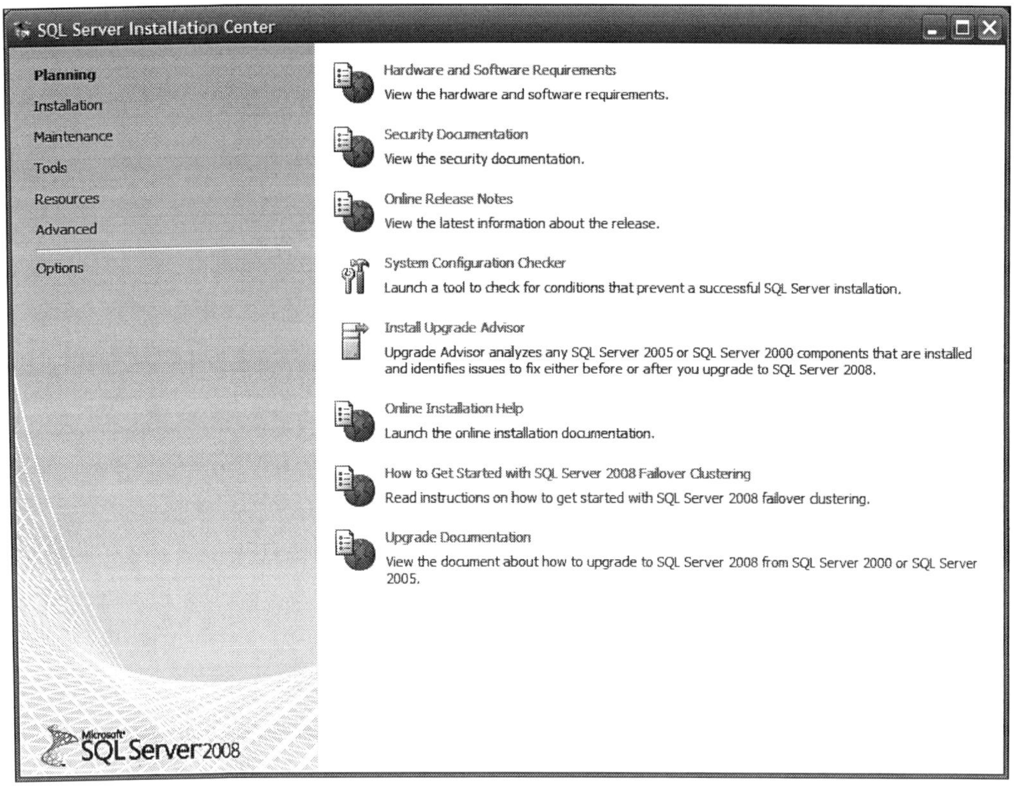

4. Click on the **Hardware and Software Requirements** link.

   This brings up the web page: `http://msdn.microsoft.com/en-us/library/ms143506.aspx`. Read the information relevant to your system. For this book the previously described hardware and software are used.

5. Click on the **Security Documentation** link.

   This brings up the web page: `http://msdn.microsoft.com/en-us/library/ms144228.aspx`. Read the information on this web page.

6. Click on the link **System Configuration Checker**.

In the following window, **Setup Support Rules**, a list of rules will appear. The 'status' for all items should be marked passed. Problems arising when any of the rules fails can be corrected and the setup can be re-run from the point where it failed last. The setup will not continue unless all failures are corrected.

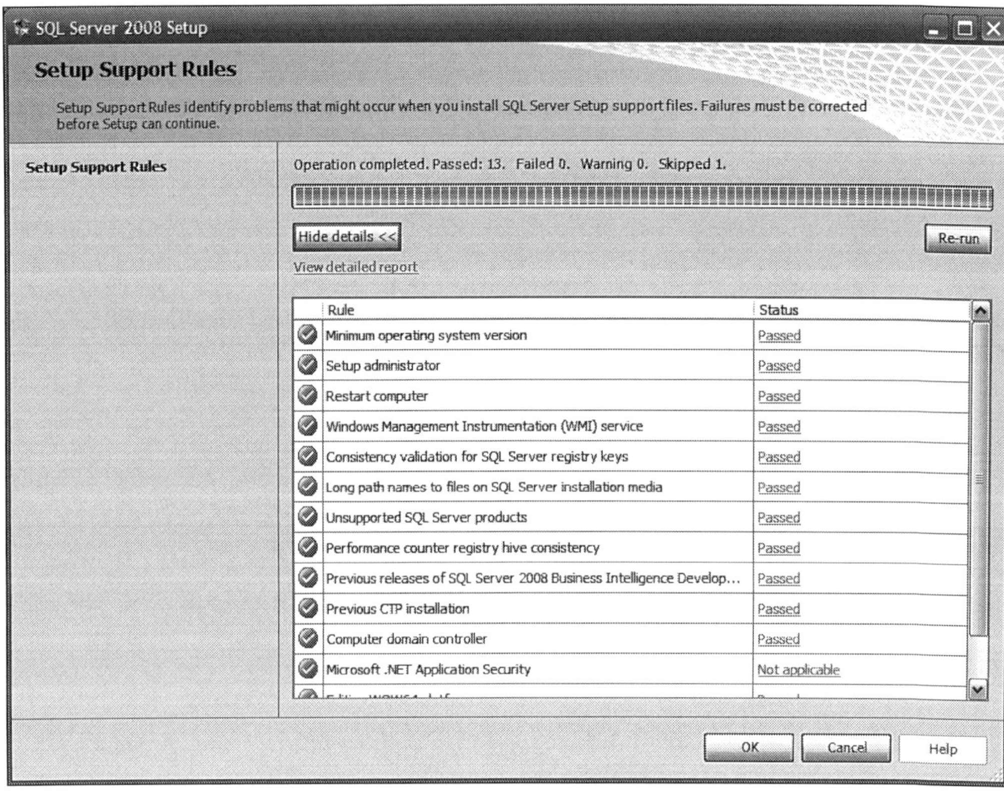

7. Click on **Installation** in the navigation (left-hand) list.

   The following **SQL Server Installation Center** window shows up again:

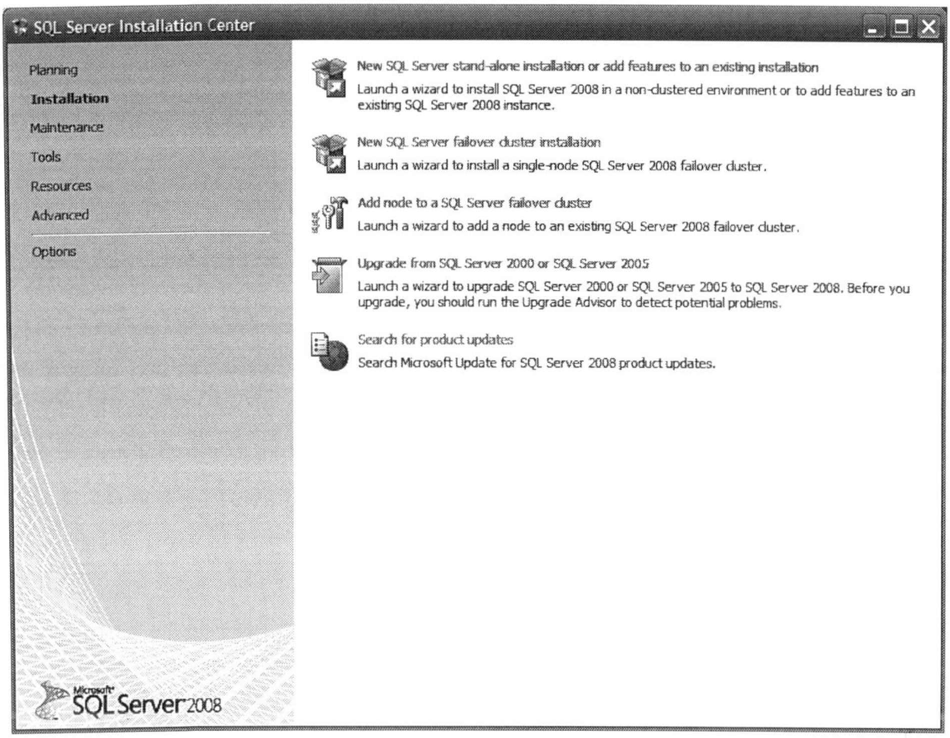

8. Click on the link **New SQL Server stand-alone installation or add features to an existing installation.**

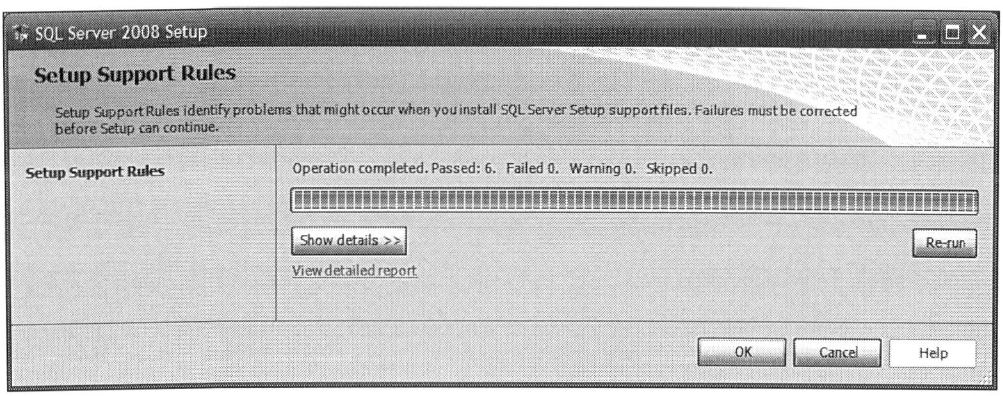

9. Click on the **OK** button.

   The **Product Key** page shows up as shown:

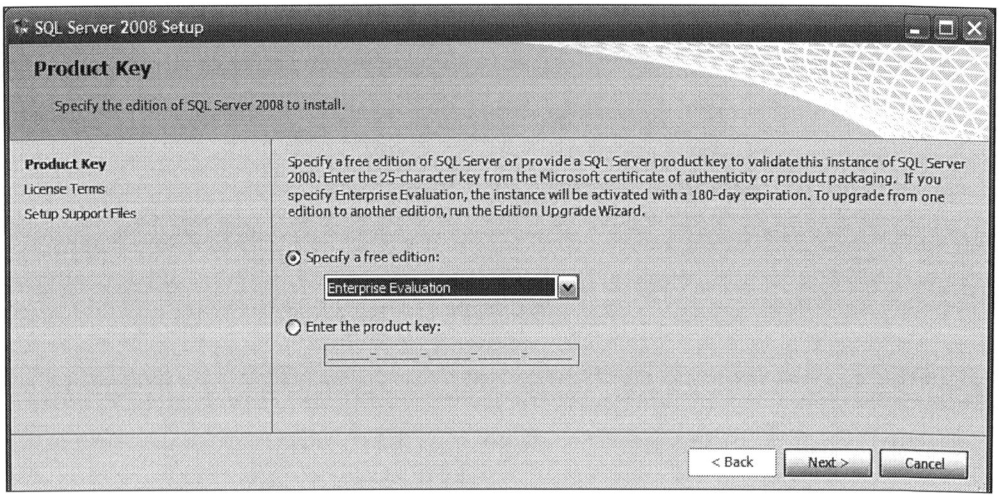

10. Accept the default and click on the **Next** button.
11. The **License Terms** page shows up as shown. Make sure you read the terms and the fine print.
12. Place check mark for **I accept the license terms** check box after reading the license and then click on the **Next** button which gets activated.

    The **Setup Support Files** shows up again as shown:

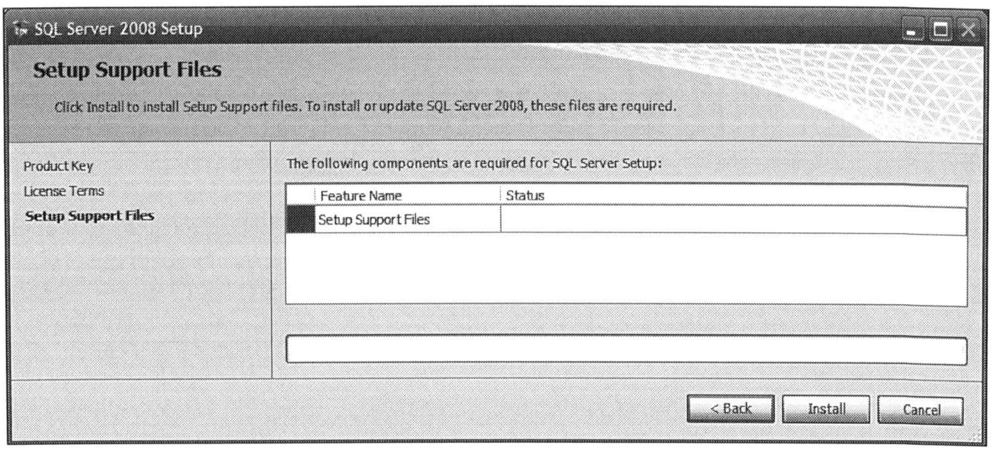

13. Click on the **Install** button.

    The setup program progress page shows up and you may need to restart the computer.

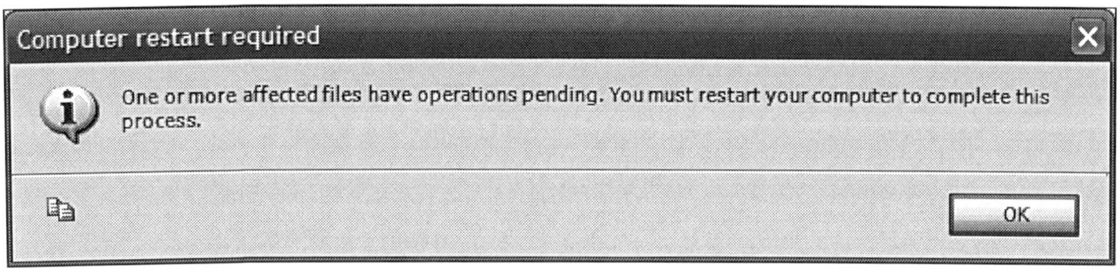

14. Click on the **OK** button and reboot the computer.

15 Click on the setup.exe file in the folder (see Step 1) after rebooting the computer.

    The **Setup Support Rules** page is displayed, checks the support files and shows the status as shown:

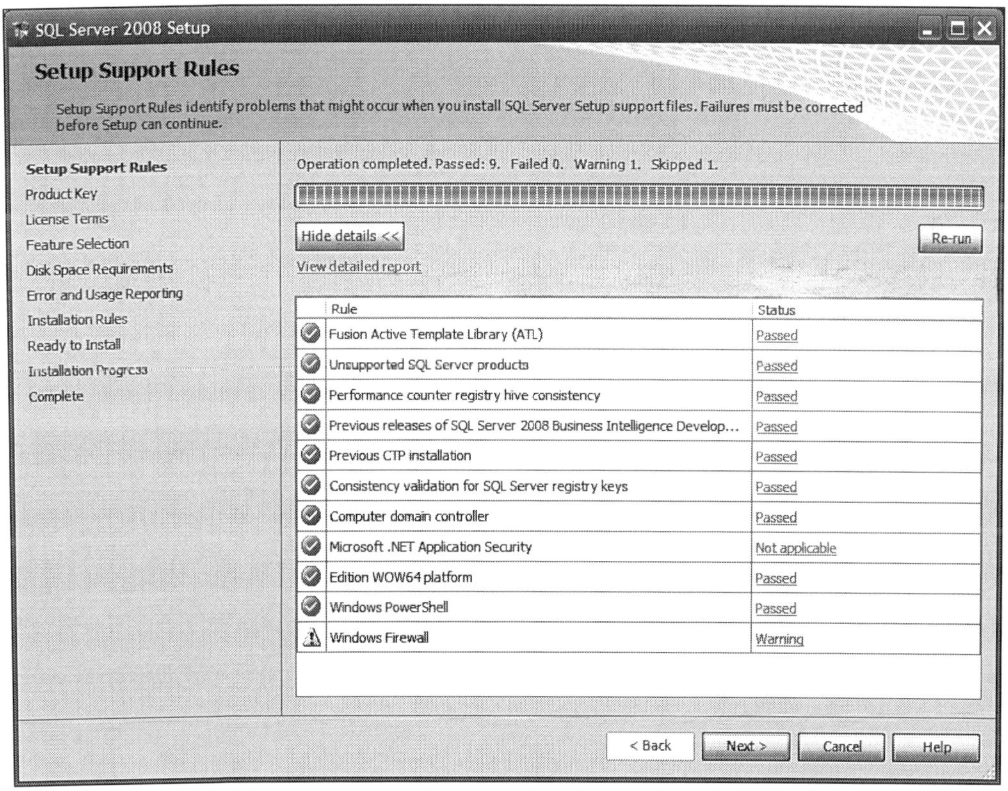

16. Click on the **Next** button on the **Setup Support Rules** page.

    The **Product Key** page shows up again.

17. Choose **Enterprise Evaluation** and click on the **Next** button.

    The **Feature Selection** page shows up as shown:

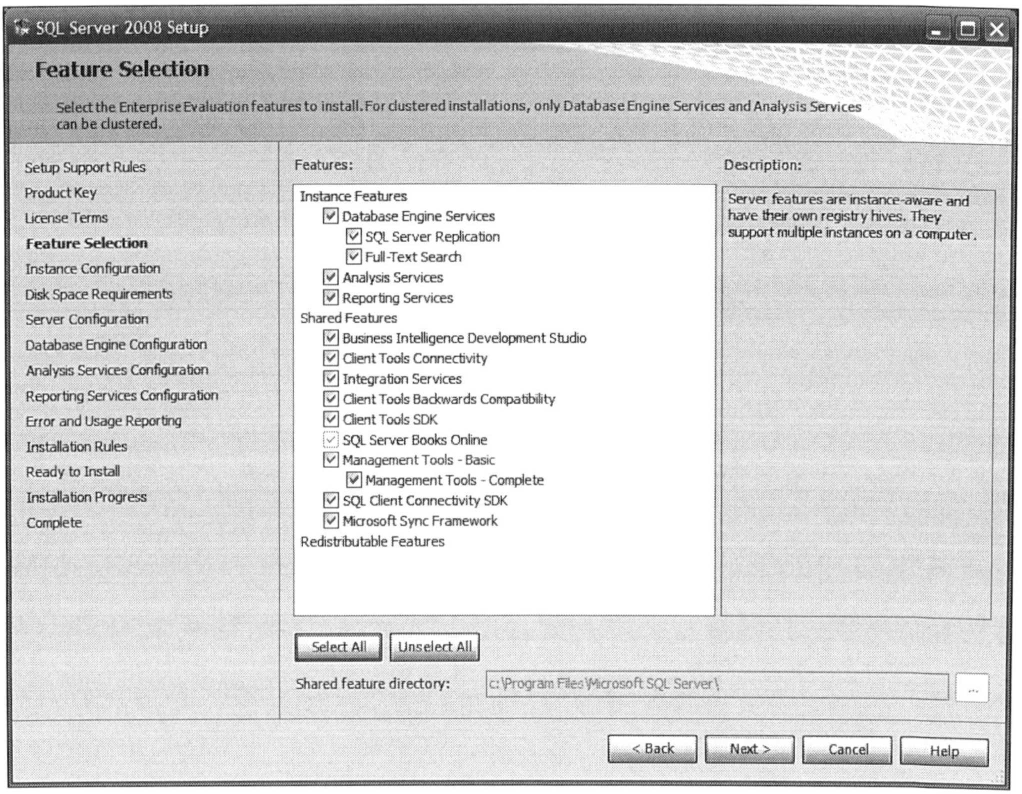

18 After clicking on the **Select All** button, click on the **Next** button.

A brief **Please Wait** window shows up.

19. In the **Instance Configuration** page that shows up, change the **Named instance** to **SANGAM** as shown. You are free to type in a name of your choice. You may also choose to install a default instance. In the installed instances you can see that there is a SQL Server 2005 **SQLEXPRESS**.

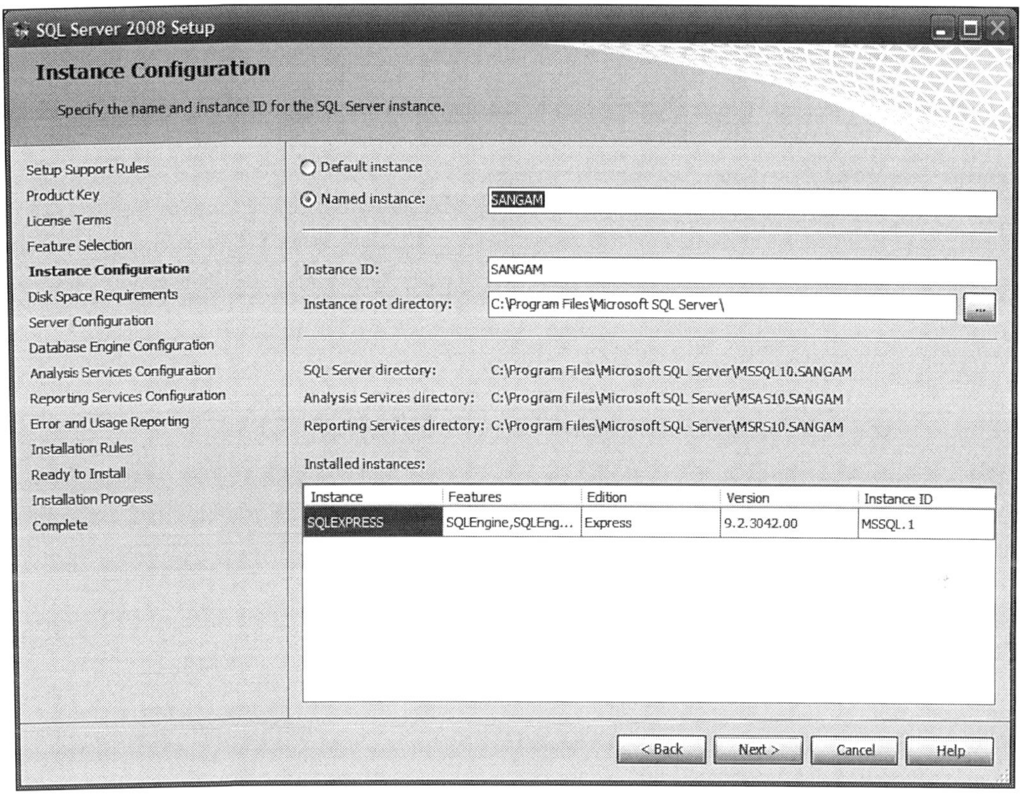

20. Click on the **Next** button.

    Again a brief **Please Wait** window shows up followed by the **Disk Space Requirements** window as shown:

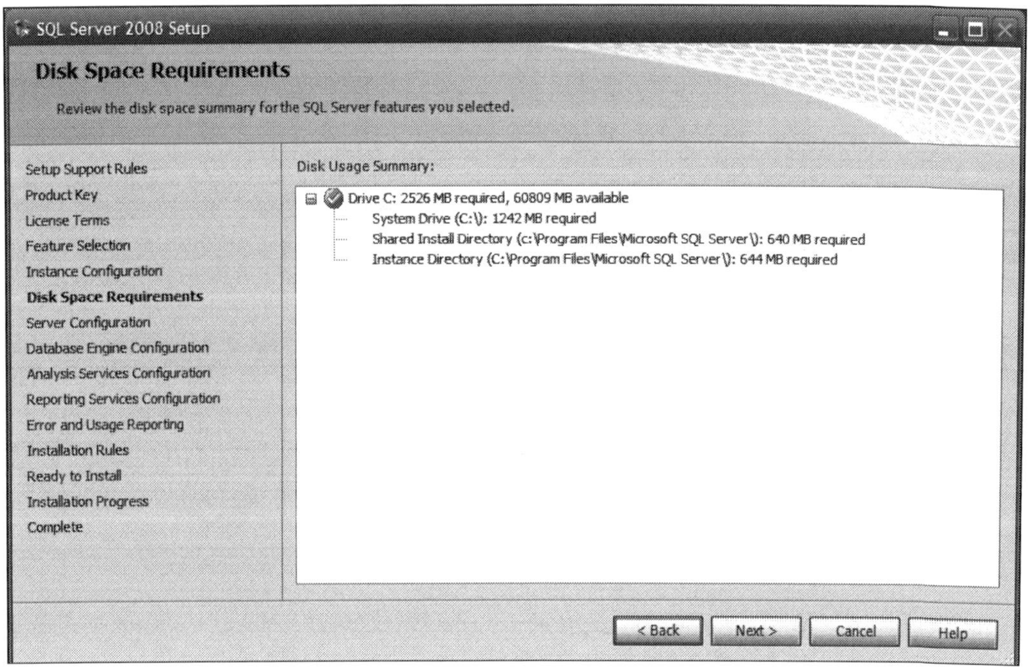

21. Click on the **Next** button.

    The **Server Configuration** window shows up with two tabbed pages, **Service Accounts** and **Collation** as shown:

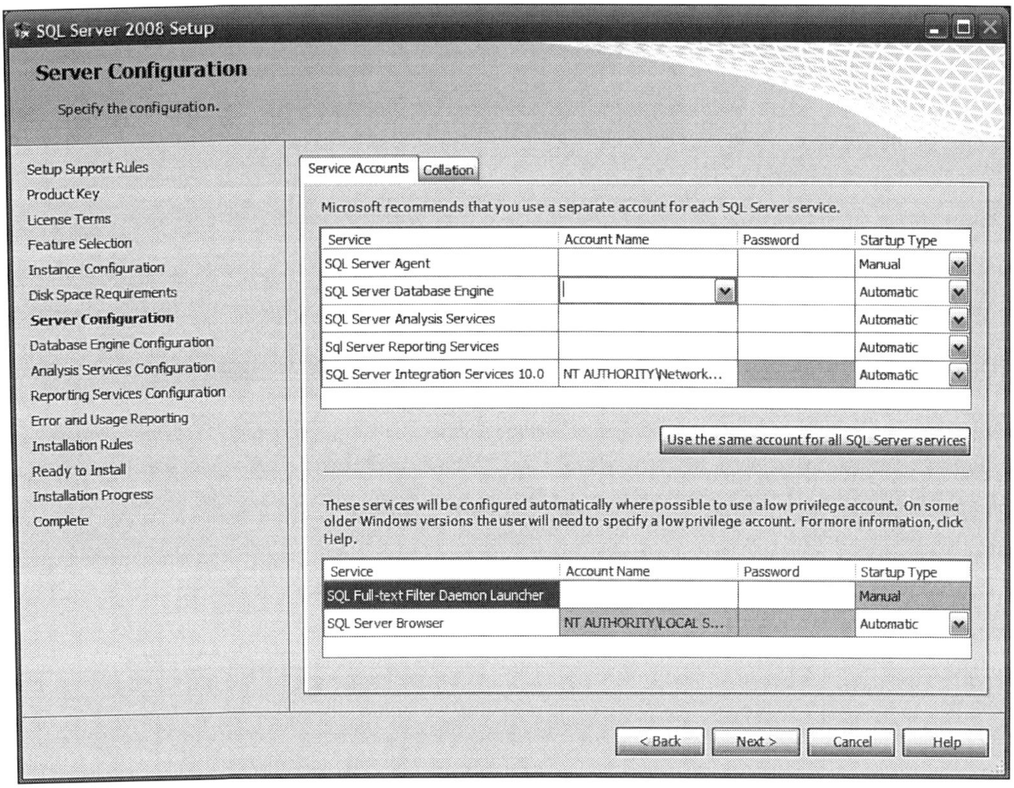

22. Click on the drop-down handle in the **Account Name** column for the **SQL Server Database Engine**. It now shows the options you have in creating an Account Name and a Password as shown:

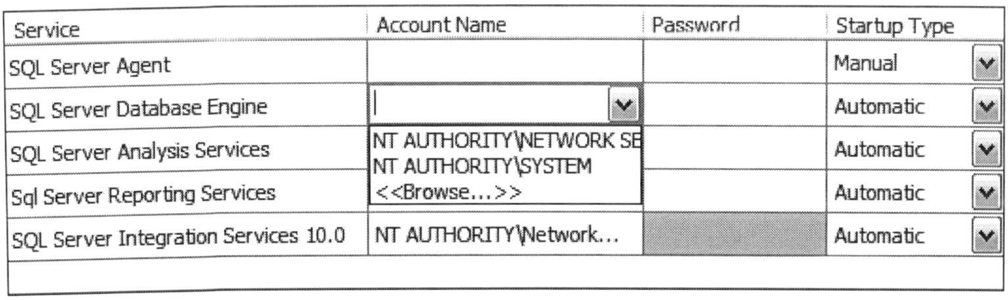

23. Click on the **<<Browse...>>** drop-down menu item.

    The **select User or Group** window shows up as shown:

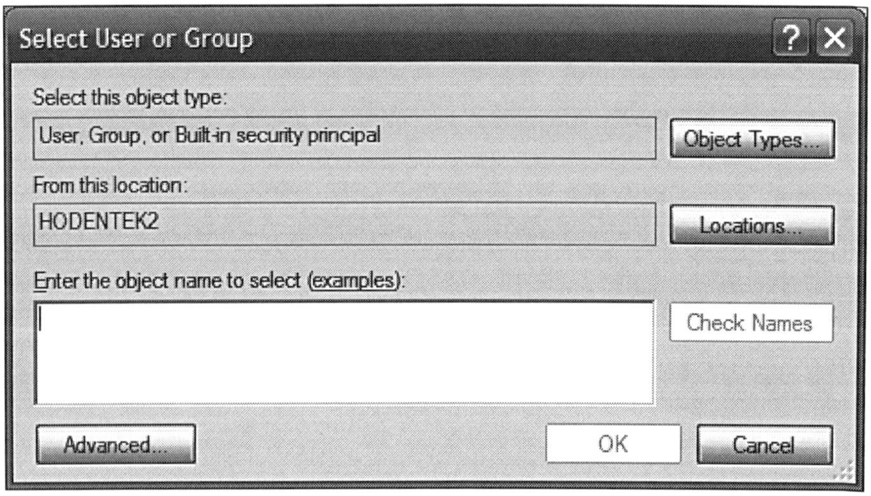

24. In the **Enter the object name to select**, type in the name of a Windows user or group. The user name gets into the **Enter the object name to select** box.
25. Click on the **Check Names** button that is enabled.

    This should verify the object name you typed in as a Windows user or group.
26. Click on the **OK** button in the **Select User or Group** window.

    This name is put into the Database Engine's Account Name. This is what you will be using for authentication. You should try to remember this or, write it down for safe keeping.
27. Click on **Use the same account for all SQL Server 2008 services** button.

    The **Use the same account for all SQL Server 2008 services** window shows up as shown:

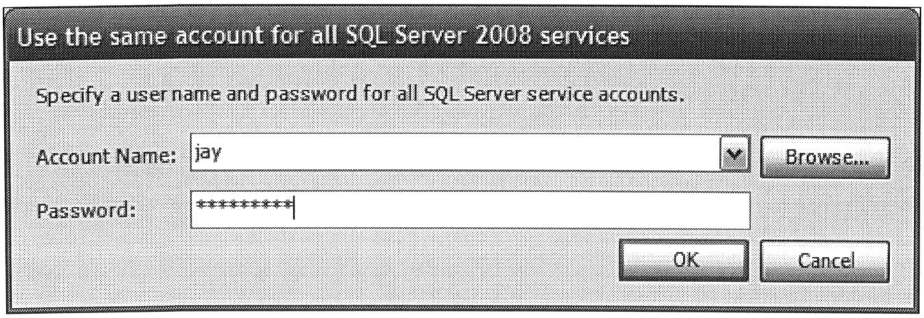

28. Enter the **Account name** you verified in the earlier step and the **Password** associated with the Windows User or Group. Click on the **OK** button.
29. All accounts get the same **Account Name** and **Password** as shown in the following screenshot:

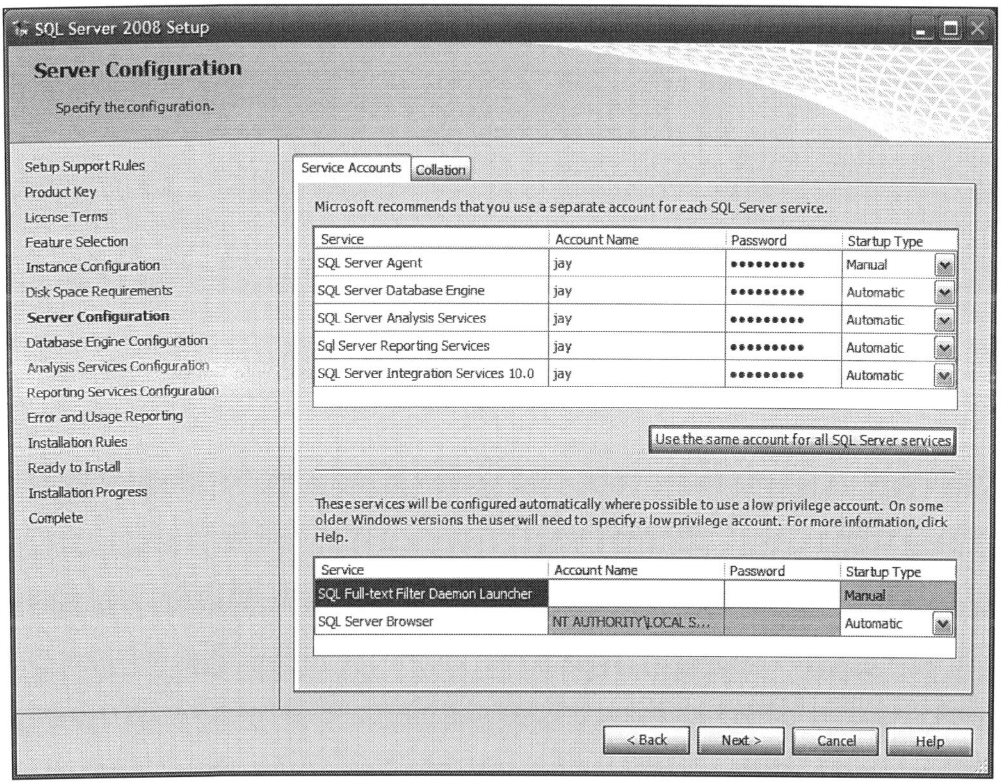

30. Make no changes to the **Collation** page and click on the **Next** button.

    The **Please wait** window shows up after which the **Database Engine Configuration** window shows up with three tabs: **Account Provisioning**, **Data Directories**, and **FILESTREAM** as shown:

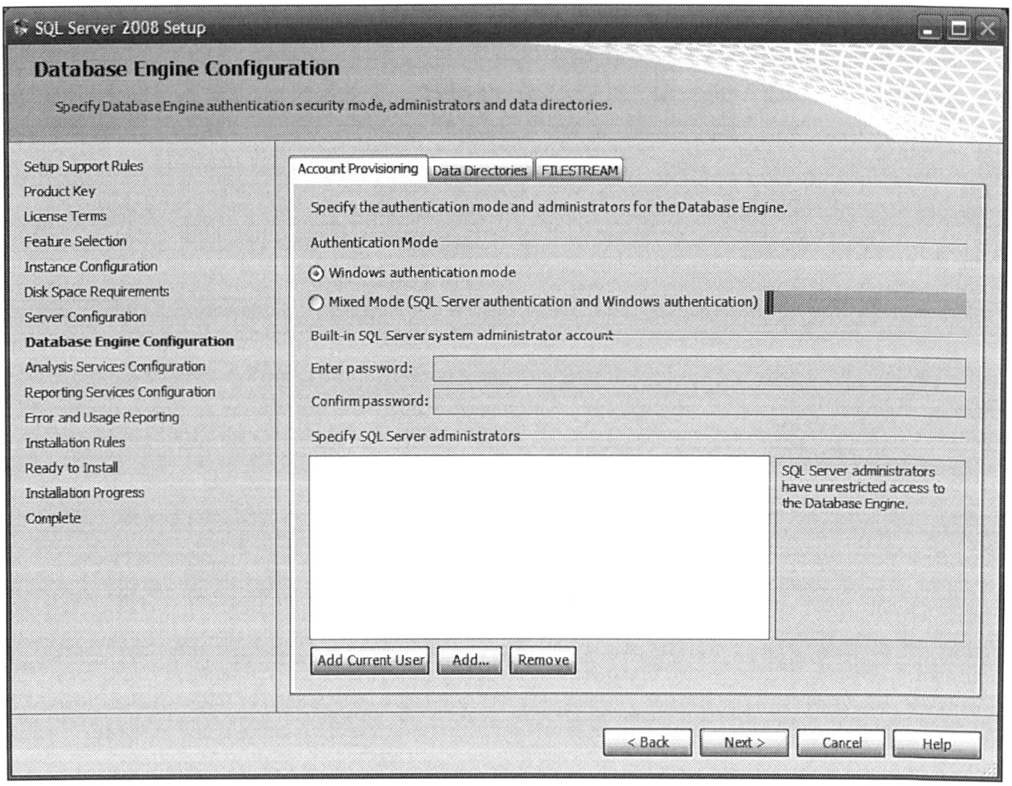

31. Accept the default authentication mode as **Windows authentication mode** and click on the **Add Current User** button. Read the instructions regarding the unrestricted privilege for this account.

    The current user's name shows up in the **Specify SQL Server administrators'** window. Here you can **Add.../Remove** names from the list. For this example only the current user was set up with this privilege.

32. Click on **Data Directories** tab.

    The **Data Directories** page shows the various directories of the Database Engine and their locations. While the default location is acceptable, a different location can be chosen. By default the directories of SQL Server Database Engine, Analysis Server, and Reporting Services are sub-directories of Microsoft SQL Server under `C:\Program Files\Microsoft SQL Server`. This could sometimes lead to errors as the wizards in applications do not necessarily discover this structure. This is especially problematic when multiple versions are installed on the same machine. A different choice for the location of the directories would avoid this problem.

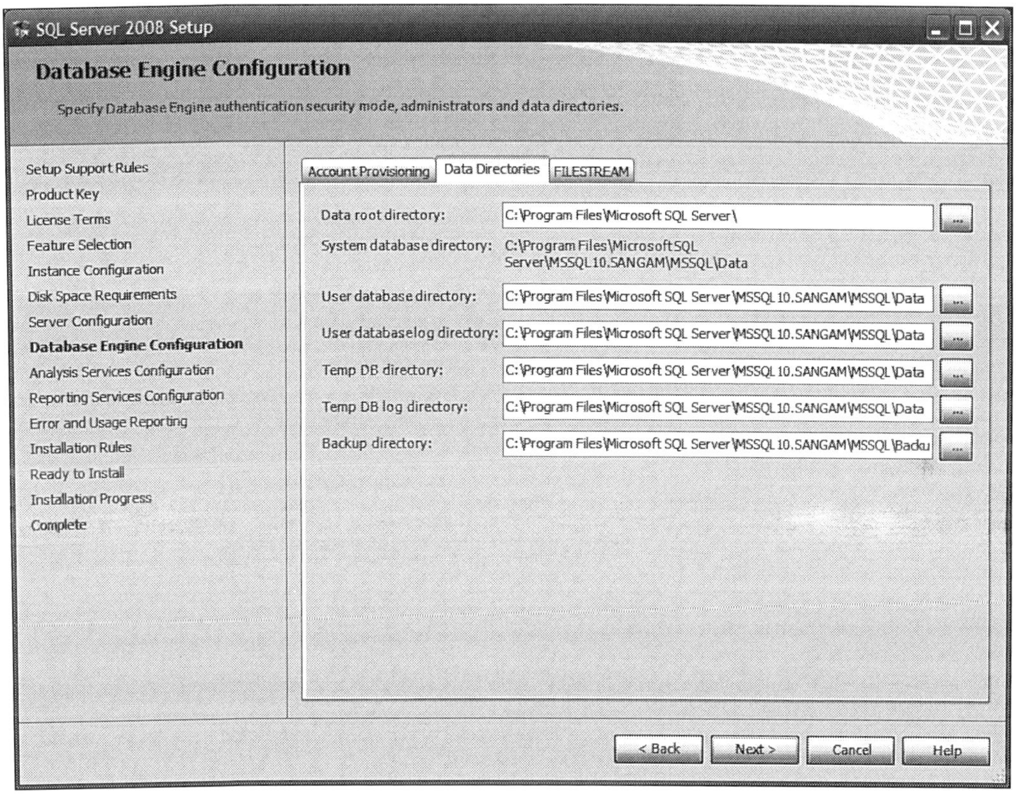

33. Click on the **FILESTREAM** tab and check the **Enable FILESTREAM for Transact-SQL access** option as well as the **Enable FILESTREAM for I/O streaming access** and fill out other details as shown. Filestream is a new feature in SQL Server 2008 that allows direct storing of large binary data to the NTFS file system while maintaining transactional consistency. This helps in storing large binary data outside of the database on cost-effective storage media. When this is enabled the **Windows share name** gets automatically entered.

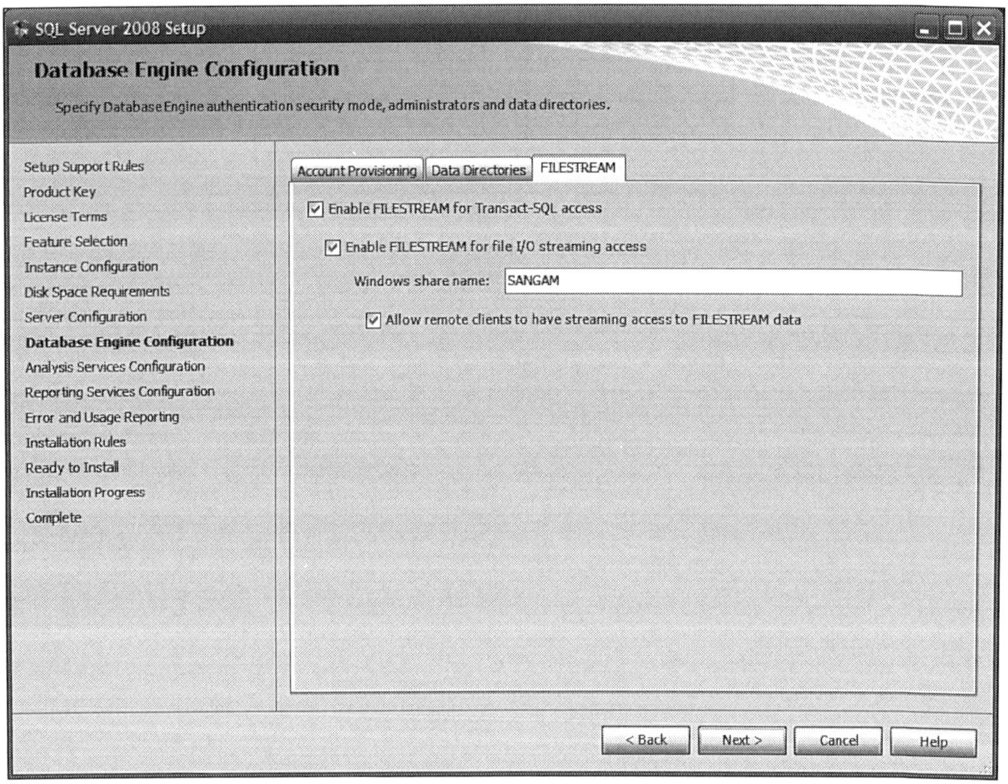

34. Click on the **Next** button.

    The **Analysis Services Configuration** window shows up as shown with two tabs: **Account Provisioning** and **Data Directories**.

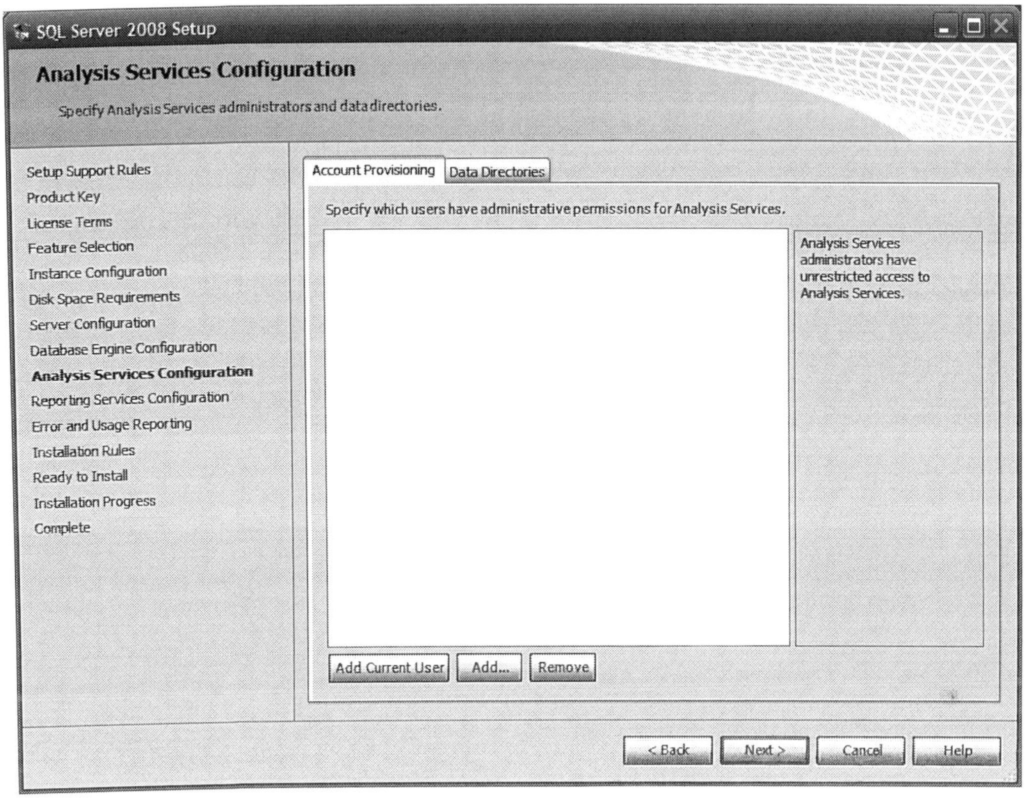

35. Click on the **Add Current User** button to add the current user as Analysis Services' administrator.

    This adds the current users name to the **Specify which users have administration permissions for Analysis Services** area above the button.

36. Click on the **Data Directories** tab.

    All the directories and their locations for the **Analysis Services Configuration** gets displayed as shown:

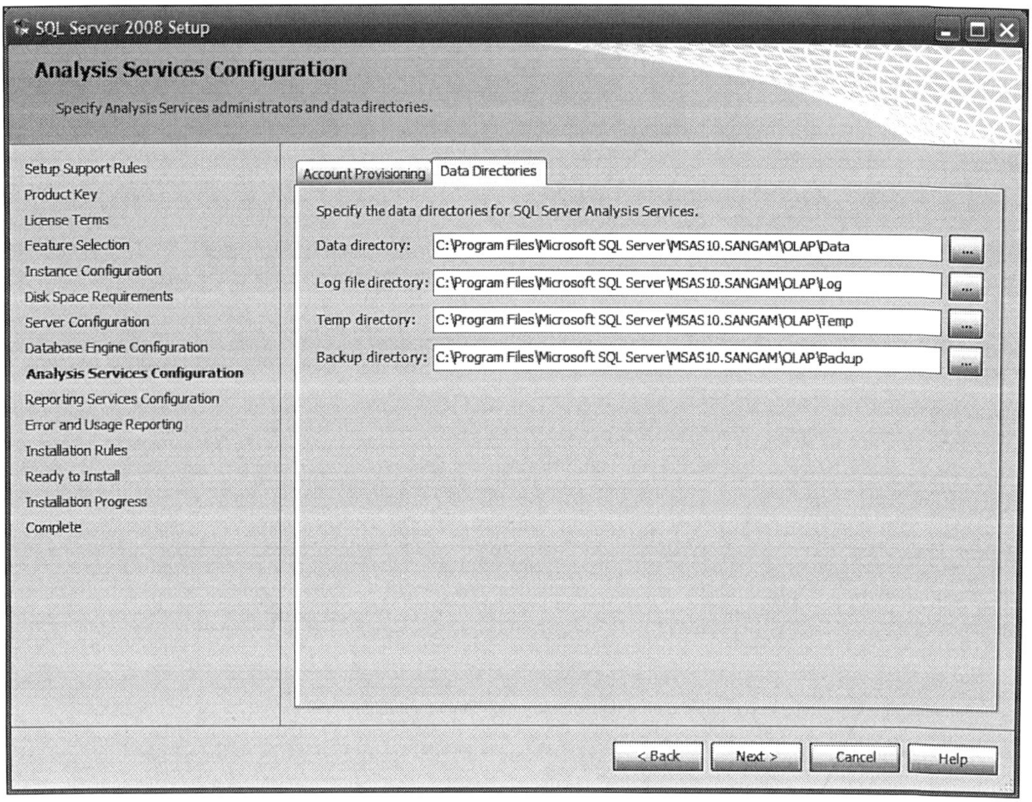

37. Click on the **Next** button.

    The **Reporting Services Configuration** window shows up with the default choice as **Install the native mode default configuration**. Note that this is the choice made for working through this book. Read about other options as well.

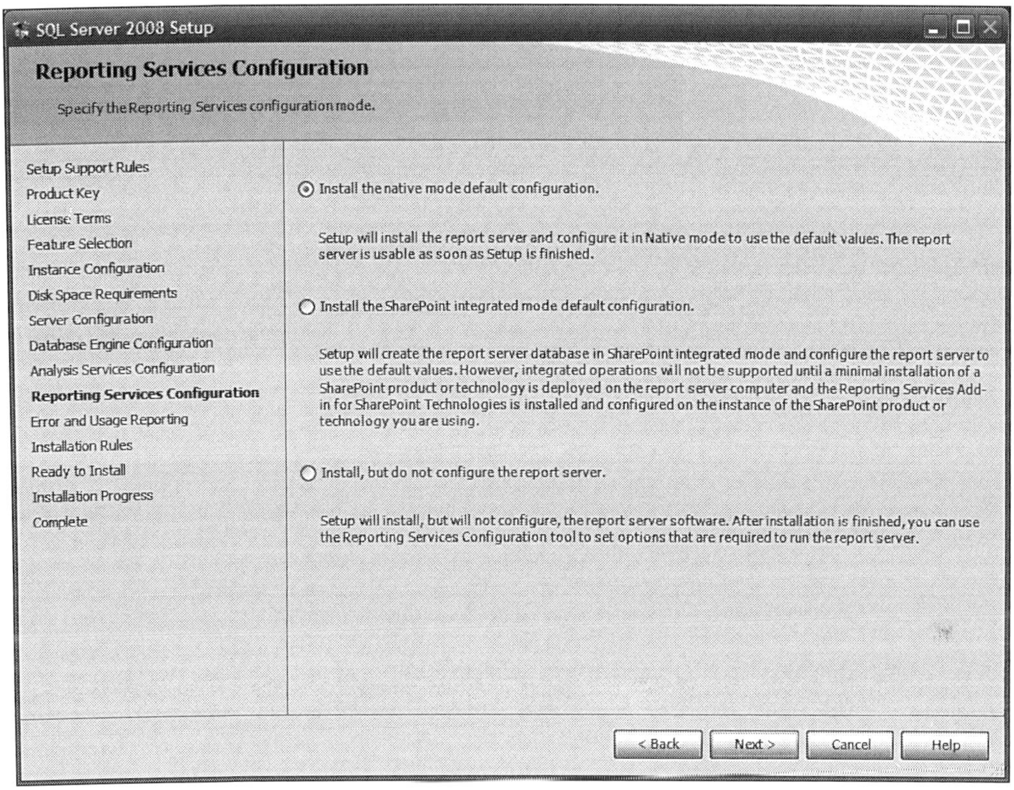

38. Click on the **Next** button.

    The **Error and Usage Reporting** page gets displayed as shown. This is optional but these have been checked for this installation.

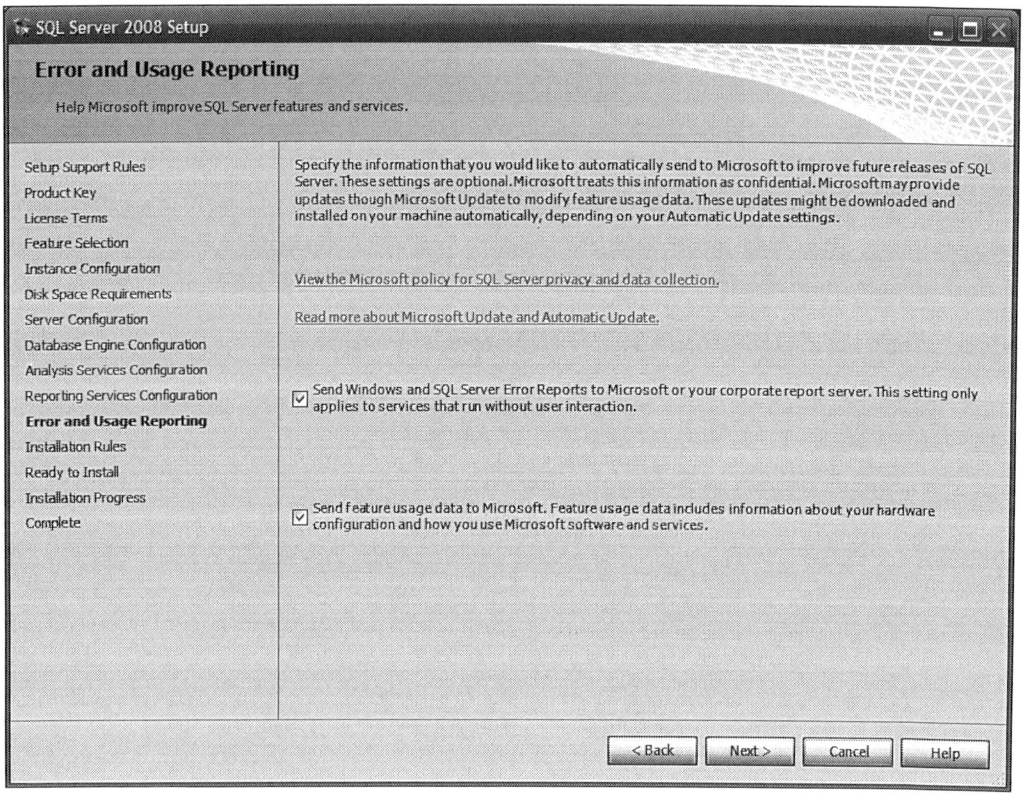

39. Click on the **Next** button.

    The **Installation Rules** page is displayed as shown. The status should be **Passed** for the rules. If any of the **Rule** items fail, the whole installation winds back. You will have to start from the beginning.

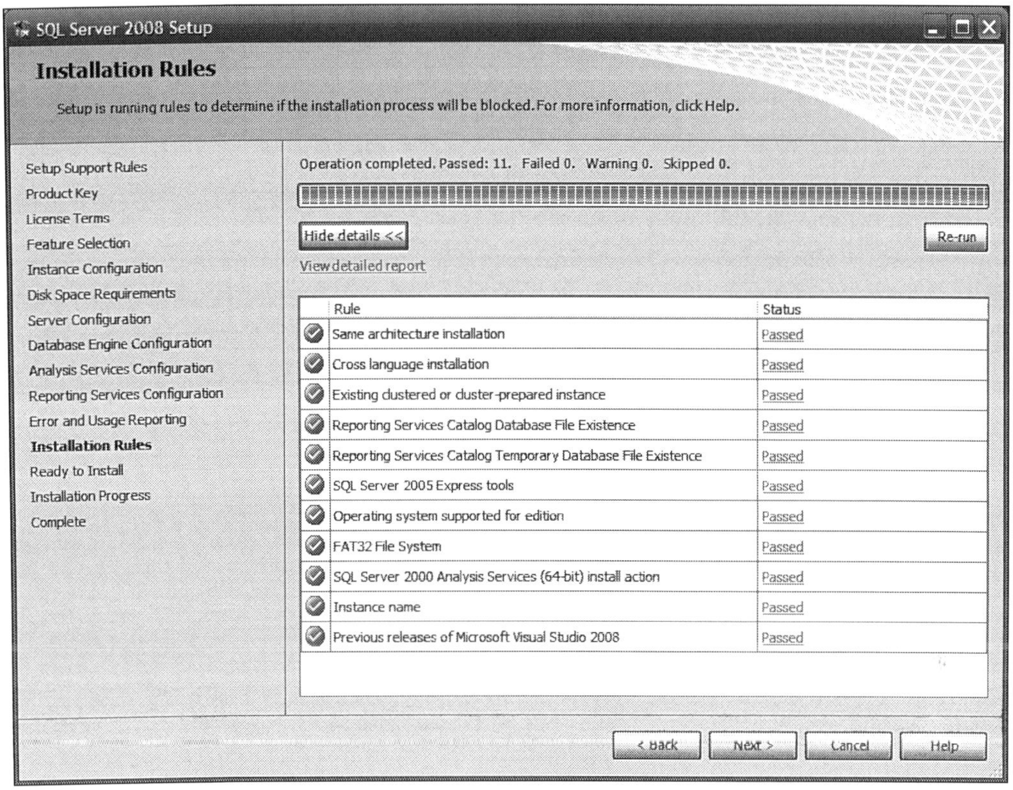

40. Click on the **Next** button.

    The **Ready to Install** page gets displayed which shows all the items chosen during this installation and the path for the `Configuratio.ini` file.

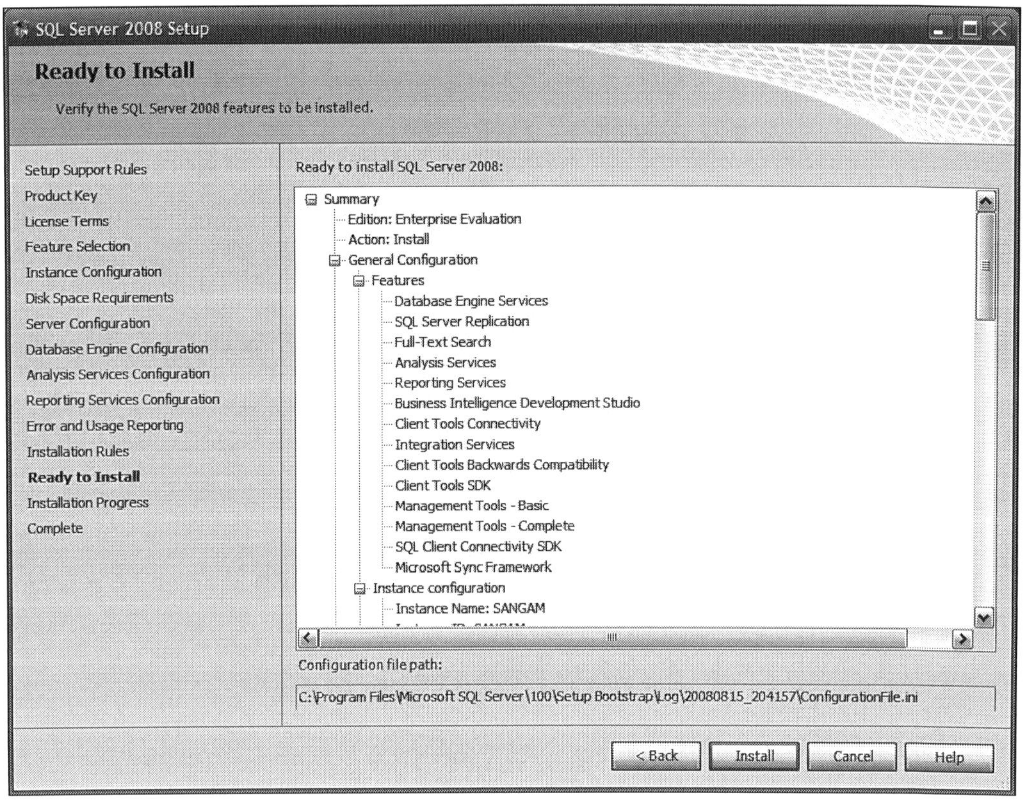

41. Click on the **Install** button.

    The **Installation Progress** window gets displayed as installation starts up. It will take quite a while. Finally the **Installation Progress** window shows up which displays that the installation was a success as shown:

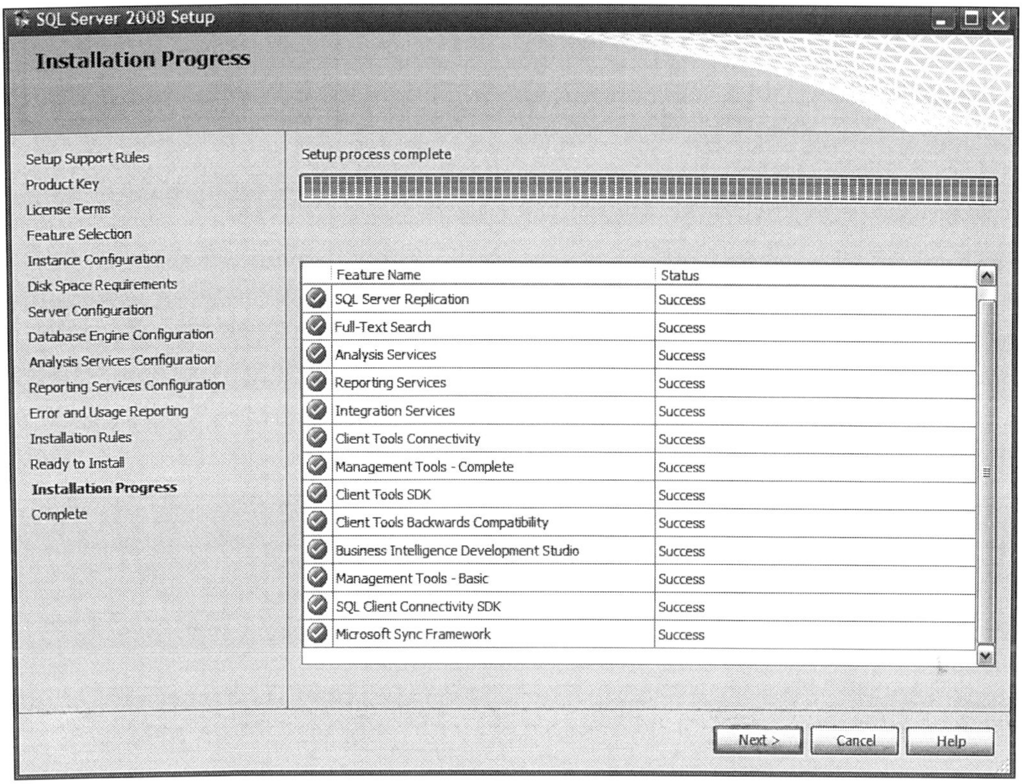

42. Click on the **Next** button.

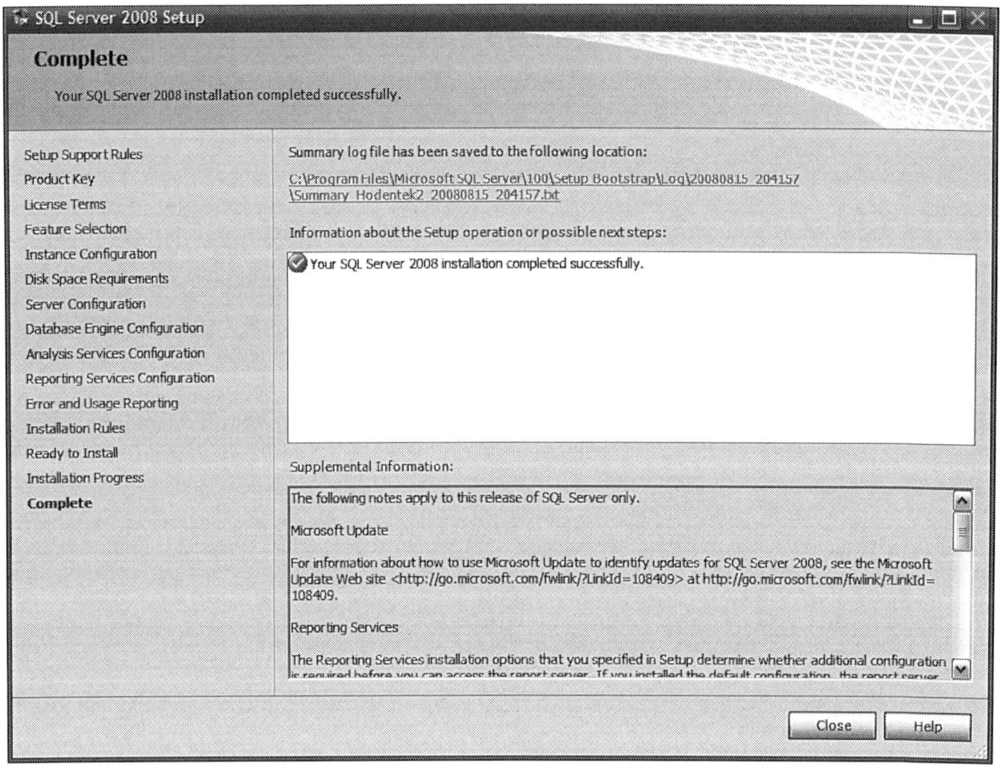

The **Complete** window shows up as shown. Read the **Supplemental information** by scrolling down. The installation log file is saved to the hard drive, which is useful if you need to look up any information.

You have completed the installation of a named instance of a stand-alone SQL Server 2008 RTM on your Windows XP Professional computer.

Installation choices and notes

Since this installation is just for working with basic Reporting Services by a single user on a single machine, the same service account was used for all of the services. Also all services were configured to start automatically except for the SQL Server Agent. During installation, the username and password chosen are of the author on this particular custom environment as it makes meaningful screen capture easier. It is not a recommended practice to make public the security arrangement except for a demo environment such as the one used here.

The author is a window's user with administrative privileges. If you want to customize, you may want to choose different locations for the data and log files, but for this book the default locations are adequate.

Windows authentication was chosen for both the Database Engine as well as the Reporting Services to keep it simple. Also to make it simple, the current user of the machine was also made the sysadmin. If necessary, one could add other SQL Server administrators using the related Database Engine page. While configuring the Database Engine, the defaults were used for Data Directories but these can be customized as well.

Regarding choices for the Reporting Services configuration mode, there are three possible modes of which the default is the native mode. It is also the simplest. Since SharePoint integration was excluded from the book, the SharePoint default mode was not considered.

The installation should proceed as described without any problem, if you are making installation of the SQL Server 2008 for the first time. However as the SQL Server 2008 and Visual Studio 2008 are tightly bound, it is essential that Visual Studio SP1 should be applied before installing SQL Server 2008. It may be noted that SQL Server 2008 can co-exist with SQL Server 2005 and that Reporting Services can be installed separately on another machine. These other installation options are outside the scope of this book. Another source of installation problems is the existence of the CTP (Community Technology Preview or Beta) installations of SQL Server 2008 (`http://www.packtpub.com/article/microsoft-sql-server-2008-installation-made-easy`). These must be completely removed before SQL Server 2008 RTM can be successfully installed.

Read the important information presented in the last installation screen regarding sample databases, late-breaking changes and many other items.

Hands-on exercise 1.2: Reviewing the installation

In this exercise you will be getting acquainted with the following:

- The program short cuts
- Reviewing installed services
- Start and Stop Reporting Services

Program shortcuts

1. Click **Start | All Programs | Microsoft SQL Server 2008**.

   This displays the submenu items as shown:

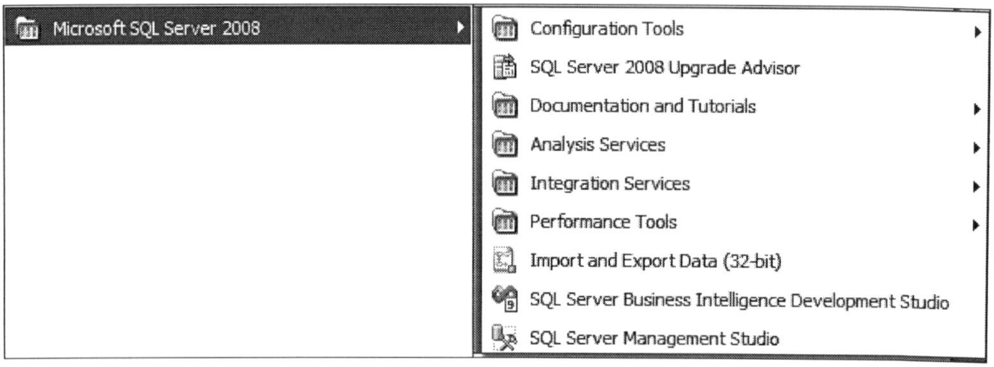

2. Click on the **Configuration Tools** submenu item to display further submenu items as shown.
   - In **SQL Server Error and Usage Reporting** you will be giving permission to Microsoft to collect information from your machine.
   - In **SQL Server Installation Center** you can carry out a number of activities (Planing, Installation, Maintenance) as described in *Hands-on exercise 1.1*.
   - **Reporting Services Configuration Manager** will open the interface where Reporting Services can be configured. This will be described in *Hands-on exercise 1.4*.
   - **SQL Server Configuration Manager** provides access to this important interface for managing the SQL Server Services, SQL Server Network Configuration, and SQL Native Client Configuration. It is also possible to stop, start, and restart several of the SQL Services including the Reporting Services from this interface.

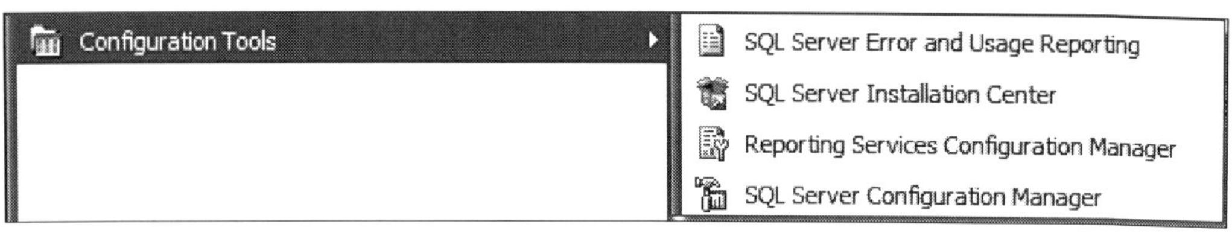

3. Click on the **SQL Server 2008 Upgrade Advisor** submenu item.

   This launches the **SQL Server 2008 Upgrade Advisor** window where you can read more about Upgrade Advisor, check for updates, launch the Upgrade Advisor Analysis Wizard, and launch the Upgrade Advisor Report Viewer.

4. Click on the **Documentation and Tutorials** submenu item.

   The following submenu item gets displayed as shown. The SQL Server Samples Overview submenu item describes code samples and sample databases and provides the following important link: `http://www.CodePlex.com/SqlServerSamples`. It also provides information on several important topics like providing feedback, and updating .NET Framework CLR samples. The other submenu items take you to the listed items.

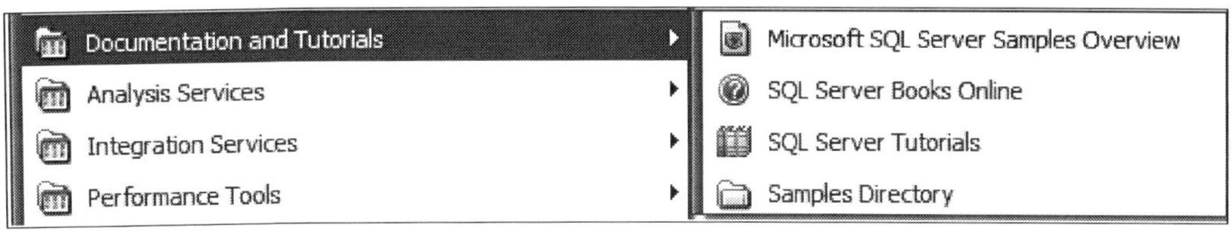

5. Click on the **Analysis Services** submenu item.

   Verify that you can access the **Welcome to the Analysis Services Deployment Wizard**.

6. Click on the **Integration Services** submenu item.

   Verify that you can access two more items in the resulting drop-down: the Data **Profile Viewer** and the **Execute Package Utility**.

7. Click on the **Performance Tools** submenu item.

   Verify that you can access the menu items, **Database Engine Tuning Advisor** and the **SQL Server Profiler**.

8. Click on the **Import and Export Data (32bit)** submenu item.

   Verify that this invokes the **SQL Server Import Export Wizard**'s Welcome screen

9. Click on the **SQL Server Business Intelligence Development Studio** submenu item.

   Verify that this invokes an instance of **Microsoft Visual Studio 2008**'s shell.

10. Click on the **SQL Server Management Studio** submenu item.

    Verify that the **SQL Server Management Studio** is invoked.

Reviewing installed services

The Database Engine, Reporting Services and SQL Server Agent are installed as Windows services. These services can be stopped and started from the **Control Panel**.

1. Click **Start | Control Panel** on your desktop. In the **Control Panel**, click on **Administrative Tools | Services** . Alternatively enter `servies.msc` in the **Start|Run command window**.

   This opens the **Services** window where you can find all the Windows services as shown in the next screenshot. This includes all the SQL Server services.

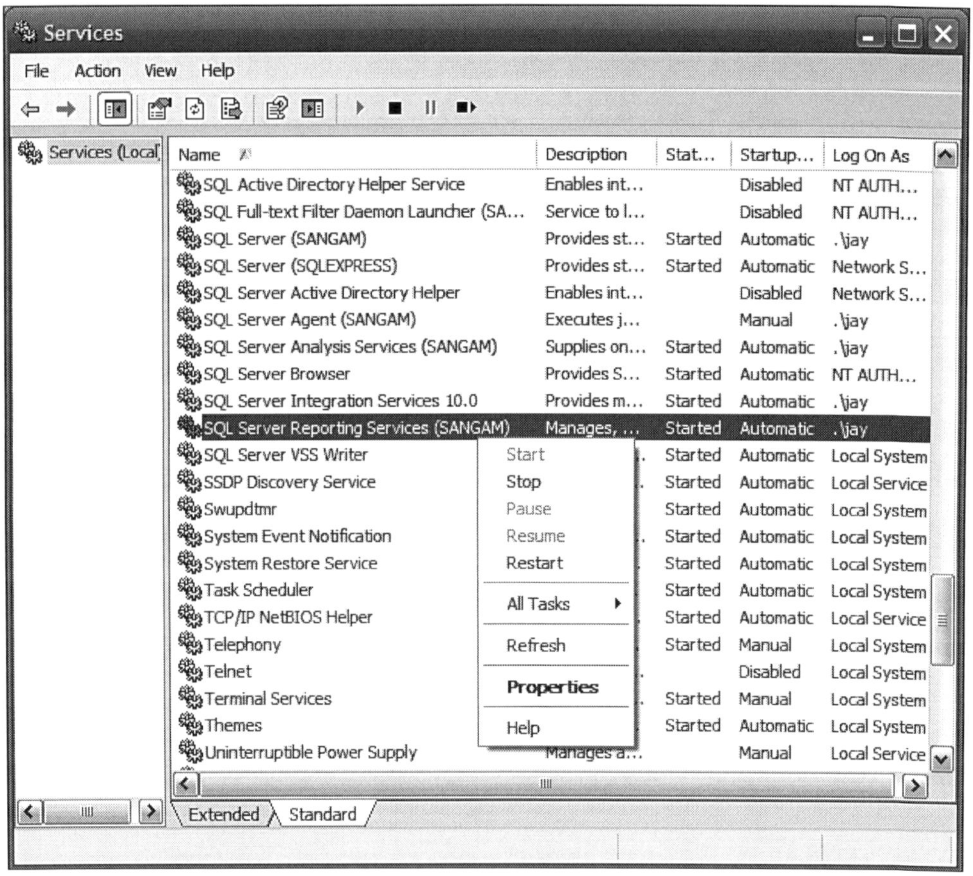

2. Review all SQL Server 2008 related services.

Starting/stopping Reporting Services

Starting, pausing, and stopping windows services are essential operations in the Windows OS for reasons that include security and performance or when the service fails for any reason. Reporting Services can be started and stopped from the SQL Server Configuration Manager, the Windows services as well as from the Reporting Services Configuration tool. Reporting Services cannot be paused. In this section you will see how it can be started and stopped from Windows services.

1. Click **SQL Server Reporting Services (SANGAM)** to change the display as shown in the following screenshot:

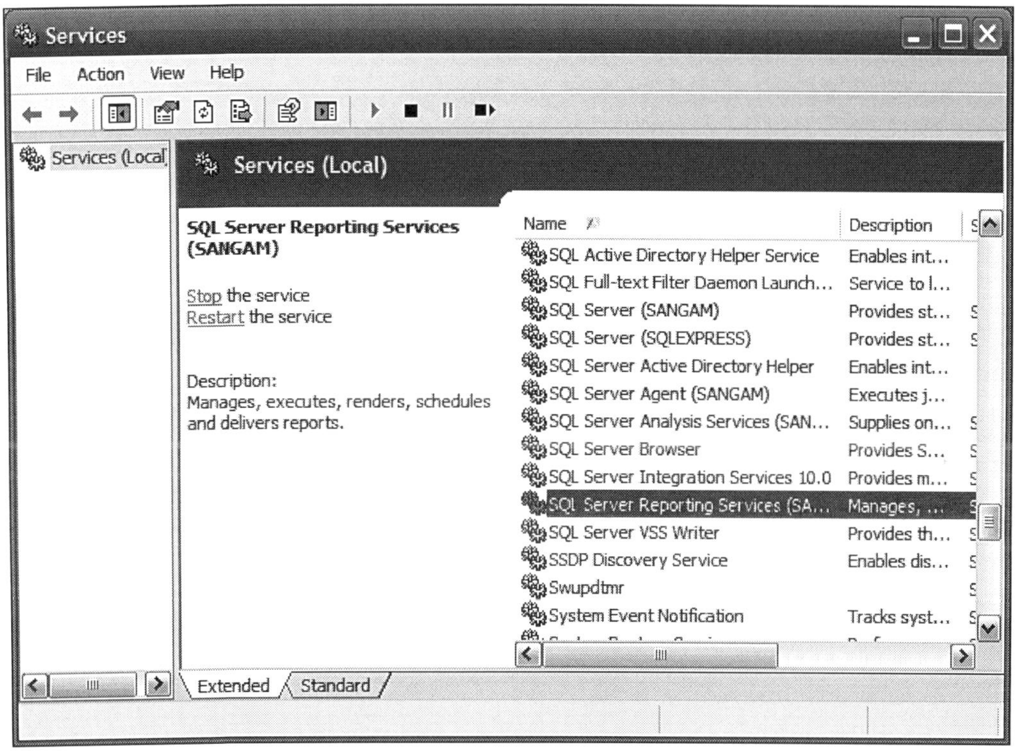

2. Click on the **Stop the service** link.

   This brings up the **Service Control** window which advises that the service is attempting to stop as shown in the next screenshot:

Reporting Services can be started in a similar manner. The other services in the **Services** window can also be similarly controlled.

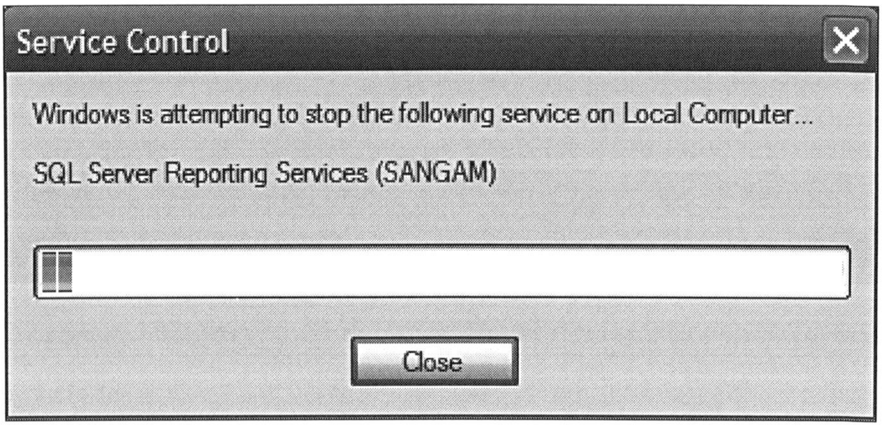

Accessing installed services from the SQL Server Management Studio

Click **Start** | **All Programs** | **Microsoft SQL Server 2008** | **SQL Server Management Studio**.

This opens up the **SQL Server Management Studio** followed by the **Connect to Server** window which immediately shows up as a modal window. The two windows are shown superposed in the screenshot:

In this screenshot the drop-down handle is activated to show the different services.

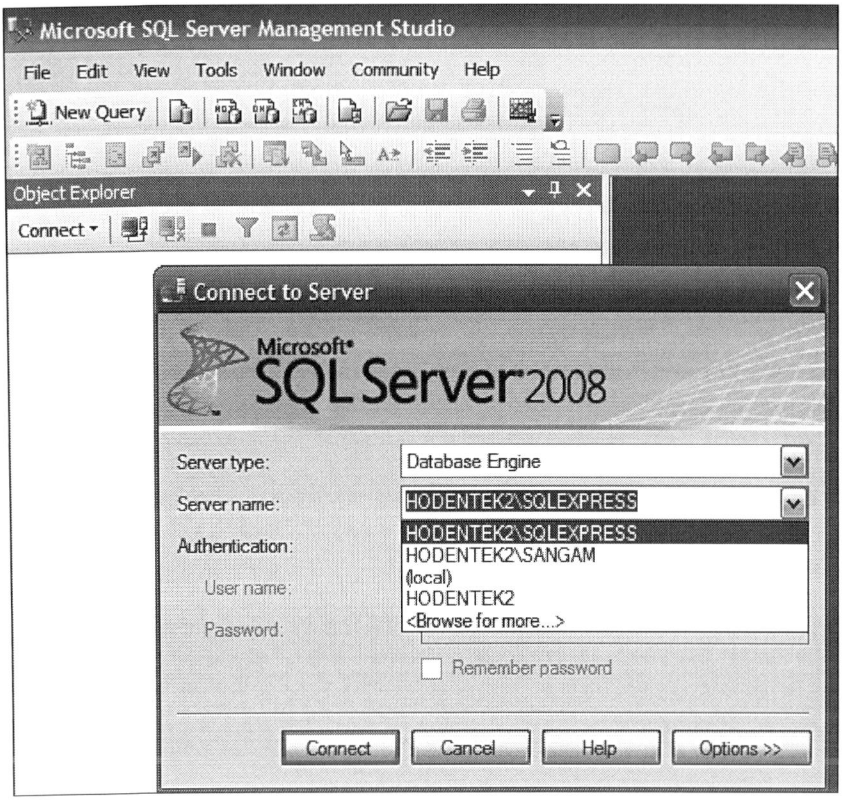

Post installation checks

Program shortcuts give one-click access to most of the tools and it is in the best interests of the reader to get acquainted with the various menus associated with it.

The configuration tools give access to the SQL Server Installation Tool, the SQL Server Configuration Manager, and the Reporting Services Configuration Manager. All of these are frequently used.

Documentation and tutorials should not be overlooked as most of what you can do with SQL Server 2008 is contained in them.

The Services collection in the Control Panel's Administrative tools folder is another very important resource that is used not only for starting and stopping services but also for trouble shooting connectivity with services. You can right-click on any item to look at the services in more detail, make changes there and look at how they depend on other constituent parts. Another way to get to the Services is to click on **Start | Control Panel | Administrative Tools | Computer Management (Local) | Services and Applications**. The following link, `http://www.aspfree.com/c/a/ASP.NET/Managing-Windows-Services-with-Visual-Studio-2005/`,describes more details regarding the use of the Services Collection in the Control Panel.

For managing objects on the SQL Server 2008 there is no better tool than the SQL Server Management Studio. You can connect to all servers, whether local or networked, using **the File | Connect Object Explorer** menu. Of course you need to know the authentication mode and authentication details. Also before you can connect to the server you must have the service started.

Hands-on exercise 1.3: Installing a test database

We will be working with the `Northwind` database tables. These tables are available if Microsoft Office is installed on the machine. In this hands-on section you will learn how to copy the `Northwind` database tables from your MS Access sample folder to the SQL Server 2008 RTM. Another option for installing the test database is to download and install a sample database from the Microsoft web site as described in the following link: `http://hodentek.blogspot.com/2008/12/northwind-database-with-sql-server-2008.html`. The installation instructions follow:

1. Click on **Start** | **All Programs** |**Microsoft SQL Server 2008** |**Import Export Data (32-bit)**.

   This displays the **SQL Server Import and Export Wizard**'s welcome page. Read the instructions on this page.

2. Click on the **Next** button.

   This opens the **Choose a Data Source** page of the Wizard. The default entries are:

   - Data Source: SQL Server Native Client 10.0
   - Server name: Installed Server Name
   - Authentication: **Windows**
   - Database: <default>

3. Click on the Data Source's drop-down handle and choose **Microsoft Office 12.0 Access Database Engine OLE DB Provider** as shown:

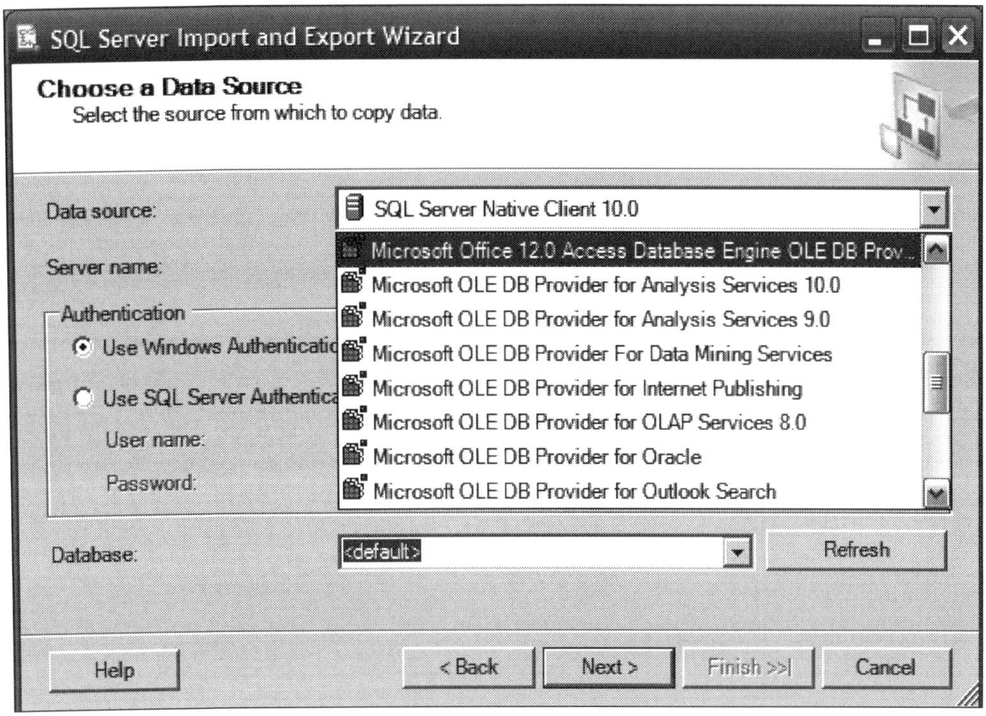

4. Click on the **Properties** button which gets displayed.

   This displays the **Data Link Properties** window where you type in the **Data Source Location**, namely, `C:\Program Files\Microsoft Office\OFFICE11\SAMPLES\Northwind.mdb` (this is the default location of the Northwind database file). Note that `Northwind.mdb` will be available only if it was part of the original installation of MS Access. If not, it can be added from **Add/Remove** programs.

5. Enter Admin for the **User name** text box and leave the Password text box blank and **Blank password** checkbox checked.

6. Click on **Test Connection**.

   Microsoft Data Link Message **Test connection succeeded** gets displayed. This tests whether the connection information provided is correct or not.

7. Click on the **OK** Button.

   This will bring you back to the **Choose a Data Source** page.

8. Click on the **Next** button.

   This opens the **Choose a Destination** page of the Wizard with the default destination displaying **SQL Server Native Client 10.0** and **Windows** authentication.

9. Click on the drop-down handle for **Server name**.

   This displays all the registered servers where you can see the recently installed **HODENTEK2\SANGAM** server as shown. This will be different depending on your installation.

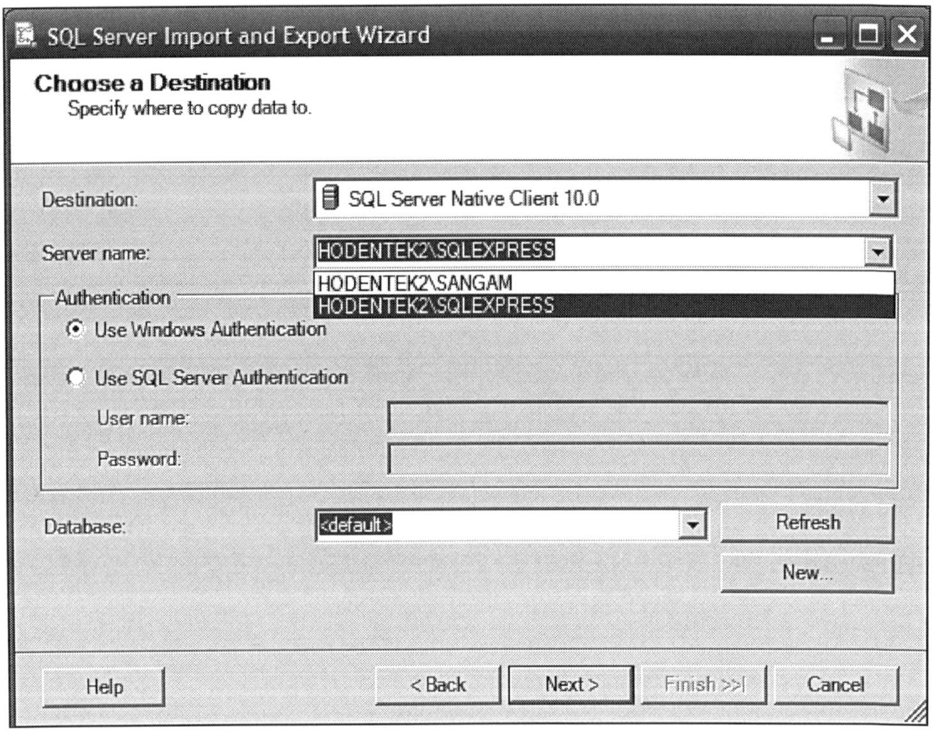

10. Click on the **New...**button below the **Refresh** button.

    This opens the **Create Database** window.

11. Provide a name in the **Name** textbox.

    In this book, the name **TestNorthwind** was provided. As you type in the name of the database, the appropriate file location information for the data and the log gets filled in. Accept the other defaults for the **Data file size** and the **Log file size**.

12. Click on the **OK** button.

    The **Choose a Destination** page gets displayed with all the information provided so far.

    - Data Source: SQL Server Native Client 10.0
    - Server name: HODENEK2\SANGAM
    - Authentication: **Windows**
    - Database: TestNorthwind

13. Click on the **Next** Button.

    The specify Table Copy or Query page of the **SQL Server Import Export Wizard** gets displayed with the default choice set for **Copy data from one or more tables or views**.

14. Accept the default and click on the **Next** button.

    This displays the **Select Source Tables Views** page of the Wizard as shown.

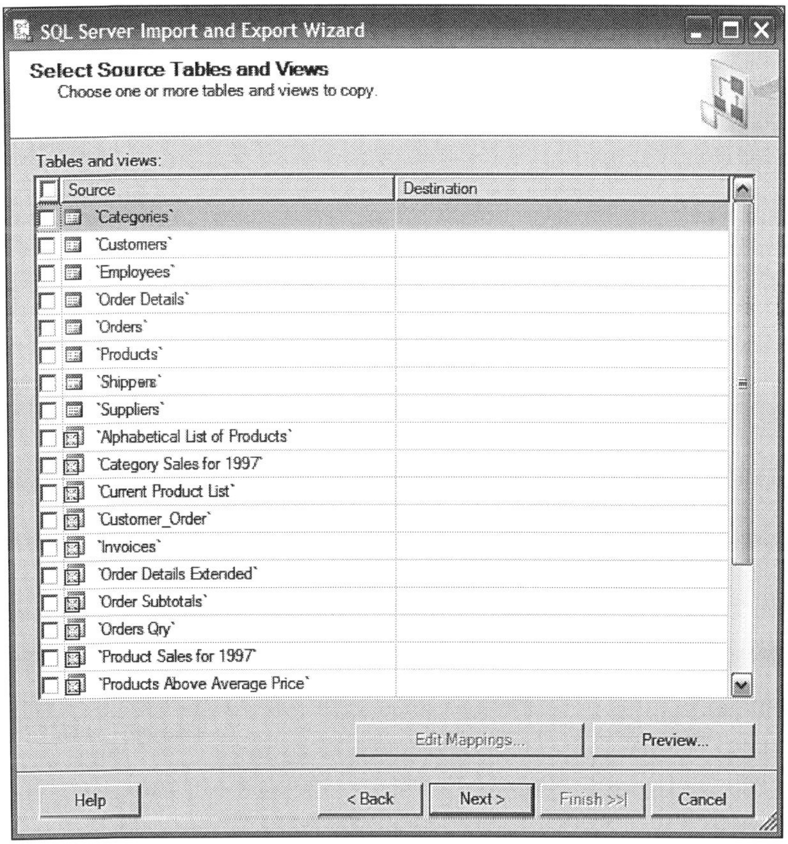

15. Place a check mark for the **Source** at the very top of the above window.

    This places check marks for all the items in this window as well as providing default names for these objects in the column heading **Destination.**

    Make no other changes and click on the **Next** button.

    This displays the **Save and Run Package** page of the Wizard.

16. Accept the **Run Immediately** default choice and click on the **Next** button on the page.

    This brings up the **Complete the Wizard** page displaying the source and destinations' location, and provider information as well as the details of the copying as shown in the following screenshot:

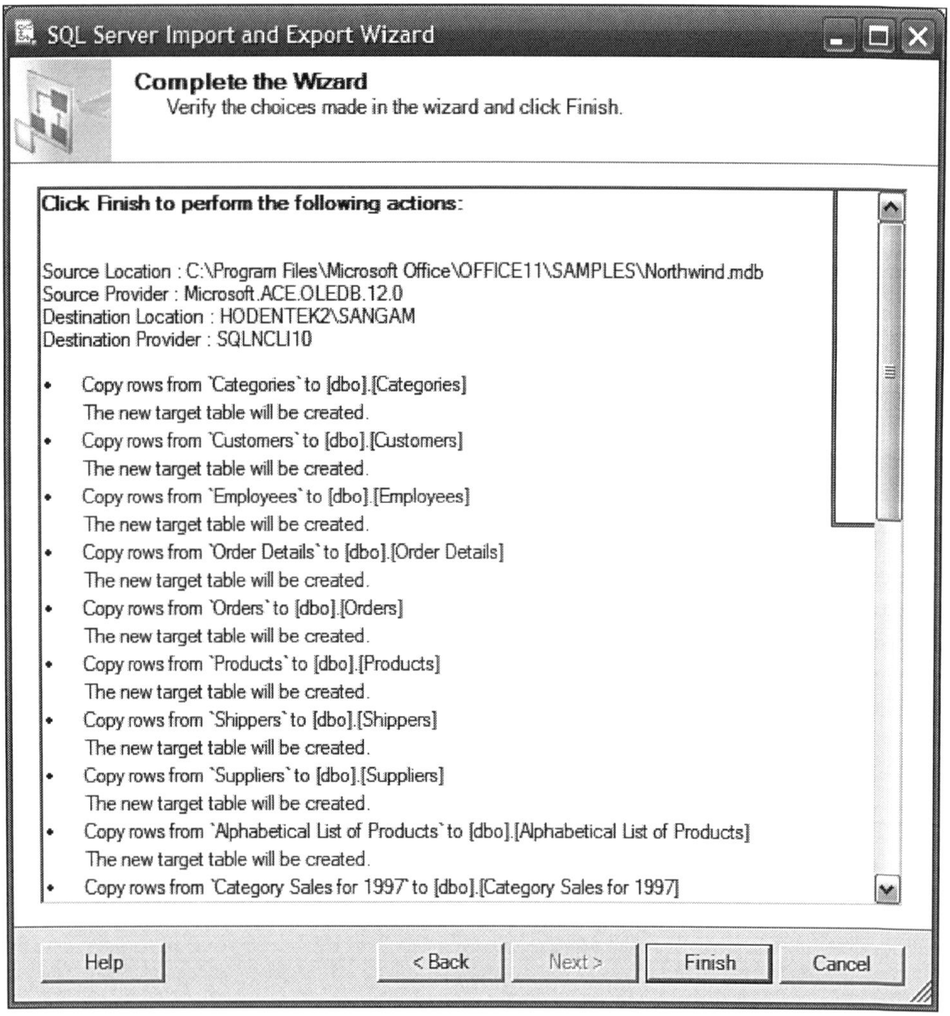

17. Click on the **Finish** button.

    This takes you to the next page, **Performing Operation...**Here you can watch the progress of the Copying of the obejcts chosen previously from the Source to the Destination. Finally you will get an execution successful message as shown:

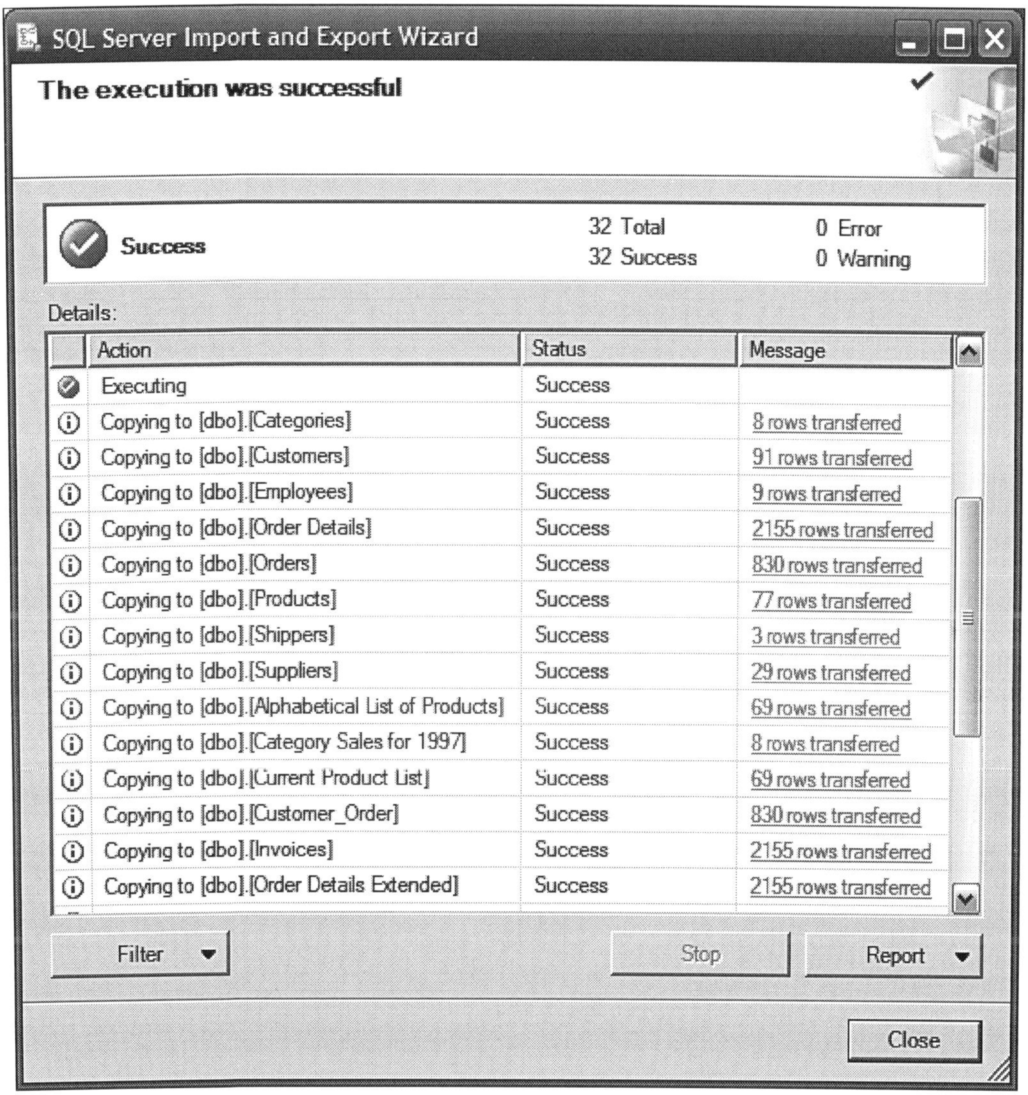

18. Click on the **Report** button with the down arrow and review how the copying took place. Close the **SQL Server Import and Export Wizard** window.
19. Open the **SQL Server Management** window from the shortcut and connect to the **SQL Server 2008** instance **HODENTEK2\SANGAM**.
20. Refresh the **Databases** node and verify that the **TestNorthwind** database has all the objects (only few shown in the following screenshot) copied as shown:

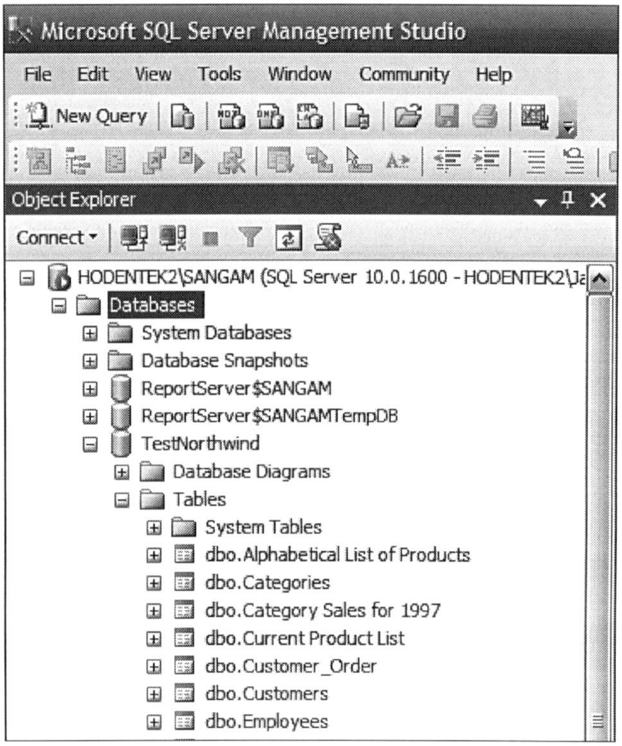

Getting sample databases into the server

Sample database(s) are needed for working with Reporting Services. There are several ways of doing this .One such way is to use the Copy database Wizard in SQL Server 2008 (`http://www.packtpub.com/article/copying-database-sql-2008-copy-database-wizard`) just discussed. You can also use the attach/detach methods (`http://www.packtpub.com/article/moving-a-database-from-sql-server-2005-to-sql-server-2008-in-three-steps`) either using the GUI in the SQL Server Management studio or by scripts. But these methods only work for copying between SQL Server databases. Export/Import database tool, which is installed with the SQL Server 2008 installation, is a very easy to use tool and works well for copying between even non-Microsoft databases.

For the hands-on here, the **Export/Import** wizard is used. It can copy the needed database files by creating a database on the fly from an existing MDB file using the OLEDB provider for the Access Database Engine.

The `Northwind` database file should be in its default location on. If it is not found there, search for `Northwind.mdb` on the computer.

Make sure you use the Microsoft Office 12.0 Access Database Engine OLEDB Provider.

All tables and views from the Access database were copied over. The destination tables and views (queries on MS Access go over to views) and their names can all be edited by mapping all, though the defaults were used in this exercise to keep it simple. It is also possible to use a subset of the tables/views.

The copying of the tables using the **Export/Import** wizard will not copy the Primary Key/Foreign Key relationships which can be established in the SQL Server 2008 Management Studio. The following link shows how it can be done: `http://hodentek.blogspot.com/2008/08/on-establishing-primary-key-foreign-key.html`.

Hands-on exercise 1.4: Configuring the Report Services

From SQL Server Reporting Services 2005 to 2008 there has been a major architectural change—removing the dependency on IIS Server. For SSRS 2008 you do not need an IIS web server. This independence has been a feature desired by many as it was considered inimical to have IIS on the same machine as SQL Server for security reasons. Microsoft has provided this change in SQL Server 2008 heeding to this request and as a consequence the way the Reporting Services is configured has changed as well. In SSRS 2008 the reporting databases are part of the SQL Server 2008 and the security is also managed by the SQL Server. The Report Server is used only for Reporting Services objects.

The Report Service is configured as a web service which can be accessed by a reserved URL (`http://hodentek.blogspot.com/2008/06/http-configuration-utility-and-windows.html`). This is achieved using the `HTTP.sys` API. While a discussion of this is outside the scope of this book, this is the feature that makes it possible to access the reports from the Report Server by making an URL request. This is also the feature that makes it possible to reuse the ports, although, presently this is only possible in the Windows 2003 OS. On Windows XP the IIS web server and the Reporting Services cannot share a port.

When installing the SQL Server 2008 we also chose to install the SQL Server Reporting Services in the native mode so that it can be used readily after finishing the installation of SQL Server. One of the reasons for choosing this mode was to keep it simple and have a quick start. Also, if native mode is not chosen then there will be additional configuration tasks both for Reporting Services Configuration as well as for the Report Manager.

In this exercise, the various steps involved when using the Reporting Services Configuration tool will be described. These steps will enable you to:

- Start the Reporting Services Configuration.
- Configure a Service Account for Reporting Services by specifying an account name and password for the Report Server Service.
- Register a Service Principal Name (SPN) manually for a Report Server.
- Configure a URL so that Report Server Web Service and Report Manager can be accessed by specifying a URL.
- Create the Report Server Database so that the Reporting Service can be deployed.

1. We will begin by starting the Reporting Services Configuration: Click **Start | All Programs | Microsoft SQL Server 2008 | Configuration Tool** and from the drop-down, click on **Reporting Services Configuration Manager**.

   This opens the **Reporting Services Configuration Manager** window followed by the **Reporting Services Configuration Connection** modal window shown in the following screenshot (shown with the drop-down for the **Report Server Instance** activated). There is only one instance of Reporting Services made during SQL Server 2008 RTM Installation (*Hands-on Exercise 1.1*).

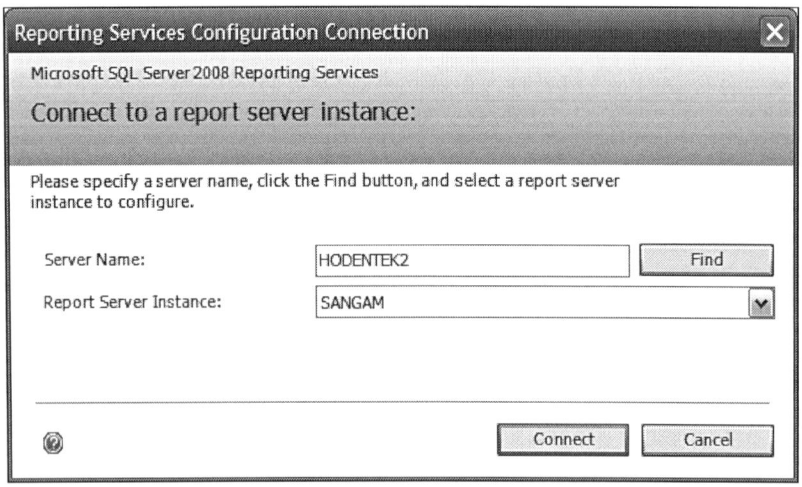

2. Click on the **Connect** button.

   This opens the **Reporting Services Configuration Manager** window which displays a list of items on the left as shown with the first item in the default view.

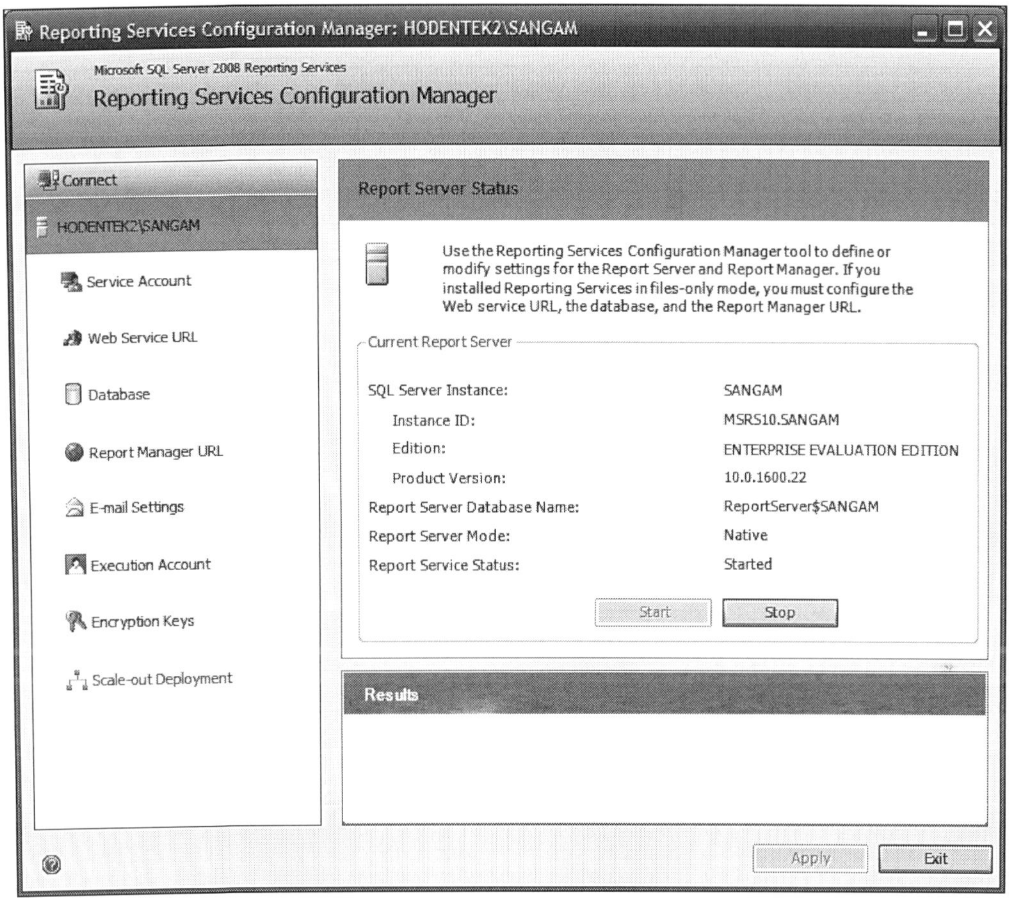

3. Click on the **Stop** button.

   This stops the Report Server and displays the status in the **Results** window in the above screenshot as shown:

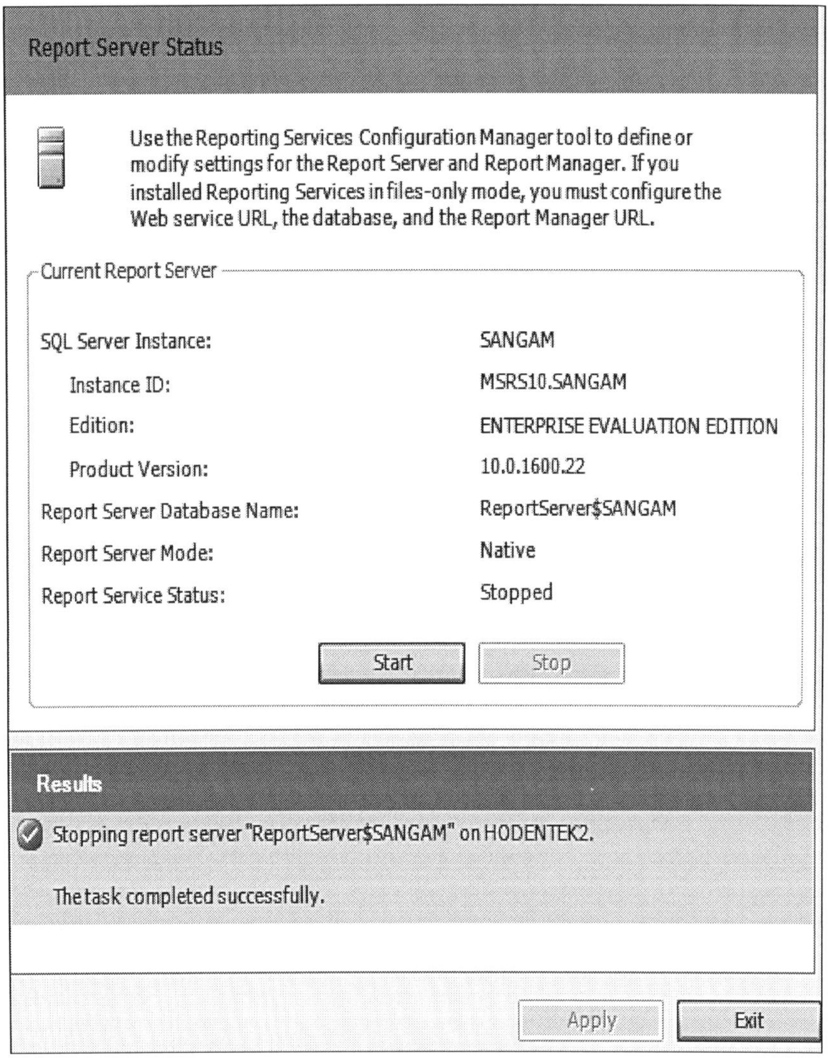

In the following steps only the right-hand portion of the **Reporting Services Configuration Manager** is shown. This is to aid in the readability of the graphics.

4. Click on the **Start** button.

5. Click on the **Service Account** item on the left after making sure that the Report Server has started.

   This brings up the **Service Account** details on the right as shown. During installation of the SQL Server 2008, the service account is already configured and this is displayed in the window.

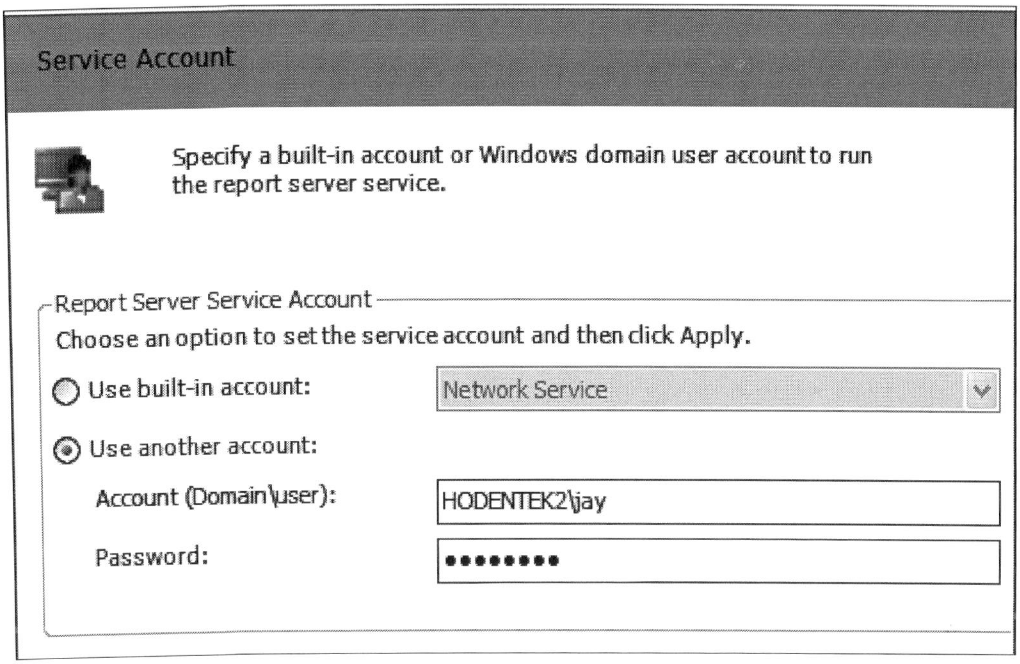

6. Click on the **Web Service URL** on the left.

   This brings up the **Web Service URL** details on the right as shown.

   If any changes to the entries are made, make sure that you hit the **Apply** button at the bottom right of the **Reporting Services Configuration Manager**'s Page.

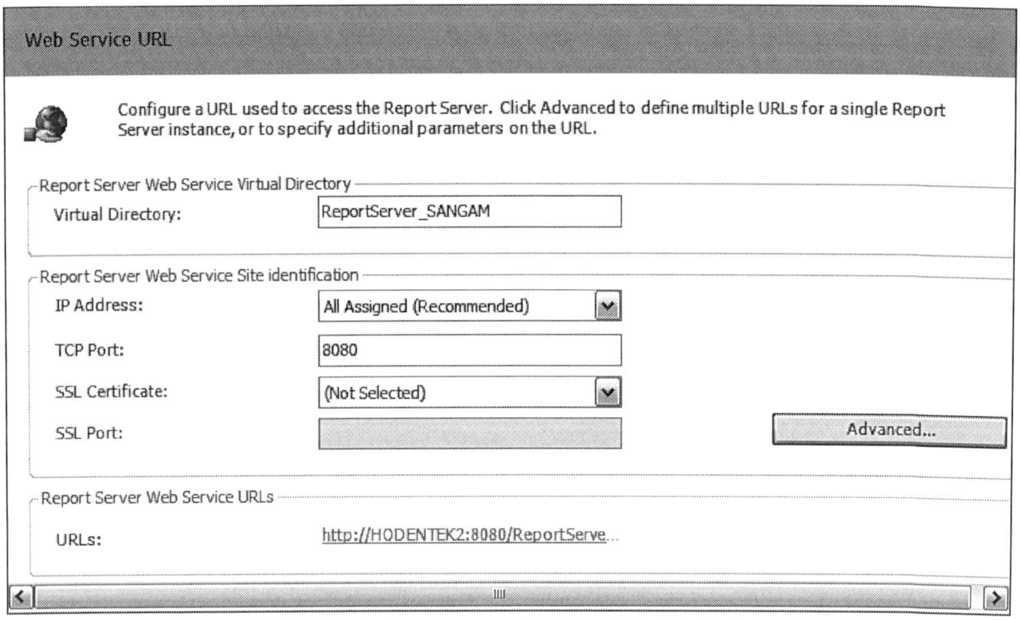

7. Click on the hyperlink in the **Web Service URL** window.

   The server authentication window comes up as shown in the following screenshot. You need to provide the account name/password you provided while installing the SQL Server 2008 RTM.

8. Now click on the hyperlink in the Web Service URL window.

   This brings up the Web page for the web service as shown in the following screenshot. We will be using this URL in several exercises of the book.

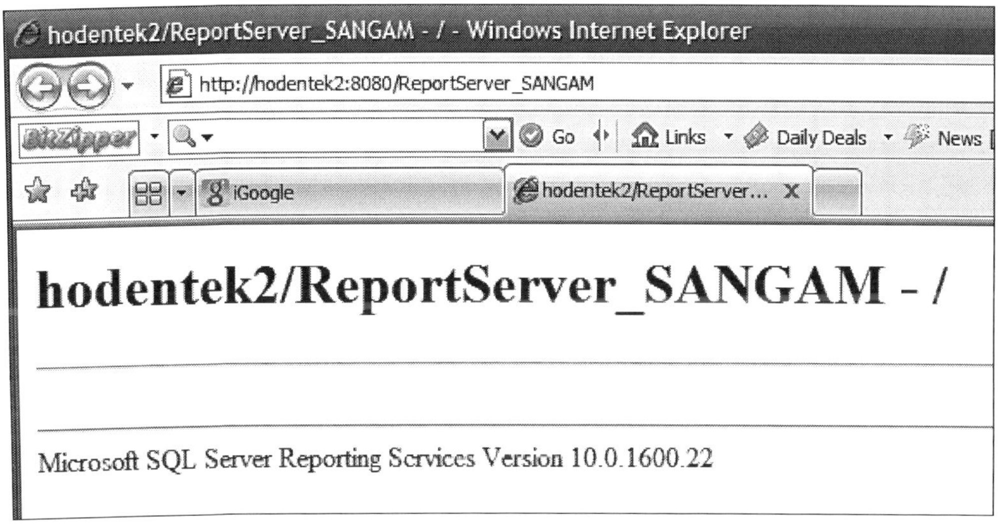

9. Display the IE Browser and type in the URL `http://localhost:8080/ReportServer_Sangam` (in your case the URL appropriate to your installation) and refresh the web page.

   This should display the same web page you saw in the previous screenshot.

10. Click on the item **Database** on the left.

    This brings up the database related details page on the left as shown. This page displays the default **Current Report Server Database** and the default **Current Report Server Database Credentials**.

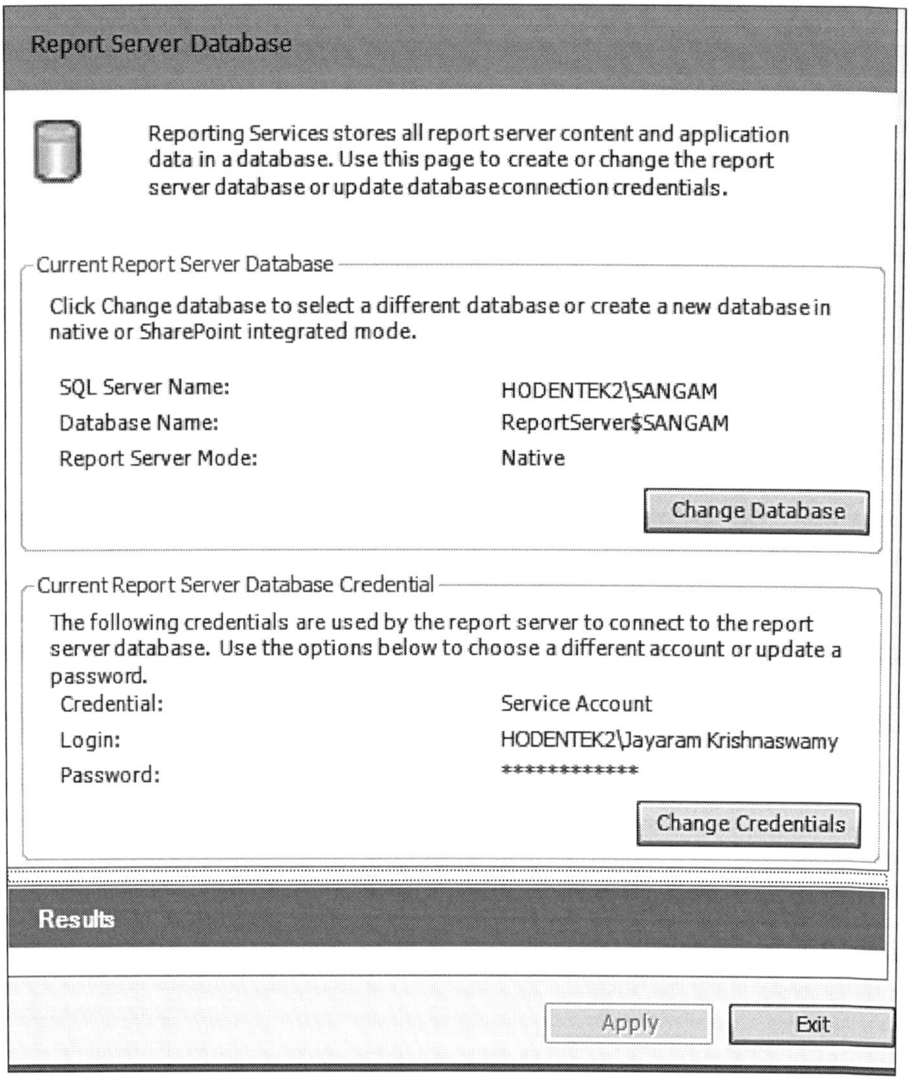

11. Open the **Microsoft SQL Server Management Studio**. Connect to the database engine and expand the **Databases** node. Expand the **ReportServer database** node as shown:

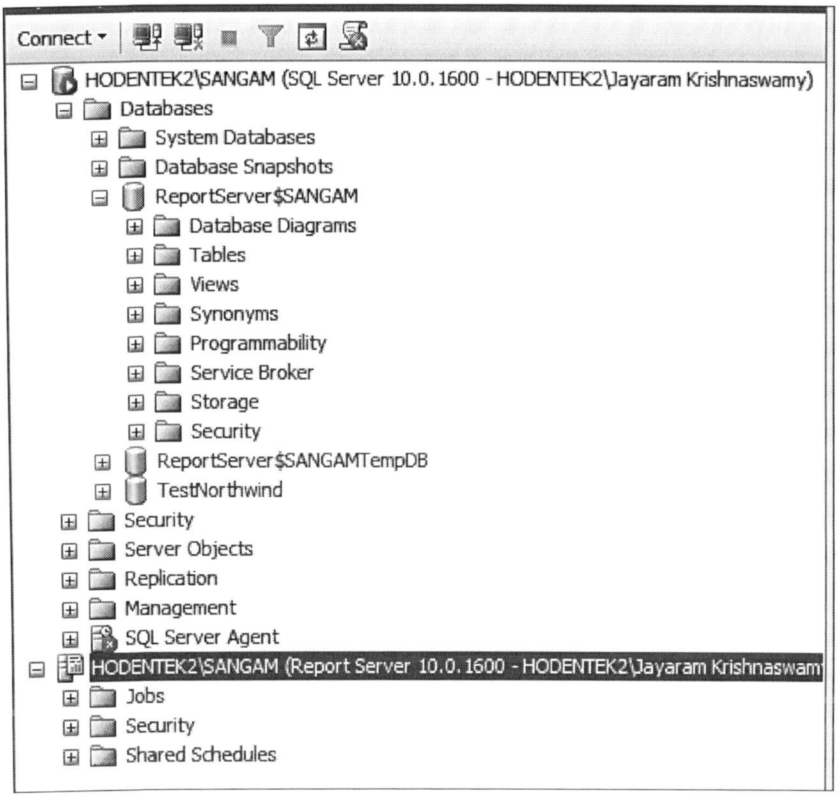

12. In the **Report Server Configuration Manager**'s page click on the **Report Manager URL** on the left.

    This brings up the Report Manager URL related information on the right as shown in the following screenshot:

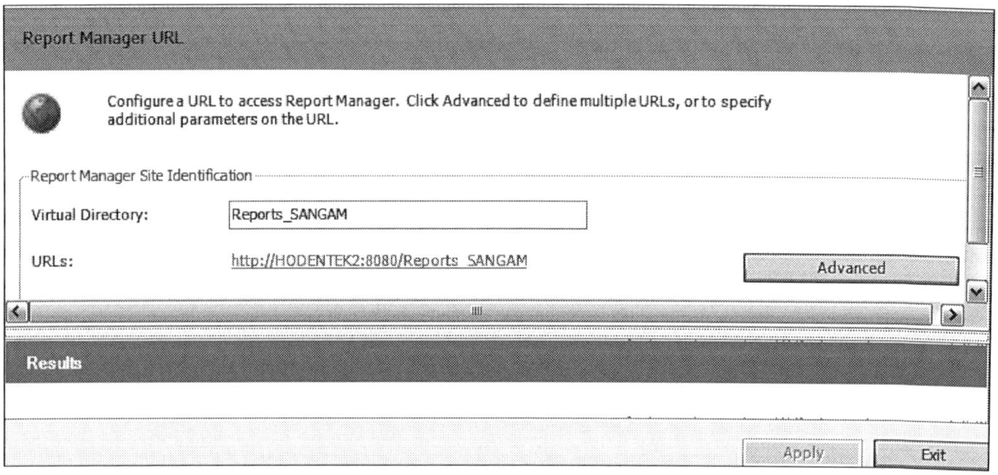

13. Click on the hyperlink, `http://HODENTEK2:8080/Reports_SANGAM`.

    The hyperlink details will depend on your chosen names but the above action will bring up the Report Manager's web page (`http://Hodentek2:8080/Reports_SANGAM/Pages/Folder.aspx`) as shown. If the SQL Server has not started, you may get a **rsReportServerDatabaseUnavailable** error since the Report Manager needs access to the Report Server database. In this case you need to start the SQL Server Instance from the Control Panel as described earlier.

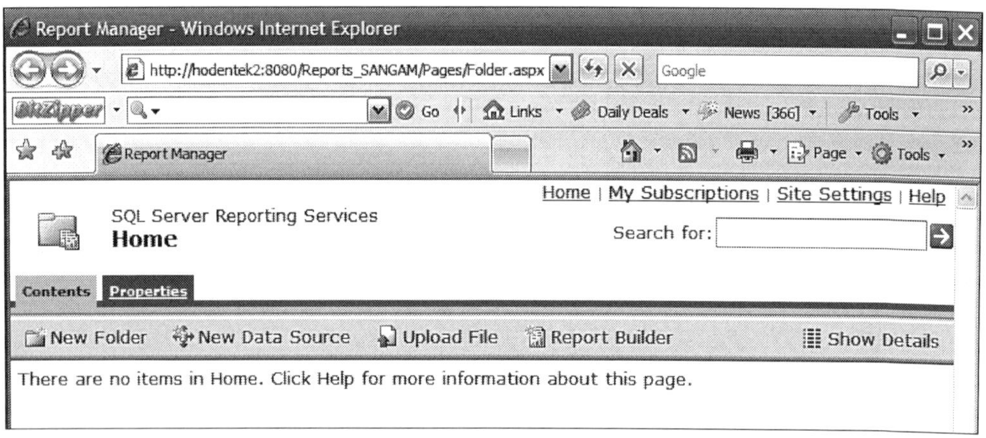

14. Click on **Email Settings** on the left.

    This opens the **Email Settings** detail page on the right as shown. Read the instructions at the top on this page.

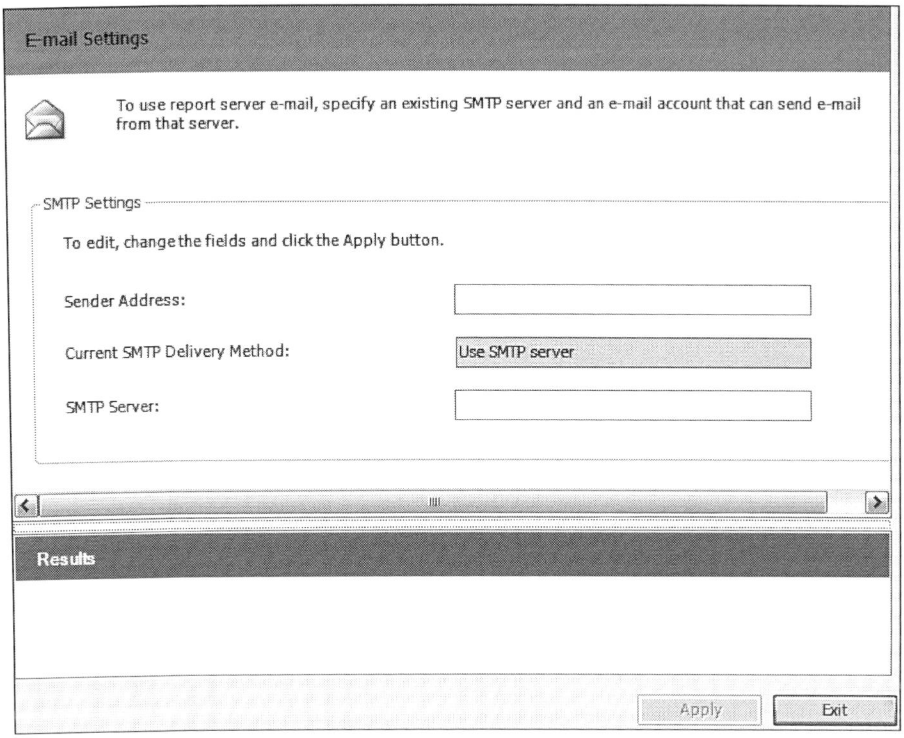

15. Fill in the details for the Sender's (email) address and the full name of the SMTP Server and click on the **Apply** button at the right-hand bottom of the **Reporting Services Configuration Manager**'s window.

    This should return a message in the **Results** pane directly below the Email Settings page as shown:

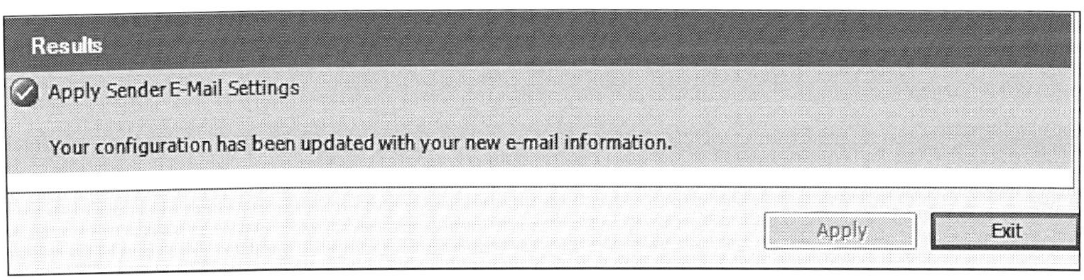

16. Click on the **Execution Account** on the left.

    This brings up the **Execution Account** related information on the right as shown:

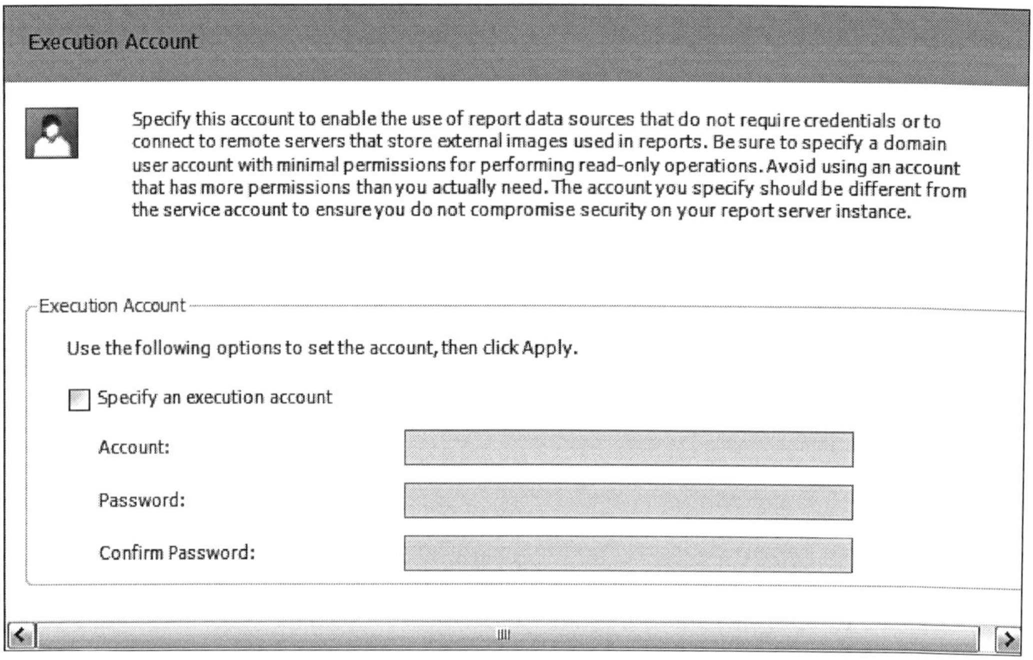

17. Make no entries in the Execution Account window. Click on **Encryption Keys** item on the left.

    This opens the Encryption Keys related information and management page on the right as shown. Read the notes on this page.

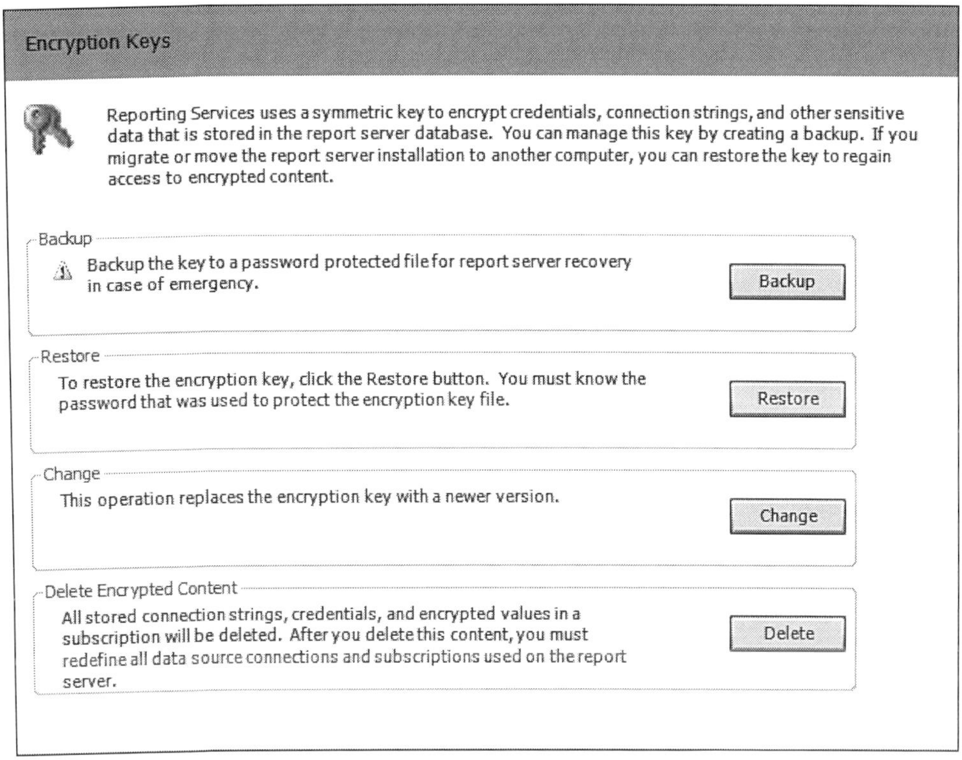

18. Make no changes. Click on the **Scale-Out-Deployment** option on the left.

    This brings up the related details page on the right as shown in the following screenshot. Read the notes on this page.

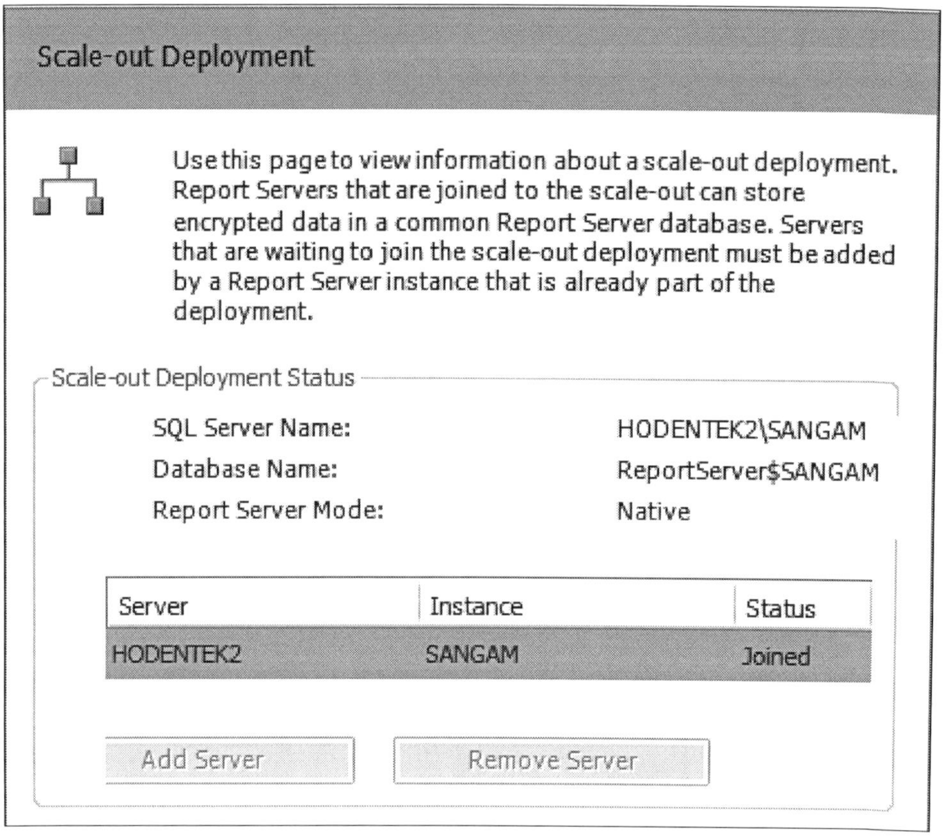

19. Click on the **Exit** button

    This completes the Report Server Configuration.

Report Server configuration options

You could configure multiple Report Servers. In this exercise there is only one Report Server SANGAM. The name of the Report Server is the one you provided during the installation of SQL Server 2008.

The Report Server mode you chose dictates most of what you see in the rest of the Report Server configuration. Most of the defaults will be configured at the end of the SQL Server installation, like whether the Service is started automatically when Windows starts, the authentication details and so on. However, it is also possible to start and stop the Report Server, make changes to authentication, access the Report Server and Report Manager URLs, and so on from the configuration tool. Using the Configuration tool is the recommended practice if you need to make changes to the Report Server installation.

The service account provided during installation is used by the Report Server as well. It is possible to change the password or to, use a different account. For the purposes of this book the default account will be used. Also as the Report Server will not be deployed on a network we will not be concerned with registering a Report Server Service Principal Name with the domain user account. Interested readers who may want to pursue this should look up "Register a Service Principal Name (SPN) for a Report Server" in the Books Online.

Reporting Services uses an encryption key to secure data in the Report Server database. Changing the account or password involves saving the backup encryption key related information. We will be using the service account and password we supplied during the SQL Server installation and do not intend to change them. This is the reason no changes were made in the Encryption details related page.

Using URLs, you can access the Report Server Web Service as well as the Report Manager. To use any of these at least one URL should be configured for each instance of Report Server and Report Manager. Since the native mode for Reporting Services was chosen during the SQL Server 2008 installation, the reserved URLs are configured with default values automatically as shown. You may also choose custom values. For this book, however, the defaults are accepted. Since Port 80 is used by IIS 5.1 on this computer, the program has assigned Port 8080 for the Web Service URL. Make sure that no other service is using this port. Note that the Virtual Directory name is a part of the URL as well. In addition to the Virtual Directory, the IP Address, the TCP Port, and the SSL related items are unique for each Report Server instance. Setting the default IP Address to All Assigned is recommended. The SSL Port and SSL Certificate related information (optional) can be configured as well. These are not configured in this book. Clicking on the **Advanced...** button brings up the window for configuring multiple web site configurations. Here multiple HTTP and SSL identities for the Report Server web service can be configured. No such identities were created for the examples in this book.

Regarding the Report Server databases, the native mode installation chosen during the SQL Server 2008 installation creates two relational databases (together called the Report Server Catalog), ReportServer (Primary) and ReportServerTempDb for storing Report

Server META data and objects. If this option was not chosen you need to manually create the catalog using this page. Using the Change Database and Change Credentials buttons, you can invoke the Wizards to make your desired changes. Regarding credentials to access the Reporting Services Catalog, the Windows Integrated Security login specified during SQ Server 2008 installation is used. The Windows User Account for the local machine (Domain account for remote) and SQL Server logins can also be used for the credentials.

Although SQL Server 2008 on the local machine hosts the database, the Report Server Catalog can be hosted on a remote machine or on a SQL Server 2005 instance. For this book the default databases are accepted. The Catalog schema is not public and applications should not run queries against this catalog. The recommended procedure is to use the Reporting Services API to access the databases.

Just like the Report Server, the Report Manager can also be accessed by a URL. The virtual directory of the Report Manager is very similar to the virtual directory of the Report Server and shows the instance name. Since the native mode installation option was chosen, it is configured with the default. The Advanced button on the Report Manager URL will bring up the Advanced Multiple Web Site Configuration window. Here you can configure various identities for Report Manager. These options are not used in the book.

Regarding email delivery, SMTP (Simple Mail Transfer Protocol) is chosen for the mail transfer and you must supply the correct information when configuring this screen. SMTP needs a Sender's address as well as a SMTP server for sending out the mail. You need to fill in the information appropriate to your environment. Advanced email settings can be made using the configuration file. For this book no further configuration of email is made apart from the basic configuration.

Configuration of the Execution Account is optional. The related screen in the hands-on describes most of the details. This account is, ideally a Windows User account and if this account is configured, it should be maintained to avoid accessing errors. For the purposes of this book this is not configured as we neither send connection requests over networks nor try to retrieve external image files for use in the reports while making requests when logged in anonymously.

Although creating a backup copy of the symmetric key used in encrypting sensitive information is an important part of Report Server configuration, we do not envisage a use for the purposes of this book since:

- We do not intend to change the Report Servers Windows Service account name or reset the password.
- We do not intend to rename the computer that hosts the instance or the name of the instance.

- We do not intend to migrate the Report Server installation.
- We do not expect to have a Report Server installation failure due to hardware failure.

A scale-out deployment model of running Reporting Services is needed when multiple Report Servers use a shared Report Server database. All action buttons are disabled in the related screen as there is only one reporting service. We do not intend to use this model of operation since we have no intention of having multiple Report Servers.

Summary

Business Reporting and its importance in the context of an Enterprise are described in this Chapter. The key players in Business Reporting are listed along with links to their sites. Overviews of the major highlights of SSRS 2008 are described with special reference to Reporting Services. The Hands-on Exercise 1.1 describes in detail the installation of SQL Server 2008 (starting from getting the download to verifying the installation). Another detailed hands-on exercise shows how to install the sample database and provides alternative approaches to installing the sample database. The Report Server configuration needed to work with the book is described in detail in yet another hands-on exercise. This is a mandatory chapter to read in order to use the rest of the book.

2

Overview of SSRS 2008 Architecture and Tools

In this chapter, we will review some salient architectural details of SQL Server Reporting Services 2008 as detailed in the Microsoft Reporting Services documentation. It is essential to understand how the different components of the architecture fit together for end-to-end support for reporting activities. This will be followed by a description of various tools and their roles in reporting services. In particular, we will look at the details of Report Server, the Report Manager, the Model Designer, Report Builder (presently there are two Report Builders available: versions 1 and 2), and other extension components that include authentication, rendering, scheduling and delivery. As every one of these tools and their specifics are detailed in the Reporting Services configuration file, we take a brief look at this file created by the configuration chosen for the installation in Chapter 1.

We will also look at the Visual Studio 2008 design interface details that are related to Business Intelligence Projects in general and Reporting Services in particular. We will then look at SSRS 2008 in relation to the Database Engine and the support provided by the SQL Server Management Studio.

Architectural details and components

Reporting services architecture has undergone a number of changes from the 2005 to the 2008 version. It is necessary to understand some architectural background information for Reporting Services 2005 users, those upgrading to Reporting Services 2008 and first time SQL Server 2008 users as some references to these will be made in the book. This section, while it describes the various features, does not deal with making changes to the default setup.

In SQL Server Reporting Services 2005 there were two services, one unattended windows service and an on demand web service. The Windows service looked after report processing, scheduling and delivery, database maintenance and extensibility. The web service, on the other hand, worked with SOAP, URL access, Report Manager, Report processing, Report Models and extensibility. These services worked with tools such as Report Builder 1.0, SQL Server Management Studio, Report Designer, the Reporting Services Configuration Tool, Sharepoint v3 and other third party applications. The underlying data resided in reporting services databases, the SharePoint databases and configuration files. Adding, removing and modifying Report Server configuration information was carried out by the WMI provider for reporting services which is built on Windows Management Instrumentation.

In SSRS 2008, there is just one Windows service and there is no dependence on IIS. Everything that was in the web service is now present in the Windows service. This was achieved by replacing the functionality provided by IIS with native SQL Server components (SQL OS, SQL CLR and SQL networking interface) leveraging .NET Framework of varying versions in several of the CTP's (Feb CTP required 3.0 and RC0 requires 3.5) including the RTM.

The reporting services (Windows service) are comprised of the web-based Report Manager Client, the Web Server Web Service and the background processing.

While the Report Manager provides the ASP.NET and UI pages, the Report Server web service works with ASP.NET, SOAP, and URL interfaces. It is also responsible for Report Processing as well as working with Report Models. In addition, the Report Manager and the Report web service have their own extensions. The background processing caters for Report Processing, Report Models, scheduling, subscription and delivery. The database maintenance is also handled by background processing.

The support tools like Report Builder, Report Designer (it's a part of the Visual Studio and BIDS), SQL Server Management Studio, the Configuration tool, the SharePoint v3 and third party applications play a similar role in SQL 2008 as they did in SQL Server 2005. The versions of these tools are of course different.

WMI provider functions in a manner similar to its function in SSRS 2005 by leveraging the classes in the `System.Management` namespace. This is especially useful when changes have to be made on systems having multiple Report Server instances.

Details of Reporting Services service architecture can be found at the following link: `http://msdn.microsoft.com/en-us/library/bb630409.aspx`.

Report Server

Report server is at the heart of Reporting Services which is implemented as a Windows service. It consists of:

- Windows Service (Provides report scheduling and delivery services).

  Both services are used in designing, saving, executing, managing and publishing the reports. Reporting Services hosts the Report Manager, the Repot Server web service and background processing features running in their own application domains.
- Report Manager:

  Provides front-end for Report Server items and handles their management.
- Web Service: (Provides access to Report Server via Report Builder)

  Report and Model processing, authentication, data, and rendering.
- Background processing:
  - Report processing
  - Model processing
  - Data processing, rendering, authenticating extensions
  - Scheduling
  - Subscription and delivery
  - Database maintenance

Report Server and HTTP

Reporting Services use a HTTP listener (implementing HTTP1.1 protocol) that handles incoming requests directed to a specific `HTTP.sys` on a specific port on the local computer. The presence of `HTTP.sys` is therefore a must for the reporting services. The host name and port reservation were described in Chapter 1 under *URL Reservation*.

Report processing

Report server has two core processors, the Report Processor and the Scheduling and Delivery Processor. The core processors cannot be modified or extended as they maintain the integrity of the reporting system. Report server also has extensions that are specialized to handle authentication, data processing, rendering and delivery operations. Extensions are also processors but are specialized for a particular kind of function. Out of the box, there are default extensions for every type of supported extension.

Report server processes requests for reports after authentication from the authentication layer and retrieves report related items such as report properties, its formatting and the data. Report server also blends in the formatting information with the data before rendering the report. A single instance of Report Server can provide end-to-end processing from handling an initial report request to a finished and rendered report. A short note (`http://hodentekhelp.blogspot.com/2008/07/how-are-reports-processed-on-report.html`) describes this process in some detail.

The programmatic interface in the Report Server is the web service components. Both this interface and the report processor access the Report Server database.

Report Server backend

Report server also stores folders and files just like a computer file system. The report you create exists as a file in the file system with the extension .rdl. When it is published (the same thing as saving to the Report Server), it will be stored on the Report Server Database. The report can be retrieved from the Report Server Database for use in applications or presentations.

Reporting services deployment uses two SQL server relational databases for internal storage. By default, the names of these databases are ReportServer (Primary) and ReportServerTempdb.

ReportServerTempdb stores:

- Temporary data
- Session information
- Cached reports

T-SQL commands, database command prompt utilities, the `rs.exe` script utility, and the Reporting Services Configuration Tool can all be used for reporting services database-related activities (backup, restore, copy and move). These databases, being considered internal, cannot be renamed. The ReportServerTempdb has stored procedures that contain the name of the primary database and therefore, renaming would throw exceptions.

Reporting Services and the database engine

Both the Report server items and Reporting Services databases can be accessed using the SQL Server Management Studio by clicking **File | Connect Object Browser...**. This displays the **Connect to Server** window as shown:

From here you can connect to any of the displayed items. The database engine and the reporting services of the named instance **SANGAM** are shown together in the next figure. The Report Server Databases are in the database engine. By default, the Report Server users are:

- Everyone
- BUITIN/Administrators
- NT Authority/System

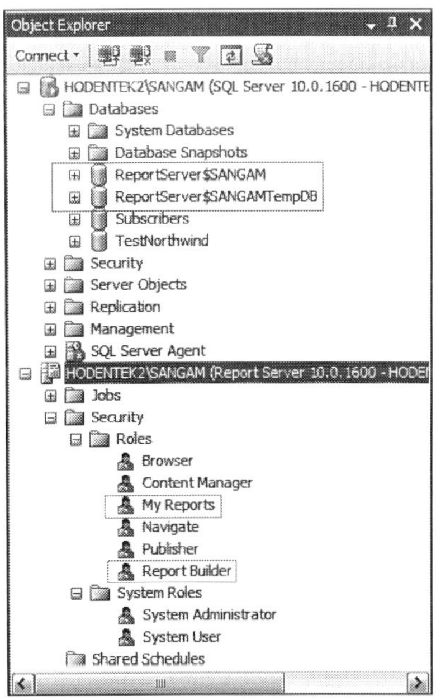

SSRS uses a role-based security and authentication subsystem. The roles for Reporting Services are shown in the Report Server's **Security** node. The built-in roles cannot be deleted. They are sufficient for almost all activities on the Report Server as you will see in the rest of the book. Also, as you will see later, the **My Reports** role is not enabled but you can enable it in the SQL Server Management Studio as described in Chapter 6. The **Navigate** custom role shown in the figure is created as described in Chapter 5. The built-in roles are found in a fresh installation. Each role shown in the **Security** node is permitted to carry out only certain tasks. While the **Browser** role can view reports and resources, manage individual subscriptions and view models, no other activity is permitted. On the other hand, **Content Manager** can do everything as shown in the **Content Manager Properties** page (right-click **Content Manager** and choose **Properties**). It is possible to customize a role by choosing items to be included. The Report Manager can then be used to assign the role to the user as you will be doing in Chapter 5. Readers interested in getting further details on role assignments in deployments (multiple instances, scale-out-deployment) other than the one described in the book should review the material in the Books Online.

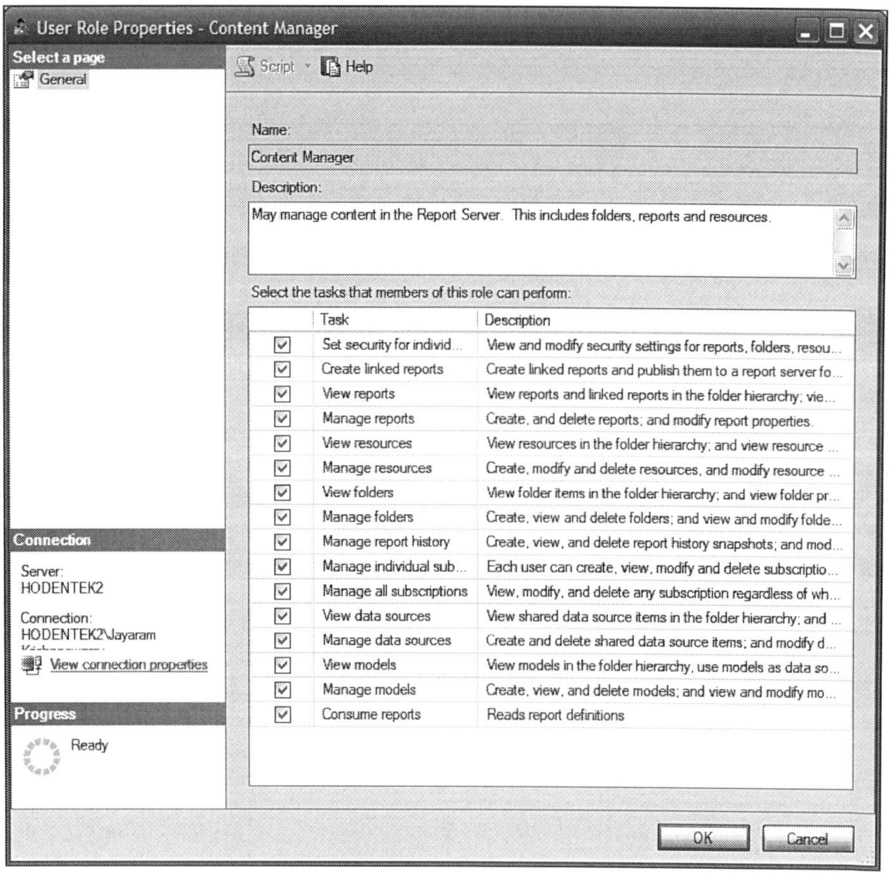

Report Manager

Report Manager is a web application for administering a single Report Server instance from a remote location over HTTP and is covered completely in Chapter 5 with numerous hands-on exercises. It is a SOAP client for the Reporting Services web service. You need IE 6.0 or later and it is only available for Report Servers installed in the native mode.

There are many uses of Report Manager:

- Organizing items on the server by creating, securing and maintaining folder hierarchies.
- View reports and print them, as well as search and set up subscriptions for them.
- Configure report related items such as execution properties, histories and parameters.
- Create report models that feed off Analysis Services and Relational data sources.
- Set security of models and set up access to specific entities in the model.
- Create linked reports to reuse existing reports for use in different scenarios.
- Create shared subscriptions and shared data sources.
- Create data-driven subscriptions to cater to larger number of clients.
- Launch Report Builder to create ad hoc reports that can be saved to/run from Report Server (as of this writing, it launches only Report Builder 1.0 which can still be used to connect to SQL Server 2008 but does not allow to work with the reports. It was originally designed for Reporting Services shipped with SQL Server 2005). This is not to be confused with Report Builder 2.0, which is a separate standalone program and is described completely in this book.

Starting Report Manager

One way to start the Report Manager is by invoking the Reporting Services Configuration Tool (see Chapter 1). Use **Start | All Programs | Microsoft SQL Server 2008 | Configuration Tools | Reporting Services Configuration Tools** to invoke the configuration tools. After connecting to the Report Server instance you can bring up the **Reporting Services Configuration Manager** page as shown in the next figure. For the native mode installation, the URL shown in the screenshot is a link to the Report Manager:

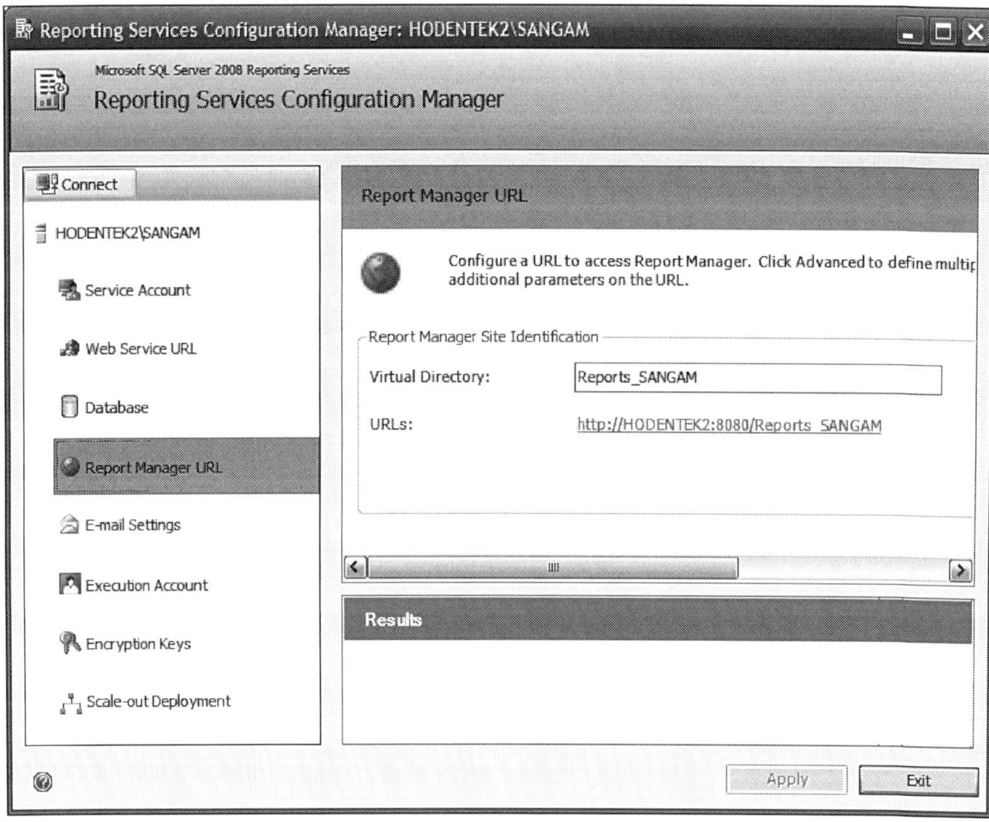

Clicking on the hyperlink **http://Hodentek2:8080/Reports_SANGAM** (which will be different for your installation) will bring up the browser displaying the **Folder.aspx** page as shown:

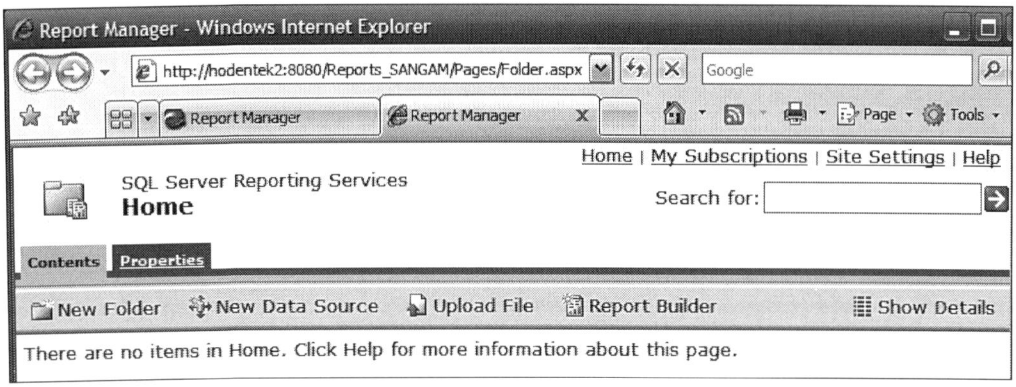

This web page can also be displayed by typing in the following URL in the IE browser: `http://hodentek2:8080/Reports_SANGAM`. The SQL server is on a machine that cannot be accessed from the intranet and hence this is not the **FQDN** (Fully Qualified Domain Name). It is for local access only. Instead of `hodentek2` you can use `localhost` or the "IP Address" of the local network. Port 8080 has been used for HTTP requests, as the default port 80 is used by the installed IIS. If you are configuring HTTPS, then you have to use port 443.

By default, the Report Manager's Home page gets displayed. From here you can:

- Create a new folder
- Create a new data source
- Upload a file
- Invoke the Report Builder 1.0 tool

The current computer user (computer administrator) is also the dbo with Content Manager Role and therefore he has the maximum accessibility to carry on all activities on this page. Besides the Content Manager there are four other built-in roles described earlier that a user can be assigned. We will see the other roles and what they can access in a Chapter 6.

The **Site Settings** link on this page will allow you to carry out such important settings as:

- Report History settings:
    - Limit the copies of Report History, or keep unlimited copies of snapshots in Report History
    - Set Report Execution Timeouts
    - Set Custom Report Builder launch URL
- Security settings:
    - Create New Role assignment. One default editable role, BUILT-IN/Administrator—the System Administrator will be the only role in a fresh install.
- Scheduling:
    - Allows you to create a new schedule

Model designer

For empowering business users who are not conversant with SQL and who would like to generate ad hoc reports, working with report models provides an easy and flexible solution. Report model, while encapsulating all of the database technology, hides the complexity at the same time providing an easy-to-handle view of the data. The model designer interface is used in creating report models.

Model designer is not a separate tool. You invoke the *Model Designer* wizard when you create a BI project of type, Report Model Project (see the section Reporting Support in Visual Studio 2008). Model designer can only generate report models from SQL Server Databases or Oracle databases version 9.2.0.3 or later. You can also create a model based on an Analysis Services Cube. While running a model designer wizard, you can create a data source and a data source view and generate the model based on them. Once a model is designed, it can be further fine-tuned using the Model Design Window. By adding roles to the model, you can establish the accessibility of the model based on roles. You can also delete items if you wish to do so.

Well, what is a Report Model? A Report Model takes a data source and builds a metadata description using the relationships it finds in the data source. The Report Model is a container for the model. The Report Model project will consist of:

- One or more data source files (with `.ds` extension)
- One or more data source view files (with `.dsv` extension)
- One or more Report Model files (with `.smdl` extension)

The Report Model file can be referenced by only one `.ds` and one `.dsv` file.

You can fine-tune the model after it is created by rearranging the model items and add additional model items in the project as shown in the following table:

Item	Description
Entities	A logical collection of model items including source fields, roles, folders and expressions presented in familiar business terms.
Folders	Used for organizing entities, perspectives and other folders to expose frequently used model items, group-related items and archive rarely used ones to aid in user navigation.
Perspectives	A perspective may be created to support role-based access. For example, a subset that is visible to all and a subset that may only be accessible based on role.
Roles, source fields, and expressions	While roles indicate how two entities are related cardinally, source fields are the familiar columns within the database. A source field usually references a single item such as, Employee name. An expression. on the other hand. represents a calculated value `[discount=cost*0.01] discount` using constants and functions utilizing various operators.

Once models are built, they can be published to a Report Server or a SharePoint library. To access the models on the server, users must have permissions to use them in the Report Builder.

Report Builder

SSRS 2008, like its previous version SSRS 2005, is built to address the needs of three different audiences. One audience is the business decision maker (or Business user). The Report Builder is targeted for Business users. These are users who have a deep knowledge of their data but may have either no detailed database knowledge or no serious programming experience. However, they are very much involved in slicing and dicing the available information to get a better handle on their business activity for decision making, analysis or forecasting. Report Builder is an ad hoc report design tool that utilizes a business model built using the available data.

Report Builder in SSRS 2005 was accessed from the Report Manager. You have seen in Chapter 1 that the Report Manager is accessible from the Reporting Services Configuration Manager. The Report Builder interface has the look and feel of Microsoft Office 2007 products such as Excel, Access and Word. Reports built using the Report Builder use the familiar report templates and are no different from reports built otherwise. They also have the same RDL structure. They are managed and secured by the same API. One main difference is that the META data of the model is saved with the report definition file. Drill-through reports created by this model give a fine-grained view of the data to its finest details. This capability is only limited by how finely the model is created and the path that is available from the location in question. Full description and usage of this tool to build reports will be described in Chapter 6.

Report Builder 1.0

Report Builder 1.0 in SQL Server 2008 (accessible from Report Manager) is very much like it was in SSRS 2005. The next figure shows the Report Manager from which you can access the Report Builder.

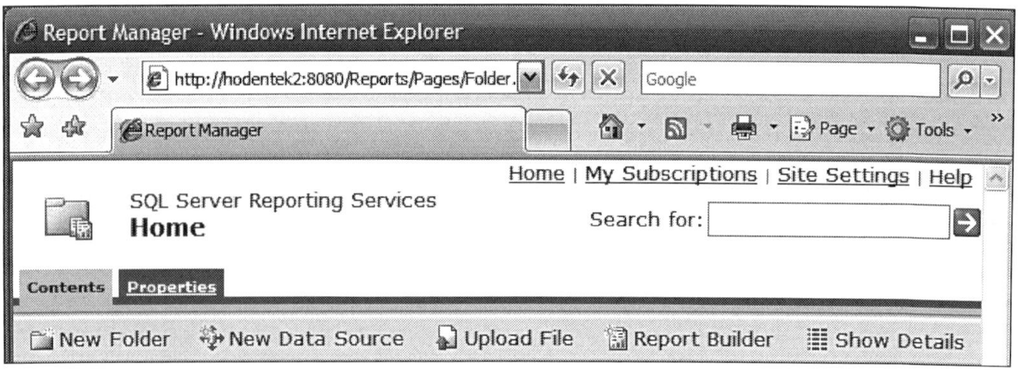

When you click on the **Report Builder** icon in the above window you will launch **Report Builder** window shown in the next screenshot. You will notice that SSRS 2008's Report Manager was invoked to access the Report Builder, but the Report Builder launched is still the version 1.0. This is probably for backward compatibility with SSRS 2005 (remains as an undefined (TBD [to be defined]) item).

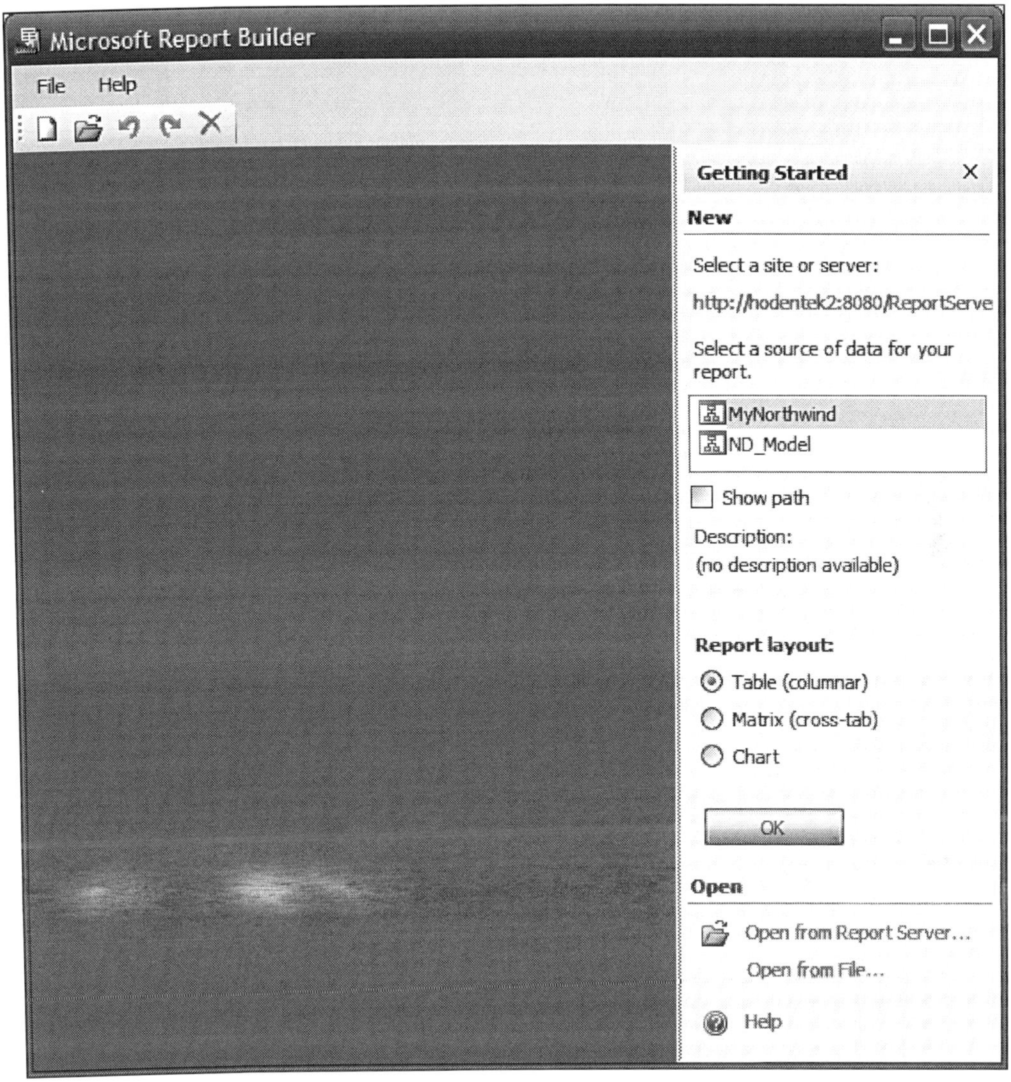

The Report Builder has all the necessary ingredients to fashion a report, such as the data source for the report and the Report layout elements. This tool actually brought into its design environment existing Models (RulePubsx, PubsxModel) created in Visual Studio. It may be noted that as of the RTM, Report Builder 1.0 does not provide any of its intended functionality (`http://hodentek.blogspot.com/2008/06/elaborating-on-report-builder-in-sql.html`).

Report Builder 2.0

Report Builder 2.0 is a feature-rich, client-side report authoring application which fully supports creating and designing reports. Report Builder 2.0 can be used for authoring reports by business and power user audiences. After the report is designed, it can be saved to a chosen location with the default extension `.rdl`. The process of report generation and deployment consists of:

- Define data to be used
- Define a layout for the data display
- Preview to test display
- Save report
- Publish report to a Reporting Services Server or SharePoint site

Report Builder 2.0 is installed when you install SQL Server 2008 RTM. It used to be a separate install in the CTP and RC0 versions. In the latest version of SQL Server 2008 Enterprise edition the Report Builder is a separate installation as well (`http://hodentek.blogspot.com/2008/10/improved-report-builder-20.html`)

Report Builder features

Report Builder 2.0 is fully described in Chapter 6. In this section an overview of the essentials are presented. Report builder is fashioned after the Office 2007 design concept with a "ribbon" that consolidates frequently accessed commands in an easy to follow visual layout. It provides a number of features such as:

- Flexible connection to data
    - Relational data
    - Multidimensional data
    - XML data
    - Custom data
- Connectivity to a variety of data source providers
    - Microsoft .NET managed data providers
    - OLE DB data providers
    - ODBC data sources
    - Table-valued functions and custom data

- Support of a variety of vendor data
    - Oracle
    - Hyperion
    - SQL Anywhere 11
    - Others
- Provide an Improved Report layout scheme
    - Page Orientation, Page Layout, margin sizing and so on are all supported
    - Tabular ---> Column based
    - Matrix --> Summarized--> Use Aggregations
    - Tablix= Table + Matrix
    - Chart --> Graphical
    - Gauges-->Dynamic web-based
    - Free-form
    - Subreports
    - Lists
    - Graphics-->Database based or external graphics
- Support Ad-hoc reporting
    - Create and save reports on the fly.
    - Drillthrough reports and interactive reports
    - Links to subreports and drillthrough reports
    - Parameter based filtering
    - Model based reports providing fine-grained click through reports
- Provide Multiple Presentation/display formats
    - Web and desktop oriented application formats
    - Support HTML, MHTML, PDF, CSV, TIFF, WORD, XML, EXCEL
- Allow Integration with custom or third part controls
- Aid Report Navigation
    - Add bookmarks and document maps for navigating large reports

Extension components

Reporting Services modular architecture is designed for extensibility (`http://msdn.microsoft.com/en-us/library/ms152934.aspx`). The data processing capability, the rendering capability and so on can be extended through the extension components that are integrated with the .NET Framework architecture. Here follows a brief description of these extensions.

Data processing

The Reporting Services data processing extension is a component included with the SQL Server 2008 installation which also installs a configurable Reporting Services instance. It is designed to retrieve a specific type of data source and provide extended functionality during report design and processing. This is the same interface as *System.Data* in the .NET Framework. Since it is data processing only, the read-only mode is implemented.

Rendering

Rendering extensions support the export formats that are available in SSRS. There are three such extensions:

- Data renderers: data only display (support CSV and XML)
- Soft page-break renderers: Maintain format and layout (support MS Excel, Word, MHTML, and ReportViewer Controls)
- Hard page-break renderers: support TIFF and PDF

Scheduling and delivery

Report Server delivery extensions included with out-of-the-box SSRS 2008 to support scheduling and delivery of reports are:

- Report server E-Mail: Uses SMTP Server to email reports
- Report server File Share: for local distribution inside an organization with network file sharing
- Custom extensions are also possible using the API
- Create Subscription and Create Data-Driven Subscription are used to create subscriptions using the delivery extension

Support for reporting in Visual Studio 2008

Visual Studio 2008 is tightly integrated with SQL Server 2008, both of which leverage the .NET framework. Visual Studio 2008 provides all the functionality available in BIDS as well as the ability to integrate reports with both web and Windows programs.

Visual Studio 2008 and BIDS both support report authoring with the capability to work with both reports and report models. The reports authored have the extension RDL and need a Report Server to process them.

However, Visual Studio also supports developing applications that can be hosted on Internet Information Services servers. They can then be processed locally without the need for Report Server. These client processed reports with the extension RDLC can be immediately deployed for intranet-wide distribution from IIS Servers. This support is provided by making available the ReportViewer controls. There are two ReportViewer controls available in Visual Studio, one for web applications and another for Windows applications. The usage of these controls makes it possible to create reports that can be viewed (inside the application) without going through the Report Manager (or Report Server). As described in the earlier sections on Report Manager and Report Server web service, Report Manager is one of the main tools to access Reports deployed on the Report Server.

Reporting Services also makes it possible to go from RDLC to RDL and RDL to RDLC, so that both kinds of reports can be hosted on either IIS or Report Server. This conversion may not be available for all kinds of reports presently as we will see later in *Appendix B*. Also support for converting from RDL to RDLC is not available in the present version of SQL Server 2008.

ReportViewer controls

The reports in Windows or web applications using the ReportViewer controls can be deployed to the Web Server or to the Report Server. Also reports on the Report Server can be integrated with web and Windows applications. We will be seeing the utility of the ReportViewer control in viewing reports in the next chapter with a number of examples. In this section, we look at the report related features of these controls in Visual Studio IDE.

ReportViewer controls have two modes of processing reports. The remote processing mode is the preferred way of processing reports on a Report Server. In the local mode, reports can be processed even if Reporting Services are not installed but a copy of the report is accessible. In this case, the data processing is not handled by the control but by the hosting site. The rendering and viewing of the report are carried out by the control. In the present version of SQL server, the runtime version of these controls is the same as in Visual Studio 2005.

ReportViewer control for Windows applications

You need to start a Windows project by going to **File | New | Project...** in Microsoft Visual Studio 2008. This opens the **New Project** window as shown:

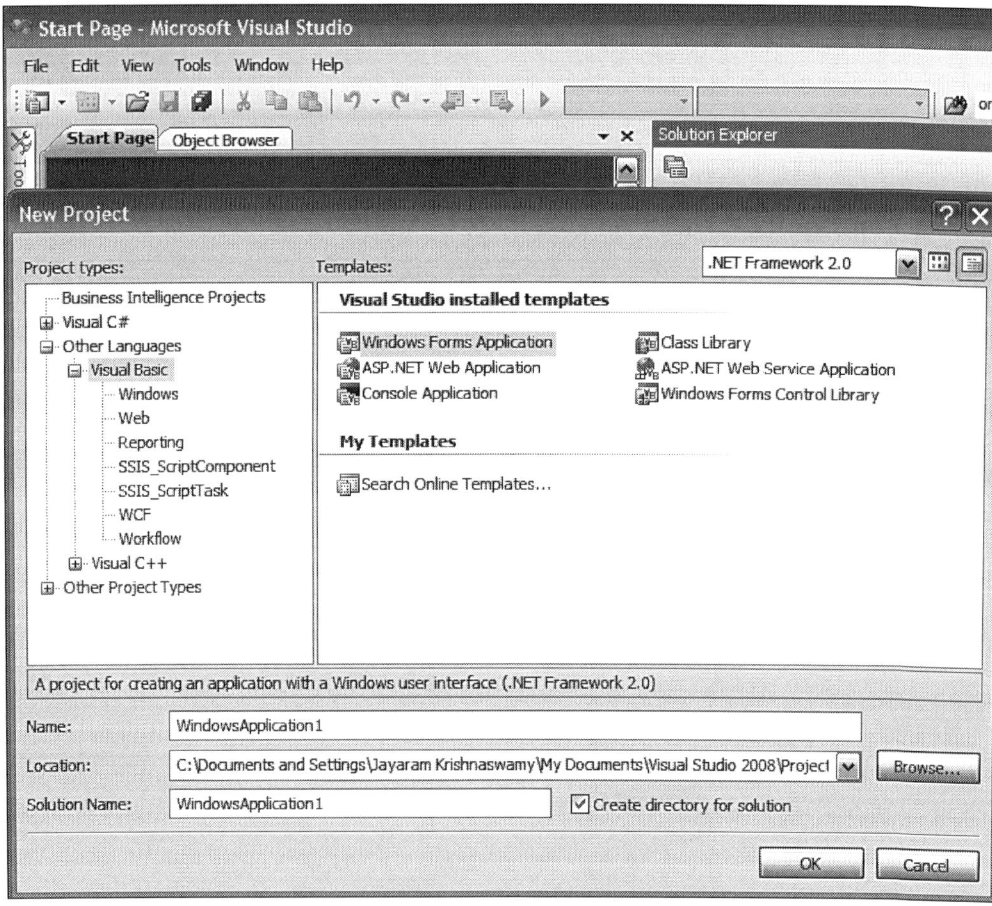

You may change the default name of the application to something of your choice (herein named TestApp). Notice that the application is being setup for .NET Framework 2.0 by default. There are two other options possible, .Net Framework 3 and 3.5. In what way each of these impact SSRS 2008 is largely undocumented (`http://forums.microsoft.com/MSDN/ShowPost.aspx?PostID=3609742&SiteID=1`). It appears that .NET Framework 3.5 is needed for the Reporting Services to perform better.

After you accept the other defaults regarding the .NET Framework and the location, a project folder will be created with a Windows Form, Form1.vb, as shown:

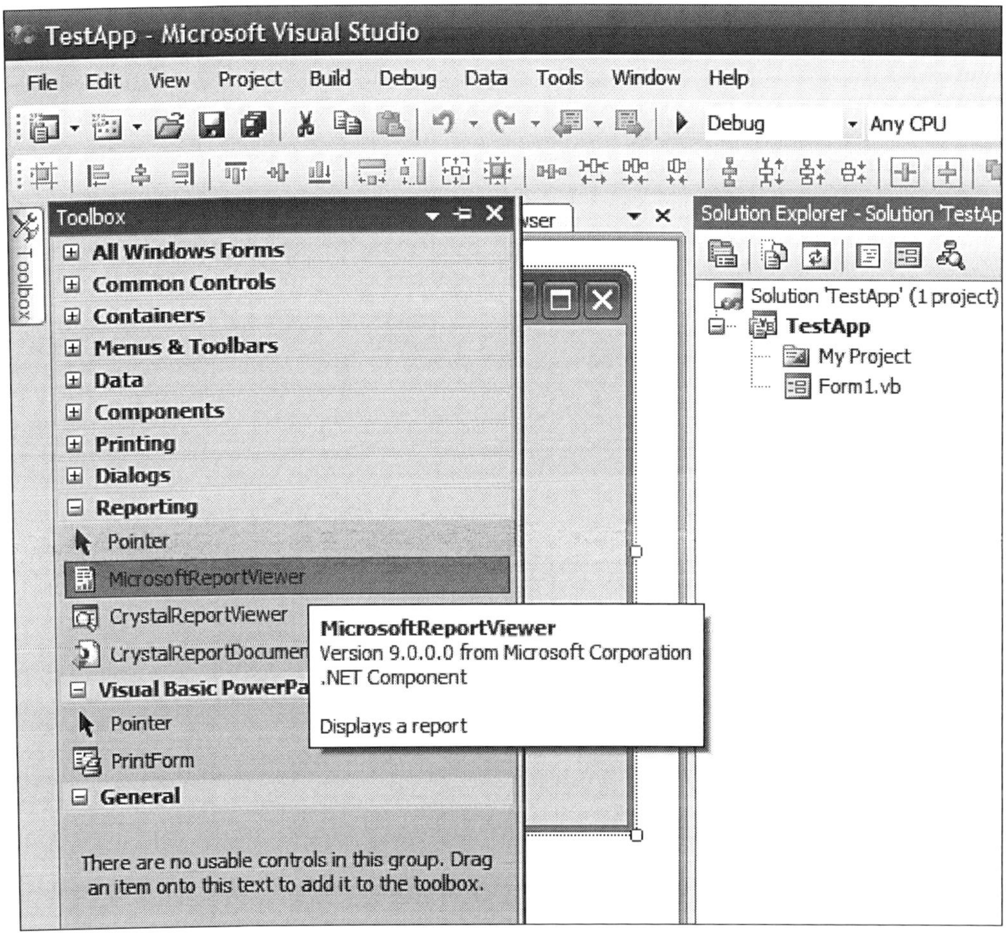

You can bring in the **MicrosoftReportViewer** control by double-clicking the control in the **Toolbox** or dragging-and-dropping it onto the form. This places the control on the form. The screenshot shows the control on the form with the items in the *Smart Tasks* revealed. Notice that in addition to Microsoft ReportViewer there are Crystal Report add-in controls. Using Crystal Reports add-in is yet another option for reporting applications. This will be discussed in Chapter 9.

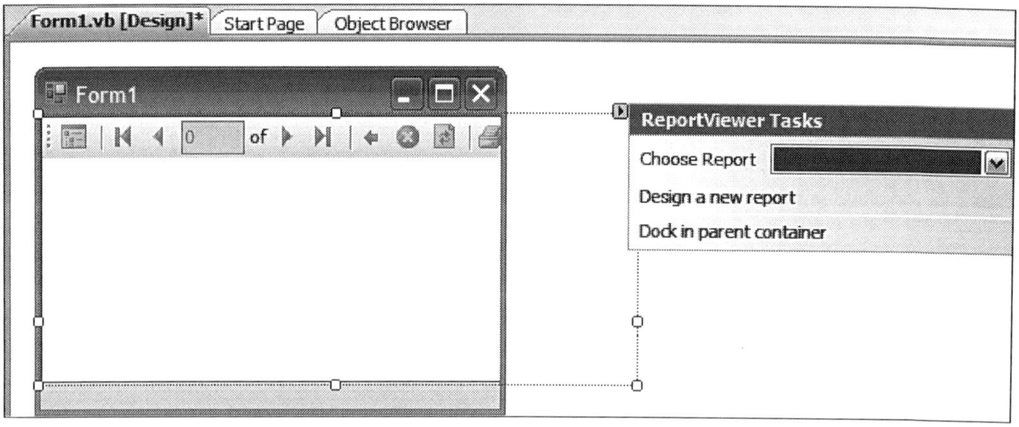

The design-time choices you make are all accessible from the control's properties (partially shown in the next screenshot) as shown in the **Properties** window. The properties window is accessible by right-clicking on the control in **Form1** and choosing **Properties** from the drop-down.

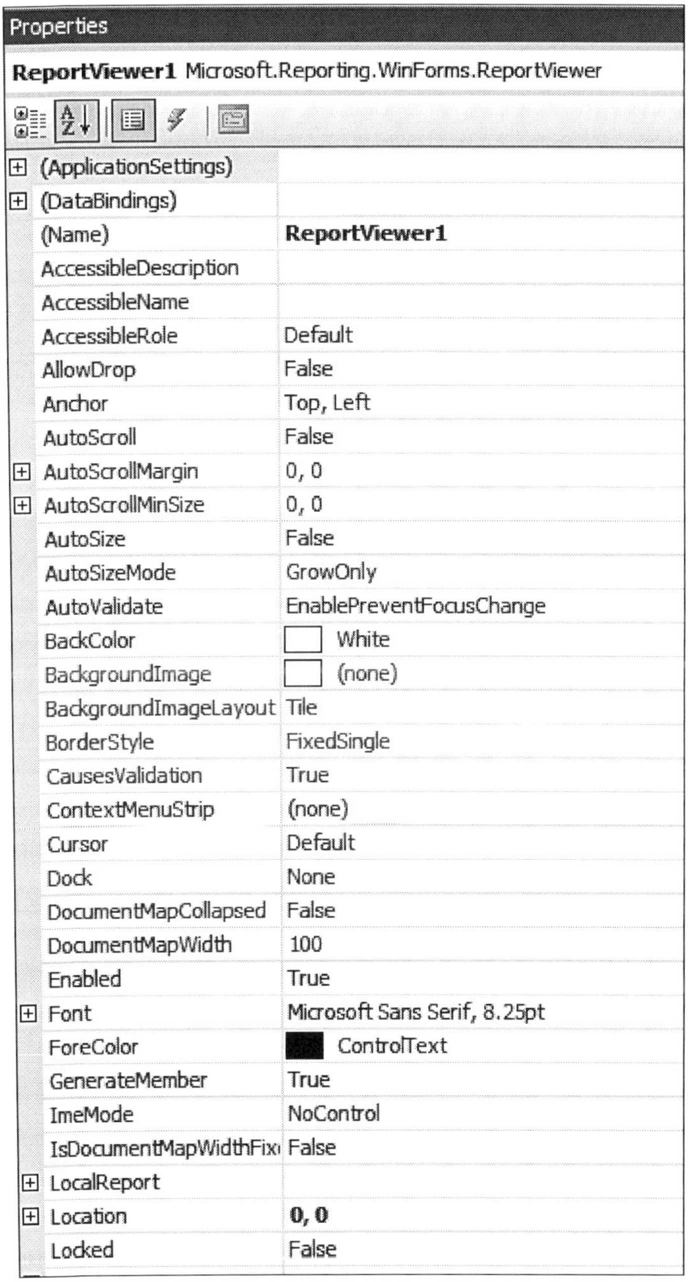

The **Object Browser,** which can be accessed from the **View** menu item, provides a complete picture of the relevant namespaces and classes as shown. This is one of the most important resources that a user must always keep in view, especially if he or she is interested in a programmatic approach to designing reports.

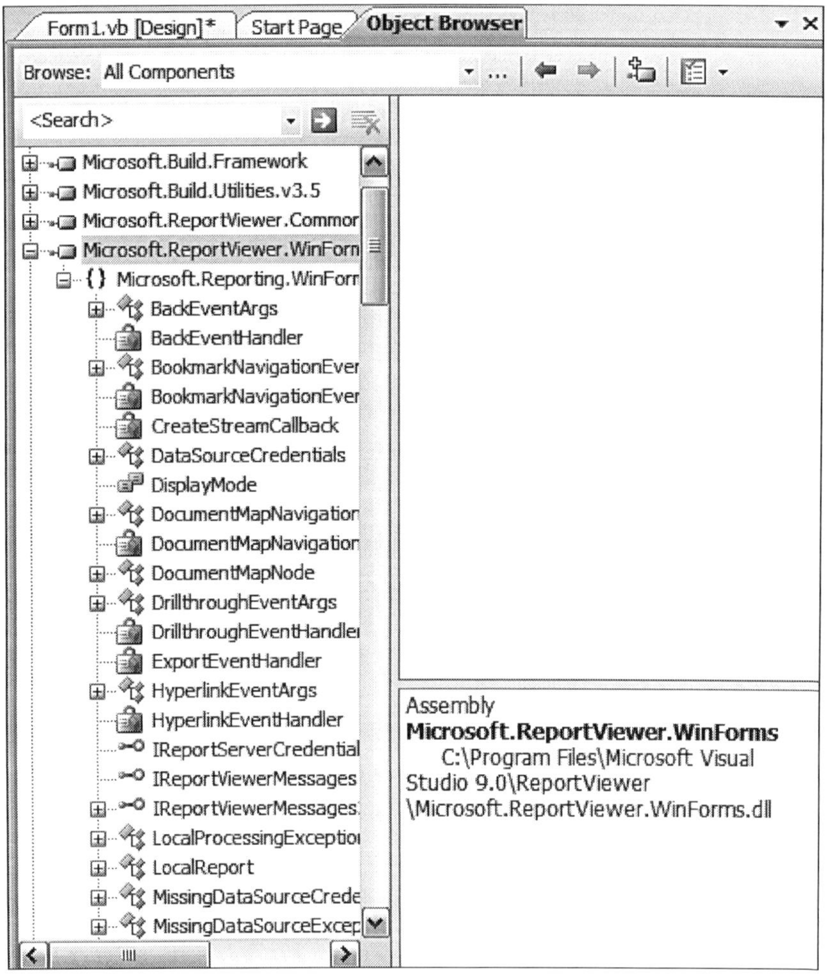

ReportViewer control for Web applications

You need to start a web site project by choosing **File | New | Web Site...**, after you have started Microsoft Visual Studio 2008. This opens the **New Web Site** window as shown:

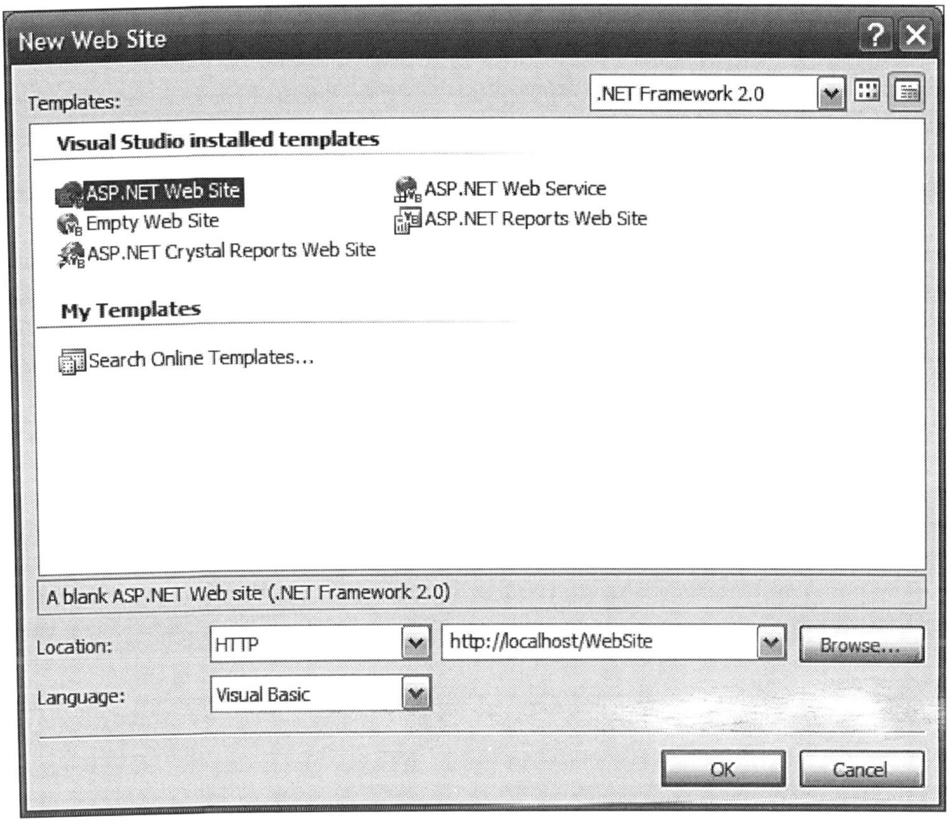

In addition to an ASP.NET website onto which you can place a Microsoft ReportViewer control, you have two other options for reporting: the ASP.NET Reports website and the ASP.NET Crystal Reports website.

As in the case of Windows forms, you can drop a Microsoft ReportViewer control from the toolbox which works in the web environment. The next screenshot shows the **default.aspx** page with the **Microsoft ReportViewer** control. This is a server control. We will see some authoring examples in the next chapter.

Again users will greatly benefit by paying close attention to the properties of the control as well as the information available from the **Object Browser**.

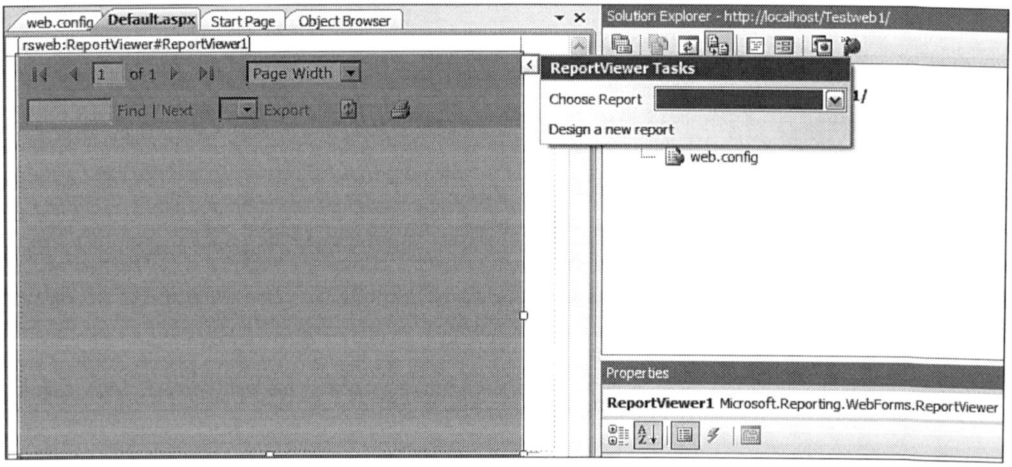

Business intelligence support

The interface that gets displayed when you activate BIDS from the Microsoft SQL Server 2008 shortcut (**Start | All Programs | Microsoft SQL Server 2008 | SQL Server Business Intelligence Development Studio**) is the same as when you create a project from **File | New | Project...** and choose the *Business Intelligence Project*'s **Visual Studio installed templates** as shown:

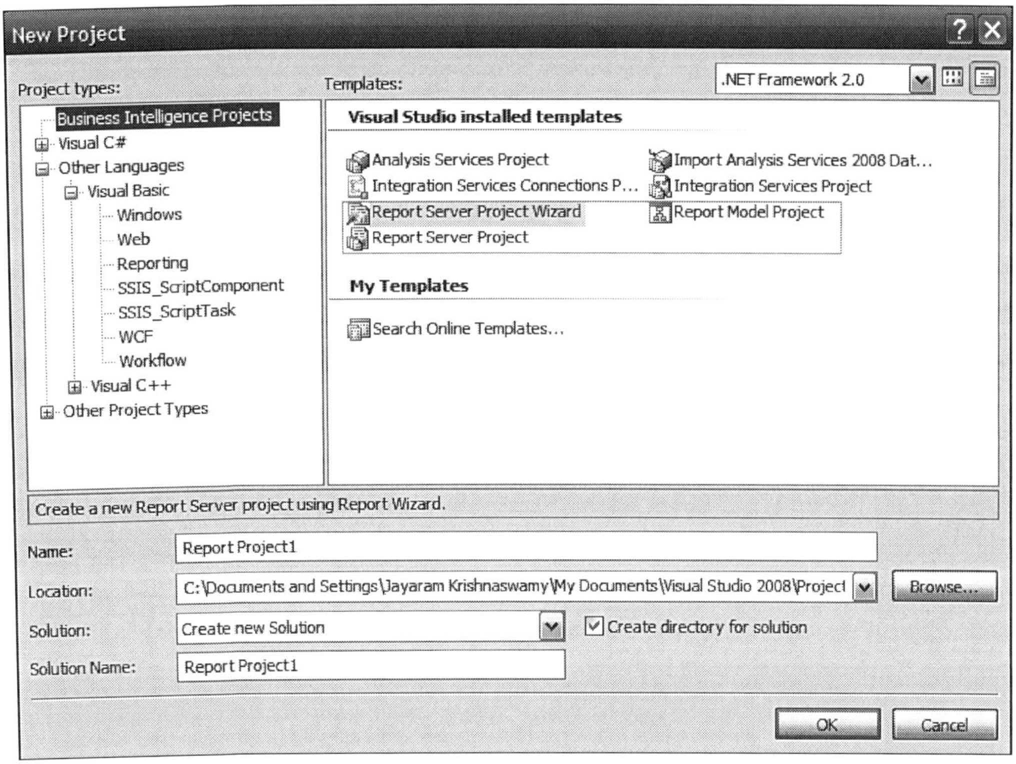

Both the **Report Server Project** and **Report Server Project Wizard** result in a Report Project. In one case it is driven by a wizard. The **Report Model Project** results in creating a report model which can be used for authoring ad hoc reports using the report designer tool, Report Builder 2.0, discussed earlier. Authoring examples created by these project types will be described in future chapters.

Reports from these projects are processed by the Report Server. These can be integrated into applications by three methods:

There is URL access, if ReportViewer controls are not available for some reason. Also URLs are easily sent as links by email for users who wish to view the reports.

Report Server web service (web services SOAP API) is the standard way for developing reporting applications. Report Manager, for example, is a web client that consumes the Report Server web service. The API exposes everything that is needed for not only accessing reports but also modifying reports.

ReportViewer controls help in accessing reports that are deployed to a server or not as described in the earlier section.

Reporting Server configuration file

The information about the Report Server web service, the Report Manager, and background processing are stored in an XML configuration file—`rsreportserver.config`. If you have installed and removed several prior versions of SQL server you must look up the configuration file appropriate for your installation. All reporting services run within a single process and look into this "config" file. This file can be found at the location: `C:\Program Files\Microsoft SQL Server\MSRS10.<Your instance name>\ReportingServices\ReportServer\rsreportserver.config`.

The following table describes what is contained in the `rsreportserver.config` file for the Report Server installed on the machine used in the book. You should look up the details for your installation. The third column shows the values for the nodes in the present installation.

Configuration Item	Description	Present Installation
DSN	This provides the connection string to the database engine that hosts the Report Server databases. This has an encrypted value and gets added to the Config file when the Report Server database is created. For a native mode, it is added to the config file when SQL Server is installed.	

Configuration Item	Description	Present Installation
Connection type	There are two kinds, the Default and Impersonate. The former is appropriate when the SQL Server login or the service account is used to connect to Report Server database. The latter when a Windows user is configured to connect to the Report Server database.	`<ConnectionType>Default` `</ConnectionType>`

LogonUser, LogonDomain and LogonCred	They store the information used to connect to a Report Server from a domain account.	`<LogonUser>`
		`</LogonUser>`
		`<LogonDomain>`
		`</LogonDomain>`
		`<LogonCred>`
		`</LogonCred>`

InstallationID	An identifier used for the Report Server installation. This is not to be modified.
	By default this value is `MSRS10.<Instancename>`
		`<InstanceId>`
		`MSRS10.SANGAM`
		`</InstanceId>`

Configuration Item	Description	Present Installation
SecureConnectionLevel	This relates to the security level chosen for Report Server as well as the Report Manager. The value for this is set by the type of setting you used for URL (HTTP or HTTPS). It has three values, of which 0 is least secure.	`<Add Key= "SecureConnectionLevel" Value="0"/>`
CleanupCycleMinutes	Specifies minutes after which the old sessions or expired snapshots are removed from the Report Server database.	`<Add Key= "CleanupCycleMinutes" Value="10" />`
SQL Command Timeout Seconds	This sets the SQL Command Timeout in minutes.	`<Add Key= "SQLCommandTimeout Seconds" Value="60" />`
MaxActiveReq ForOneUser	Maximum number of reports a user can process at the same time. The default Value 20 is used.	`<Add Key= "DatabaseQueryTimeout " Value="20" />`
RunningRequests ScavengerCycle	Specifies the number of seconds after which expired requests are cancelled.	`<Add Key= "RunningRequests ScavengerCycle " Value="60" />`
Running RequestDbCycle	Checks periodically (default 60 seconds) whether the running jobs exceeded report execution timeout time.	`<Add Key= "RunningRequestsDbCycle" Value="60" />`

Configuration Item	Description	Present Installation
RunningRequestsAge	Specifies interval in seconds (default 30 seconds) when the status of a running job changes from new to running.	<Add Key= "RunningRequestsAge" Value="30" />
MaxScheduleWait	Specifies the number of seconds the Report Server windows service waits for a schedule update by SQL Server Agent service when the Next Run Time is requested.	<Add Key= "MaxScheduleWait " Value="5" />
DisplayErrorLink	When an error occurs this specifies whether a link to more details of the error is available as a hyperlink.	<Add Key= "WebServiceUseFile ShareStorage " Value="false" />
Watson Flags, WatsonDump Onexceptions and WatsonDump ExcludeIf Contains Exceptions	These are used for diagnosing problems, exceptions, storage of log files and so on.	

Configuration Item	Description	Present Installation
URLReservations	This was described in Chapter 1. URL reservation defines HTTP access to the Report Server Web Service and the Report Manager for the current instance. These are reserved and stored in HTTP. SYS when the reporting services are configured.	<URLReservations> <Application> <Name>ReportServerWebService </Name> <VirtualDirectory> ReportServer_SANGAM </VirtualDirectory> - <URLs> - <URL> <UrlString>http://*:8080 </UrlString> <AccountSid>0-0-0-00- 000000000-0000000000- 0000000000-0000</AccountSid> <AccountName>HODENTEK2\\ account_name </AccountName>name </URL> </URLs> </Application> </URLReservations> * SID here is a dummy

Configuration Item	Description	Present Installation

Authentication types	The different types of authentication allowed for the Report Server is specified here. Default settings are added automatically. Custom values may be set by editing with a text editor. Valid values are RSWindows Negotiate, RSWindows Kerberos, RSWindowsNTLM, RSWindowsBasic and Custom.
	
	RSWindowsBasic and RSWindows Kerberos can also be added to have a cumulative effect. Multiple authentications will support different kinds of clients with varying authentications. For accessing from different kinds of browsers it is necessary to keep the RSWindows NTLM.
		`<Authentication>`
		`<AuthenticationTypes>`
		`<RSWindowsNTLM />`
		`</AuthenticationTypes>`
		`<EnableAuthPersistence>true`
		`</EnableAuthPersistence>`
		`</Authentication>`

Configuration Item	Description	Present Installation
Service	This specifies the service settings applicable for the service as a whole. A number of the terms in `Service` are self defining, while others or not. Some of them were explained during the installation. The details for any specific item must be obtained from Microsoft's latest documentation. The enabling and disabling of Reporting Services functionality can be managed using the SQL Server Management Studio.	<Service> <IsSchedulingService>True </IsSchedulingService> <IsNotificationService>True </IsNotificationService> <IsEventService>True </IsEventService> <PollingInterval>10 </PollingInterval> <WindowsServiceUse FileShareStorage> False </WindowsServiceUseFile ShareStorage> <MemorySafetyMargin>80 </MemorySafetyMargin> <MemoryThreshold>90 </MemoryThreshold> <RecycleTime>720 </RecycleTime> <MaxAppDomainUnloadTime>30 </MaxAppDomainUnloadTime> <MaxQueueThreads>0 </MaxQueueThreads> <UrlRoot /> - <Unattended ExecutionAccount> <UserName /> <Password /> <Domain /> </UnattendedExecutionAccount> <PolicyLevel> rssrvpolicy.config </PolicyLevel> <IsWebServiceEnabled>True </IsWebServiceEnabled> <IsReportManagerEnabled>True </IsReportManagerEnabled> -<FileShareStorageLocation> <Path /> </FileShareStorageLocation> </Service>

Configuration Item	Description	Present Installation
UI	This refers to the Report Manager and is not modified for accessing the Report Server in the current instance and should be modified if you are accessing a Report Server in another instance. The PageCountMode refers to the rendering of the report by the Report Manager. There are two possible settings with **Estimate** being the default. The other setting is "Actual". With **Estimate** the page count calculation is made during the viewing of the report, as it is rendered. With Actual, the entire report needs to be processed before it is rendered and may delay in rendering.	<UI> <ReportServerUrl /> <PageCountMode>Estimate</PageCountMode> </UI>
Extensions	Summarized in the next table	

If you want to know the URL reservations for your installation you can run the **Httpcfg** tool. This is generally found at `C:\` or `C:\windows\Support\Tools\Support.cab`.

You can run this from command line as in:

```
C:\>query
```

This will provide a help file shown here:

```
C:\>httpcfg query

Usage: httpcfg ACTION STORENAME [OPTIONS]

    ACTION                         - set | query  | delete

    STORENAME                      - ssl | urlacl | iplisten

    [OPTIONS]                      - See Below

Options for ssl:
    -i IP-Address                  - IP:port for the SSL certificate (record key)

    -h SslHash                     - Hash of the Certificate.

    -g GUID                        - GUID to identify the owning application.

    -c CertStoreName               - Store name for the certificate. Defaults to
                                     "MY". Certificate must be stored in the
                                     LOCAL_MACHINE context.

    -m CertCheckMode               - Bit Flag
                                        0x00000001 - Client certificate will not be

                                                     verified for revocation.
                                        0x00000002 - Only cached client certificate
                                                     revocation will be used.
                                        0x00000004 - Enable use of the Revocation
                                                     freshness time setting.
                                        0x00010000 - No usage check.

    -r RevocationFreshnessTime     - How often to check for an updated certificate
                                     revocation list (CRL). If this value is 0,
                                     then the new CRL is updated only if the
                                     previous one expires. Time is specified in
                                     seconds.

    -x UrlRetrievalTimeout         - Timeout on attempt to retrieve certificate
                                     revocation list from the remote URL.
                                     Timeout is specified in Milliseconds.

    -t SslCtlIdentifier            - Restrict the certificate issuers that can be
                                     trusted. Can be a subset of the certificate
                                     issuers that are trusted by the machine.

    -n SslCtlStoreName             - Store name under LOCAL_MACHINE where
                                     SslCtlIdentifier is stored.

    -f Flags                       - Bit Field
                                        0x00000001 - Use DS Mapper.
                                        0x00000002 - Negotiate Client certificate.
                                        0x00000004 - Do not route to Raw ISAPI
                                                     filters.

Options for urlacl:
    -u Url                         - Fully Qualified URL. (record key)
    -a ACL                         - ACL specified as a SDDL string.

Options for iplisten:
    -i IPAddress                   - IPv4 or IPv6 address. (for set/delete only)

C:\>
```

The Httpcfg query provides the following information for the current installation.

```
C:\>Httpcfg query urlacl
    URL : http://*:2869/
    ACL : D:(A;;GX;;;LS)
------------------------------------------------------------------------------
    URL : http://+:8731/Design_Time_Addresses/
    ACL : D:(A;;GX;;;IU)
------------------------------------------------------------------------------
    URL : http://+:80/Temporary_Listen_Addresses/
    ACL : D:(A;;GX;;;WD)
------------------------------------------------------------------------------
    URL : http://*:8080/ReportServer_SANGAM/
    ACL : D:(A;;GX;;;S-1-5-21-163234558-2721018899-1066107519-1005)
------------------------------------------------------------------------------
    URL : http://+:8080/Reports_SANGAM/
    ACL : D:(A;;GX;;;S-1-5-21-163234558-2721018899-1066107519-1005)
------------------------------------------------------------------------------
    URL : http://+:10243/WMPNSSv3/
    ACL : D:(A;OICI;KA;;;NS)
```

[ACL for ReportServer and ReportManager have been removed in the above.]

Summary of Extensions

There are several extensions as shown below in the <Extension/> node:

```
<Extensions>
+ <Delivery>
+ <DeliveryUI>
+ <Render>
+ <Data>
+ <SemanticQuery>
+ <ModelGeneration>
+ <Security>
+ <Authentication>
+ <EventProcessing>
  </Extensions>
```

The following table provides an overview of these extensions. Microsoft documentation should be followed to configure them for custom use.

Extension	Summarized Description
Delivery	Report Server FileShare, Report Server Email, ReportServerDocumentLibrary and Null are the various extensions in delivery.
DeliveryUI	Report Server Email and Report Server FileShare are provided in this installation.
Render	The rendering extensions provided in the out of the box installation are XML, NULL, CSV, PDF, RGDI, HTML4.0, MHTML, EXCEL, RPL, IMAGE and WORD.
Data	The default data processing extensions which include the following: SQL, OLEDB, OLEDB-MD, ORACLE, ODBC, XML, SAPBW, ESSBASE, SSIS and SAP.This section should not be modified except to insert a custom extension.
SemanticQuery	The semantic query processing provides support for three of the following data providers: SQL Server, ORACLE, TERADATA and OLEDB-MD (Analysis Server). This section should not be modified.
ModelGeneration	This extension supports creation of model generation with Server, TERADATA and OLEDB-MD (Analysis Services Multidimensional data). This is not to be modified.
Security	This extension works together with the Authentication node described earlier. This is also not to be modified except when a custom extension is created.
Authentication	This includes both default and custom extensions. In the current installation there is only the default Windows Authentication extension.
EventProcessing	This extension is for the default event handling and is used internally. This is not to be changed. SnapShot, Time Subscription and CacheUpdate extensions are found in the current installation.

Summary

The salient features of the architectural details of the SQL Server Reporting Services 2008 were summarized. The various components and tools that enable an end-to-end support for all reporting activities were described.

3
Report Integration with Microsoft ReportViewer Controls

ReportViewer controls, which are freely redistributable, are a part of the VS 2005 \VS2008 software suites. They can embed reports into both window and web-based applications. They can be dragged and dropped into reports like any other Microsoft control and assist in designing reports by using the Report Designer, (included in Standard Edition and above) an integral part of Visual Studio. They are supported by .NET Framework versions 2.0 and above. Report templates are available for all versions, although 2.0 is the most popular. ReportViewer controls do not require the installation of an SQL Server.

Reports in Visual Studio 2008 can be created using the links to report wizard provided by Microsoft ReportViewer controls in the toolbox or from predefined templates for both windows and ASP.NET applications.

There are two types of ReportViewer controls in Visual Studio 2008 toolbox:

- ReportViewer Web Server control for ASP.NET Pages for web hosting
- ReportViewer Windows Forms control for report display in Windows Forms applications

The type of control depends on the project type chosen in Visual Studio. These controls also provide interfaces to create reports facilitated by wizards or by features in templates. We will be looking at authoring reports and previewing them using Visual Studio 2008. The reports you will be creating in the hands-on exercises are barebones reports, as the objective is to get started with the essentials of retrieving data and displaying it. You will be creating a variety of reports beyond what you see in this chapter in Chapter 7.

In the Visual Studio 2008 IDE there are two ways a report-based Windows Application Project can be created. The Reports application project is a windows project containing a Windows form which contains an embedded ReportViewer control. It starts off with a Report Designer as soon as it is created. In the other option, a ReportViewer control is dragged by the user to begin the Report generation using a Report Wizard.

The ASP.NET Reports web site provides a default web page containing a ReportViewer control. It also starts off with a Report Wizard creating a report definition file to be associated with the ReportViewer control.

ReportViewer features

ReportViewer controls are tools used by any user to view reports generated using the SQL Server Reporting Services' Report Builder tool. They are also used to view desktop and intranet web hosted reports generated by Report Wizards in Visual Studio. In this case, they automatically wake up the wizards as soon as they are instantiated on a windows form or a web page.

ReportViewer controls have a view area to display the report and a configurable toolbar in a typical report, the like of which you will be designing in this chapter as well as in others. This is the report you will be designing in *Hands-on 3.1*.

Toolbar

The toolbar, configurable both in design and at run time, provides a large number of features both in windows as well as in the web versions. All features in the Windows version are enabled to display by default, and two of the features are disabled in the web version. Some of the features, such as a document map, navigation (the interactive features like Document Map are described in *Hands-on 7.2* in Chapter 7), controls for a multi-page report, zoom, print, export functionality, and so on are shown in the following screenshot. Some features may be enabled (or disabled) depending on the type of report and the one shown here corresponds to the report you will be creating in the hands-on exercises.

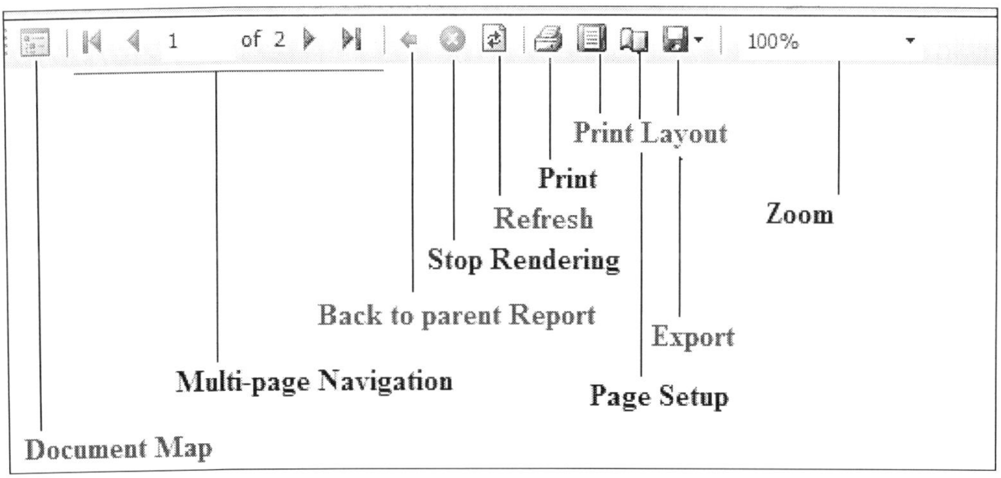

The toolbar items may be modified using the **Property** window of the **ReportViewer** control shown in its default state (for a Windows ReportViewer control). The processing mode enables you to specify whether the report is processed locally, or in the remote mode. Processing modes have been described in Chapter 2. For remote processing, a **Report** file should exist on the report server as you will see in Chapter 8.

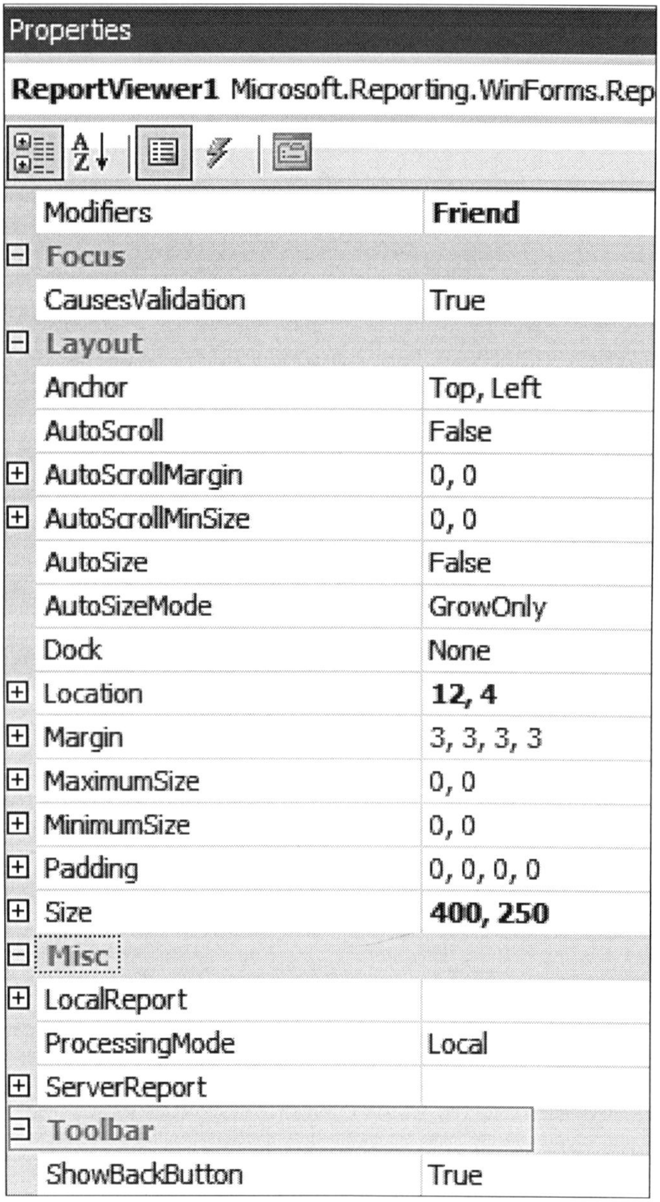

Like other Visual Studio controls, the IDE provides programmatic interfaces to interact with the ReportViewer control using code as shown. A dummy procedure is used to display the accessible properties and methods of the control in the intellisense drop-down menu. The accessible properties of ReportViewer can be displayed as in the code, if a ReportViewer is instantiated. Using the programmatic interface to customize a report at run time can be achieved as you will see in Chapter 8.

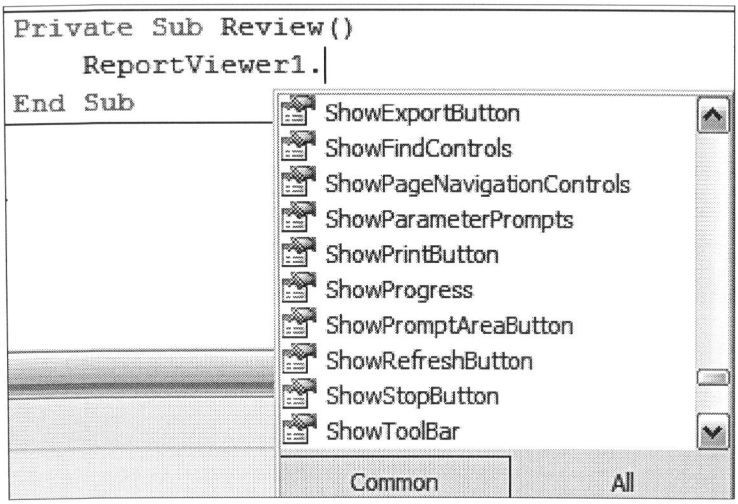

Difference between web server and Windows forms versions

While both types of controls have the same name, Microsoft ReportViewer and are available in Visual Studio 2008, there are obvious differences because of the differences in the environment in which they are used. These differences replicated from the Microsoft web site (`http://msdn.microsoft.com/en-us/library/ms251771.aspx`) are shown in the following table:

Function	RV Web Control	RV Windows Control
Where used	Designing an ASP.NET web application	Designing a Windows Application
Default Presentation Format	HTML	Graphic Device Interface
Report Processing	Configurable for asynchronous processing	Local report processed as a Windows Background Process Configurable for asynchronous processing

Function	RV Web Control	RV Windows Control
Printing	Uses an ActiveX Control for reports on remote server For locally processed reports, use report export functionality to other formats	Uses print functionality of OS
Deployment	Deployment should take session information and web farm configuration For reports on a remote server, user authentication and access to report data sources should be provisioned	Like any windows application
Browser requirement	IE 6.0 or above with scripting enabled to use full functionality of the control	No need of a browser

Hands-on 3.1: Using ReportViewer control for Windows

In this section you will be working with the ReportViewer control for a Windows Forms application. While the ReportViewer control appears to be the same for Windows and the web, they are slightly different.

Getting ready

To display a report in a desktop application you need to embed a ReportViewer control on a Windows Form. In this hands-on exercise, the usage of a Microsoft ReportViewer control in a Windows environment will be described in a step-by-step procedure. Make sure that you have installed Visual Studio 2008 SP1 (not the beta version).

Follow the steps

The following steps are necessary to complete this activity:

- Create a windows project
- Add a ReportViewer Control to the form
- Configure the report using the Report Wizard
    - Configure the data source
    - Design the layout of the report
    - Preview the report

Create a Windows project

1. Open the Visual Studio 2008 IDE from its shortcut accessible from **Start | All Programs | Microsoft Visual Studio 2008.**
2. Click on **File | New | Project...** to open the **New Project** window as shown.

   Click on **Windows Forms Application** under **Visual Studio installed templates**. Change the default name **WindowsForm1** to **MRVWin**.

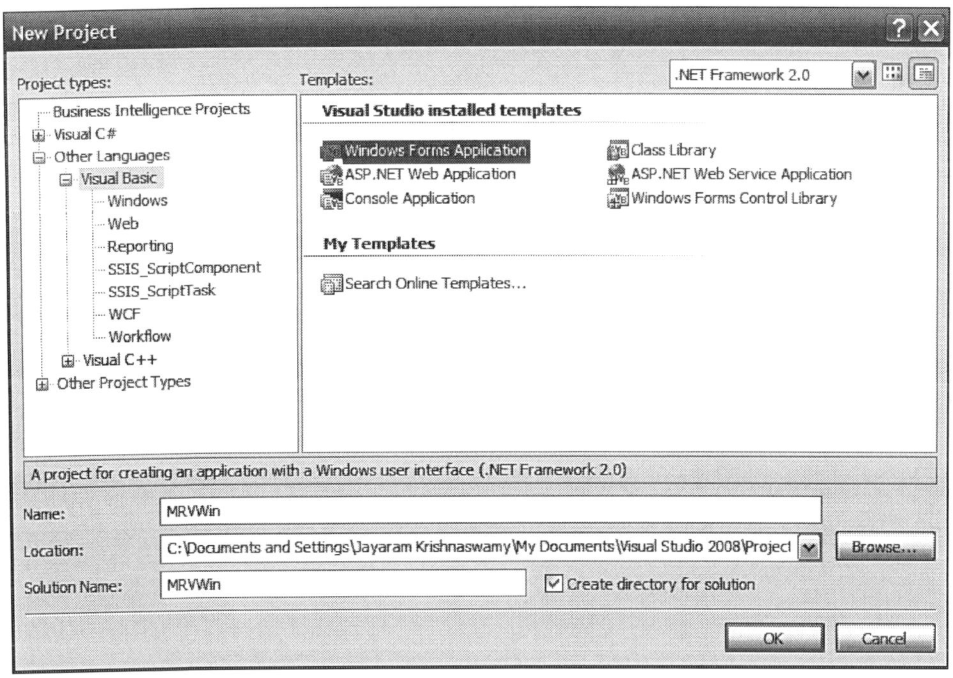

3. After providing a name, use the **Browse...**button to select a location for your application. Click **OK**.

   This creates a project with the chosen name and creates a tree structure for the project with a default Windows form **Form1** as shown.

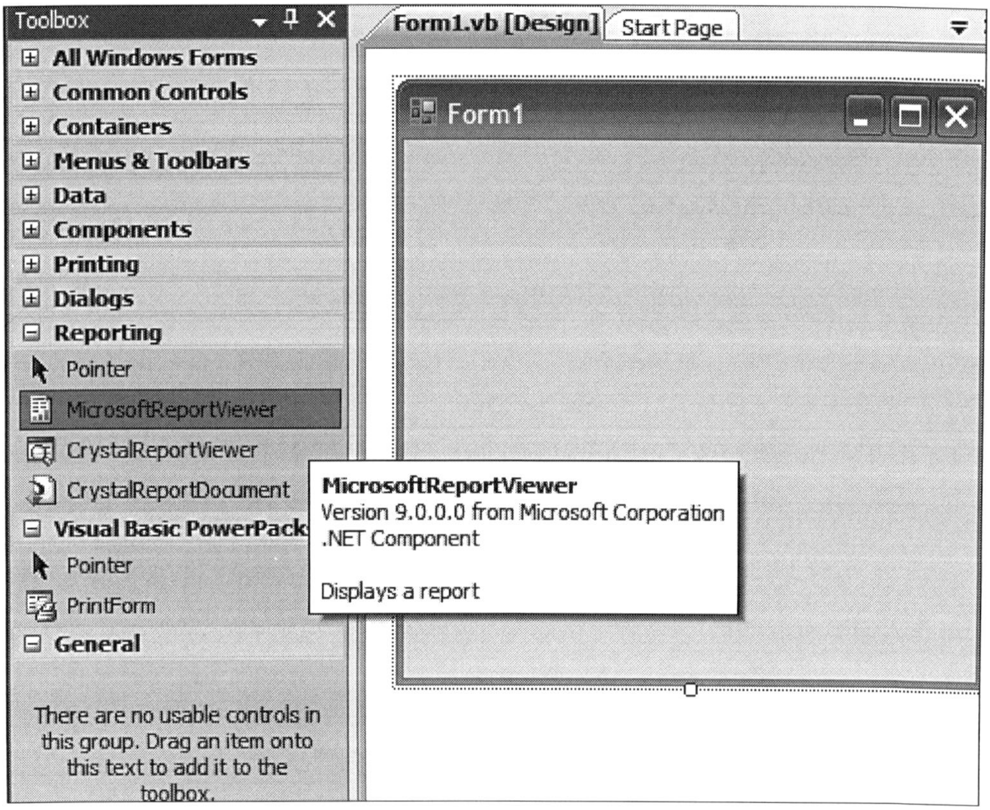

Visual Studio 2008 supports targeting projects on three different .NET Framework versions (see `http://hodentek.blogspot.com/2008/01/multi-version-support-in-vs-2008.html`). The project in this exercise is targeted to .NET 2.0. You can change the targeted version in the Project properties' advanced compiler options. To learn about creating a report application with 3.5 enabled and its effect, read this post on MSDN: `http://forums.microsoft.com/MSDN/ShowPost.aspx?PostID=3609742&SiteID=1`.

Add a ReportViewer control

4. In the **Toolbox,** double click the **MicrosoftReportViewer** Control.

   After a little while, the Microsoft ReportViewer control, **ReportViewer1**, is inserted into the form.

5. Click on the *Smart Tasks* arrow to display the **ReportViewer Tasks** as shown:

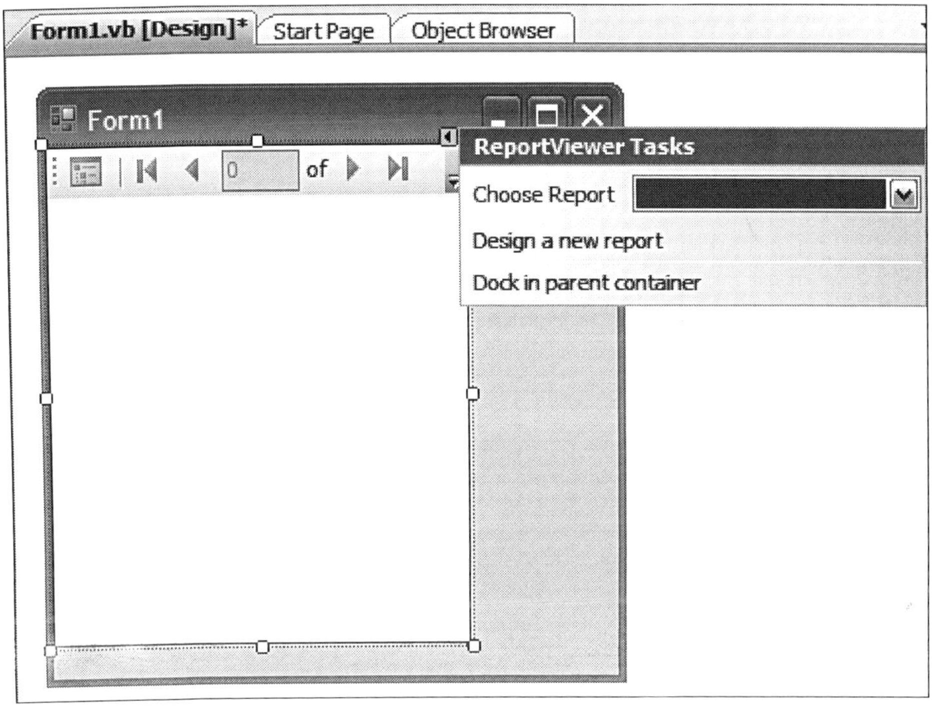

[The Smart Tasks menu can expand or collapse depending on the choices you make. You need to adjust the ReportViewer control size and the Form1's size as needed, depending on the number of columns you bring into the report. You can access and change the form's size and report size from their properties windows.]

Configure the report using the Report Wizard

6. Click on **Design a new report** in the **ReportViewer Tasks** drop-down menu.

   This opens the Welcome to the Report Wizard page of **Report Wizard** as shown in the next figure.

7. Read the notes on this wizard which explains the steps involved in generating a report.
8. Click on the **Next** button.

   This brings up the **Data Source Configuration Wizard**'s **Choose a Data Source Type** page as shown:

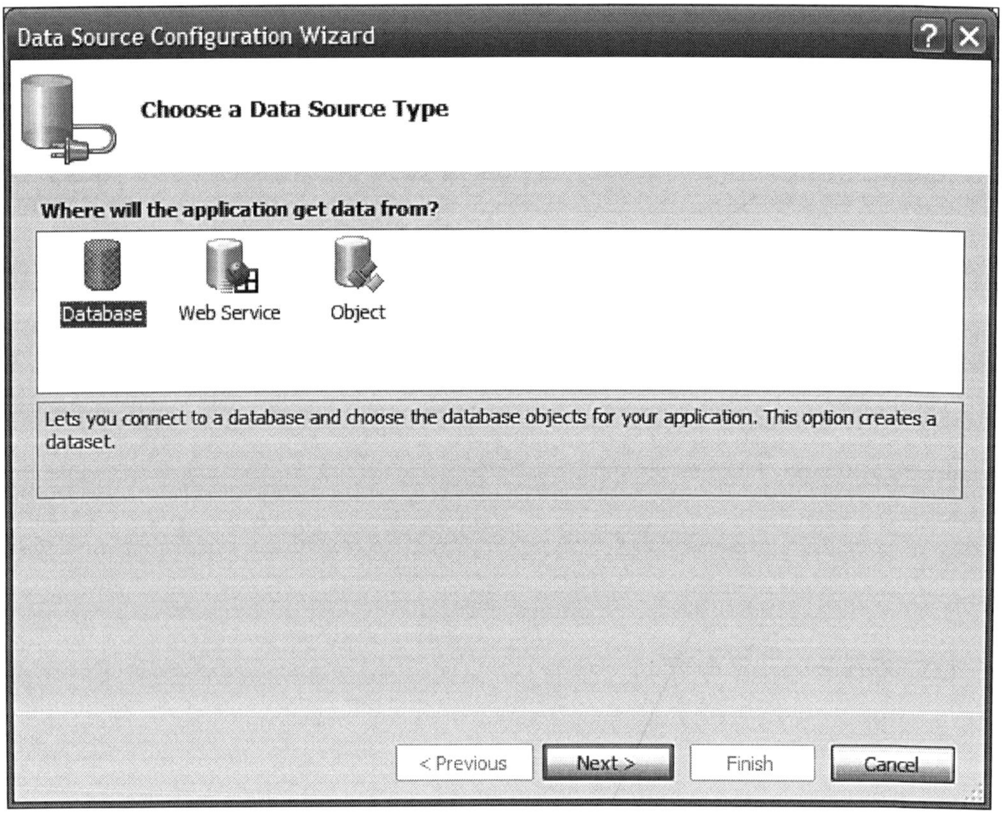

Configure the Data Source

The data can come from a variety of sources. In this cases you will be using data from database. After getting connected to the database you will also retrieve the required information from the database and you will be doing these in the next few steps:

9 Accept the default **Database** as the source of data and click on the **Next** button.

This brings up the **Choose Your Data Connection** page. This is in case there are some existing connections of which one of the connections may show up as the default connection.

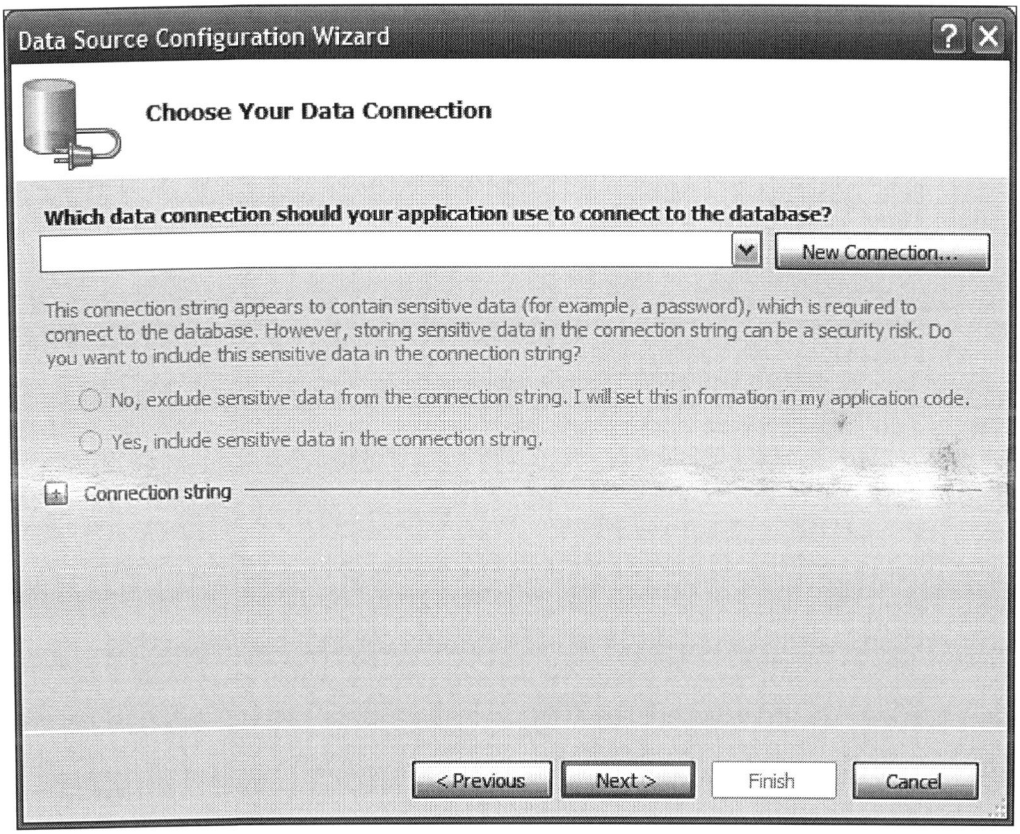

10. Click on the button, **New Connection...**

    The **Add Connection** window is displayed as shown with the default data source **Microsoft SQL Server Compact 3.5(.NET Framework)**. You will be using the `TestNorthwind` database in the named instance of SQL Server 2008 (see Chapter 1).

11. Click on the **Change...** button.

    This brings up the **Change Data Source** window which displays the default data source.

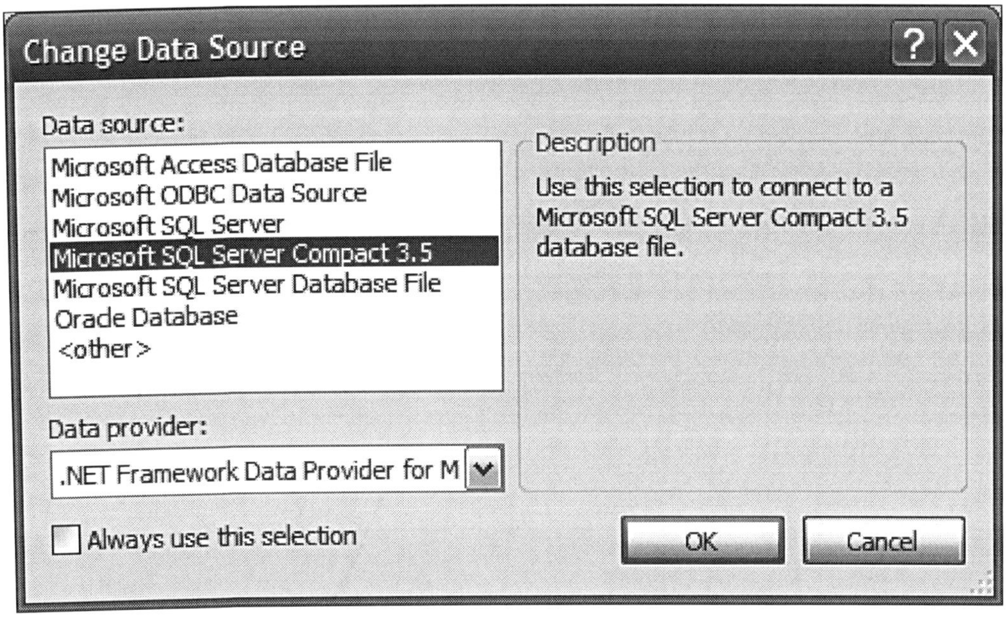

12. Highlight **Microsoft SQL Server** and click on the **OK** button.

> Provider Selection:
>
> This selection uses SQLOLEDB, a .NET Framework data provider for OLE DB. It is also possible to use an ODBC source, but the default SQLOLEDB provider is recommended as it provides optimum performance.

This displays the **Add Connection** window with **Microsoft SQL Server (OLEDB)** as the source as shown:

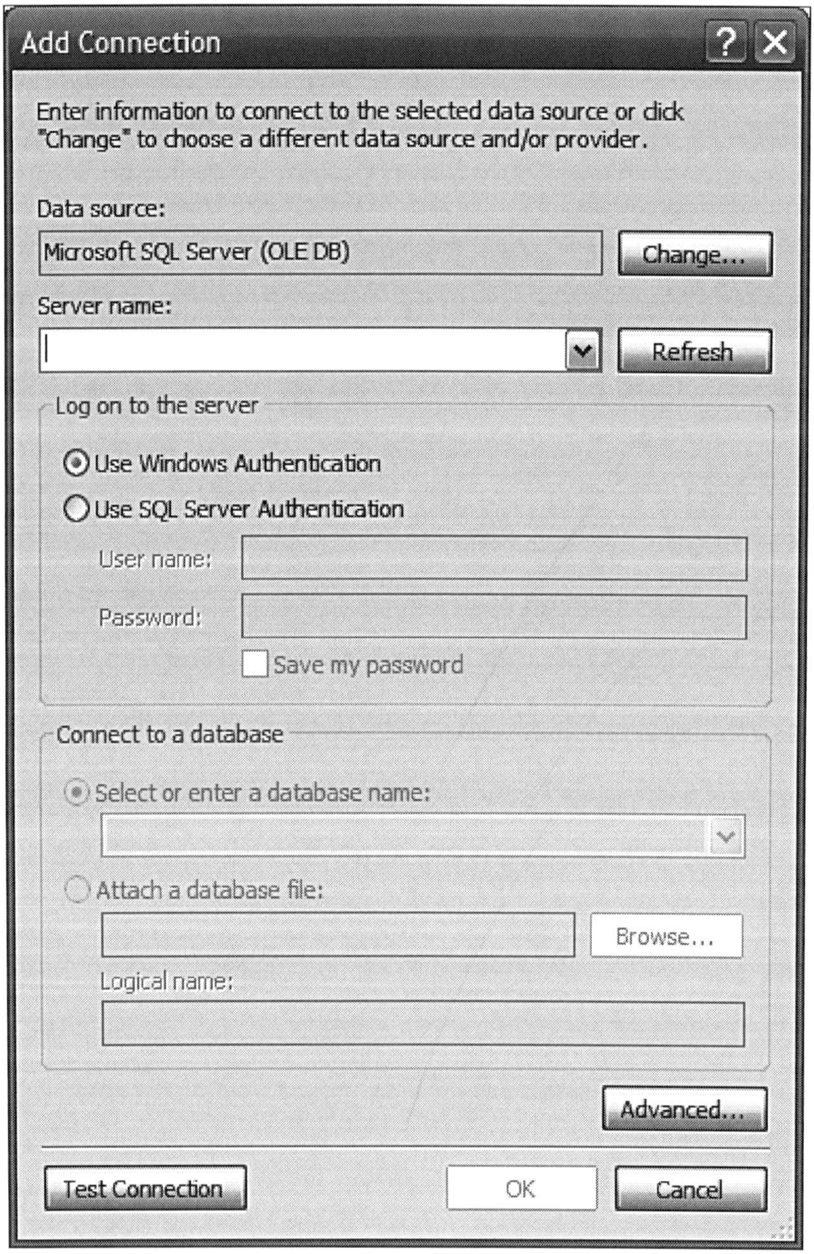

13. Click on the drop-down handle corresponding to **Server name**.

    The drop-down shows a list of SQL Server instances (local as well as networked) that are available. You may have a different list depending on the SQL Servers on your machine.

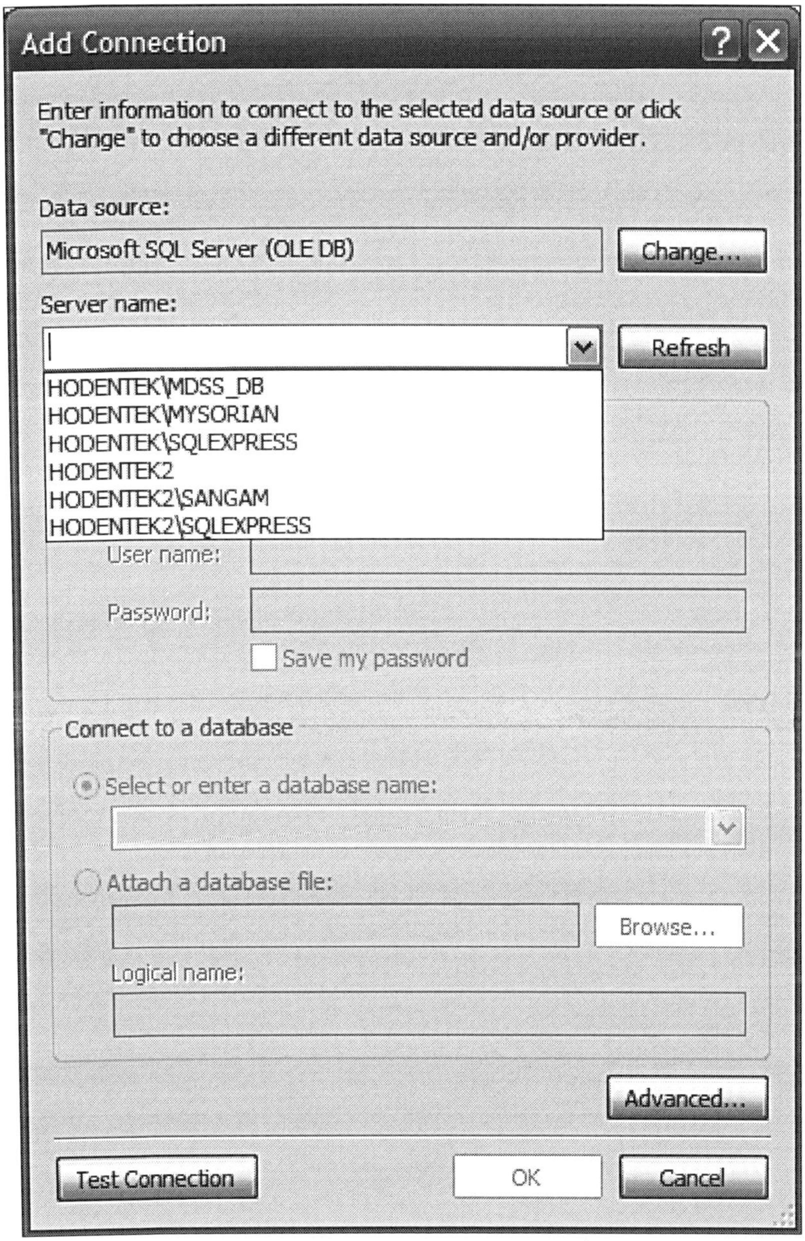

14. Click on **HODENTEK2\SANGAM**, the named instance of SQL Server 2008 (local).

    This gets entered into the **Server name** field.

15. Accept the default **Use Windows Authentication** and click on the drop-down handle corresponding to **Select or enter a database name** field.

    This displays a list of databases on the SANGAM Server as shown. If your server's authentication mode is set to **Use SQL Server Authentication**. You need to have the authentication information (you would have this if you installed the SQL Server) or you should obtain this form your DBA.

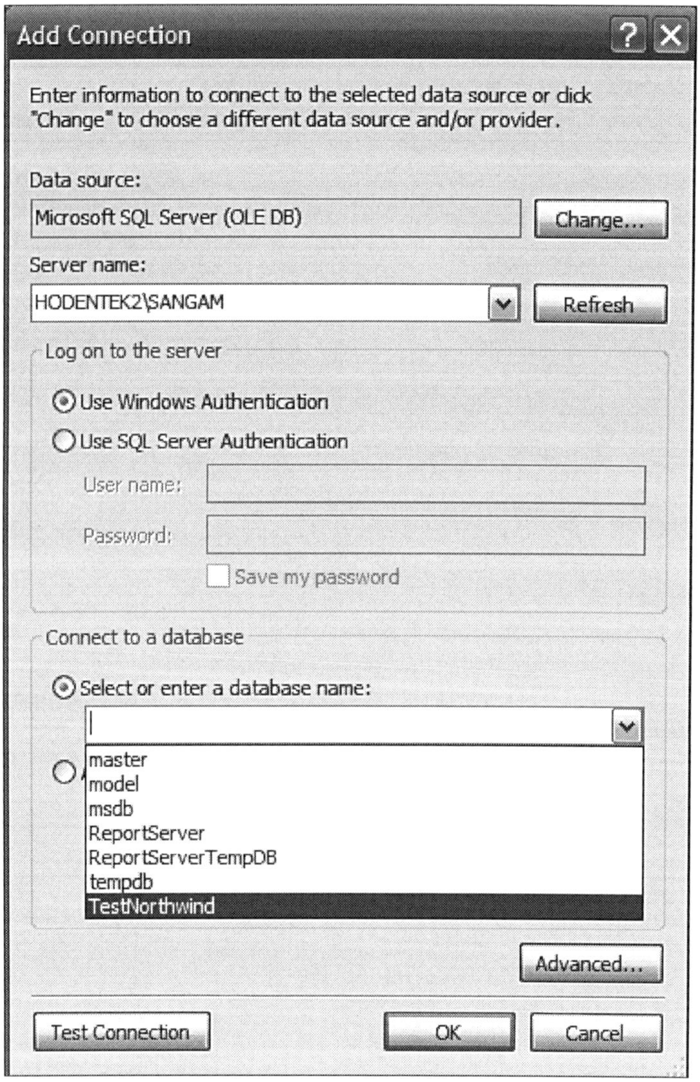

16. Choose **TestNorthwind** and click on the **Test Connection** button.

    The success of this connection will be displayed in a **Microsoft Visual Studio** message box. As long as the connection information is correct (the server is available and the authentication information is correct) there is little chance of encountering a problem. If the server is stopped for any reason make sure it is restarted. For correctness of authentication you may need to check with your DBA.

17. Click the **OK** button in the message box as well as **OK** button in the **Add Connection** window.

    This will bring you back to the **Data Source Configuration Wizard** window with the connection information you configured earlier displayed in the **Connection String** field (shown expanded).

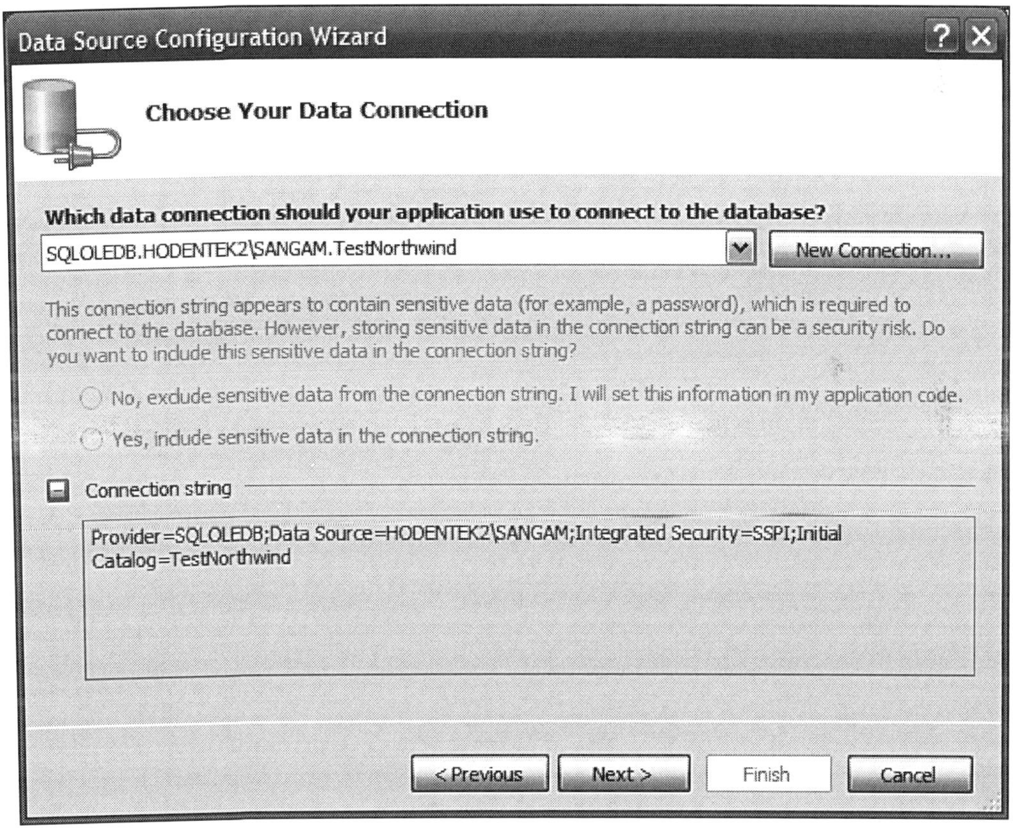

18. Click on the **Next** button.

    This will display the **Save the Connection String to the Application Configuration File** window as shown. Read the instructions in this window.

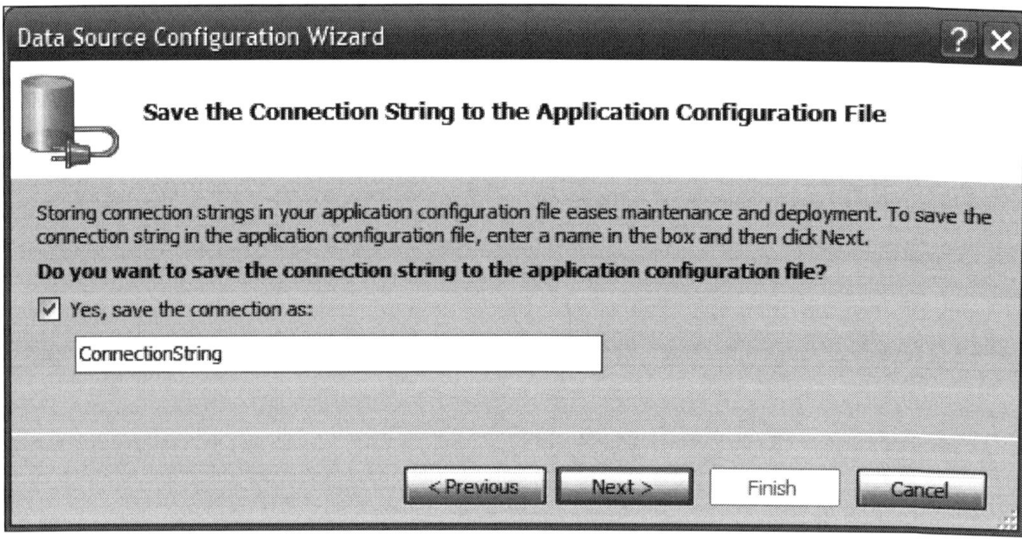

19. Click on the **Next** button.

    After a few seconds the accessible objects in the `TestNorthwind` database will be displayed in **the Choose Your Database Objects** page of the **Data Source Configuration Wizard** as shown:

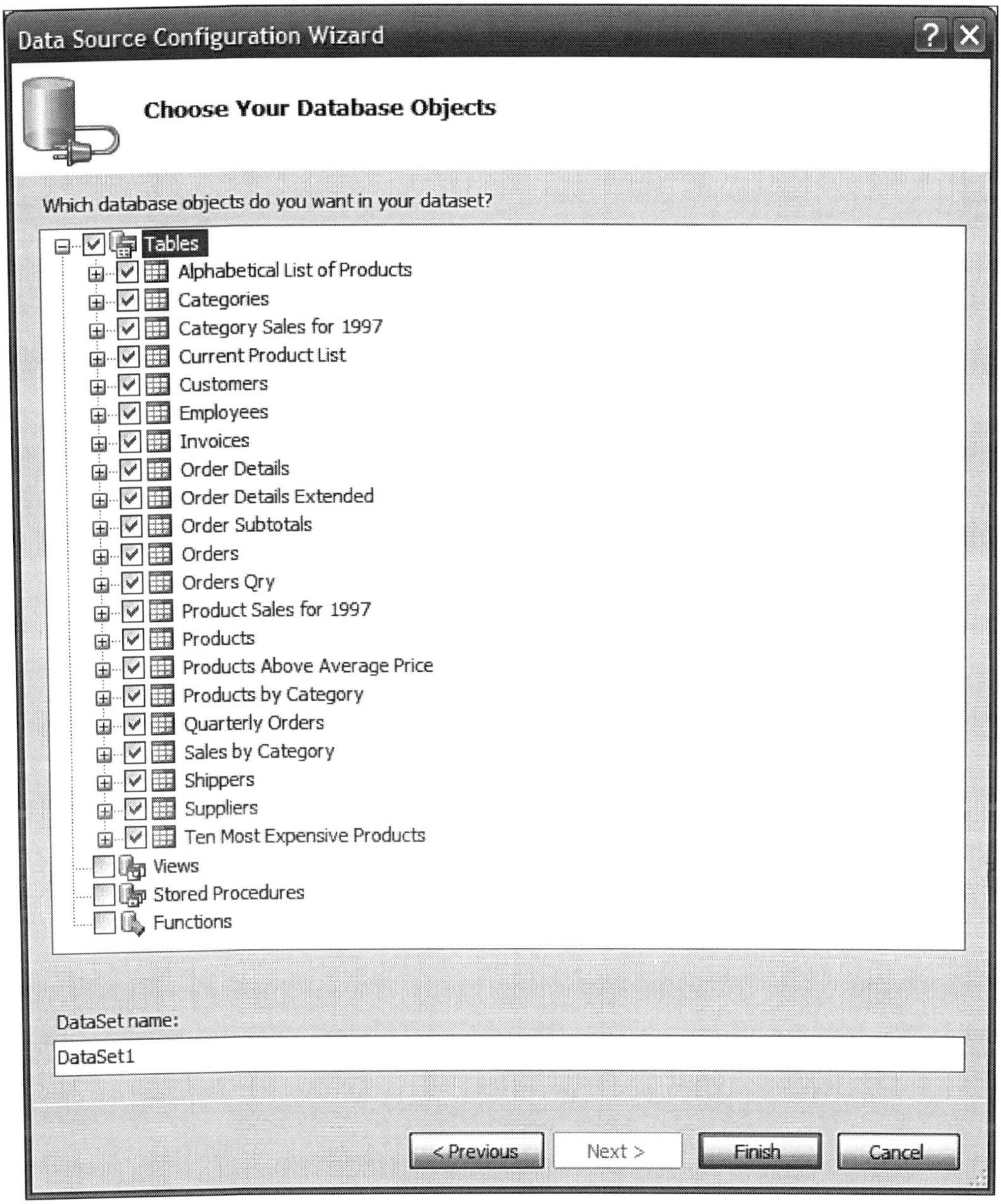
Data Source Configuration Wizard
Choose Your Database Objects
Which database objects do you want in your dataset?
Tables
Alphabetical List of Products
Categories
Category Sales for 1997
Current Product List
Customers
Employees
Invoices
Order Details
Order Details Extended
Order Subtotals
Orders
Orders Qry
Product Sales for 1997
Products
Products Above Average Price
Products by Category
Quarterly Orders
Sales by Category
Shippers
Suppliers
Ten Most Expensive Products
Views
Stored Procedures
Functions
DataSet name:
DataSet1
< Previous
Next >
Finish
Cancel

20. Click on the checkbox **Tables** to remove the check mark which deselects all tables. Choose only the **Customers** table (or any table, as we are just generating a report based on a single report in the present exercise) by placing a check mark for this item. An example which uses two tables is described in *Hands-on 3.4*.
21. Change the **DataSet name** from **DataSet1** to something different of your choice.

    In this book, **DsWin** is chosen for the name.
22. Click on **Finish**.

    This brings up the **Select Data Source** page of the **Report Wizard** as shown. The table details have been expanded to show the columns in the table.

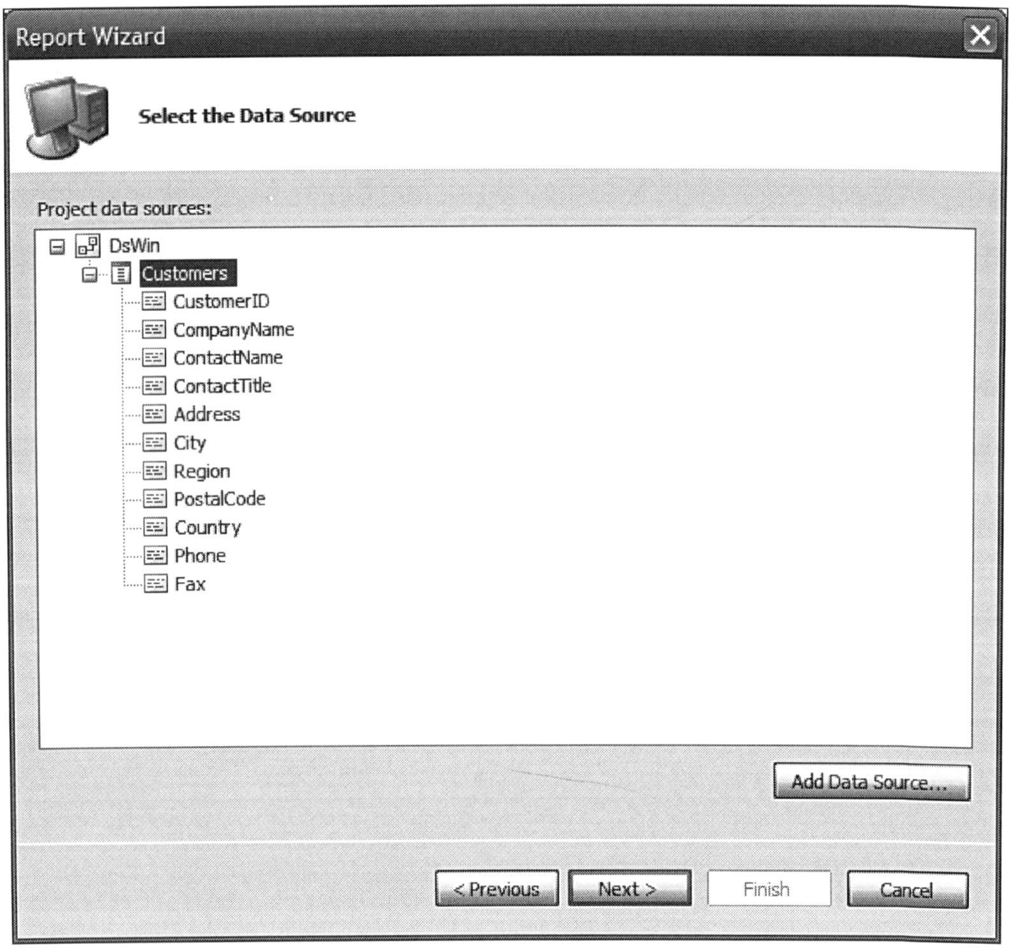

> Data Source Configuration:
>
> Although this exercise uses a connection to SQL Server 2008, there are lots of other Microsoft and third party vendor sources some of which are accessed natively and others through ODBC and OLE DB technology.
> To access any of the data sources, the authentication and permissions are important. In this exercise since the author, the computer owner and the database owner are all the same person, having Windows authentication access is simple. In production this can be vastly different.

Design the report

In the previous section the data that gets into the report was addressed. In this section you will work with the next essential tasks used to create a report, namely designing the layout, choosing the style and so on.

23. Click on the **Next** button.

    This brings up the **Select the Report Type** page of the **Report Wizard**. This has two options. For the columnar report the default **Tabular** is appropriate.

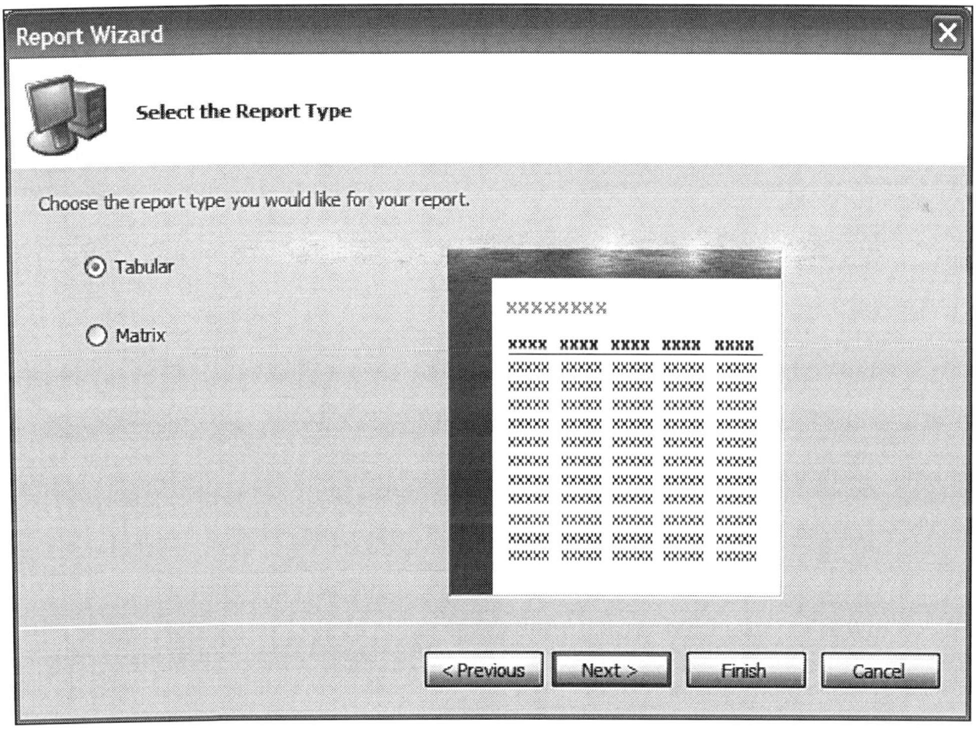

24. Click on the **Next** button.

    This brings up the **Design the Table** page of the **Report Wizard** as shown. This is an interactive window where you can choose the columns to be displayed from among the available columns. You may also group them. For this exercise you will use only a couple of columns (fields). You can easily move columns between **Available fields** and **Displayed fields** using the buttons **(Page, Group, and Details)** in the centre.

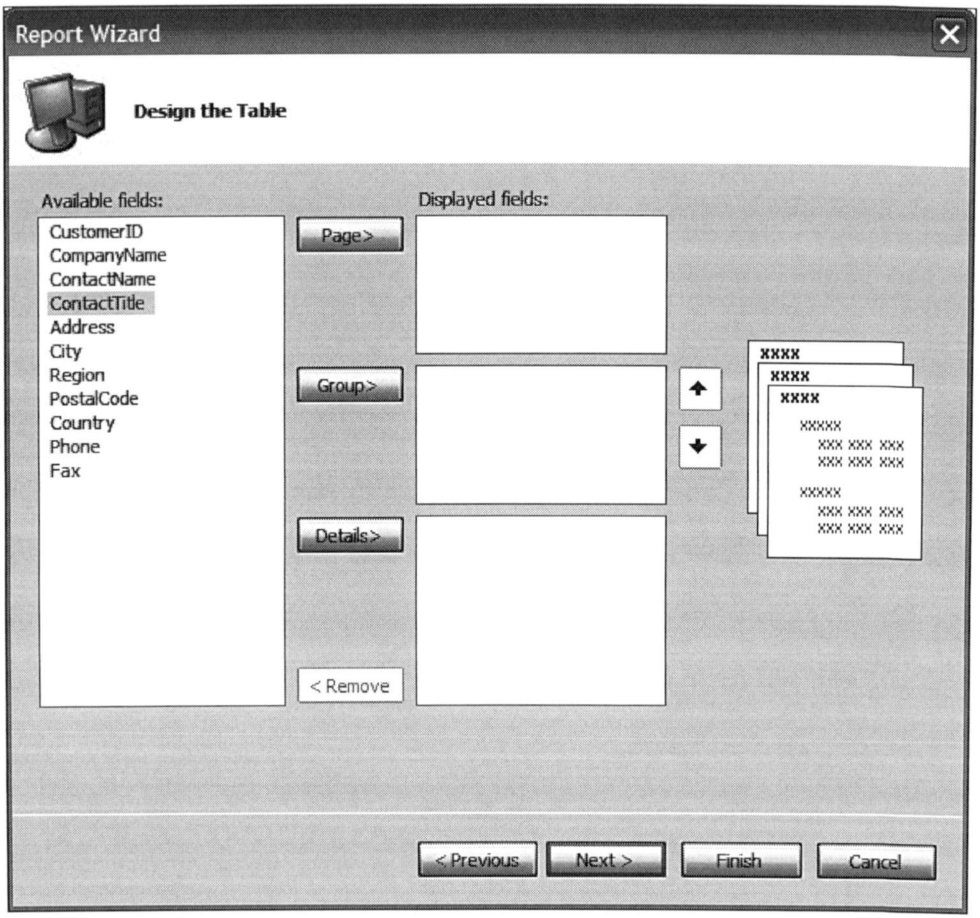

25. Click on **CompanyName** from the **Available fields** area and click on **Details**. This brings the **CompanyName** to the **Displayed fields** area on the right as shown:

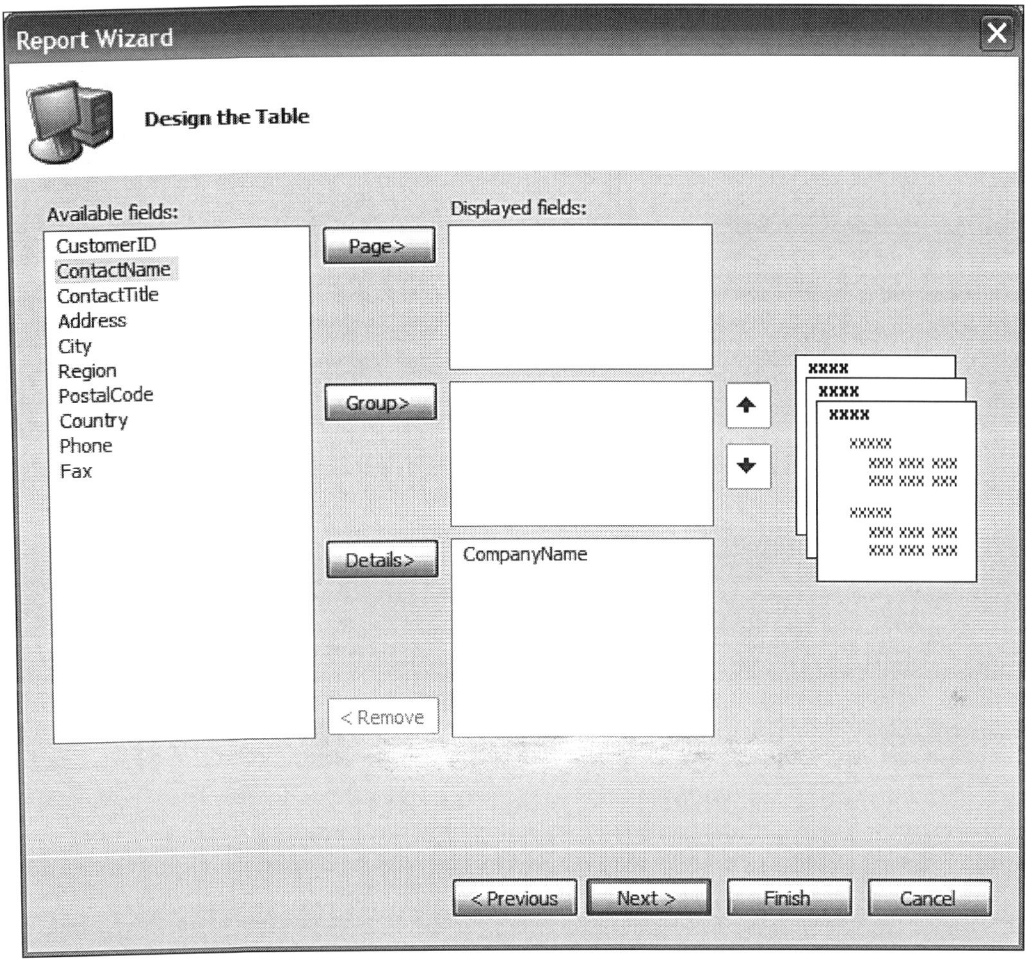

26. In a similar manner transfer **Address, City, Country**, and **Phone** from the left to the right into the **Details** area. Click on the **Next** button.

    This brings up the **Choose Table Layout** page of the Report Wizard.

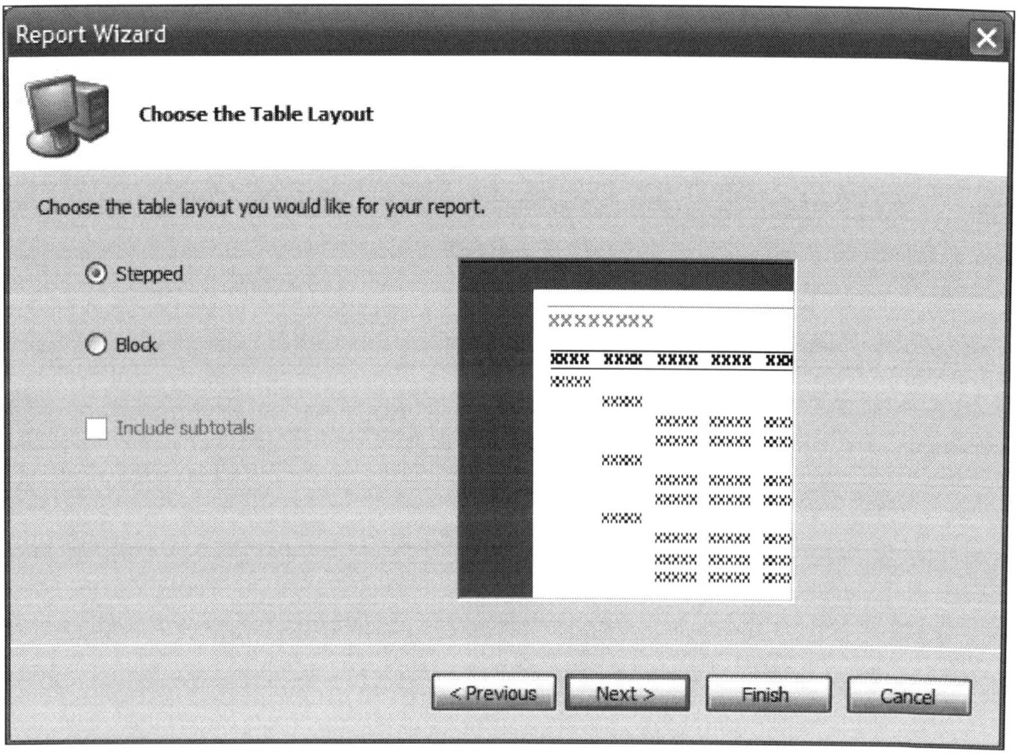

27. Accept the default layout and click on the **Next** button.

    Accepting the default layout produces a report in which the grouping information produces a step, clearly delineating the step. On the other hand, a blocked report will produce a report where the step is absent. This brings up the **Choose the Table Style** page of the **Report Wizard** as shown:

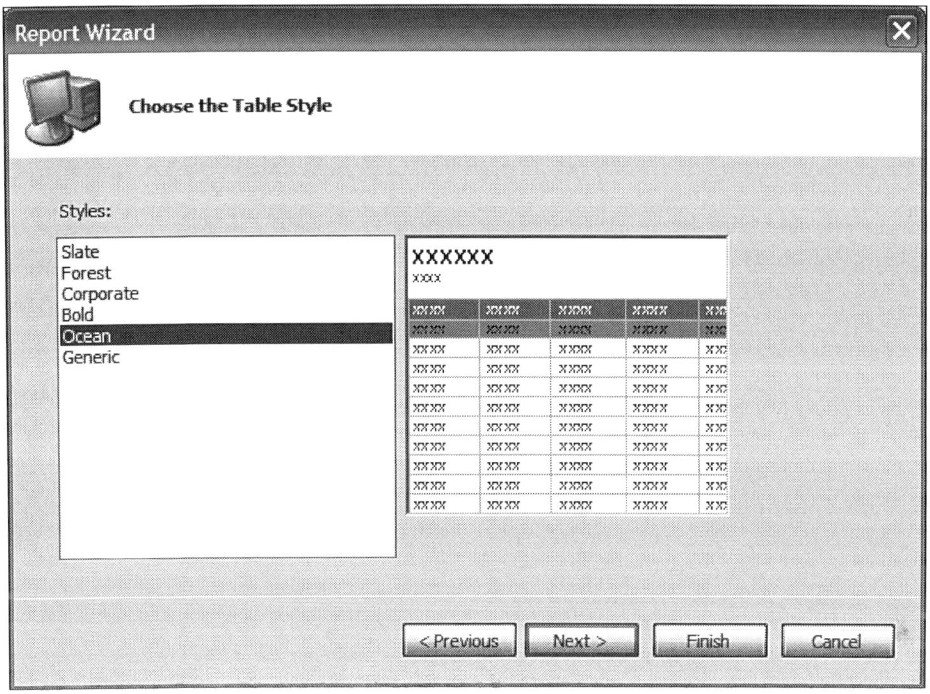

28. Choose a style (here the style **Ocean** is chosen) and click on the **Next** button.

    This brings up the **Completing the Wizard** page of the **Report Wizard** which displays items chosen during this wizard driven report authoring process.

29. Click on the **Finish** button.

    This brings of the Visual Studio 2008 IDE which displays a number of items such as the dataset **DsWin** on the left, the **Report1.rdlc [Design]** in the middle, and additional items added to the project folder in the **Solution Explorer**.

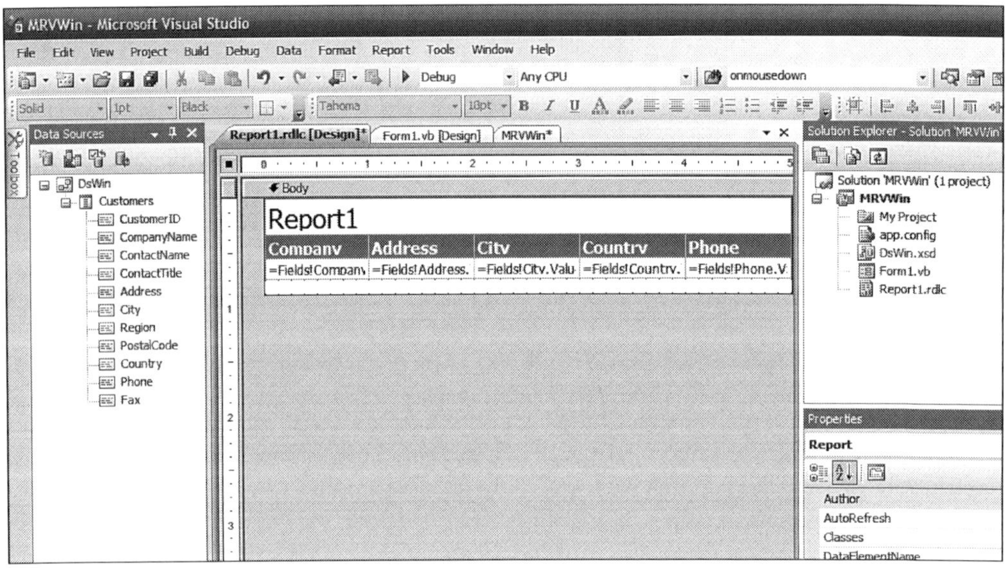

> **Report Wizard:**
>
> The designer part of the wizard uses familiar Microsoft technology which can even be found in some of the older MS Access applications. If you are trying to prototype a report, this is the fastest option.

Preview the report

30. Click on the menu item **Build** and choose **Build MRVWin** as shown.

    The **Output** window is displayed with the output ending with the line:

    Build: 1 succeeded or up-to-date, 0 failed, 0 skipped

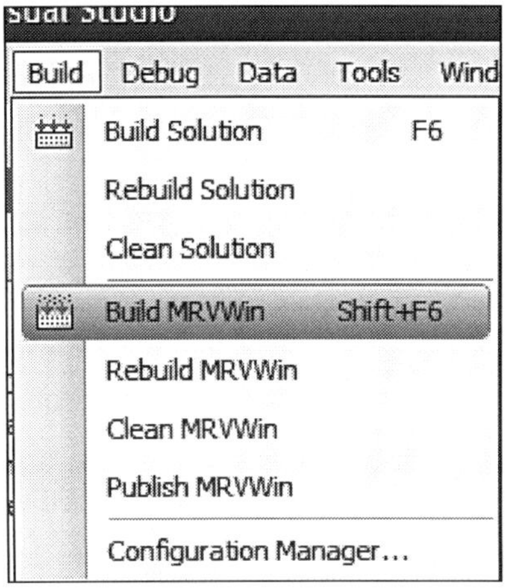

31. Click on the menu item **Debug** and choose either **Start Without Debugging** or **Start Debugging (**as shown). The green arrow in the main menu can also be used to run the form in which case it will start with debugging.

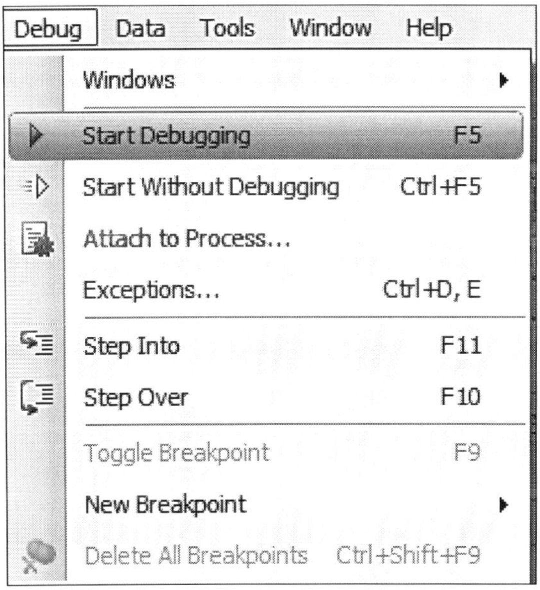

This runs the program and **Form1** gets displayed as shown. The form is empty and the reason for this is that while the data for the report has been defined, the Report Viewer Control's report source has not been set.

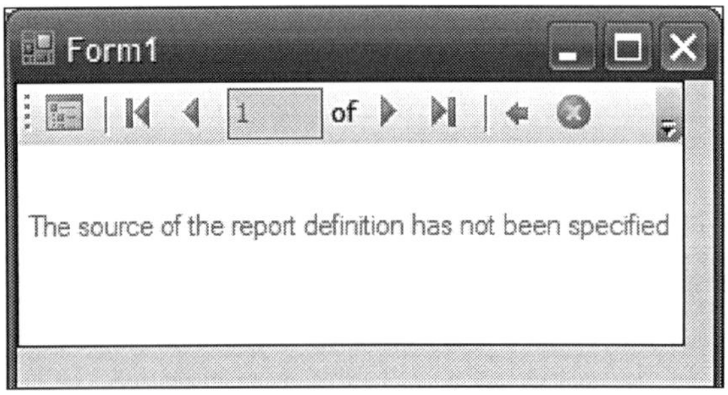

32. Close the displayed **Form1** in the above and click on **Form1** in the design view.

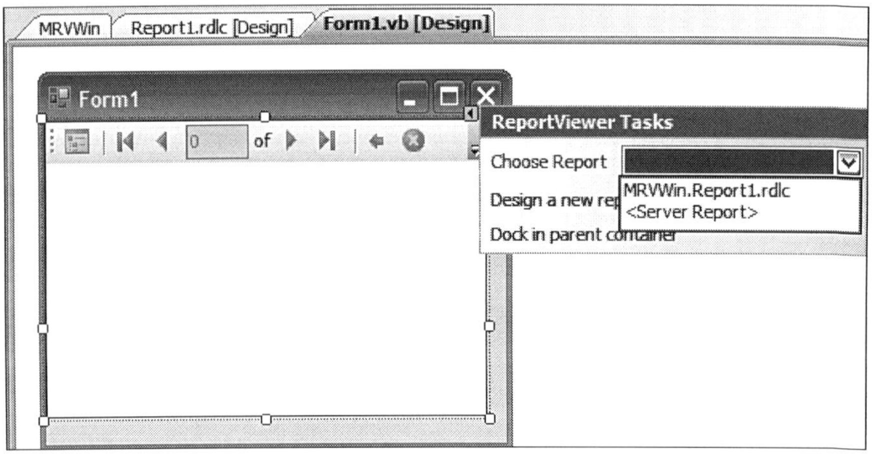

33. Click on the **Smart Tasks** (design aid for Microsoft controls) and choose the report, **MRVWin.Report1.rdlc** as shown above.
34. Click on **Build** and then click **Start Debugging**.

    The program will run and after a while the report will be displayed. It starts out with a rotating progress icon and then finally displays **Report1** as shown.

Report details of the RDLC file

While the steps to create a report were easy enough to follow, a lot of details are hidden in authoring the report. In order to understand how the report is structured, the best place to look for is the `Report1.rdlc` file shown in the next figure (abbreviated screen shots are shown to keep the displayed area small). An understanding of this structure will be useful in order to work with the programmatic access to report discussed in Chapter 8.

In the above figure, only the **<DataSources>** node is expanded to show the connection string. The details of the connection string were chosen to be saved to the application settings. These may be reviewed by opening the **app.config** file in **Solution Explorer**.

The dataset **DsWin** is defined against the database referenced in the Connection String. The next part of the **Report1.rdlc** file shows this detail.

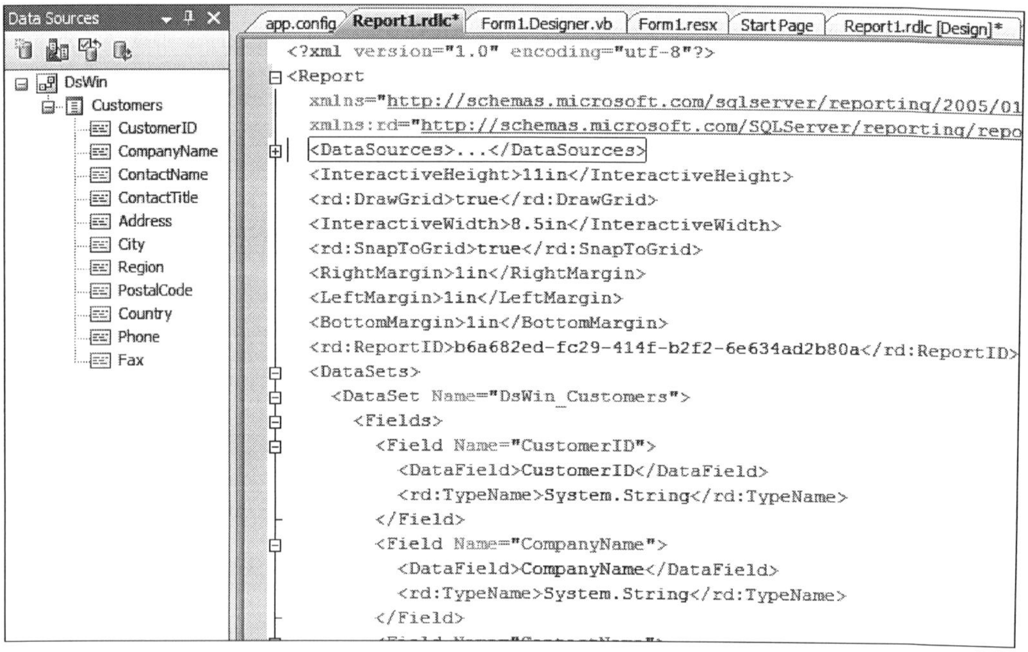

The **<DataSets>** node lists out all the fields (only two are shown) in the chosen table. It displays the data type as well.

Using the connection string specified, the Data Source Configuration Wizard provides the dataset that makes it to the report. The elements in the dataset get bound to the report when you associate the report with the `MRVwin.Report1.rdlc`. Review the design view of **Form1** as shown in the next figure.

The body of the `Report1.rdlc` file is shown in the following figure:

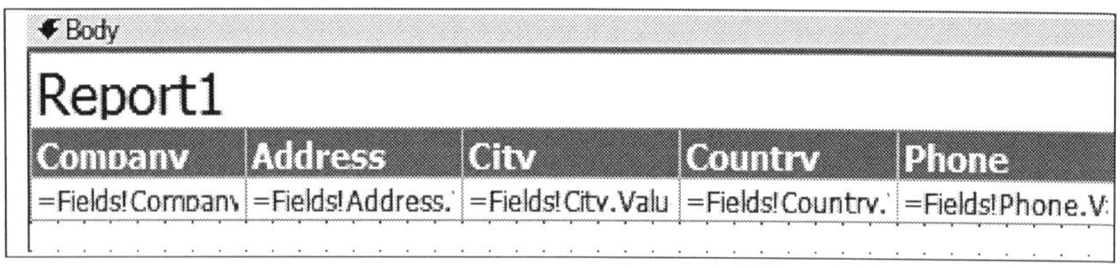

The<**Body**> node in the **Report1.rdlc** file shows the contents of the Report1.

```
<Body>
  <ReportItems>
    <Textbox Name="textbox1">...</Textbox>
    <Table Name="table1">
      <DataSetName>DsWin_Customers</DataSetName>
      <Top>0.33in</Top>
      <Details>
        <TableRows>
          <TableRow>
            <TableCells>
              <TableCell>...</TableCell>
              <TableCell>...</TableCell>
              <TableCell>...</TableCell>
              <TableCell>...</TableCell>
              <TableCell>...</TableCell>
            </TableCells>
            <Height>0.19in</Height>
          </TableRow>
        </TableRows>
      </Details>
      <Header>...</Header>
      <TableColumns>...</TableColumns>
      <Height>0.41in</Height>
    </Table>
  </ReportItems>
  <Height>0.875in</Height>
</Body>
```

The above figure really shows the report's UI formatting features. These consist of a text box which contains the report name. It also has 5 table cells in a row of the table contained in the **<Details>** node of the report. The data from the table after the column selection is routed to the details section. The **<Body>** is also a container for the **<Header/>** and the **<TableColumns/>**. The **<TableColumns/>** contains just the design details of the table columns but the **<Header/>** contains the information for the table column headers and their formatting.

The following figure shows one of the **<TableCell>** from the **<TableCells/>** node expanded:

```
<TableCells>
  <TableCell>
    <ReportItems>
      <Textbox Name="CompanyName">
        <rd:DefaultName>CompanyName</rd:DefaultName>
        <Style>
          <BorderColor>
            <Default>LightGrey</Default>
          </BorderColor>
          <BorderStyle>
            <Default>Solid</Default>
          </BorderStyle>
          <FontFamily>Tahoma</FontFamily>
          <FontSize>9pt</FontSize>
          <PaddingLeft>2pt</PaddingLeft>
          <PaddingRight>2pt</PaddingRight>
          <PaddingTop>2pt</PaddingTop>
          <PaddingBottom>2pt</PaddingBottom>
        </Style>
        <CanGrow>true</CanGrow>
        <Value>=Fields!CompanyName.Value</Value>
      </Textbox>
    </ReportItems>
  </TableCell>
  <TableCell>...</TableCell>
  <TableCell>...</TableCell>
  <TableCell>...</TableCell>
  <TableCell>...</TableCell>
</TableCells>
```

While Visual Studio was used to create this RDLC file, it can also be created programmatically or by converting a RDL file by processing it in the local mode. You will see this in Chapter 12.

Features of report binding to form

The data displayed in the Windows from Form1 was retrieved by the Data Source Configuration wizard based on a dataset DsWin. The data bindings for the form are from the generated **CustomersBindingSource** (`System.Windows.Forms.BindingSource`) and the data is in the **CustomersTableAdapter** *(represents connection and command used to retrieve and save data).*

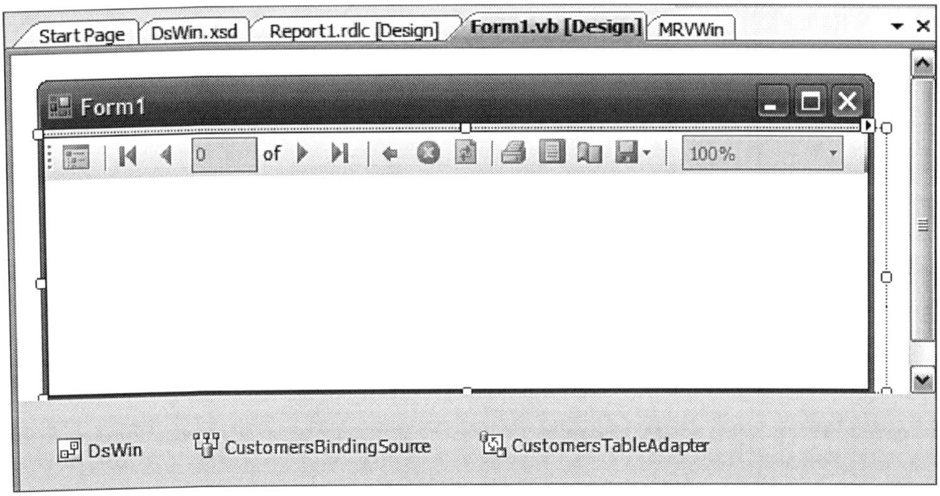

The **DsWin** dataset, the **CustomersBindingSource** and the **CustomersTableAdapter** are added to the form when you finish the *Data Source Configuration*. You will also notice that a *Schema Definition* file **DsWin.xsd** is added to the project. The following figure shows schematically how the form gets bound to data through the *Binding Source*. In the appendix on Dataset you will learn more about the schema (`DsWin.xsd`) file.

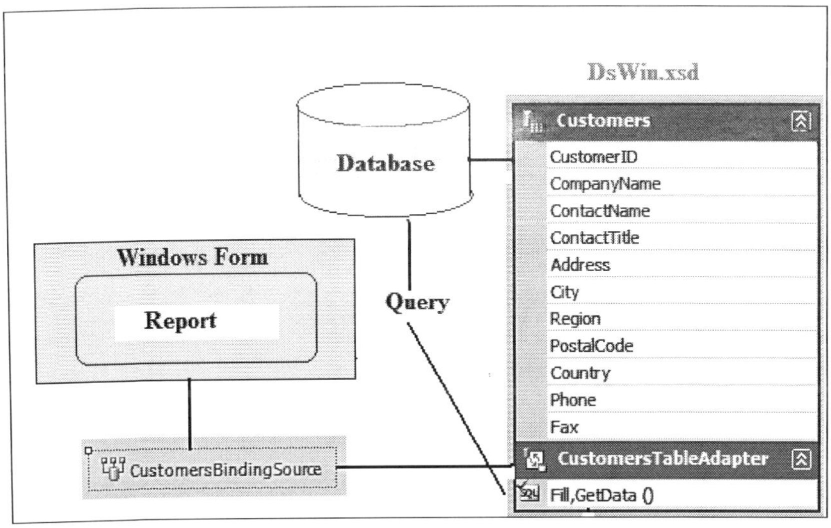

Hands-on 3.2: Modifying the previous report

The report created in *Hands-on 3.1* is just a barebones report displaying a chosen number of columns from a database table. As you might have observed, there were options in most of the steps of the wizard under whose guidance the above report was designed. You can make changes to the data beginning with your connection (not only to Microsoft SQL Servers but also from other vendors) as well as whether you use data from a single table or a number of related tables. You can also modify how the data is displayed by making changes using proper options in the report design.

In this exercise you will be using the same connection and data, but you will make changes to the report design (of course you can start a new project and do the same).

You might have also noticed from the data that customers in the `TestNorthwind` database reside in different cities and countries. The design changes you make will result in a report where each page displays a different country and in each country the customers are shown grouped under the cities where they live.

Follow the steps

In this activity you will be modifying your previous report while retaining several of the features. You will also be carrying out some enhancements to the report.

Modifying an existing report

It is a reality of the business environment that there is often a need to modify an existing report by changing the data, layout, or style. Microsoft controls are well suited for the task and in this section you will be modifying a report.

1. Add a form named `Form2` to the project. In the **Smart Tasks** click on **Choose Report** and accept to use the **MRVWin.Report1.rdlc**.
2. Click on **Design a new report** to display the **Report Wizard**.
3. Click on the **Next** button in the **Welcome to Report Wizard** Page.
4. Click on the **Next** button in the **Select the Data Source** page of the wizard.
5. Click on the **Next** button in **the Select Report Type** where **Tabular** is the default.

6. Make changes to the **Design the Table** page in the **Report Wizard** as shown. First, transfer the **Country** from left to right by clicking on the **Page** button. Next, move the City by clicking on the **Group** button, and then move the other fields by clicking on the **Details** button.

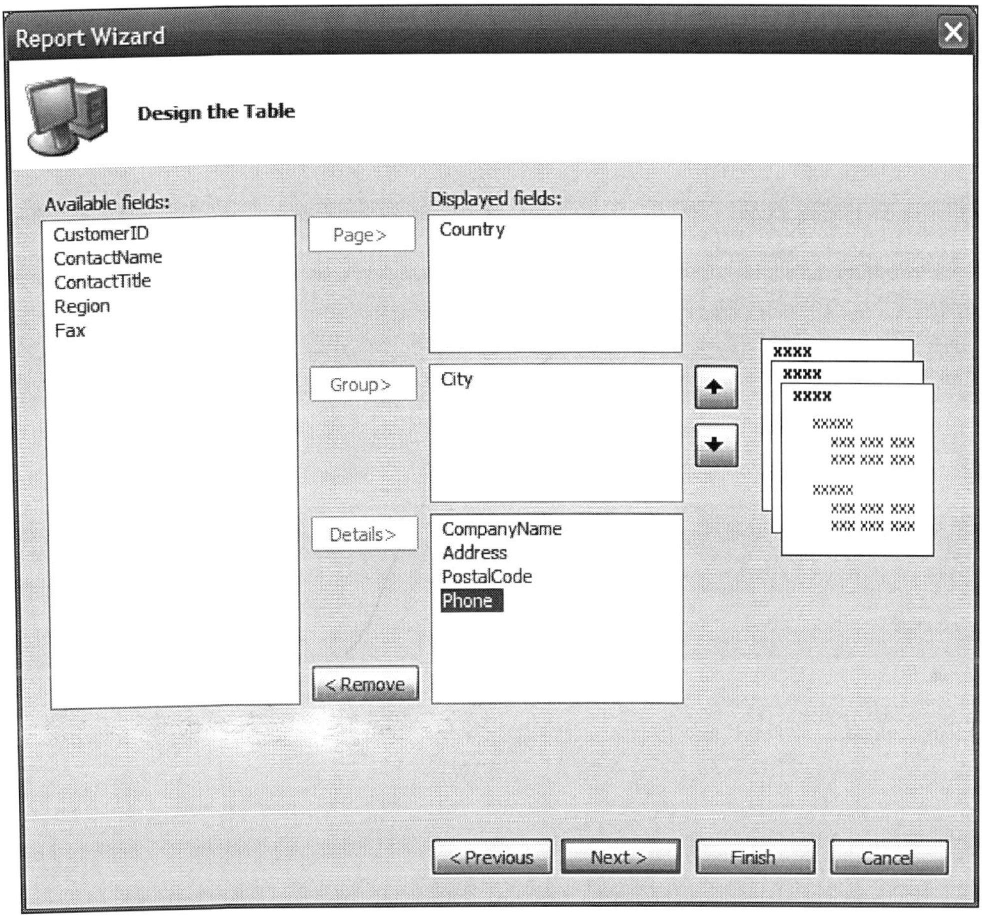

7. You may click on the UP/DOWN (arrows) buttons on the right to arrange the order of the items in the **Details** displayed fields. Click on the **Next** button.

8. Choose a style in the **Styles** list by highlighting it and then clicking on the **Next** button.

9. In the **Complete the Report Wizard**, change **Report2** to something different (**ModifiedReport** in the present example) and click on the **Finish** button.

   The new report, **Modified Report** appears as shown in the following figure:

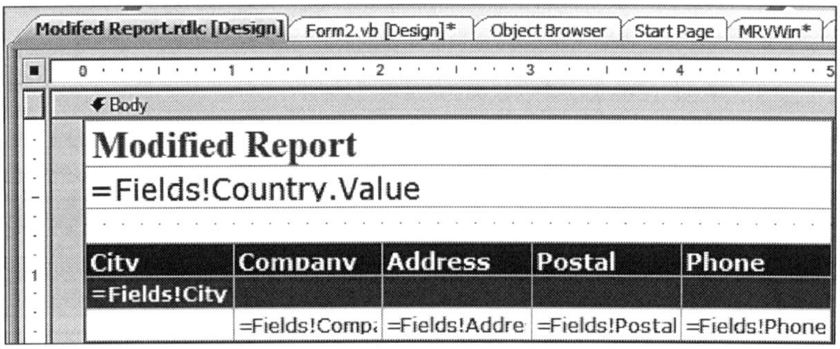

10. Build the project and click on **Debug | Start Debugging (F5).**

    After a little while the **Form2** is displayed (the navigation button was used to come to this record in the figure after the report was displayed).

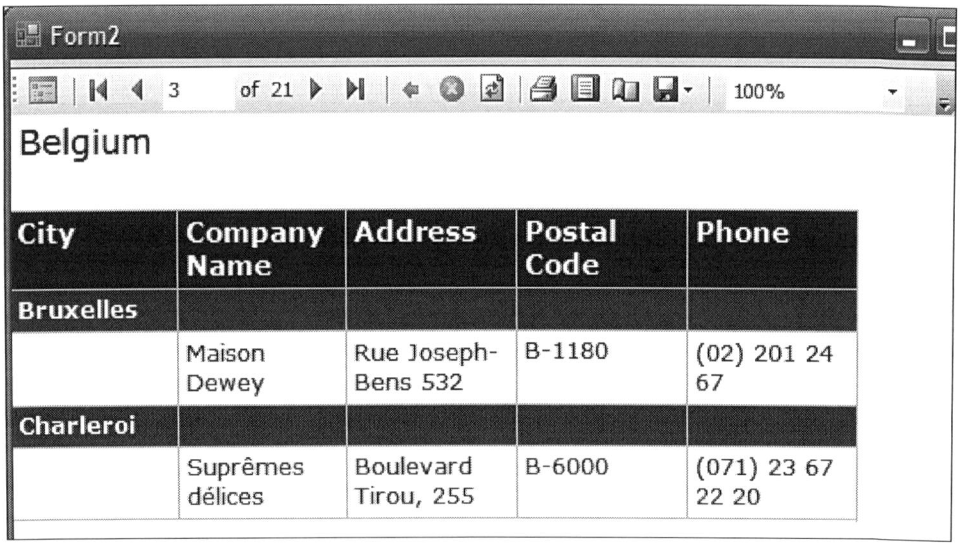

Hands-on 3.3: Adding a graphic to the report

Images greatly improve the displayed report and often times they are necessary. Images can originate from external sources or from a database. Images like logos or banners are most common.

Follow the steps

In this activity you will add an external image to the report. It is assumed the image is available as a file with the supported extensions (`*.jpg`, `*.bmp`, `*.png`, `*.gif`, `*.jpe`).

1. Click on the **textbox** where **Modified Report** is displayed and reduce the width of the textbox (by dragging the left edge of the box towards right).

   The image is going to occupy a position to the left. The image cannot be contained in the same textbox as the **Modified Report**.

2. From the **Toolbox** (with the Report in design view) drag-and-drop an image control onto the space created by reducing the width as shown:

3. Click on the **Report** menu item and from the drop-down click on **Embedded Images...**

   This brings up the **Embedded Images** window.

4. Click on **Images** and browse your hard disk to pick an image and then click on the **OK** button.

   The following figure shows what image was picked on this machine. You may need to pick the right **Mime Type** as well (this depends on the image file extension you are planning to use) and an image of appropriate size. If the image is too large, use a reduced size image.

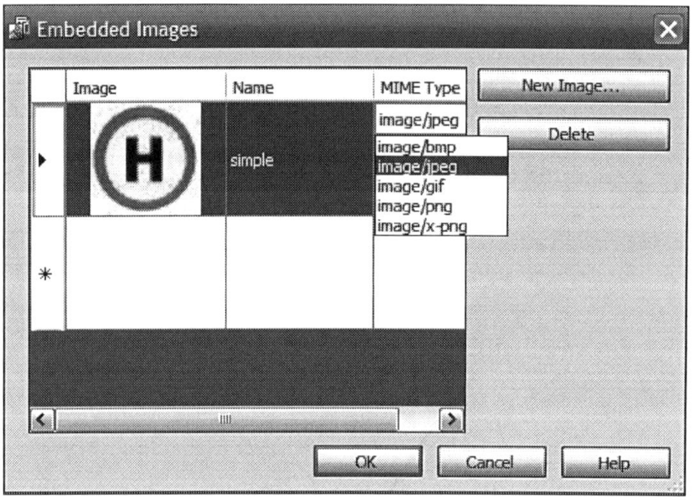

6. Click on **Image1** on the report and review its properties and make the following changes:
   - Change source from **External** to **Embedded**
   - Click in an empty space by the side of **value** and from the drop-down pick up the name of the image file (in this case, **simple**)

   With these settings your design view of the report should appear as in the following figure:

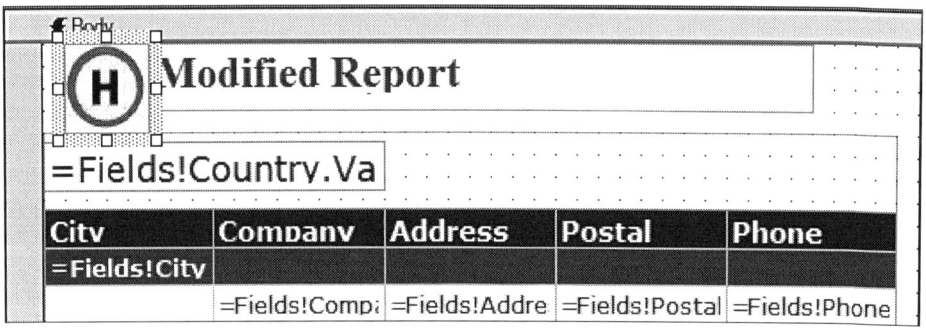

7. Build the project and click on **Start Debugging** (*F5*). The form gets displayed with the embedded image as shown:

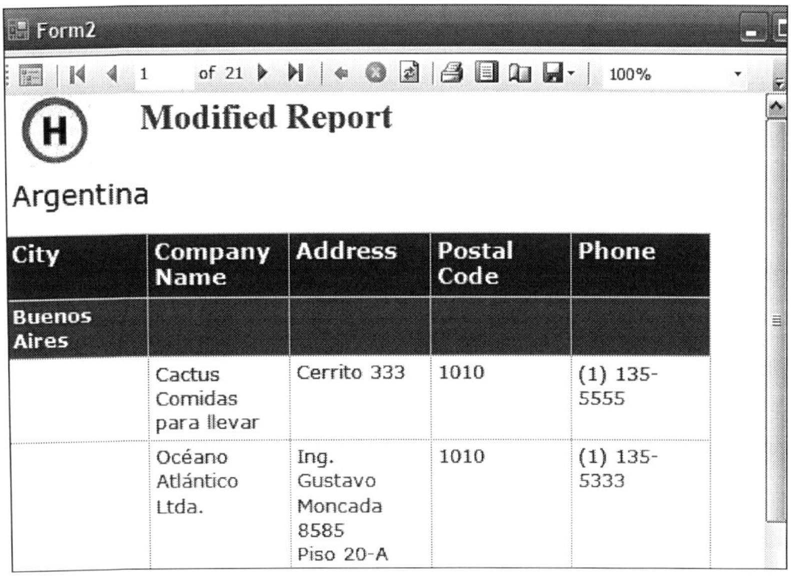

8. Open the `ModifiedReport.rdlc` file in an XML editor and review how different this file is from the `Report1.rdlc` file.

> **RDLC and images**
>
> Use the XML editor in the Visual Studio IDE (right-click the file and choose the **openwith...** option to access the XML Editor). If you want the logo to appear on every page of the report, you need to place the image file in the textbox that contains the value `Fields!Country.Value`.

9. While the above procedure works for embedded images, what about external images? Not a problem! In order to bring in an image from an external source, store it on a web server. For the image property's source **value**, use the web address (`http://localhost/simplex.jpg`). You also need to set the **EnableExternalImag** property (expand **LocalReport**) to **true** in **ReportViewer**'s **Properties** window.

Hands-on 3.4: Using ReportViewer control for a web application

Enabling reports to be displayed in a web page is a much desired feature. The ASP.NET web site project template in Visual Studio helps you in getting access to your corporate data on the Intranet.

Getting ready

As a preparation for this, a local web server installation will be necessary. However, for testing the report access, the run-time web server that Visual Studio provides is adequate. In a production server a web server will be needed. In the exercise to follow the local IIS 5.1 web server is used.

Follow the steps

The following two steps are necessary for completing this task:

- Creating an ASP.NET Web Site Project
- Adding a data set to the project using the Query Builder Tool

Creating an ASP.NET web site project and adding a dataset using the Query Builder Tool

To host a report on a web server, a web page is needed in which the ReportViewer Control will be embedded. This section shows you how. This section also describes another important tool, the Query Builder.

1. Click on **File | New | Web site...** (*Shift+Alt+N*) to open the **New Web Site** window as shown:

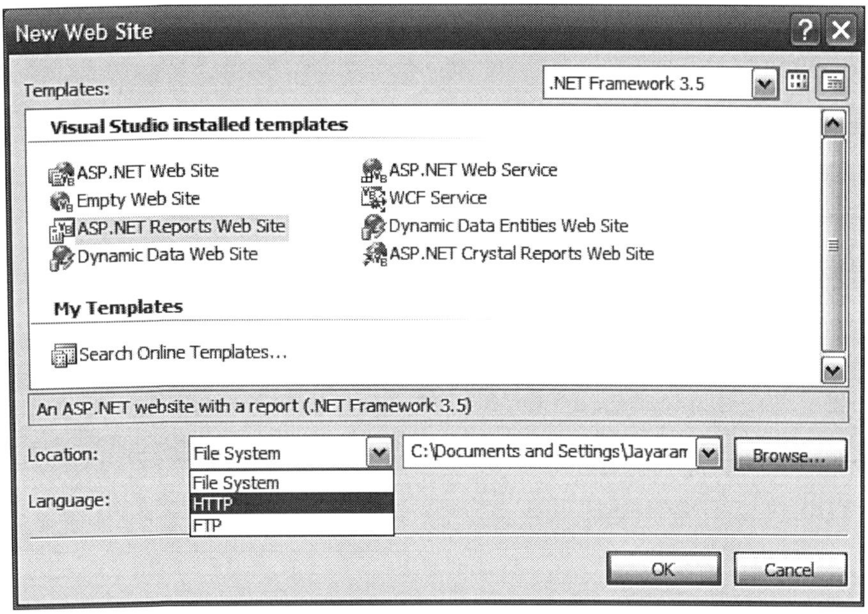

2. Highlight **ASP.NET web site** in **Templates**, click on the drop-down handle for **Location** and choose **HTTP**. Provide a name for the web site (like **MRVWeb**) and click on the **OK** button.

   This creates a web site folder with three items: **Default.aspx, App_Data** and **web.config**.

3. Click on the menu item **Website | Add New Item...** to open the **Add New Item - http://localhost/MRVweb** window as shown:

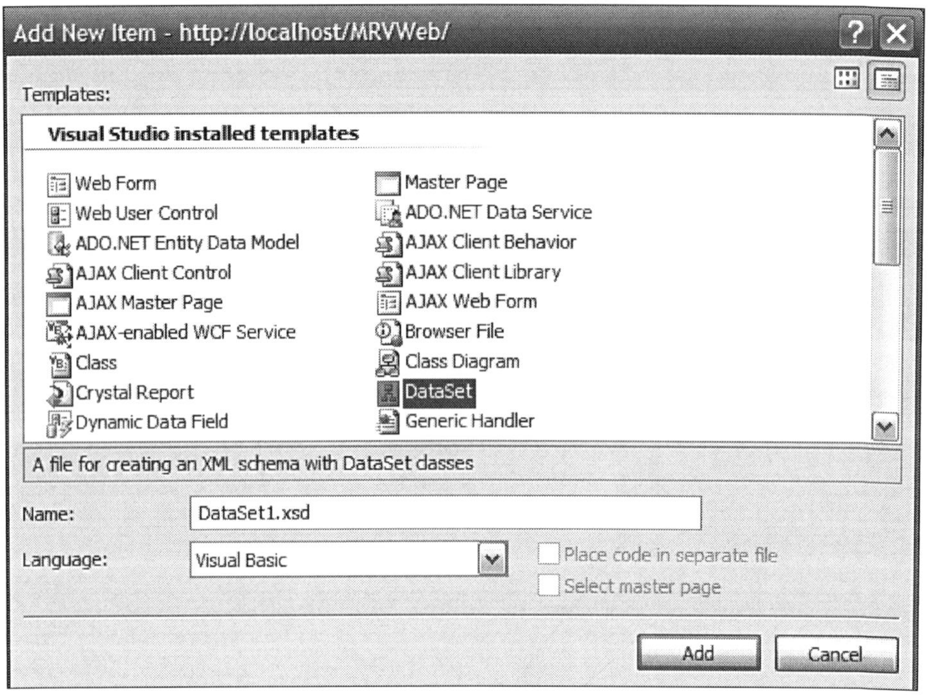

4. Click on **DataSet** in the **Templates** and change **DataSet1.xsd** to something different (like **DsWeb.xsd**). Click on the **Add** button.

   You get the **Microsoft Visual Studio** message, "*You are attempting to add a special file type (dataset) to an ASP.NET web site. In general, to use this type of item in your site, you should place it in the App_Code folder. Do you want to place the file in the App_Code folder?*" with **Yes**, **No** and **Cancel** buttons.

5. Click on the **Yes** button.

   This adds the **App_Code** folder containing the **DsWeb.xsd** file to the web site. Also, the **DsWeb.xsd** item is displayed in the designer as shown in the next screenshot:

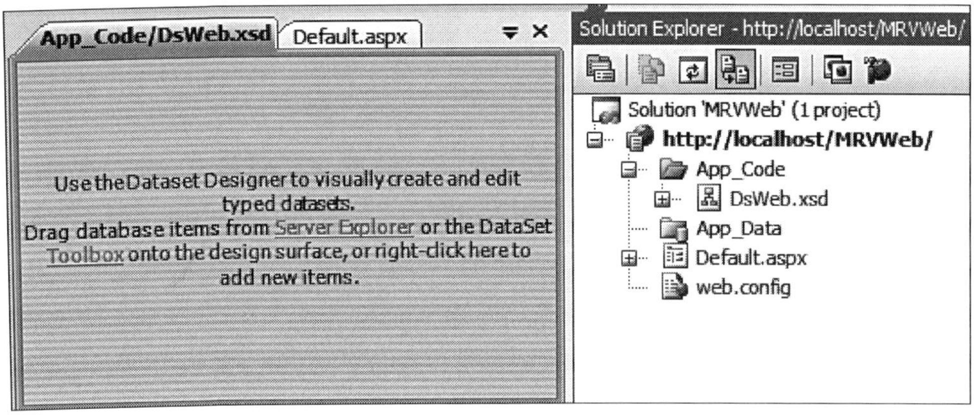

Read the instructions.

6. In the tabbed page **App_Code/DsWeb.xsd**, right-click and from the drop-down menu choose **Add | Table Adapter...**.

   This adds **DataTable1** to the design area and pops up the modal window **TableAdapter Configuration Wizard** which is shown together superposed in the following screenshot:

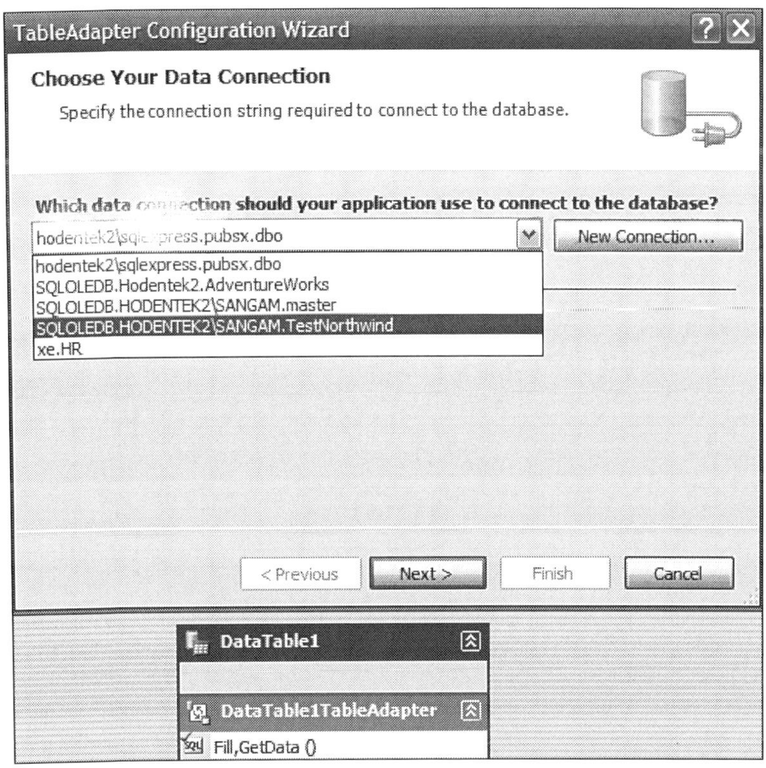

7. Choose the **SQLOLEDB.Hodentek2\SANGAM.TestNorthwind** (will be different in your case) regarding the connection and click on the **Next** button.

   This may bring up the SQL Server login page where you need to provide the authentication information. You had to have these when you installed the SQL Server 2008 (here a trusted connection was used).

8. Provide the information and click on the **OK** button.
9. In the **Save the Connection String to the Application Configuration** page that gets displayed, accept the default choice and click on the **Next** button.
10 In the **Choose a Command Type** page of the wizard, accept the default choice **Use SQL statements**. Read the details and click on the **Next** button.

   This opens up the **Enter a SQL Statement** page of the wizard as shown. You need to describe the data to be loaded into the table.

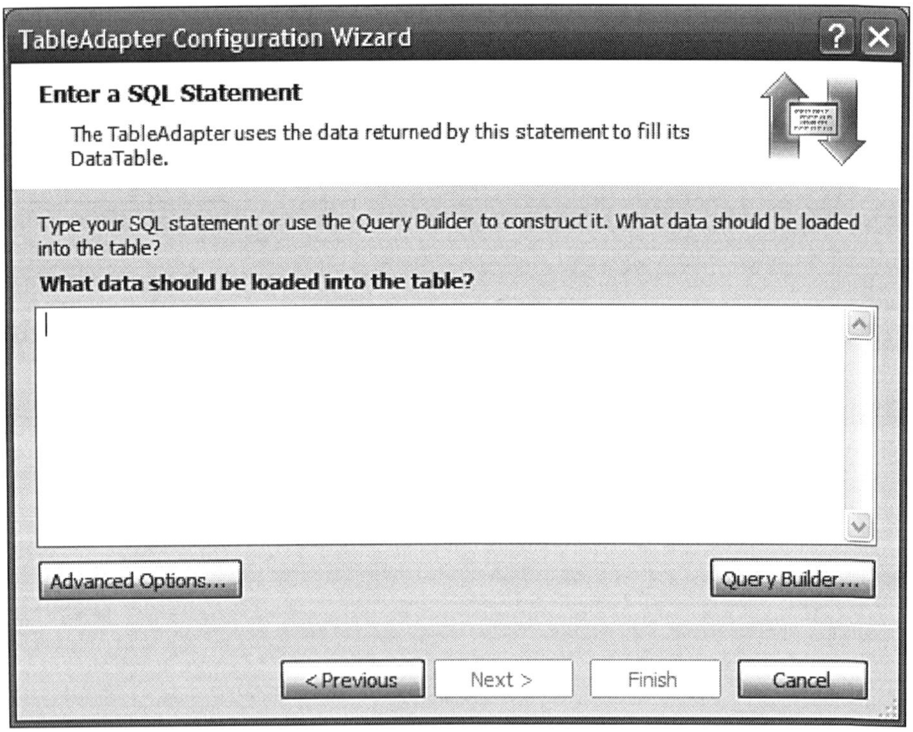

11. Click on the **Query Builder...** button to open the **Query Builder** interface.

    The Query Builder is described in detail at this link, `http://aspalliance.com/819`. The **Add Table** window gets displayed (the Add table window is not shown here) together with the **Query Builder** window. The article also describes the next several steps of designing a query with the query builder.

12. From the list of tables choose the **Categories** and **Products** tables and add them to the **Query Builder** by clicking the **Add** button. Then close the **Add Table** window by clicking on the **Close** button.

13. In the **Query Builder**, from the **Categories** table, choose **CategoryName** and in the **Products** table choose **ProductName**, **QuantityPerUnit**, **UnitsInStock**, and **Discontinued**.

    The **Query Builder** should now appear as shown in the following screenshot:

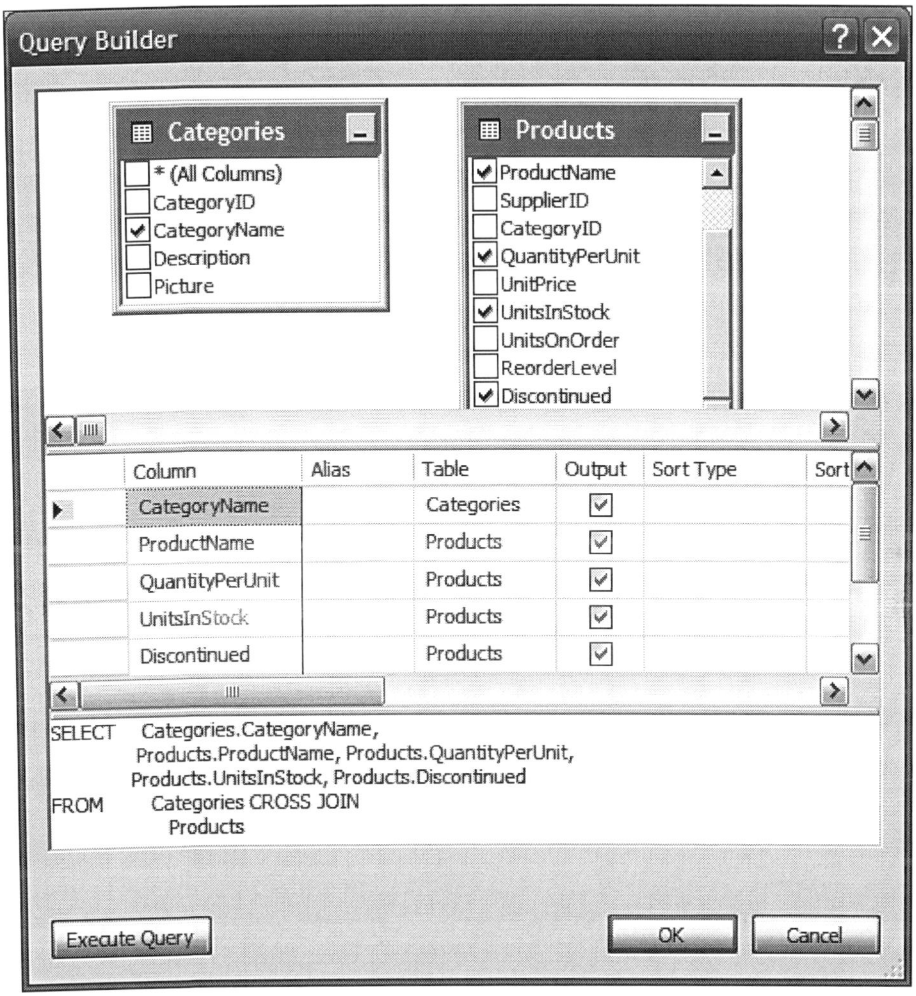

14. Place cursor on **CategoryID** in the **Categories** table and drag it out to **CategoryID** in the **Products** table to establish a **join** which by default is an **inner join** of the two tables.
15. Impose the **Where** condition by typing in **0** in the filter for the column **Discontinued** as shown:

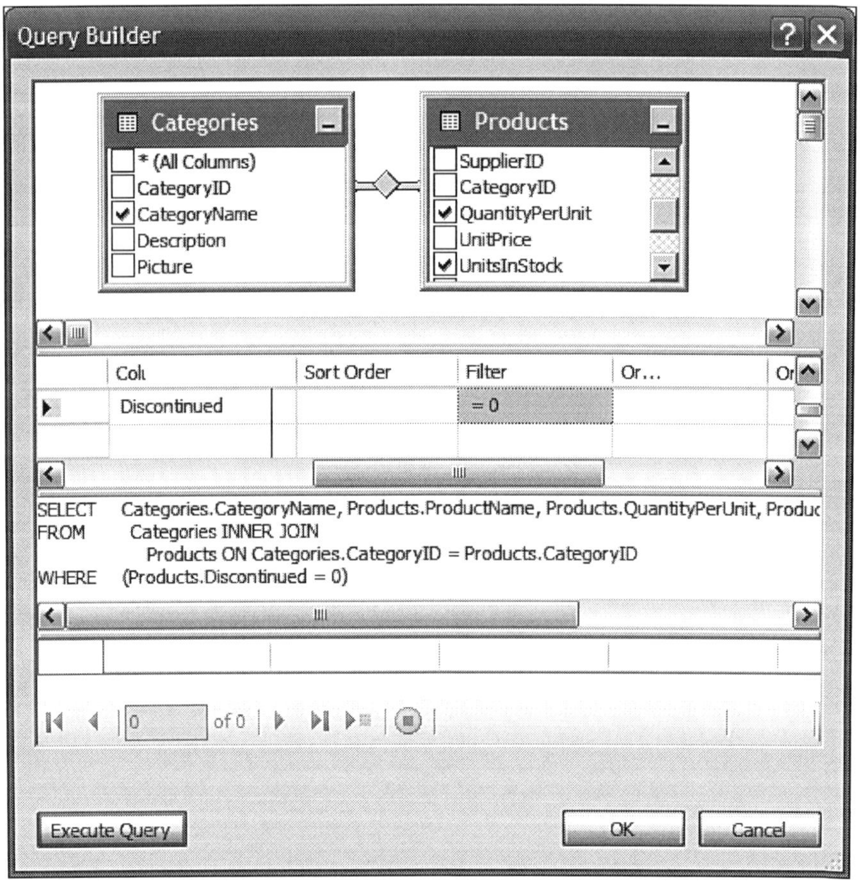

16. Now click on the **Execute Query** button and verify that the SQL statement returns 69 rows of data. The data can be seen in the bottom pane of the **Query Builder**. Click on the **OK** button.

    You will now be back in the **TableAdapter Configuration Wizard**'s **Enter a SQL Statement** page displaying the query you just created.

17. Click on the **Next** button.

    This opens the **Choose Methods to Generate** page of the wizard as shown. Read the details carefully.

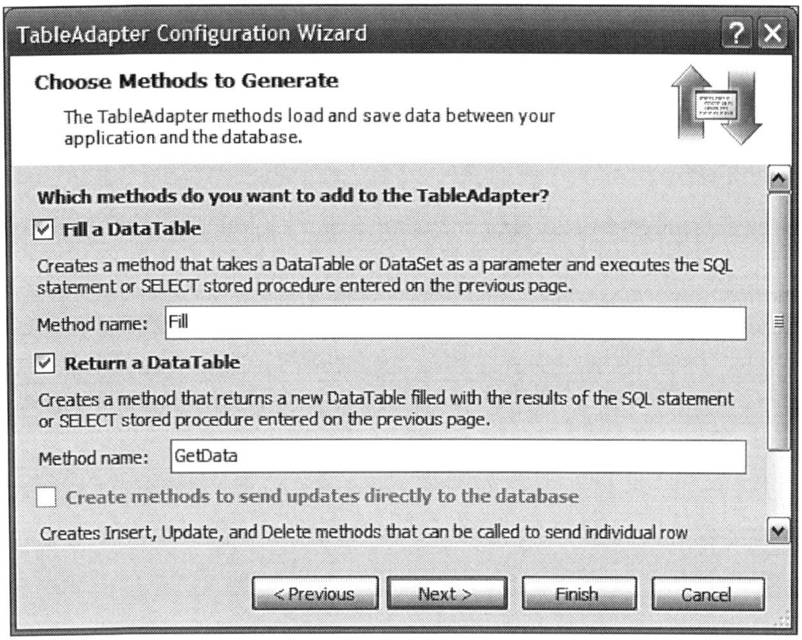

18. Accept defaults and click on the **Next** button. In the **Wizards Results** page (not shown) that is displayed click on the **Finish** button.

    The configured **DataTable1** now appears in the **App_Code /DsWeb.xsd** designer as shown:

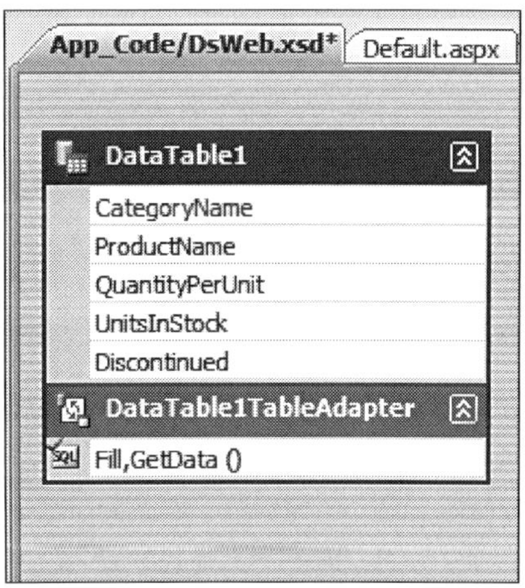

Adding a report template

The report template is the canvas on which you will be placing the other report items such as table, list and matrix. The template provides the body of the report. In this section you will be adding report items to the body of the report and configuring them to display the data:

1. Click the menu item **Website | Add New Item...** to open the **Add New Item - http://localhost/MRVWeb**. Choose **Report** in the **Visual Studio Installed templates**. Name **Report1** something different (**Web Products)** and click on the **Add** button.

   This adds the **Web Prodcuts.rdlc** file to the **App_Code** folder in the web site as well as exposing the report design area in the tabbed page as shown. Right now the report has only the **Body** of the report.

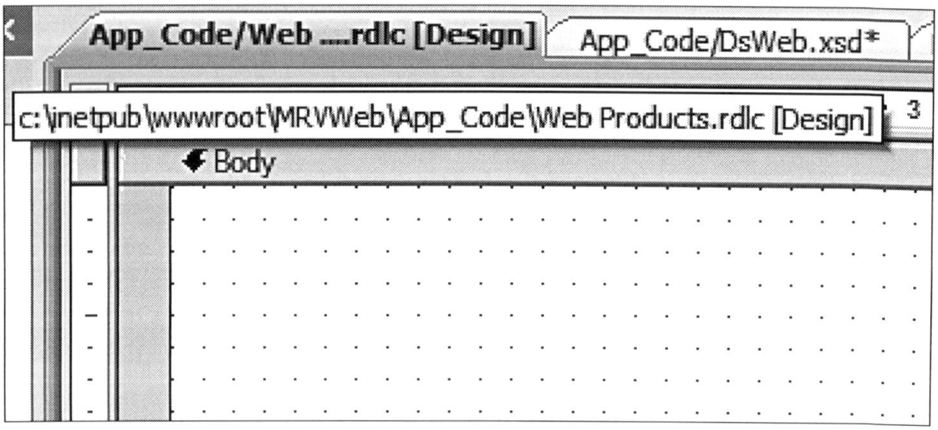

2. Drag-and-drop a **Textbox** from the **Toolbox** to the top of the body and type in **Products and Categories** inside the textbox. Expand the textbox to occupy the full width of the report.
3. Drag-and-drop (or double-click inside the toolbox) a **Table** from the toolbox just below the textbox you created in the previous step.

The design surface now appears as shown:

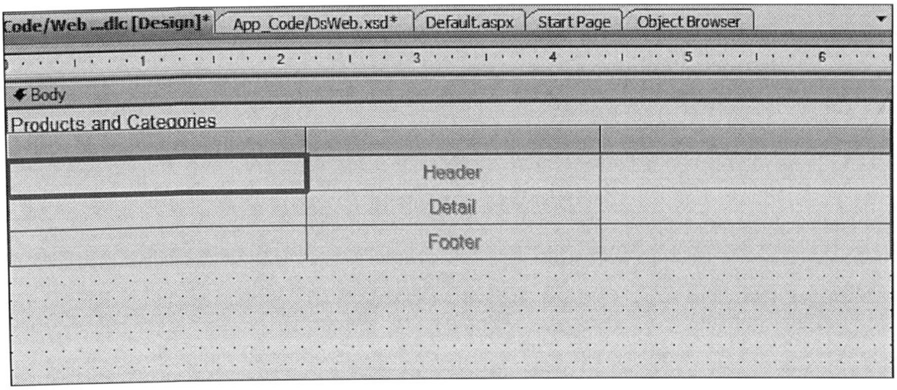

4. Click on the menu item **Report** (you must be in report designer) and **choose Data Sources...**

   This opens the **Report Data Sources** window displaying the data source created earlier.

5. Click on the **Add to Report** button.

   This adds the chosen data source to the **Report Data Sources** area displaying the **Name**, **Type**, **Data Set** and **Table** details directly below as shown. Click on the **OK** button.

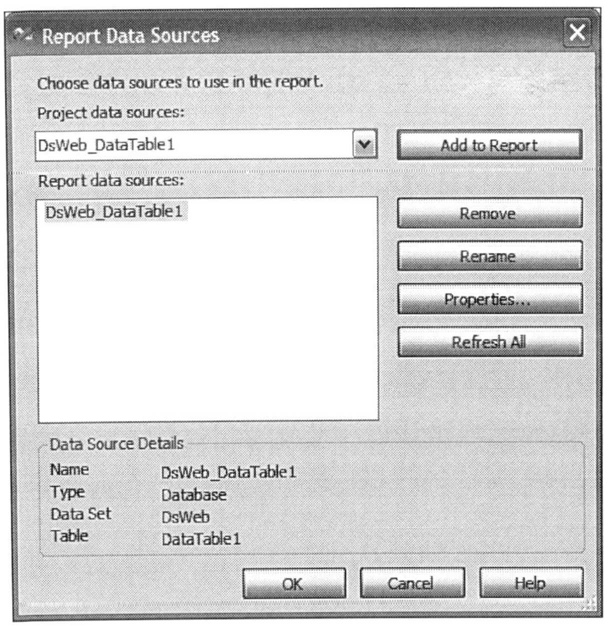

6. Click on the menu item **Data** and from the drop-down click on **Show Data Sources** (*Shift+Alt+D*).

   A floating window **Website Data Sources** gets displayed. It can be parked anywhere and displays the **Data Table1** in the DataSet, **DsWeb** as shown:

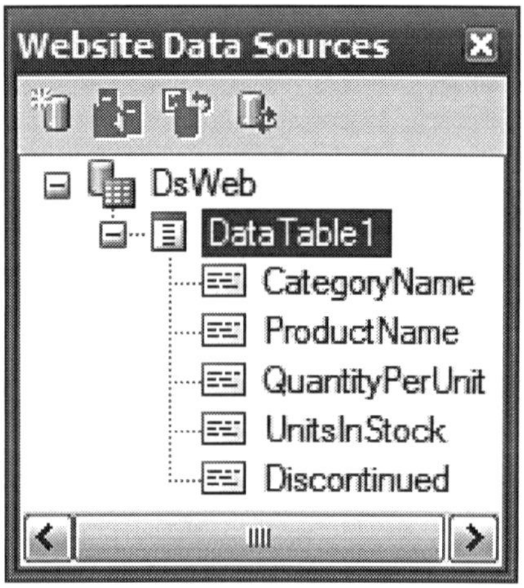

7. Click on **CategoryName** in the **Website Data Sources** window and drag it over to the **Body** of the report and drop it into the first column and second row of the table as shown:

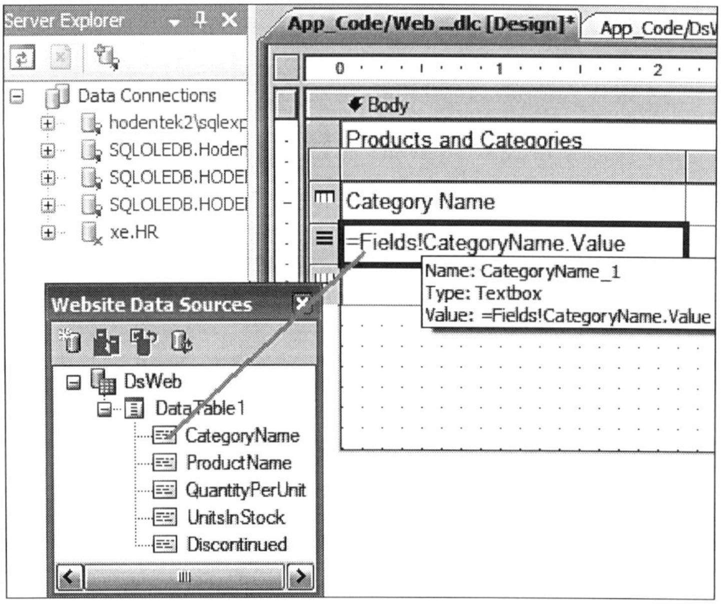

8. In a similar manner, drag-and-drop **ProductName** into the second column, second row followed by **UnitsInStock** into the third column, second row. Click on the columns and from the properties set the individual columns widths to **1.5in** and make changes to fonts (size and font weight) as required.

   The following screenshot shows the report design with all elements added and changes to the font made:

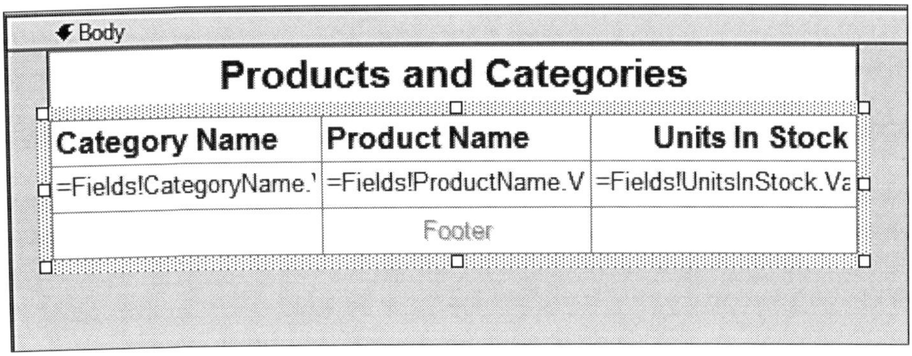

9. Drag-and-drop a **Microsoft ReportViewer** control from the **Toolbox** onto the **Default.aspx** page. From the *Smart Tasks* on this control, choose to add the **Web. Products.rdlc** as shown:

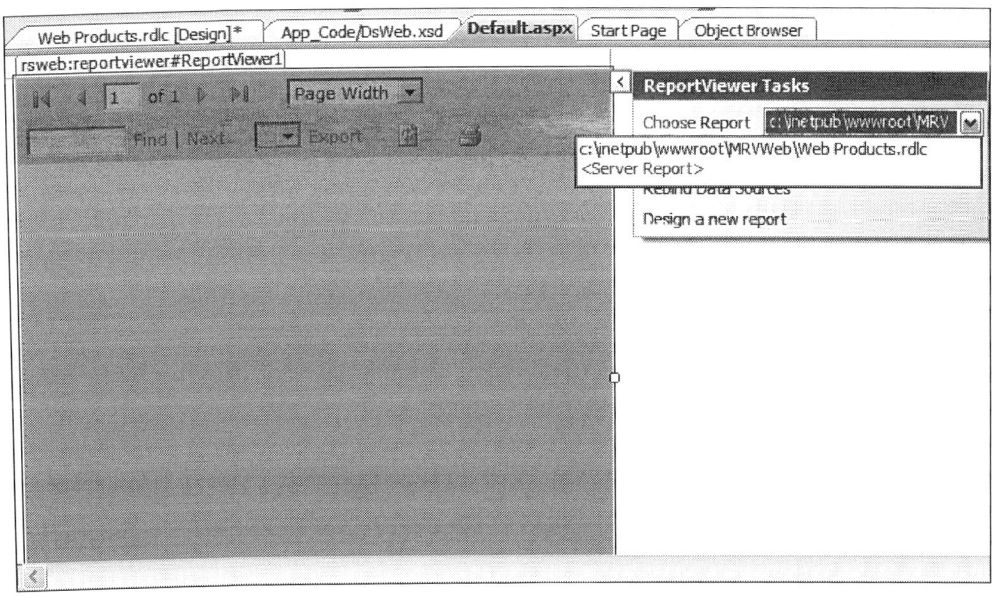

10. Build the web site and display the **Default.aspx** page by right-clicking **Default.aspx** page and choosing **View in Browser**.

    After a little while the **Default.aspx** page gets displayed in the IE browser as shown:

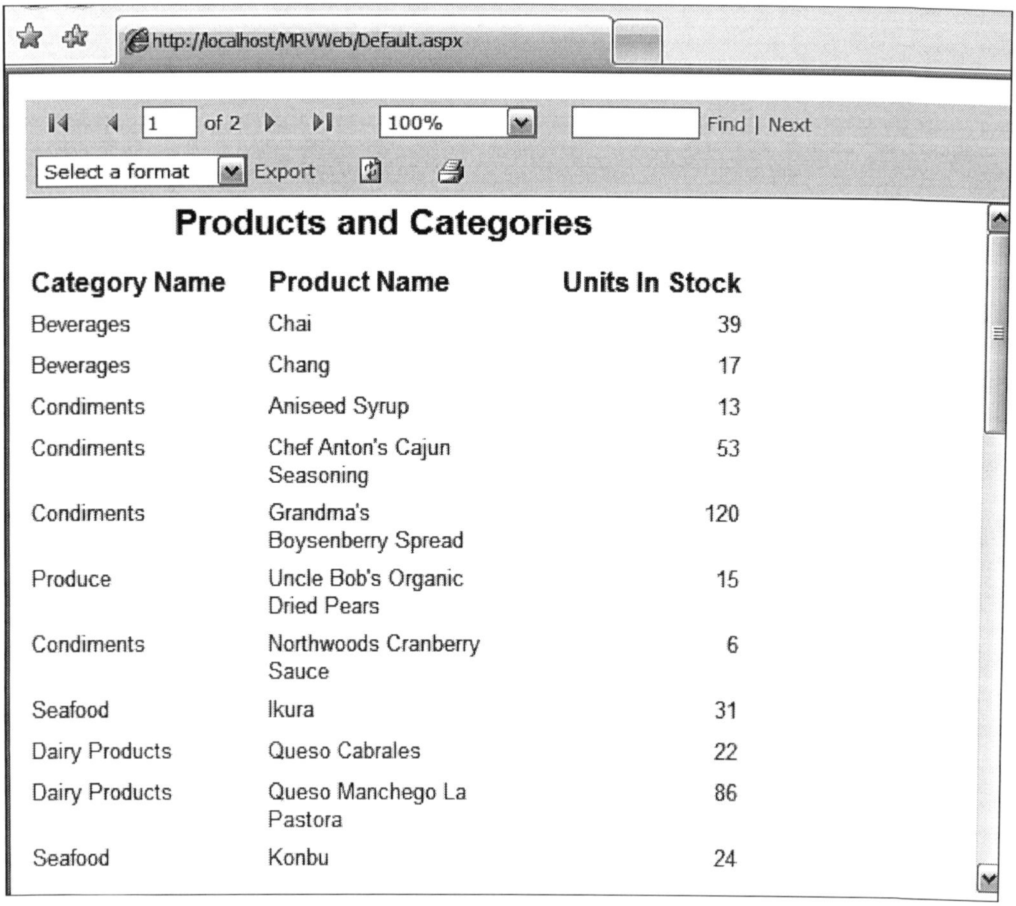

> **Web-based report:**
> The web report can be accessed by providing its URL address in a browser, as the report is hosted on the local web server.

In case the web page does not show up and complain about access failure (to the database), you must add the ASP.NET as a login to the SQL Server 2008 security logins. This is because you are trying to access the database from an ASP.NET application.

In this exercise you used the built-in Query Builder to create an SQL Statement. However, if you know enough of SQL you could directly type-in the statement and reduce the number of wizard steps you may need to take. For beginners, the Query Builder is an invaluable tool.

Summary

Two types of ReportViewer controls were described with examples, one for the Windows environment and the other for the web. While each of them has two processing modes, a local mode and a remote mode, only the local mode has been described. In Chapter 8, the remote mode processing will be described.

As far as report authoring is concerned, you have seen the use of a report wizard in the first example, and report authoring starting from scratch using the report template in another exercise. Each of these authoring options has capabilities beyond those described in the hands-on exercises especially as related to their interactive nature and the variety of rich formatting options they provide. You will work with these features in Chapter 7.

Charts and gauges provide a great deal of visual information to reports and you will see them in Chapter 6.

4

Visual Studio 2008 Business Intelligence Template Projects

In Chapter 3, we worked with Visual Studio's built-in features to generate reports and to embed them in either Windows forms or web forms. In the case of web forms, the reports were available for URL access on the intranet web server. These reports were generally processed on the client side. In addition to this, Visual Studio also has Report Server projects that are available in the **Business Intelligence Development Studio** (**BIDS**). Furthermore there is also the Report Builder 2.0 stand-alone tool for generating (authoring) reports.

In this chapter, we will work with the Visual Studio 2008's Business Intelligence Template projects. The reports created using these templates are hosted on the Report Server by a process called **deployment**. You will also deploy the report on the report server you configured in Chapter 1. Hosting reports on Report Server will allow you to work with the reports in meaningful ways as you would do in a business environment. Another topic you will learn about is Report Model and its deployment on the Report Server. The deployed models can then be used by Report Builder 2.0 to generate stand-alone as well as ad hoc reports. This is shown in Chapter 7. Importing MS Access reports is discussed towards the end of the chapter. It provides a great tool for those interested in report authoring and also for those who are interested in migrating reports.

Visual Studio 2008 Business Intelligence Projects

When you create a project in Visual Studio 2008, you can choose the Business Intelligence Projects category. In this category you will find the following project templates. These are the same templates you would find in BIDS.

- Report Server Project
- Report Server Wizard Project
- Report Model Project

Using the Report Server project template

When you choose to start with a Report Server Project, the program creates two blank folders, Shared Data Sources and Reports, in the project. From each of these folders you can begin the process of creating a report.

Right-clicking the **Shared Data Sources** folder provides the following options:

- **Add New Data Source**—brings up the Shared Data Source window where you can begin configuring a shared data source.
- **Add | New Item...**—brings up the Report Project Category Add New Item report category window which consists of Report wizard, Report and Data Source templates.
- **Add | Existing Item...**—allows you to browse your file system for `.rdl` and `*.rds` file types.

Right-clicking the **Reports** folder gives you the following options:

- Add a New Report—brings up the **Report** wizard.
- **Add | New Item...**—brings up the Report Project Category which consists of the Report wizard, Report and Data Source templates
- **Add | Existing Item...**—Allows you to browse your file system for *.rdl and rds file types
- **Import Reports | Microsoft Access**—Allows you to import an MS Access Report. You will be working on this in *Hands-on 4.5*.

Therefore, you can see that there are a number of ways of doing the same thing. In summary, to create a report for the report server, you need to create a data source and you need to work with the report wizard or create from scratch (starting from a blank report) by setting up the data source to feed this report.

Using the Report Server wizard project template

When you start with the Report Server wizard project, you create the same two empty folders. Simultaneous with the creation of the folders, the Report wizard pops-up and you will be guided by the wizard through the report authoring process including the data access and the design of the report.

Using the Report Model project template

When you create a Report Model project from the template you will be creating a project with three empty folders, Data Sources, Data Source Views and Report Models. You create a data source by right-clicking the **Data Sources** folder. You then reference this data source to create a Data Source view. The Data Source view created is then used in creating the Report Model. This is completely a wizard-driven activity which you will be doing in *Hands-on 4.3*. The report which you made using the Report Builder will be based on the model you created.

Report authoring

The basic steps in report authoring consists of connecting to data sources and running queries against the database, retrieving data (essentially columns from a table or related tables), applying filtering and sorting to control the data, and embellishing with any necessary aggregations before displaying the data in an appropriately designed report. The **Query Designer Tool** comes in handy in retrieving the data from the database. While the Query Designer can also apply filtering, sorting and aggregating, the *Hands-on exercise 4.1* uses the tool to extract the dataset (set of data retrieved from the database). The report wizard uses its built-in capability to filter, sort and aggregate the results.

Data sources used in reports

There are two ways you can define connections to the data sources. Data sources can be embedded or shared. The difference lies only in the way the connection data is stored and managed. The Visual Studio templates support creation of these data sources by wizards that allow you to set up your connections.

Embedded data sources

The embedded data source connection is report-specific and this information gets embedded in the report definition or stays internal to the subscription. You can make an embedded connection only in the Report Designer. You cannot use the Report Manager.

In order to bring up the wizard you need to click on **Reports | Add New Report.** In the displayed **Report Wizard** page, click on the **Next** button. You will be presented with the **Select a Data Source Page** of the wizard as shown. The default is the **Shared data source** if you have a previously defined shared data source; otherwise the option **New data source** will be enabled.

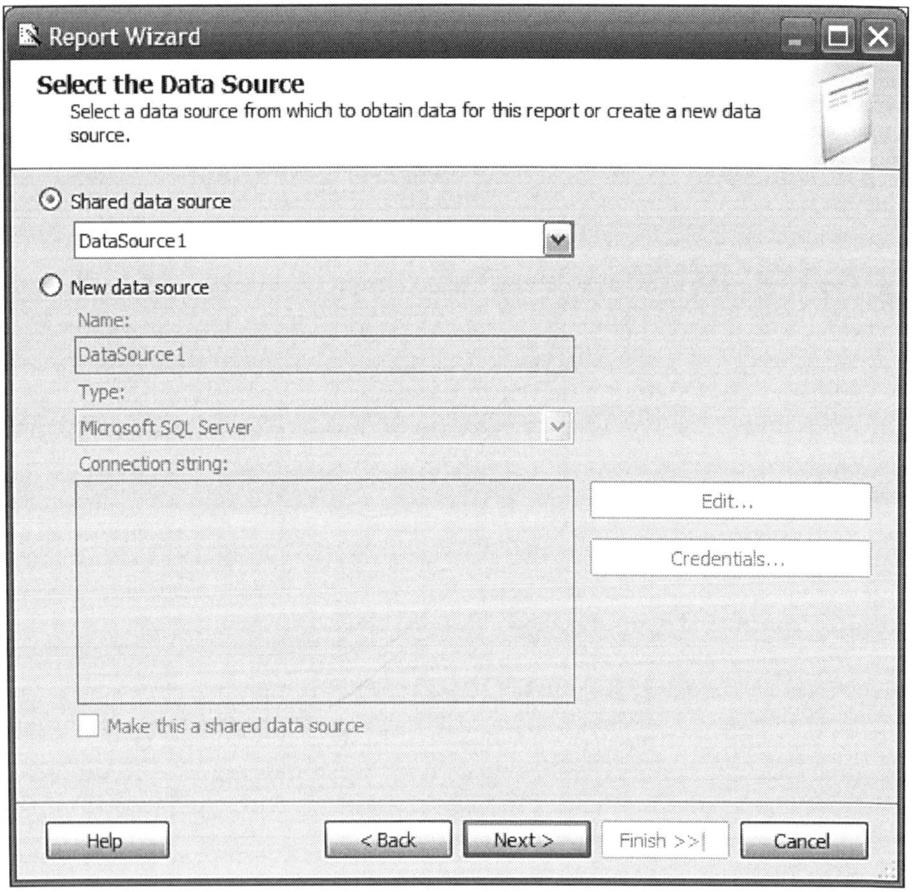

Shared data sources

Unlike an embedded data source, a shared data source, as the name implies, is shared among a number of reports. It can also be defined inside or outside the Visual Studio 2008 IDE. The default data source type option is shared, as discussed previously. When you accept the default in the previous screenshot, you will have created a shared data source. An `.rds` file is then added to the **Shared Data Sources** folder in the Report Server project.

Report Data and Query Designer

The query designer will be described during its usage in *Hands-on exercise 3.2*. It is also explained briefly in the *Hands-on exercise 4.1*. Once the query that is going to be bound to the report is finalized, the data used in the report will be available from the **Report Data** window. It can be accessed from the **View** (*Ctrl+Alt+D*) menu. An example of a **Report Data** window is shown in the next screenshot.

In addition to the database fields in the **DataSet**, you also have the **Built-in Fields** folder which contains some of the report properties, folders for report **Parameters** and report **Images**.

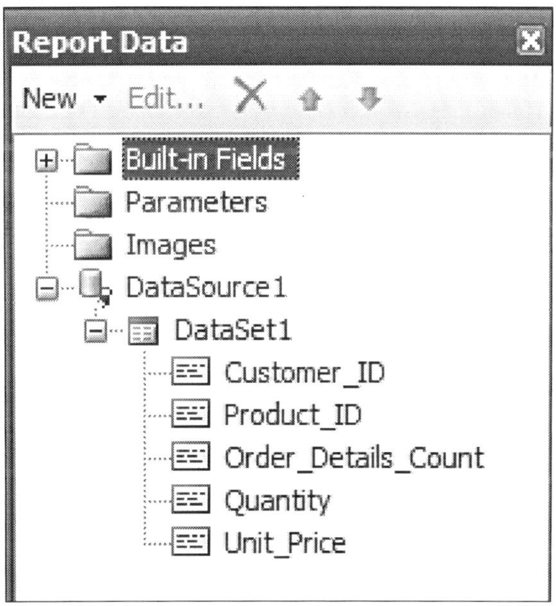

Report designer

When you choose to create a Report Server project and add a report, the design interface also gets displayed. The design interface, also called the Report Designer, consists of a **Toolbox** with report related items, **Design and Preview panes** and a **Report** menu items drop-down, all shown in the same figure. To get the Report menu items you need to click on **Reports**. These completely take care of the physical layout and formatting of the Report.

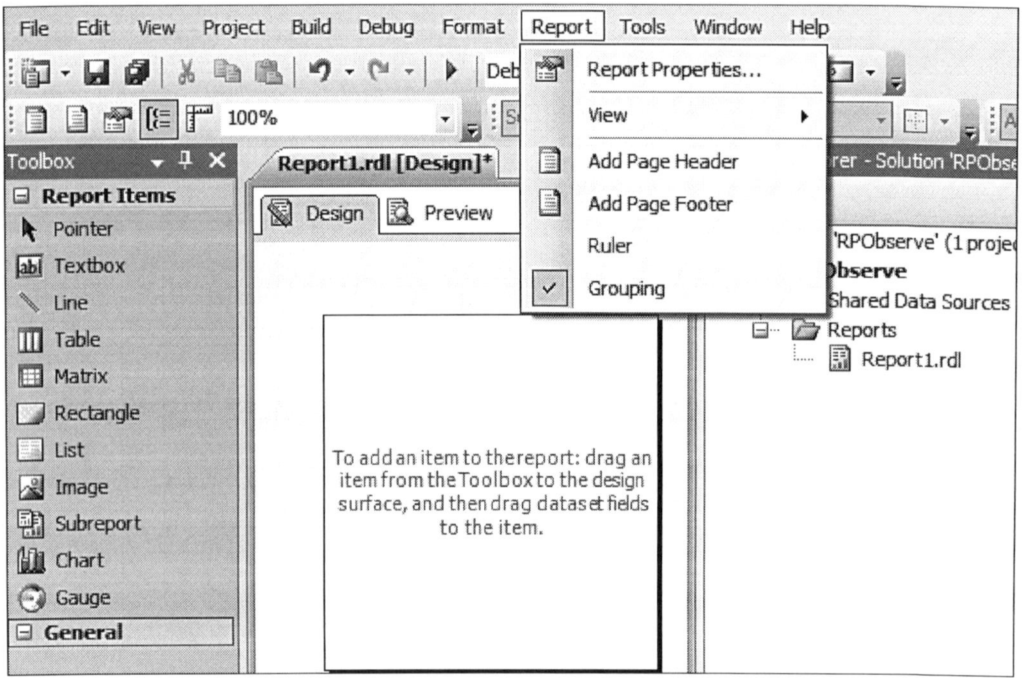

The process of building up the report begins by placing (drag-and-drop) controls that can display data on to the body of the report, which, to begin with, is empty. Then you drag-and-drop the Report data items one-by-one into the controls that can bind to the data. When you use the Report Wizard however, the above activities will take place under the wizard's guidance.

Report items toolbox

The Report items may be roughly classified as follows:

Report Item	Function
Table, Matrix, List, Chart, Gauge	These are the data regions of a report and each links to a data set. Table, Matrix, and List together are called Tablix. When they are placed on the body of a report, they immediately call up the Data Source Wizard. Report definition is incomplete without the data source.
Text Box	This is a container for plain text such as a column header. It can also contain data or a built-in data field. Table cells contain textboxes.
Image	Links to an embedded, external or database referenced image. The MIME type is an important property that must be specified.
Line and Rectangle	These are graphical elements to improve the report design. However, rectangles can contain data regions.

All report items have their own property pages and provide exhaustive support for developing highly interactive reports. Some of these features you will be using in the next chapter.

Expression builder

Report menu items can be used to add page headers and footers. These can contain textboxes which can contain other Report features such as page number, execution time and so on. These can be dragged-and-dropped into the textboxes placed in headers and footers from the **Built-in Fields** in Report Data, contain expressions bringing in other values such as date and sometimes data from the database. The next figure shows a text box that may be populated by database fields using the expression builder which is invoked when it is chosen from a contextual menu in the text box. In the next screenshot, the empty textbox will be used to invoke (by right-clicking inside the textbox) the query builder to fill the textbox with the full name (**First Name, Last Name**).

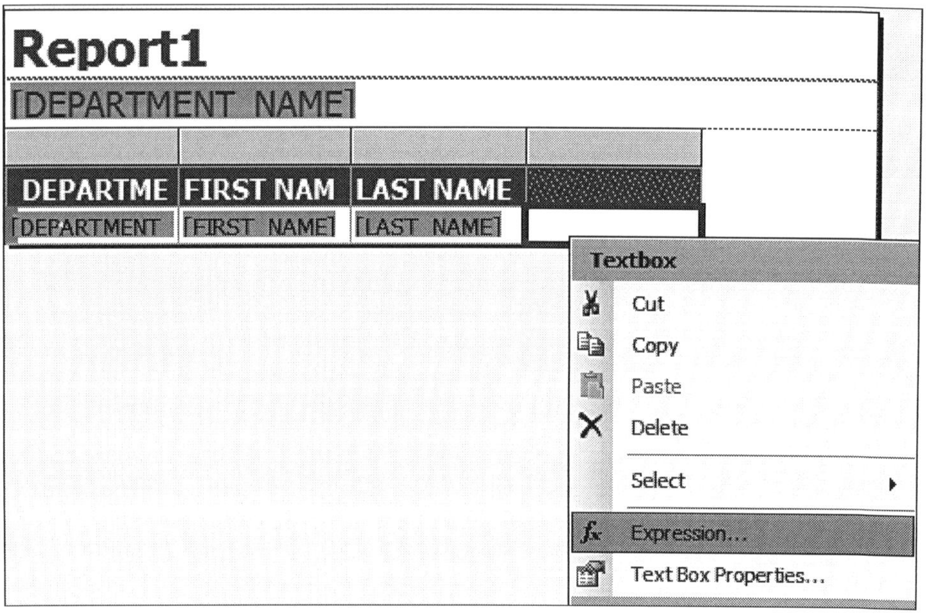

The **Expression...** menu item is a common tool whenever you are required to build an expression consisting of built-in fields, database fields and others. This utility has a long history of usage in Microsoft Access from its earliest versions.

As shown in the next figure, two database fields are concatenated together to provide a value to be placed in the textbox by creating an expression. The expression is set by choosing **Category** | **Item** | **Values** in that order and any logical or mathematical operators chosen again from the **Operators**.

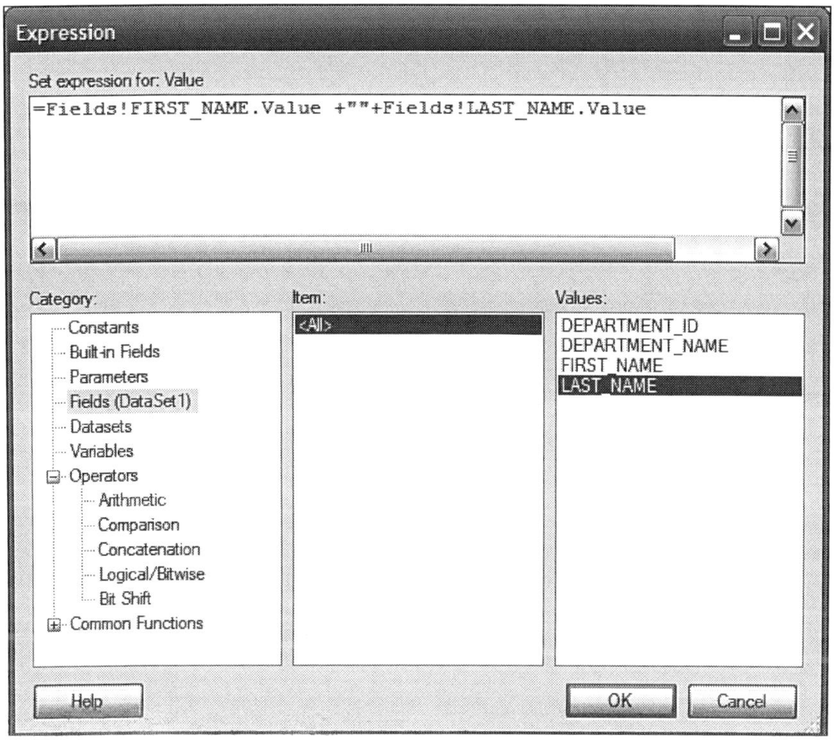

After fomulating the expression, you will be seeing the expression that populates the empty textbox as shown in the following design view:

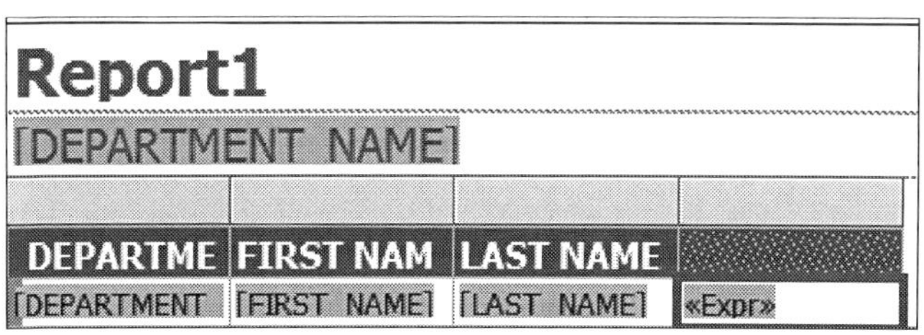

Other design tools

Visual Studio also provides other design help items like object handles, rulers, object grouping, and snap-to-grid alignment features. Some of these features become visible when you are dragging and aligning objects with respect to each other on the design surface. The design surface is shown in the following screenshot as a blank report with no data defined. These design tools must be utilized to get an aesthetically pleasing report.

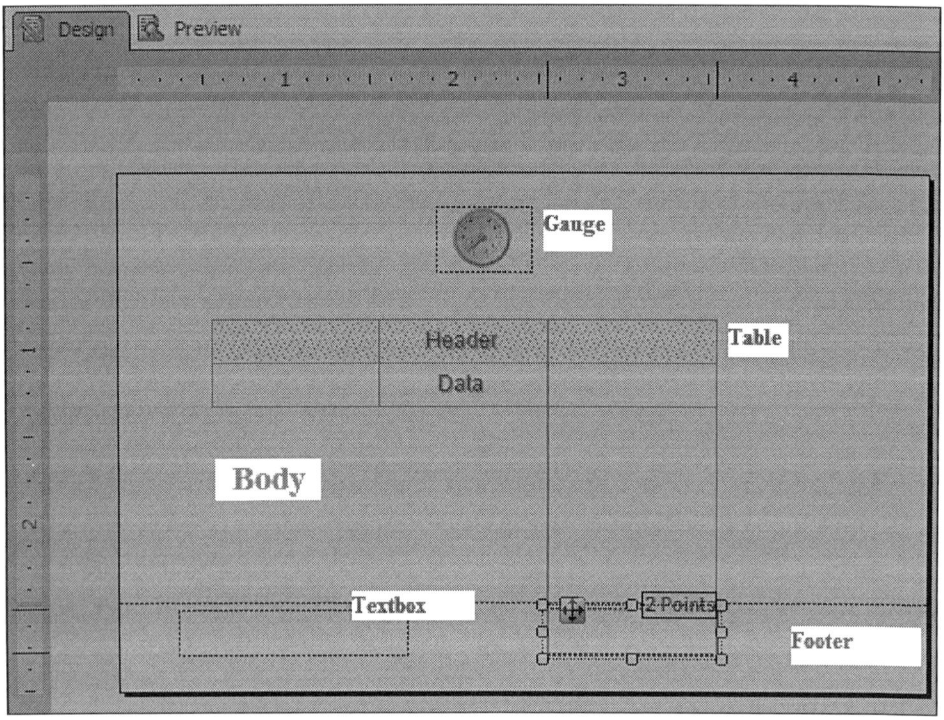

Hands-on exercise 4.1: Creating a Report Server project using the Report Server Wizard project

In this hands-on exercise you will be creating a Report Server Wizard project. This wizard will guide you through the following steps in authoring a report after you create the project:

- Creating a Report Server Wizard project
- Connecting to a data source

- Building a query
- Designing the report

In order to create a Report Server project we must start the Visual Studio 2008 from it shortcut and choose to create a Business Intelligence project. You will be doing this in this section.

1. Click **File | New | Project...** to display the **New Project** window as shown in the next screenshot.
2. Select **Report Server Project Wizard** under **Visual Studio installed templates** from the **Business Intelligence Projects**. Provide a name for the project (herein **RSPW08**) and if needed change the location for project files on your hard disc by using the **Browse...**button. Then click on the **OK** button.

   You create the project with two folders: **Shared Data Sources** and **Reports**, which you can see displayed in the Project folder in **Solution Explorer**.

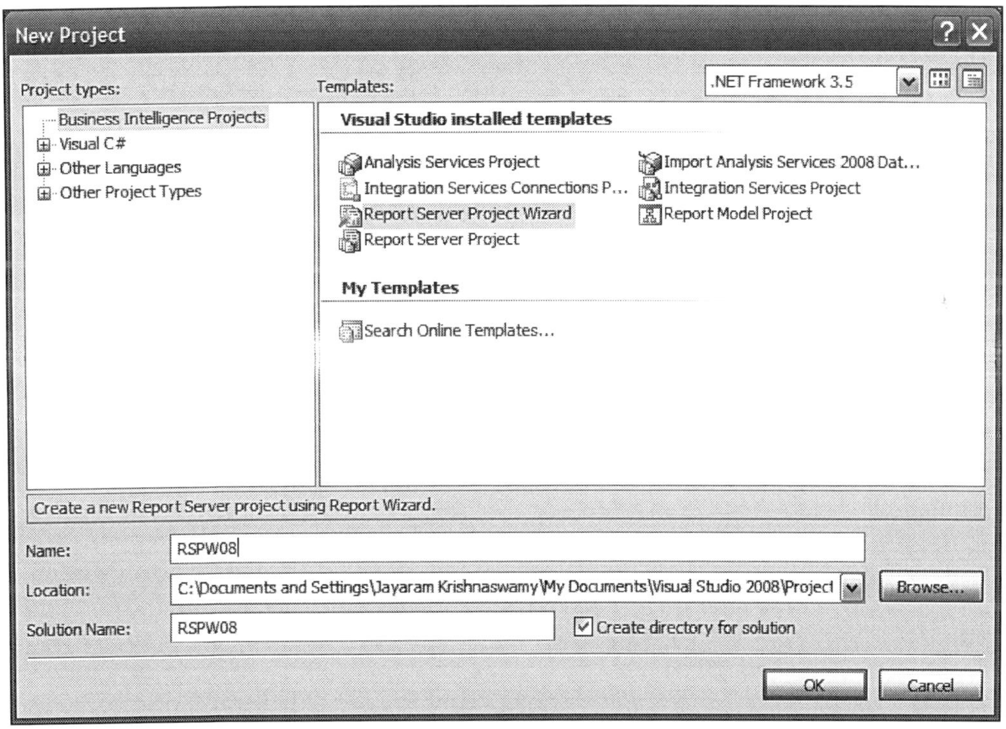

   You will also bring up a modal **Report Wizard** window (**Welcome to the Report Wizard**). Read the notes on this page.

Connecting to a data source

Once the project is created the very first thing to do is to connector a data source.

1. Click on the **Next** button.

   You will open the **Select the Data Source** page of the wizard as shown:

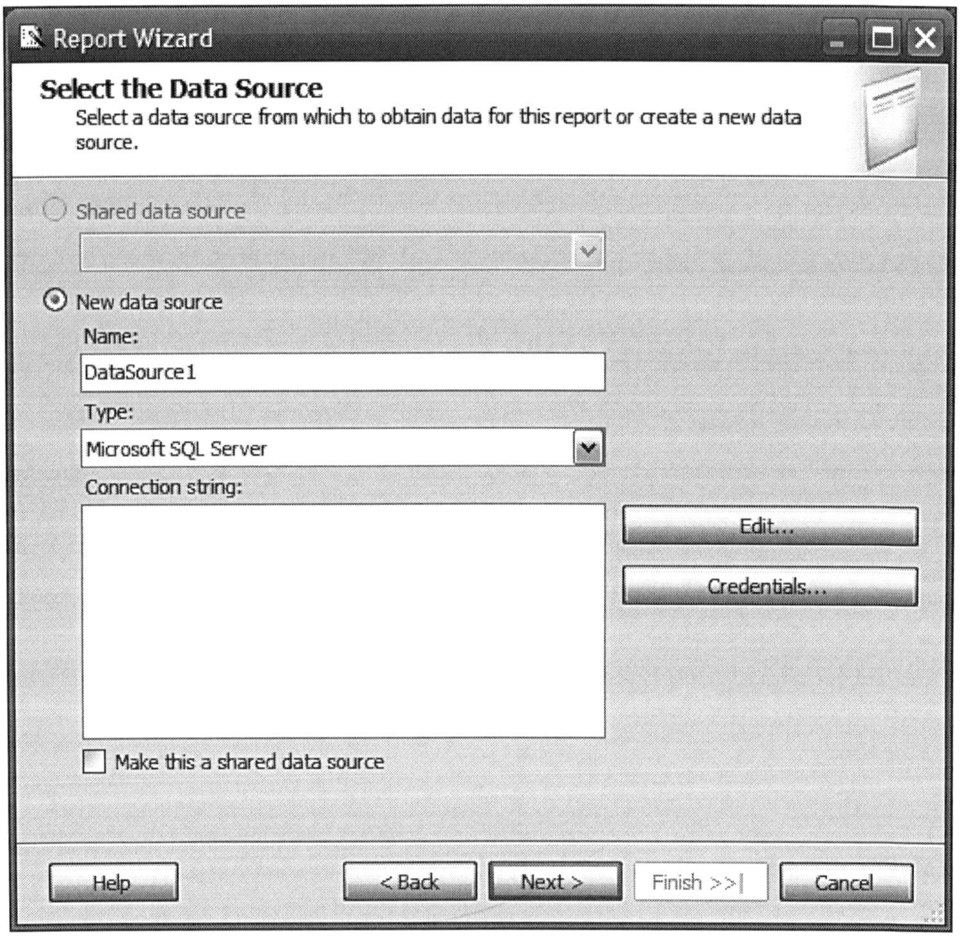

For the new data source, **DataSource1,** you could choose from among a number of sources in the drop-down list as shown in the next screenshot (**Hyperion EssBase** and **Teradata** are also in this list). The default is Microsoft SQL Server.

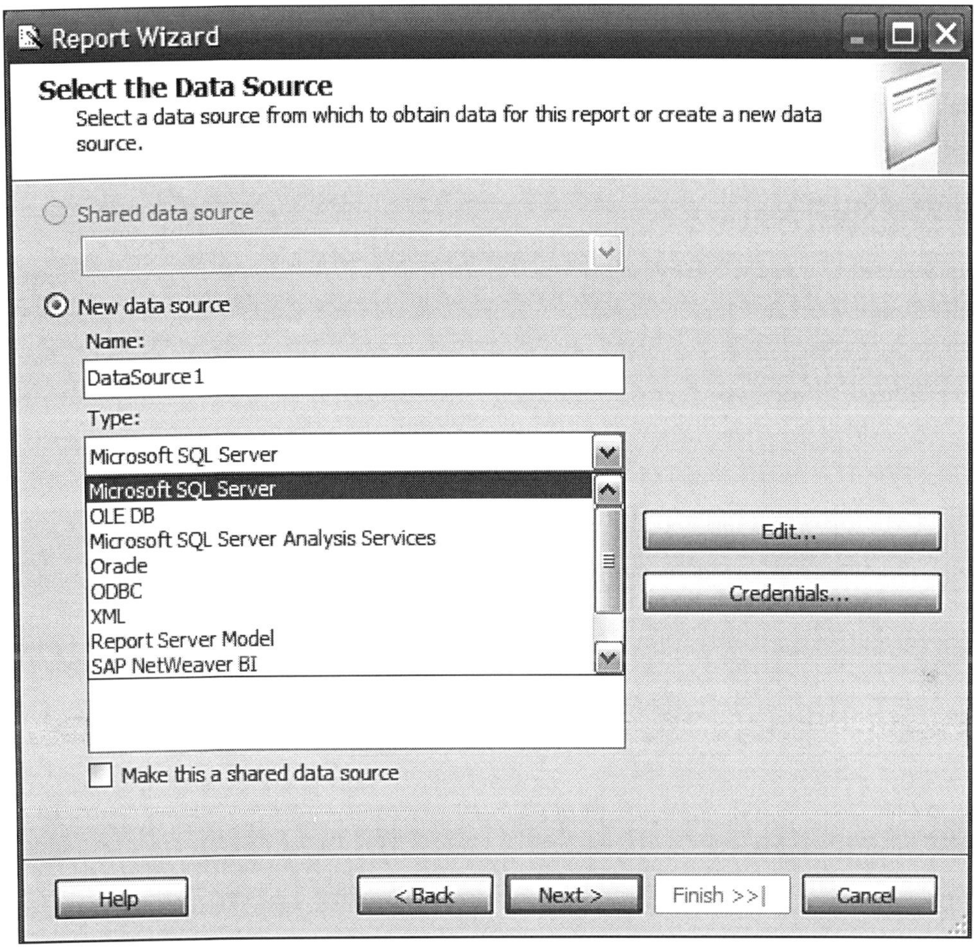

2. Accept the default for the data source type (Microsoft SQL Server) and click on the **Edit...** button.

3. In the **Connection Properties** window that gets displayed, click on the **Refresh** button for the **Server name**.

   In the drop-down list you will get to see all the accessible servers as shown:

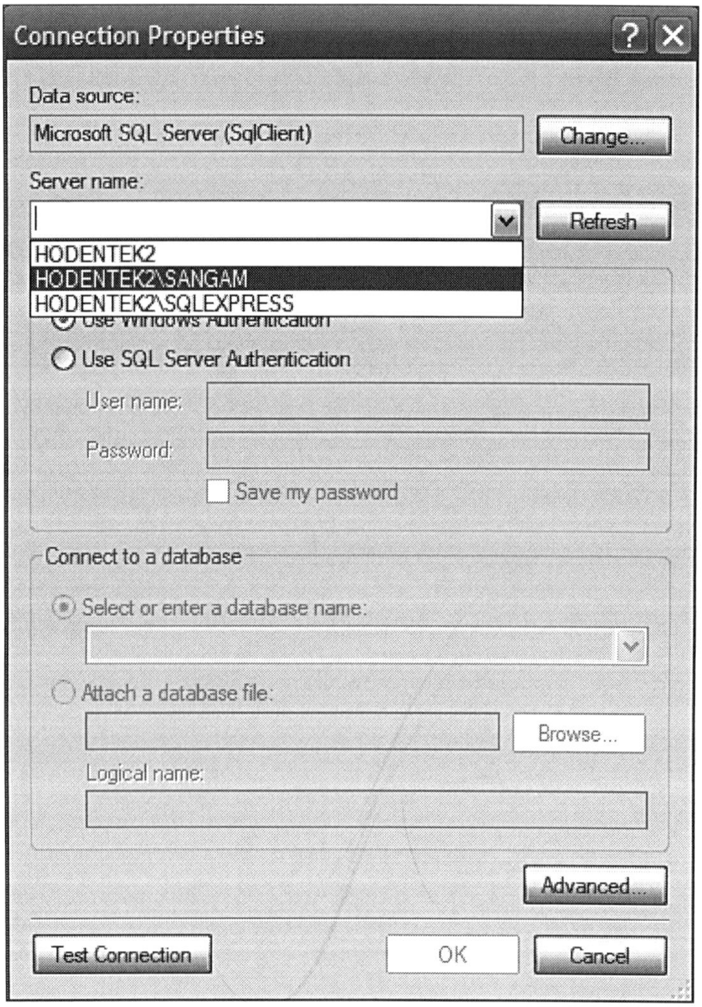

4. Click on **Hodentek2\SANGAM** (this will be your choice of the SQL Server that you are able to access on your machine).

   The default **Use Windows Authentication** is appropriate for the **Hodentek2 \ SANGAM** server. If you configured **SQL Server Authentication** you should use the appropriate **User Name** and **Password** to proceed further.

5. Click on the drop-down handle for **Select or enter database name** which gets enabled and from the list click on **TestNorthwind**.

6. Click on **Test Connection** button to verify that your connection information is correct. You should get a **Test Results** window displaying a **Test Connection succeeded** message.
7. Click on the **OK** button in the **Test Results** window as well as in the **Connection Properties** window.

   You will be returned to the **Select the Data Source** page of the wizard, which now displays the connection information in the **Connection string** field of this page as shown:

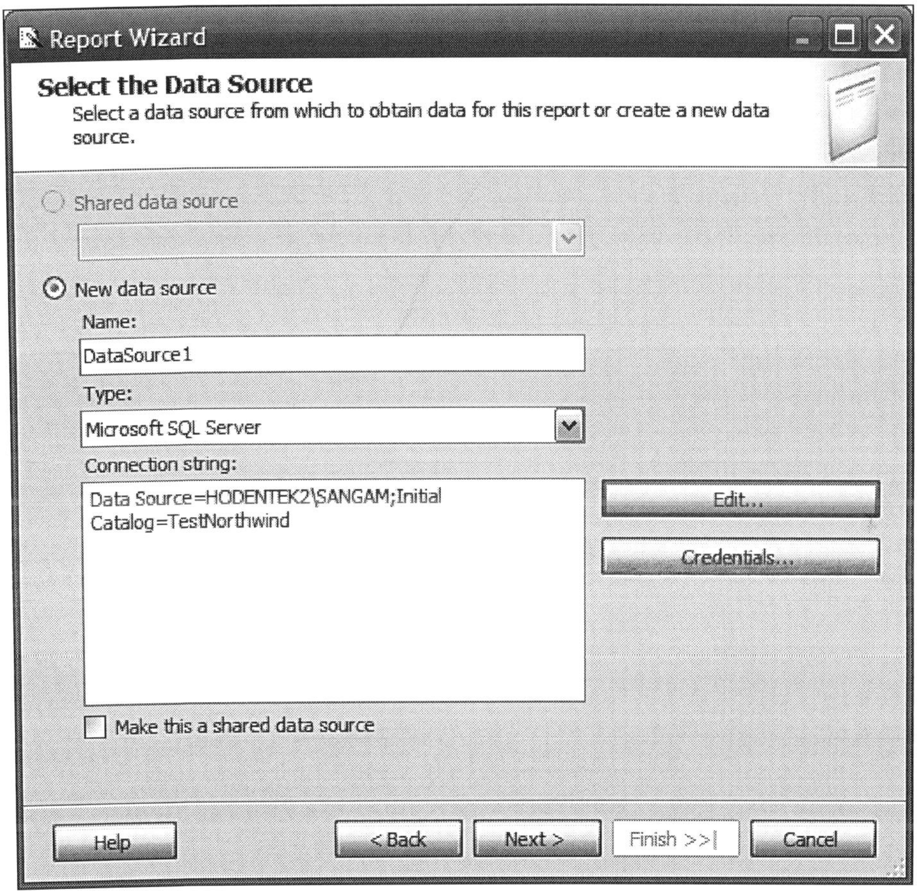

The Connection String may be different in your case.

Building a query

After connecting to the data source you need to retrieve a set of data that you want to show in your report. You will be doing this in this section.

8. Click on the **Next** button.

This opens the **Query Designer** window as shown. There are two options. You can use the Query Builder or enter the SQL statement directly. If you want you may type in the query statement in the window that gets dsisplayed when you hit the icon **Edit As Text** at top left. You may even **Import** a file with extension SQL or RDL, if you have saved copies of the query files you want to work with.

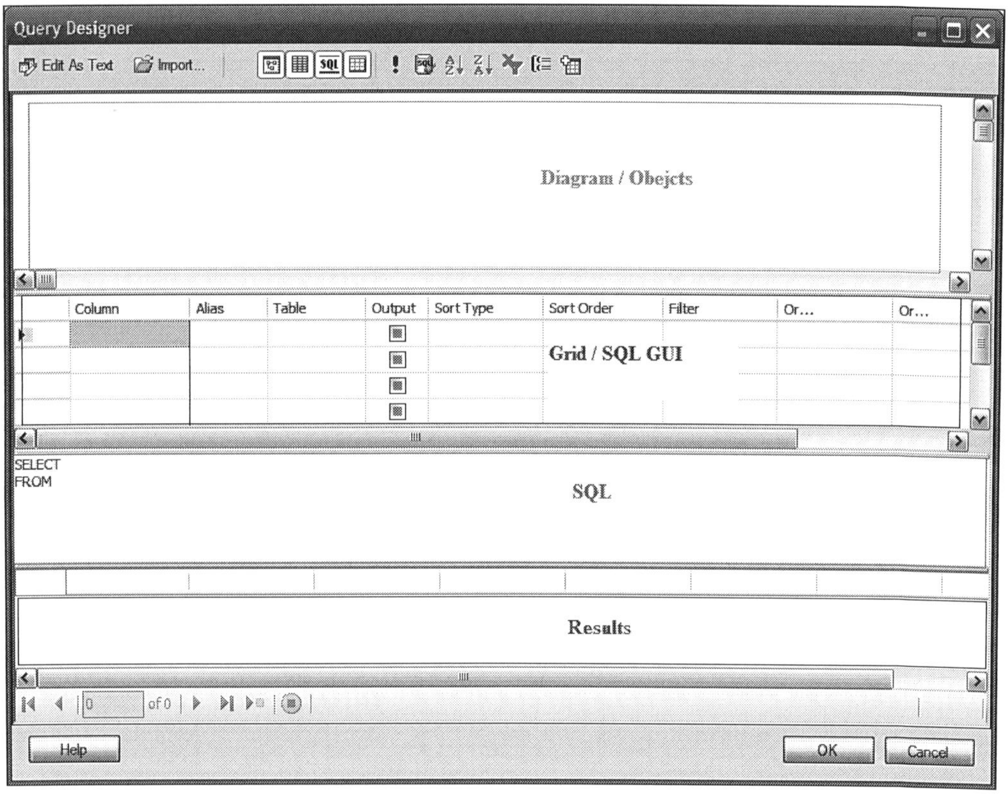

9. In the pane marked **Diagram/Objects,** right-click and from the drop-down choose the **Add Table...** item to display the **Add Table** window as shown:

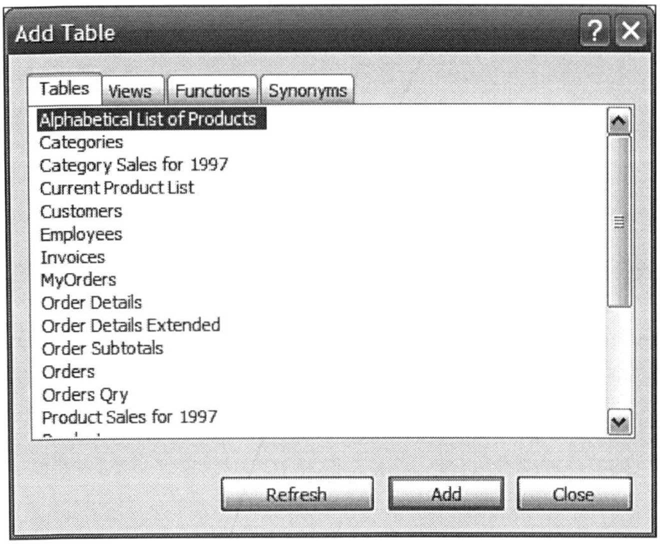

10. Click on the **Customer** and **Orders** tables while holding down the *Ctrl* key. Then click on the **Add** button to add the two tables to the **Diagram / Objects** pane of the Query Builder.
11. Close the **Add Table** button by clicking on the **Close** button.
12. Click (do not place check mark in the **CustomerID** check box) on the **CustomerID** column in the **Customers** table and drag it over. Then click on the **CustomerID** column in the **Orders** table to make a **join**.

    You will observe that this establishes a join between them as shown. The SQL text changes to reflect this action.

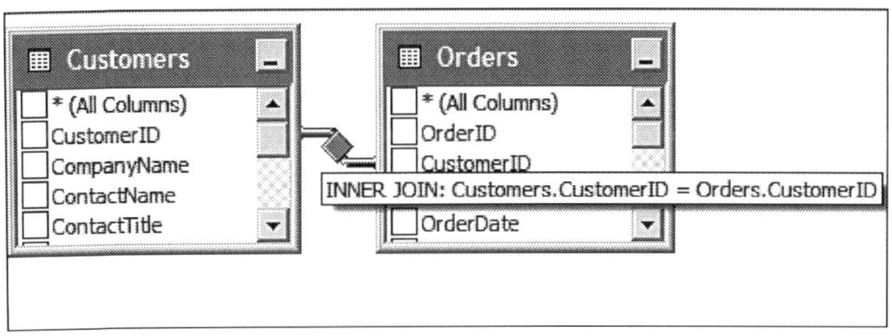

13. Place a check mark in the columns **CustomerID**, **CompanyName**, **Address**, **City** and **PostalCode** in the **Customers** table and **OrderDate**, **RequiredDate**, **ShippedDate**, **Freight** and **EmployeeID** from the **Orders** table.

    The Query Builder reconfigures the SQL statement and the grid gets filled up with the choice of these columns.

14. Right-click in any of the panes and choose the **Execute SQL** option. This executes the SQL statement and the result appears in the **Results** pane as shown. Only a few of the 830 records returned are shown:

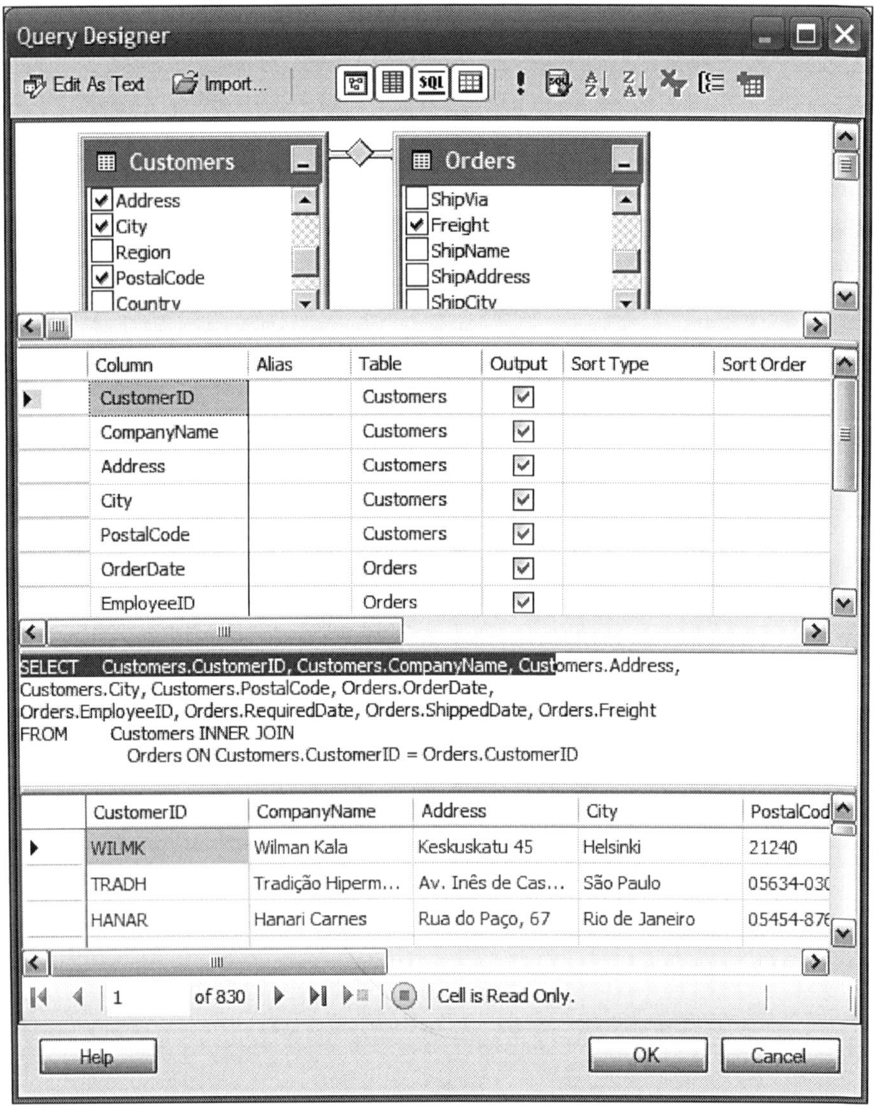

15. Click on the **Next** button.

    The Report Wizard's **Design the Query** page gets displayed again, this time the Query String box gets filled up with the following SQL Statement built by the Query Builder Tool.

```
SELECT Customers.CustomerID, Customers.CompanyName, Customers.
Address, Customers.City, Customers.PostalCode, Orders.OrderDate,
Orders.EmployeeID, Orders.RequiredDate, Orders.ShippedDate,
Orders.Freight
FROM Customers INNER JOIN Orders ON Customers.CustomerID =
Orders.CustomerID
```

16. Click on the **Next** button.

Designing the report

This brings up the **Select the Report Type** page of the wizard.

17. Accept the default **Tabular** and click on the **Next** button.
18. In the **Design the Table** page, select **CompanyName** by clicking the **Page** button. Then select the CustomerID and EmployeeID by clicking on the **Group** button. Select the remaining items in the **Available fields** by clicking the **Details** button. Now, add these items to the **Displayed fields** on the right-hand side as shown. Click on the **Next** button.

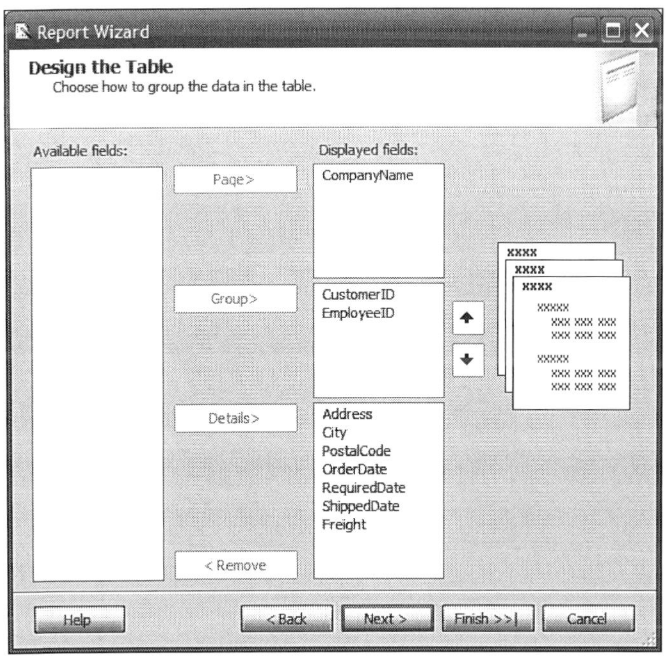

19. In the **Choose the Table Layout** page that follows, accept the default choice **Stepped**. Place check marks for the **Include Subtotals** and **Enable drilldown** check boxes and click on the **Next** button.
20. In the **Choose the Table Style** page that follows, choose a style that you like (here **Corporate** is chosen) and click on the **Next** button.
21. In the **Choose the Deployment Location** page, delete the default entries in both the **Report server** and **Deployment folder** text boxes and click on the **Next** button.

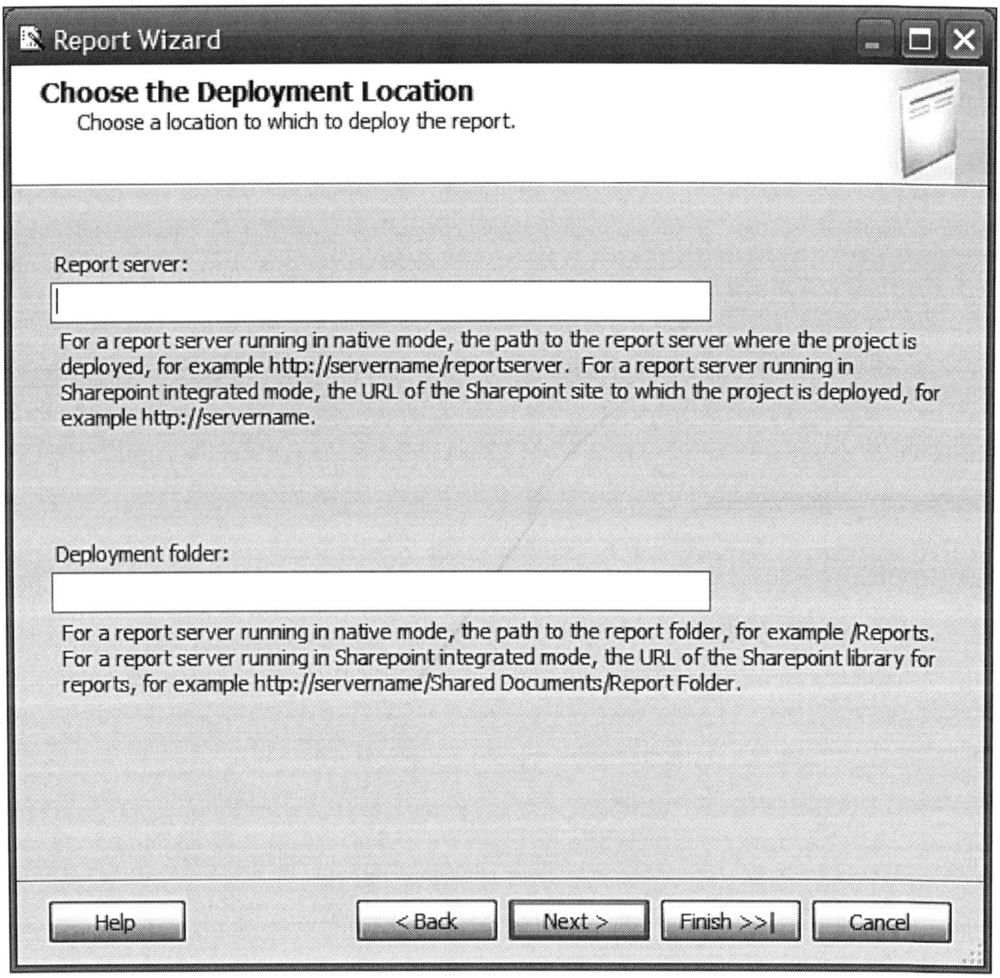

22. In the **Completing the Wizard** page, change the default report name from **Report1** to something meaningful. Here it is named **OrderInformation.** Click on the **Finish** button.

    After a little while the **OrderInformation** report appears in the **Report Designer** tabbed page as shown. Also a file **OrderInformation.rdl** gets added to the project folder in the **Solution Explorer**.

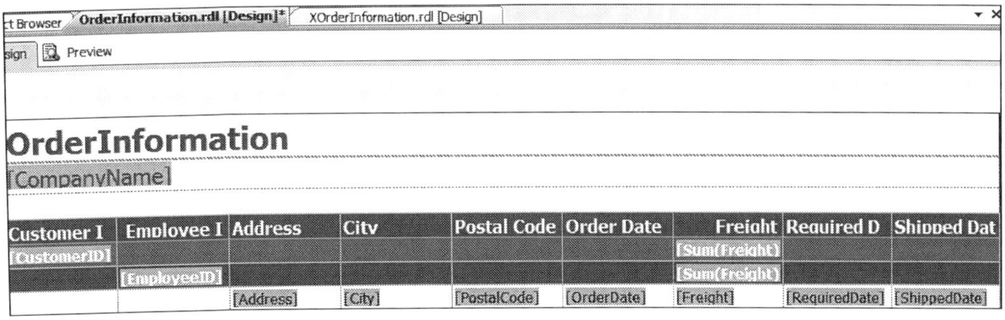

23. Click on the **Preview** tab of the **Report Designer**.

    The program starts running and displays a progress icon **Report is being generated**. Shortly thereafter it displays the report as shown. In this display one of the grouping columns is expanded to show the drill down option chosen during the design.

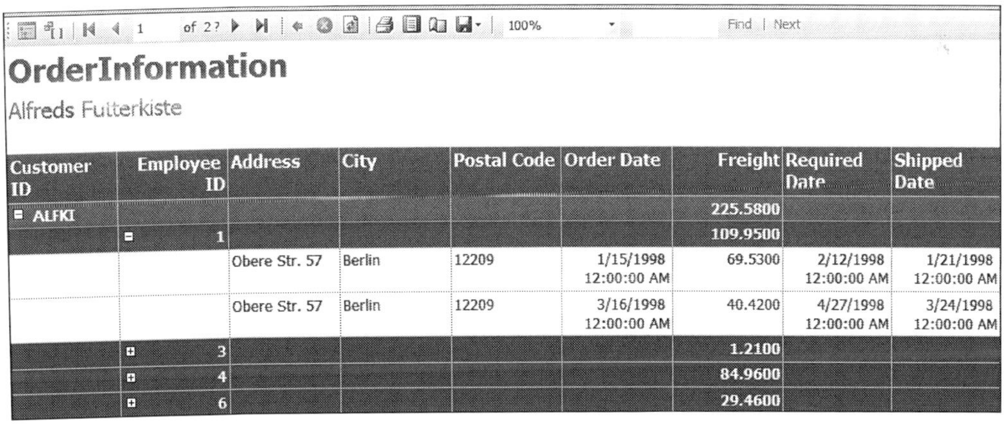

Deploying the report to the Report Server

The report created by using the Report authoring templates in BIDS is a server report and is to be hosted on the Report Server. In SQL Server 2008, the reports with the extension `.rdl` are hosted on the Report Server.

The **Choose the Deployment Location** page of the wizard in *Hands-on 4.1* was skipped. But if you were to fill-in the following details for the two text fields on that page the report would have deployed to the Report Server at the conclusion of the wizard.

Report server: `http://hodentek2:8080/ReportServer_SANGAM`

Deployment folder: This could be any name of your choice and this could also be an existing folder on the Report Server.

Methods of deploying reports to the Report Server

There are two ways you can deploy reports to the Report Server. They are:

- Starting with the Report Server Project Wizard and providing deployment information during the deployment step of the wizard as discussed previously.
- Right-clicking the report definition file and choosing **Deploy** from the drop-down menu.

Hands-on exercise 4.2: Deploying and viewing the report designed in Hands-on 4.1

You will start with no deployed reports on the server (a situation if this is the first time you are deploying a report) and then you will deploy a report to the server. You will then review changes to the report server after deploying a report.

1. Open the IE browser and type-in (you may need to type-in information specific to your configuration) the URL of your Report Server.

   After a little while the above server shows up in the IE browser as shown. As there are no deployed items, you will see an empty server.

2. From **Project | RSPWIz08Properties...**, open the **RSPWIz08 Property Pages** Window as shown.

   The values for the **TargetDataSourceFolder** and **TargetReportFolder** are the defaults, but these can be changed. The **OverwriteDataSources** by default is set to **False**. This can be changed as well if changing the option is acceptable. The **TargetServerURL** is the URL appropriate for your installation.

3. Accept defaults for the first three deployment options and type in the **TargetServerURL** as shown. Click **OK**.

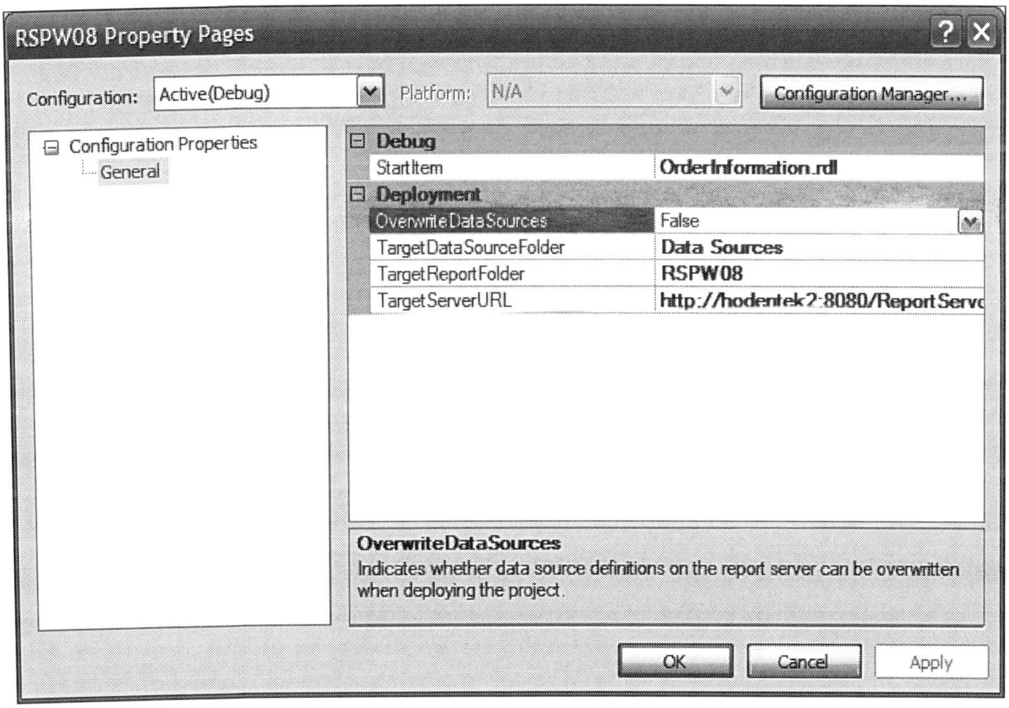

4. Right-click the **OrderInformation.rdl** file and from the drop-down choose **Deploy**.

   After a little processing, the report gets deployed to the Report Server. This is assuming you provided the correct **TargetServerURL**. You should now see the following message in the **Output** window.

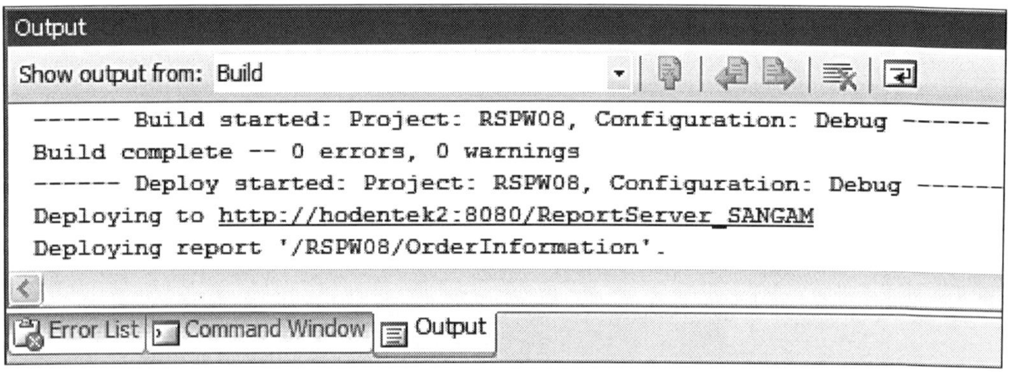

5. Refresh the IE browser while making sure the address shown is the Report Server URL.

   Now you will see the deployed report on the Report Server when you access it in IE.

6. Now click on the link **RSPW08** in the IE browser.

   This will send a URL request. This is a request to list all the reports in this project. The following screenshot shows what is displayed in the browser. The access to reports is controlled by roles that are assigned to authenticated users as you will see in Chapter 5. In this hands-on, the authenticated user is accessing the objects allowed for his role specified in the server.

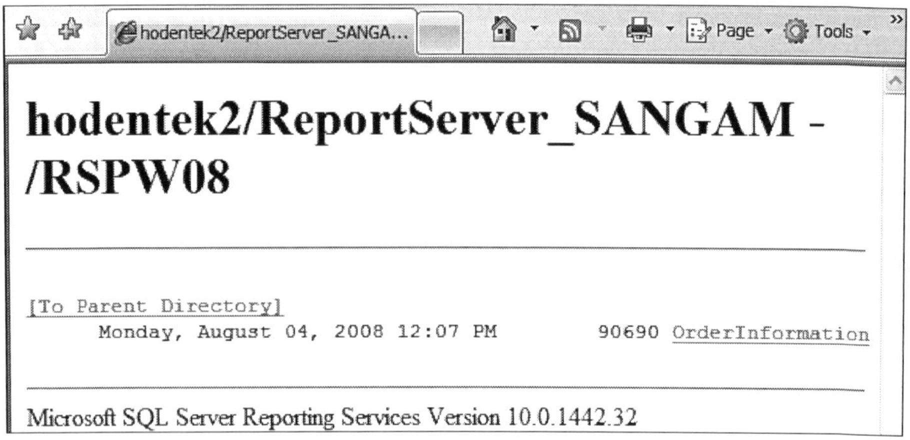

7. Now click on the link **OrderInformation**.

   The **OrderInformation** report gets rendered in the browser.

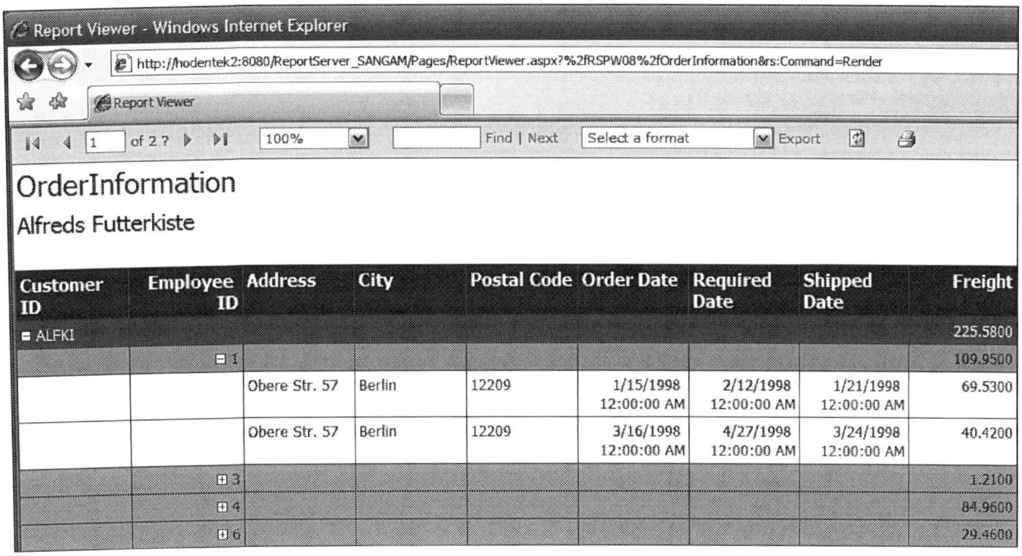

Report Model

Enterprise data residing in its backend database is generally a relational database with data in tables. But the business user does not usually possess a good knowledge of the underlying data in the enterprise databases. For example, a manager in charge of **orders** visualizes orders as related to **inventory**, **customers who ordered a product**, the **latest source price from a vendor source** and so on. This kind of information may not necessarily exist in the *orders* table but would exist dispersed among several tables and views. This is what the Report Model would create for the business user so that he can make business decisions using the Report Model rather than a whole lot of tables about which he knows very little. The model gets built in such a way that the report author, in this case the business user, need not know the intricacies of report authoring such as connecting to data, running queries, filtering, sorting, using parameters and so on. All these come packaged in the model and all that the business user needs to do is to drag-and-drop the items of interest and presto, he has a report. Visual Studio 2008 builds this model with maximum flexibility for Microsoft SQL Server back-end data as well as Oracle data version 9.2.0.3 and above. A less flexible model can also be built using the Report Manager (described in Chapter 5) and Office Sharepoint server (This is outside the scope of this book).

The Report Model is data representation, a level higher than the underlying data but describing the data in business terms. In constructing the Report Model there is therefore a mapping from the tables (views) in the database to the model entities.

Using the Report Model project template

When you choose to create a Report Model Project using the template, the program creates three empty folders: Data Sources, Data Source Views and Report Models. You start adding a data source, and once you are connected you get the objects from the database that you want in your Data Source Views. You must remember that the model only uses relational data in your database tables having Primary/Foreign keys relationships. Once the Data Source View is defined then the report model is generated readily guided by the wizard. In *Hands-on 4.3*, you will be designing a Report Model and reviewing some of its features. You will also deploy it to the Server. Although Visual Studio 2008 was used to craft the Report Model, it can also be created using the Report Manager. You will see this in Chapter 5.

Hands-on exercise 4.3: Creating a Report Model using the Visual Studio 2008 template

The Report Model template is one of the built-in templates under Report Server projects in Visual Studio. In this section, you will start off with this template and following the wizard steps create a Report Model after connecting to the data source.

Getting ready

You need the following:

- SQL Server reporting Services should be running in native mode
- `TestNorthwind` Database available on the SQL Server 2008
- Visual Studio 2008 or BIDS available
- In order to deploy or publish the Report model you should have Content Manager or Publisher Role
- You should have permissions to objects on `TestNorthwind`

Follow the steps

The process of creating a Report Model consists of the following steps:

- Creating a Report Model Project
- Defining a data source for the Report Model
- Defining a data source view for the Report Model
- Defining the Report Model

Creating a new Report Model Project

In order to create a Report Model project we can use the built-in template of the project from BIDS. The model building is completely driven by the wizards. Modifications and changes to the model can be made after the model is built. Here are the steps to follow when creating a new project:

1. Click on **Start | All Programs | Microsoft SQL Server 2008 | SQL Server BIDS**.
2. Click on **File | New | Project...**.

   The **New Project** window gets displayed.
3. In the **Visual Studio installed templates**, click on **Report Model Project**.
4. Replace the default name ReportModelProject1 with one of your own. Here it was replaced by MyReportModel as shown.
5. Click the **OK** button on the **New Project** window.

   The project MyReportModel gets created with three empty folders: **DataSources**, **DataSourceViews** and **ReportModels** as shown:

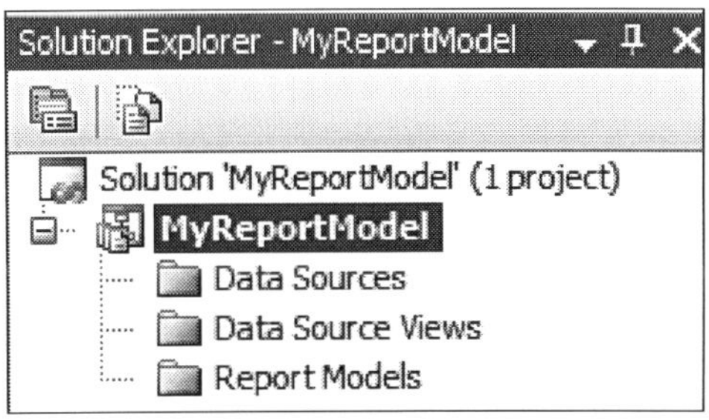

Defining a Data Source for the Report Model

Report Model is built on top of the relational data in a relational database and the first step is to define what this database is going to be. In this section you will be connecting to the data source.

1. Right-click the DataSources folder and from the drop-down choose Add New Data Source.

   This brings up the Data Source Wizard's welcome page. Read the notes on this page.

2. Click the Next button on the Welcome to the Data Source Wizard page.

   This takes you to **Select how to define the connection page** of the wizard as shown:

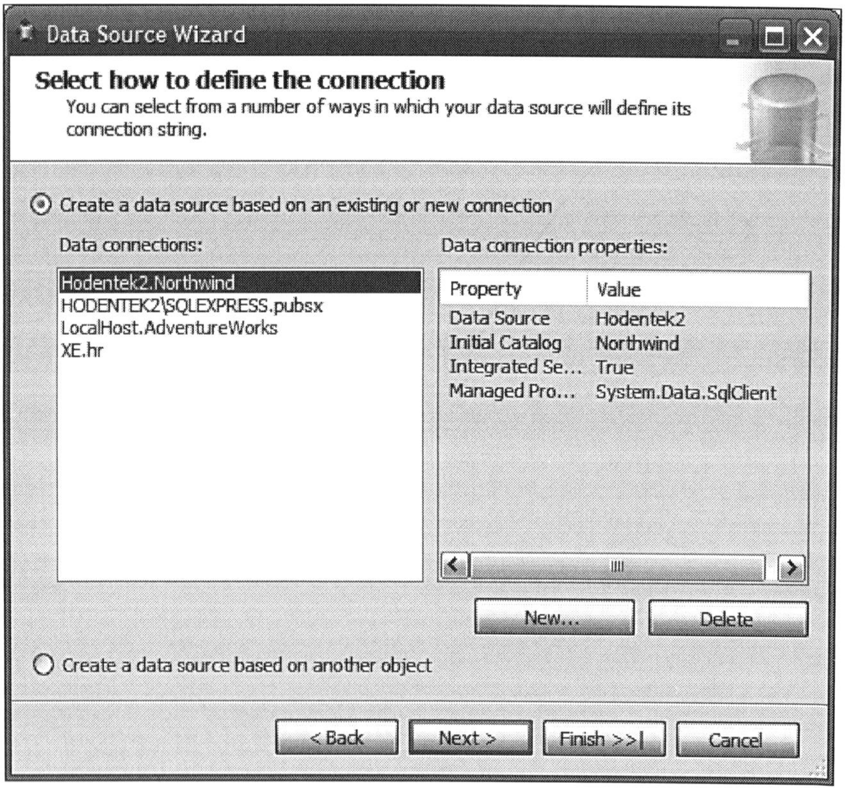

   There are two primary options. One is to create a data source based on an existing or new connection. The other is to create a data source based on another project. For example, there are four existing connections that may be used, or create a new connection as described in the steps.

3. Click on the New... button.

   This brings up the **Connection Manager** window as shown:

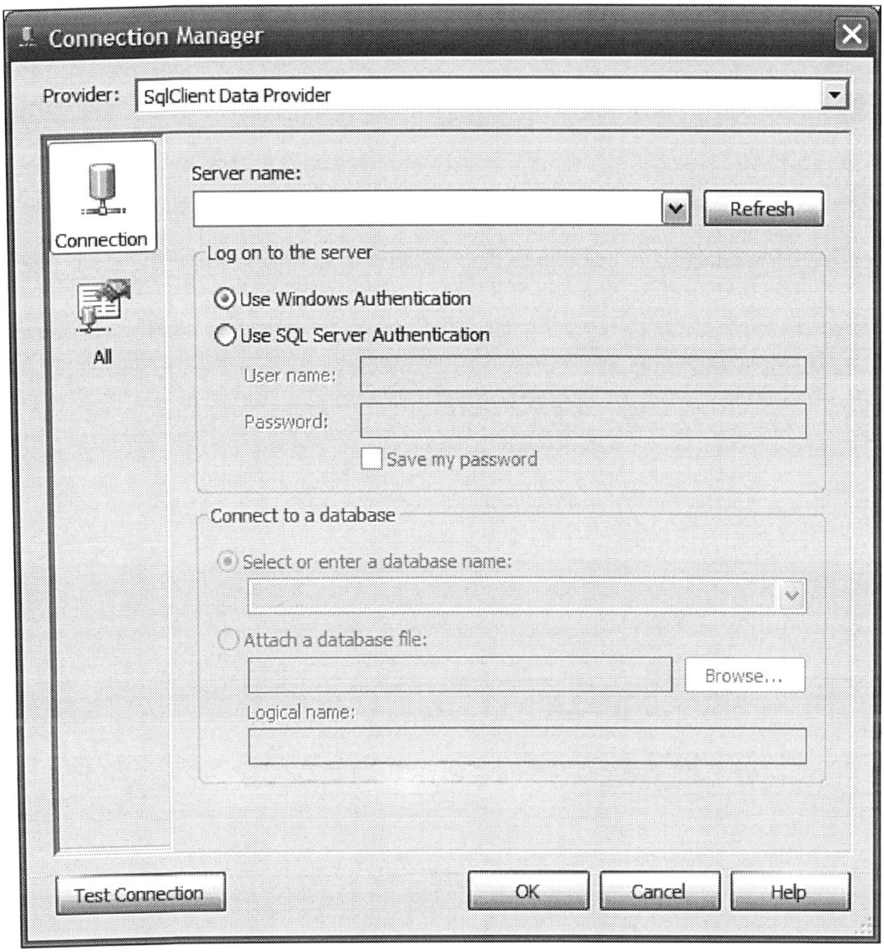

4. Click on the Refresh... button and then click on the drop-down handle by its side.
5. Choose Hodentek2\SANGAM (a server appropriate for your machine), accept Windows authentication (authentication appropriate for your installation) and click on the handle to Select or enter database name.

6. Choose **TestNorthwind** from this list and click on the Test Connection button to verify the connection as shown:

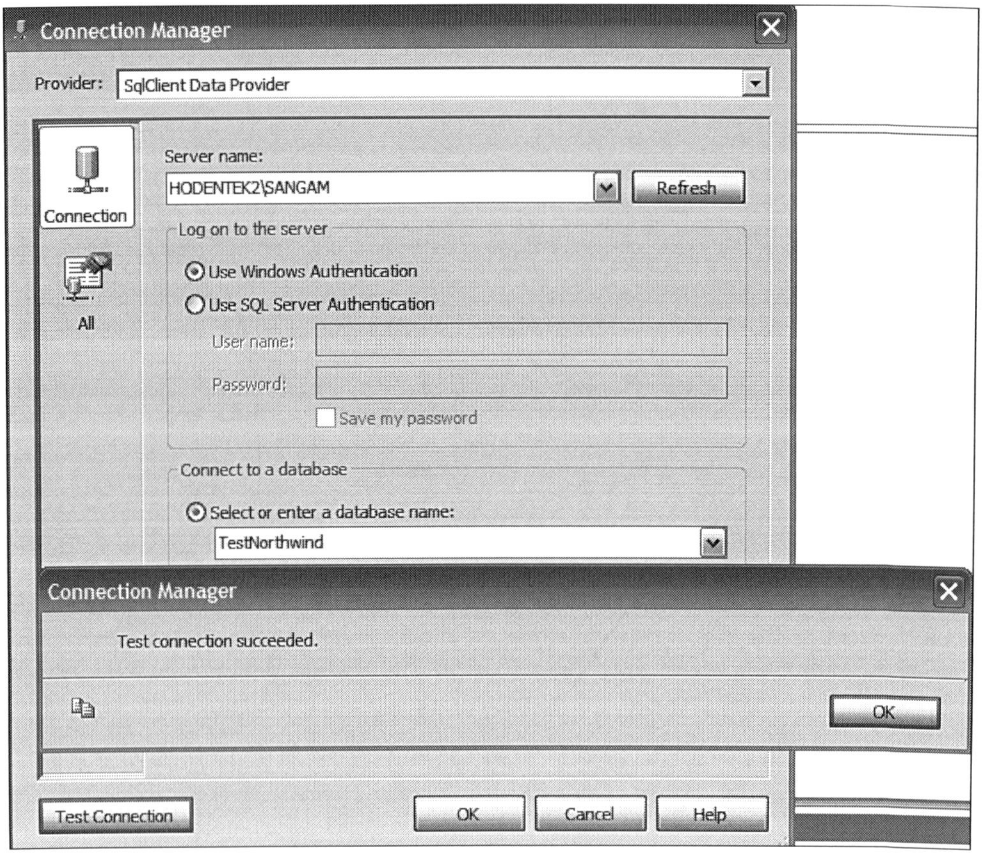

7. Click the OK button on the message box as well as on the Connection Manager window.

   This adds the connection information created into the **Data Source Wizard**'s page as shown. Notice that there could be other existing connections.

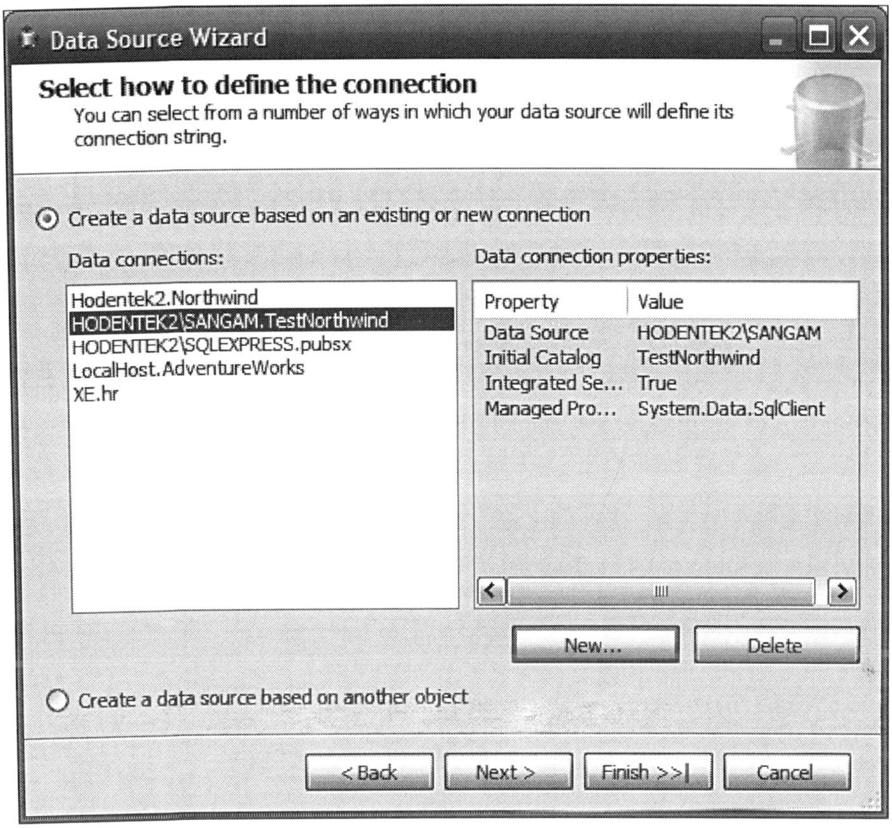

8. Click the **Next** button on the **Select how to define the connection page.**
9. In the **Completing the Wizard** page of the wizard, change the default **Data source name** to something different, (here it is **MyFirstNorthwind**). Make sure the connection string information is correct.
10. Click on the **Finish** button.

    The `MyFirstNorthwind.ds` file gets added to the **Data Sources** folder as seen in the Solution Explorer.

Defining a Data Source view for the Report Model

Data source view is a logical model created out of one or more data sources. It is built on top of data sources and encapsulates the tables and views and provides for named calculations and named queries created separately outside the data source. With the view created you do not need to be connected with the data sources to work with the model.

1. Right-click the **Data Source Views** folder. From the drop-down pick **Add New Data Source View.**

   The **Welcome to the Data Source View Wizard** page of the **Data Source View Wizard** gets displayed. Read the notes on this page.

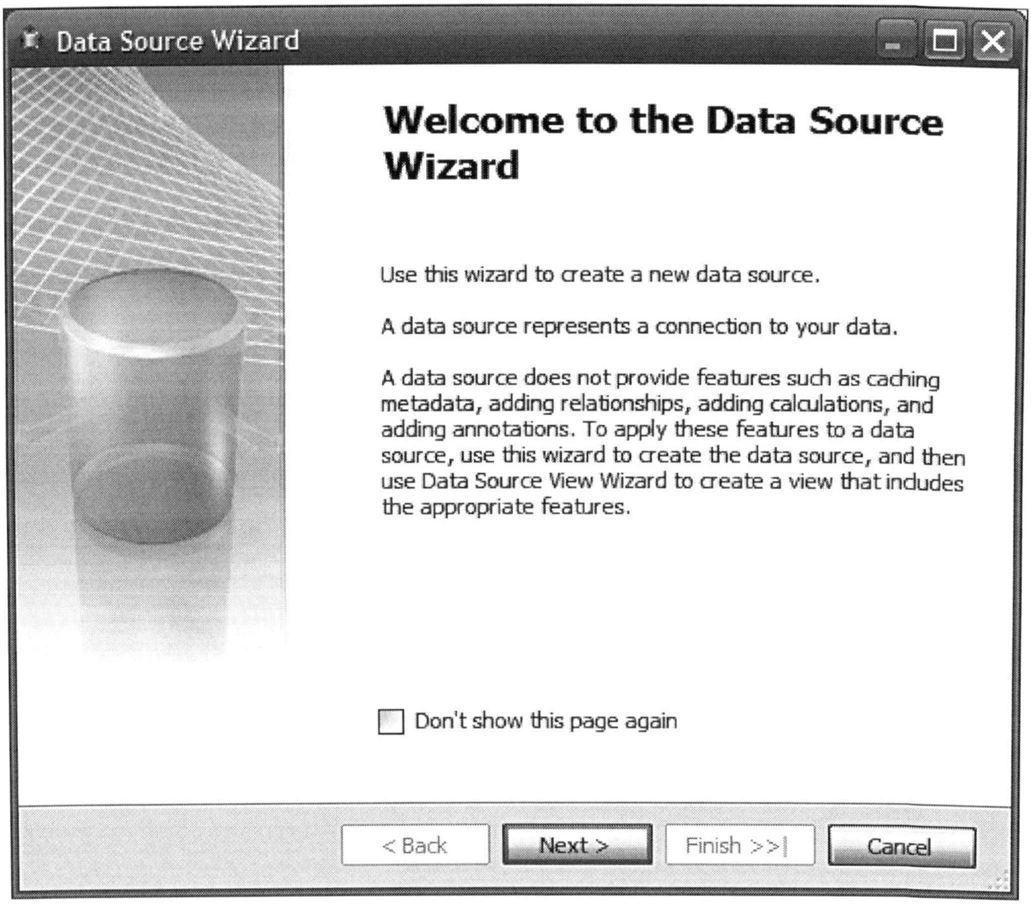

2. Click on the **Next** button

   The **Select a Data Source** of the wizard gets displayed showing **MyFirstNorthwind** created earlier in the **Relational Data Sources** field as shown with some of its properties.

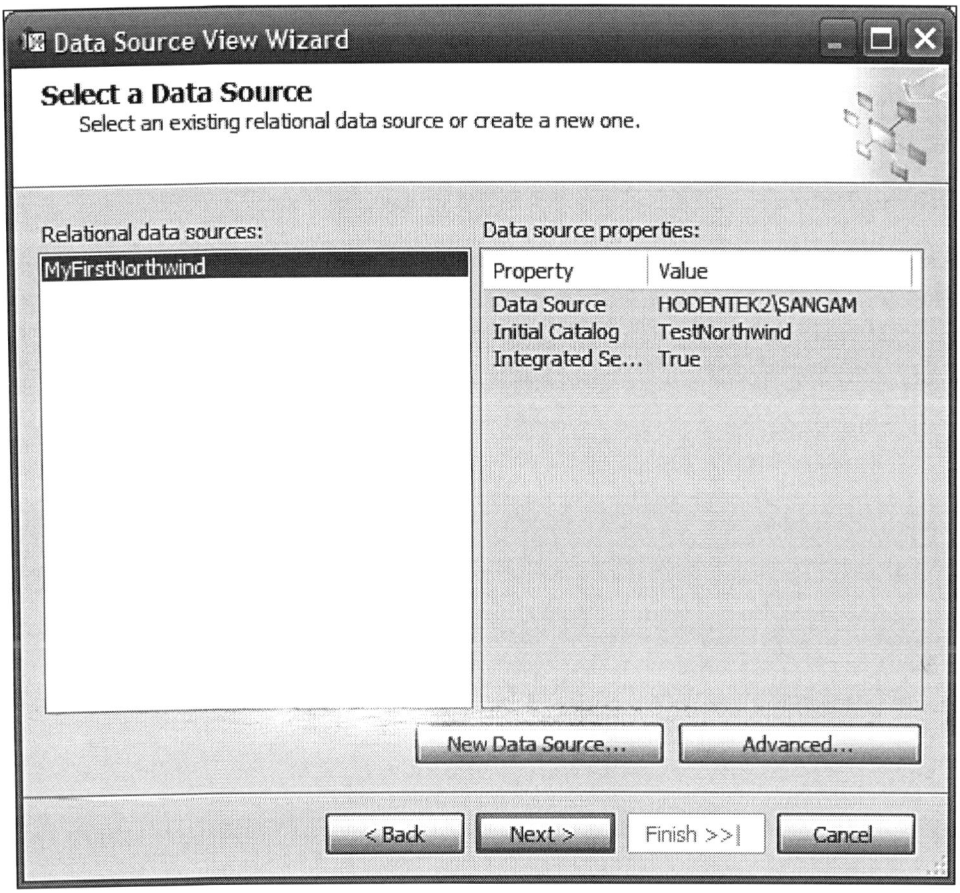

3. Click on the **Next** button.

   The **Select Tables and Views** page of the wizard gets displayed as shown:

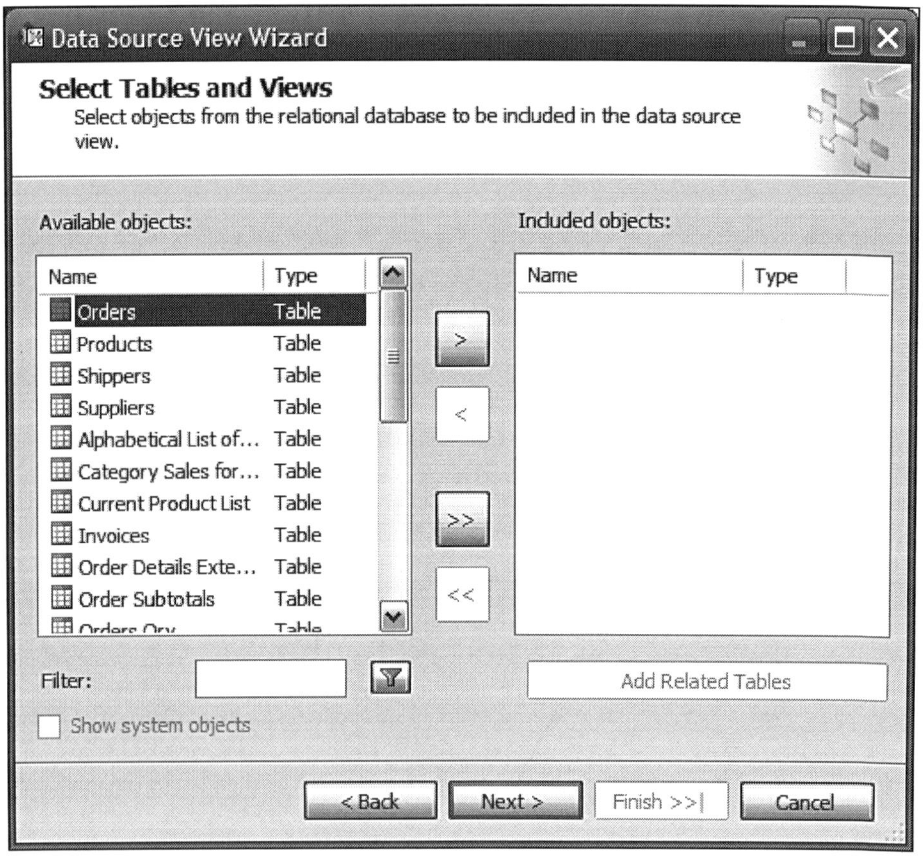

4. Select all from the **Available objects** to the **Included objects** area by clicking on the "**>>**" button.
5. Click on the **Next** button.

6. In the **Completing the Wizard** page of the wizard, change the default name to something different of your choice. Here, it is changed to **MyNorthwind**.

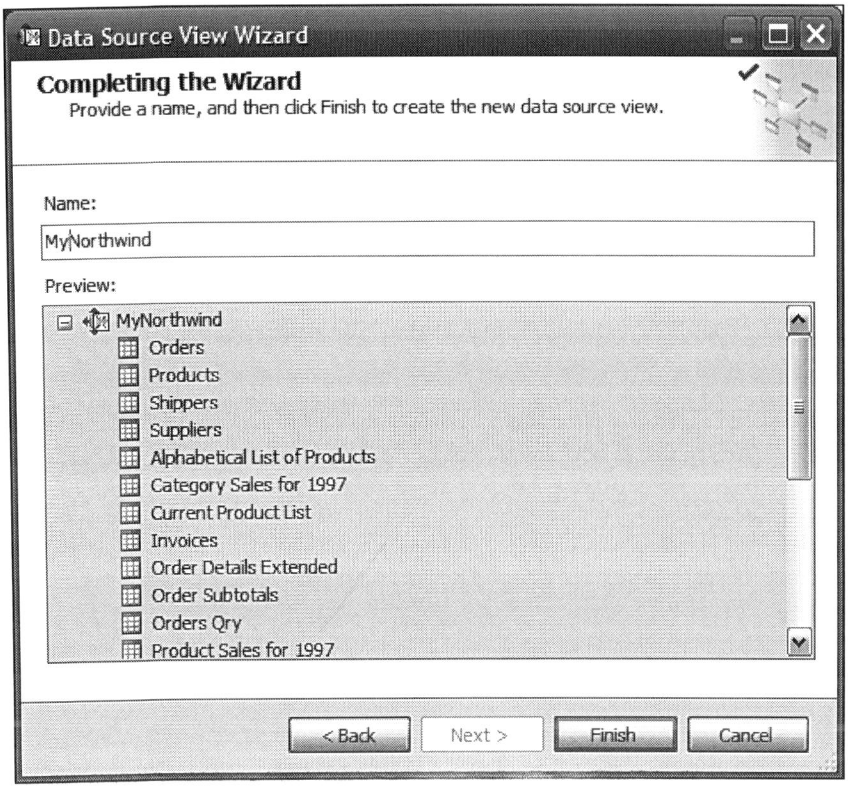

7. Click on the **Finish** button.

   After some processing, the file `MyNorthwind.dsv` gets added to the **Data Source Views** folder of the project as shown:

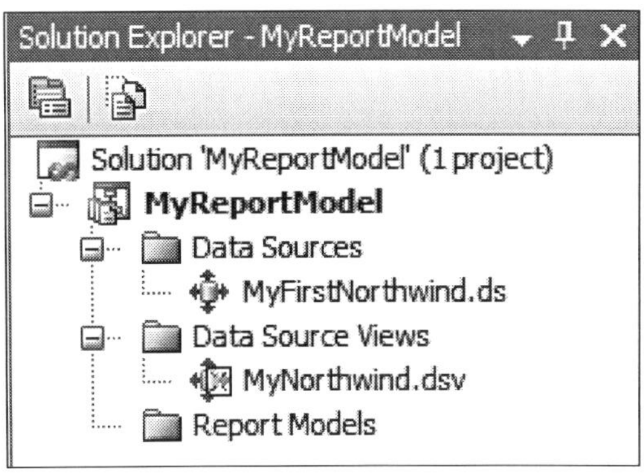

Defining the Report Model

Report Model hides the complexity of the underlying data by presenting a user friendly interface to access the data. It consists of entities—groups of report items with a friendly face, predefined calculated values and with predefined relationships in the data.

1. Right-click on the **Report Models** folder and from the drop-down choose **Add New Report Model.**

   The **Welcome to the Report Model Wizard** page of the **Report Model Wizard** shows up (read the notes on this page).

2. Click on the **Next** button.

   In the **Select Data Source View** page of the wizard, the Data Source View created earlier is displayed.

3. Click on the **Next** button.

   The wizard's **Select report model generation rules** page gets displayed as shown in the next figure. These rules dictate how the Meta data is generated from the data source.

4. Accept defaults and click on the **Next** button.

   This brings up the **Collect Model Statistics** of the wizard as shown (read the notes on this page).

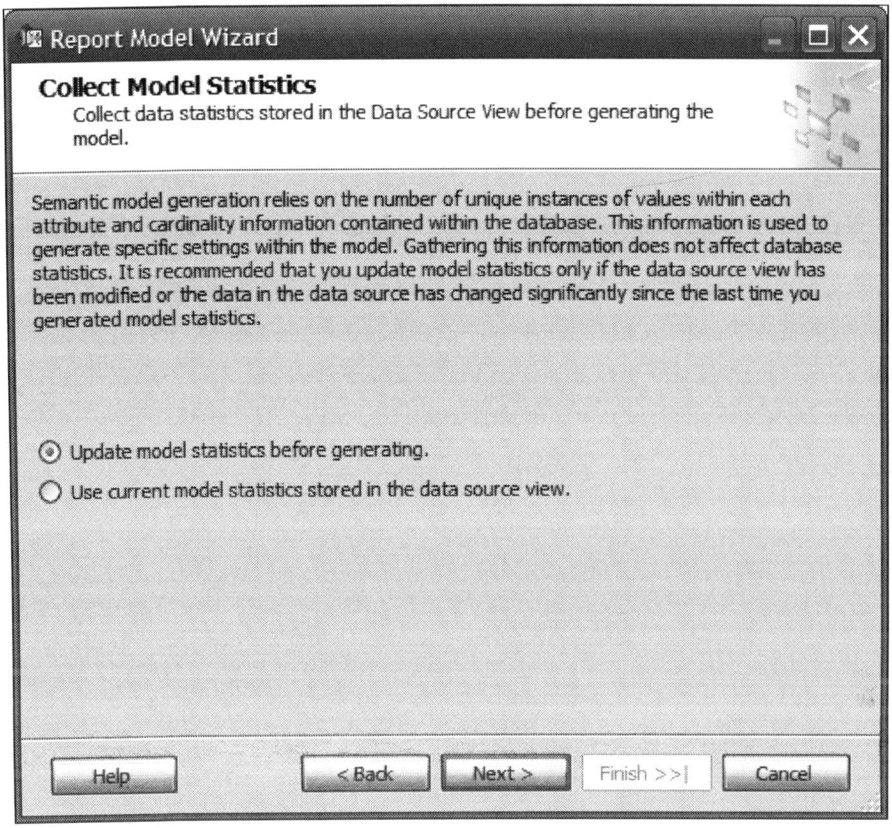

5. Accept the default choice and click on the **Next** button.

   This brings up the **Completing the Wizard** page.

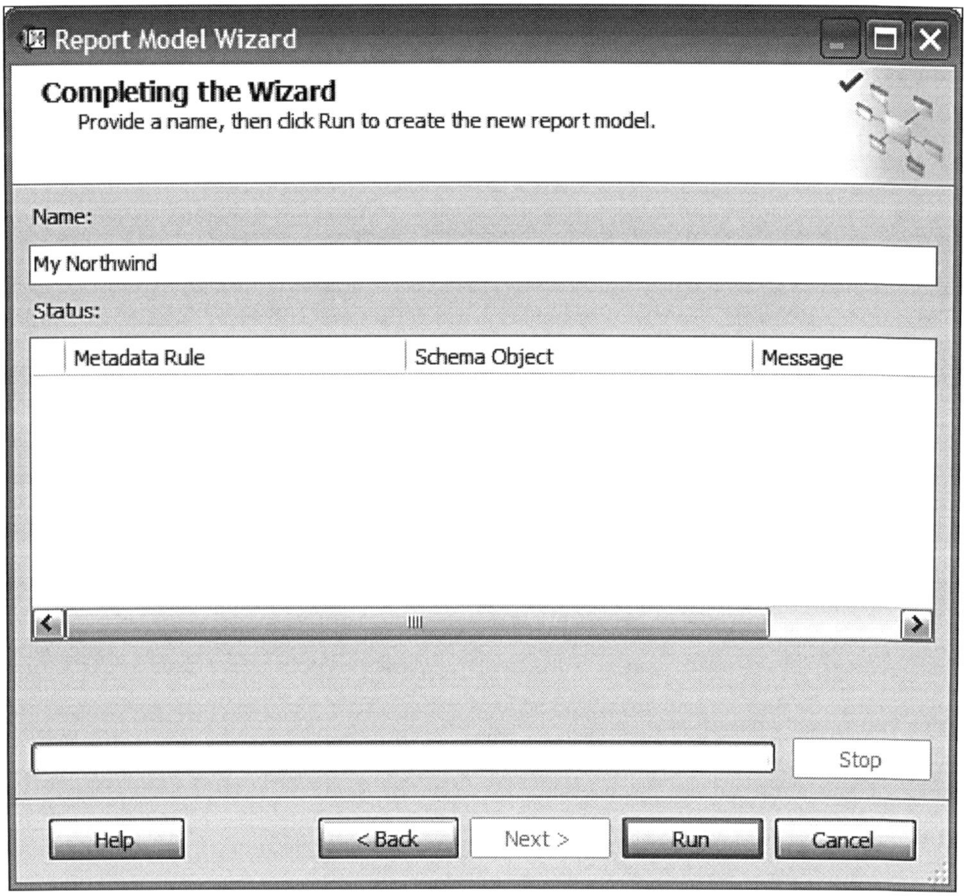

6. After providing a name (**My Northwind**), click on the Run button. After some processing, the following screen shows up with some warnings.

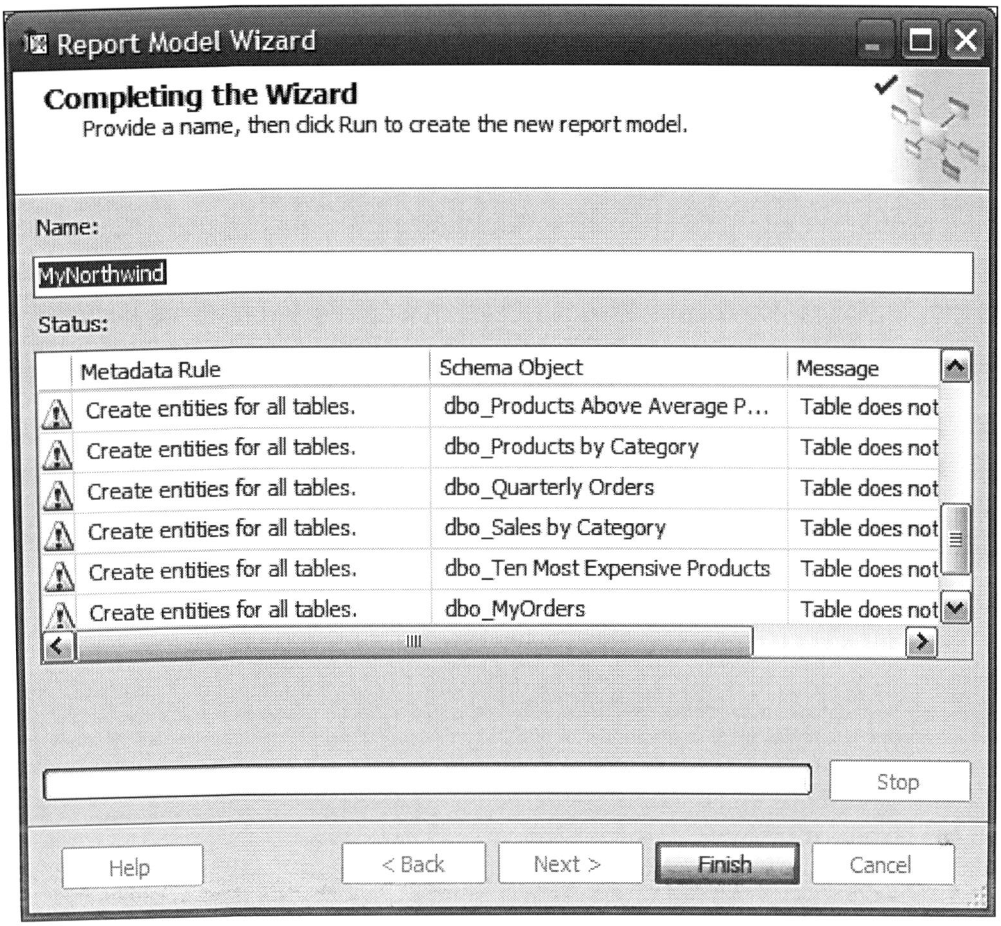

The program is flagging the tables, which will not be part of the Report Model as they fall short of requirements (relational). These warnings may safely be ignored.

7. Click on the **Finish** button.

   You get a Microsoft Visual Studio message asking you if you want to reload the `MyNorthwind.dsv` as the file was modified outside of the source editor.

8. Click on the **Yes to All** button.

   The file **MyNorthwind.smdl** gets added to the **ReportModels** folder as shown:

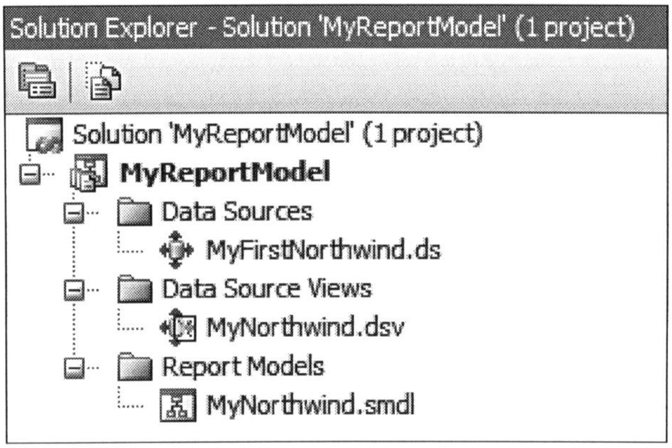

The **ReportModel** tabbed page gets displayed as shown. This page lists all the entities in the model.

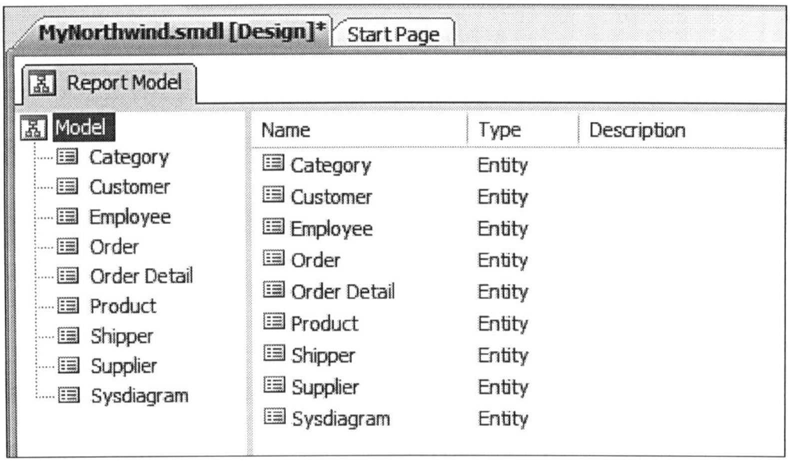

The **Data Source View** tabbed page in the design view displays both relational and non-relational data as shown. The objects have been zoomed out so as to display all of them. The connected objects belong to the relational data which can be traced back to the way they are related in the database. As the warnings were ignored in an earlier step, some of the other tables also got into the Data Source View. These in no way interfere with the usage of this model.

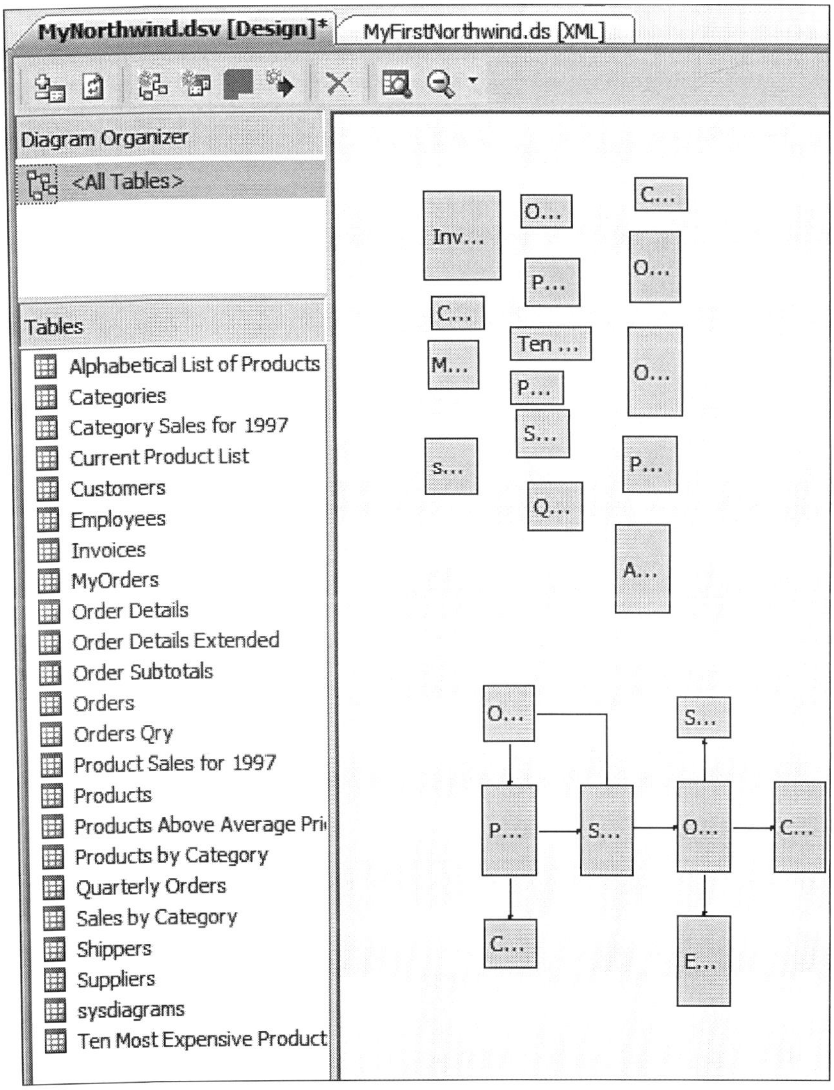

An enlarged view of the relational tables is shown in the following screenshot:

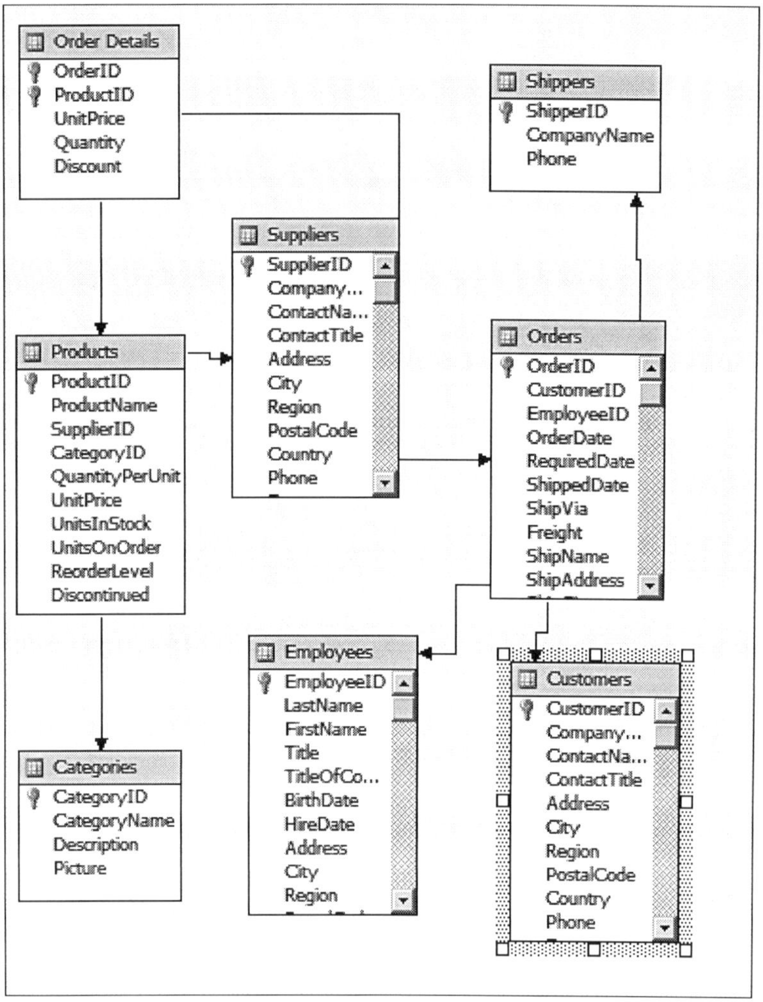

Deploying the Report Model to the Report Server

The Report Model developed in the previous hands-on should be available to the end user so that he/she can generate reports based on the model. For this to happen, the Report Model must be accessible on the Report Server to the end user. The deployment of the Report Model is similar to how the report was deployed to the Report Server. It may be noted that database changes get automatically updated in the model when you access the model after the changes to the underlying is made.

Hands-on exercise 4.4: Deploying the Report Model

Before making use of the Report Model to generate reports, it is necessary to make it accessible from the Report Server. In this section you provide information about the Report Server to deploy the model on the Report Server.

1. Click on **Project | <ReportModelName> Properties....**

   The ReportModelProject Name is **My Report Model.** This opens the Project's property pages as shown. **TargetServerURL** is the URL of your Report Server which you should know from the *Configuration Tool* described in Chapter 1. Except for **TargetServerURL,** all other items are defaults. You need to provide the URL.

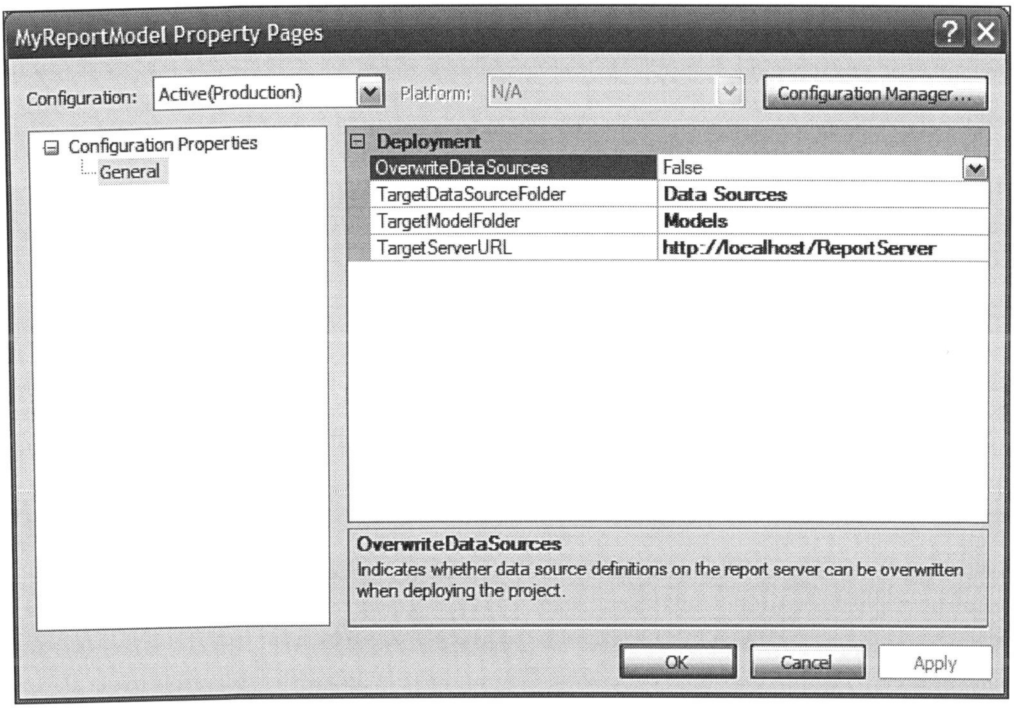

2. Type in the **TargetServerURL** name as shown above.

   If you need, you can change the option **OverwriteDataSources**. Here, the default is accepted.

3. Click on the **Apply** button and click on the **OK** button.
4. Right-click the Report Model file `MyNorthwind.smdl` in the Project, choose **Deploy**.

   You should get a reply that the deployment was successful in the **Output** window.
5. Type in the URL of the Report Server and browse with IE.

   The Report Server web page gets displayed showing the **Models** folder. There is only one model in the folder.

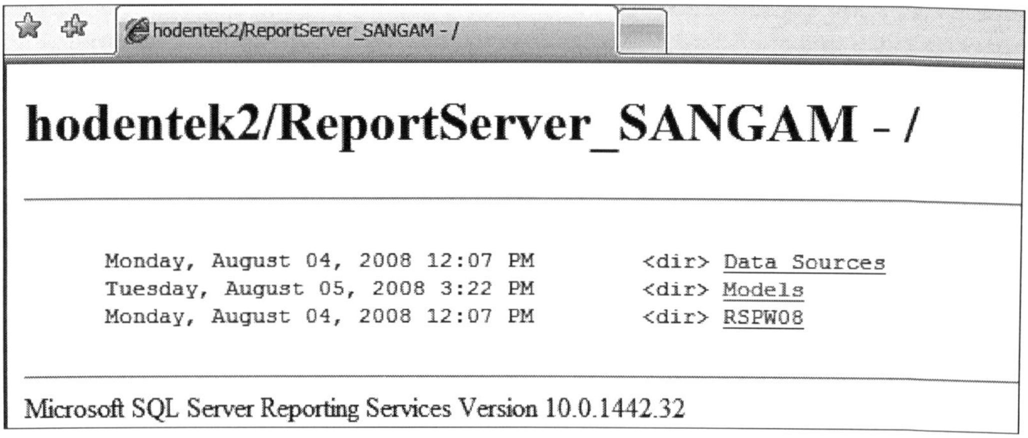

6. Click on the **Models** link in the browser to open the following web page:

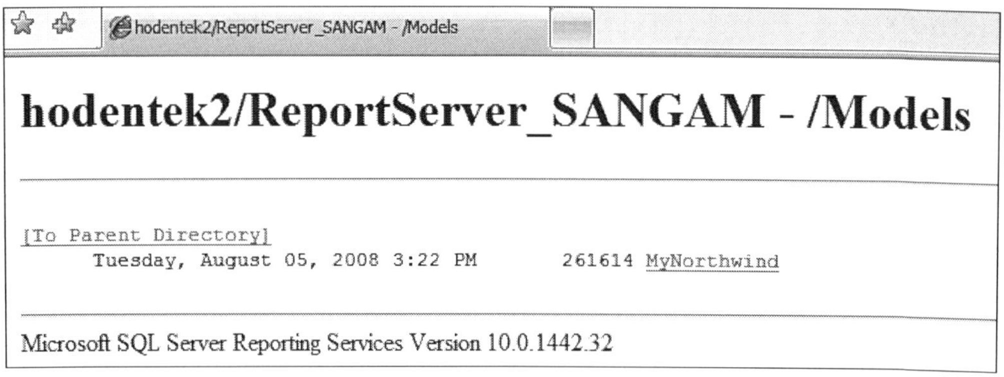

7. Click on the **MyNorthwind** link in the above display.

   You should see the semantic model in the XML format which shows all the details of the model.

Hands-on exercise 4.5: Importing reports from MS Access 2003

As mentioned in the very beginning, you can import reports created in Microsoft Access into the Visual Studio 2008 IDE. This provides an excellent example of how reports can be authored using the sample reports (Report objects in an MDB Database). The reports in Northwind database are an excellent resource that can be imported into Visual Studio.

Getting ready

You need the following:

- SQL Server Reporting Services should be running in native mode.
- Access 2003 should not be running, or the database file used by other users. In case Access 2007 is also present, the export function may try to access from Access 2007. It is assumed that only Access 2003 is installed.
- Visual Studio 2008 or BIDS available.
- Northwind Sample should be accessible.

Follow the steps

Migrating reports is just one click away with Visual Studio 2008's Report Server project. All you need to do is to point to the source of your Access reports on your machine.

1. Create a Report Server Project as described in **Using the Report Server Project** template and provide a name for the project. Here, the project name is **RPImportAccess.**

   This provides a `Reports` folder and a `Shared Data Sources` folder which are both empty.

2. Right-click the **Reports** folder and choose **Import Reports | MS access.**

   This brings up the **Open** windows dialog where you browse for the file `Northwind.mdb`. The Northwind database with all the objects, including the reports, is in the `Northwind.mdb` file. It is usually found at the default location: `C:\Program Files\Microsoft Office\OFFICE11\SAMPLES`. Note that the acceptable file types have the extensions ACCDB, MDB and ADP.

3. Browse to the file `Northwind.mdb` and click **Open**.

   After some processing, all the reports in the Northwind database will appear as Report Server RDL files as shown in the following screenshot:

You can start using these examples as the starting point for your learning experience by deploying them to the server, reviewing how the reports are structured or using them as templates for authoring your own reports.

Summary

The salient features of Visual Studio 2008/BIDS interface for developing report server projects and deploying them to the Report Server was described. The five hands-on exercises cover all aspects of this IDE for developing Reports to be deployed to the Report Server. Creating a Report Model using the data in a Northwind relational database was also described. Importing Microsoft Access reports has the special significance for those who are interested in learning how to author, how report items are placed on the report, how they are bound to data. It is also useful for those interested in migrating reports as it provides an immediate source of reports for deployment. However, as the imports are from an older version, some of the new features of SSRS reports are not available in these reports.

5 Working with the Report Manager

In Chapter 2, Report Manager was briefly introduced. To recapitulate, Report Manager is a management tool for the Report Server. It acts as a middle man between users and the Report Server. Also recall the many tasks that can be performed by the Report Manager.

In this chapter, we will look at some of the basic tasks that one can perform with the tool. Specifically the following hands-on exercises allow you get a good handle on working with this very important tool:

- Creating, deleting, and modifying folders
- Assigning users (or group) to roles and permissions to access reports
- View, print, and search
- Windows user access to a report on the Report Manager
- Deploying reports
- Creating a new data source and generating a model using Report Manager
- Downloading a report definition file from the Report Server
- Working with report cache
- Working with standard, email, fileshare, and data-driven subscriptions

The first step in working with reports is to get them on to the Report Server, a process called deployment (published). Once your report is deployed (published), the detailed information about all objects will get into the Report Catalog as shown. You will find the Report Catalog node in your Report Server in the SQL Server Management Studio. You should take a look at it after you have a couple of reports. The figure shows a listing of the objects in the `dbo.Catalog` table of the Report Server database, `ReportServer$SANGAM`. As you can see, there are only a few objects deployed on the Report Server that are used in the hands-on exercises. There are several ways of deploying reports as we will see later. Most of the objects in the catalog were deployed from the Visual Studio 2008 IDE in Chapter 4. The project **ReportPush** containing a single report **Push** was pushed (deployed) from Visual Studio 2008 to the Report Server. The project is similar to the project **RSPWiz08** but uses a single table `Employees` from the `TestNorthwind` database.

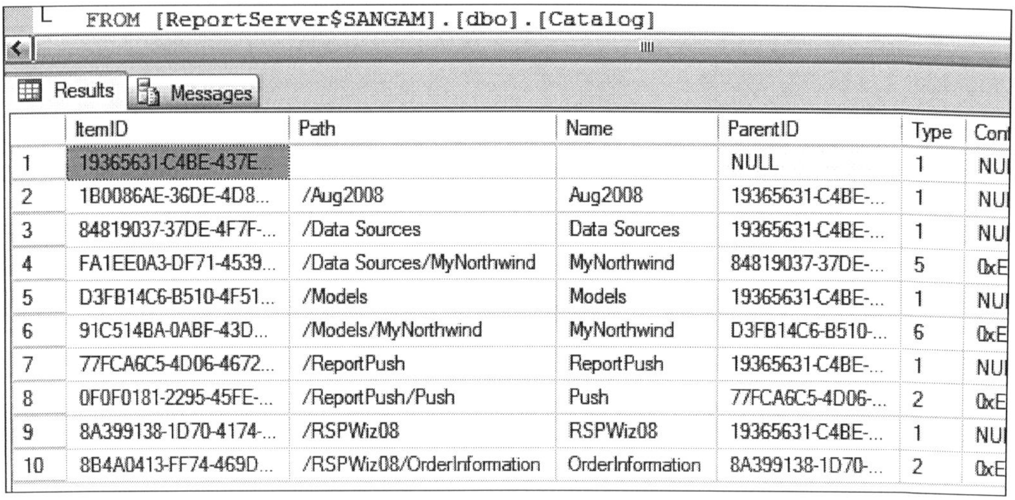

Once the Reports are deployed to the Report Server it is the Report Manager who manages, schedules, and delivers. Report Server's security features will determine the user's access to the reports using roles created by the Report Manager. The Caching and Report History features determine the report execution when a report is requested. The hands-on in this chapter gives you a grip on the details of working with the more essential features of Report Manager.

Report Manager components

When the Report Manager is accessed for the first time from the Reporting Services Configuration Manager, it is empty except for the features you see displayed in the following screenshot. It is assumed here that the user who is typing has the credentials described in Chapter 1 (in this case the author is the computer owner who configured the reporting services).

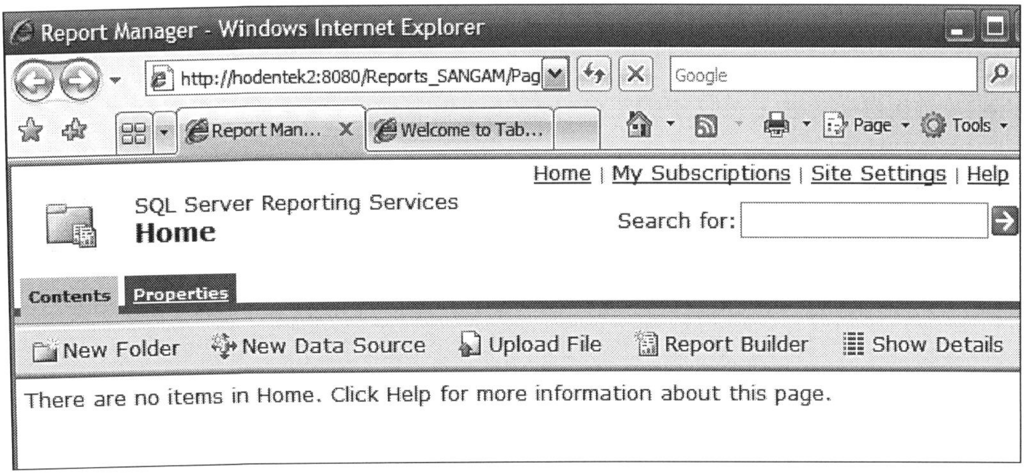

The look of this page is controlled by a stylesheet, a CSS style page (`ReportingServices.css`), which is located in the Report Manager's folder in the original SQL Server installation directory. Customization of the look of this page is possible if desired.

In this page, the Home page, you can carry out a number of activities such as:

- Create a new folder
- Create a new data source
- Upload a file from your file system to Report Server
- Start up Report Builder 1.0

You will be doing hands-on with most of these activities. The Report Builder you launch from this page is the version 1.0. This can still work with SQL Server 2008 created Report Models. More about this and the brand new Report Builder 2.0 will be considered in Chapter 6. **Show Details** is a toggle which changes over to **Hide Details** revealing **Edit** options for most of the items. In addition to these activities you can also access:

- **My Subscriptions**
- Link back to the **Home** page
- **Site Settings**
- **Help**

My Subscriptions shows all subscriptions created for the Reports including the Standard and Data-Driven subscriptions where you can create, edit, delete and check the status of subscriptions. The **Home** page link will bring you back from wherever you are presently to the Home page. In **Site Settings**, the Report Manager title can be set by providing a name in the **Site Settings** page. The default for this is **SQL Server Reporting Services**.

You can also select the default settings for report history on this page. Each report carries with it a separate report history. The limit refers to the number of copies of each report in history. You can change this at the report level. When you add more reports, the older reports will be removed and new ones added. The total number of reports should not exceed the specified limit. Report execution timeout after a number of seconds can be set here as well. The report timeout is the time it takes on the Report Server to process reports. The security page shows the roles that can access and modify the site settings. Users are normally not given permission to alter the settings. On the schedules page you can predefine shared schedules that users can select for their reports and subscriptions.

There is also a choice for **Custom Report Builder launch URL** for which there is no adequate documentation from Microsoft at the present time (place holder probably for future enhancements).

The **Help** page is an important link that takes you to the online help file for Report Manager which was installed with the original SQL Server 2008 Installation.

Folder structure and hierarchy

When you access the Report Manager you will be directed to the **Home** page of Report Manager as described earlier. The Report Manager is folder-based with sub-folders which in turn may contain *Reports*, *DataSources*, *Models*, and other folders. The folder structure in Report Manager is similar to the folder structure in the Windows file system except that Report Manager folders are not found in the file system but instead in the Report Server database. Each of the objects in a Report Manager folder has their own properties as seen in the table. When you deploy a project from Visual Studio 2008 to the Report Server, they appear as folders with the project name in the Report Manger. You can create new folders, delete existing folders or modify any folders. In the next hands-on, you will be carrying out a number of operations with folders on the Report Manager.

Sub-items in folder hierarchy

Report Manager folders are hierarchical and each folder has further properties that refer to its contents and these have to be properly understood to work with the Report Manager. The following table shows what these properties are. Here, you can observe that security is a common feature.

Item	Sub-items
Home | Properties	Security
Folder | Properties	General, Security
Report | Properties	General, Datasource, Execution, History, Security
DataSource | Properties	General, Security
Model | Properties	General, DataSources, Clickthrough, Model Item Security, Security

The reader should review the details of each of the items shown in the table for his Report Manager, as it is the central management console for all report related activities after deployment. It is a very flexible interface for managing reports.

Hands-on exercise 5.1: Creating, deleting, and modifying folders

At the topmost level is the **Home** page which is a root folder for all other folders. In addition to some reserved folders such as DataSources and Models, there could be many folders created during deployment or created in the Report Manager. As you will see later, the security that you provide for the folders propagate to its contents.

Creating a folder

Creating a folder in Report Manager is very easy. The steps to create a folder are listed here:

1. Start Report Manager from its URL.
2. In the **Home** page of Report Manager, click on **New Folder** toolbar item.
3. Provide a **Name** for the folder (herein **Sept08**) and an optional **Description** as shown, and place checkmark for the **Hide in list view**. The name cannot contain the characters (? : @ & = + , $ / * < >) as these are also used in querying the URL.

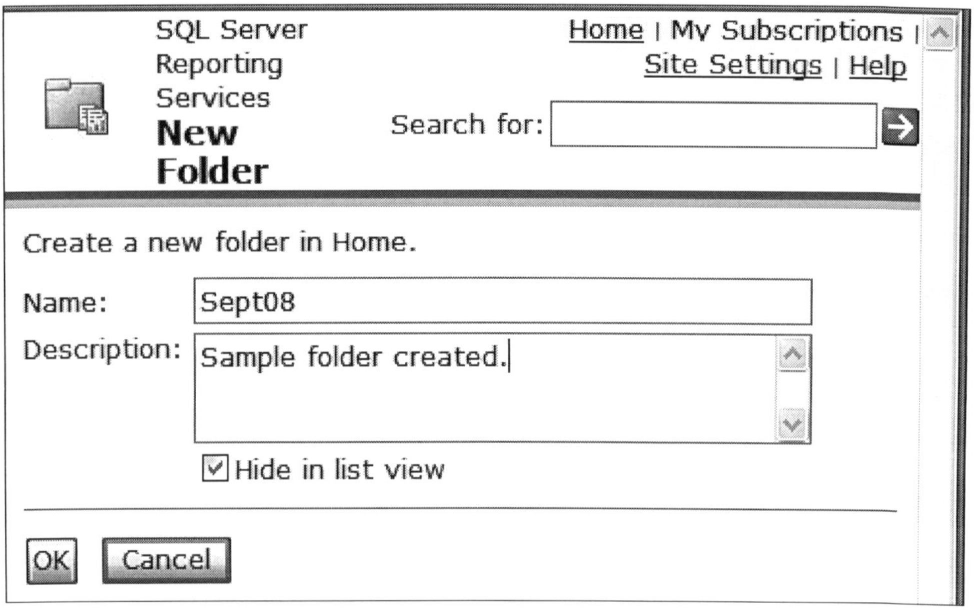

4. Click on the **OK** button.

   The new folder **Sept08** gets created in the **Home** page, but will not be seen in the list view.

5. In the **Home** page, click on **Show Details** to see this folder as shown. The **!New** added to the folder name disappears after 48 hours.

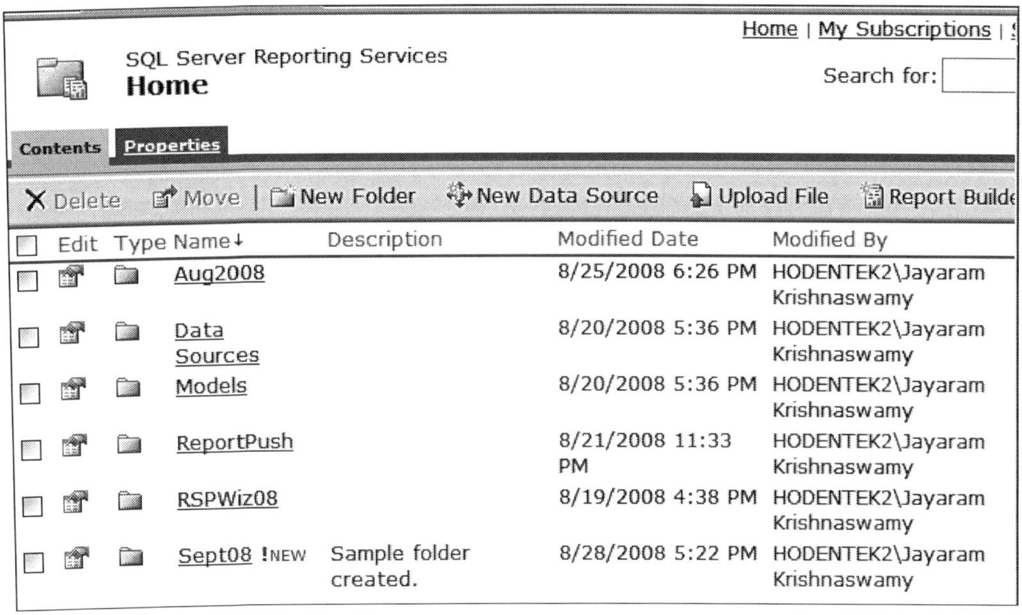

Deleting a folder

Deleting a folder is simpler than creating a folder. However, exercise caution while deleting.

1. Now place a checkmark for the **Sept08** folder.

   The **Delete** button gets enabled.

2. Click on the **Delete** button to remove this folder.

   You get a Windows Internet Explorer message asking whether you want to delete this item.

3. Click **Yes** to the message.

   The folder is deleted.

Moving a folder

While organizing your folders there are occasions when you may want to move out a folder and place it elsewhere. In Report Manager you can very easily move folders. The **Aug2008**, as you see here, is an empty folder created just like the **Sept08** folder. You may independently create another empty folder for this exercise.

1. In the **Home** page, click on the **Show Details** toolbar item.
2. Place a checkmark for the **Aug2008** folder.

   Both the **Delete** and **Move** buttons get enabled.

3. Click on the **Move** button.

   The **Move Aug2008** page shows with a text box where you would indicate the folder into which you desire **Aug2008** to be moved to as shown. The location should be the ones that are available. You cannot create a new folder here.

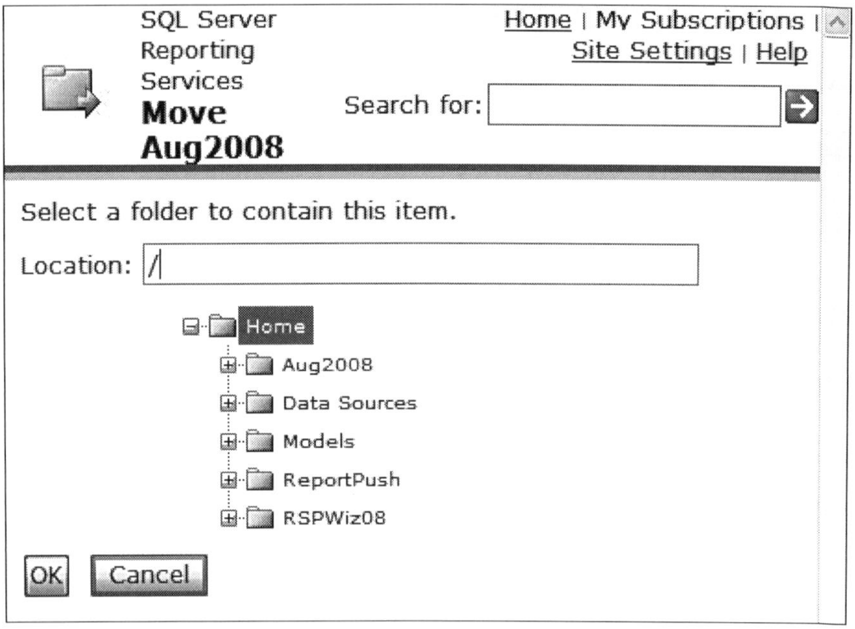

4. Click on one of the existing folders, **RSPWiz08**.

   This becomes the location into which **Aug2008** will be moved to and this name goes into the **Location** textbox.

5. Click on the **OK** button.
6. Click on the **Hide details** button and in the **Home** page click on the **RSPWiz08** folder.

   Verify that **Aug2008** folder has moved to the **RSPwiz08** folder.

Modifying a folder

You can click on a folder and choose the **General** tab of the **Properties** page. You can make changes to the name and description and click on the **Apply** button to save changes made.

Report management

Two main features of report management on a report server are: security that the reports should have and how well the reports perform. Reports depend not only on report security, but also on the access to the data in the Database Engine. Therefore before a report can be rendered on the Report Manager, report permissions must be in place and data access to the report data must be unimpeded.

Reporting Services, as we have seen in previous chapters, is a Windows service and so it depends on Windows user authentication and does not store its own user names and passwords. However, Windows users must have permissions to access objects on the Report Server. These permissions are set up in Reporting Services and managed by the Report Manager in the **Security** tab of most objects. The next section deals with permissions and only a few of the many scenarios possible are explored with the hands-on. However, these basic hands-on could be used for most of the usual cases. Permissions in Reporting Services can be very fine grained and permissions can be set for individual report, if needed. It may be noted that Windows Servers and Windows XP Professional have different security features and the hands-on here are specific to Windows XP.

Permissions in Reporting Services

Access to Report Server Content is controlled by permissions that depend on roles users can assume. By assigning roles to users you can limit the visibility to reports or otherwise allow them work with Report Server items. In order to assign roles to users you must have administrative privileges.

There are two types of roles: system-level and item-level. **System-level** role assignments apply to system wide tasks whereas **Item-level** role assignments range over tasks that covers all content related tasks like, publishing reports, viewing reports, creating subscriptions and so on. The following screenshot shows the global view of Report Server's **Security** node (expanded) for the Report Server in the Management Studio.

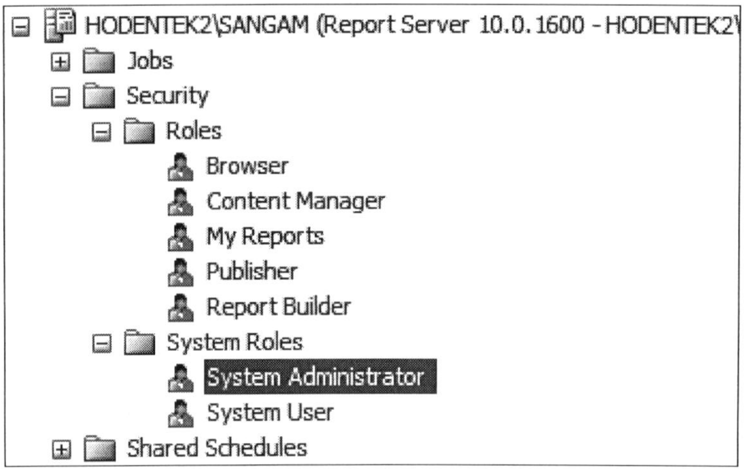

You can see by double-clicking each item and looking at its properties what each role assignment would permit the user. For example, a user who is assigned to the **Browser** role would be able to carry out the tasks shown in the following screenshot:

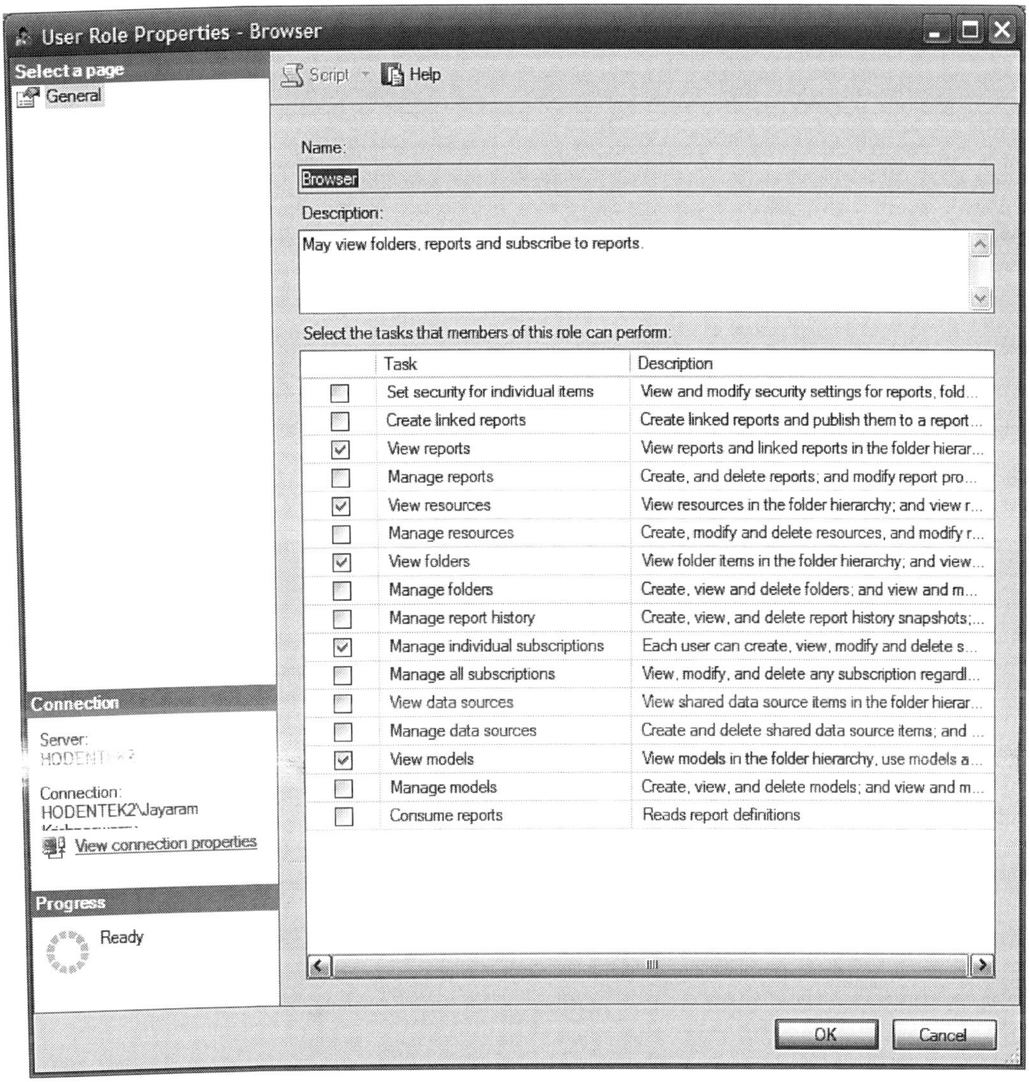

As can be seen in the above screenshot, the **Browser** role can only carry out a limited number of tasks. This is the default task list and may be modified. The following table shows the different roles and a description of the type of tasks that they have permission to carry out. If you are in doubt, you must always check in the **Security** node of the Reporting Services about what a role is permitted to carry out and based on that you can assign the role.

Role	Description
	System
System User	View system properties and shared schedules.
System Administrator	View and modify system role assignment, system role definitions, system properties, and shared schedules.
	Content (Item)
Browser	May view folders, reports, and subscribe to reports.
Content Manager	May manage content in the Report Server including folders, reports, and resources.
My Reports	May publish reports and linked reports, manage folders, reports, and resources in a user's **My Reports** folder.
Publisher	May publish reports and linked reports to the Report Server (manage models, manage data sources).
Report Builder	May view report definitions.
Custom Role	Pick and choose tasks.

The above roles (except the Custom Role) are the roles out of the box. An administrator can set up new roles and customize them. By right-clicking the **Roles** folder in the **Security** node you can bring up a new role Window by clicking on the drop-down item **New Role...**.

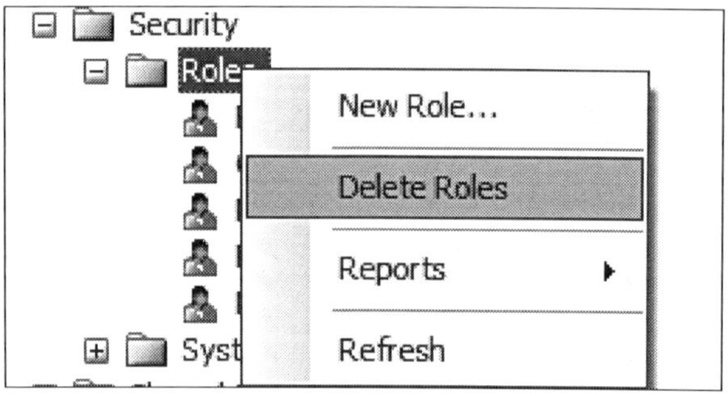

In the New Role Window, you can pick and choose the tasks the role can have permission to carry out and then save it with a custom name. Creating new roles can only be done in Management Studio by the administrator. The assignment of users to roles is however carried out in Report Manager. In the next hands-on you will be creating users and assigning them to system-wide and item-level roles. The permissions in Reporting Services are fine-grained and are not just limited to these roles. Even permissions to individual folders and files (Reports, Data Source, and Model) within the folder can be configured.

The custom role you will be creating will get into the `Roles` table in the Report Server Database as shown in the following screenshot. For example the `RoleName` **Navigate** is a custom role created for testing while the rest of them are default roles in the Reporting Services.

```
FROM [ReportServer$SANGAM].[dbo].[Roles]
```

Results | Messages

	RoleID	RoleName	Description	TaskMask	RoleFlags
1	5D555AA1-EBD0-48ED-A5...	Browser	May view folders, reports an...	001010...	0
2	CE527202-AB5F-4E32-8272...	Content Manager	May manage content in the ...	111111...	0
3	989F95D2-29A6-41FB-8E59...	Model Item Browser	Allows users to view model i...	1	2
4	42B292F8-5B32-4B79-A724...	My Reports	May publish reports and link...	011111...	0
5	7DEDBA37-95D0-4F5E-9AB...	Navigate	View Folders	001000...	0
6	619557B1-60EC-4D77-BB8...	Publisher	May publish reports and link...	010101...	0
7	8CFA4E6F-71F0-4A0F-8009...	Report Builder	May view report definitions.	001010...	0
8	B719C12F-A0B1-4159-A337...	System Administrator	View and modify system role...	110101...	1
9	34E3249F-8D41-4002-9CDF...	System User	View system properties and ...	001010...	1

Hands-on exercise 5.2: Assigning users (or groups) to roles and permissions to access reports

In order to work with any item on the Report Manager, computer users (or groups) must be assigned roles according to the security details discussed earlier. In this hands-on, you will create two Windows users and assign one of them to the System Administrator and the other to the item-level role—the browser role. In addition, you will also be configuring permission to a specific item on the Report Manager.

Getting ready

In order to practice with this exercise, you must satisfy the following:

- You are the administrator of the computer and know how to access and work with administrative tools on the computer
- The Reporting Services must be installed in the native mode
- You can create reports in Visual Studio and deploy them to the Report Server (review Chapter 4)
- You must know how to work with objects in the SQL Server Management Studio
- IE browser version greater than 6.0 installed

> In the following hands-on many users will be added to the computer. Although all of them have different names, all of them have the same password that never expires. This was to keep things simple and easy to work with. In a production system the user names and their passwords will all be different.

Hands-on 5.2.1: Assigning a Windows user to System Administrator role

This is the very first thing that must be in place in order to work with the Report Manager. This is because the Reporting Services is funtioning within the Windows Operating system.

Creating a Windows user

In order to have access in Windows the user should be a Windows user or should belong to a group. Herein only users are considered. But you could also provide access to Windows groups.

1. Go to **Start** | **Control Panel** | **Administrative Tools** and click on **Computer Management.**
2. In the **Computer Management** window, right-click on **Users** and from the drop-down menu choose **New User....**
3. In the **New User** window that pops-up provide a **User name, Full name,** and a **Description**. Also provide a **Password** which you can remember and clear the checkmark for **User must change password at next logon**. Place checkmark for the other two. Do not disable the account. This is just for this hands-on exercise and click on the **OK** button.

For the hands-on exercise the user name was **RSMax**.

The new user **RSMax** gets added to the list of users as shown in the following screenshot (part of list shown):

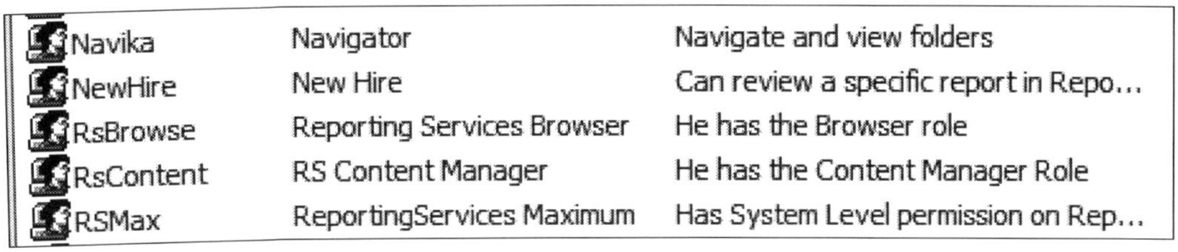

You have successfully created a window user.

Assigning a user to the System Administrator role

The role of System Administrator is important because they manage the majority of the tasks. Here, the BUILTIN\Administrator role is assigned to the System Administrator.

1. Log on to the Report Manager from the Reporting Services Configuration tool or by typing in the Report Manager URL in the IE browser.
2. In the **Report Manager**'s window, click on the **Site Settings** link at the top right. This opens the **Site Settings** page of **Report Manager.**
3. Click on the **Security** link on the left hand side.
4. Here you will find **BUILTIN\Administrators** assigned to the **System Administrator** role as shown:

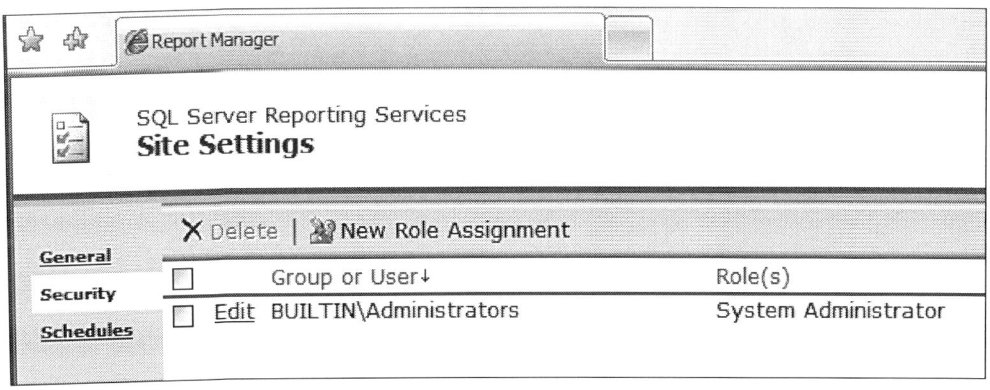

5. Click on **New Role Assignment**.

6. The **New System Role Assignment** page gets displayed as shown:

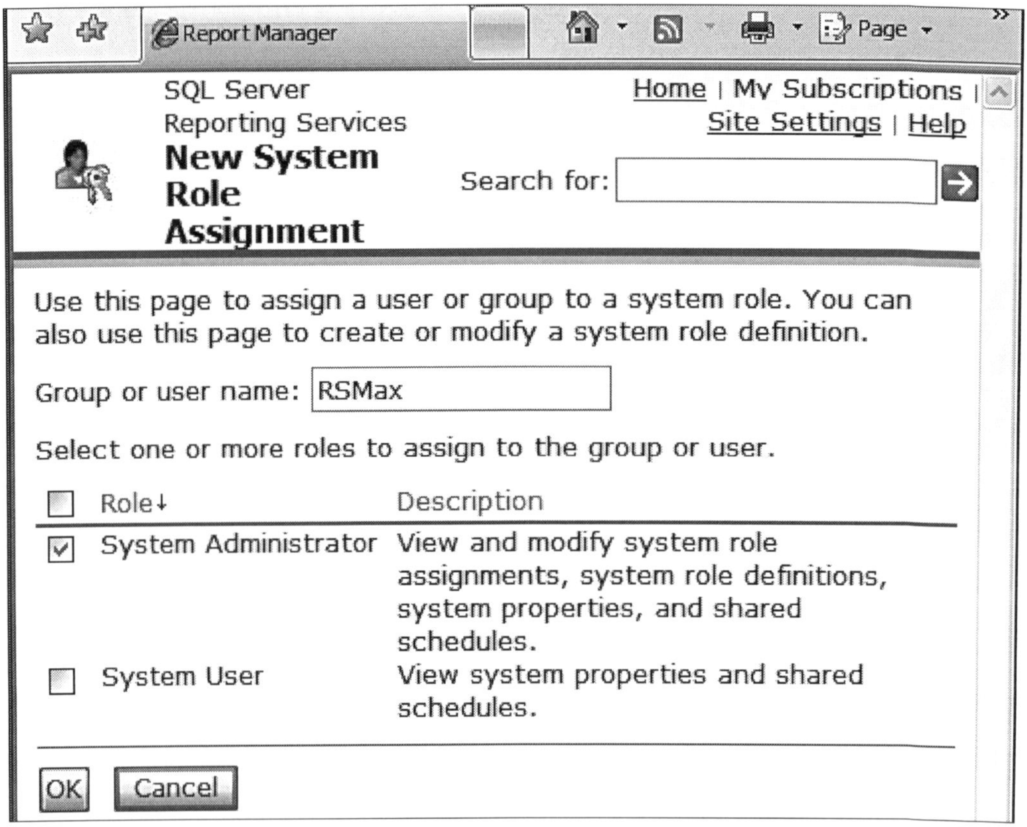

7. Enter **RSMax** for (**Group** or) **user** name and place a checkmark for **System Administrator** and click on the **OK** button.

8. This takes a pretty long time to process at the end of which you will see the following display:

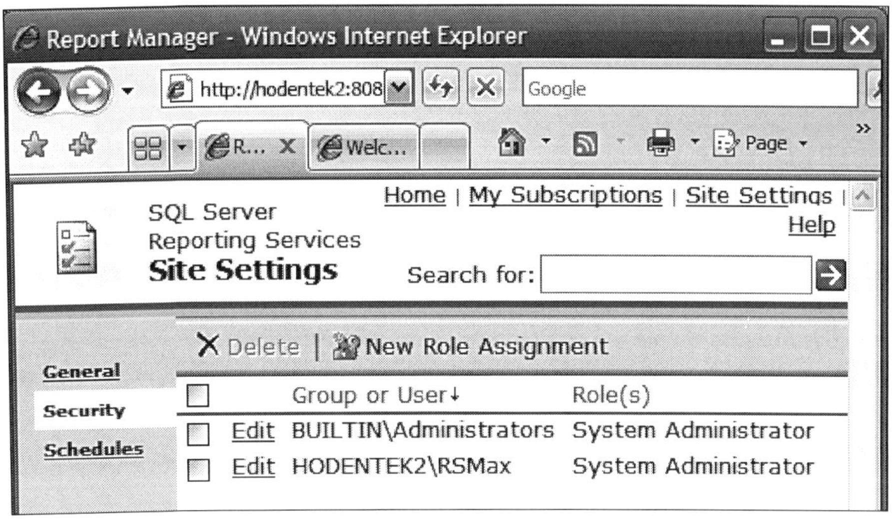

You have successfully assigned the role of System Administrator to the new user **RSMax**.

Hands-on 5.2.2: Assigning users to item-level roles

In the following, you will create a Windows user **RsBrowse** and assign the role of *Browser* to the user. RsBrowse will have limited capability compared to RsContent.

Creating a Windows user

This is similar to the previous case. The user will be assigned to an item level role in this case.

1. Create a windows user *RsBrowse,* as in the previous hands-on exercise, by providing a suitable password with appropriate descriptions and set the password to **never expire**.
2. The user will be added to the **Local Users** account as shown in an earlier screenshot.

Assigning users to roles

Both Windows users and groups can be assigned to roles although users are considered here. The procedure is similar for groups. You need to add a windows user to the group and the user will have the permissions for the group.

1. Open the IE browser to access the **Report Manager** by typing in the URL as in the previous case.

> As described in Chapter 1, the Report Server is using port 8080. Make sure that the port is (in this case 8080) available for the Report Manager and no other service is running. If there is any other service, stop that service; and stop and start the Reporting Services.

2. Click on the **Properties** tab on the **Home** page.
3. The **Properties** page opens as shown in the following screenshot:

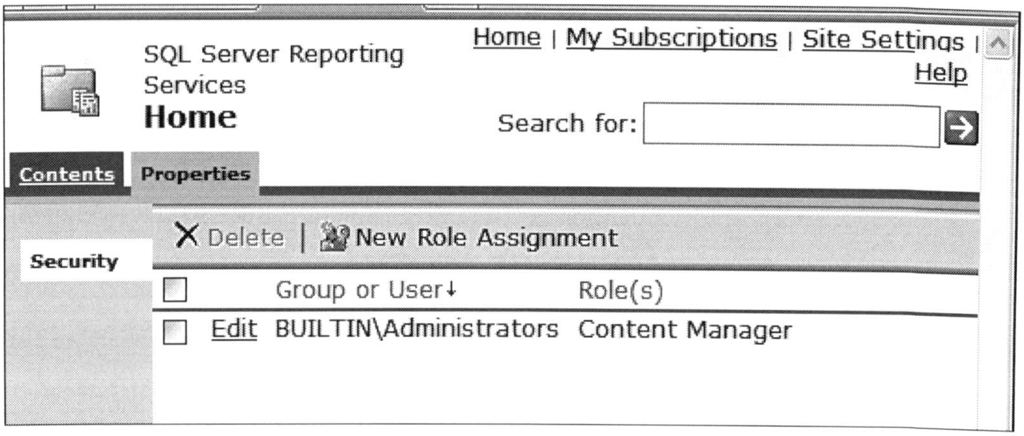

4. Click on the **New Role Assignment**.
5. The **New Role Assignment** page gets displayed as shown.

> To assign roles to users you must have administrative privileges to the computer.

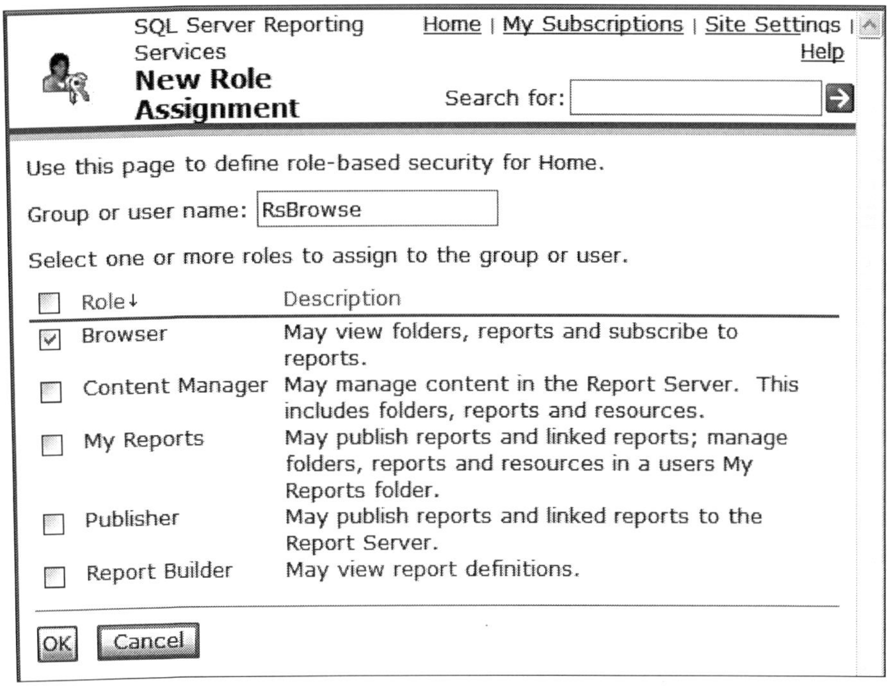

6. Enter **RsBrowse** for **user name** as shown above and place a checkmark for the **Browser** role and click on the **OK** button.

7. You will be back in the **Properties** showing **Hodentek2\RsBrowse** user as having the **Browser** role. The **Properties** page of **Home** page appears as shown in the following screenshot. The user **RsContent** has the role of a **Content Manager**.

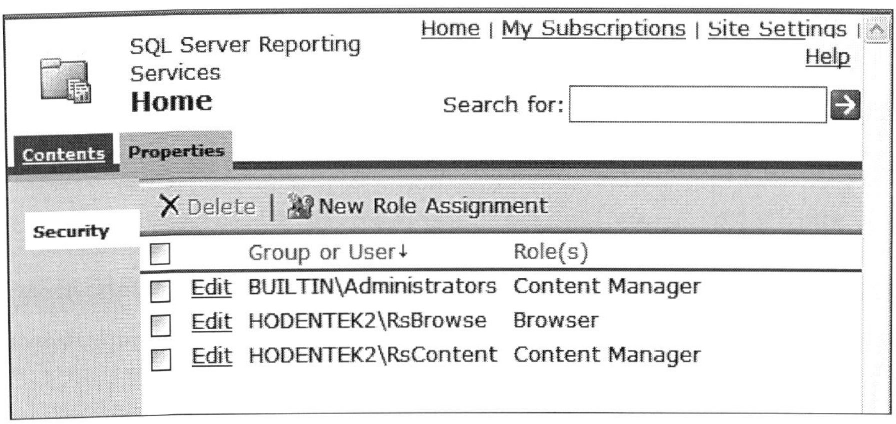

You successfully assigned Browser Role to the Windows user RsBrowse.

Hands-on 5.2.3: Assigning a user to a custom role

1. Create a new user with the name **Navika** with a password as described previously.
2. Logon to Reporting Services in SQL Server Management Studio, expand the **Security** node and right-click on **Role** to display **New User Role** window as shown:

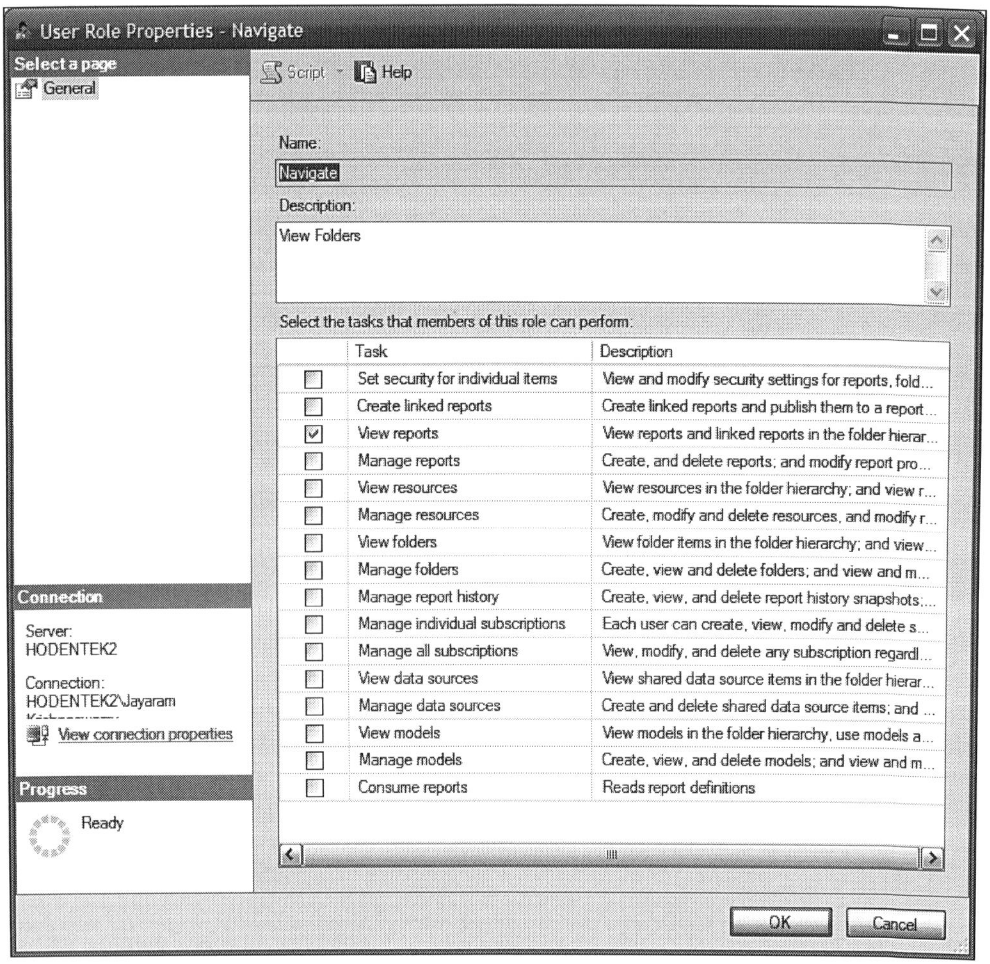

3. Provide a name (herein **Navigate**) and check only **View reports** and click on the **OK** button.

   The role *Navigate* gets registered in the Security/Roles in the Report Server.

4. Open the IE browser and type in the *Report Manager URL*. In the display page click on **Properties** tab.
5. Click on **New Role Assignment** and assign the role *Navigate* to a windows user *Navika.*

   The role **Navigate** gets registered in the ReportServer$SANGAM/Tables/Roles in the *Database Engine*.

Hands-on 5.2.4: Creating a permission to a specific report

The permissions work by inheritance. The **Home** folder is like the root folder and everything under it will be subfolders and will inherit from **Home**. For example, the **RSPWiz** folder will inherit from the **Home** Folder. The report **OrderInformation** will inherit from its parent, **RSPWiz**. However, the security of this page can be edited. This way we can set up permissions to a specific item by editing the security for the parent folder. In this section you will permit the only user **Navika** to view the **OrderInformation** report.

1. In **Report Manager**, click on **RSPWIz08** and click on **Properties**.

   The **Properties** page appears as shown. Since all these roles were added to the *Home* page (*Home* folder) they are all inherited from the **Home** folder.

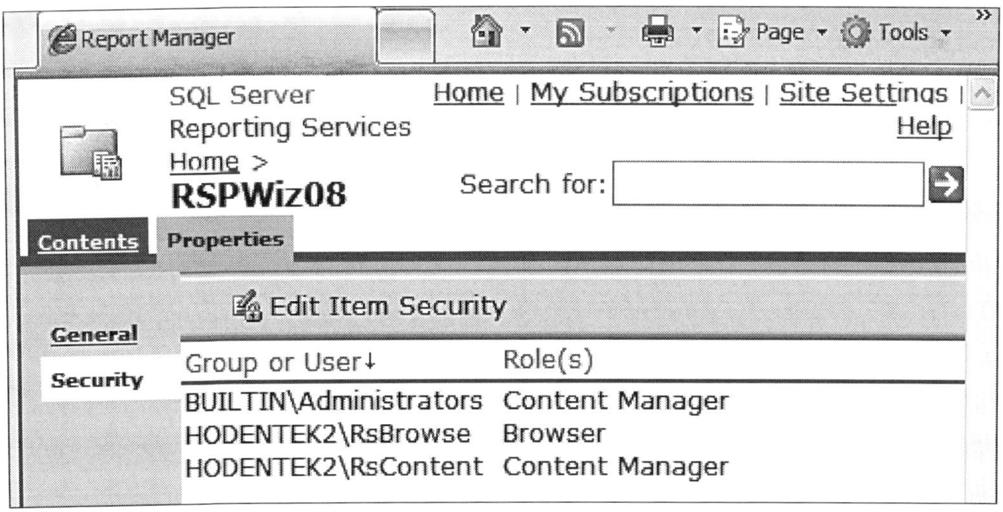

2. Click on **Contents** and then on **OrderInformation**. Follow it up by clicking on **Properties** and **Security** in the **Properties** of **OrderInformation**.

   The **Security** page of the **OrderInformation** report gets displayed as in the following screenshot. You will observe that the **OrderInformation** report inherited the security details from its parent **RSPWiz08**.

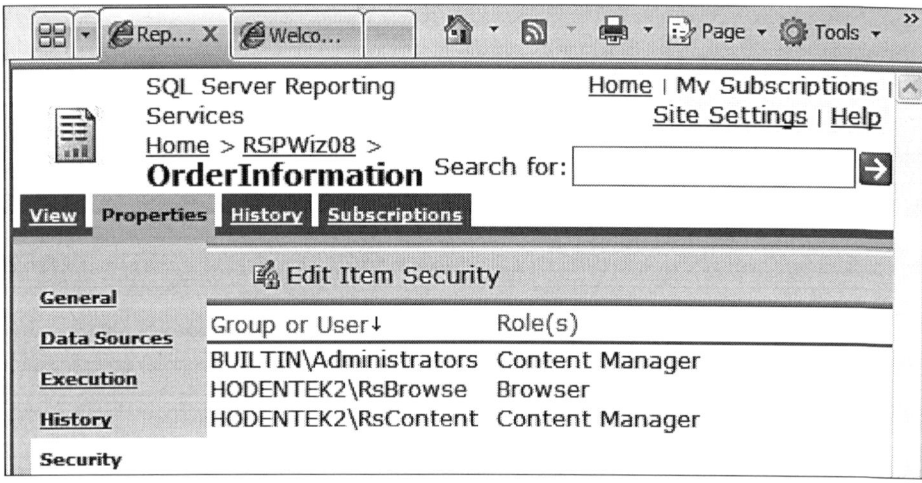

Permitting only the user Navika to this report

In this section you will provide custom permission to a Windows user Navika configured earlier.

1. Click on **Edit Item Security (previous figure).**

   You get a Windows IE message that says:

   Item security is inherited from a parent item. Do you want to apply security settings for this item that are different from those of the parent item?

2. Click on the **OK** button for this window.

   The **Properties** page changes to the one shown in the following screenshot:

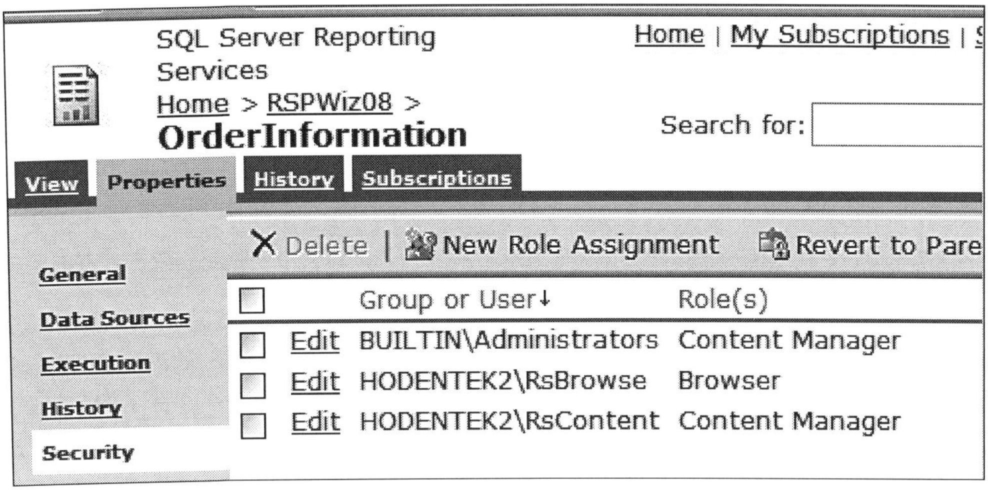

   You can remove all of them (or any of them if you want, except **BUILTIN\Administrators**) by placing a checkmark and clicking the **Delete** button which will get enabled when the choice is made.

3. Click on **New Role Assignment**.

   In the **New Role Assignment** page (which you have seen earlier) type in **Navika** for the user name and place a checkmark for the **Navigate** role and click on the **OK** button. The user **Navika** gets assigned to this specific report as the custom role **Navigate**. You may also verify that Navika will not be found in the parent, **RSPWiz08**.

Report Data Sources

Data that gets into a report is central to a report without which report is meaningless. Data comes from data sources obtained from the databases in the Database Servers. Clicking **Home** | **RSPWiz08** | **OrderInformation** | **Properties** | **DataSources** will display the following window:

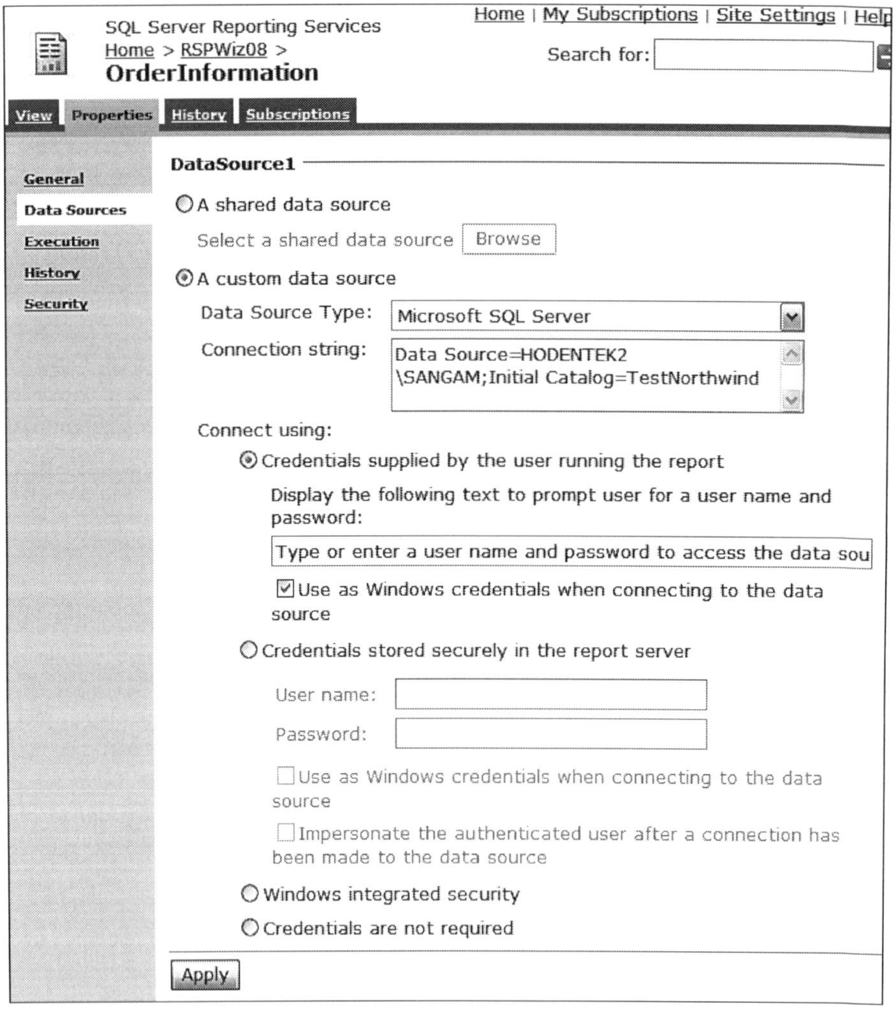

There are basically two ways data sources can be configured for reports: embedded and shared. In Chapter 4, we used the embedded (custom) data source. In this case, the data source connectivity information accompanies the report and is specific to that report such as the one we are working with. The RDL report file carries this information with it.

In this case, you see **Data Source Type** and the **Connection string** for **DataSource1** that came with the report created in Chapter 4 deployed to the Report Server. This was a custom data source pulling data from a SQL Server, the server that was installed in Chapter 1. Now this report has four options as to how it can connect to the Server data. They are:

- Using credentials supplied by the user running the report
- Credentials stored securely in the report server
- Windows Integrated Security
- Credentials are not required

The user needs to choose one of the options and click on the **Apply** button to make that option effective. For this particular report the first option has been chosen.

Report viewing and printing

Viewing reports and printing the reports are some of the major activities that most organizations do on a daily or, scheduled basis. Reports are generated electronically and during printing they must be transformed into as desired by the user specific formats. The reports generated by the Reporting Services accommodate several different formats both for print and for web. Both reports on demand as well as reports for which subscription is provisioned, support the several print format options. For example, a user can subscribe to a report to be sent to him by email in a Word format for printing, and in an HTML format for easy browsing.

In a business environment, the number of reports created can be very large and overwhelming. Searching for reports in a large archive is a must. In addition to report search, there must also be a tool for searching within reports for some specific information. This is accomplished by the **Find** tool.

Viewing of reports is tightly bound to security. The following Hands-on exercise enables the administrator to see reports and other objects that he finds on a report server. The administrator needs to set up roles to users so that their access is limited by their role. These roles also have to comply with accessing data on the server on which the report is based.

Hands-on exercise 5.3: View, print, and search

In this hands-on, you as an administrator will be carrying out a number of activities such as viewing, printing, and searching on the Report Manager. As you are the computer owner, who installed the SQL Server and configured the Reporting Services, you have the maximum power not only to view reports, but also carry out all other activities. It is assumed that you have reporting services running and some reports have already been uploaded (pushed to the server) from BIDS, or from the Visual Studio IDE.

In Chapter 4, you deployed a Report and a Report Model. You will be using them in the hands-on exercise.

Viewing reports

Viewing a report after it is deployed will be the first activity. After making sure the report completely satisfies the requirements, you will consider other activities such as scheduling delivery and so on.

1. Click on **Start | All Programs | Microsoft SQL Server 2008 | Configuration Tools | Reporting Services Configuration Manager.**
2. In the **Reporting Services Configuration Manager** connect to the Report Server. In the **Report Server Status** page click on **Start** if it has stopped.
3. In the navigational list on the left in the **Reporting Services Configuration Manager,** click on **Report Manager URL.**

   The **Report Manger URL** page gets displayed as shown:

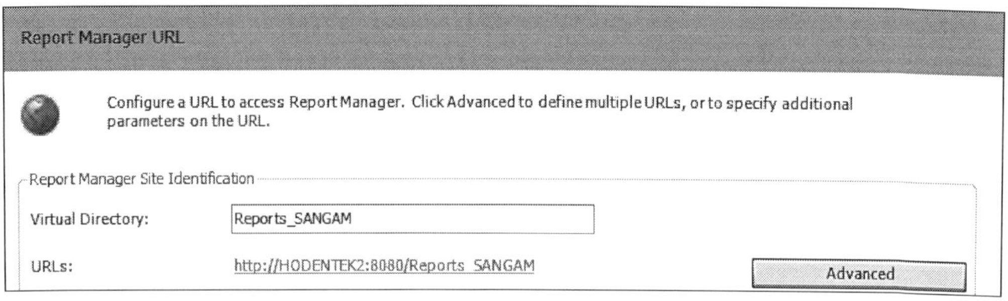

4. On the **Report Manager** page, click on the hyperlink for the URL of the Report Manager (in the present demo `http://Hodentek2:8080/Reports_SANGAM`).

5. This opens up the Report Manager's **Home** page. It is assumed you are using IE 6.0 or above. The URL you type in redirects you to the `Folder.aspx` page as shown:

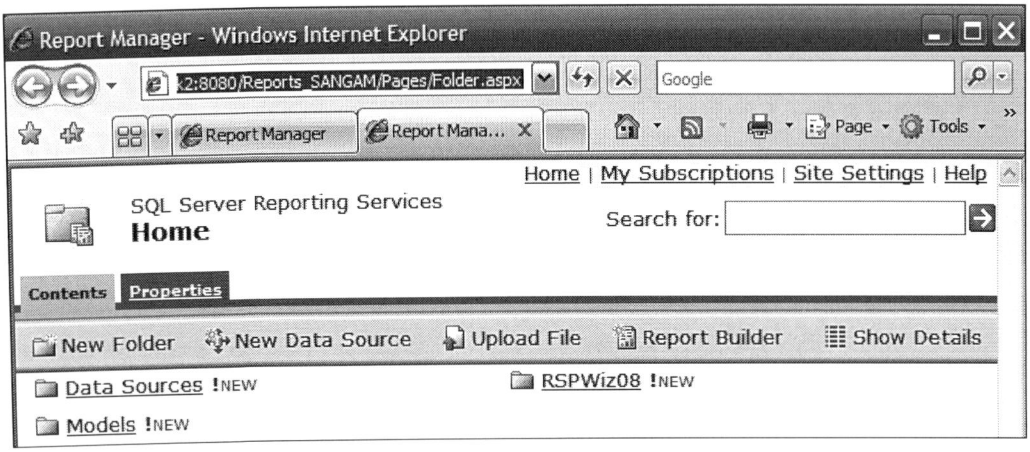

6. **Click on the item RSPwiz08 !New.**
7. The hyperlink takes you to the following page. RSPWiz08 was the name of the project you created in the Visual Studio IDE in Chapter 4. The !New tag refers to a newly created item which lasts for 48 hours after which the tag disappears. There is only one report in the project.

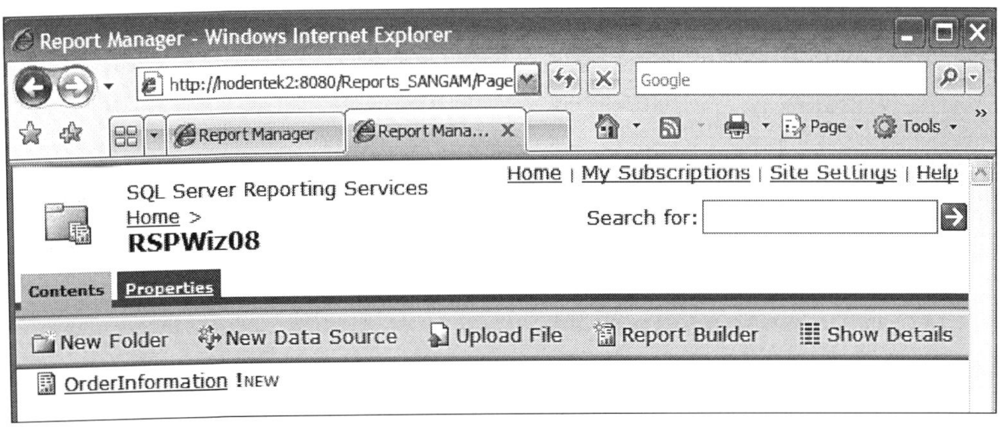

8. Click on the hyperlink OrderInformation !New.

9. At first the 'Report is being generated' progress icon gets displayed after which the Report gets displayed in the Report Manager as shown. In the URL of this page you would find the following:

```
http://hodentek2:8080/Reports_SANGAM/Pages/Report.aspx?ItemPath
=%2fRSPWiz08%2fOrderInformation
```

10. The itemPath points to the path of the chosen report in the Project.

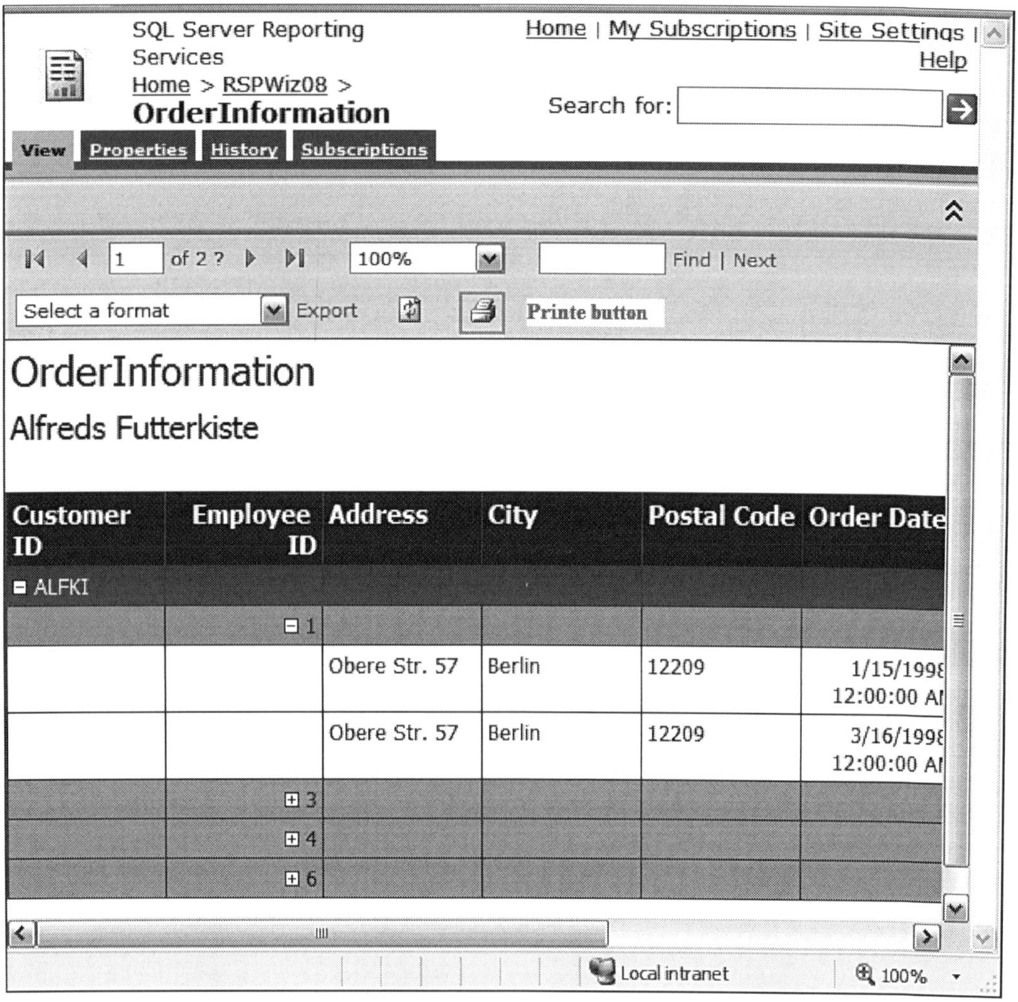

The **OrderInformation** report opens in the **View** tab as in the above screen-shot. You could also access the **Properties**, **History**, and **Subscriptions** by clicking on the other tabs shown on the report.

Printing reports

The report in the previous page is an HTML page and it can be printed from the IE browser.

1. Click *Alt+R* followed by *Alt+P*.
2. This brings up the following **Print** window as shown. From here you can pick the printer available to you. You may need to work on properly arranging the report dimensions to fit the paper size with margins that you may be able to specify. Not all printing devices (printers shown in the following screenshot) give a choice in paper orientation. Often only the portion of the report viewable on the browser will be printed.

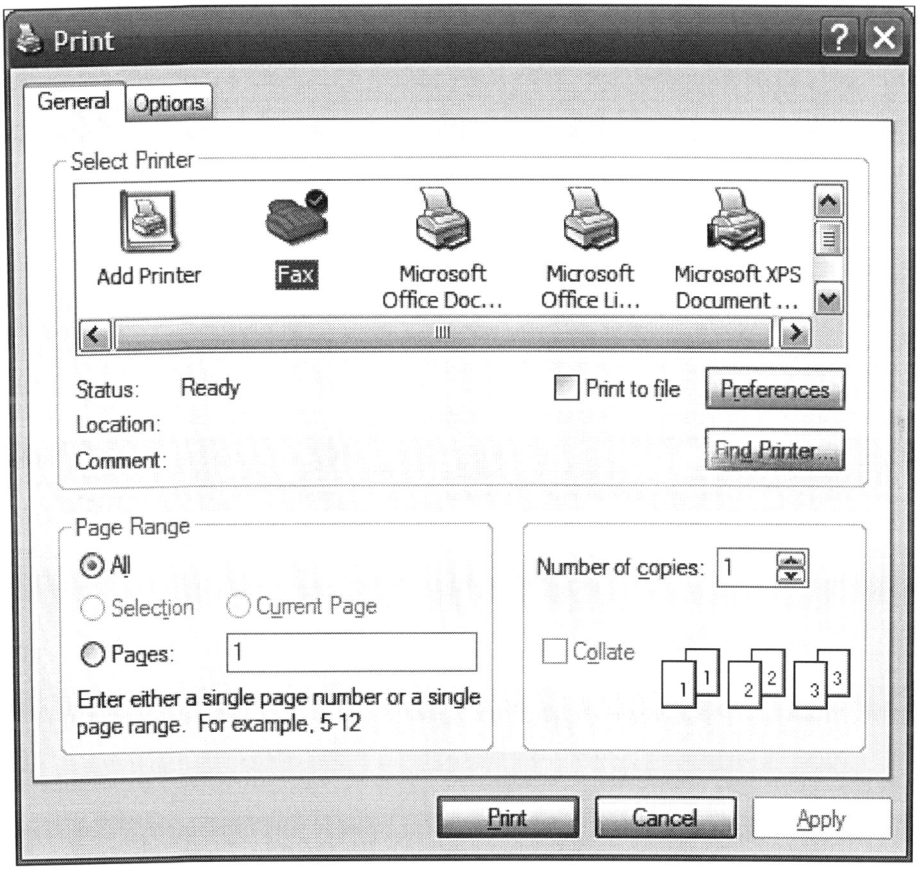

Another option, where the client viewing the report page can print directly from that page, is to use the **Print** toolbar item on the report.

Printing report from the Print button on report

While viewing the report on the Report Manager or Report Server is sufficient to access the report for verification and checking, hard-copy reports are needed for presentation and in some cases for archiving purposes. Reporting Services provides a number of options for printing.

1. **Click on the Print** button (for example, on the OrderInformation Report in Report Manager).
2. You get a SQL Server 2008 message asking if it is alright to download a file. Click on the **Yes** button, the printer interface (an ActiveX component) gets installed which is the Fax control as shown. Hit the **Preview...** button to view the report. Using the **Properties...** you can set the printer properties that you want to use.

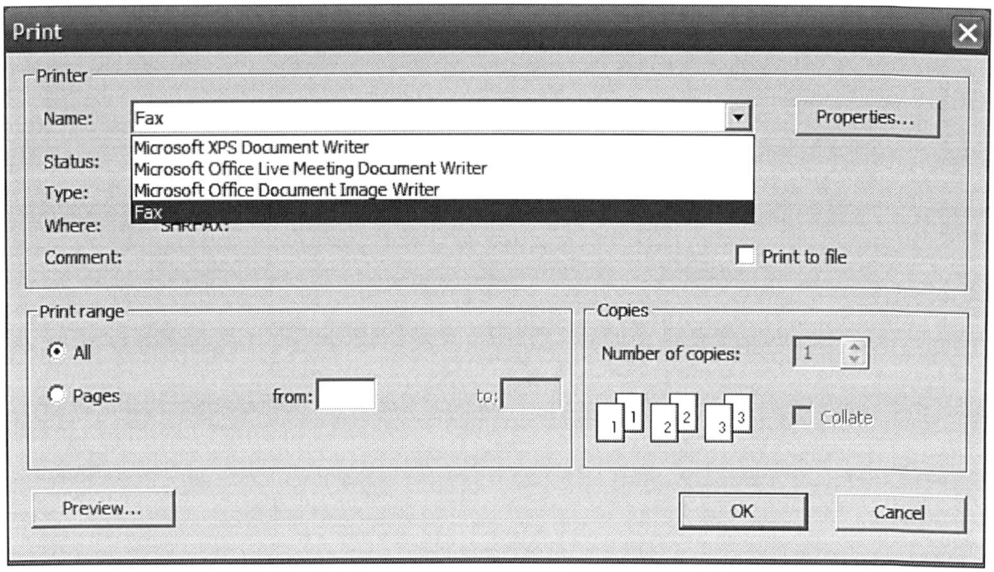

> Microsoft XPS Document Writer prints the report to an XPS (XML Paper Specification) file which is a competitor for Adobe's PDF format. XPS provides excellent Print support. As the report gets printed, it does not add the XPS extension. After renaming with the XPS extension it can be opened up in the IE browser. This is convenient for emailing. This file can also be printed using the .NET Framework and Visual Studio 2008.
>
> Microsoft Office Document Image Writer also writes to a file and saves it as a file with the extension TIF or TIFF. Although the Preview... would show all the pages in the report, the saved file shows only one page.
>
> Microsoft Office Live Meeting Document Writer also writes to a file which is saved with the MDI extension and can be viewed with Microsoft Office OneNote.

Not all of these have all the features and you should verify which of these works best.

Yet another option for printing reports is to convert the file to another format as in the next step.

Changing report format for printing

Reports can be printed in different formats. While some users may require Word format, others may need it in PDF. Reports in Reporting Services have a couple of report formatting options.

1. Click on Select a format (for example, on the OrderInformation Report) drop-down list and choose PDF (or any of your choice) and click on the export link by its side.
2. The file will be saved as a PDF file (or your chosen format) to a location of your choice which you can later print. Another choice is of course Microsoft Word format.

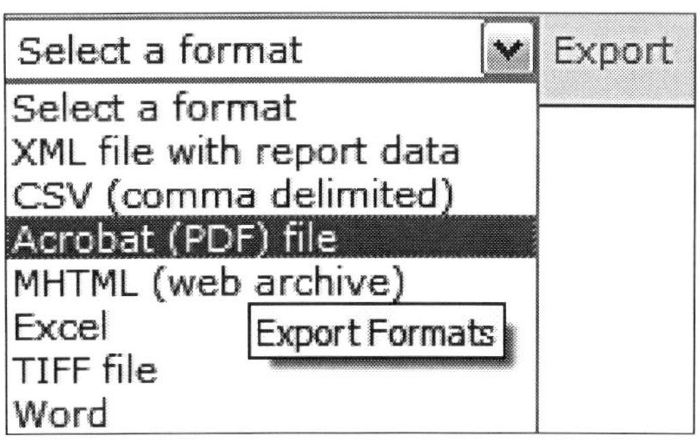

Search for reports

Although this Report Manager has just one report and a report model, it can contain a large number of reports, models, and data sources. In order to locate a report it will be necessary to have a search routine available. The search for text box can be used to search the contents in the Report Manager.

1. Type in **Order** in the **Search for** text box and click on the arrow by its side.
2. The search takes you to the **OrderInformation** report page. Even **Ord** or **rd** can locate the **OrderInformation** report. Similarly **My** would locate the **MyNorthwind** data source. After the search you can always hit **Home** to return to the home page.

Find text in a report

After finding a report you may need to look in the report by searching for a piece of text, a keyword, or something specific. This is a very common scenario as the report title itself may not be sufficient.

Once you have searched for a report (object), you may also want to find a certain text contained in the report. This is often required when you are looking for a specific name or a date inside a report as you do not want to go through the report page by page. The Find and Next buttons on the report help you locate the text you are looking for.

1. Type in bot or BOT inside the text box to the left of the Find button and click on Find.
2. It immediately takes you to the location where it locates the text. You can click on the Next button to take you to the next occurrence of the same text if it exists. Of course Find will not find text if it is part of a drill-down report.

Managing data source connections with Report Manager

In the case where Reporting Services is installed in the native mode (which is true for the hands-on used in this book as described in Chapter 1), the report data sources can be managed using the Report Manager. In the case where the report is deployed using the SharePoint Integrated Mode, you will have to use the application pages on a SharePoint site. SharePoint related discussion is outside the scope of this book. Interested readers should review the material at `http://technet.microsoft.com/en-us/library/bb326358.aspx`.

As you can see from the previous screenshot, the data source related management is carried out by the administrator or anyone, who is granted permission to manage reports on the Report Server. The administrator can perform the following data source related tasks:

- Change connection strings—useful while changing computer or moving from a test database to a production database. Both static and dynamic connection strings can be managed while the latter is limited to replacing it with a static connection string.
- Change credentials—useful while providing access to users so that they can manage reports with their credentials. For subscription to reports, the credentials need to be stored in the Server.
- Create or change a shared data source on a Report Server.
- Change an embedded data source to a shared data source.
- Control access to data source properties by permitting permissions on the reports, models, or any shared data source.

Connecting to report data sources

Having permission to access a report on Report Manager is not sufficient to render it and one should be able to connect to the data source from which the report derives its data. The credentials to access the data source are present in the report file and are defined at the time the report is authored for custom data sources (as distinguished from a shared data source). For example, for the report **OrderInformation** the data source was created with Windows authentication. If you look at the **DataSources** information (clicking on **Home | RSPWiz08 | OrderInformation | Properties | DataSources**), you will see the information displayed in the following screenshot. Hence, when the user logged in with the service account and accessed the report on the Report Manager, the report got immediately rendered. This is because the service account was also the the account used for all the services with Windows authentication.

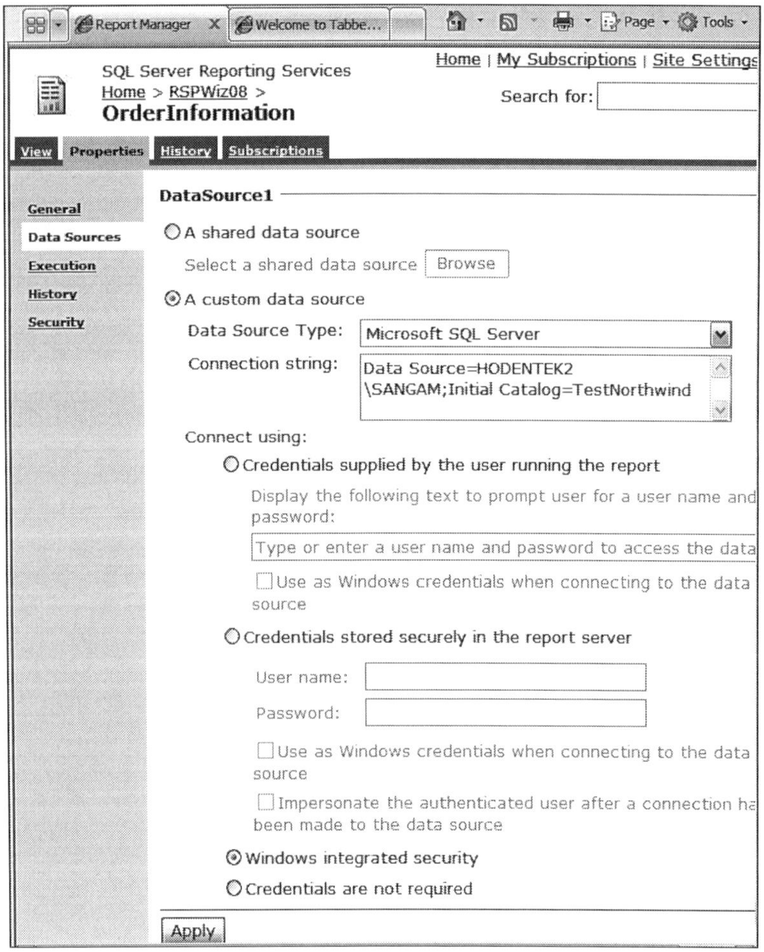

Now this report has four options as to how it can connect to the Server data. They are:

- Using credentials supplied by the user running the report
- Credentials stored securely in the report server
- Windows Integrated Security (currently configured for the **OrderInformation** report)
- Credentials are not required

The credentials needed to access the OrderInformation, when the report was originally designed, used Windows authentication. It can, however, be modified by the user to access by supplying his credentials. He/she, however, must specify how he/she may establish (strictly the report the user is trying to run) connection to the data source as we see in what follows.

Connect using user supplied credentials

If this option is chosen, the user must provide the credentials for the data source each time he runs a report. When the user tries to run a report, the user gets a prompt and will be asked to type in the user name and password as required, shown in the following screenshot:

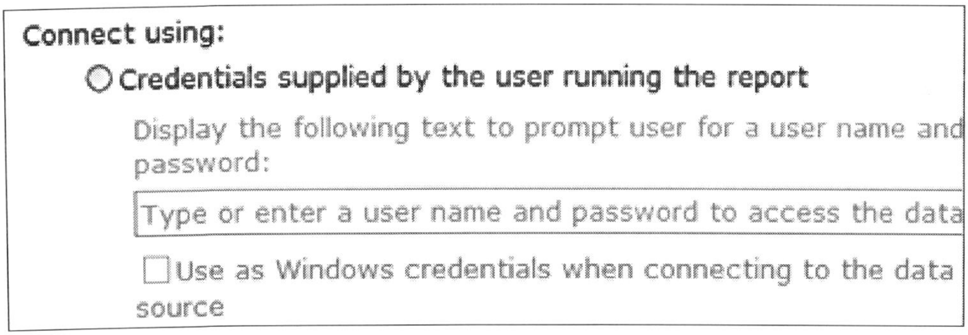

In addition, if the checkbox for the item **Use as Windows credentials when connecting to the data source** is checked, then his credentials will be treated as a Windows login. If this is not checked then it will be treated as a database login. This is the most secure way of giving user access to reports although, the user has to enter (remember securely) his credentials each time (a user unfriendly option). If the security policy demands such a method then this is the preferred option.

Connect using stored credentials

In this option, where the stored credential specification is chosen in the data sources property of a report, the credentials are to be stored in the report server database. The user name and password are encrypted on the report server and the password entry box does not reveal the password. This is more user friendly than the previous option and has adequate security due to encryption. The specification part is shown in the following screenshot:

The **Use as Windows credentials when connecting to the data source** checked option was considered earlier.

On the other hand, if the checkbox for the item **Impersonate the authenticated user after a connection has been made to the data source** is checked, the data source uses the credentials to impersonate this user. Support for this impersonation depends on the database server product, some do and some do not.

Connect using Windows integrated security

Windows integrated security does not demand that the user provide credentials. It takes the Windows login credentials that the user uses to access the Report Manager and passes them along to the database server. It is up to the database server to accept these credentials. Integrated security works on the basis of **hops** across a network if the data source and the report server are not on the same SQL Server. Please look up Windows Integrated Security in the **SQL Server 2008 Books** Online at the following link: `http://msdn.microsoft.com/en-us/library/aa984236.aspx`.

Connection that does not require credentials

This is not recommended by Microsoft. Except under certain constraints, the remote data may not need credentials (some XML data for example). The exception holds for secure connections, where the credentials are part of the connection string, or in the case of a sub-report which gets its credentials from its parent.

Hands-on exercise 5.4: Windows user access to a report on the Report Manager

Provided a user has been assigned to some role, he/she can access reports on the Report Manager. Depending on the assigned role, he/she can manipulate the reports.

Getting ready

If you are a user accessing the Report Manager, you may need to work with the DBA to complete this hands-on. You should have the credentials of the user **RsBrowse** you created in *Hands-on 5.2*.

In the Report Manager, the user RsBrowse was assigned the browser role for the `RPSWiz08` folder. The report OrderInformation inherited this role from the folder. The OrderInformation report gets its data from the report source Data Source1, which is derived from a database table on the SQL Server using the connection string `Data Source=HODENTEK2\SANGAM; Initial Catalog=TestNorthwind`. When the report was created, the Windows authentication credentials was used. The user RsBrowse does not have login credentials to the database server, although he has permissions to access the Report Manager. With this kind of credentials what does the user see when he logs on to the computer and accesses the Report Manager? You will find the answer to this in this hands-on and you will also find how he may view the data.

1. Login to the computer using the credentials created for the user RsBrowse in *Hands-on 5.2*.
2. Open the IE browser and type in the URL access for the Report Manager.
3. If you are unable to access the Report Manager, it means that you have not assigned the user an appropriate role to access the Report Manager.
4. Click on the folder RPSWiz08 and then follow it by clicking OrderInformation.

5. The following message gets displayed in the Report Manager.

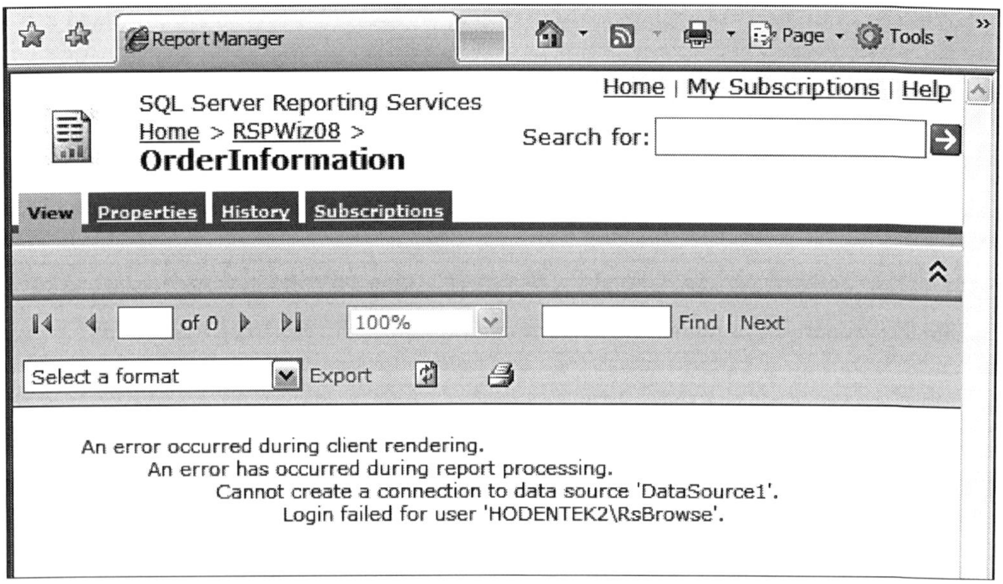

6. Ask your DBA to give the user **RsBrowse** login credential to the server, access permissions to the database, and **Select** permission to the `Orders` table on which the report **OrderInformation** is built.
7. Log on to the computer with the credentials of the user **RsBrowse** and access the Report Manager by typing in the URL address. In the Report Manager, access the report **OrderInformation.**
8. Verify that the report **OrderInformation** is rendered correctly as shown:

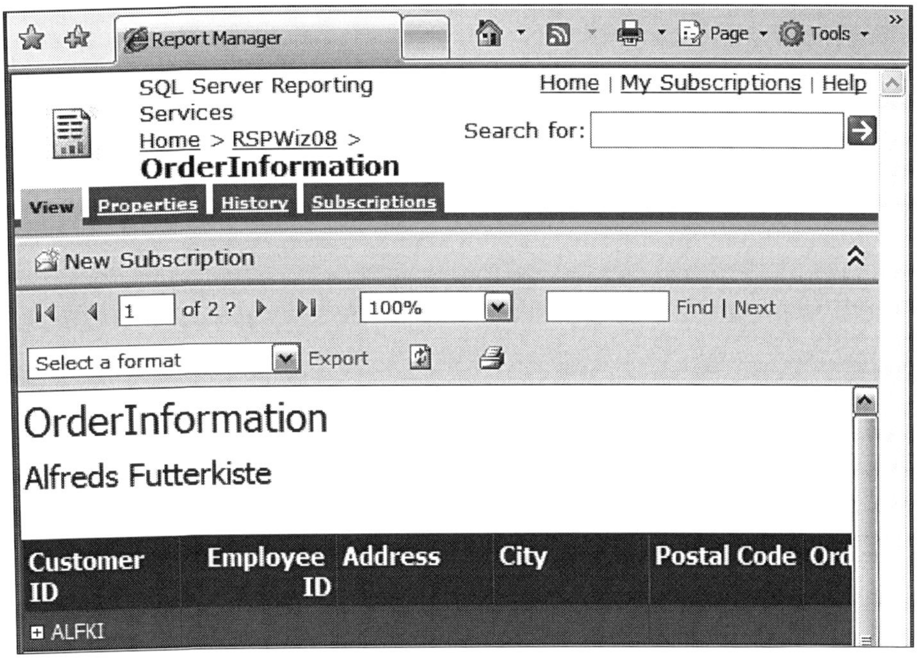

9. Log out of the computer using **Start** | **Log off** | **Switch user** to get back to the computer with the Administrator login.
10. Access the Report Manager by typing the URL in the IE browser.
11. Access the report OrderInformation and change the data source properties in the properties of the order from Windows Authentication to connect using the credentials supplied by the user. Also place a checkmark so that the credentials will be treated as Window credentials. Click on the Apply button.
12. Log out as **Administrator** and login as the user **RsBrowse**. Open the Report Manager in the IE browser by supplying the URL. Click on the **RSPWiz08** folder and follow it up by clicking **OrderInformation**.

The following page gets displayed wherein you are asked to supply the credentials:

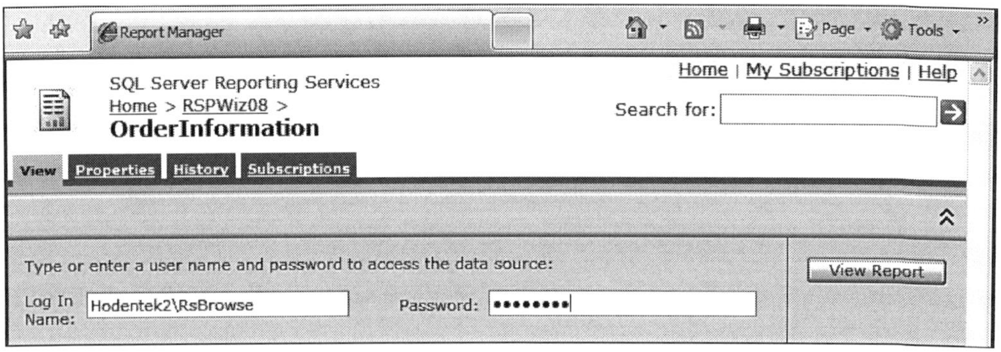

13. Enter the credentials as shown above for Log In Name and Password. Click on the View Report button.
14. You should see the Report Manager interface as shown in the following screenshot:

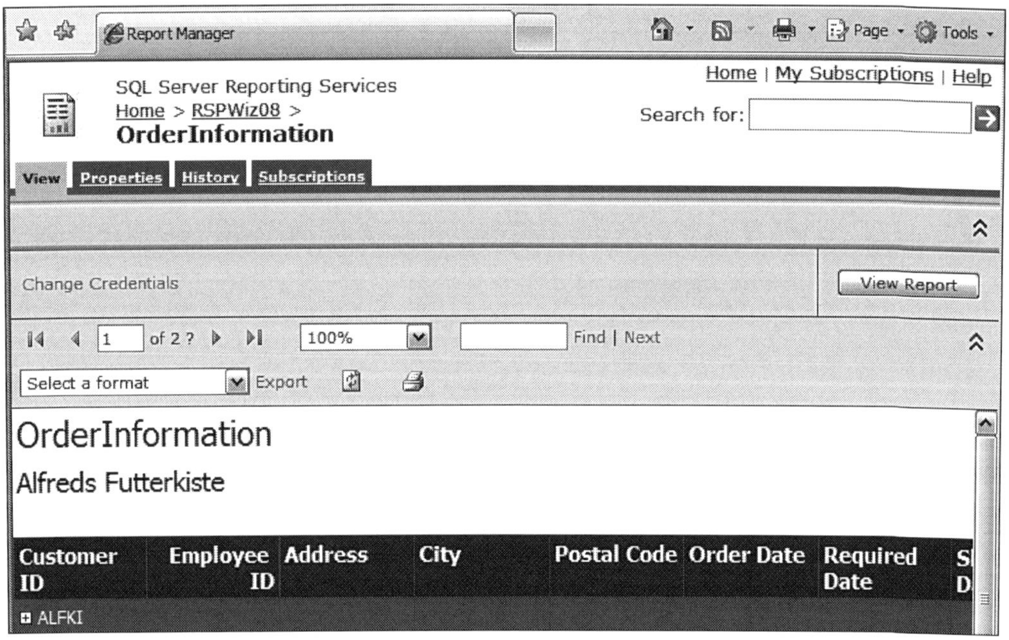

Deploying reports

You have already deployed a report containing an embedded data source to the Report Server in Chapter 4 using the standard way to deploy reports, namely using the Deploy support in Visual Studio. You have also deployed a Report Model to the Report Server. When the project was deployed, a folder with the project name was created in the Report Server containing the report.

The deployment works the same way for reports that use a shared data source. It is also possible to deploy a single report instead of the whole project. While deploying a report from Visual Studio to the Report Server may be called a "push" method, uploading a report to the Report Manager may be called a "pull" method. You will be doing examples of the "push" method of deployment in the next hands-on.

Hands-on exercise 5.5: Deploying reports

In this hands-on you will be 'Pushing' a report from VS 2008 to the Report Server. You will also deploy a report using a shared data source to the Report Server.

Deploying a single report

In here you will be deploying a report which is already in a Report Server project. Important points to know beforehand are the target folder into which you want to deploy (in case you do not want the default) and the target URL of the Report Server.

Make sure you have completed the Chapter 4 *Hands-on* and that the report server has started

1. Create a new folder and provide a name for it, here it is **MSAccess**.
2. Open the project **ImportMSAccess** from Chapter 4 in VS 2008.

3. Click on **Project | ImportMSAccess Properties....**

   This opens the **ImportMSAccess Property** pages as shown. This project has many reports.

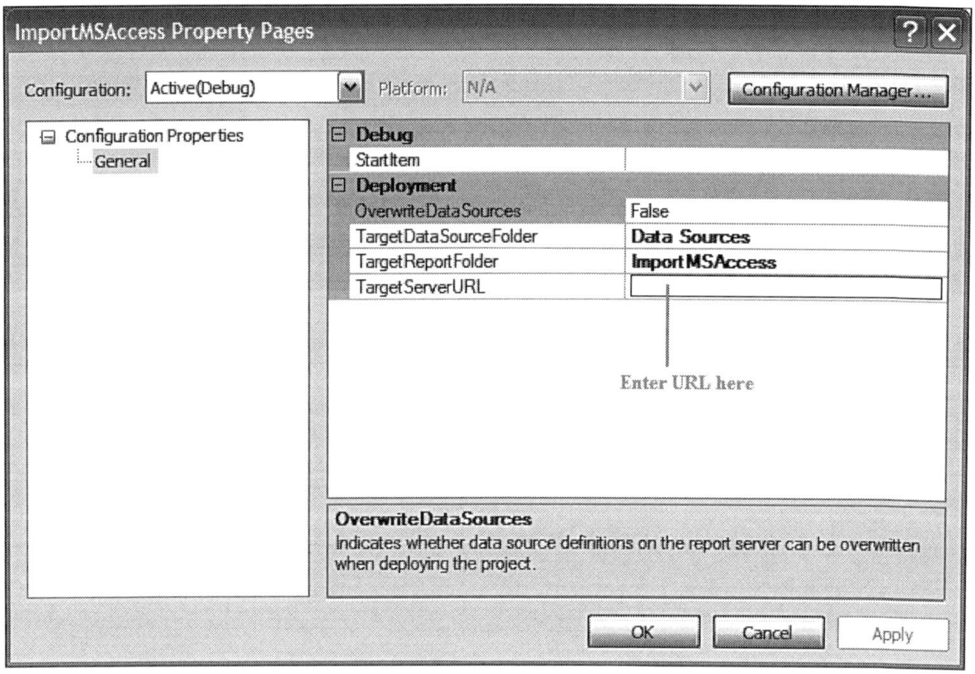

4. Type in the URL of the Report Server in the **TargetServerURL** field on this window at the indicated location.

   You may need to change the **OverwriteDataSources** from **False** to **True** if you have made changes to the data source.

5. Click **Apply** and click on the **OK** button.
6. Right-click **ByOrders.rdl** in the `Reports` folder and click on **Deploy** in the drop-down menu.

7. The report gets deployed to a named folder as seen in the **Output** window of Visual Studio.

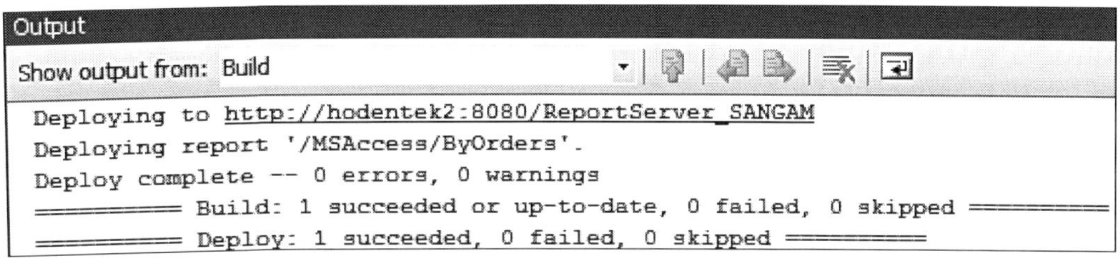

8. Access the Report Manager and verify that the **ByOrders** report is in the **MSAccess** folder as shown.

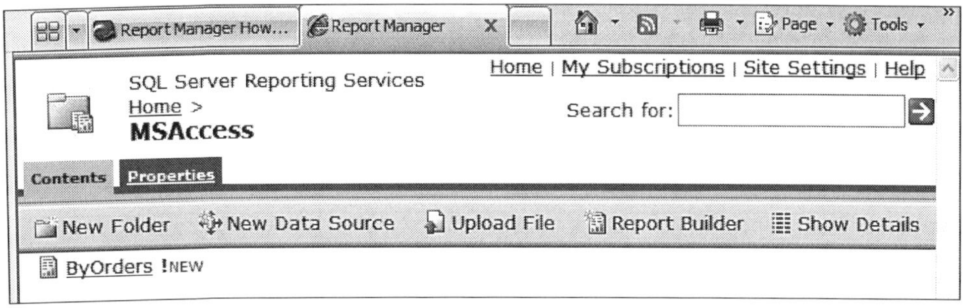

9. Click on the **Properties** tab of the **ByOrders** report.
10. Click on the **DataSources** link to open the **DataSource1** page.
11. Choose **Windows Integrated Security**.

12. Click on **Contents** and then click on **ByOrders.**

    The report gets rendered as shown:

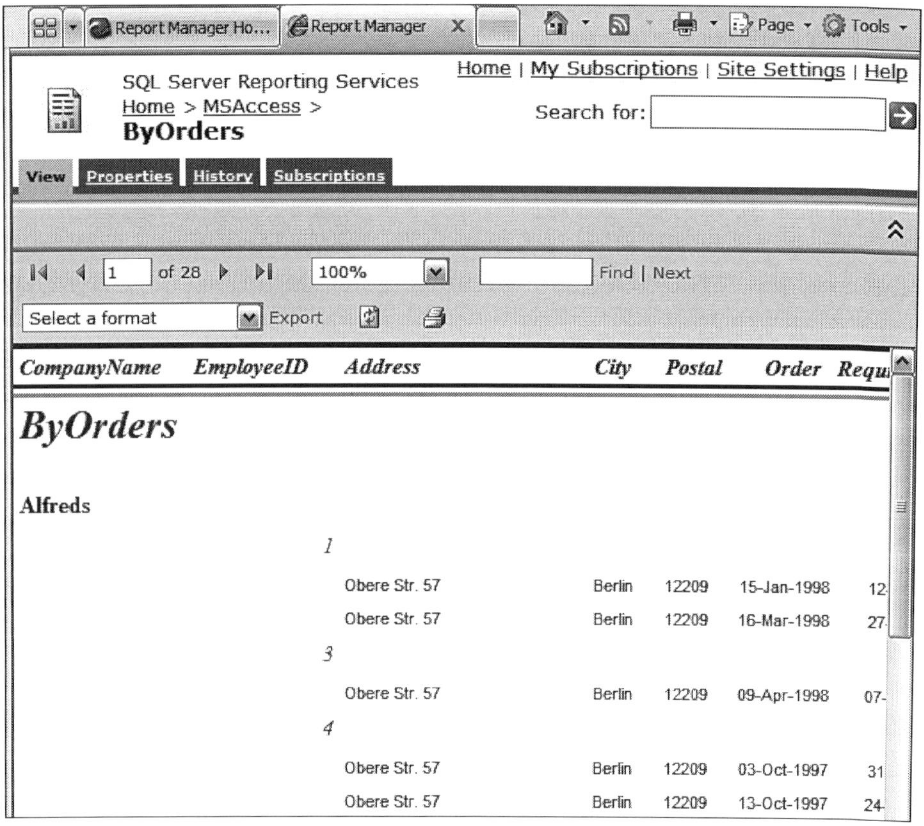

Deploying a report with a shared data source

In Chapter 4, we created a report using data from an Oracle database in VS 2008 project Shared Data that uses an Oracle Database as a Shared Data Source.

Make sure the Oracle services are running as described in Chapter 4. You can do this in the control panel using the **Services** under **Administrative Tools**.

1. Open the **Project SharedData** in Visual Studio or BIDS.
2. Click on **Project | SharedData Properties....**

3. **SharedData Property** page opens.

   Shared data is normally used by more than one report and so you do not normally overwrite the data. Overwrite DataSources false (which is the **default) is therefore acceptable. Enter the Target Server URL** (`http://hodetek2:8080/ReportServer_SANGAM`).

4. Click on the **Apply** button and click on the **OK** button.
5. Right-click the **Project SharedData** in **Solution Explorer** and from the drop-down menu click on **Deploy**.
6. The project gets deployed to the Report Server as displayed in the **Output** window:

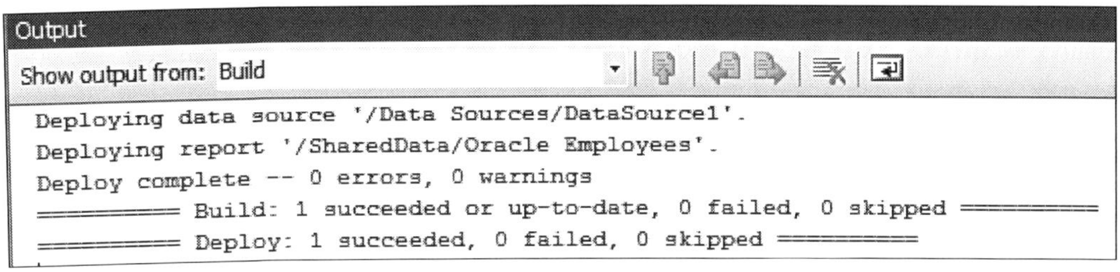

7. Access the Report Manager in the IE browser.
8. The **SharedData** folder appears in the Report Manager as shown:

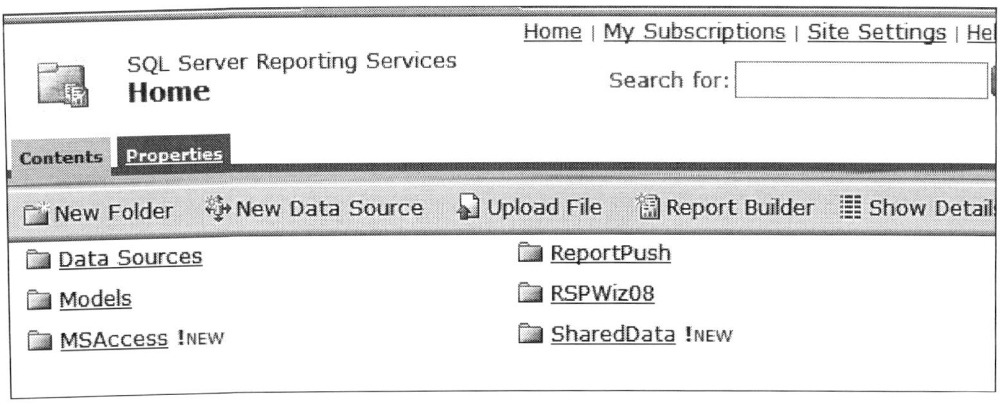

9. The shared data source has been deployed to the Data Sources folder as shown:

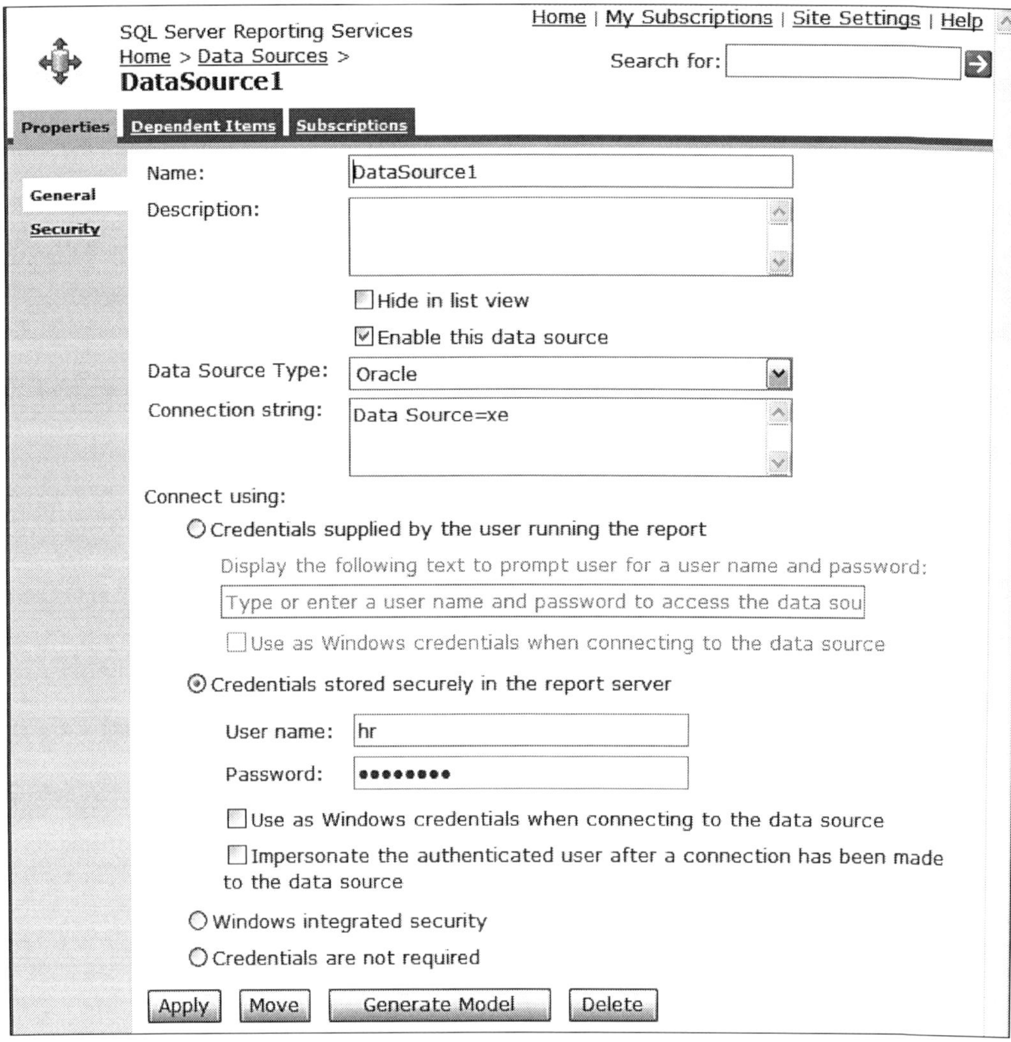

Note that the data source details get stored on the Report Server in the **dbo. DataSource** table as shown. This data source may be shared by other reports. The username and password are encrypted.

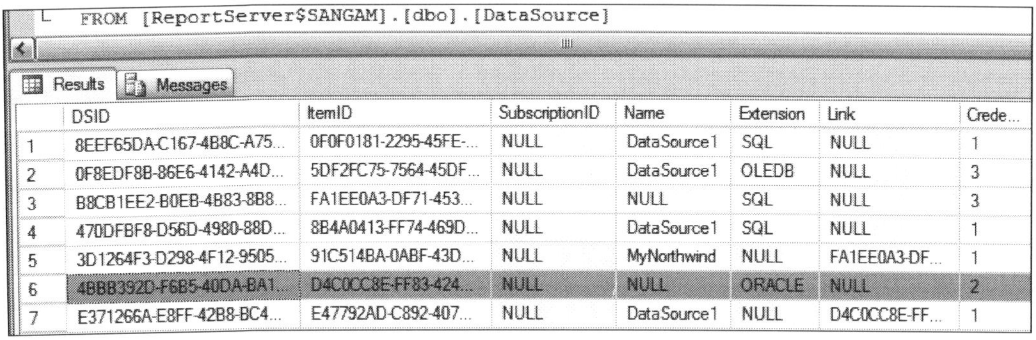

10. The Oracle Employees report will appear in the SharedData folder as shown:

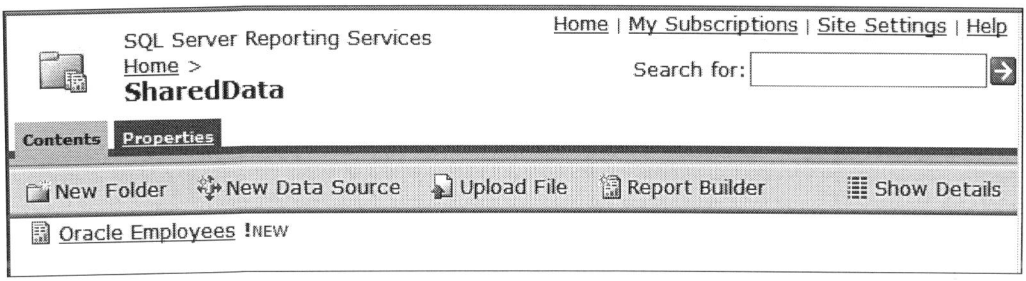

Uploading a report using the Report Manager

In a scenario where the report author is not the Report Server administrator, the report can be saved to a file by the author and then uploaded by the Report Server administrator after verifying that the report meets the requirements. For this section of the hands-on you will upload a file from your ImportMSAccess project created in Chapter 4.

Make sure you have the Products by Category file on your machine.

1. Open Report Manager in the IE browser and create a new folder and name it **Uploads**.
2. Click on **Upload File** icon.

   Upload File's page gets displayed as shown:

3. Click on **Browse...** and search for the `.rdl` file (**Products by Category** or any other file) you want to upload.
4. Place a checkmark for **Overwrite item if it exists**. Click on the **OK** button.

   The **Products by Category** file is uploaded into the Report Manager in the **Uploads** folder as shown:

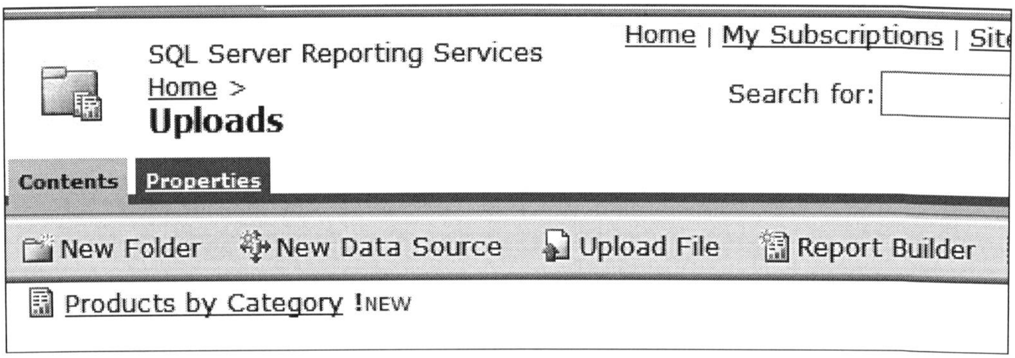

   Since files can be moved around it is not necessary that you should already be in the folder before uploading.

5. Click on the **Products by Category** report followed by clicking its **Properties**.

6. Click on **DataSources**.

   The **DataSource1** page appears as shown. The **Connect using** credentials supplied by the user running the report is chosen by default as MS Access files require authentication (Contrast this with the earlier one where the file was deployed from Visual Studio.)

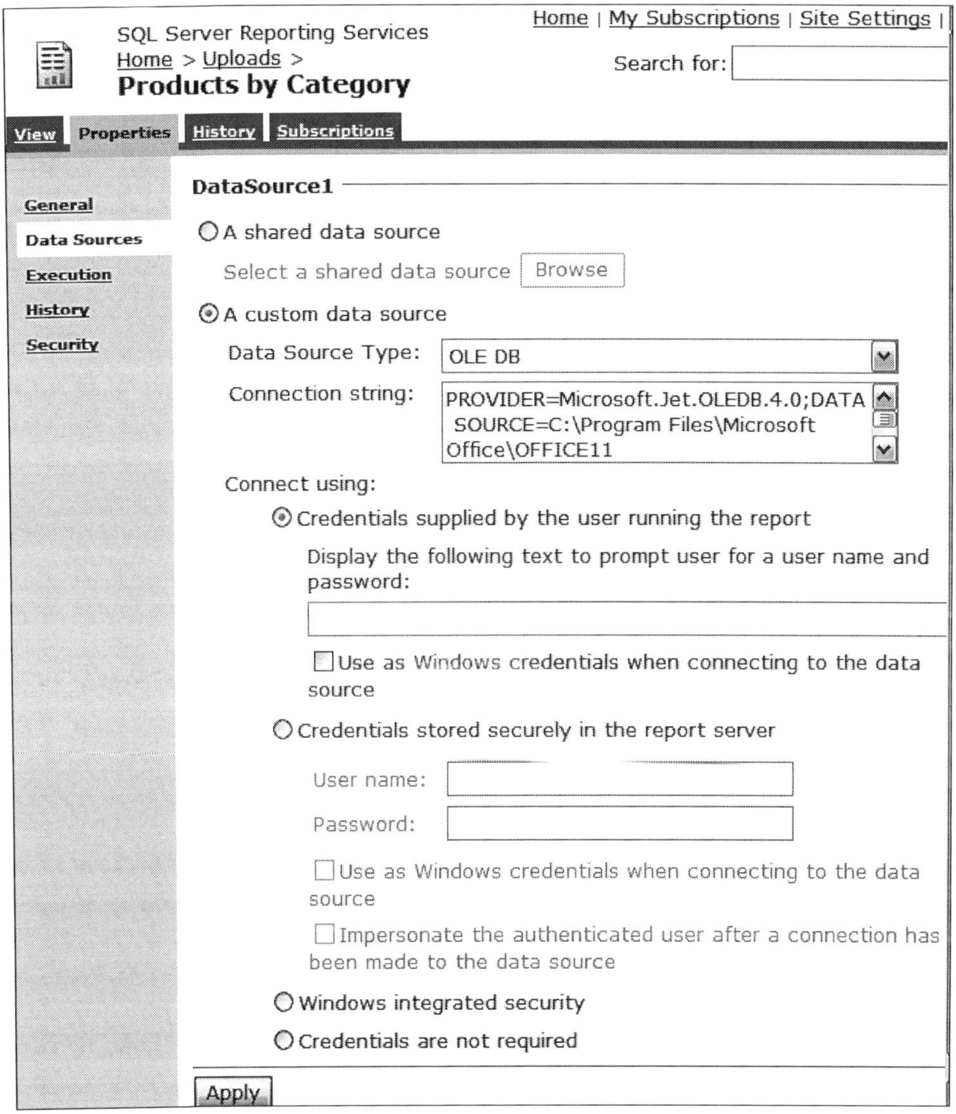

7. Click on the **View** tab.
8. The **View** page gets displayed requesting user input of credentials.
9. Enter **Admin** for **User Name** and leave **Password** empty and click on the **View Report** button.

   The report gets rendered in the Report Manager as shown:

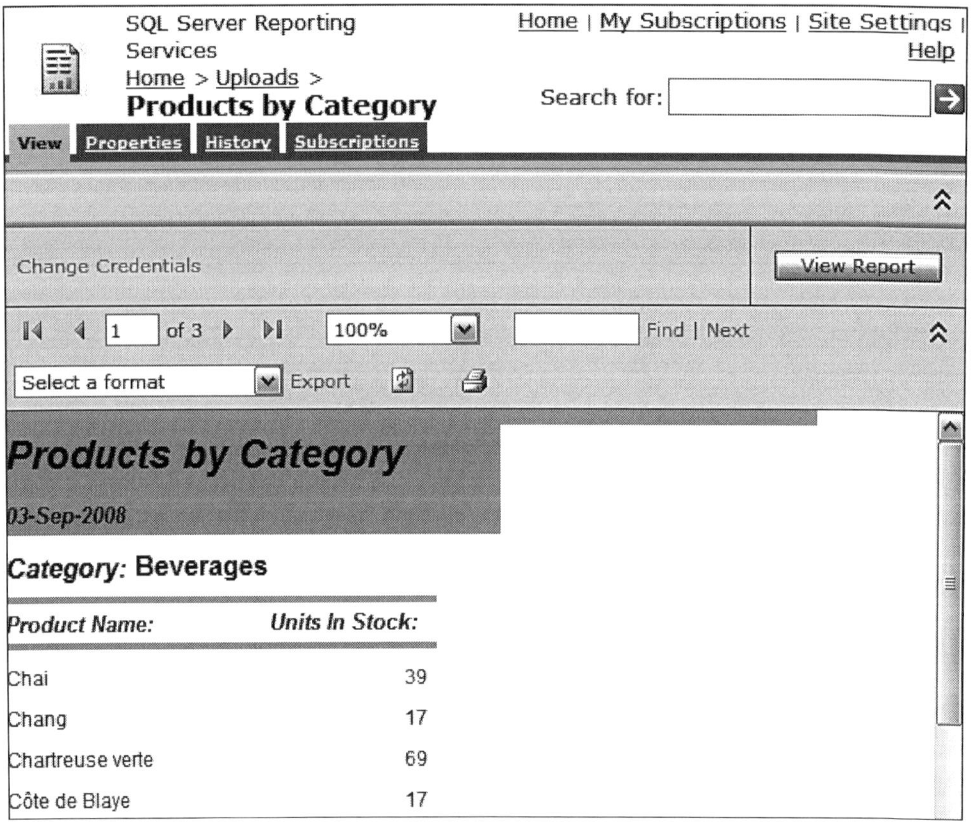

If you prefer, you may store the log in name by modifying the **DataSouce1** property for the report with the option to store credentials on the Report Server.

Creating a new data source in Report Manager and generating a model from the data source

In Chapter 4, you created a Report Model using the Visual Studio template which is completely driven by a wizard. Report Manager can also create a report model.

Report Manager supports creating new data sources as well as new models. These can be created in any folder using the **New Data Source** tool. After it is created a model can be generated from the data source. These models and data sources can be used by designers for report authoring using the Report Builder. These will be discussed in Chapter 6. Some of the features work only with SQL Server 2008 Enterprise Server for reports created using Report Builder 2.0, especially for the *clickthrough* items referenced in the Report Models generated by Report Manager.

Hands-on exercise 5.6: Creating a new data source and generating a model using Report Manager

While Visual Studio 2008 can be used to create a Report Model using the Report Model template, Report Manager can also be used for creating a Report Model. In this hands-on you will be creating a report model using the Report Manager. However, Visual Studio has lot more control over the model than the Report Manager.

Create new data source

Creating a data source for a report model is no different from creating a data source for a report. You will start off by creating a new data source in this section.

1. Access Report Manager by providing its URL in an IE browser.
2. In the **Home** page, click on the **Data Sources** folder to open it.

3. Click on the **New Data Source** toolbar item.

   The **New Data Source** page gets displayed as shown. Enter details as shown. There is no interface to obtain the connection string. You have to know it beforehand (see the table from Microsoft documentation later in this section).

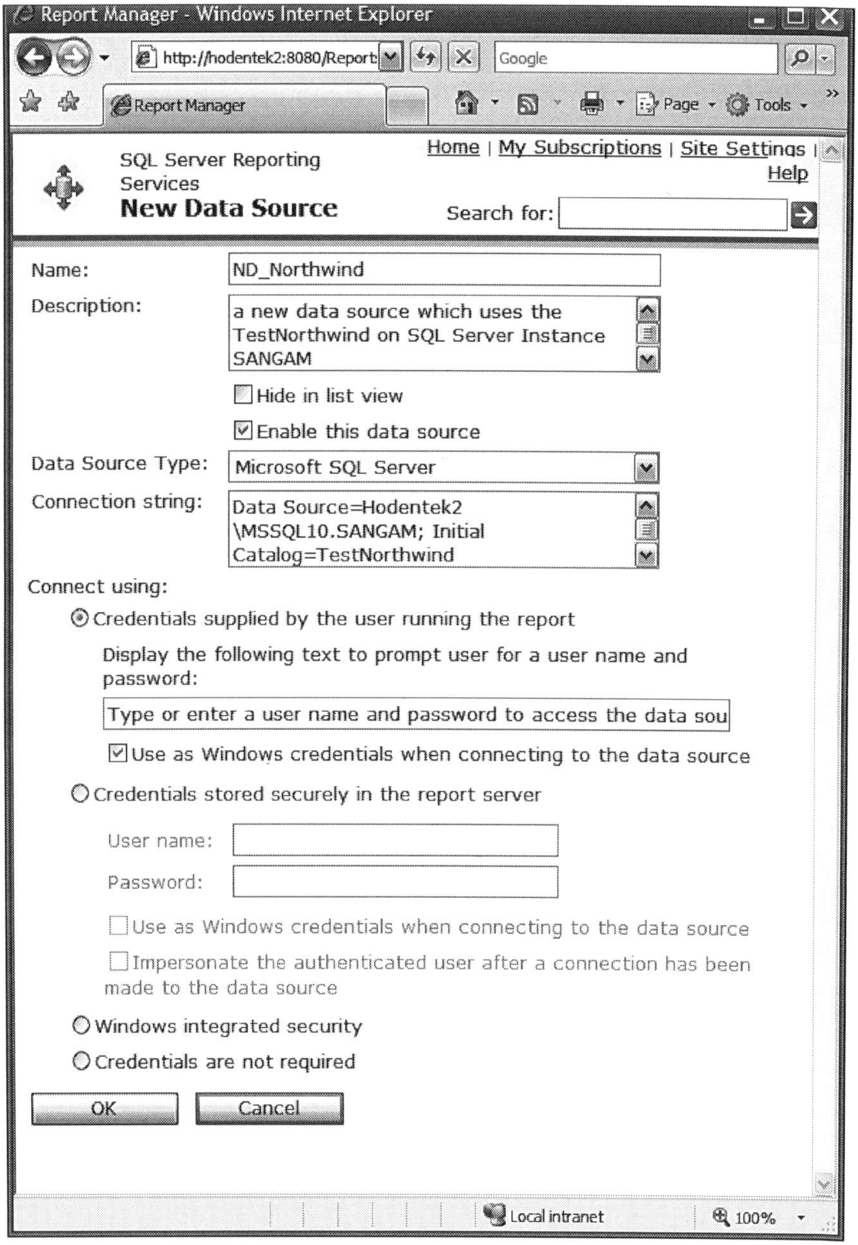

4. Change the **Connect using** option to **Windows Integrated Security**, the recommended secure connection.
5. Click on the **OK** button.

   The new data source gets added to the **DataSources** folder as shown:

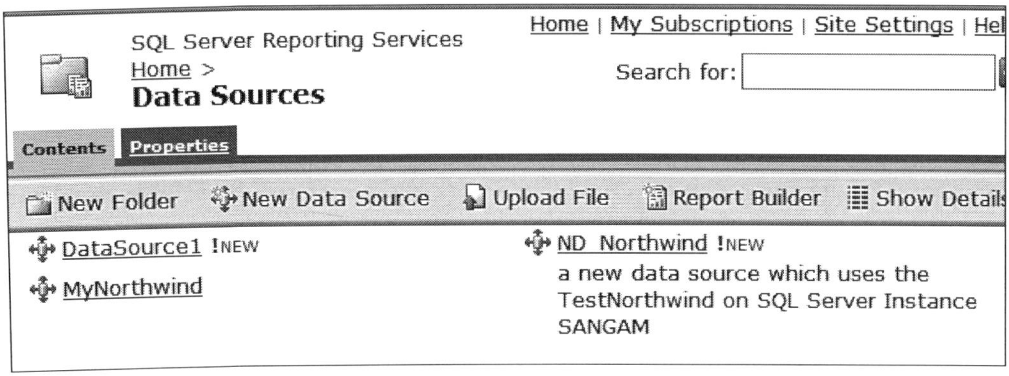

You can create a new data source from a number of different servers as shown here.

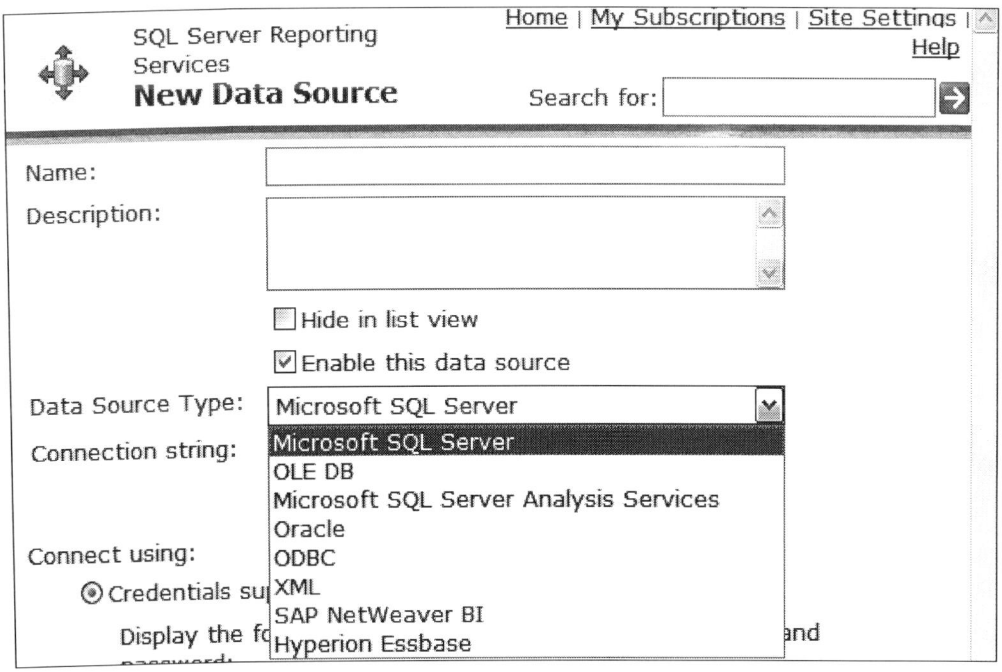

Each data source type you choose requires you to specify the connection string. Report Manager has no hooks (wizard) to generate a connection string and you will have to know where the data is located. It is also necessary that you have adequate credentials to use the data. You have already worked with the connection strings for SQL Server 2008 and Oracle 10G XE server in the previous hands-on exercises.

The following (partial list excerpt from Books Online) is the connection string that you would specify in the new data source page for the different servers. The entry for the SQL Anywhere 11 is not in the Microsoft documentation. The full list of all the supported types can be found in the Books Online (`http://msdn.microsoft.com/en-us/library/ms156450.aspx`).

Data Server	Data Source (connection string)	Description of Data Source Type
SQL Server Instance database	`Data Source=localhost\MSSQL10.InstanceName; Initial Catalog=AdventureWorks`	Set data source type to SQL Server.
SQL Server Express database	`Data Source=localhost\MSSQL10.SQLEXPRESS; Initial Catalog=AdventureWorks`	Set data source type to SQL Server.
SQL Anyhwhere 11	`Dsn=SQL Anywhere 11 Demo`	ODBC DSN of the Sample database
Analysis Services database on the local server	`Data source=localhost; initial catalog=Adventure Works DW`	Set data source type to SQL Server Analysis Services
Report model data source on a report server configured in native mode	`Server=http://myreportservername/reportserver; datasource=/models/Adventure Works`	Specify the report server or document library URL and the path to the published model in the report server folder or document library folder namespace.

Generating a model using Report Manager

Although a new data source can be created from any of these products, the models can only be generated from:

- Oracle
- Microsoft SQL Server
- Microsoft SQL Server Analysis Services

The report model is based entirely on the schema of the shared data source. Everything in the database gets into the model and these are not editable, as is possible in Visual Studio. However, after the model is created, it is possible to set properties and role assignments.

1. Click on **ND_Northwind** data source in the **Data Sources** folder.

   The **ND_Northwind** data source gets displayed as shown:

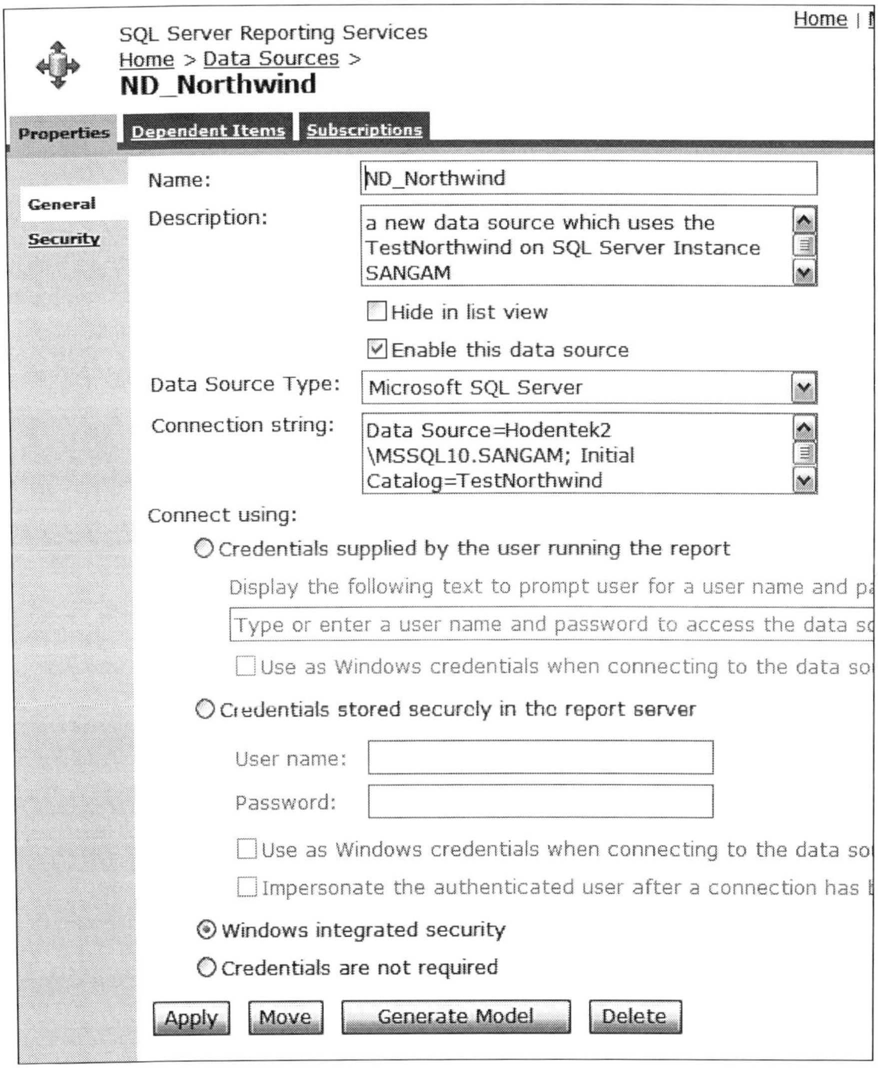

2. Click on **Generate Model** button.

   The following page gets displayed:

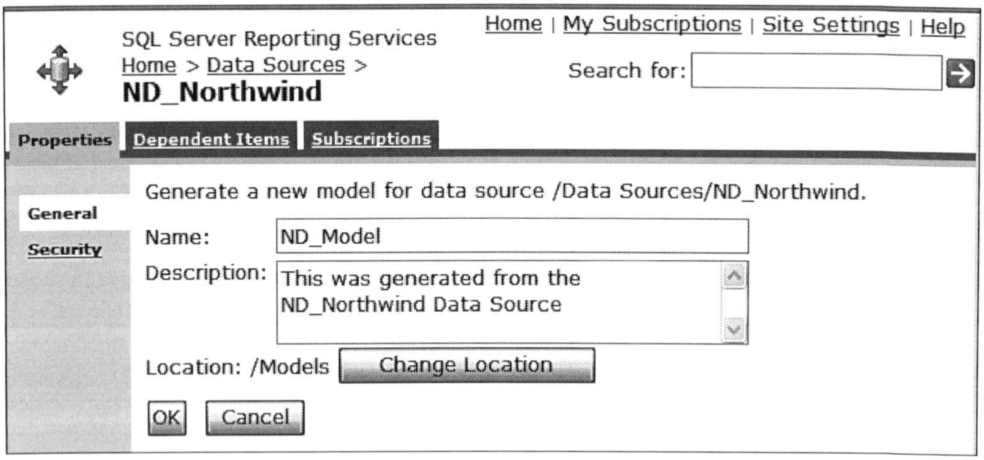

3. Provide a **Name** for the model and a **Description** as shown:
4. Click on **Change Location** button and choose the **Models** folder to save the model and click on the **OK** button.

   It takes a while for processing and the next page is displayed:

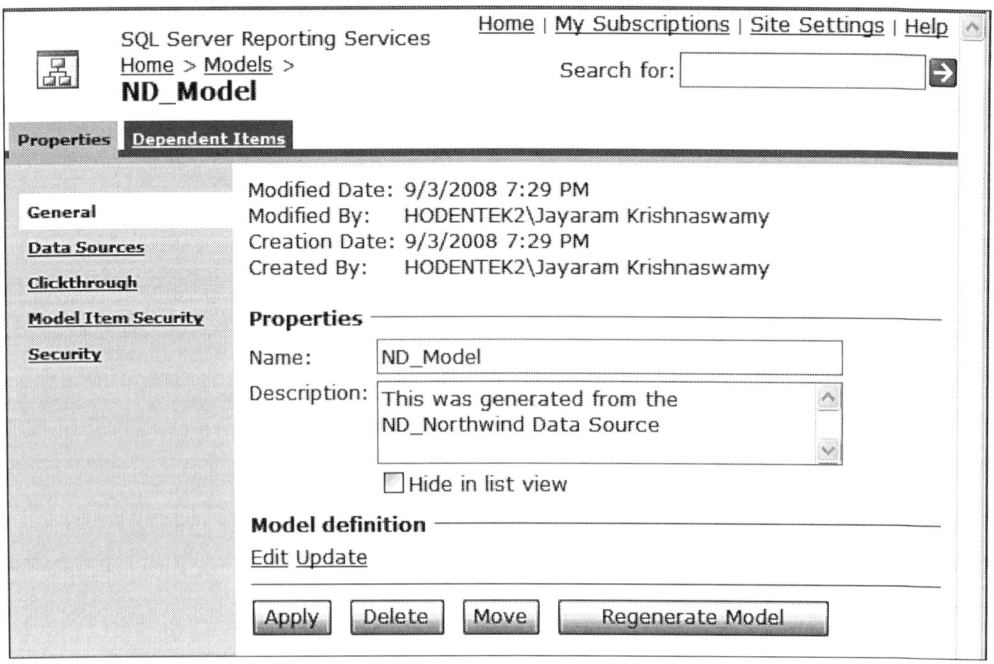

5. Click on **Clickthrough.**

   The entities page gets displayed as shown. Compare this to the method of creating a model from a Visual Studio Report Model Project in Chapter 4.

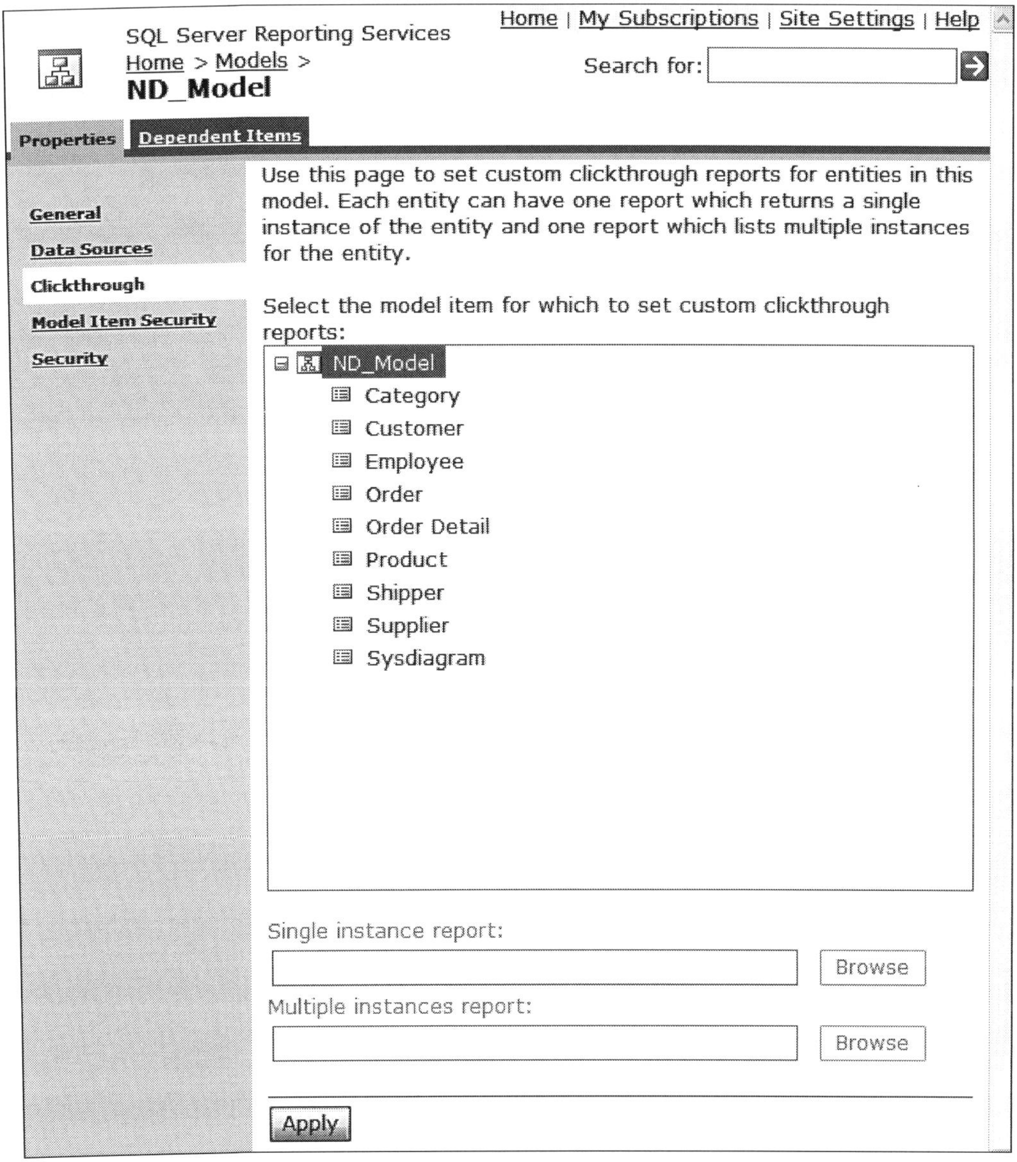

Clickthrough reports will be described in Chapter 6.

Modifying reports on a Report Server and creating linked reports with Report Manager

In this section you will be downloading and modifying a file on the Report Server. You will also be learning about creating linked reports using Report Manager.

Modifying reports

There could be instances where the Report Server has a report but the persisted report definition file is unavailable and the report needs modification. In this case it is possible to download the file to the hard drive, modify if necessary with BIDS and upload it to the server.

One way to modify a report definition file is described schematically in the following figure:

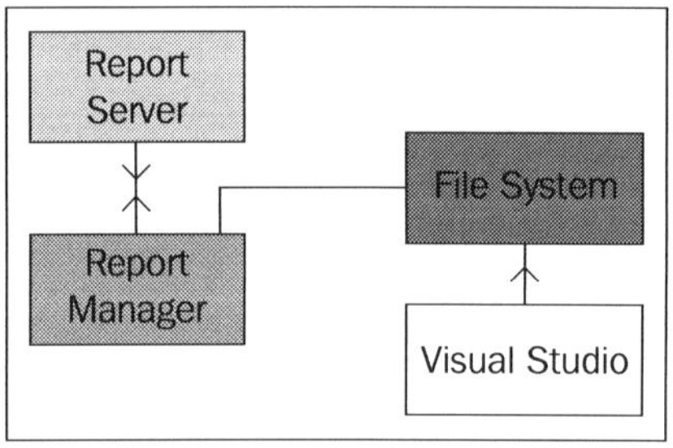

The process consists of the following:

- Downloading the file from the report server using the Report Manager to the computer file system
- Pulling the report file (using **Add New Item**) to a Visual Studio Project and saving the project files
- Uploading the report back to the report server from the Report Manager

The last two of the activities were described in Chapter 4 and the earlier hands-on exercises. In this section, you will be downloading a file from the report server to a location on the file system using Report Manager.

Linked reports

There are occasions when the same report is needed by different users who are assigned to different roles. Instead of creating reports for each of them, it is possible to create a single report and create links to it which controlled by a hidden parameter that restricts the report content based on the user's role. This will be described in detail in Chapter 7.

Hands-on exercise 5.7: Downloading a report definition file from the Report Server

Herein you will be downloading a report on the Report Server and persisting it to the hard drive.

1. Access the Report Manager using its URL in an IE browser.
2. Click **Home** | **RSPWiz08** | **OrderInformation.**
3. Click on **Properties** | **General.**

   The **OrderInformation** page gets displayed as shown:

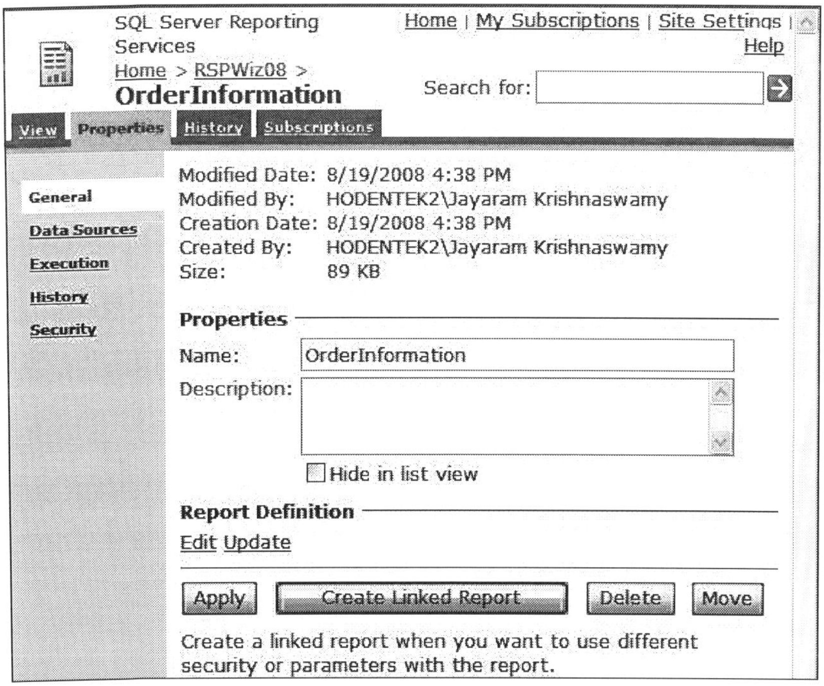

4. Click on the **Edit** hyperlink above the **Apply** button.
5. The **File Download** message box gets displayed.
6. Save the file to a known location which can be later pulled into a Visual Studio Project or uploaded to the Report Server.

Report delivery (new or cached)

Delivering the report after it has been developed is also one of the main tasks of the Report Manager. The delivery of reports can be scheduled or they can be delivered on demand. In case of scheduling delivery, Report Manager has an extremely flexible interface. In this section, you will be working with all aspects of report delivery.

On demand

When a report is executed the report gets the latest data from the database. This could present a problem in managing reports, especially if the number of users accessing the reports is large. It will also depend on the complexity of the reports being accessed. This can be mitigated in some cases where the latest data is either not needed or where data for a previous fixed period (weekly, monthly) is all that is necessary. These are handled in reporting services by report caching. Report services also takes care of handling parameters that may be needed for executing parameter-based reports by storing parameter information in the cached report.

Report caching

This can be turned on for individual reports by the user. Since the cached information is retrieved from the temporary location, where it was stored the first time it was requested, the turnaround is very fast as no data is required. The idea of report caching is very much analogous to web page caching. There is a cache lifetime that can be specified as you do not need the same report for ever. Also it can have a bearing on resources. The report cache can also bring in problems of security breach and to mitigate this, the report should only be available to the user or group that created the cache in the first place. Hence the user who creates the cache must have the report data source configured to **store** his credentials. This has been described in the previous section. Report cache is a step before the final rendering and therefore, it is in an intermediate format internal to reporting services and can be rendered in a chosen format at the time of printing. The cached report has a finite lifetime after which it is removed. It may also be removed if the underlying report is updated to reflect new information.

While access to the cached report has been taken care off by storing the credentials of the user creating the cache, the permissions to change the cache properties must also be covered by security. These are secured by permissions that are only given to some of the roles such as Content Manger, Publishers and so on. Refer to the Books Online for details.

Report cache is created by the user but it can be created automatically by execution snapshot. Execution snapshot can be used to create cache on a scheduled basis. This feature needs to be turned on for each report. Execution snapshot lends itself to handling cache expiration by proper scheduling.

Hands-on Exercise 5.8: Working with the report cache

The Execution navigational link for a report gives you access to how you may want the report executed, with the most recent data, from the cache or render a report from an execution snapshot. You can also change the report execution timeout. You will be working in this hands-on with the report cache.

Make sure your report data source is configured for the credentials being stored on the Report Server.

Turn on cache and cache a report

In here you will choose to cache a report for the default duration of 30 minutes. You should also try other options on your own while you are trying out this hands-on.

1. Access Report Manager and access the Properties of the report **OrderInformation.** Click on the **Properties** tab and then click on the **Execution** link on the left.

   The cache-related page shows up. The options are self-explanatory.

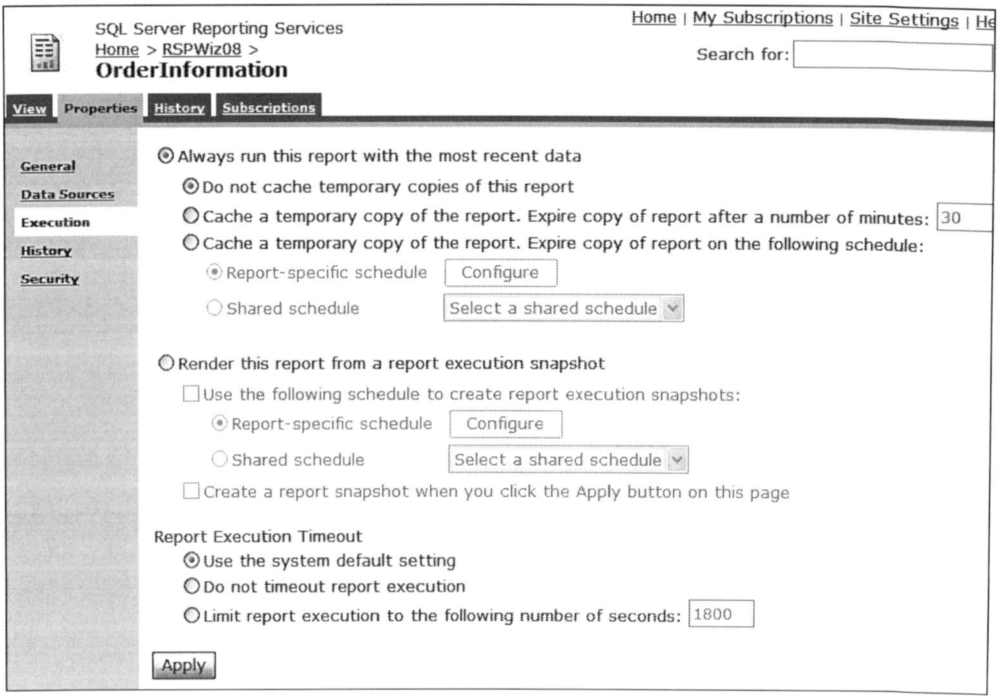

2. Change the default to **Cache a temporary copy...** and keep default expiration of **30** minutes.
3. Click on the **Apply** button.

   A cache created will be active for 30 minutes (default expiration) after which it disappears and the report will send the query to the database if the report is requested again.
4. Click on the **View** button.

   A cached copy will be rendered in default format. The copy can however be exported in any of the available formats.
5. Return to the **Execution** link page from **Properties** (the same page as the above) for the same report.

Schedule a report cache

You need to access the **New Schedule** or **Edit Schedule** page on the Report Manager to schedule a report. The idea of scheduling can be used for subscriptions, refresh cached reports, and to create snapshots as stand alone items in the repository. Since a report is scheduled it is unattended and therefore the the data source credentials must be stored in the Report Server database.

> Report Manager will not allow you to schedule a report if database credentials are not stored on the Report Server database.

1. Choose the option **Cache a temporary copy of the report. Expire, copy of report on the following schedule**. In the default choice, report-specific schedule that gets enabled, click on **Configure**.

   The schedule set up page gets displayed as shown:

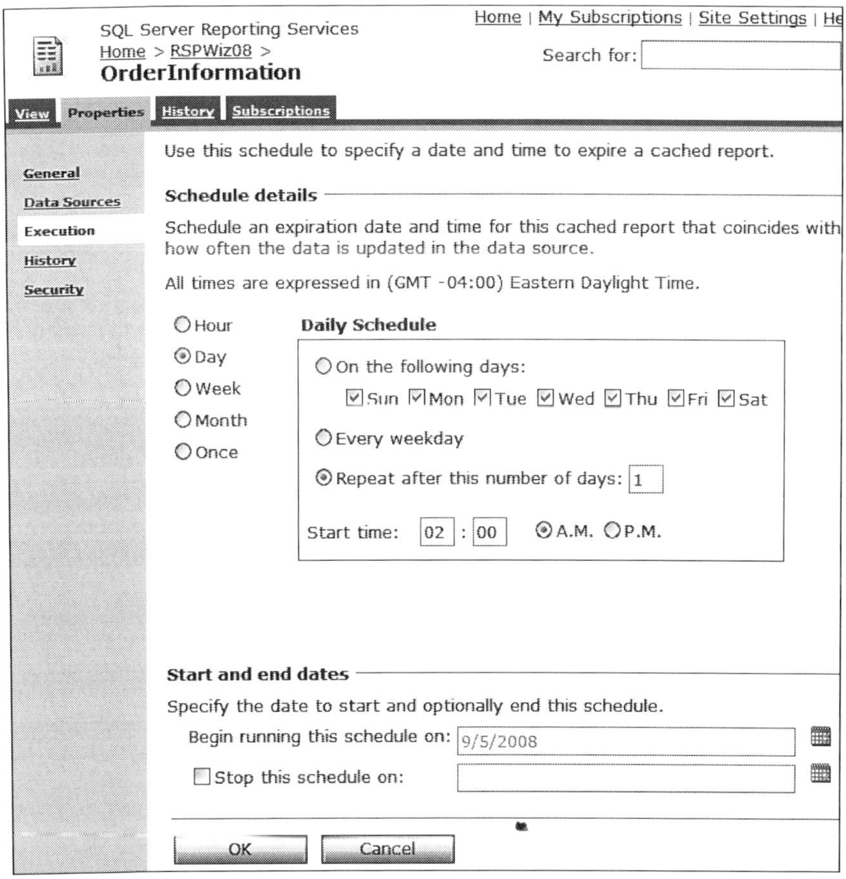

There is wide flexibility available in scheduling.

2. Choose a schedule and click the **OK** button

Create a cache from execution snapshot

Return to the execution link page from **Properties** (the same page as the above) for the same report. Choose the option **Render this report from a report execution snapshot**.

The page changes to reflect this choice as shown:

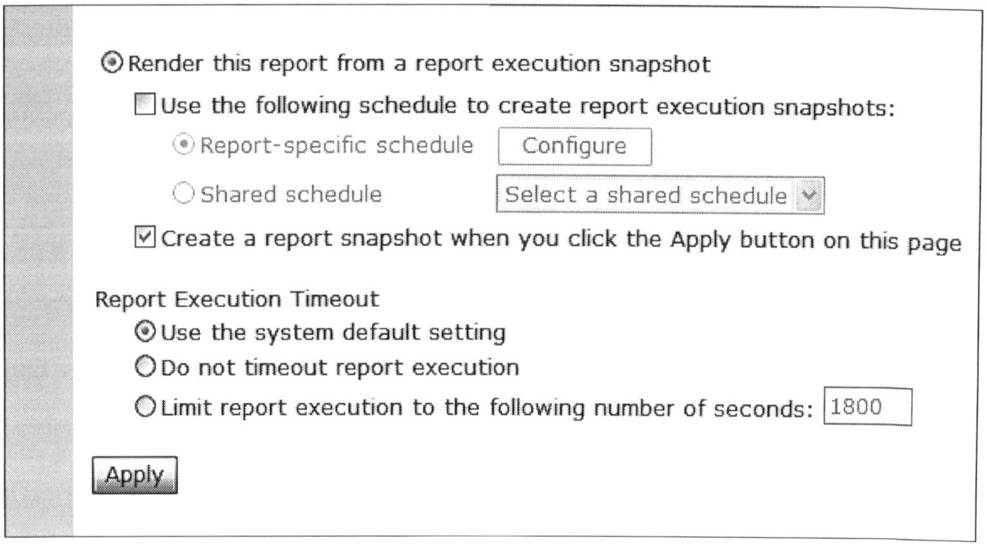

There are two choices for rendering of the report and there is a wide flexibility if the report snapshot is scheduled.

Report subscription

Reports can be pulled from the Report Manager by finding the report the user wants to have. You can then execute it or cache it, as discussed earlier. Another way to deliver reports at a specific time, in a specific format to the user is to use subscriptions. This is achieved by a timer or an event. This takes the form of a **push**, wherein the reporting services initiates the execution of the report and sends it out to the user. Report subscriptions are processed on the Report Server. They reach end users through delivery extensions that are deployed on the Report Server.

There are two kinds of subscriptions:

Standard: Managed by individuals and has only one set of presentation, parameter and delivery options.

- Data-driven: This kind of subscription is query-based, and requires knowledge of parameters. Report server administrators create and manage these subscriptions. This is normally used when there are a large number of recipients.

There are two ways a report can be delivered:

- By email: There are several ways the reports are delivered by email:
    - Through a hyperlink to the generated report
    - By sending a notification in the subject line containing the Report name (`@ReportName`) and Execution time (`@ExecutionTime`)
    - Embedding or attaching a report
- Send report file to a shared folder

In order to create a subscription, a report must have stored credentials. The user must have permission to view the report and create individual subscriptions. Scheduled events and report delivery must be enabled on the Report Server.

> Email addresses are not checked and users must correctly enter email addresses.

Hands-on exercise 5.9: Working with standard email, fileshare and data-driven subscriptions

In this section you will be working with the two different ways of creating subscribing to a report, email and file share.

Creating an email subscription

In here you will be creating an email subscription. Before you begin, make sure the SQL Server agent service is running. If it is not, start it from **Start | Control Panel | Administrative Tools | Services.**

1. Open the **OrderInformation** report and change its DataSource properties so that **credentials stored securely in the report server** is enabled with **use windows credentials when connecting to the data source** checked. Use credentials that has the Content Manger role. Click **Apply** button.
2. Click on the **Subscriptions** tab and click on **New Subscription.**

   The **Subscription: OrderInformation** page gets displayed as shown with several default choices. The **Email** delivery option is set by default in addition to several others. The drop-down menu for rendering format displays several options as well. The "**To**" address line may bring up some default, but it should be properly entered. In this case, the local service name comes up which is not in correct email format (`johndoe@tcm.com`). This must be changed.

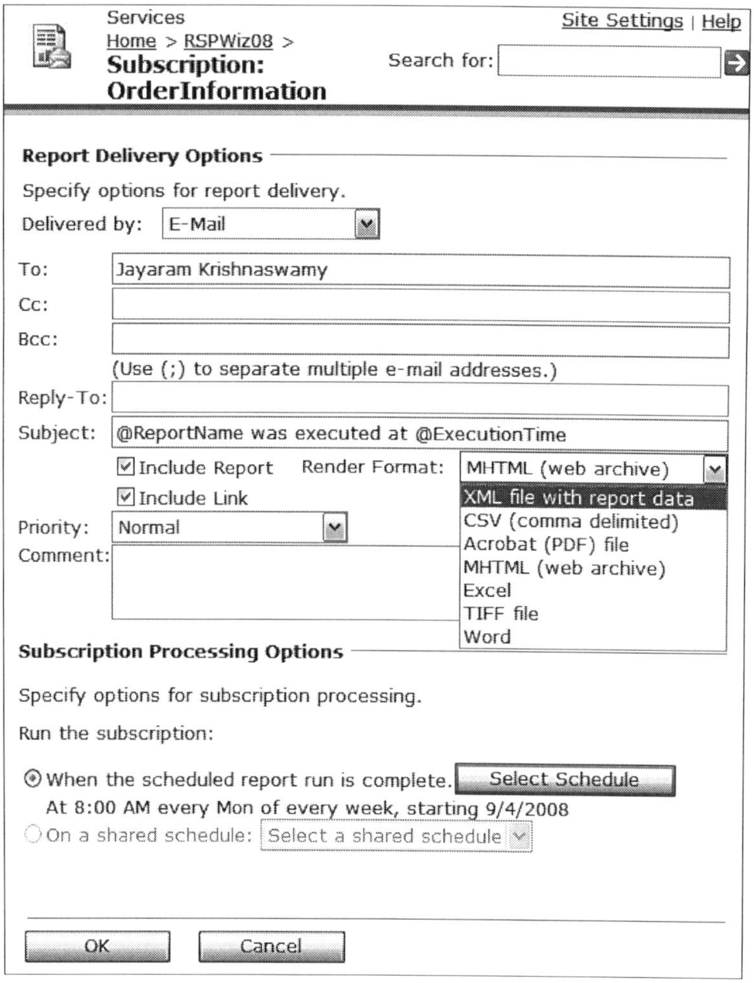

3. Click on the **Select Schedule** button.

   The schedule setup page gets displayed as shown:

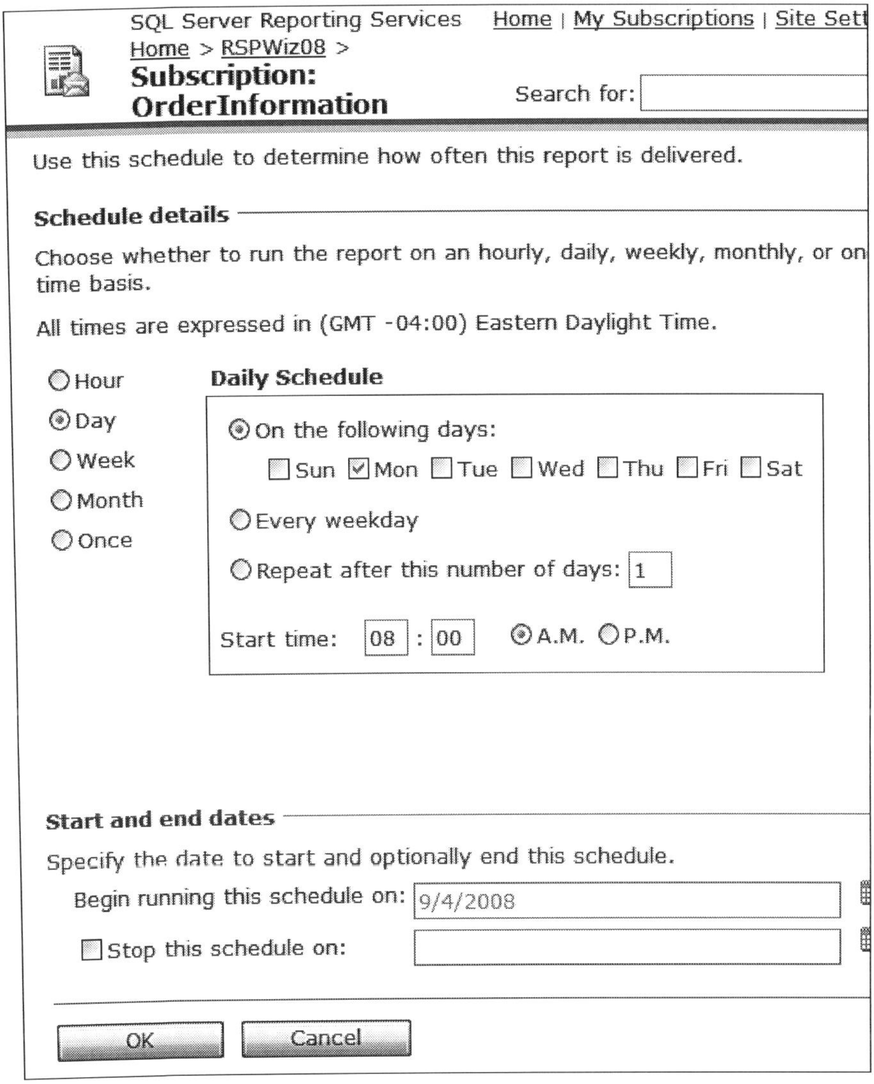

   This is very comprehensive and will suit any fancy scheduling. The next step just shows one example:

4. Choose the option "**Once**" and set the time for the report to be scheduled. Click on the **OK** button. This schedule information gets recorded in the **Report Delivery Options** page.

5. Click on the **OK** button.

   If the SQL Server agent service is not running, you will get an error message.

6. Click on the **Subscriptions** tab in the **OrderInformation** report.

   The subscriptions list gets displayed. There is just one subscription created. After the report is delivered you can check by clicking on the **Status**. This subscription can also be edited or deleted from this window.

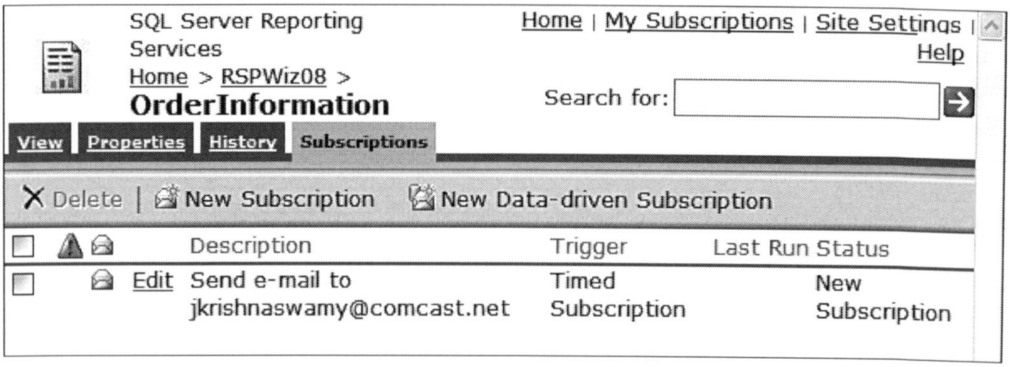

7. Wait for the specified time and click on the **Status** list column in the **Subscription** that you created.

   The email delivery status gets updated as shown:

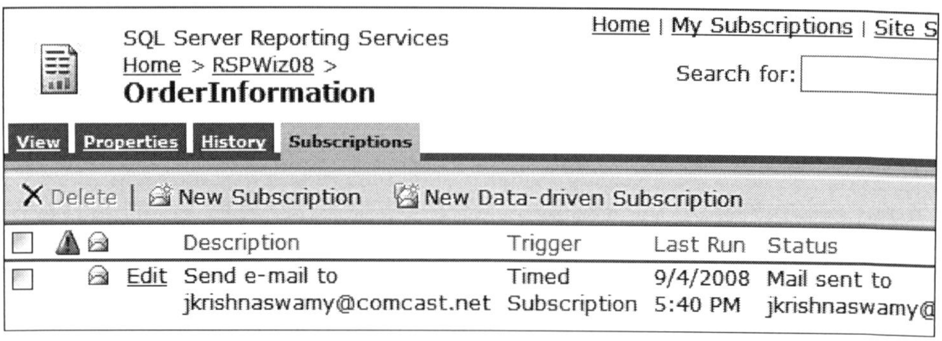

Another place where you can see the subscription delivery is in the Microsoft SQL Server Management Studio under SQL Server Agent under Jobs | Acitvity monitor as shown:

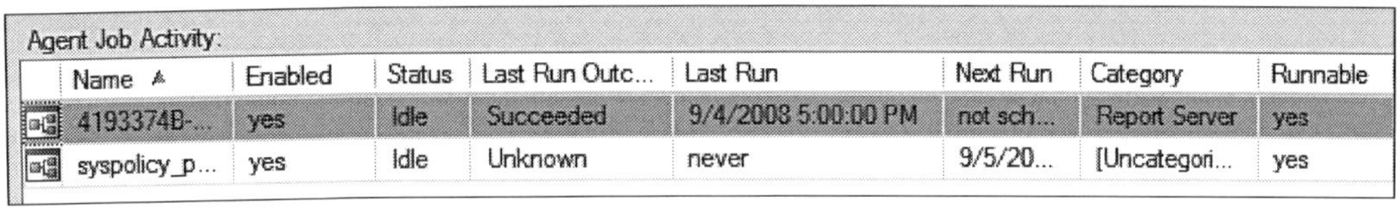

Creating a file share subscription

Before you begin with this activity create a shared folder on the hard drive. For the folder permissions list, add the same user who will generate the report (he or she should have credentials stored in the Report Server) to have **full** permission on this folder. For the other users provide **read** permission only.

1. Access Report Manager by providing the URL. Click the report you want to subscribe to and open it.
2. Click **Subscriptions** tab, and then click **New Subscription.**

   The **Subscription: OrderInformation** page gets displayed as shown:

3. Click on the drop-down handle for the item, **Delivered by**. Choose **Windows File Share** and click on the **OK** button.

   The **Report Delivery Options** and **Subscription Processing Options** page gets displayed as shown:

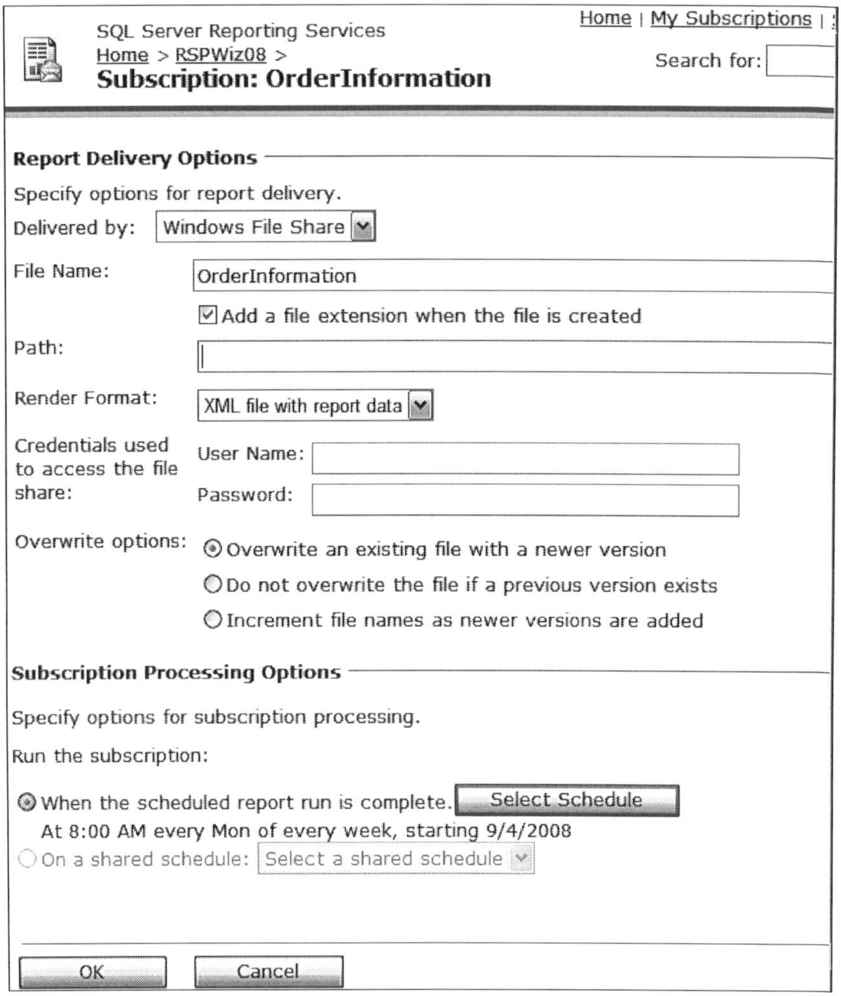

4. Fill out the details. For **Path** provide the UNC path for the shared file you created earlier (`\\machine_name\sharename`). Also fill in the credentials.

   If the credentials are not stored you will get a warning message alongside the credentials.

5. Click on **Select Schedule** button and in the displayed page choose the **Once** option as well as the scheduled time in the adjoining box. Click on the **OK** button.

   The schedule information is put into the **Report Delivery Options** page.

6. Click on the **OK** button.
7. Click on the **Subscriptions** tab.

   The file share subscription you created gets displayed.

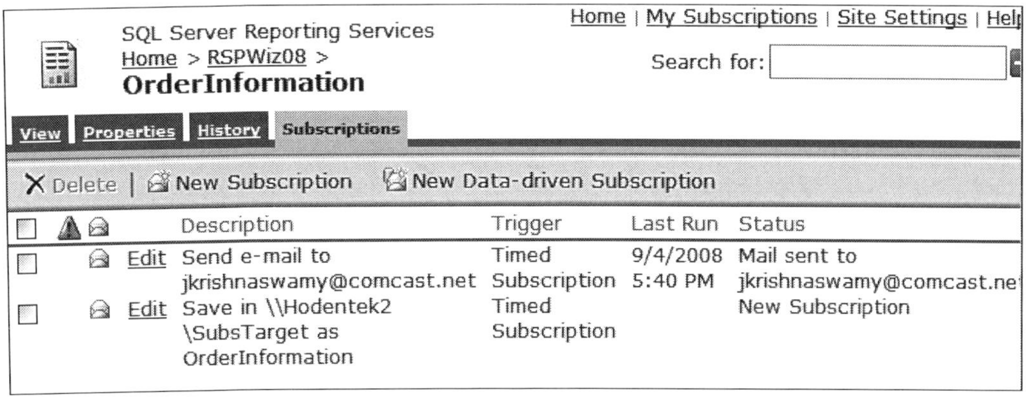

8. After the scheduled time expires verify the status as you did in the email delivery example. Also go and verify that the report has arrived in the shared folder.

Creating a data-driven subscription

Data-driven subscriptions send out reports to not just one individual or two but to a large number of recipients whose desired format (among other details) are maintained in a database on the server. This is report delivery targeted at mass distribution. In order to work with this hands-on exercise you need to have a database of recipients ready. When the subscription is processed, the Report Server customizes the output for each of the recipients maintained on the database. The example shown sends out reports to multiple recipients by email.

Create a Subscriber database in SQL Server 2008

Before you can send out the email to a number of recipients you need to have information about their email addresses in the correct format in your SQL Server database which stores subscriber information. This activity guides you through this.

1. Connect to the database engine (**Hodentek2\SANGAM** in this case) in the SQL Server Management Studio.
2. Right-click the **Databases** node and select **New Database.**
3. In the **New Database** window type in **Subscribers** for the **Database Name** and click on the **OK** button (accept all other defaults).

Populate a table in Subscribers database

After creating the Subscribers database you must create a table in the database to hold recipient information. This you will do by executing a Transact-SQL statement.

1. Copy the following Transact-SQL statements into the empty query window and **Execute (!)** the query:

   ```
   Use Subscribers
   CREATE TABLE [dbo].[RecipientInfo] (
   [SubscriptionID] [int] NOT NULL PRIMARY KEY,
   [RecipientID] [int] ,
   [Email] [nvarchar] (50) NOT NULL,
   [FileType] [bit],
   [Format] [nvarchar] (20) NOT NULL ,
   ) ON [PRIMARY]
   GO
   INSERT INTO [dbo].[RecipientInfo] (SubscriptionID, RecipientID,
   Email, FileType, Format) VALUES ('1', '289', 'John@ixy.net', '1',
   'IMAGE')
   INSERT INTO [dbo].[RecipientInfo] (SubscriptionID, RecipientID,
   Email, FileType, Format) VALUES ('2', '284', 'dona@pix.com',
   '1', 'MHTML')
   INSERT INTO [dbo].[RecipientInfo] (SubscriptionID, RecipientID,
   Email, FileType, Format) VALUES ('3', '275', 'mysorian@gmail.com',
   '1', 'PDF')
   GO
   ```

2. Refresh the **Databases** nodes, expand the **Subscribers** database and right-click the table **RecipientInfo** to verify that the table has been populated.

Creating the data-driven subscription and testing it

After creating and populating the table as described in the previous section, you can now create a data-driven subscription. You will choose the option to send out an email to the recipients, an activity you performed earlier.

1. Access Report Manager by providing the URL. Click the report (here **OracleEmployees** in **SharedData** folder was used) you want to subscribe to and open it.
2. Click the **Subscriptions** tab and then click **New Data-Driven Subscription.**

   The **Subscription: Oracle Employees** page's **Step1-Create a data-driven subscription: Oracle Employees** is displayed.
3. Provide a description and accept the default, **Specify for this subscription only**. Choose **E-Mail** from the drop-down list for **Specify how recipients are notified** and click on the **Next** button.

> The other options in the drop-down list are **Windows File Share** and **Null Delivery**. Null Delivery will not deliver, but if **Report Cache** is enabled then the result of executing the subscription with this setting will end up here. This may be useful in cases where you may want to keep copies of a report that depends on various parameter settings.

The page for **Step 2** gets displayed as shown:

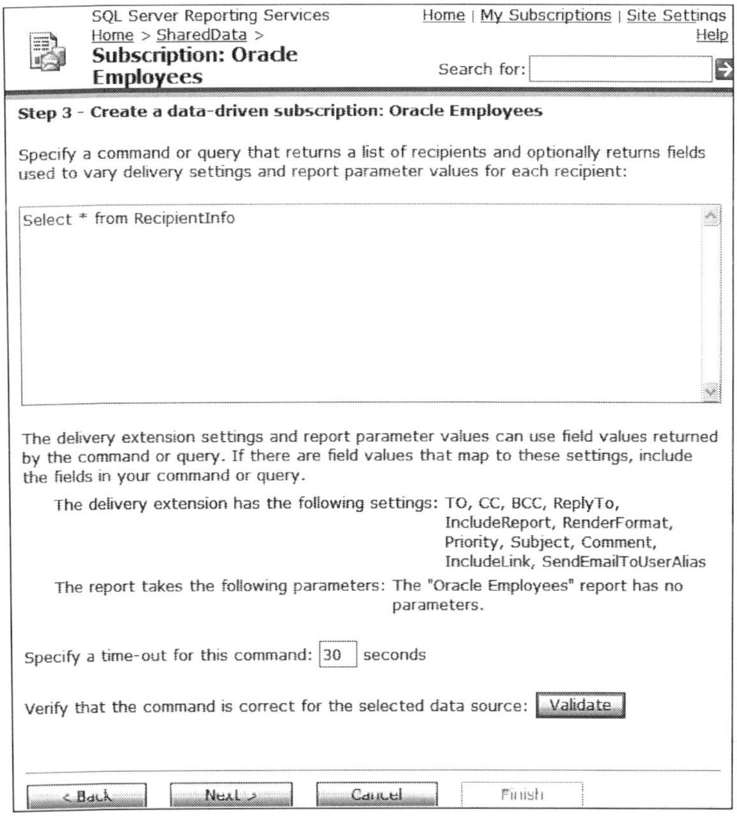

4. For the connection string type in **Data Source=Hodentek2\SANGAM; Initial Catalog=Subscribers**. Enter credentials (these should be the stored credentials for the report). Place checkmark for **Use as Windows credentials when connecting to the data source** and then click on the **Next** button.

   The page for **Step 3** gets displayed as shown:

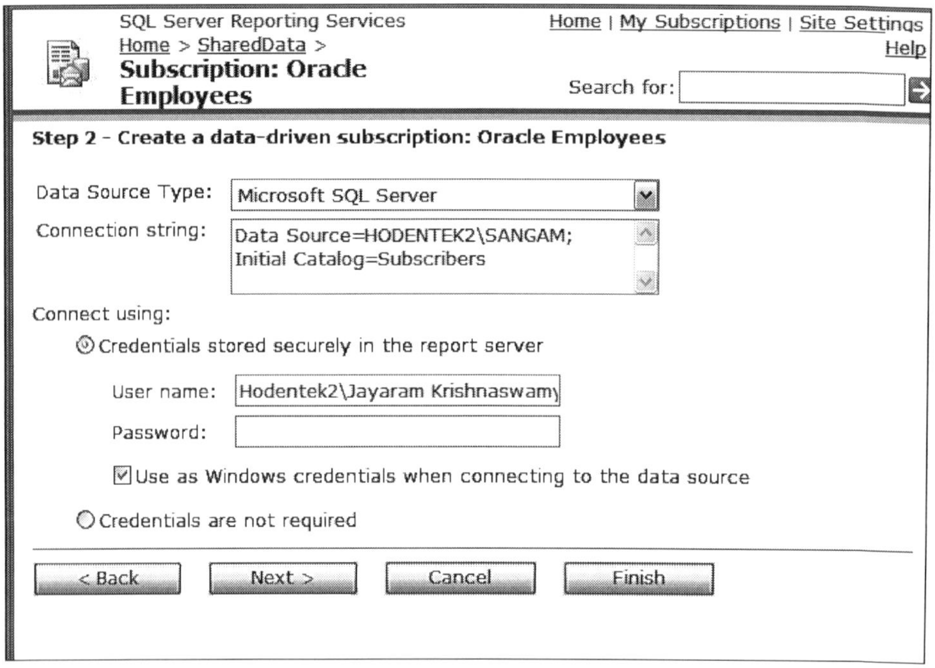

The delivery extension settings are the ones that the program will pull out from the `RecipientInfo` table in the `Subscribers` database. The **Oracle Employees** report is not parameter-based.

5. Type in **Select * from RecipientInfo** as the command (shown typed in), accept default time-out and click on the **Next** button.
6. For each of the delivery extension settings for the Report Server **Email** choose the suggested options, herein the following were chosen:

TO Get the value from the database **Email**

Cc **No value**

Bcc **No value**

Reply-To No value

Include Report **True**

Report Format **Get the value from the database** Format

Priority Specify a static value **Normal**

Subject Specify a static value **@ReportName was executed at @ ExecutionTime**

Comment **No value**

Include Link specify a static value **True**

7. Click on the **Next** button after making the above choices.
8. In **Step 5**, click on the **Next** button.
9. In **Step 6**, choose the option "**On a schedule created for this subscription**" and click on the **Next** button.
10. In **Step 7,** choose the option "**Once**". In the one-time schedule box click on a desired time (**herein 12:30 P.M.**) and click on the **Finish** button after making sure the SQL Server Agent Service is running. If the service is not running start it from **Control Panel | Administrative Tools | Services.**
11. The **Subscriptions** tabbed page gets displayed as shown:

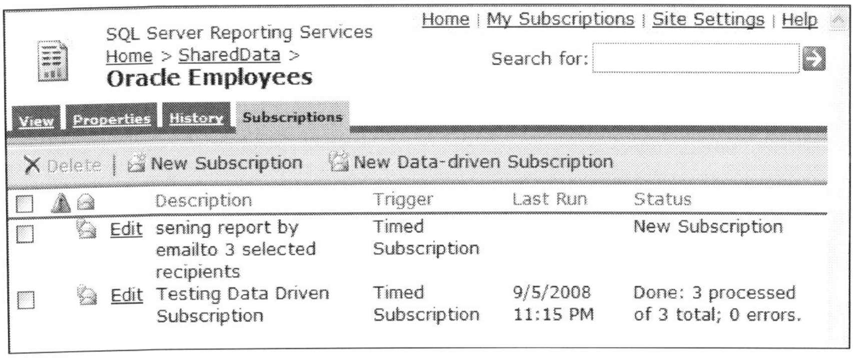

12. Check the status of the subscription after the specified time.

Summary

Report Manager, the one stop user interface to interact with the reporting services, is described in great detail by highlighting its salient features. The hands-on exercises will help a user in finding his way around with this important tool in Microsoft SQL Server Reporting Services 2008. Individual hands-on exercises deal with the many tasks this web client has been designed to carryout on the Report Server such as managing folders, assigning roles to users, deploying reports, viewing and printing of reports, uploading and downloading reports, managing scheduling of reports, managing delivery of reports in several ways, linking up reports, creating datasources, creating models and many others. In order to work with reporting services the reader should master the ins and outs of Report Manager.

6

Working with the Report Builder

The Microsoft SQL Server 2008 Reporting Services Report Builder 2.0 tool can be installed from a standalone installer available at this Microsoft site, `http://download.microsoft.com/download/a/f/6/af64f194-8b7e-4118-b040-4c515a7dbc46/ReportBuilder.msi`. The same file is also available from a collection of download files when you access the Microsoft SQL Server 2008 Feature Pack, October 2008 at `http://www.microsoft.com/downloads/details.aspx?FamilyId=228DE03F-3B5A-428A-923F-58A033D316E1&displaylang=en`.

Report Builder 2.0 is feature-rich reporting tool with the latest Microsoft Office look and feel. It provides an extremely flexible GUI with user friendly wizards for creating the Tablix data regions, a versatile construct that includes tables, matrix, and charts and gauges. Report Builder 2.0 supports server resources such as shared Data Sources, works with SQL Server Data Sources and many third party products, and can directly open and edit server hosted reports. Report Builder together with Report Manager provides powerful support for building and managing a bewildering array of report types.

Report Builder overview

In the present version of SQL Server 2008 [Enterprise Evaluation edition] there are two Report Builders available. Report Builder 1.0, which has remained as a program that can be launched from the Report Manager, and the new Report Builder 2.0, which is a stand alone report authoring tool that needs to be independently launched.

Although Report Builder 1.0 can access Report Models built with Visual Studio 2008 and the Report Manager, it cannot be used to create reports using those models. It also does not work with Reports generated by Visual Studio 2008 / BIDS / Report Builder 2.0. The errors can be summarized as follows:

- When you try to access the Report Server 2008 from the link provided on the Report Builder 1.0 interface you get the following error message:

  Specifying credentials in a URL is not supported

- When you try to open a report created using VS2008/BIDS/Report Builder2.0 using the **Open Report...** and **Open File...** navigational items in Report Builder 1.0 you get the following error message:

  System.IO.StreamReader: The Report element was not found.

- Report Builder 1.0 allows you to access Report Models created with VS2008/BIDS/Report Manager and even allows you create a report in design view but this report cannot be processed on the Report Server. If you try to do so, you get the following error message:

  MemoryStream length must be non-negative and less than 2^31 - 1 - origin. Parameter name: offset; Remote GDI stream version: ?. Expected version: 11.0.1.

In this chapter the Report Builder 2.0 interface will be described along with the new features that are incorporated into this version. Report Builder 2.0 is admirably suited to address all items in the Report Definition Language of 2008. The *Hands-on exercise 6.1* describes enabling My Reports, which allows each user to save his reports in his own folder helping the author to make his reports available after verifying that the report meets all the requirements. *Hands-on exercise 6.2* describes how you can take an existing report authored with Report Builder 2.0 or otherwise (VS2008) and modify its formatting and other features using Report Builder 2.0. *Hands-on exercise 6.3* shows how you may create a report from scratch and embellish with charts and gauges.

One of the important features of Report Builder 2.0 is the empowerment it provides business users to create ad hoc reports using the Report Models built on the databases they use. Building these models was discussed in Chapters 3 and 5. In the next chapter, you will be creating ad hoc reports based on the models you created earlier using Report Builder.

In this chapter, you will be learning mostly about the Report Builder 2.0 interface details and working with it to create reports or modify them. It may be noted that Report Builder generates 2008 compliant RDL files as described in `http://download.microsoft.com/download/6/5/7/6575f1c8-4607-48d2-941d-c69622e11c32/RDL_spec_08.pdf` and therefore, cannot work with reports generated using 2005 technology.

Report Builder 2.0 user interface description

Report Builder is a report authoring tool and the basic procedure for authoring a report consists of the following steps:

- Report planning
- Connecting to a source of data
- Extracting a dataset from source
- Designing the report and data binding
- Previewing the report

Although deploying the report is not included in the above, Report Builder can deploy the report as well. It is not always necessary to deploy a completed report, as any part of a report definition file can be deployed. This makes modifying a report on the server very flexible.

In the following sections, the various parts of the Report Builder interface will be described starting at the very top and going to the bottom of the interface.

The menu for file operations

Report Builder 2.0 can be accessed from **Start | All Programs | Microsoft SQL Server 2008 Report Builder| Report Builder 2.0.**

This brings up the Report Builder Interface 2.0 as shown with the design area containing two icons: **Table** or **Matrix** and **Chart.** Each of these will launch a related wizard which will step you through the various tasks. The Report Builder 2.0 interface is very similar to Office 2007. More than one instance of Report Builder can be launched.

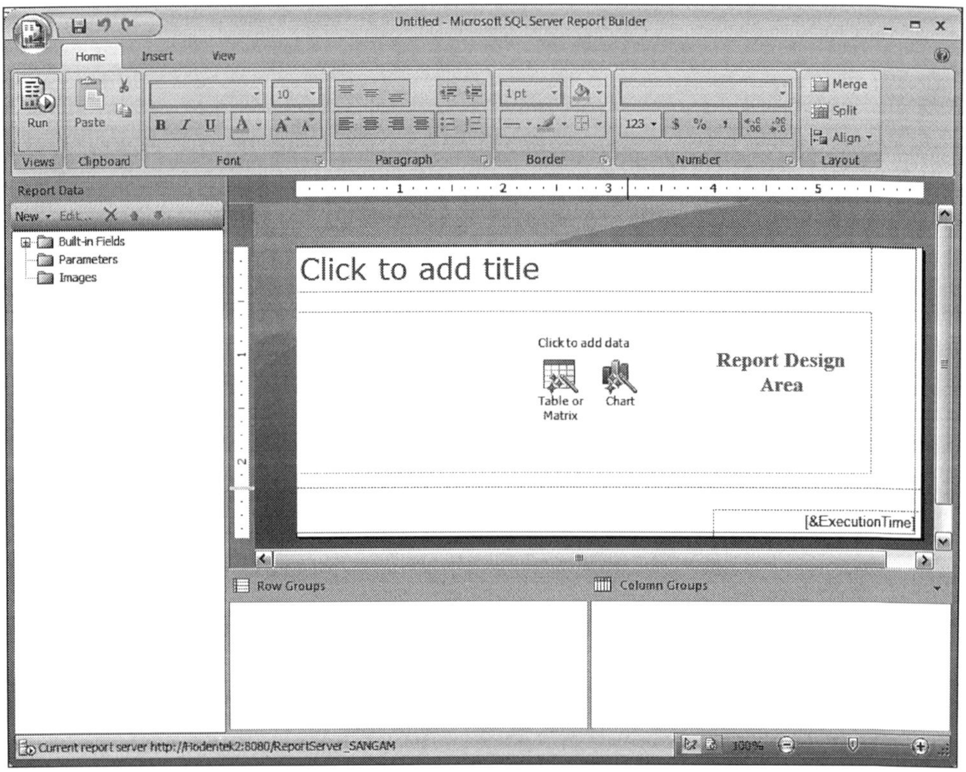

At the very top of the following screen shown you have the *undo* and *redo* controls as well as a *save* icon.

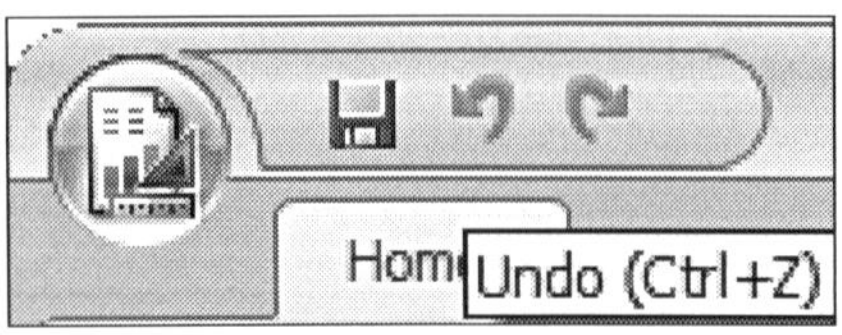

When you click on the *save* icon the **Save as Report** window gets displayed as shown. Here you provide a name for the report. The default save extension is `*.rdl` and it will be saved to the report server. It may also be persisted to a folder on your machine.

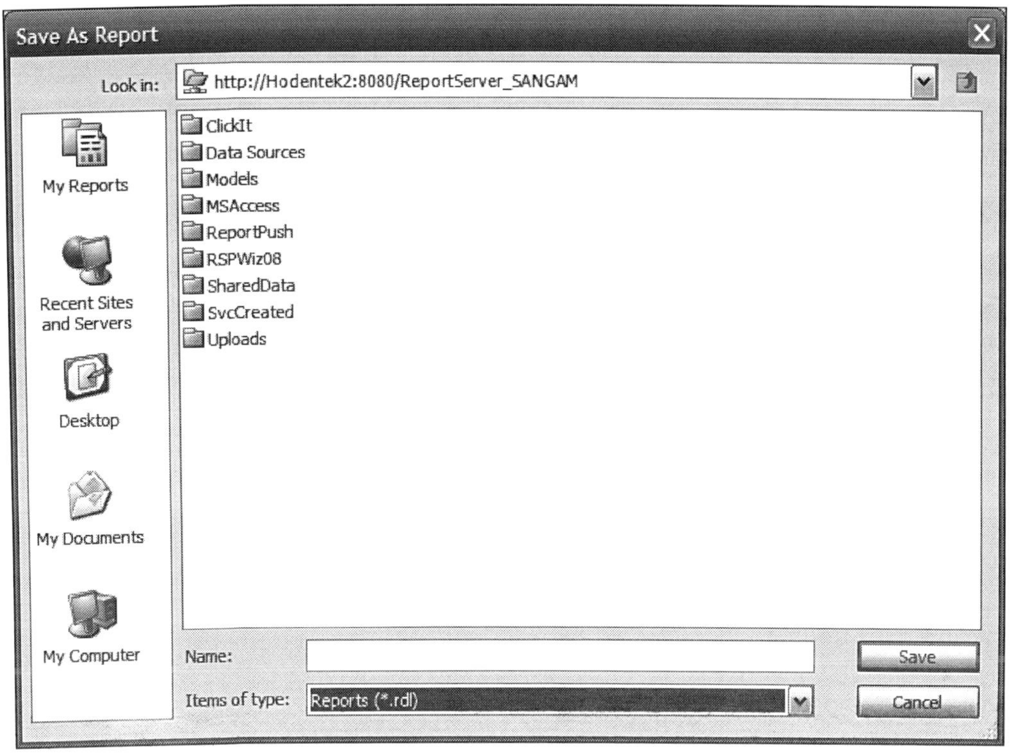

Clicking on the **Office button** (top left) opens a drop-down window shown in the following screenshot:

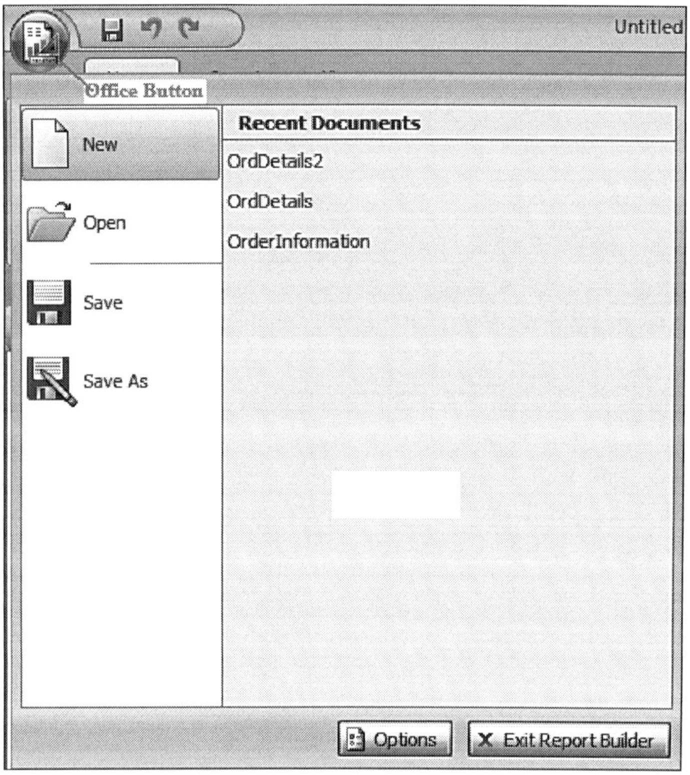

In this window, you can carry out a number of tasks such as creating a new report, opening an existing report, saving a report, and saving a report with a different name.

The **Save** button saves it to the default location seen earlier and **Save as** invokes the same window to save the report with a different name as seen earlier displying the report server instance as the **Save to** location.

The **Recent Documents** pane shows the more recent reports created with this tool.

New allows you to create a new report. When you click on **Open**, the following **Open Report** window gets displayed with the default location `http://Hodentek2:8080/ReportServer_SANGAM/My Reports`. You will also notice the message: This folder is not available because the My Reports feature is not enabled on the computer. Also the **Open Reports** window allows you look for reports with the extension `.rdl`.

Therefore, unless the **My Reports** feature is enabled, this window is unusable. This is supposed to be possible from Report Manager but there are no controls in Report Manager that would do this. An alternative was suggested by one of the MSDN forum moderators (see `http://social.msdn.microsoft.com/forums/en-US/sqlreportingservices/thread/6c695160-29e8-4185-be6d-5fe027a6975c/`). *Hands-on exercise 6.1* describe how you may enable My Reports. The idea of *My Reports* is similar to **My Documents** where each user can keep his reports.

When the Options button (in the previous screenshot) is clicked it opens the window **Report Builder Options** window with two tabbed pages **Settings** and **Resource** shown as follows:

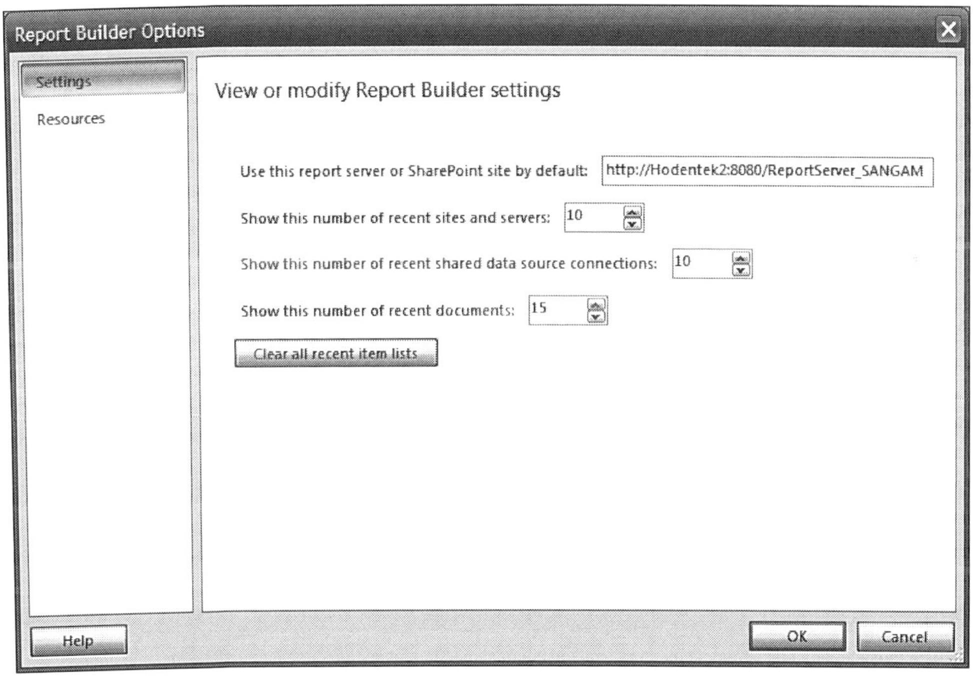

Here you can view, as well as modify, Report Builder settings. The defaults are more than adequate to work with the examples in this book.

Clicking on the **Resources** button brings up this interesting window which enables you to interact with Microsoft regarding SSRS activities, concerns, community, and so on. If you are serious about Reporting Services, these are very valuable links. The **About** button when clicked can provide you with Report Builder version information.

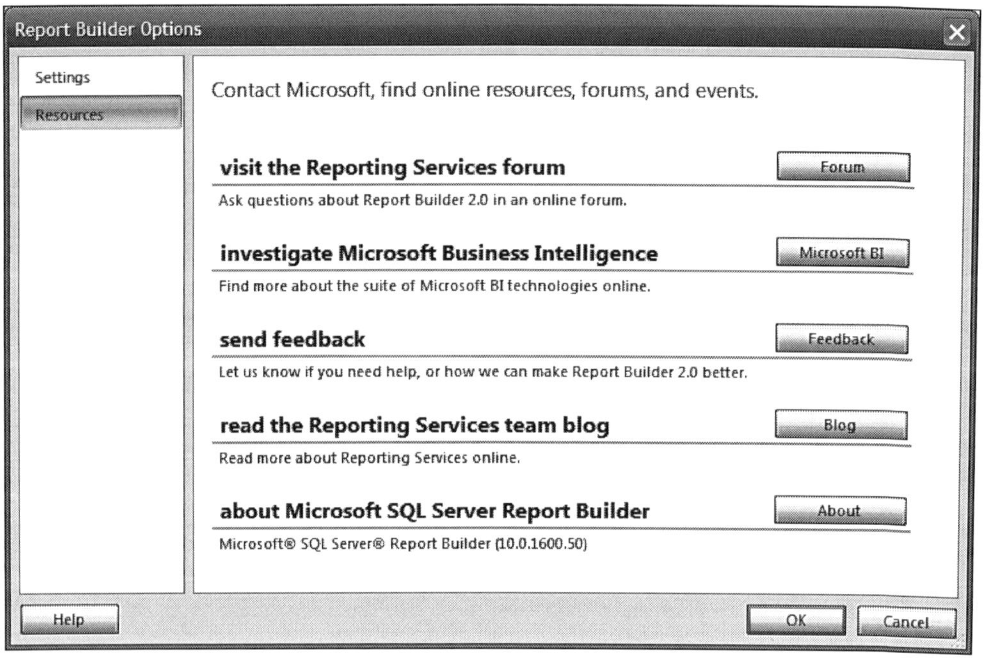

The ribbon

The main menu consists of **Home**, **Insert**, and **View** menu items which are part of the "ribbon". The ribbon introduced by Microsoft in Office 2007 is actually a container for other toolbar items. The ribbon is the replacement for the classic menus, toolbars, and is supposed to be more efficient and discoverable by the user. In fact you see a lot more on the "ribbon" than in the classic menu.

Home

The next figure shows the **Home** menu with its toolbar arranged from left to right and divided into sections. The **Run** toolbar item with the title **Views** when clicked would run the report open in the design view (in fact, even without a report open in the design view, the report can be run. The result would be the current date and time getting displayed in the center of the screen of an untitled report which has just ExecutionTime as the only item in the report).

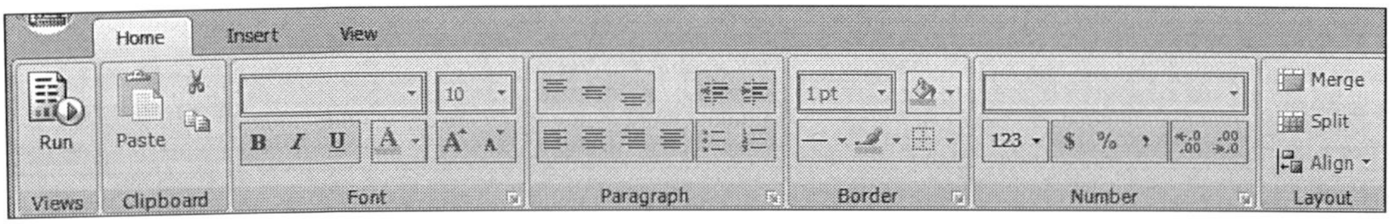

The **Font, Paragraph, Border,** and **Number** toolbar sections become enabled if parts of a report need editing. The formatting of textboxes in the report, the formatting of numbers in the report, and the alignment of components in the layout can all be independently managed using these toolbar items.

Insert

When you click on the **Insert** menu item on the "ribbon", the tabbed page for this item is displayed as shown in the following screenshot:

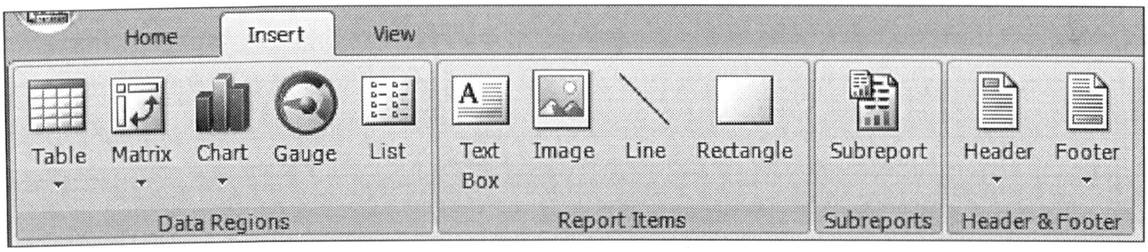

It has four sections: **Data Regions**, **Report Items**, **Subreports**, and **Header & Footer**. These are all the normal items that are used either individually or together to make up a report. There can be more than one data region in a report.

Data Regions

In the **Data Regions** section you have both the Tablix (**Table, Matrix, and List**) and the graphic controls that can be bound to data—the **Chart** and the **Gauge**. **Gauge** is new in SQL Server Reporting Services 2008. Chart and gauge implementations are the off shoot of collaboration with Dundas (`http://www.dundas.com/`). Report Builder is built in such a way that the dataset must be defined before any of the data regions are added to the report body. For the purpose of describing the various data regions in this section, it is assumed (in order to get the screen shots shown here) that a dataset has been defined and the default wizards on the design surface have been removed.

Table

The Table is meant for displaying data retrieved from a database either all data detailed in groups or a combination (some grouped and some detailed) of both. It has a fixed number of columns which can be adjusted at design time. The table length expands to accommodate the rows.

Data can be grouped by a single field or by multiple fields. Expression designer can be used in grouping as well. The grouping is carried out by creating row groups. Static rows can be added for row headings (labels) and totals. Aggregates for groups can be added. Both detailed data as well as grouped data can be hidden initially and the user can interactively reveal the data needed by drill downs.

When you click on **Insert | Table | Insert Table** and then click on the design surface you can add a table to the design area. The table appears as shown with handles to adjust its dimensions. The table can be dragged to any other location on the design surface (the body of the report) as well.

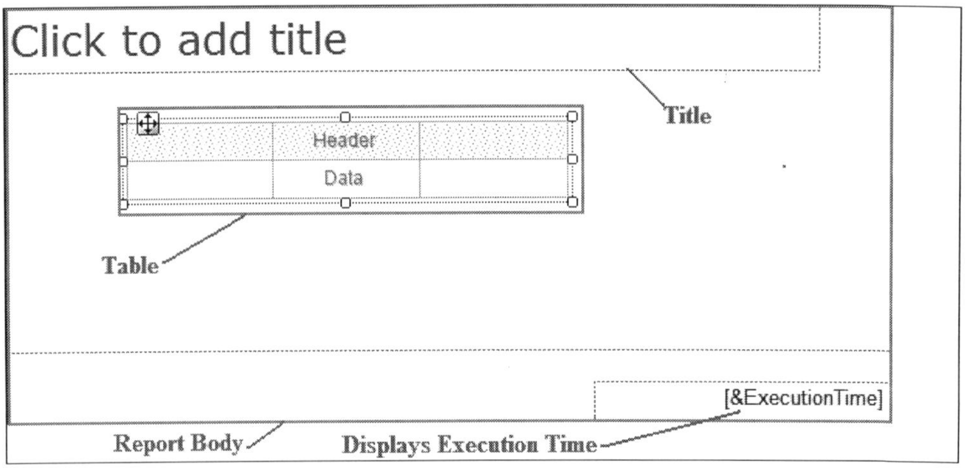

After placing the table, which by default has three columns and two rows, when you click on any other part of the design area you will see the table as shown. When you hover over the cell marked **Data** on the table you will see a little icon. This icon is a minimized version of the dataset fields. The grayed out feature that surrounds the table indicate the position of the rows and columns of the table. It also shows such other features as whether it is a detail, or whether it is a group. In the case of group, within a group the feature would indicate the nesting schematically as well. When you want to increase the size of a column or a row you can drag the double headed arrow that gets displayed when your cursor is placed between two columns or between two cells as shown.

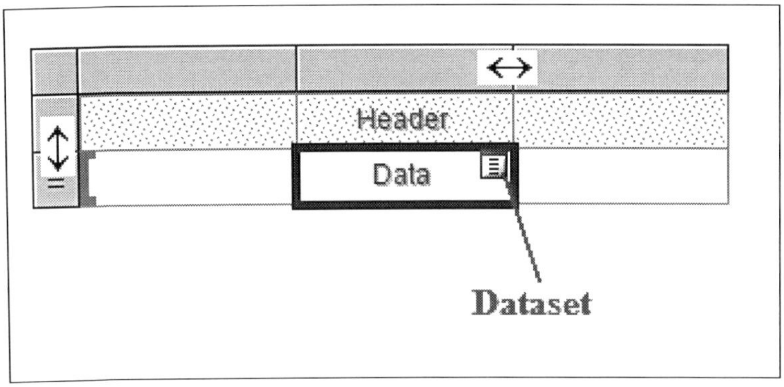

When you click on the dataset icon in the cell **Data** you get a drop-down list containing the fields in the dataset as shown. You can choose any of the fields to occupy the cell you clicked and the corresponding header will be added to the table. In this particular dataset there are nine fields and you can choose any of them to occupy the cell.

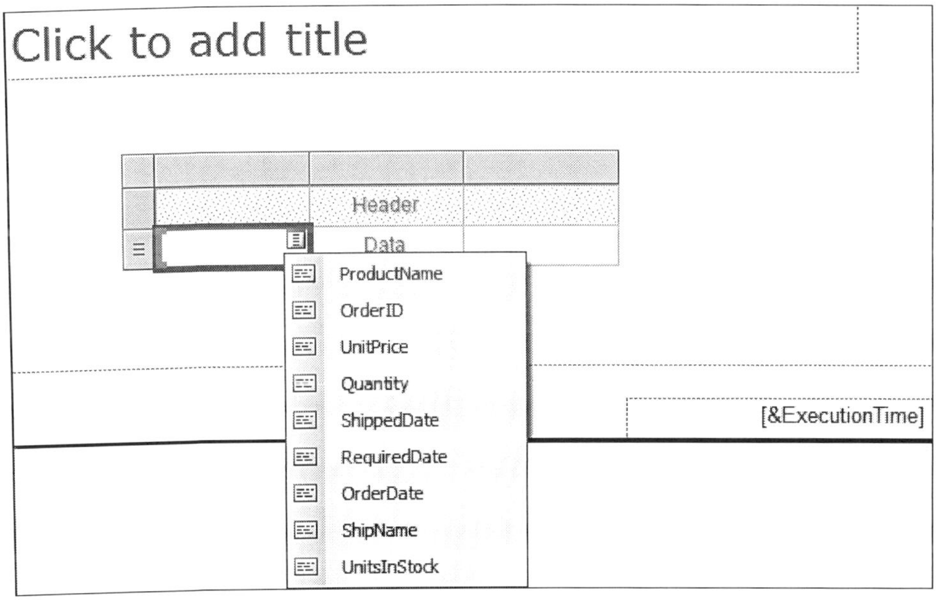

When you right-click on a cell, a drop-down menu will be available. It can be used for the following:

- Work with the highlighted textbox (each cell of the table is a textbox) including to copy, cut, delete, and paste contents.
- Work with the properties of the Textbox.
- Populate the textbox with an expression using the expression builder. The expression builder gets displayed when *fx* **Expression** is clicked.
- Use **Select** to select the body or the Tablix.
- Insert a new column or a new row. Columns can be added to the right or the left of the clicked cell and rows can be added above or below the clicked cell.
- Delete columns and rows.
- Add a group. Both row and column groups can be added.

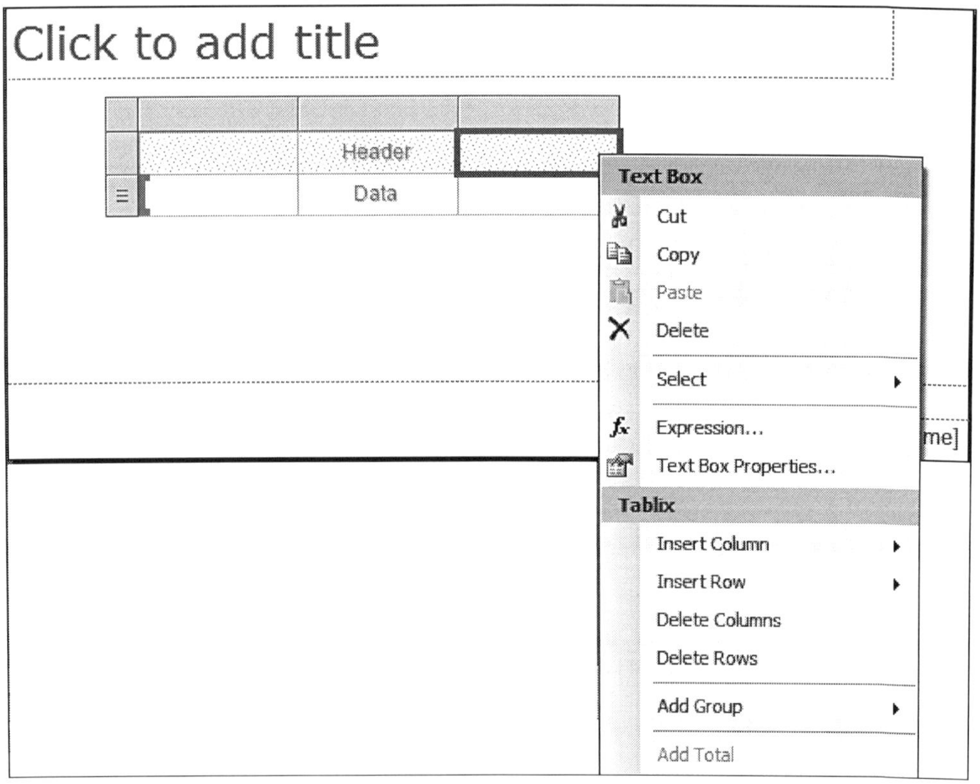

When you click on the properties of the textbox, the **Text Box Properties** window is displayed. The textbox has several properties which are arranged on the left as a list with each item having its own page as shown. The **Help** button on any of the pages will take you directly to the definition of the properties and is extremely useful.

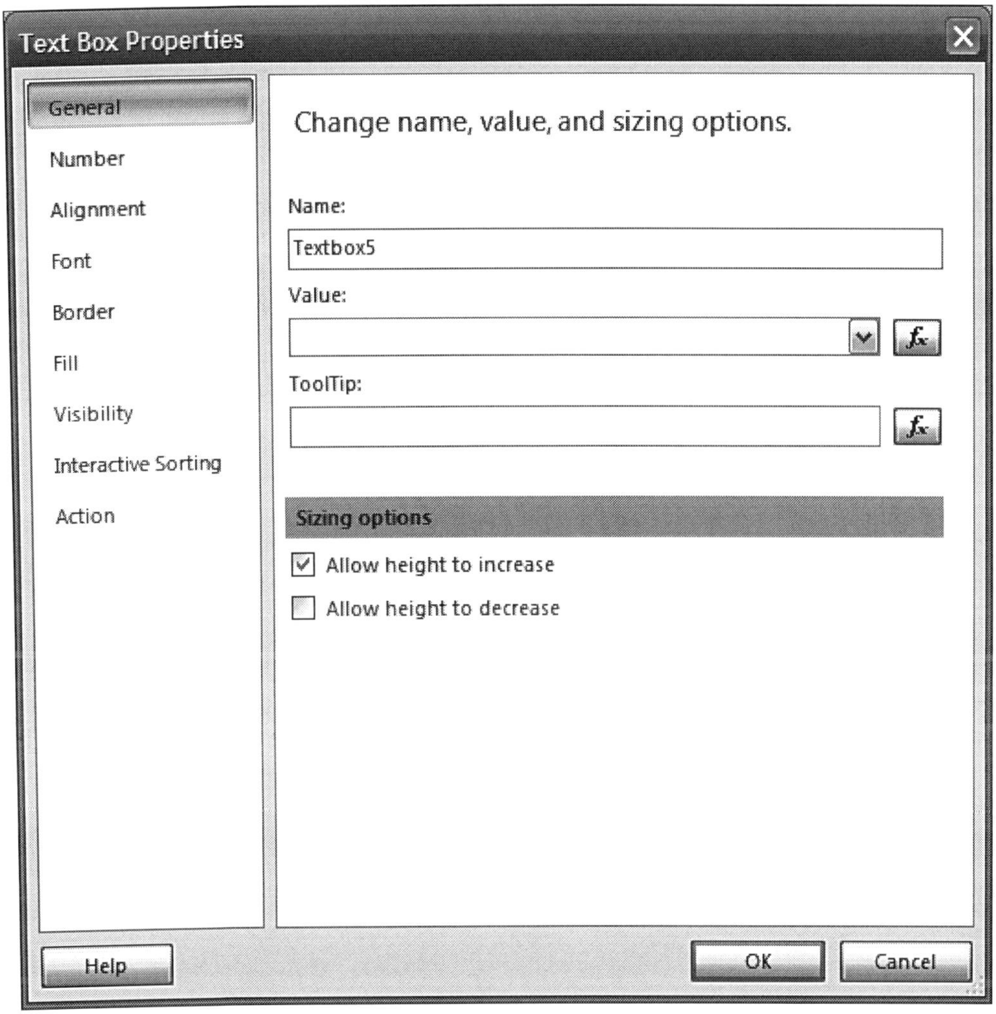

In the **General** page, you can make changes to the elements in the **Name, Value,** and **Sizing options** page as shown. The **Value** is one which you choose among the column values (from the drop-down) from the dataset. You may also add a text for the **ToolTip**, which will display this text when the report is generated and this cell is accessed by hovering over it in the report. Alternatively you can set the **Value** and **Tooltip** using *fx*—the button that brings up the **Expression** window.

In the **Number** page you can set the number and date data type formatting options for the cell that contains a number or a date. This is what you normally would find in most Microsoft products such as Excel and Access.

In the **Alignment** page you can choose the vertical and horizontal alignments as well as the padding of the textbox content from the edges of the cell.

Similarly the **Font** and **Border** properties are the same ones you find in most Microsoft products.

The **Fill** property lets you add or change background color to the report as well as add a graphic element. The graphic element can be **embedded, external**, or originate from a **database** (being one of the fields accessed). Expressions can be developed to set a desired color for the **Fill**.

The **Visibility** of the textbox can be any of **Show, Hide, Show or Hide based on an expression**. In each of these cases the visibility can be toggled when another table cell is clicked (which can be chosen). This page also gives access to the **Expression** window which is similar to the MS Access expression builder.

The **Interactive Sorting** page allows you to define interactive sorting options on the textbox.

Matrix

Matrix provides a similar functionality (roughly speaking rows against columns) to cross-tab reports in MS Access (`http://aspalliance.com/1041_Creating_a_Crosstab_Report_in_Visual_Studio_2005_Using_Crystal_Reports.all`) and Pivot Table dynamic views (`http://www.aspfree.com/c/a/MS-SQL-Server/On-Accessing-Data-From-An-OLAP-Server-Using-MS-Excel/3/`). The matrix should have at least one row group and one column group. The matrix can expand both ways to accommodate the data, horizontally for column groups and vertically for row groups. The matrix cells (intersection of rows and columns) display summary information (aggregates).

When you click on **Insert Matrix** in the **Insert** menu and drop it on the design area of Report Builder 2.0, it gets displayed as shown in the next figure.

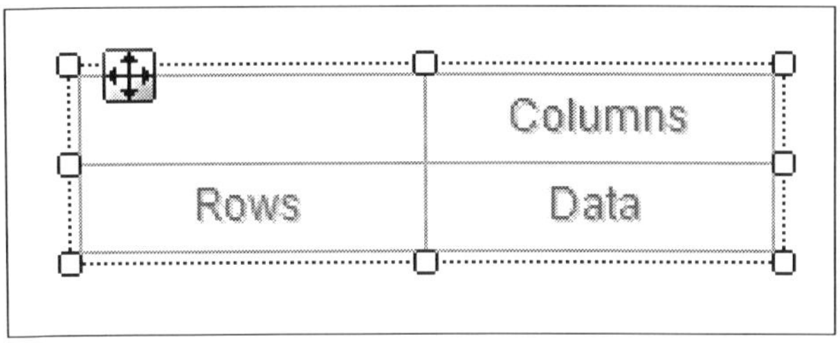

Now if you click inside the boundary of the (2x2) empty matrix you will see more features of the matrix as shown in the following screenshot. The basic elements are the **ColumnGroup** (Column Groups), the **RowGroup** (Row Groups), and the **Data**. The group information is also displayed as shown by overlaid lines pointing to them. There needs to be a minimum of one group and one column for the matrix and there could be a hierarchy of column and row groups.

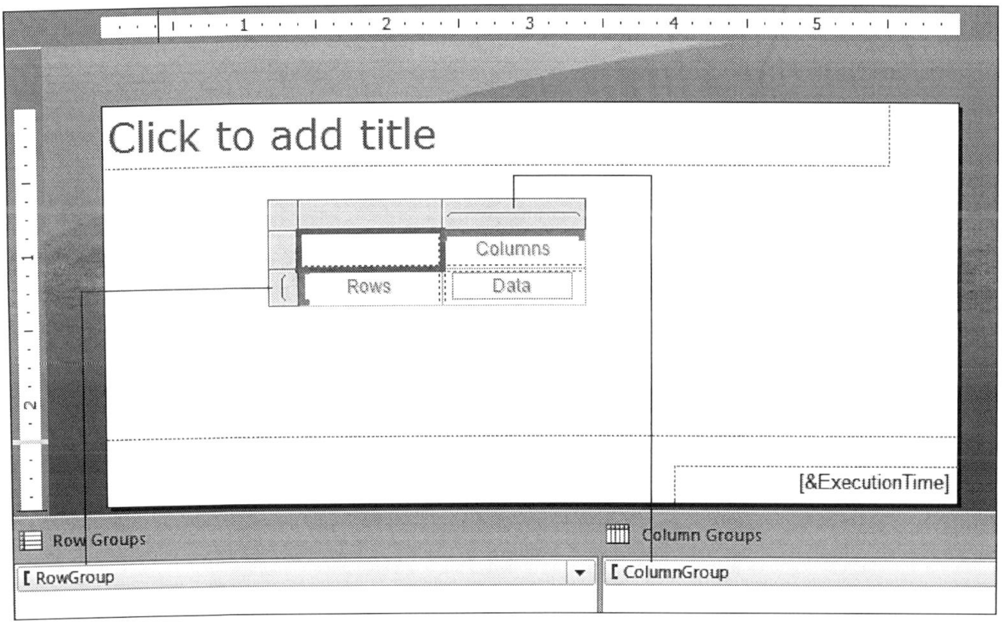

The row and column group cells have their own properties which can be displayed when you right-click on them as shown in the next screenshot for the row group. When you right-click on the cell marked **Rows**, the following drop-down menu pops up.

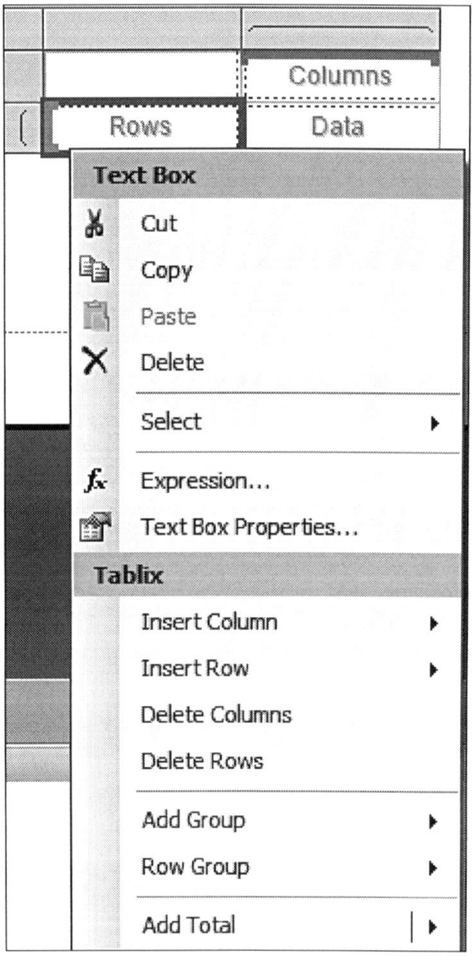

In addition to the properties that you can set for the textbox in that cell, you have additional submenu items that work with the grouping and totaling. These are part of representing data in a matrix.

Each of the Tablix for the **Rows** and **Columns** has the additional submenu items which are shown here for the **Rows**. Similar ones apply for the **Columns** as well. These are useful when you want to create nested groups as you shall see in the hands-on exercises in Chapter 7. With the Matrix design interface in SQL Server 2005 this would not have been possible.

Add Group

- Row Group
    - Parent Group...
    - Child Group...
    - -------------------
    - Adjacent Above
    - Adjacent Below

Row Group

- Delete Group
- Group Properties

Add Total

- Before
- After

In addition to the above, each of the items **Rows** and **Columns** cells has the following items as well. These specify how new columns and rows are inserted with reference to the current cell as shown. The differences are due to the geometrical positions that are allowed for the new columns or rows as shown.

For the "Columns" cell:

Insert Column

- Inside Group-Left
- Inside Group-Right
- -----------------
- Outside Group-Left
- Outside Group-Right

Insert Row

- Inside Group-Above
- Inside Group-Below
- -----------------
- Outside Group_Above

For the "Rows" cell:

Insert Column

- Inside Group-Left
- Inside Group-Right
- ------------------
- Outside Group-Left

Insert Row

- Inside Group-Above
- Inside Group-Below
- ------------------
- Outside Group_Above
- Outside Group_Below

Besides using a cell as a starting point, one could also use the rows as a whole or column as a whole to add further structure as shown in the next figure. Of course you need to use the proper submenu option to arrive at a particular matrix structure. Clicking at the indicated points would let you choose the structure you want for your matrix. If you click at the location shown for the Tablix you could choose to the delete the whole matrix. The Tablix graphical arrangement gives you the maximum flexibility in extending the matrix in 2-dimensions.

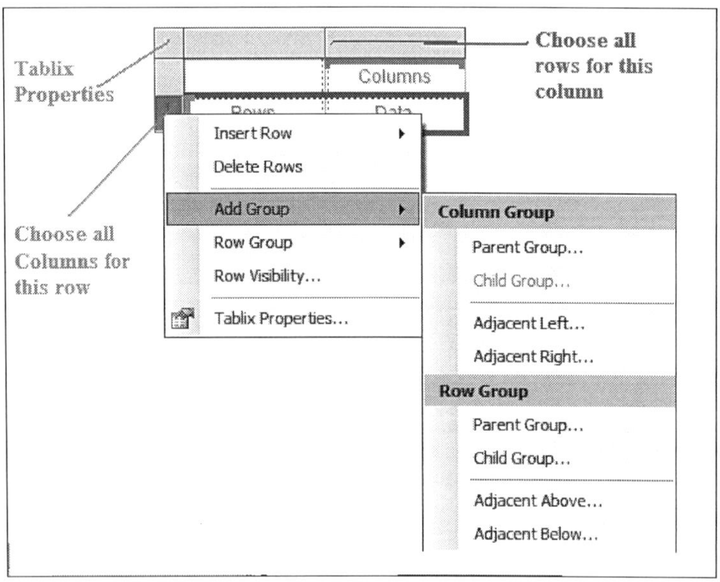

List

The list data region repeats for each row of data. List element provides a single container for the data which can be used to generate what are called *Free Form Reports*. In this kind of report there is no rigid structure such as a table for the data. You can also place a list inside another list or even a chart inside a list. You can drag a column from a dataset and drop it into the list. You can work with the list using the properties of the **Rectangle** it contains as well as its Tablix properties.

As described earlier, the design interface is very flexible and you can leverage all features provided by the Tablix structure like displaying details and adding groups either independent, or nested. The properties pages described earlier allow you to sort and filter grouped data.

When you drop a **List** on the design surface you will see just a single cell as shown. You can change its dimensions to suit your needs.

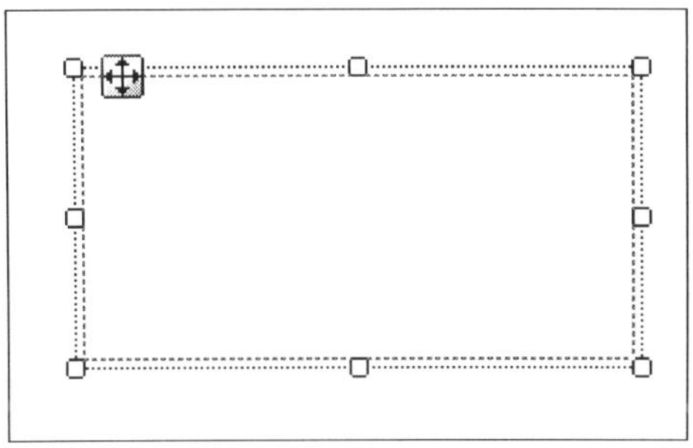

When you click on the List you can access its handles as shown.

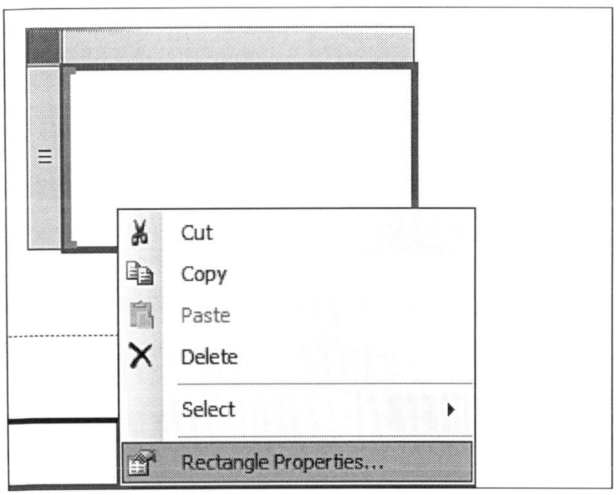

When you add a List, there is one column and one row (just one cell). This can be extended in both directions by choosing the appropriate submenu items. These can be displayed by right-clicking on the handles as shown.

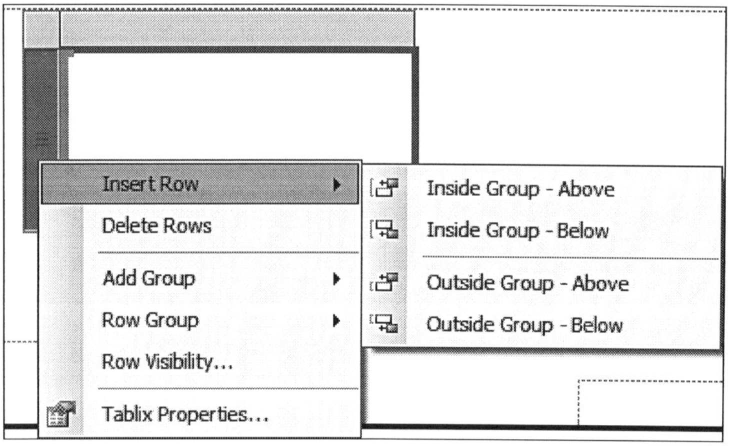

In Chapter 7, you will be creating free form reports using the List data region.

Chart

A picture tells lot more than a bunch of numbers, and charts (graphs) aggregate the whole range of data that is highly informative and aesthetically pleasing. Charts have a myriad of properties, both with regard to how they are linked to data as well as their visual properties that it is hard to justify describing them in an abbreviated fashion. This section and the hands-on exercise deal mostly with the basic principles of implementing charts in Report Builder 2.0.

Charts are basically used while creating a graph from the data to summarize important and relevant information. There are two ways you can work with chart in Report Builder 2.0. The easiest is to use the **Chart Wizard**. The other way is to start with a chart template and then associate it with a dataset.

There are many chart types such as bar charts, column charts, line charts, pie charts, area charts, polar charts, range charts, scatter charts and so on. The following screenshot schematically shows the various supported chart types. The chart type would depend on the data that it represents. Generally a chart should help visualize the data. A chart has its data region as well, its Tablix properties.

You can insert a chart on the report body by clicking **Insert | Chart | Insert Chart** and clicking again on the body of the report. This brings up the **Select Chart Type** window as shown:

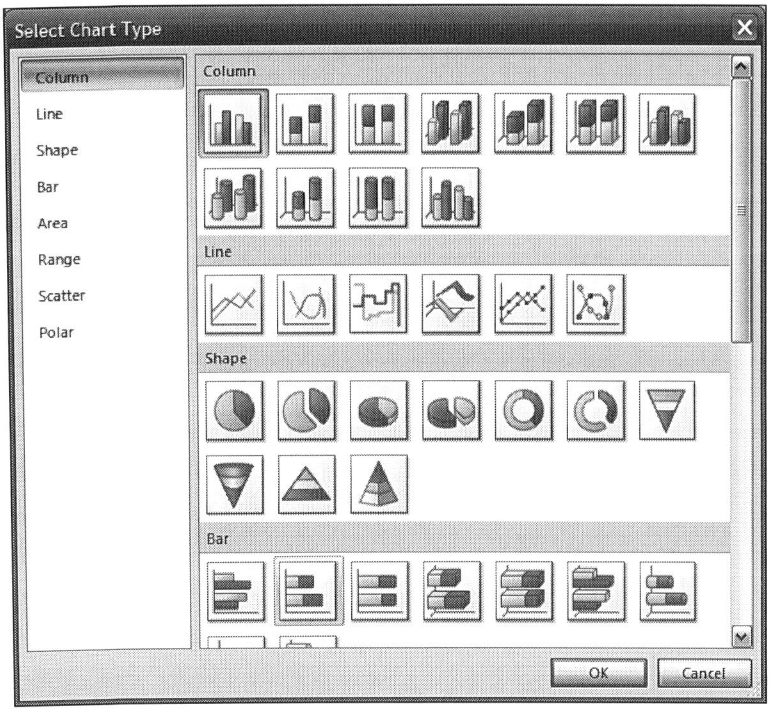

Here you have number of options as shown. For each of these choices you have a number of other options as shown on the right-hand side when you choose the **Column** type.

Assuming you choose the default (the one highlighted in the above figure) and click on the **OK** button, the type of chart you chose gets added to the design area of the report as shown. You can increase the size of the chart both ways by dragging the handles.

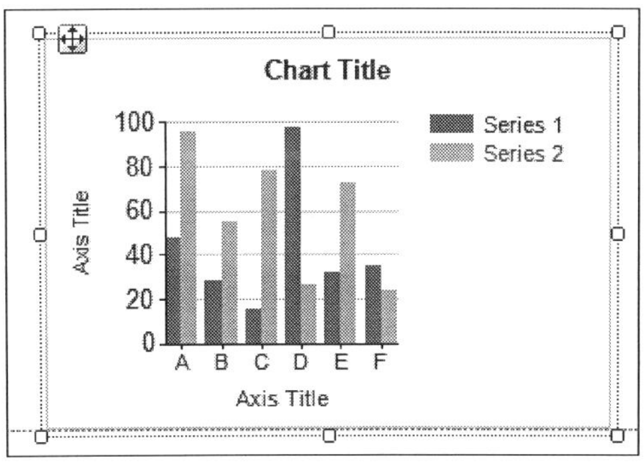

When you double-click inside the chart, you see the drop-zones on its three sides as shown. These are the areas into which you can drag-and-drop columns from the Dataset or use the minimized dataset icon that gets displayed when you hover over this area.

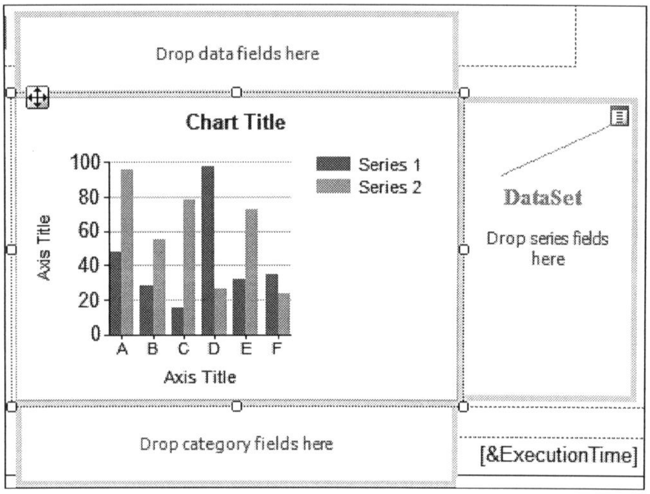

When you right-click on any of these areas, you can access the various ways you can work with the charts as shown:

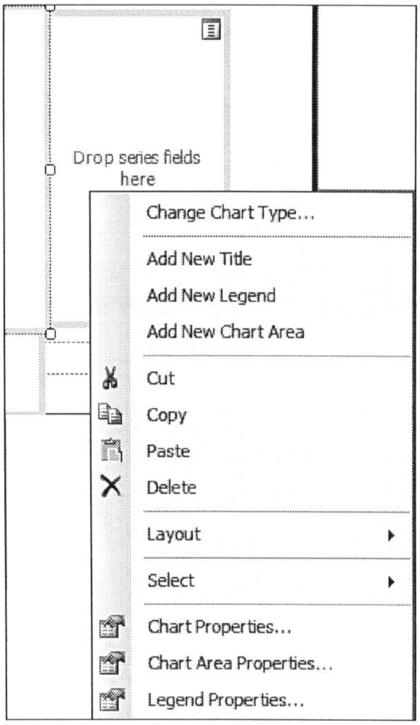

The important chart related items are category fields, series fields, and data fields. You can work with all properties of the chart from this drop-down menu and even change the type of chart you want to develop.

In *Hands-on exercise .6.3*, a rather long one, you will be creating a chart and modify some of its properties and use the *Expression* tool to set the number of properties. It is not necessary to complete this exercise in one sitting as you can save the report to the report server and bring it back and forth to work on it.

Gauge

This is new in Reporting Services 2008. Like chart, gauge is also a data region. Gauge has only a single data region unlike a chart. It has the look of any industrial meters (measuring instrument) with a range of values and the indicator showing the present value or some configurable value. They can be used together with both table and matrix elements.

When you add a gauge to a report, it comes up positioned within a gauge panel. The properties of this can be accessed when you click outside the boundary of the gauge. When you want the gauge to display data, you should associate its data property with the dataset. Gauge, like chart also has a myriad of properties which can be accessed from its **Properties** window.

In *Hands-on exercise 6.3*, you will be adding a **radial** gauge to display the data and a **linear** gauge to display an average.

Report Items

Textbox, image, line, and rectangle are the items you find in the **Report Items** section of **Insert**. You will be using textbox and image both of which may be bound to related as well as unrelated database variables. In the case of textbox, you have an option to use a static text, a field from the built-in fields, or connected to one of the fields from the dataset. A table added to a report has textboxes in its cells, but you can add a textbox outside the table and bind it to an aggregate value related to the dataset.

Similar to the textbox, an image added to the report can be embedded, originate from an external source; or being one of the dataset fields. An image can be added to the current report by right-clicking the **Images** folder in **Report Builder** and picking an image from your hard drive which can then be simply embedded in the report using the **Image** report item. This way you can add a logo to your report.

A line cannot be bound to the dataset. Its purpose is purely to provide support as a graphic separator element. The rectangle is also used to improve the visible appeal. However, it can contain other items, even data regions. You can control the rendering behaviour of items placed inside a rectangle (parent control) for the controls placed inside the rectangle. The rectangle will be an anchor for the items placed within it and move when the rectangle is moved in the report design.

When the line or the rectangle is used inside data regions you may use their **RepeatWith** property to allow them to be rendered when the report gets displayed.

In the next chapter you will use images in a database to get displayed in the report.

Subreports

A subreport is a child of a main report. The main report is a container for the subreport (s). The **Subreport** section in the **Insert** menu item of the "ribbon" allows you to add a subreport. The parent report and the subreport are stored usually in the same folder on the report server. The main report can be designed to pass parameters to the subreport. The parameter then filters the subreport for it to be displayed in a data region of the main report. You will be doing a hands-on, where you will be designing a Main Report/Subreport pair to learn about passing parameters in the next chapter.

Subreports can be separated from main data region of the main report or they can be placed within the data region of the main report. A report can contain more than one subreport.

As described above, the subreport may be placed inside the main report several ways as shown in the following screenshot:

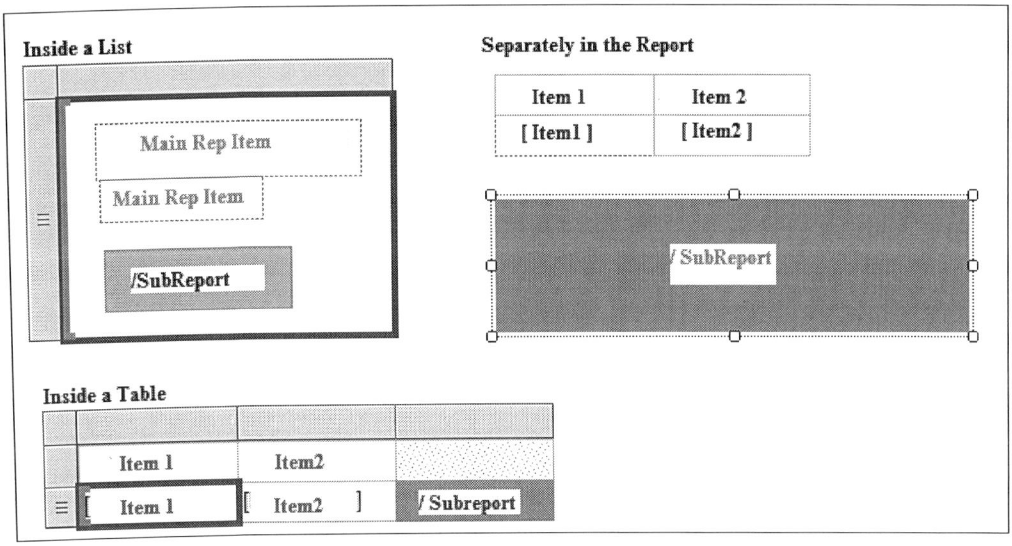

Header and footer

A report page can contain a header and footer. In Report Builder 2.0 there is page footer by default which contains the built-in parameter `ExecutionTime`.

Some of the common features of page headers and footers are the following:

- Headers go at the top of the page and footers go to the bottom and they repeat on each page of the report.
- They both can contain static text, images, lines and rectangles, borders, expressions (lookup the properties of these in Report Builder 2.0).The expressions can include field references for reports from the dataset.
- You can easily add headers and footers from the **Insert** menu item in the "ribbon". You can just, as easily, remove them by right-clicking the item and choose to remove the item.
- The most common use of headers and footers is to display page numbers, report titles, and so on. There are number of built-in fields such as **Page Number, Execution Time, Report Name, Total Pages** and so on, which can be dragged-and-dropped on to headers and footers.
- To display variable data from a dataset in headers and footers you place a textbox and set the value for the textbox using an expression. Choose the appropriate field from the dataset. In a similar manner you can display aggregate values from the expression builder. For data from multiple datasets you cannot reference the fields, rather you should reference the objects in the report.

- You can suppress these on the first and last pages of a report using the `PrintOnFirstPage`, `PrintOnLastPage` properties which can be accessed from their properties.
- Report headers and footer are not the same as the page headers and footers.
- Reports that you see with a browser are rendered by the HTML renderer, but the report can be delivered in different formats. Each of them has their own renderer and you should optimize the report for the format you want to deliver.

You will be getting some practice adding headers and footers and working with them in the next chapter.

View

The **View** menu has very few items as shown:

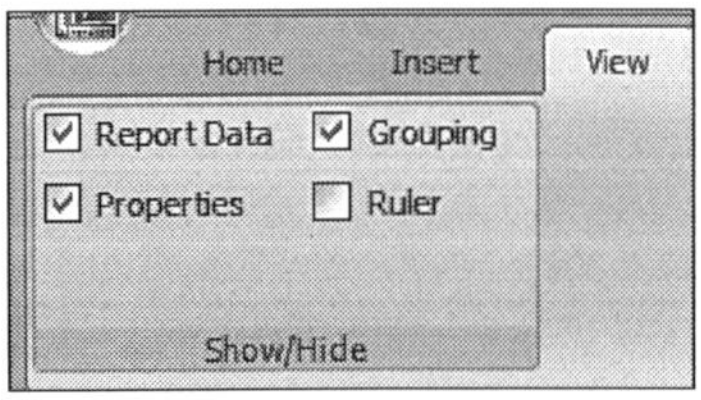

Report Data and **Grouping** are checked by default. If you want to review or make changes to the properties of objects you place on the report, you should first place a checkmark for the **Properties**. Otherwise you will see only the **Properties** pop-up window that comes up when you right-click an object to look at its properties. In *Hands-on 6.3*, you will be accessing properties for some of the items, such as the bookmark property.

Place checkmark for the **Rulers** if you want to design measured placement of objects on the report. The rulers become visible when you move around or adjust object sizes.

Report Data, the Report Designer, and the properties

These are the items that you will find just below the "ribbon" assuming you have not disabled **Report Data** and **Properties** (these are enabled by default) as shown in the following screenshot. The properties will be that of the object highlighted in the report body.

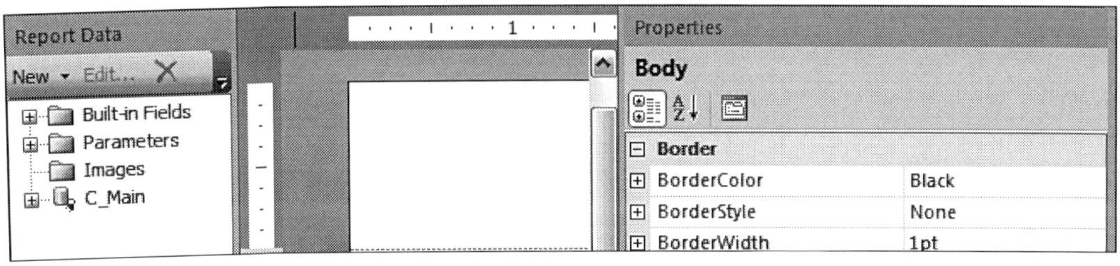

Report Data

As seen in the previous figure, you can create **New** report data; **Edit** an existing report data (the figure above has an existing report data in the **C_Main**. It also has three main folders. The built-in fields we saw earlier. The parameters will contain parameters associated with the report. The images folder contains images that can be imported into this folder, which you can embed in a report from your hard drive.

The **Report Data** is an excellent starting point to create a report from scratch without using wizards displayed in default. When you click on the drop-down handle **New** the following menu will be displayed.

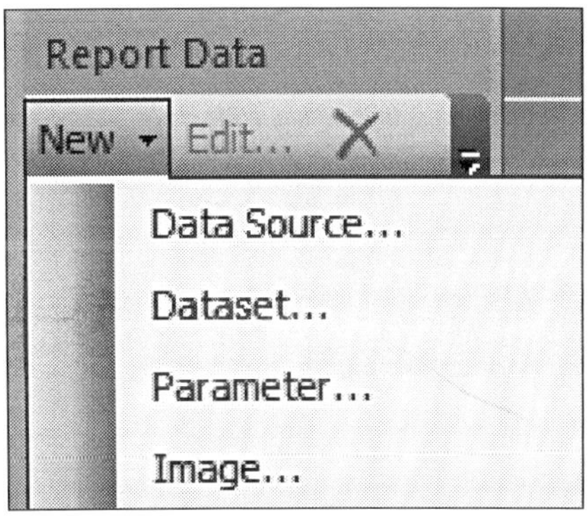

All you need to do is to go and configure each of the items from top to bottom as follows:

- The **Data Source...**will bring up a window where you establish the connection to the datasource.
- After this, you click on **Dataset...**to create a query to extract a set from the database which you want to display in your report. When you click on **Dataset...**you will display the properties of **Dataset** which you can use to design a query visually (only for SQL Server databases), an SQL Statement or import a saved SQL query or RDL file.

- You can then define parameter(s) by clicking on **Parameters...** to create a parameter from its **Properties** window. You add a parameter if you want to filter your query further to produce a smaller and morer manageable set of pertinent information.
- Click on **Images...** to choose images from your machine if you need to embed them in the report.

On the other hand, if you already have these you can edit them or delete them.

Report Designer pane

The various parts of this pane are shown in the following screenshot. This has been described earlier. The choices you make in the **View** pane will show or hide the **Groupings** at the bottom as well as in the **Ruler**. When you want to create a report from scratch and do not want to use the wizards, you can delete everything on the report and start from scratch.

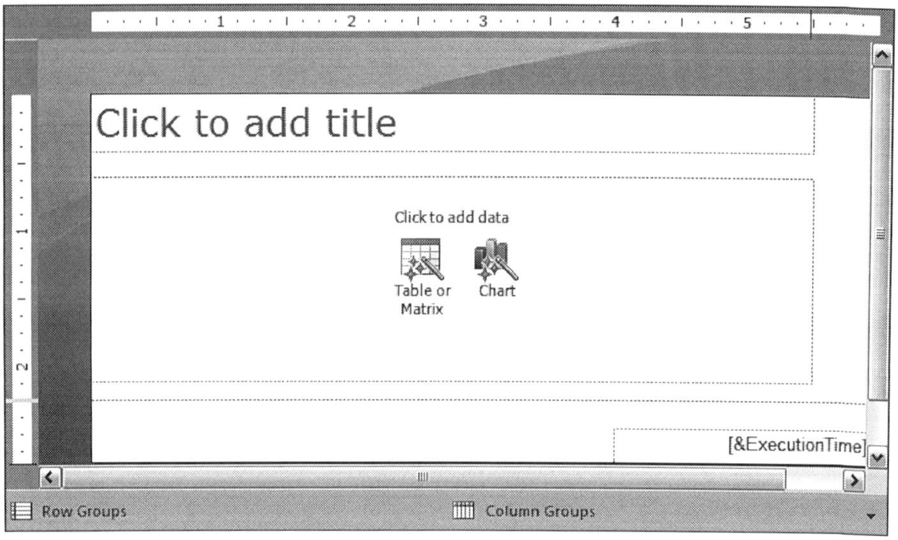

For displaying groups of data, the underlying data must support this structure and it is necessary that there exists hierarchical relationships within the data. An example is shown in the following screenshot from the `TestNorthwind` database used in the exercises.

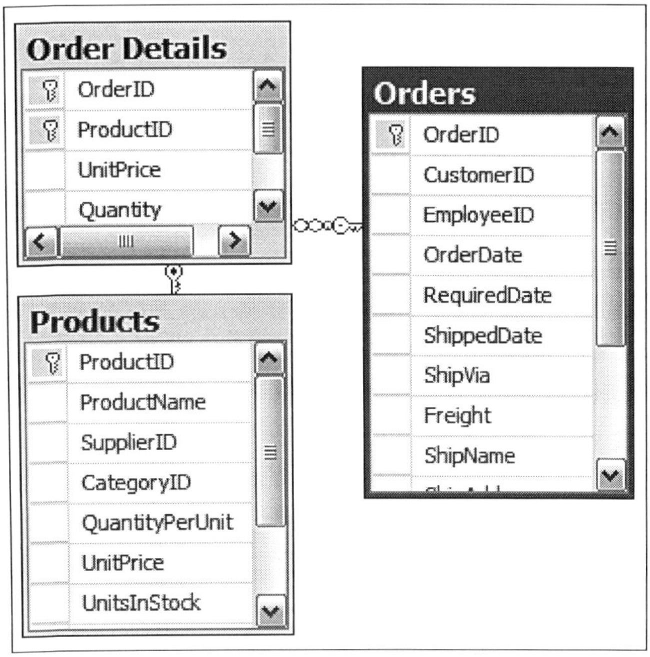

In Report Builder 2.0, groupings show both row groupings as well as column groupings. If you are starting from the wizard, you will be setting up the row groups as well as column groups as seen in the **Arrange Fields** page of the wizard. The available fields were moved into column groups and row groups. One of the shortcomings of this wizard is that once you move a field from the available to any of the other three, you cannot move it back. However you can only move between the three. If you go **back** and return, you have the same arrangement. If you **Cancel**, you need to start the wizard again. Another problem with this wizard step is that you must add a field to the **Value** field. What if one wants to show only a few columns of data in a table? However, it is well suited for matrix design. The above shortcomings in the earlier SQL Server 2008 RC0 version have been rectified in the latest version of Report Builder 2.0 bundled with the Feature Pack (`https://connect.microsoft.com/SQLServer/feedback/ViewFeedback.aspx?FeedbackID=371356`).

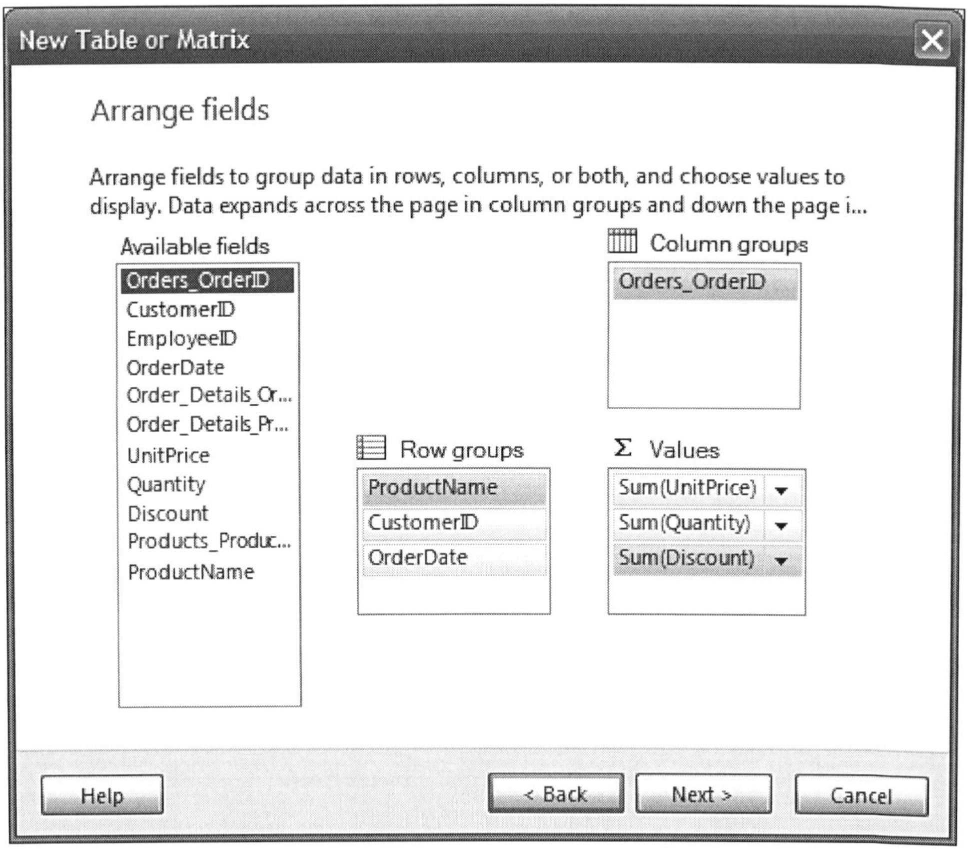

The above arrangement would lead to a report's grouping as shown here:

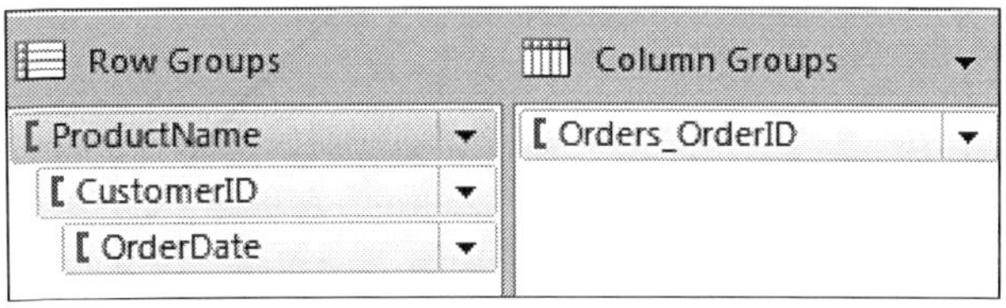

Each of the groups shown above has its own properties which can be accessed by right-clicking the group. For example, the row group **[ProductName]** in the above. You can then review its **Group Properties** window as shown in the two following screenshots:

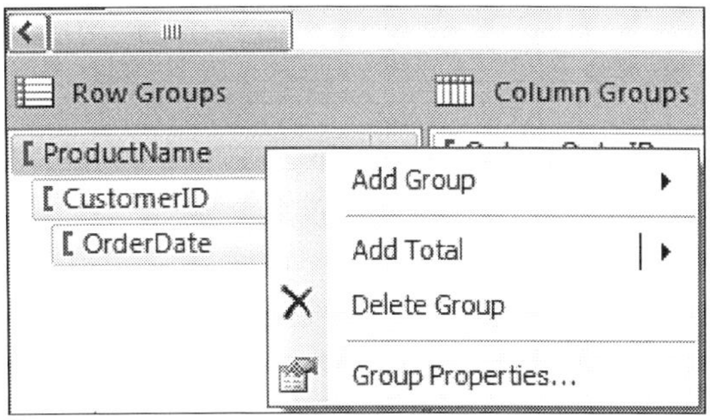

When you click on the drop-down item, **Group Properties**..., the **Group Properties** window shows up.

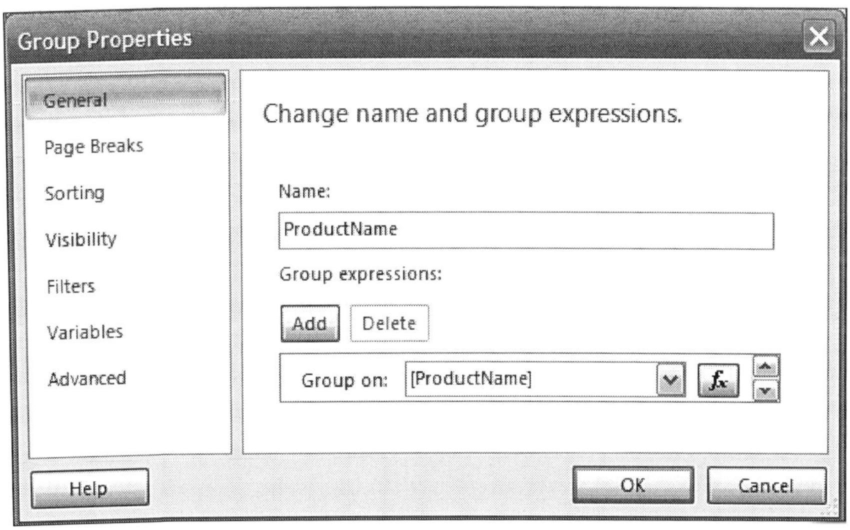

Clicking on the Next button in the **New Table or Matrix** wizard's **Arrange Fields** page takes you to the window where you can arrange to show the group aggregates. You can show them in several ways depending on the choice you make as shown in the following screenshot:

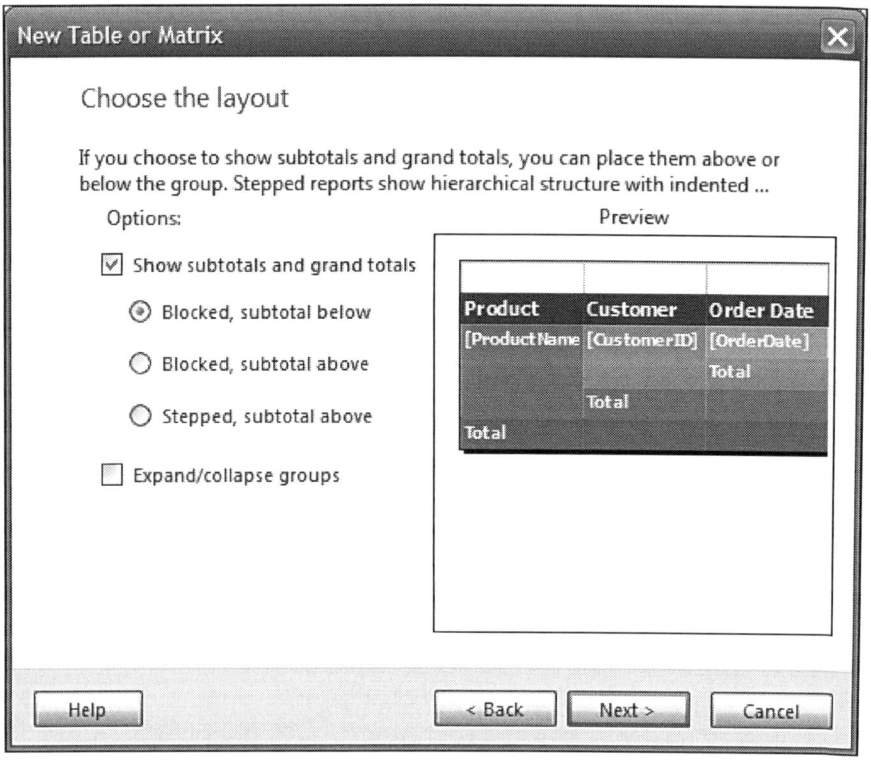

You will be working with the groups and grouping in the next chapter.

Properties

This window appears, by default, at the right of the report designer pane. It shows all configurable properties of the objects on the report body. You only need to click on the object. Most of the properties become effective as soon as you complete the property and leave that property or move to the next property in the **Properties** window. If you add custom assemblies, these are also shown in this window.

Server status and tools

At the very bottom of the Report Builder you will get an indication as to the Report Server you are connected to (present case there is only one running) and its status as shown in the following screenshot. You can also change from design to run (preview) by clicking on the respective icons in this figure. You can also enlarge or reduce the size of the report both in design and in preview using the zoom slide.

Hands-on exercise 6.1: Enabling and reviewing My Reports

As described previously the My Reports folder needs to be enabled in order to use the folder or display it in the Open Report dialogue. The RC0 version had a documentation bug which has been rectified (`https://connect.microsoft.com/SQLServer/feedback/ViewFeedback.aspx?FeedbackID=366413`).

Getting ready

In order to enable the My Reports folder you need to carry out a few tasks. This will require authentication and working with the SQL Server Management Studio. These tasks are listed here:

1. Make sure the Report Server has started.
2. Make sure you have adequate permissions to access the Servers.
3. Open the **Microsoft SQL Server Management Studio** as described previously.
4. Connect to the Reporting Services after making sure you have started the Reporting Services.
5. Right-click the **Report Server** node.

   The **Server Properties** window is displayed with a navigation list on the left consisting of the following:

   - **General**
   - **Execution**

- **History**
- **Logging**
- **Security**
- **Advanced**

In the **General** page the *name, version, edition, authentication mode,* and *URL* of Reporting Service is displayed. Download of an **ActiveX Client Print** control is enabled by default. In order to work with Report Builder effectively and provide a **My Reports** folder for each user, you need to place a check mark for the check box **Enable a My Reports folder for each user**. The **My Reports** feature has been turned on as shown in the next screenshot.

In the **Execution** page there is choice for report timeout execution, with the default set such that the report execution expires after 1800 seconds.

In the **History** page there is choice between keeping an unlimited number of snapshots in the report history (default) or to limit the copies allowing you to specify how many to be kept.

In the **Logging** page, report execution logging is enabled and the log entries older than 60 days are removed by default. This can be changed if desired.

In the **Security** page, both Windows integrated security for report data sources and ad hoc report executions are enabled by default.

The **Advanced** page shows several more items including the ones described thus far as shown in the next figure.

6. In the **General** page enable the **My Reports** feature by placing a check mark.

7. Click on the **Advanced** list item in the left.

   The **Advanced** page is displayed as shown:

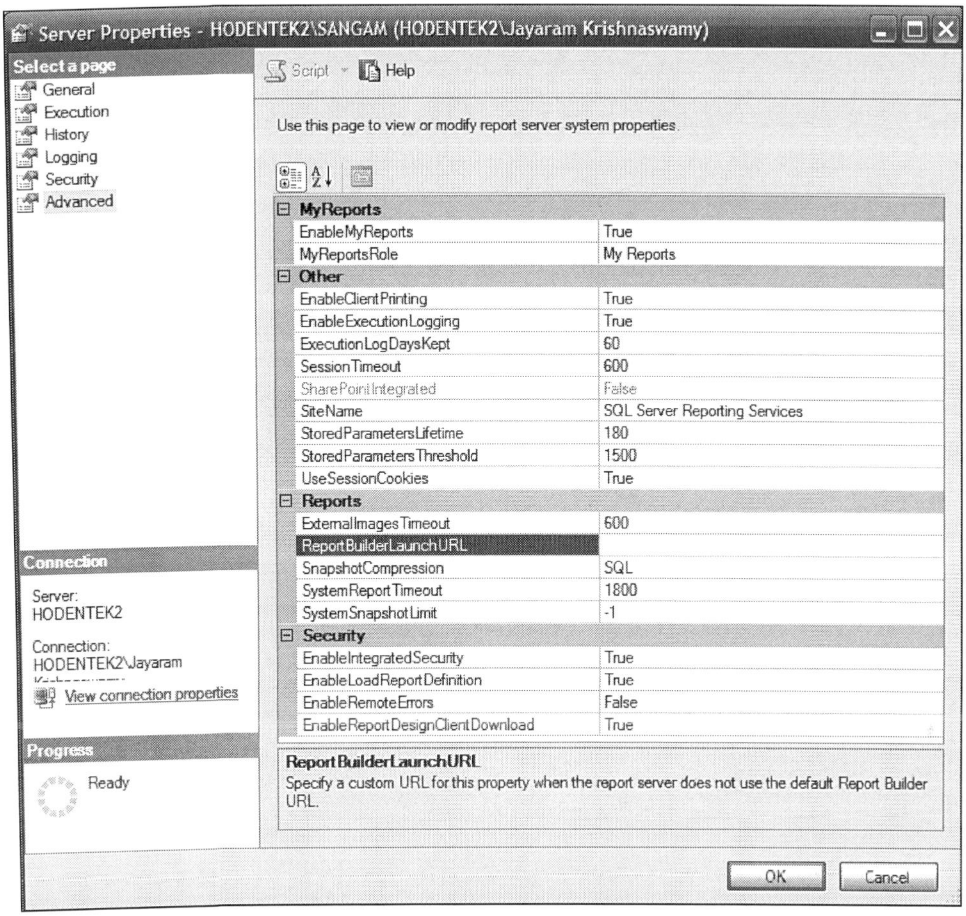

8. Now expand the **Security** node of **Reporting Services** and you will see that the **My Reports** role is present in the list of roles as shown. This is also added to the ReportServer database.

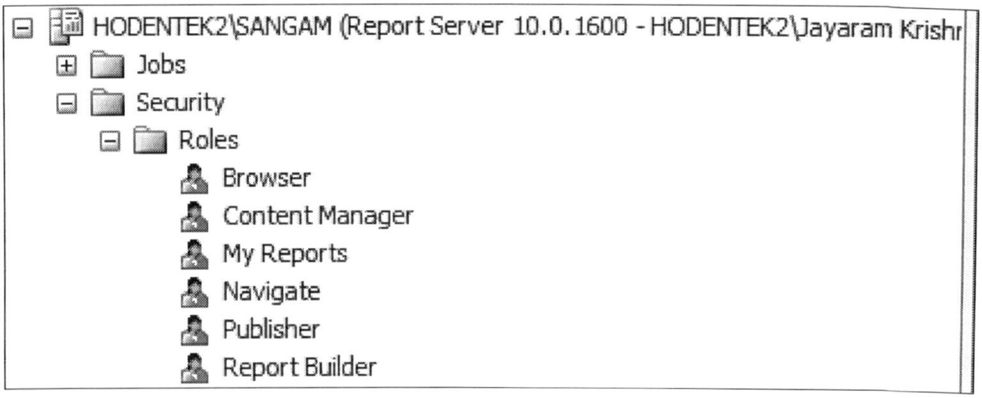

The description of everything that a user with the assignment **My Reports** role can do is as follows:

"May publish reports and linked reports, manage folders, reports, and resources in a users My Reports folder." As discussed in Chapter 5, this role may be assigned to a user in Report Manager.

9. Now bring up Report Builder 2.0 by clicking **Start | All Programs | Microsoft SQL Server 2008 Report Builder | Report Builder 2.0.**

   Report Builder 2.0 is displayed.

10 Click on **Office Button | Open.**

The **Open Report** dialogue appears as shown. When the report Server is offline, the default location is **My Documents,** like Microsoft products Excel and MS Access.

11. Choose the **Recent sites and Servers**.

The Report server that is active should get displayed here as shown:

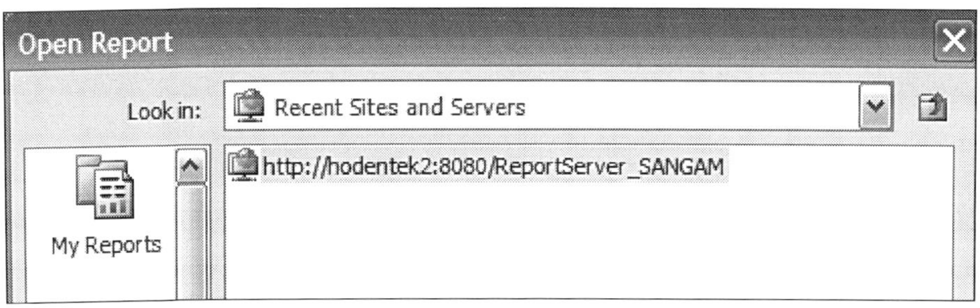

12. Highlight the Server URL and click **Open**.

    All the folders and files on the server become accessible as shown:

13. Open the Report Manager by providing its URL address.

    Verify that a **My Reports** folder is created for the user (current user). For other users you need to go into Report Manager and assign the role as discussed in Chapter 5.

> There could be slight differences in the look of the interface depending on whether you are using the RTM or the final version of SQL Server 2008 Enterprise edition.

Hands-on exercise 6.2: Modifying a basic report

In this exercise, the report created in Chapter 4 will be modified to illustrate the formatting, layout, and other capabilities built into the Report Builder. A number of other features of Report Builder will be taken up in the next chapter.

Getting ready

This hands-on will be using a MS Access report that was imported using Visual Studio in Chapter 4 and hosted on the Report Server. The MS Access report will be modified to use the new Report Items in Report Builder 2.0.

Follow the steps

You will be carrying out the following steps:

1. Open Report Builder and open the **ByOrders.rdl** report imported in Chapter 4.
2. Review the imported MS Access report.
3. Modify the properties.

Open Report Builder and open the ByOrders.rdl report

You will be accessing the ByOrders.rdl file from the Report Builder in order to modify it in the Report Builder. The steps are listed here:

1. Start Report Builder from its shortcut.
2. Click the **Office button** and in the drop-down window click on **Open.**

   The **Open** dialogue is displayed.
3. Click on **Recent Sites and Servers** in the left navigation area.

   The Report Servers' URL is displayed.
4. Highlight the Report Server URL and click on the **Open** button.
5. Click on the MS Access folder and click on the **Open** button.

6. Highlight the report **ByOrders** and click on the **Open** button.

   The **ByOrders** report gets displayed in the Report Builder as shown:

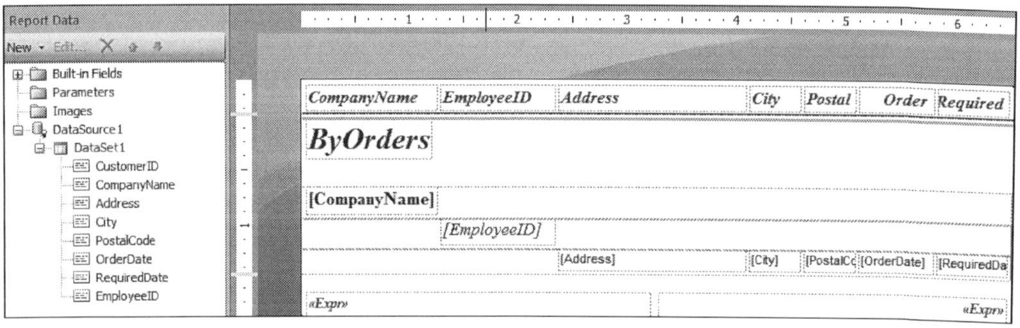

Review the imported MS Access report

The dataset for the report is **DataSet1** on the left and the report body is in the design area. The various report items and their data binding will be examined for one such control, the **CompanyName**. It will be instructive to study the others as well. In order to review the report we will follow these steps:

1. Highlight **CompanyName** and right-click on it.

   The properties of **CompanyName** are displayed as shown. **CompanyName** is inside a container textbox inside the Tablix and it is a place holder. You should also notice the large square bracket on the left ranging three rows. This is the grouping symbol.

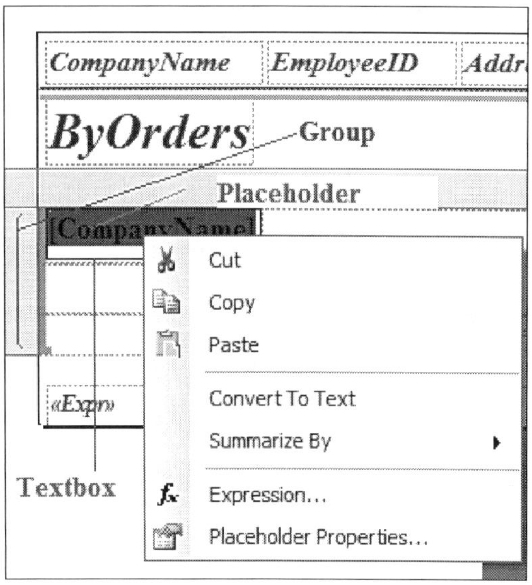

2. Click on **Placeholder Properties....**

   This opens the **Placeholder's Properties** page as shown:

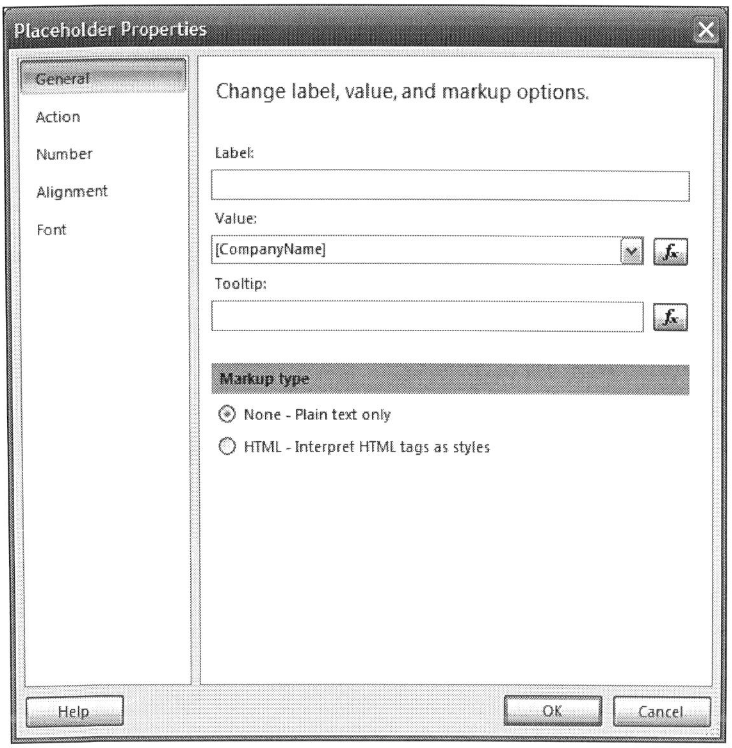

3. Change the **Markup type** to **HTML – Interpret HTML tags as styles**.
4. Click on the *fx* symbol (which opens an **Expression** window) along the **Value**.

5. In the **Expression** window that is displayed, modify the expression as shown in the following screenshot:

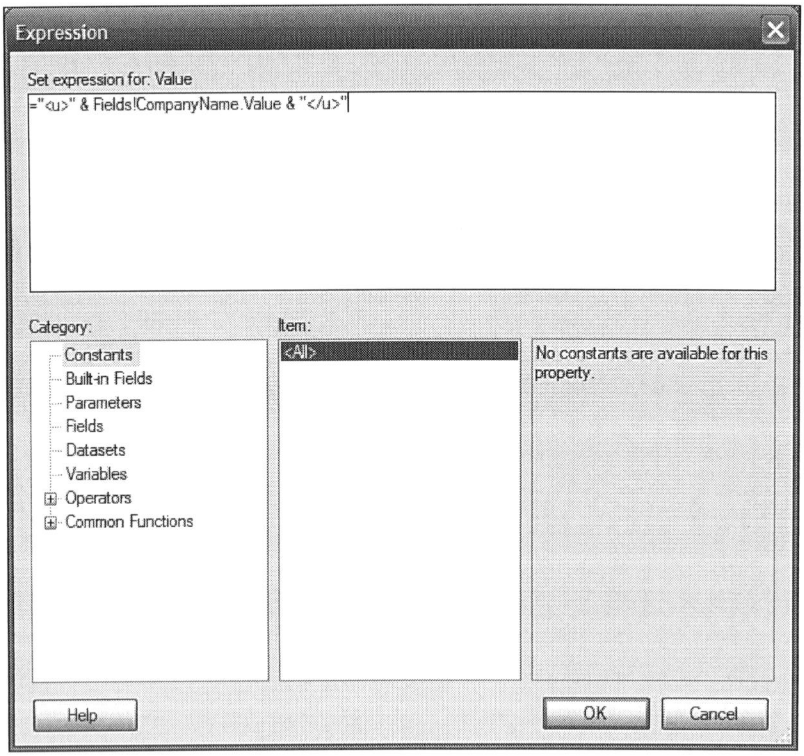

You have added the HTML tags `<u>` and `</u>` on either side of the original **CompanyName** data that came from the dataset. Now it is slightly more than the data and in the design view (CompanyName) it is replaced by this expression. A placeholder is the holding place of an expression. You can make a textbox into a placeholder by designating the textbox to hold an expression. For example there are two place holders for the time `Now ()` and the expression `="Page" & Globals.PageNumber & " of "& Globals.TotalPages`.

6. Click on the **OK** button on the **Expression** window as well as the **Placeholder Properties**' window.

7. Click on the **Run** button in the **Home** menu.

   The report gets processed and you may need to provide the login for this report. The username is **Admin** and there is no **password**.

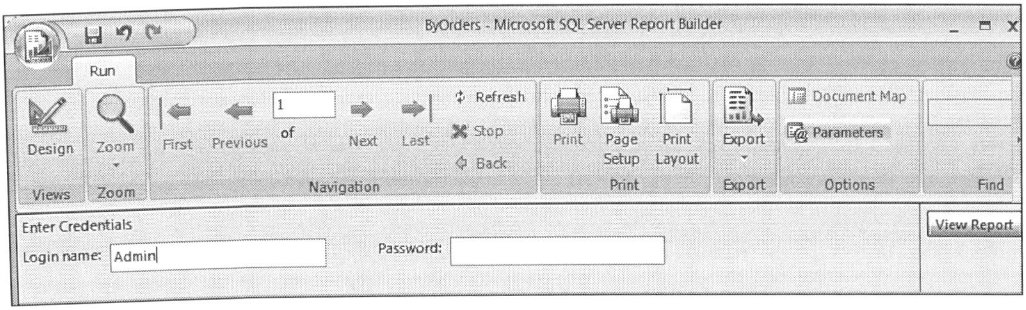

8. Click on the **View Report** button.

   The report is displayed in the Report Builder as shown:

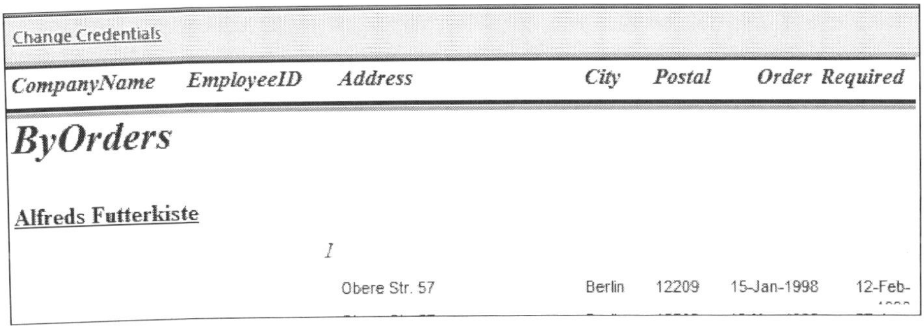

9. Click on the **Address** field in the report design.

   The **Address** field is highlighted in the report as shown:

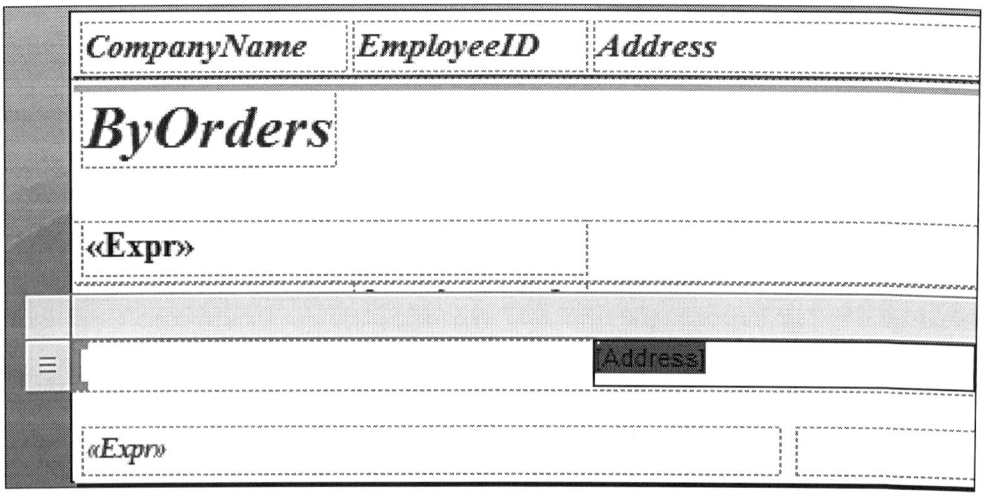

   You can see that this represents the detail (the data that comes in each of the rows). It is also a placeholder and its value is that of "Address". You can apply Rich Text formatting by using HTML tags for textboxes as well as placeholder values.

   Note that only certain HTML tags and CSS attributes are supported. For the supported HTML tags refer to `http://msdn.microsoft.com/en-us/library/dd207048.aspx`. For an example of CSS rendering, refer to `http://hodentek.blogspot.com/2009/01/can-you-use-css-style-attributes-in.html`.

10. Change Report title **ByOrders** to **Orders** by editing the textbox.
11. Extend the length of the **<<Expr>>** directly below the report title to accommodate a longer string.
12. Make the **EmployeeID** field left aligned as well as formatted. Set the font weight **Bold**.
13. Click on the table that has the **Address**, **City**, and so on. Extend it to the right by dragging the table handles so that the **Required Date** can be fully displayed.
14. Rearrange the positions of objects and the size of textboxes to fully display the data.

Both vertical and horizontal movements of objects can be very smooth and can be changed in **Points** as shown:

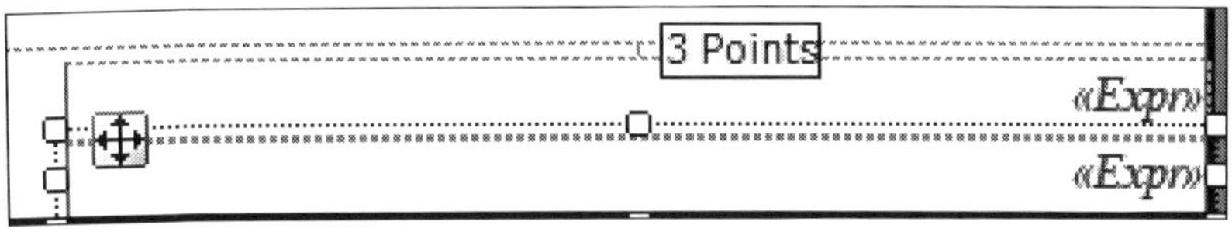

Highlighted objects can be expanded and moved using the *Ctrl* or *Shift* keys together with the arrow keys.

The modified report design is shown in the following screenshot:

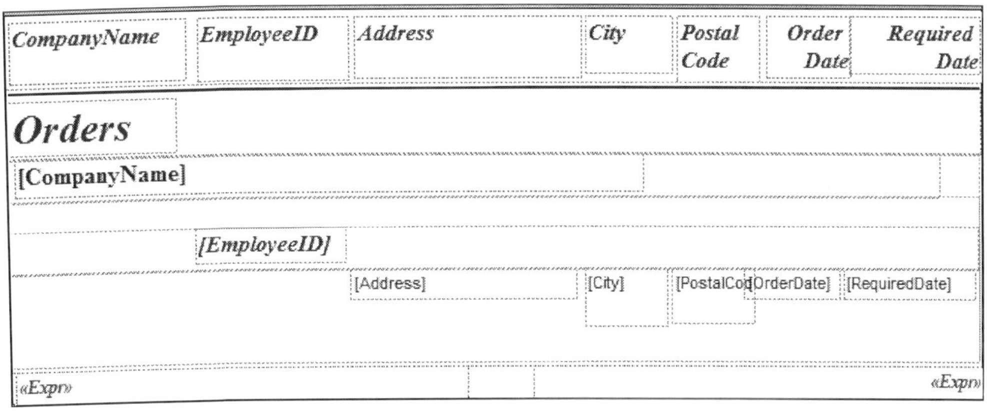

Hands-on exercise 6.3: Creating reports with charts and gauges

In this exercise you will be connecting to an Excel spreadsheet with some data and will be creating a simple report. You will also add a chart and gauge data regions to the report to display the data. In authoring the report you will be creating a report using the New Table or Matrix wizard which is supposed to lead to the creation of a table or a matrix according to the documentation. What has been noted is that this wizard can only create a matrix report and if you need a table report you need to start from scratch. However, a workaround has been adopted to use it as is. Again this was another reported bug that was fixed in the final version.

Getting ready

In order to carry out the tasks make sure you have Microsoft Excel installed on the machine and that the Report Server is running.

Follow on

In this exercise you will carry out the following steps:

1. Create a Microsoft Excel Spreadsheet with some data.
2. Create an ODBC DSN to access the data.
3. Create a datasource using this DSN in Report Builder 2.0.
4. Create a dataset based on the data in the Excel file.
5. Design a report to display the data.
6. Create a chart to display the data.
7. Add gauges to the report.

Creating a Microsoft Excel spreadsheet with some data

In order to work with this exercise we will create a simple spreadsheet with data using the MS Excel program. The chart we will be creating will use this spreadsheet.

Open an empty MS Excel file and type in some numbers as shown in the following screenshot. Delete Sheet 2 and Sheet 3 from the file. Save this file after providing a name (herein `RptChart.xls`).

The file is quite simple and you can just type in the numbers shown or makeup your own data. All data are numbers. The file gets saved to the default folder `MyDocuments` on the `C:\` drive.

	A	B	C	D
1	Time	First	Second	Third
2	1	8.5	3	-3
3	2	13.5	6	-60
4	3	18.5	11	11
5	4	23.5	18	9
6	5	28.5	27	9
7	6	33.5	38	9.5
8	7	38.5	51	10.2
9	8	43.5	66	11
10	9	48.5	83	11.85
11	10	53.5	102	12.75

Create an ODBC DSN to access the data

The MS Excel data will be accessed by creating an ODBC DSN. The details of how to do it are listed here:

1. Click on **Start | All Programs | Control Panel | Administrative Tools | Data Sources (ODBC)** to open the **ODBC Data Source Administrator.**
2. If the tabbed page is not in User DSN, change the tab to **User DSN** and click on the **Add** button.
3. Scroll down and highlight **Microsoft Excel** Driver `(*.xls)` [Version 12.00] and click on the **Finish** button.

   This opens the **ODBC Microsoft Excel Setup** window as shown.

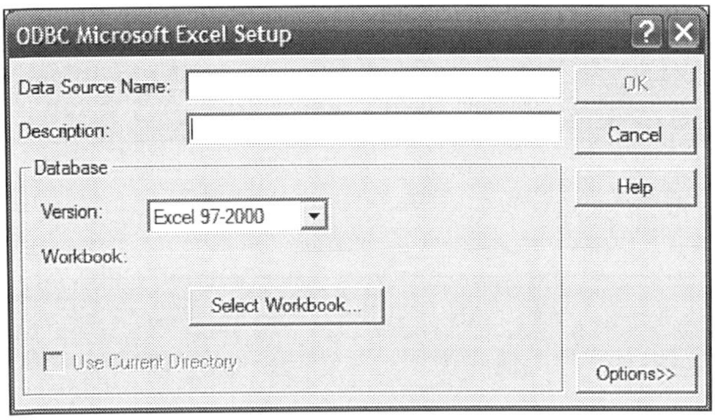

4. Provide a name (**Gauges**) and a **Description**. Click on the **Select Workbook...** button.
5. Use the controls on the **Select Workbook** window to locate the file you saved: the **RptChart.xls file**. Highlight the file. This will get the file into the **Database Name** window as shown.

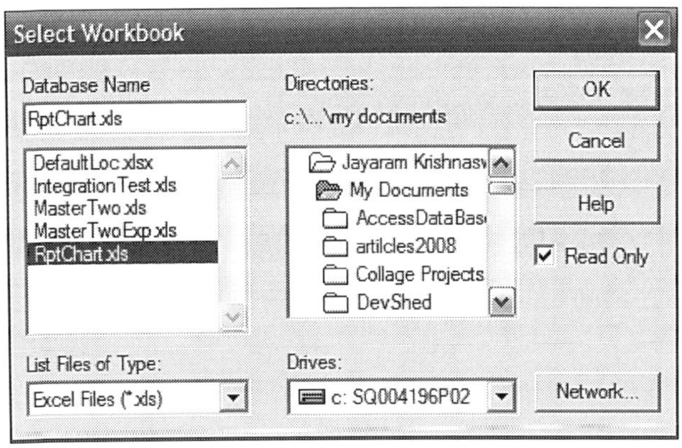

6. Click on the **OK** button.

   This creates the ODBC DSN as shown in the following screenshot. The DSN you created enters the **USER DSN** folder.

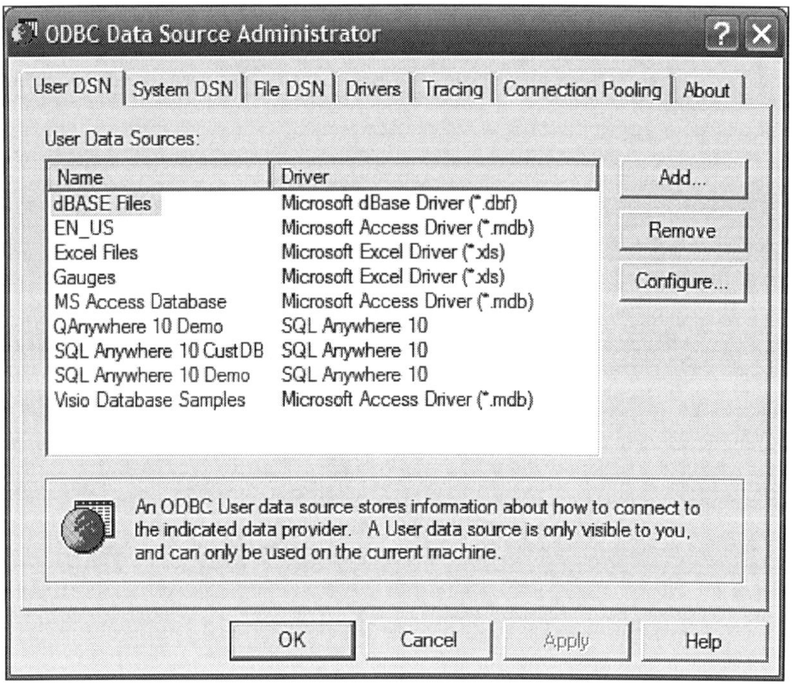

7. Click on the **OK** button to close the window.

Create a datasource using a DSN in Report Builder 2.0

After creating the ODBC DSN it will be possible to access the data using Report Builder. The following steps show how you may carry out this task.

1. Open Report Builder 2.0 just as you have done in other exercises.
2. Click on the **Office button** and choose **New** in the drop-down.

   The design surface displaying the body of the report with the two wizards will be displayed.

3. Click on the **Table or Matrix** wizard to open the **New Table or Matrix** window.
4. Click on the **New...** button to open the **Data Source Properties** window.
5. Provide a name for the datasource and replace the default **DataSource1** (Herein **GaugesSource**).
6. Click on the handle for **Select connection type** and choose **ODBC** as shown:

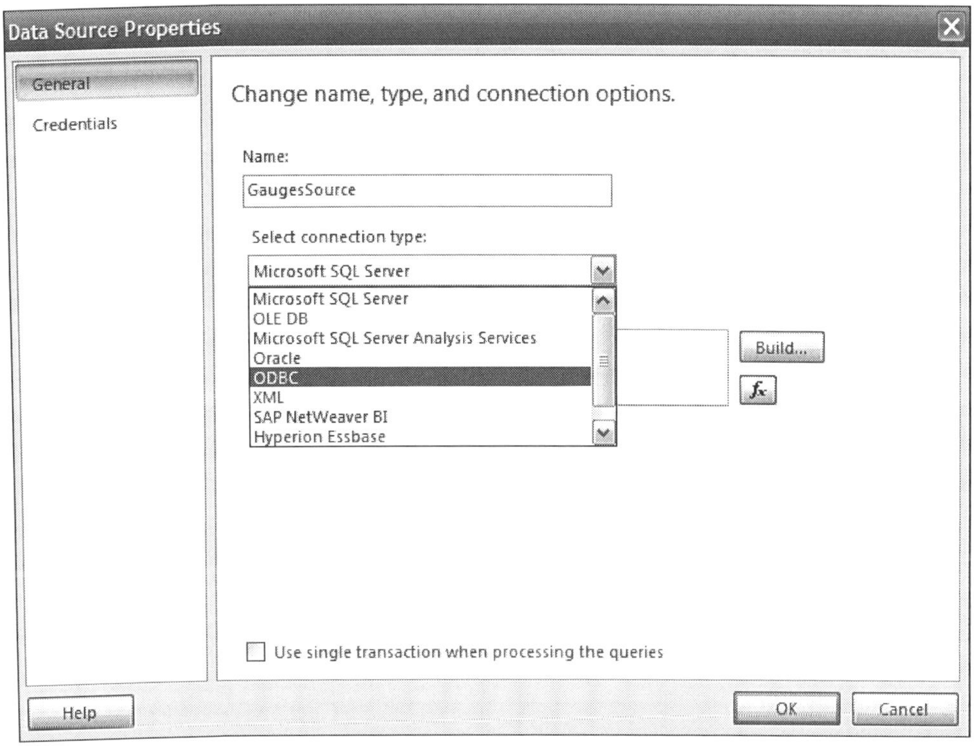

7. After choosing **ODBC** in the drop-down click on the **Build...** button.

   The **Connection Properties** window is displayed as shown:

8. Click on the **Build...** button in the **Connection Properties** window.
9. The **Select Data Source** window with the **File Data Source** tabbed page will be displayed.
10. Change over to the **Machine Data Source** window. Scroll up/down if necessary, highlight **Gauges** and click on the **OK** button.

    The **Select Work Book** window will come up.
11. Locate the **RptChart.xls** by browsing the folders and click on the **OK** button.
12. The DSN connection string will be entered into the **Connection Properties** window.
13. Click on the **Test Connection** window to verify that the connection is good.
14. Click on the **OK** button on the **Connection Properties** window.
15. The Connection string field in the **Data Source Properties** page will be updated with the connection information.

The Connection string is as follows:

```
Dsn=Gauges;
dbq=C:\DOCUMENTS AND SETTINGS\John Doe\MY DOCUMENTS\RptChart.
xls; defaultdir=C:\DOCUMENTS AND SETTINGS\John Doe\MY DOCUMENTS;
driverid=790;fil=excel 8.0;
maxbuffersize=2048; pagetimeout=5
```

16. Click on the **OK** button in the **Data Source Properties** window.

    The **GaugesSource** datasource is added to **Data Source Connections** list in the **New Table or Matrix** window and appears at the top of the list.

Create a Dataset based on the data in the Excel file

Data that gets displayed in a report is obtained from a dataset. In this section you will see how you get a dataset by using a query.

1. Click on the **Next** button in the **New Table or Matrix** window.
2. The **Design a query** page of the **New Table or Matrix** wizard is displayed.
3. Type in the following statement and hit on the (**!**)[Query run] button.

   ```
   Select * from [Sheet1$]
   ```

   The query is executed and the result is displayed as shown:

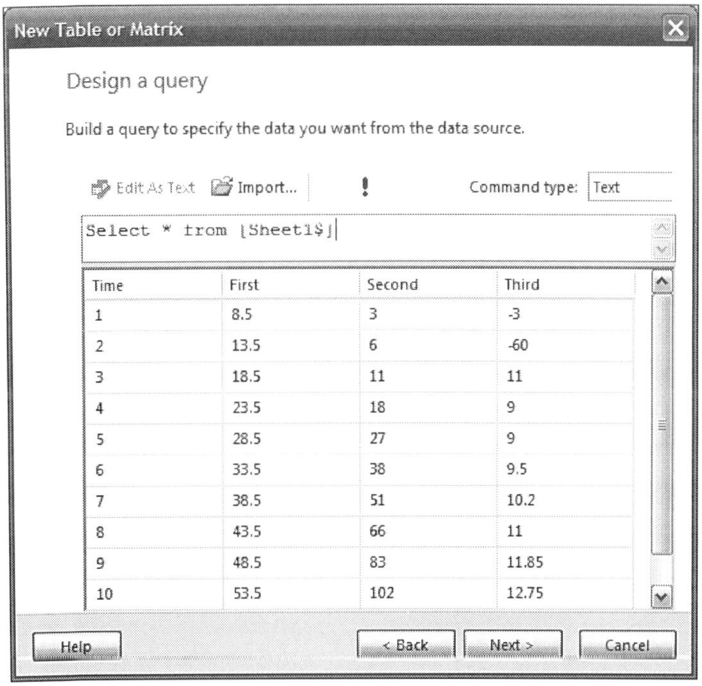

Design a report to display the data

Once the dataset is available then the report can be laid out to display this data. Again you will follow the wizard to fashion the report to display the data.

1. Click on the **Next** button.

   The **Arrange fields** page of the **New Table or Matrix** wizard gets displayed.

2. Click on **Time** and drop it on the **Values** field and drop each of **First, Second_,** (an underscore is appended to Second as it would represent a system variable otherwise) and the **Third** on the **Row groups** as shown:

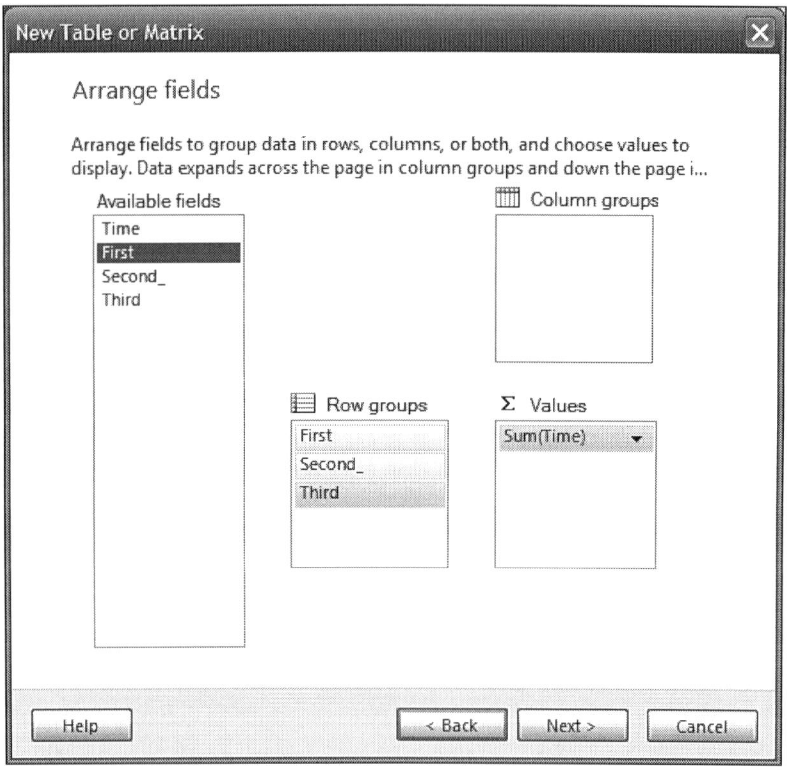

3. Click on the **Next** button to display the **Choose the layout** page of the wizard.
4. Click on the **Next** button on the **Choose the layout** page.
5. Choose a style (herein **Mahogany**) on the **Choose a style** page and click on the **Finish** button.

The report design gets displayed in the design surface of Report Builder as shown:

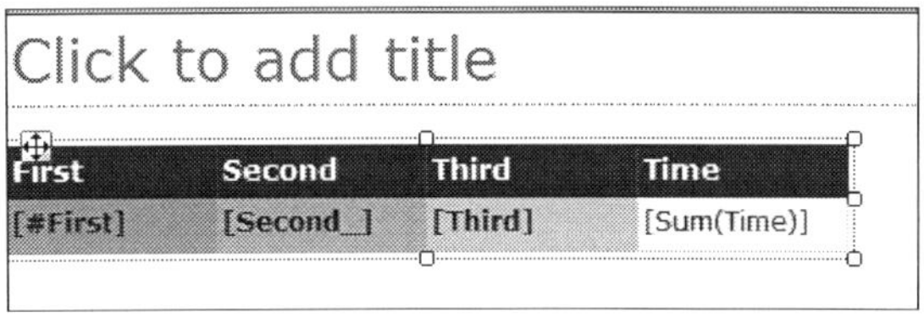

6. Run the report from **Home | Run (F5).**

   The report is displayed as shown in the following figure:

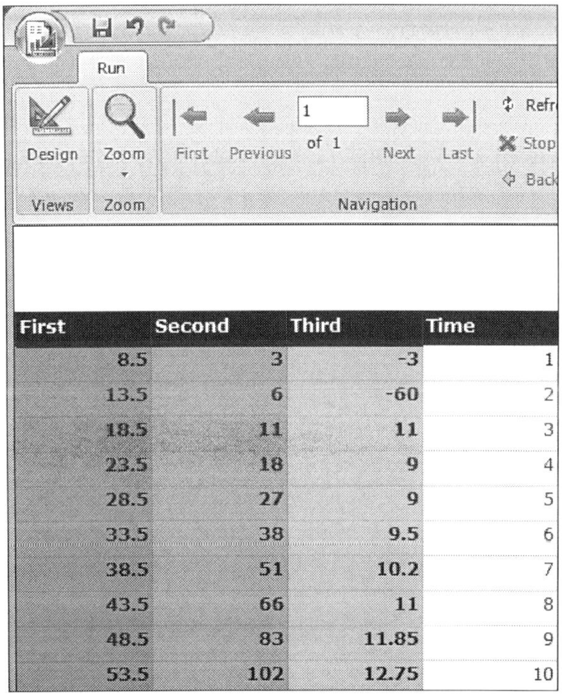

Format a column based on some criterion

In the above report in the third column, there is a wide variation in the value of the rows. The purpose of this is to demonstrate using a condition in the expression. This section shows how you may use the *Expression* to set the color of that textbox based on the value it contains when you run the report.

1. In the design of the report, select the textbox for the Third (third row second Column).

2. Right-click to access the textbox's properties.
3. In the Text Box Properties window, click on the navigation item Fill.
4. In the Fill page, click on the symbol *fx* to open the Expression window for the Fill Color.
5. In the Expression window, type in the expression as shown in the following screenshot.

   This screenshot has two windows superposed. By using this expression you are changing the background color of the textbox. The expression contains the value that will appear in the textbox. Now you are using the **Program Flow** function in the **Expression** window to coin the expression. The syntax of this function is also displayed in the **Expression** window. The expression contains a nested **IIF** function. If the value is greater than or equal to **10**, the background will be **Blue** otherwise the color will depend on another condition. If the value is greater than or equal to **1**, (must be less than 10 because of nesting) it will be **Yellow**. If less than **1** it will be **Red**.

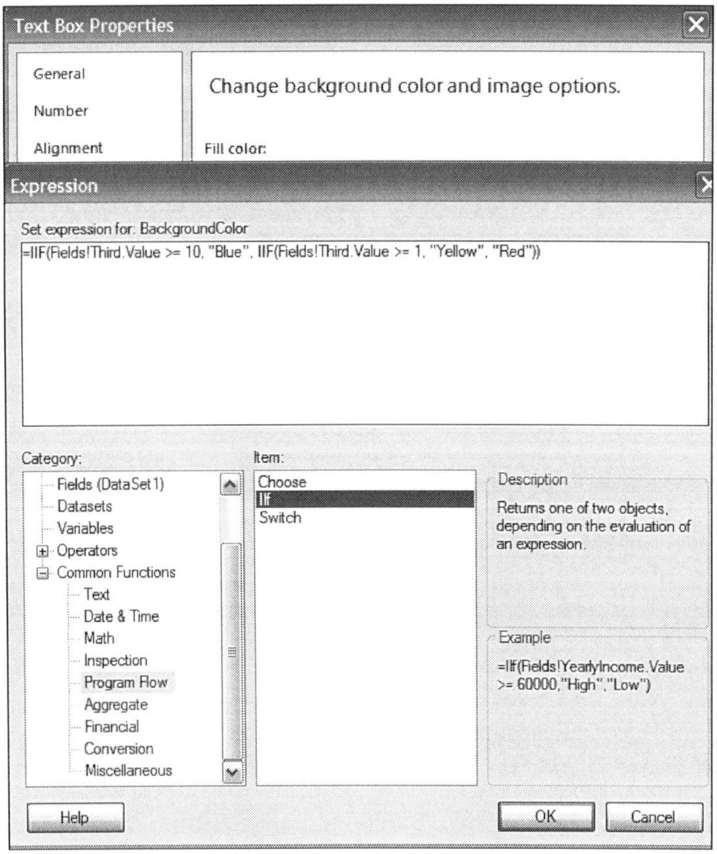

6. Click on the OK button in the Expression window and also on the OK button in the Text Box Properties window.
7. Run the report from the "ribbon".

   The report gets displayed as shown in the following screenshot:

First	Second	Third	Time
8.5	3	-3	1
13.5	6	-60	2
18.5	11	11	3
23.5	18	9	4
28.5	27	9	5
33.5	38	9.5	6
38.5	51	10.2	7
43.5	66	11	8
48.5	83	11.85	9
53.5	102	12.75	10

Create a chart to display the data

The chart you will be creating will be based on the data. You will be using the chart template to begin creating the chart. You will be using the placeholders on the chart to associate data with the details you will be displaying in the chart.

1. Return to the design view of the report by clicking on the Design button of the Run tab.
2. Enlarge the length of the report body by dragging down the bottom side of the report to create space for the chart.
3. Click on **Insert | Chart | Insert Chart** and then click in the space you created.

4. The **Select Chart Type** window gets displayed as described earlier. Accept the default choice and click on the **OK** button.

   This adds a chart template to the report as shown. All objects shown on the chart can be configured.

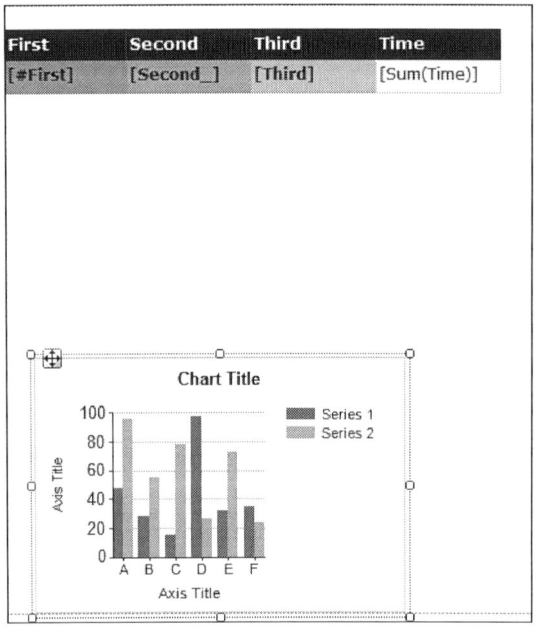

5. On double-clicking inside the chart, the drop data fields appear on the three sides of the chart as shown:

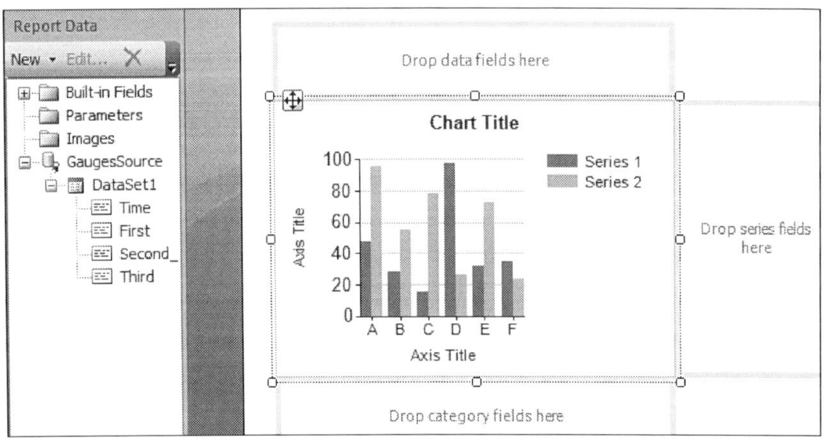

6. Click on **Time** in the **Report Data** and drag it over and drop it on the **Drop category fields here**.
7. Click on **First** in **Report Data** and drag it over and drop it on the **Drop data fields here**.
8. Repeat the previous step for the **Report Data** fields **Second_** and **Third**.
9. The design of the chart now appears as shown in the following screenshot showing the drop fields. The chart in the design view is not the data from the source but shows how the chart would look when rendered.

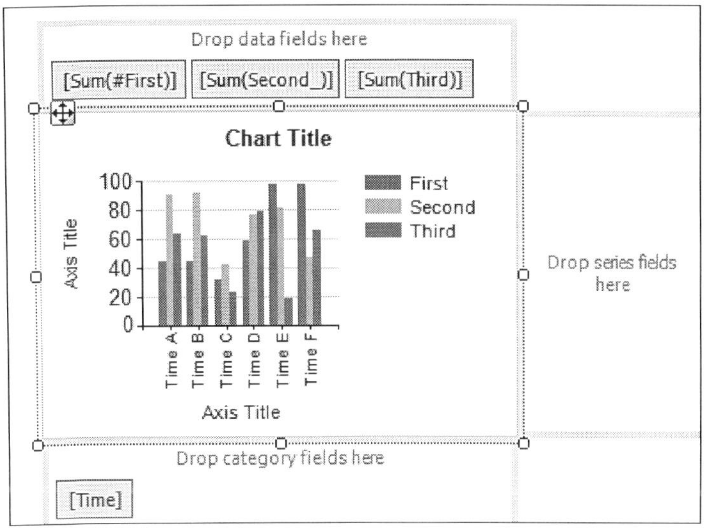

10. Run the report from the "ribbon".

    The chart in the report is displayed as shown:

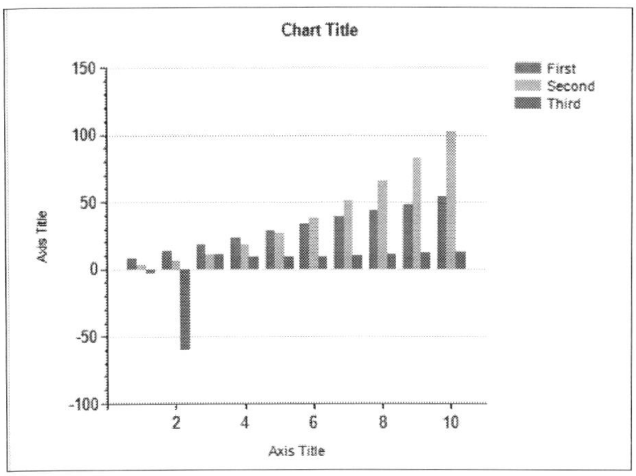

The chart data region has a large number of properties which allows you to fine tune the formatting of the chart. All properties are accessible in the design. The best place to obtain information is the online documentation (Help menu). In addition to the regular properties, the properties that you can assign using expressions provide even more options to format.

Add gauges to display the data

Gauges add visual features to enhance the aesthetic appearance as discussed earlier. However, whether gauges are more appealing than just data is a matter open for discussion. We will see how to add gauges here:

1. Click on the report to display the report handles. Right-click the last column and from the drop-down menu that gets displayed click on **Insert Column | Right.**

   This inserts an extra column on the right.

2. Click on **Insert | Gauge** and click on the **Data** cell of the new column you created.

   The **Select Gauge Type** gets displayed.

3. Accept the default that shows up and click on the **OK** button.

   A gauge gets placed in the cell as shown:

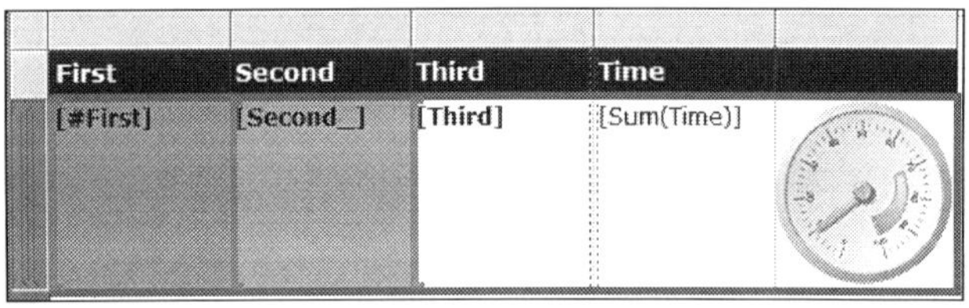

   The vertical side was extended to improve the display.

4. Double-click the gauge to display its configurable features as shown:

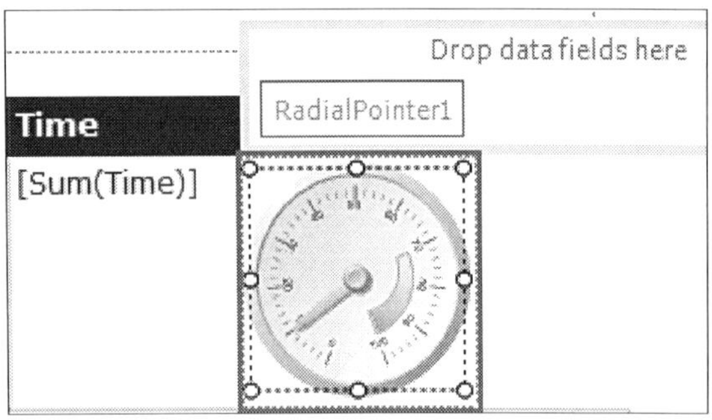

Let us say that this Gauge should represent the data in the second column of our report table.

5. Drag **Second_** from **Report Data** and drop it on the location **Drop Data fields here**.

   Alternatively you may also choose the drop-down from the data list icon that appears in that textbox when you hover over it.

6. Click on **Home | Run** to process and display the report.

   The report gets displayed as shown (only part of it shown).

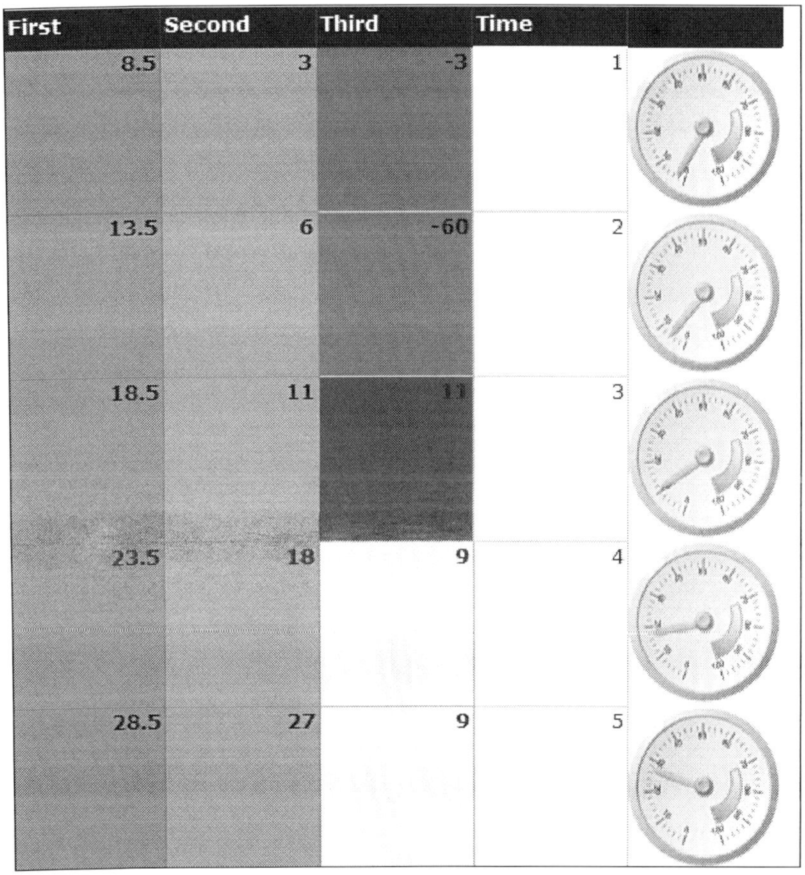

Observe that the gauge needle is pointing at the values in the **Second_**column.

Add a report item to display the average value of a column

Gauges can show not only item data but they can also be used to show aggregates such as SUM, Average and so on. In this section, you will be creating another display type of a gauge and associating the average value of a column.

1. Right-click the data cell of second column (second column, second row).
2. Choose from the drop-down menu **Insert Row | Outside Group Below.**
3. Right-click the inserted textbox to access the properties of the **Tablix** as shown and click on **Outside Group Below**.

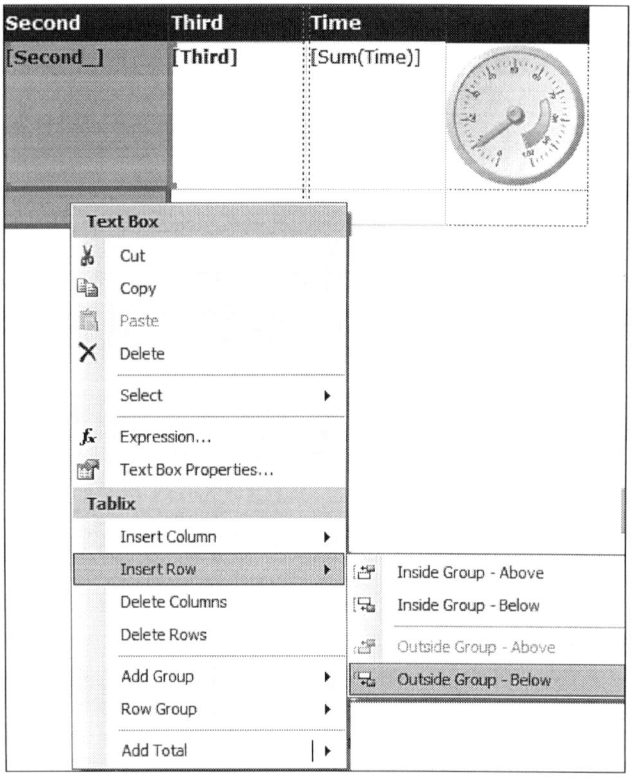

This adds a textbox outside the group for the second column as shown in the following screenshot:

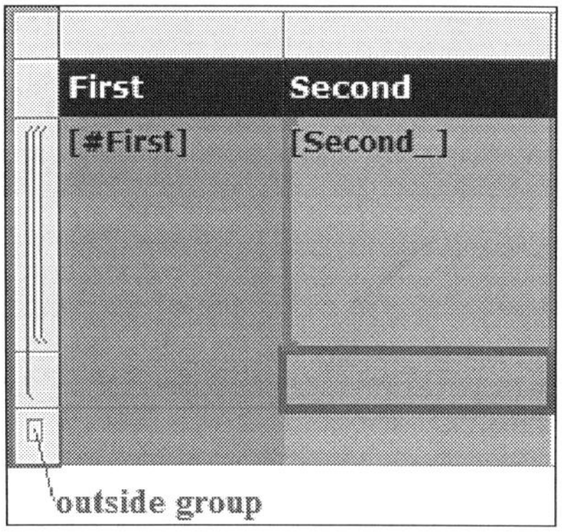

4. Right-click the inserted textbox and click on **Expression...**.
5. At the top, in the **Set expression** pane type in `="Avg= " &`.
6. Expand the category **Common Functions**. Click on **Aggregate** to expand. In the **Item** field double-click **Avg**.
7. The **Set expression for: Value** gets filed with `"="Avg= "& Avg ("`.
8. Now click on **Fields (DataSet1)** and in the **Values:** field double-click **Second_**.
9. The expression now becomes `"="Avg= " & Avg(Fields!Second_.Value"`.
10 Close the parentheses to make the expression complete as shown:

```
="Avg= " & Avg (Fields!Second_.Value)
```

11. The textbox you created now gets this expression.
12. Click **Home | Run** to run the report. It is displayed as shown in the following screenshot, on the second page of the report.

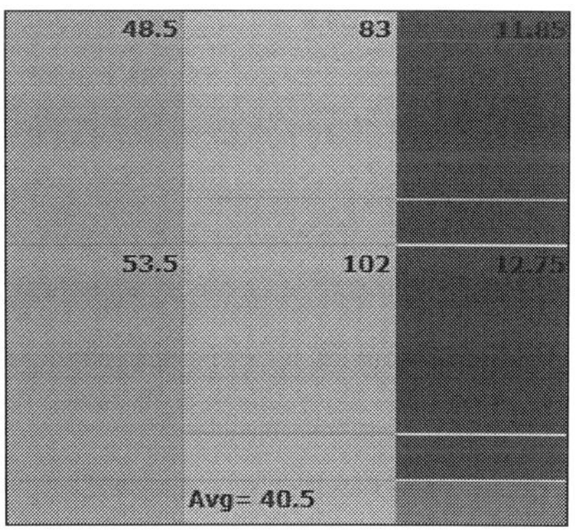

Add a gauge to display this average

In this section you will add a single gauge in the same column as the others but outside the group, and set its value to represent the group average of the second column:

1. Click **Insert | Gauge** and drop it on the intersection of the last row. This row is outside the group and the column containing the gauge from the previous section.

   The **Select Gauge Type** gets displayed.
2. Select the default **Linear** type (the first one).

   The linear type gauge gets added to the report.
3. From the dataset, click on **Second_** to add it to the gauge as shown:

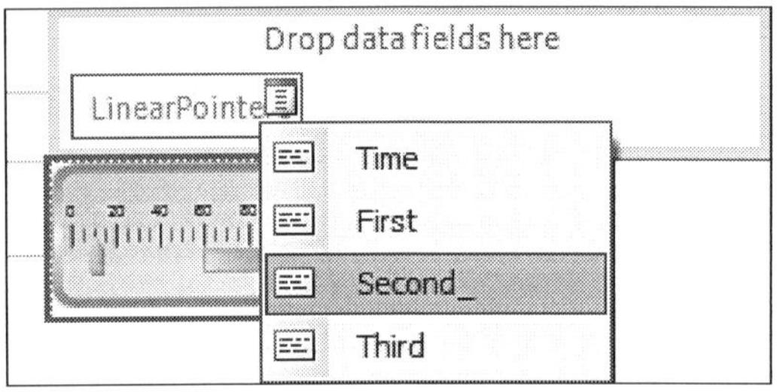

4. Now the **Linear Pointer** gets the value **[Sum (Second_)].**
5. Right-click the **Linear Pointer** and choose to review the **Pointer Properties....**

   The **Linear Pointer Properties** window gets displayed as shown:

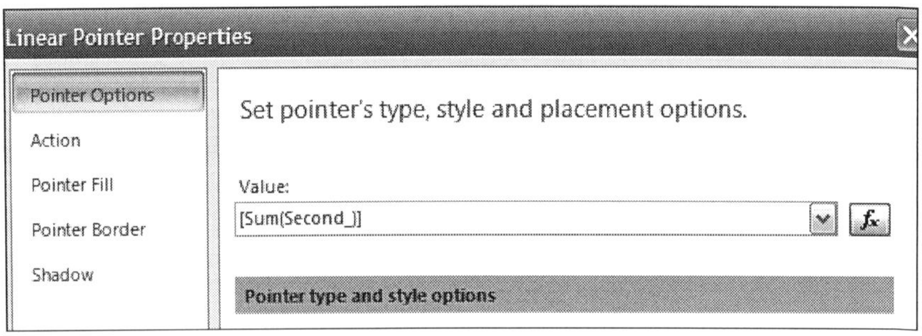

6. Click *fx* to open the **Expression** window and alter the value displayed to the following.

   ```
   =Avg(Fields!Second_.Value)
   ```
7. Close the **Expression** window and close the **Linear Pointer Properties** window.

8. Run the report from **Home | Run.**

   The report gets displayed as shown (only the relevant part is shown):

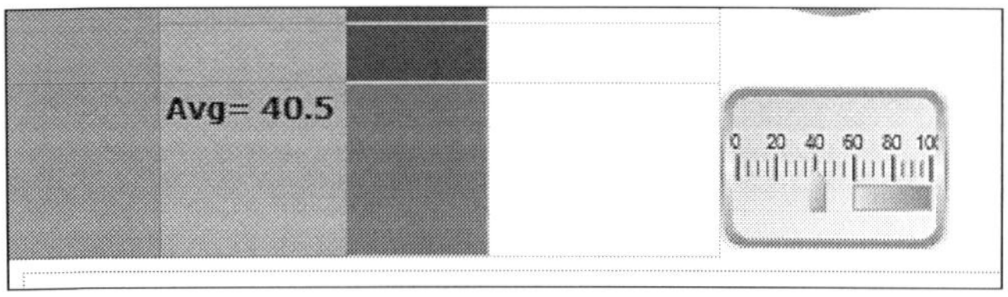

The linear gauge now displays the same average value as seen in the above screenshot. There is a row and a textbox that do not have any data shown in the above (row above and the textbox to the right of the average) and these may be prevented from showing up by using the hide property.

Create a bookmark and jump to it

Bookmarks are also like hyperlinks in web pages but they jump to another part in the same document. Microsoft Word supports adding bookmarks to several locations in the document and makes a provision to jump to them. In web pages, the same is achieved by having links and anchors (`http://www.w3.org/TR/REC-html40/struct/links.html`). In this section you will create a bookmark for the title of **Second Column**. This way when you click on the **Second** series on the chart, the display changes to the second column title.

Create a bookmark using the Bookmark property

You need to create a bookmark first:

1. Click **View** and place a check mark in the **Properties** checkbox.

   This allows you to access the **Properties** window for all objects in the report. right-clicking on an object shows only a limited number of available properties.

2. In the design view of the report click on the **Second** column title.
3. In its **Properties** window type in the text **Go to data** for its **Bookmark** property. This is shown in the following screenshot:

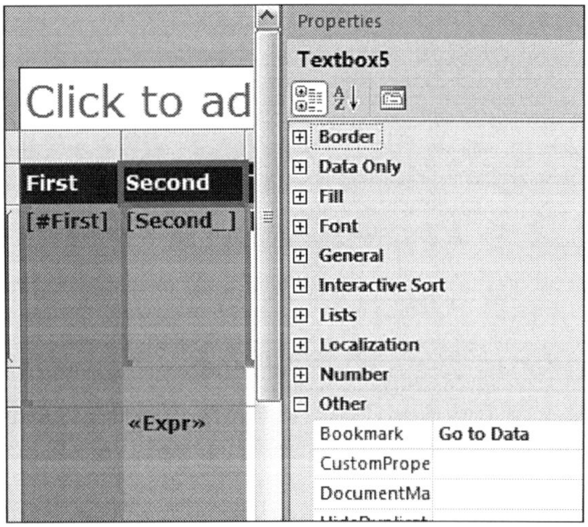

Jump to bookmark using the Action property

There are basically two steps in order to have the ability to jump to a known location. The first step is to create a bookmark and the next step is jump to it. Different parts of the report builder are used and this section shows how you may do it.

1. In the design view of the chart, click on the series **Second_** as shown and set its **Action** property to **Go to Data** as shown:

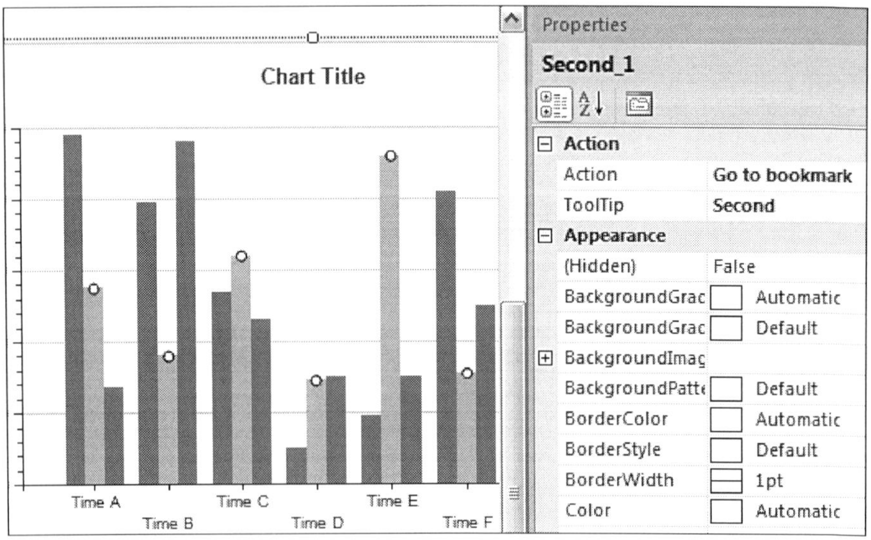

2. Run the report from **Home | Run.**
3. Verify that only the series **Second_** in the chart takes you to the top of the report.

Summary

The Report Builder 2.0 tool is described in full starting from the top to the bottom of this interface. Creating reports with this tool is described using an existing report and modifying it as well as creating a new report from data. Embedding charts and gauges are also described. Some of the interactive and rich text features are also discussed.

Report Builder 1.0 is briefly mentioned but its utility for reports models created using VS 2008 or BIDS did not warrant an example due to current limitations. It may be possible to use this tool with Report Models created with an earlier version of SQL Server. One of the main features of Report Builder 2.0 is its ability to create Ad Hoc reports and this will be described in detail in the next chapter. The reader may notice slight differences in the look of the interfaces slightly at variance depending on the version of the SQL Server 2008 and Report Builder 2.0 used.

7 Report Authoring with Report Builder 2.0

This chapter is all about Report authoring using Report Builder 2.0. In this chapter, you will be doing most of the Report authoring yourself. Sometimes you may use the wizards and sometimes you will do it from scratch. You will be building many types of reports. Of these, the snapshot and cached reports were described in Chapter 5, but you will be working with the rest of the report types in this chapter.

In the hands-on exercises you will be specifically working with the following:

- Parameterized reports
- Column grouping and creating a document map
- Sub-reports and drill-down
- Linked reports
- Drillthrough report
- Report with an XML data document source
- Ad hoc tabular report
- Ad hoc matrix report with a Report Model

As far as ad hoc reporting is concerned, it is the type of report a business user (decision maker) would like to see in order to make some decisions. Hosting a report or making a hard copy immediately is not his concern. The user wants to create his own view of the global data available to him which he wants to message to gather his intelligence in an interactive mode. The user will use the Report Model for this and you (the reader) will be working with the Report Model created in Chapter 6.

Report authoring

Report writing starts with planning like most of the other activities. Some of the key considerations are:

- Audience
- Report structure
- Look and feel of report
- Report visibility related to security
- Report delivery format
- Canned or ad hoc
- Web or desktop
- Internet or intranet

Although these considerations are separately listed they are interconnected. Details of some of these considerations are discussed in the previous chapters.

This chapter is not about planning but about using the Report Builder 2.0 tool to author reports of different kinds that are normally encountered. Of course there are others that require custom treatment. Visual Studio 2008 and Report Builder 2.0 have the same set of tools and most of what you do in one can be done with the other. Visual Studio 2008 is capable of creating both *Server* and *Client* based reports (as related to reporting activity) and Report Builder creates *Server* (hosted) reports. However, to publish server reports to the web server would require Visual Studio. You may also create a web hosted report based on a server report using Visual Studio.

Hands-on exercise 7.1: Filtering data at source using a query parameter

It is not often that you want the entire set of data from a database. In fact it is counter productive in terms of resources and bandwidths to seek a large amount of retrieved data. What is needed is a surgical procedure to get just the right data. Using parameters to filter the data is very essential. Perhaps you are looking for people with a certain last name or a social security number in a certain state. After filtering the data for the state you may filter for the person using his last name or social security number. These are the types of scenarios you associate with filtering data. In this hands-on you will be using a query parameter to filter data.

Parameterized reports

Filtering the data is an essential part of effectively retrieving relevant data in a short time.

A parameterized report depends on the report reader typing in the specific parameter to complete the processing of the report. The output of a parameterized report would depend on the parameter(s). Parameterized reports are frequently used in creating drillthrough reports, linked reports and sub-reports.

There are two kinds of parameters used in Report Builder 2.0. There are Report parameters as well as Query parameters. Query parameters are used at the source of data during data retrieval. For the query parameter, a value must be specified by the user (or a default value provided) to complete the processing of the `SELECT` statement or the stored procedure in the query. The usage of query parameters requires you to make trips to the server for processing the query as the data is first processed before it is used in the report.

Report parameters are used during report processing with most data available at hand where the filtering is made. Hence, report parameters work on a larger dataset and they are processed in the report.

Follow on

In order to proceed with this exercise you need to open Report Builder 2.0 from its shortcut. You should also make sure you have started the Reporting Services.

In the Report Builder, click on the **Table** or **Matrix** wizard at the centre of the design area.

The **New Table or Matrix** window opens. It displays the existing data sources and their folders. These were the ones you created in earlier chapters. In this hands-on a new datasource will be created.

Creating a data source

The very first thing to do is to get connected to the data source.

1. Click on the **New...** button.

   The **Data Source Properties** window gets displayed. You can choose a variety of databases from which you can use the data. The ODBC and OLEDB can support a much larger number than the others.

2. Click on the **Build...** button (the **fx** button is not useful just now).

   The **Connection Properties** window shows on top of the **Data Source Properties** window.

3. Click on the **Refresh...**button and choose the server from which you are retrieving the data (herein, **Hodentek2\SANGAM**). Use the database you are retrieving the data from.

   Enter authentication information (herein **Windows Authentication** is appropriate). Click on the drop-down handle for **Select or enter a database name** and choose **TestNorthwind**. Test the connection by hitting the **Test Connection** button.

4. Click on **OK** on the **Test Results** window and the **Connection Properties** window.

   The **Connection Properties** gets entered into the **Data Source Properties** window.

5. Click **OK** on the **Data Source Properties** window.

   You will be back in the **New Table** or **Matrix** window. Your new connection is at the top of this window.

6. Click the **Edit...** button and change the name to something different, herein **QryParam.**

Query design

1. With **QryParam** highlighted, click on the **Next** button in the **New Table or Matrix** window.

The **Design a query** page of the **New Table or Matrix** window gets displayed as shown. The figure shows the **Tables** node expanded.

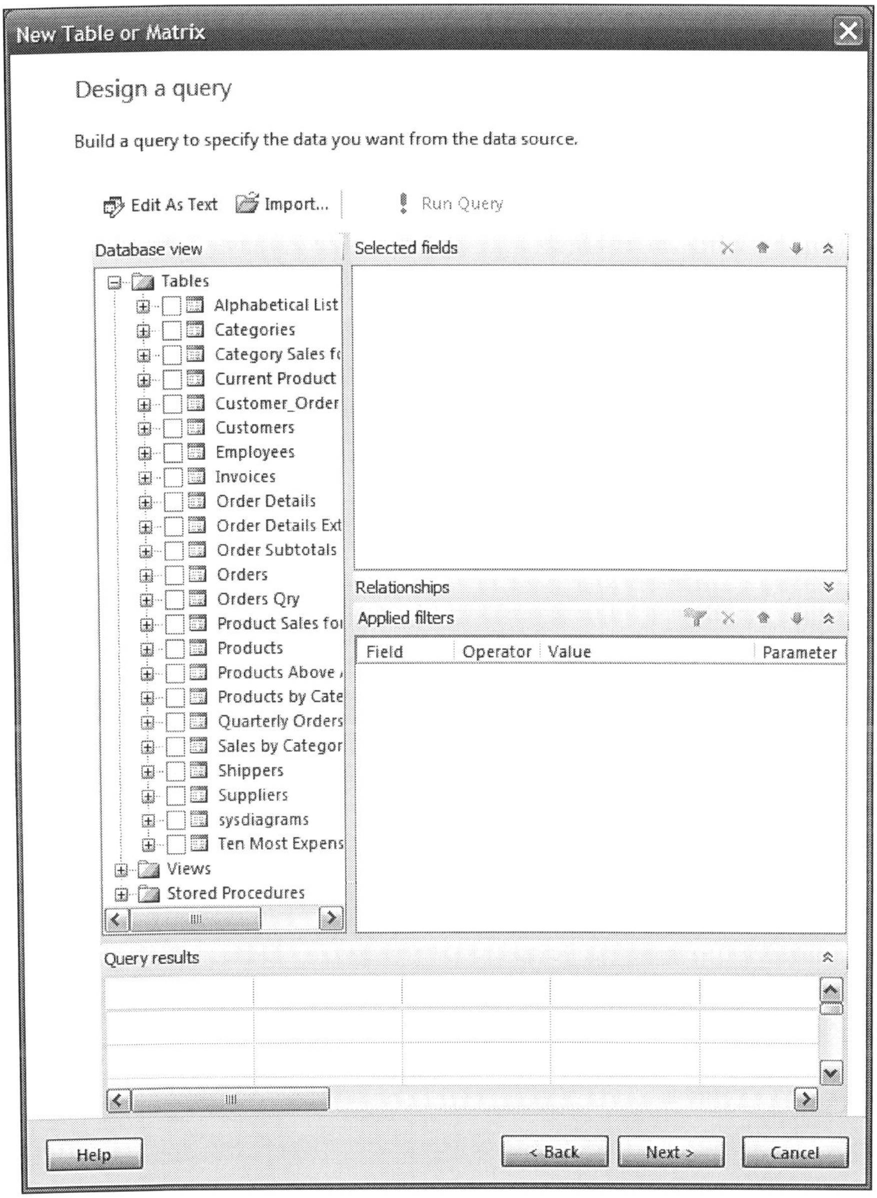

2. Click on the **Customers** table and place checkmarks for the following: **CustomerID, CompanyName, Address, City, Region, and Country**.

   As each checkmark is placed, the corresponding column gets added to the selected field's panel as shown:

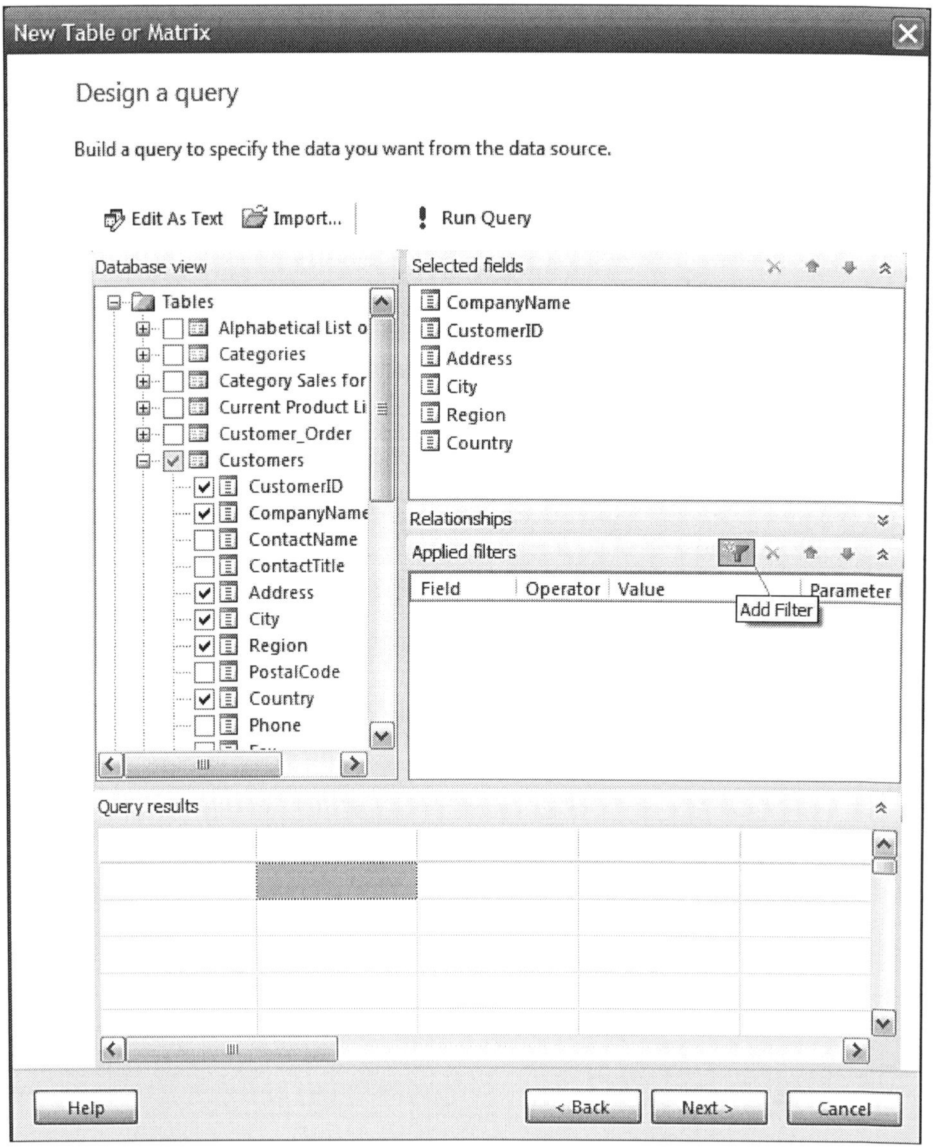

Parameter design

1. Click on the filter icon showing the text **Add Filter** just above the **Applied filters** pane.

   The table for filtering develops as shown with the first field **Company Name** as shown (only part of **New Table or Matrix** window is shown).

   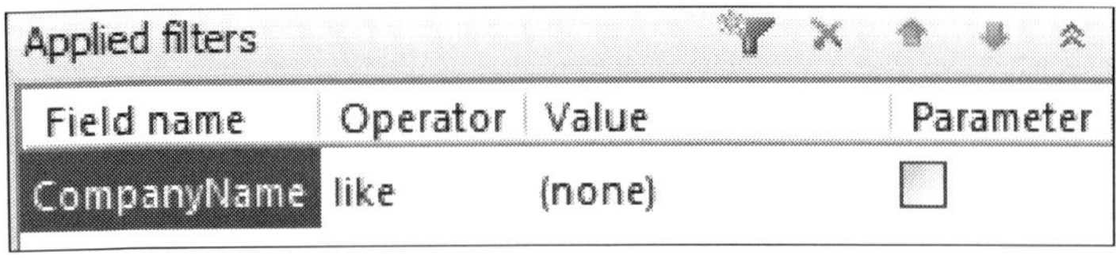

2. Click on the default **CompanyName** below the **Field** name column and then click on **City** in the drop-down menu as shown:

   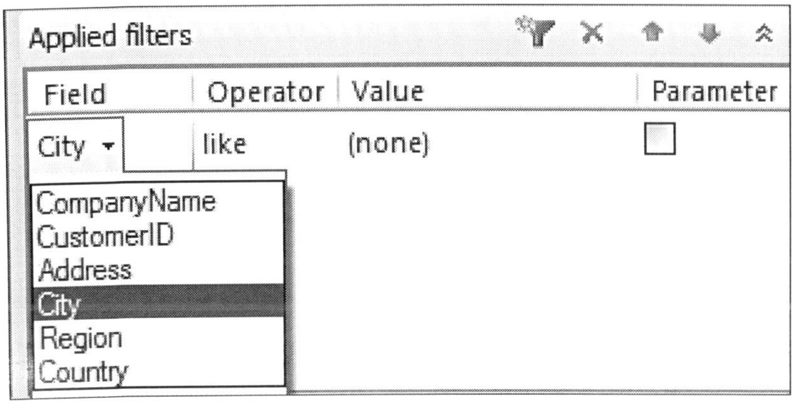

   The column, **City**, is going to be the parameter that will be used for filtering the data. You can use any other field as the parameter. You may also choose more than one parameter.

3. Click on **Like** under the **Operator** column and choose **is** from the list.

4. Click on **none** under the column **Value** and enter a city name (any name would do, herein **Japan** was entered) and place a checkmark in the **Parameter** column. This gets entered into the **Query Designer** as shown in the next screenshot. When the report gets displayed, **Japan** will appear as the default city. As **Japan** is not one of the cities there will be no data on the displayed report. But, by changing the parameter value you will be able to access the data for other cities.

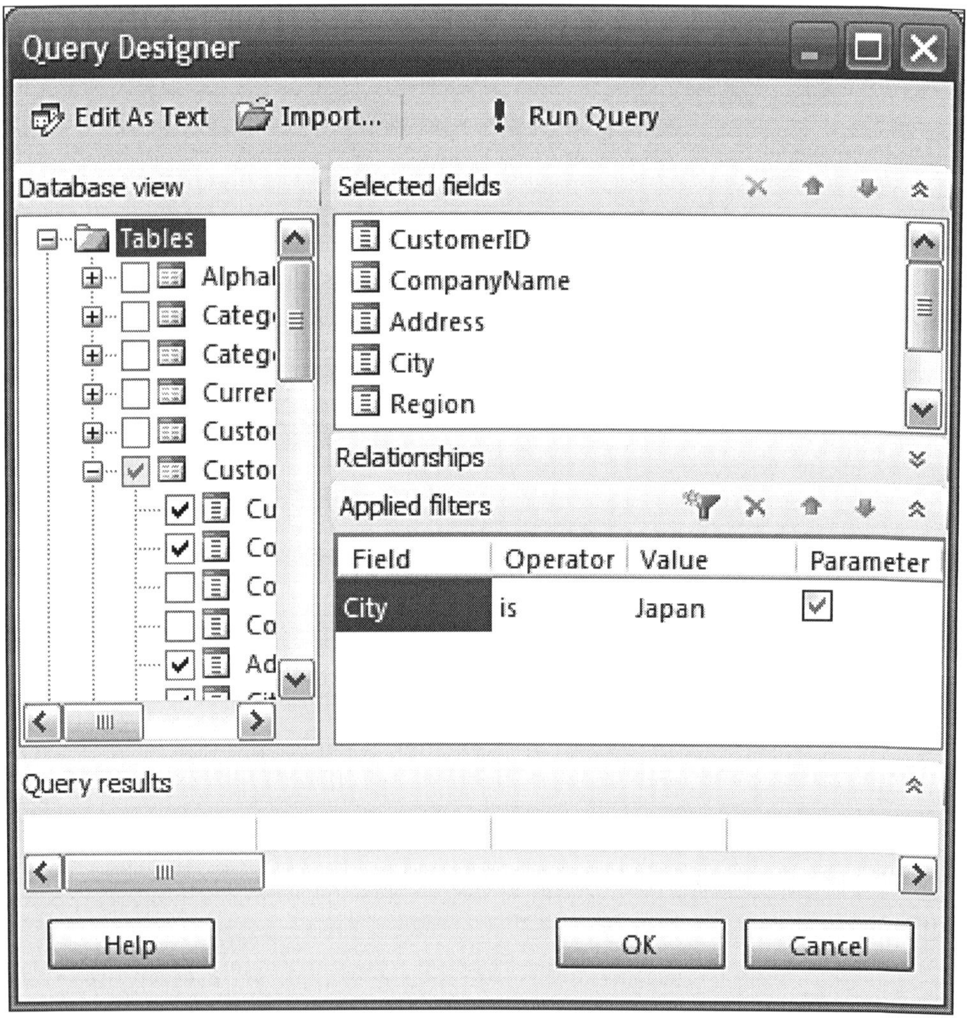

5. Click on the Next button.

   The **Arrange Fields** page of the **New Table or Matrix** wizard gets displayed showing all the available fields. Although grouping of fields can be specified here, you will be just displaying the data without grouping.

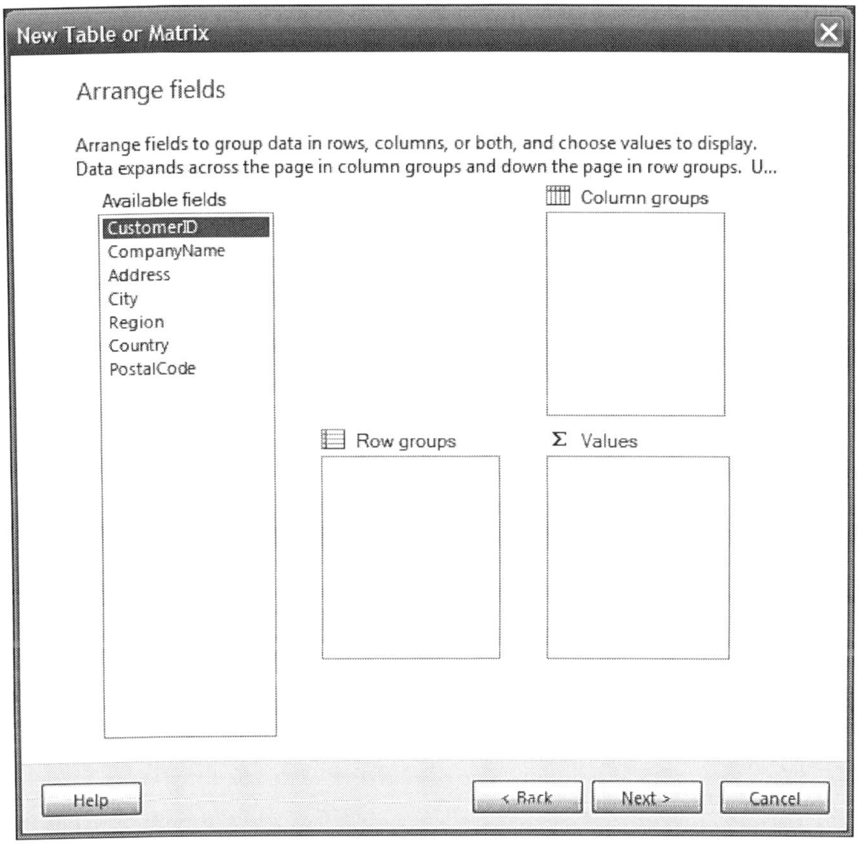

6. Click on **CustomerID** and drag it over to the **Values** panel (right bottom). Similarly drag-and-drop the rest of the available fields and drop them in the **Values** panel.

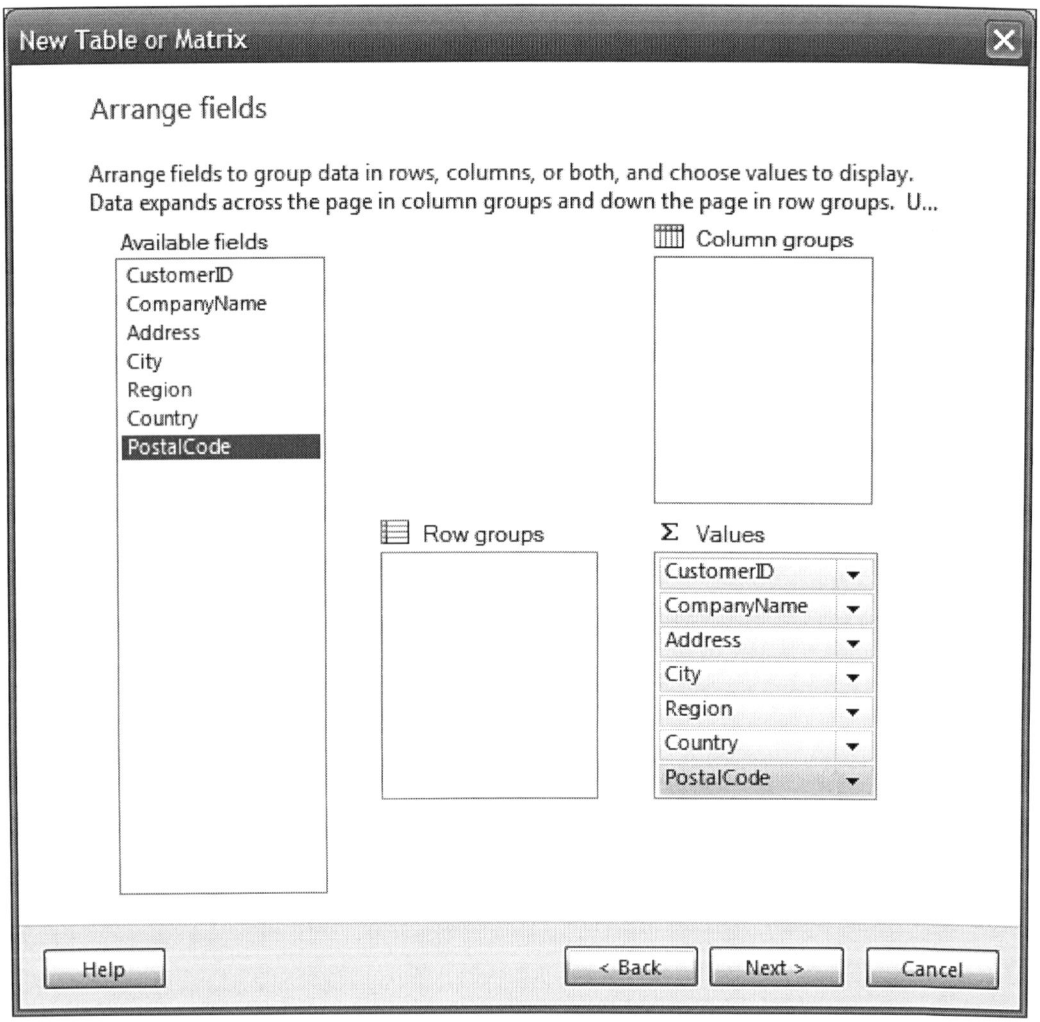

7. Click on the **Next** button.

   The **Choose the layout** page gets displayed. All options are greyed out as you will not be using them for this exercise.

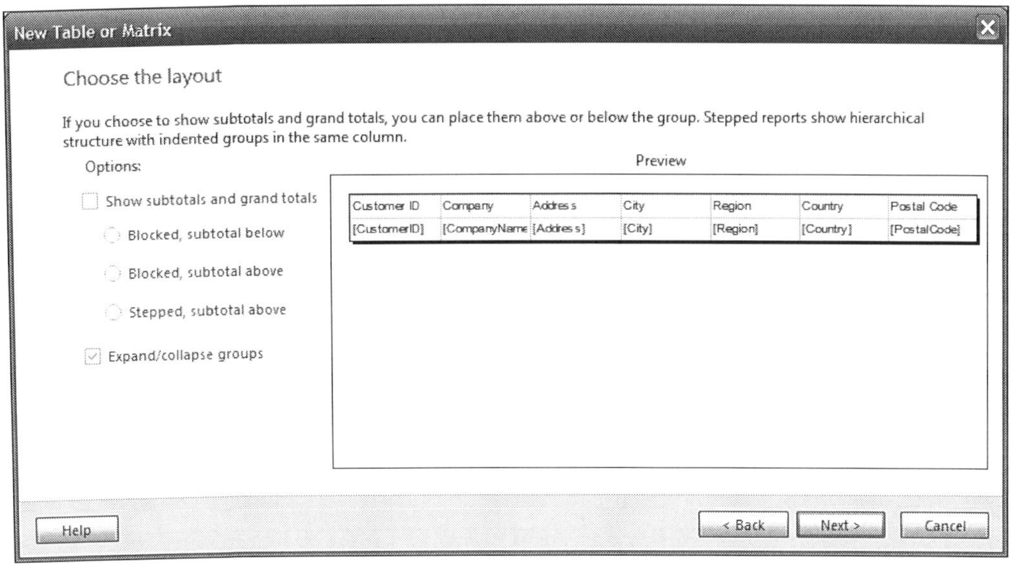

8. Click on the **Next** button.
9. In the **Choose a style** window, accept the default and click on the **Finish** button.

   The Report Builder gets displayed showing your finished report in the design area and the **QryParam** datasource on the left from which the dataset **Dataset1** has been derived by the query. Observe that there is no parameter related object in the design view.

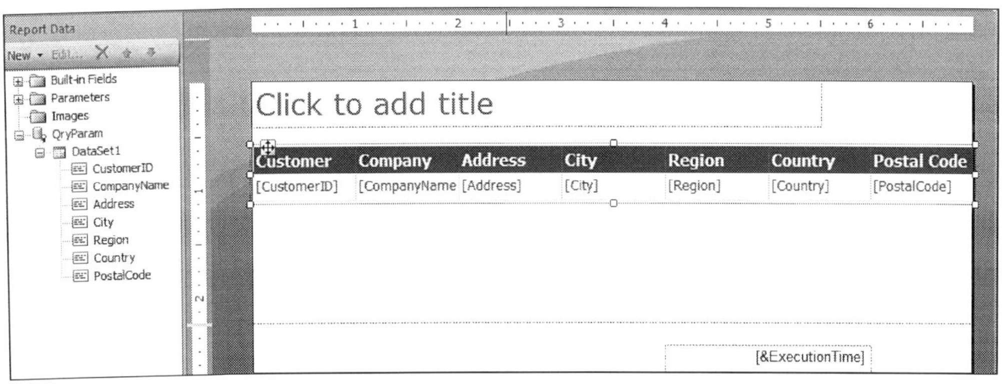

10. Right-click on **Dataset1** as shown in the following screenshot:

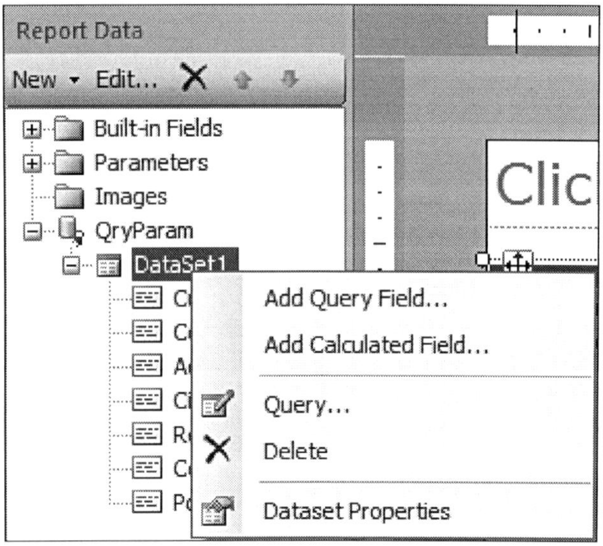

You can do a lot of modification to the dataset as described in the following section.

11. Click on the **Dataset Properties** from the drop-down.

The **Dataset Properties** window displaying the query that was prepared by the wizard is as shown. You can see that the parameter has been configured in the `WHERE` clause of the query.

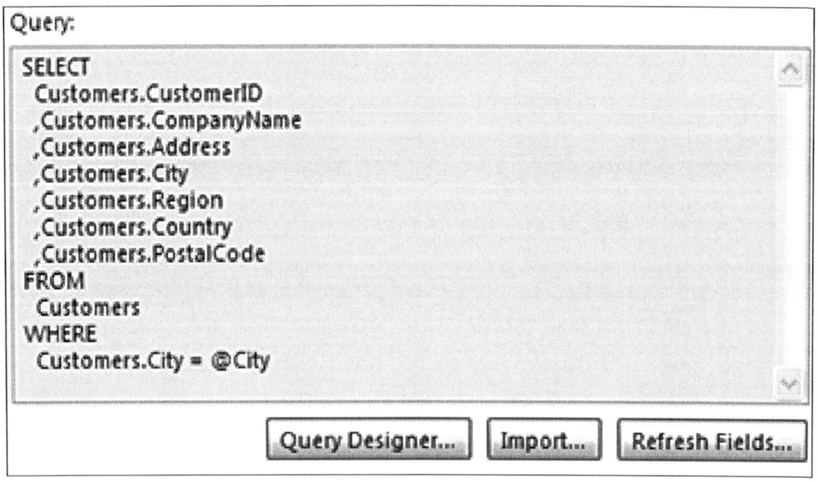

12. Click on the **Parameters** in the navigation column of the **Dataset Properties** window on the left.

    The **Choose query parameter values** page gets displayed as shown. Here you can **Add** or **Delete** parameters.

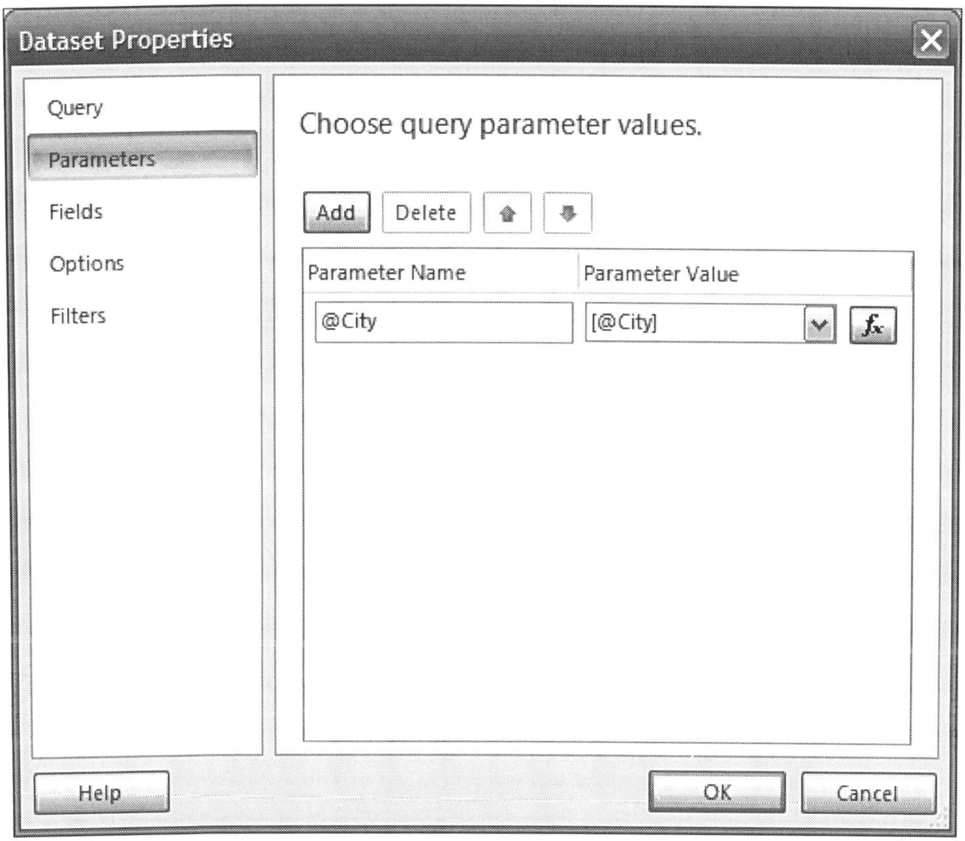

13. Clicking on **Fields** will display all the columns that are in the report. You may add or delete columns here.
14. Clicking on **Options** (collation, case sensitivity, accent sensitivity) and **Filters** (add or delete) can be used to further fine-tune the report.
15. Click **OK** for the **Dataset Properties** window.

Viewing the Report

1. In the **Home** menu, click on the **Run** icon in the **Views** section.

   After some processing, the yet to be named report is displayed as shown:

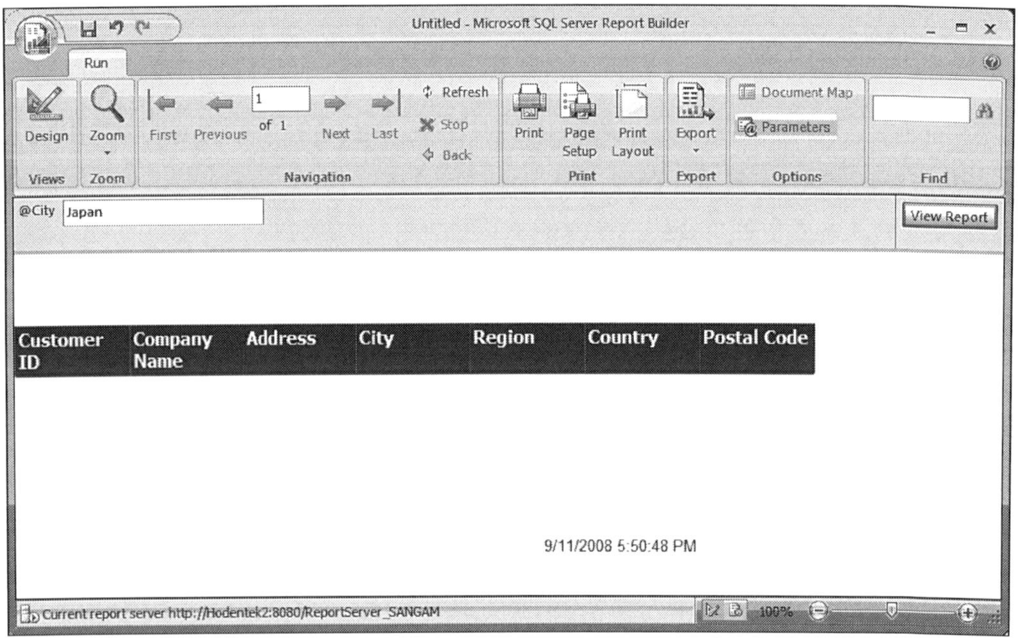

   There is no data because the table has no row where the **City** column has a value **Japan**. The parameter is shown at top left **@City**. The name of the server on which the report is processed is at the bottom.

   There is a control at the bottom right to control the size of the display. The "(100% slide bar) Zoom" in the **Run** page can be used. If there is more than one piece of data, the navigation would become enabled. It is also possible to print from this page and set up the printer.

2. Click on **Export** and verify the different formats.

   The drop-down list shows the different formats that one can use to export the report.

3. Click on **Parameters** in the **Options** section of the **Run** tab.

   The drop-down shows whether the **Parameter** pane is hidden or displayed (this toggles). Using the **Find** button you may be able to search for items on the report.

4. Delete **Japan** and enter **London** in its place and click on the **View Report** button.

   The report for the parameter **London** is displayed as shown:

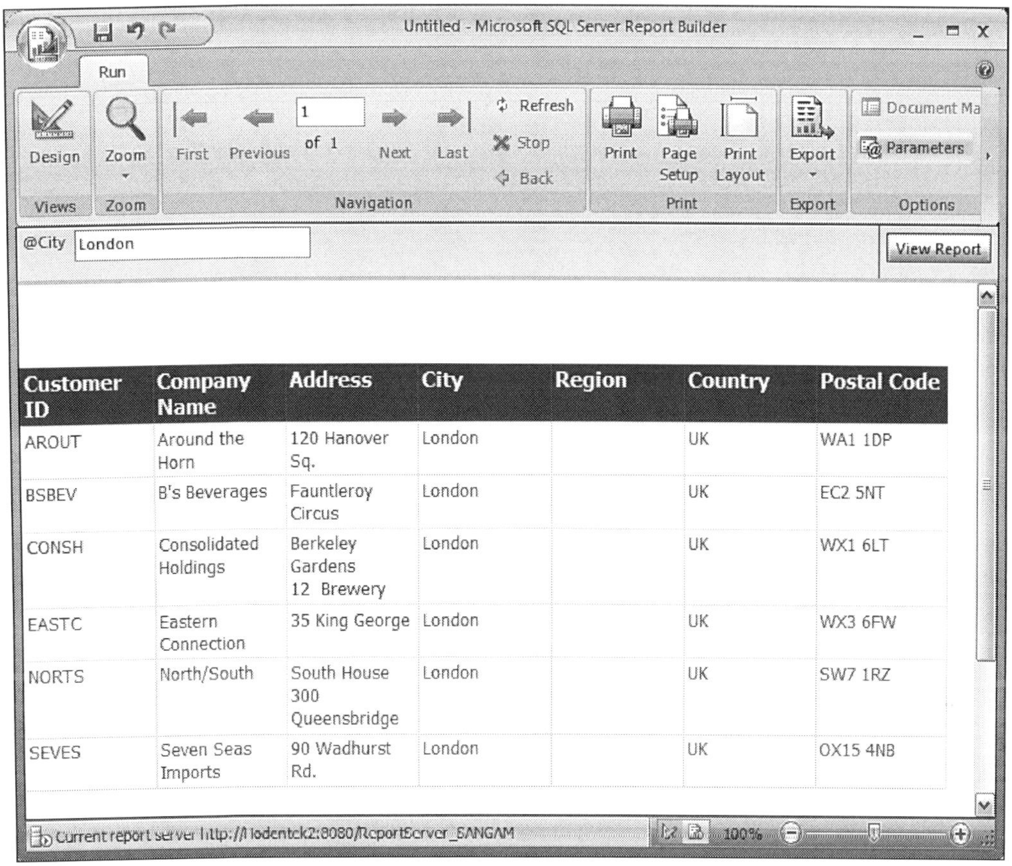

5. Click **Office Button | Save As** and save the report with some name (herein **QryReport**).

   As mentioned earlier it gets saved to the Report Server with the same default value.

6. Open the Report Server by providing its URL in the IE browser.
7. In the Report Server page you can see the **QryReport** in the listed contents.

In order to use the above report the user has to know what the query parameter is. When reports are requested with the user sending a query, it is a good practice to allow users to pick query parameters through pick lists. On the other hand, if the user is allowed to enter a query string you may be compromising the security (via SQL injection attacks). Hence, a drop-down list to select the parameter would be very helpful. This can also be designed as you will do in *Hands-on 7.3*.

Hands-on exercise 7.2: Working with a column group and setting up a document map

A group is a named set of data from the report dataset that you bind to a data region. You will use a simple example of this in this hands-on. There could be many other groups as well. The layout designer in Report Builder 2.0 assigns this intuitively. You could have groupings by rows or columns. We will be using groups in most of the hands-on without explicitly mentioning it.

In the previous hands-on you created a query which had a parameter in it. You later associated this with the report. As a first step, you will modify the query to drop the parameter. Once the parameter is dropped, you have no filtering and you will get all the rows. To work with groups, you will start with this set from a single dataset datasource.

Follow on

Here, the parameters will be removed and groupings on columns will be made. You will then "group" the data based on `City`. You will use this report for learning about document map and interactive sorting.

Removing the parameter from the previous hands-on

Parameters can be removed as easily as they can be added. This greatly helps in modifying reports after they are designed. Herein, you will start with the report and remove the parameters.

1. Double-click **Dataset1** in **Report Data.**

   This brings up the **Dataset Properties** window.

2. Click on **Parameters** in this page.

   This opens the **Choose query parameter values** page.

3. Click anywhere just below **Parameter name** field on this page.

   The parameter gets highlighted.

4. Now click on the **Delete** button.
5. Click **OK** to the **Dataset Properties** page.

   If you try to run the report you will get an error message.

6. Expand the **Parameters** folder under **Report Data** and delete the parameter **@City** by right-clicking on it and choosing **Delete**.

   This is still not sufficient to delete the parameter.

7. Right-click **Dataset1** and click on the **Query** icon.
8. In the **Applied Filters,** delete the parameter for the filter **City** using the **Delete** button (red icon next to the funnel icon for a filter).
9. Click on the **OK** button on the query designer.

Now when you run the report you will see all the data for the `Select` query without the `WHERE` clause. You have succeeded in removing the parameter.

Group the results by "City"

After removing the parameter, your report is a tabular report, which returns a number of columns. Now you will group the rows based on **City**.

1. Highlight the **City** column and right-click to delete the column **City** by choosing **Delete Columns** from the drop-down.
2. Right-click on the row handle of the table for the group and choose **Add Group | Parent Group** as shown:

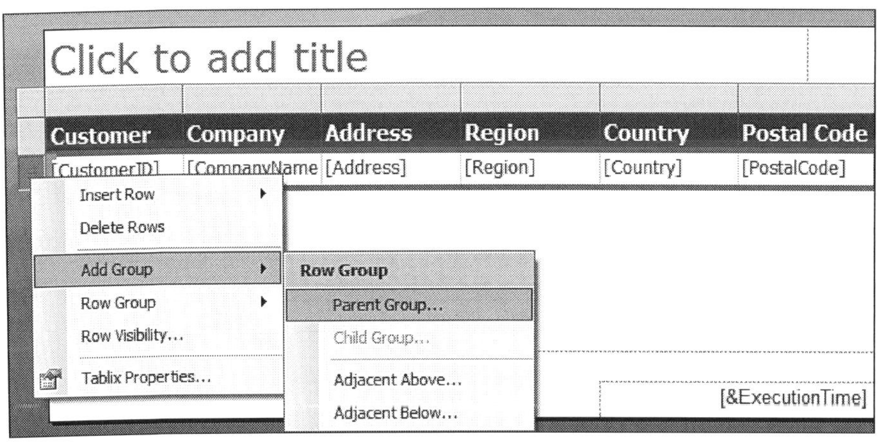

This brings up the **Tablix group** window as shown:

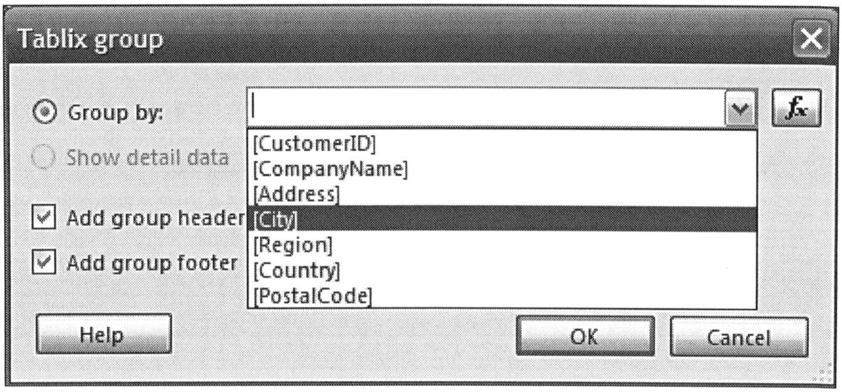

3. Choose **[City]** in the drop-down list, check both the checkboxes and click on the **OK** button.

   The report design now changes to the one shown next figure.

> Alternatively you can just drag the **City** from **Report Data** and drop it on the **Row Groups** in the Report.

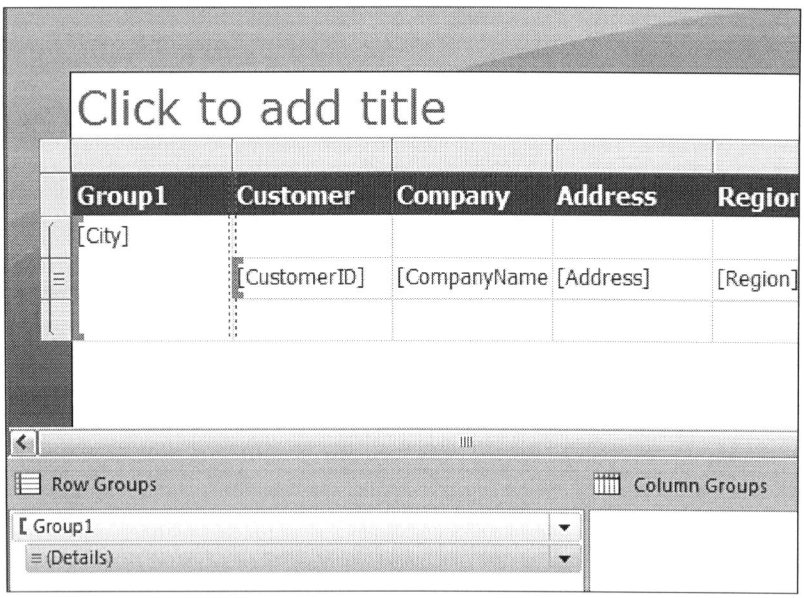

4. Click on **Home** | **Run** to run the report.

   You will see that the report has returned rows in groups of cities.

Adding a Document Map for the report

Document Map is a navigational feature that, when implemented, allows the user to navigate through the document and its hierarchies. When a document map is added, an extra side panel is added to the report much like the "List of Chapters" in a book. You can jump to a directed location from the navigation list.

1. Right-click on the row group and choose **Row Group** | **Group Properties...** as shown:

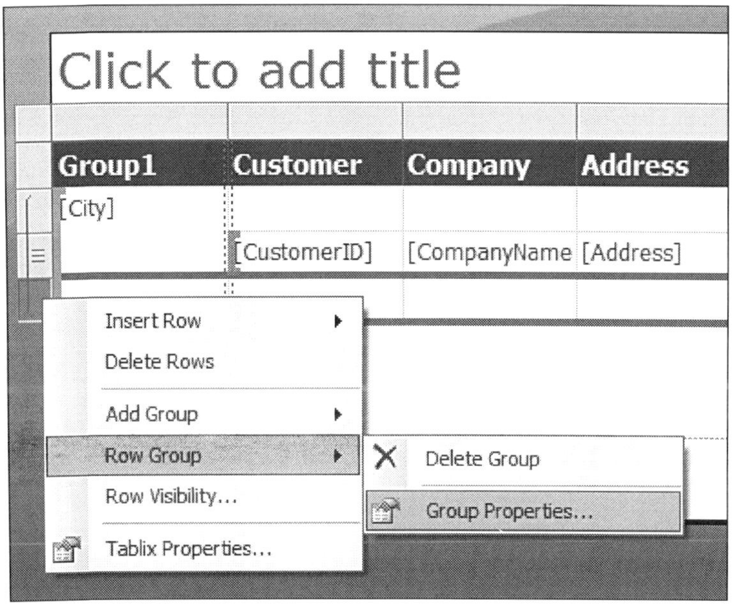

This brings up the **Group Properties** window.

- In the **General** tab of **Group Properties** you can add and delete the group on.
    - You can choose to add a group on using the drop-down list or by means of invoking the Expression window. You can delete a group as well.
- You can set up **Page Breaks** for the windows. You will set up a page break for the group. You may setup these breaks between each instance and also at the start of a group as well as at the end of a group.

- You can also setup **Sorting** options for the results
    - There are two choices, sort by the fields in the dataset, or use an expression to sort. Sorting can be **A to Z** or **Z to A**. You can sort by multiple columns as well by using the **Add** keys. You can order the sorts by the Up/down keys if you sort on multiple columns.
- You can change the **Visibility** of the group.
    - You can Show**, Hide or Show, or hide based on an expression**. You can toggle the display by clicking on another report item. You can filter further by using a combination of expression, operator and value that you specify here. For example you can choose to show only those cities which begin with the letter "M".
- You can add a group **Variable** (different from the Report Variable you define for the whole report)
    - You use a group variable defined here to calculate a value in the scope of this group. This variable is also available for the child groups.
- You can add **Advanced** properties like adding a **Document Map** or a **Recursive parent**.
    - Document Map is mostly for **HTML** rendering. Other renderers render differently.
    - PDF: Uses Bookmarks.
    - Excel: Uses named worksheet with hierarchical links. Report sections appear in other sheets.
    - Word document also has a document map like the table of contents.
    - Tiff, CSV, and XML ignore this setting.
    - Recursive data is related to the idea of self joins where the relationship between parent and child is represented by fields in the dataset.

2. Click on the **Advanced** list item in the **Group Properties** window.
3. Click on the drop-down handle for the **Document Map.**
4. Choose **City** and click on the **OK** button in the **Group Properties** window.
5. Click on **Home | Run** to run the report.

The report gets displayed. When you click on a **City** in the navigational area, you will see the report for that city at the top of the report on the right as shown.

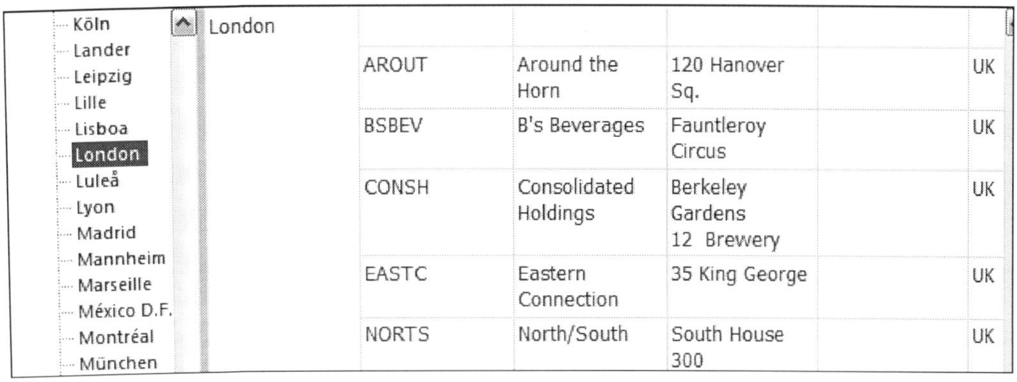

6. Save the report after providing a name. Herein, it was named **GrpReport**.

Add interactive sort

Interactive sort is one of the sort methods available. With interactive sort, the user can sort the results of the column(s) by just clicking on the column heading (usually the textbox that holds the column heading). You must implement the interactive sorting in design.

The methods available for sorting are:

- Sort data in a dataset query (use `ORDER BY` clause, see *Appendix A*)
- Define a sort expression for a data region or a group
- Provide interactive sort buttons to tables and matrices

These all can be combined in a report. The following instructions describe how you can implement this in your report. You will add interactive sort buttons to the CustomerID column of the above report.

1. Right-click the textbox (not the place holder) for the **Group1** column in the report layout and choose **Properties** from the drop-down.

   The **Text Box Properties** window is displayed as shown in the following screenshot:

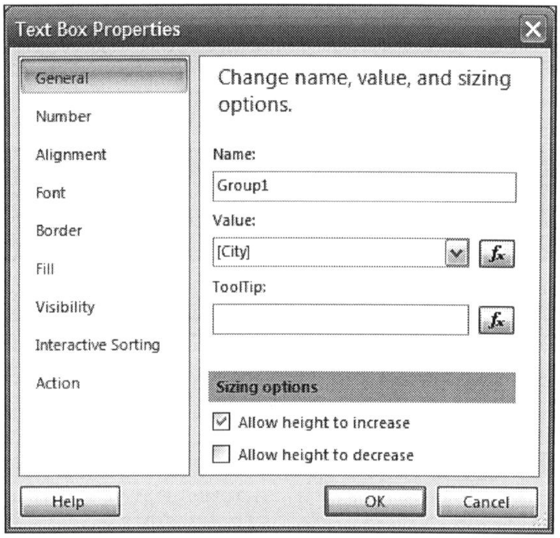

2. Click on **Interactive Sorting** and set up the window as shown in the following screenshot:

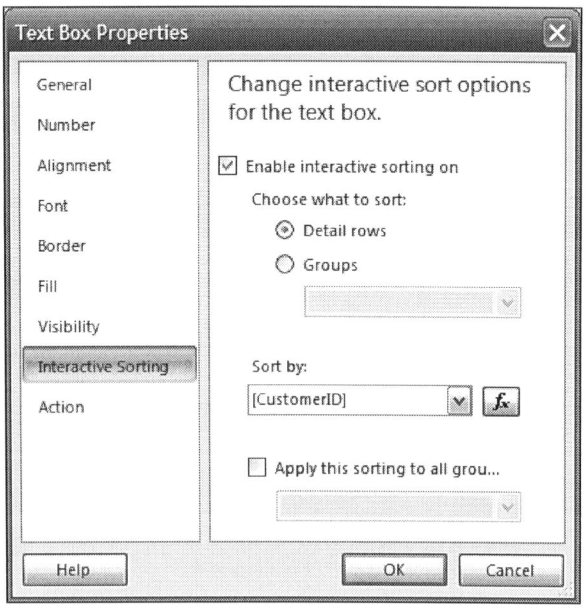

3. Click on the **OK** button. Click on **Home** | **Run** to display the report.

   The report gets displayed as shown. Notice the group column has two small up/down interactive buttons as shown:

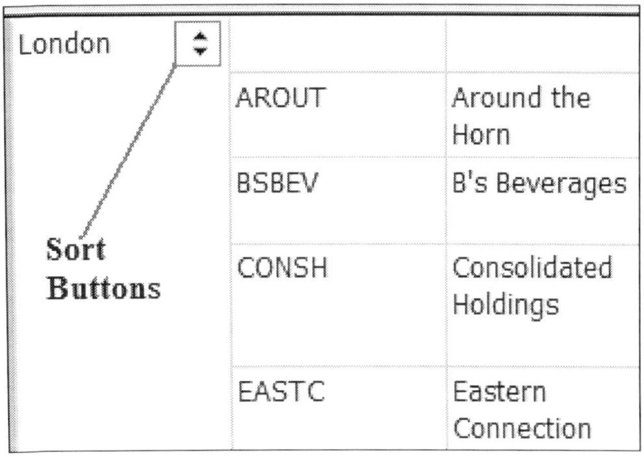

4. Click on **London** in the navigational area in the left.
5. Click on the **Sort** buttons to verify that the report can be sorted.
6. Save the report to the Report Server.

Hands-on exercise 7.3: Working with a subreport

Using subreports is an excellent method to merge several reports and produce a consolidated report. Subreports can be linked or unlinked. In the case of a linked report, there is a synchronization of information between the main report and the subreports. There is no such synchronization in an unlinked subreport. Subreports are invaluable in displaying details in master/slave tables. There is no limit on the number of subreports a main report can have. Since the subreport is going to occupy a certain physical region on the main report, its layout may have to be properly sized.

In this hands-on you will be creating two reports and will use one of them as a subreport for the other. You will also pass parameters between the two reports. For the main report you will create an additional dataset to populate the drop-down list of parameter values that you can choose to display the results. Additionally, you will add a toggle item to display the subreport. The report data source derives the data from an MS Access database on the local computer.

Follow on

First we create a parameterized subreport from the ODBC DSN created previously. We will follow it up by creating a main report to house this subreport. We will also decorate the report in such a way as to improve its readability. The main report will be a free form report, which is configured to display a subreport based on one of the parameters. We further add drill-down features so that subreport display is subject to a drill-down action.

Create a data source for the subreport

A subreport is also a report and as such you need to provide the data. The procedure for feeding data to the subreport is no different from that of the main report. Herein you will be using a ODBC datasource.

1. Click **New** under **Report Data** and choose **Data Source...**.

   In the **Data Source Properties** window, configure as follows:

   In the **General** Page:

   Name: ProductSrc

   Use a connection embedded in my report option

   Select connection type: ODBC

   Connection string: Dsn=rptDsn

   In Credentials page:

   Choose the **Prompt for credentials** option

   For **Enter prompt text:** User Name

2. Close the **Data Source Properties** window and right-click the Data Source **ProductSrc** and choose **Add Data Set**.

Add a dataset to the subreport

If a login is required, type in **Admin** for user name, then leave the password blank and click **OK**. In the **Data Set Properties** window for the **Choose a data source and create a query** enter the following:

Name: qryProducts

Data Source: ProductSrc (from previous step)

Query type option: Text

Query:

```
SELECT
  Products.ProductName
  ,Products.CategoryID AS [Products CategoryID]
  ,Products.ProductID
  ,Products.UnitPrice
  ,Products.UnitsInStock
  ,Categories.CategoryID AS [Categories CategoryID]
FROM
  Categories
  INNER JOIN Products
    ON Categories.CategoryID = Products.CategoryID
WHERE
Categories.CategoryID = ?
```

1. Click on **Parameters** in the **Data Set Properties** page.

   The parameter name **?** comes up by default.

2. Click on the drop-down handle and choose **@CategoriesCategoryID** and click on the **OK** button to close the window.
3. Expand the **Parameters** folder and right-click the parameter **@CategoriesCategoryID**.
4. In the **General** page set **Data Type**: to display **Integer**.
5. In the **Default Values** page click on **Add** and change **NULL** to **1**. Click on **OK**.

Add a table to the subreport

The Subreport is also a report and will use a table layout. You insert a table from the Insert menu item.

1. Add a **Table** to the design. Drag-and-drop **ProductName**, **UnitPrice** and **UnitsInStock** to the table columns to create a tabular report.
2. Run the report after providing credentials if needed. Test for a couple of integer values of the parameter (change default value of parameter for testing).

Changing background color of alternate rows

When a report consists of a large number of rows of data close together, it will be nice to have alternate rows highlighted in some way. This is usually achieved by making the background color of alternate rows gray. This can be implemented by conditionally formatting the background color of data rows.

1. Highlight the data row and change the background color property of the row by accessing the expression (You must have the **Properties** checkbox enabled in **View** menu in the "ribbon".)
2. In the expression, type in the following to alter the background color

   ```
   =IIf(RowNumber(Nothing) Mod 2, "Silver", "White")
   ```
3. Save the report to the Report Server with a name, **ProductsSubreport**.

The main report is the parent or the master for the subreport. There are different ways a subreport can be contained in the main report. The placement of subreports in reports was discussed in Chapter 6. They can be placed in a couple of different ways, such as both main and subreport in a table, or inside a list, or with the main report in a table and the subreport in a list.

Create a data source and a dataset for the main report

Here you will be creating a parametric query with the CategoryID as the query parameter. The report data will be filtered using this parameter.

1. Use the following information to create a report from the same datasource that was used in the previous section.

   Name of data source: **MdbCats**
2. Create a data set `MdbCatsQry` using the above source **MdbCats** and using the following information:

   Name: MdbCatsQry

   Query Type: Text

   Query:

   ```
   SELECT DISTINCTROW Categories.CategoryName, Categories.Description,
                      Categories.Picture, Products.ProductID,
                      Products.ProductName, Products.QuantityPerUnit,
                      Products.UnitPrice,Categories.CategoryID
   FROM Categories INNER JOIN Products ON Categories.CategoryID =
     Products.CategoryID
   WHERE (((Products.Discontinued)=No))and Products.CategoryID=?.
   ```
3. In the **Parameters** page set **Parameter Name:?** and **Parameter Value=[@ Parameter1].**
4. Click **OK** to close the **DataSet Properties** window.

Add a list to the main report

For displaying data in the main report you will be using a list. You can add the list to the design surface from the main menu.

1. Delete the **New Table or Matrix** and **New Chart** wizards to start with an empty report body.
2. Click **Insert** and click on **List**. Drop it on the report body.
3. Drag-and-drop **CategoryName**, **Description** and **Picture** in any location inside the list.

   This is a *free form report* design where the locations can be of your choosing.
3. Highlight the text **(Picture)** and delete it.
4. Click on **Insert** and on **Image**. Drag-and-drop it in the place from where you removed **(Picture).**
5. Right-click the image and configure its properties as follows:

   Name: **Image1** (default)

   Select the **Select the image source:** Database

   Set **Use this field:** with the Expression set to:

   ```
   =System.Convert.FromBase64String(Mid(System.Convert.
      ToBase64String(Fields!Picture.Value),105))
   ```
6. Set **Use this MIME type** to: image/bmp

   You will need to click on *fx* to set the expression shown above. The above code is needed to account for the image property data types being different in MS Access and MS SQL server. Also the MS Access application should be for English language (EN_US). This was a bug reported by the author and was resolved as reported in Microsoft Connect web site.
7. Click **Home** and **Run**.
8. The report gets displayed after processing. Verify the same for the other parameter values.

Create a second dataset

A second dataset is required to populate a drop-down list from which the Parameter to run the report is obtained at run time. If there are more parameters, more such datasets will be required. Although not described here, it is possible to cascade the parameters in such a way that a more focused set of data rows are displayed (more refined filtering).

Create a second dataset with the following and close the **Dataset Properties** window

Name: Dataset1 (default)

DataSource: MdbCats

Query Type: Text

Query: Select `CategoryID from Categories`

Get parameter list from this query

Here you will be adding report parameters based on another query. You need this to populate the drop-down list of categories.

1. Expand the **Parameters** folder and right-click on **@Parameter1.**
2. Configure the window **Report Parameters** with the following:
3. In the **General** page set **Data Type** to **Integer**
4. In the **Available Values** choose the **Get values from this query** option. Set the following for the new controls that appear:

   Dataset: Dataset1 from the drop-down

   Value field: CategoryID

   Label field: CategoryID
5. Click on the **OK** button to close the **Report Parameters** window.
6. Click **Home** and **Run** to process and display the results as shown in the next figure. You may need to provide a login name.

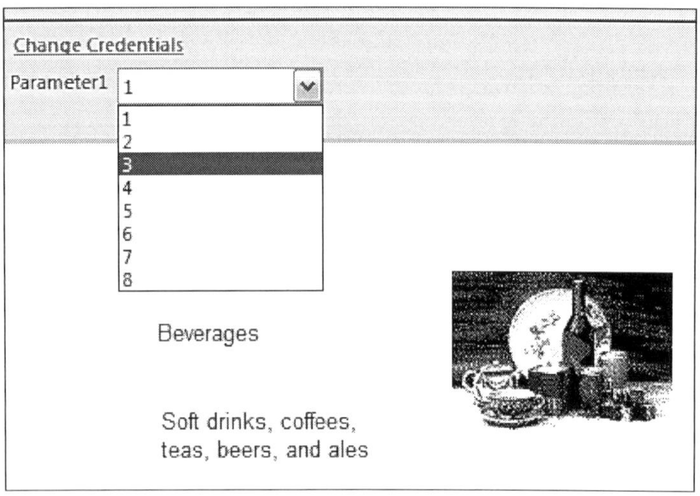

7. Test the report for other drop-down values.

Add the subreport to the report

The subreport is placed inside the main report. The subreport will occupy an area inside the list containing the main report.

1. Click **Insert**, click on **subreport** and drop it on an empty area on the List data region in the main report as shown.

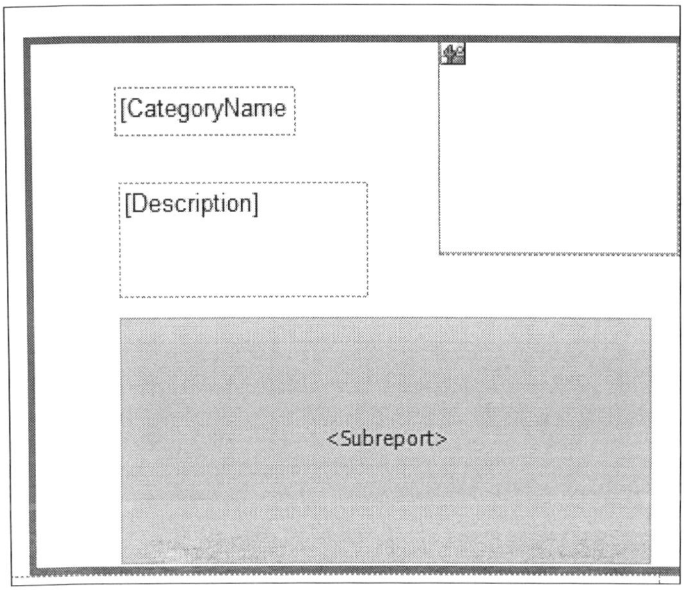

2. Right-click the subreport in the above and set its properties as follows:

   Name: Products

   Use this report as a subreport: ProductsSubreport (Browse the Report server)

   In the **Parameters** page click on Add and set the following:

   Name: CategoriesCategoryID

   Value=: [CategoryID]

3. Close the **Subreport Properties** window. Click **Home** and **Run.**

   The report gets displayed as shown in the next figure. You may need to provide login information twice, once for the subreport and once for main report.

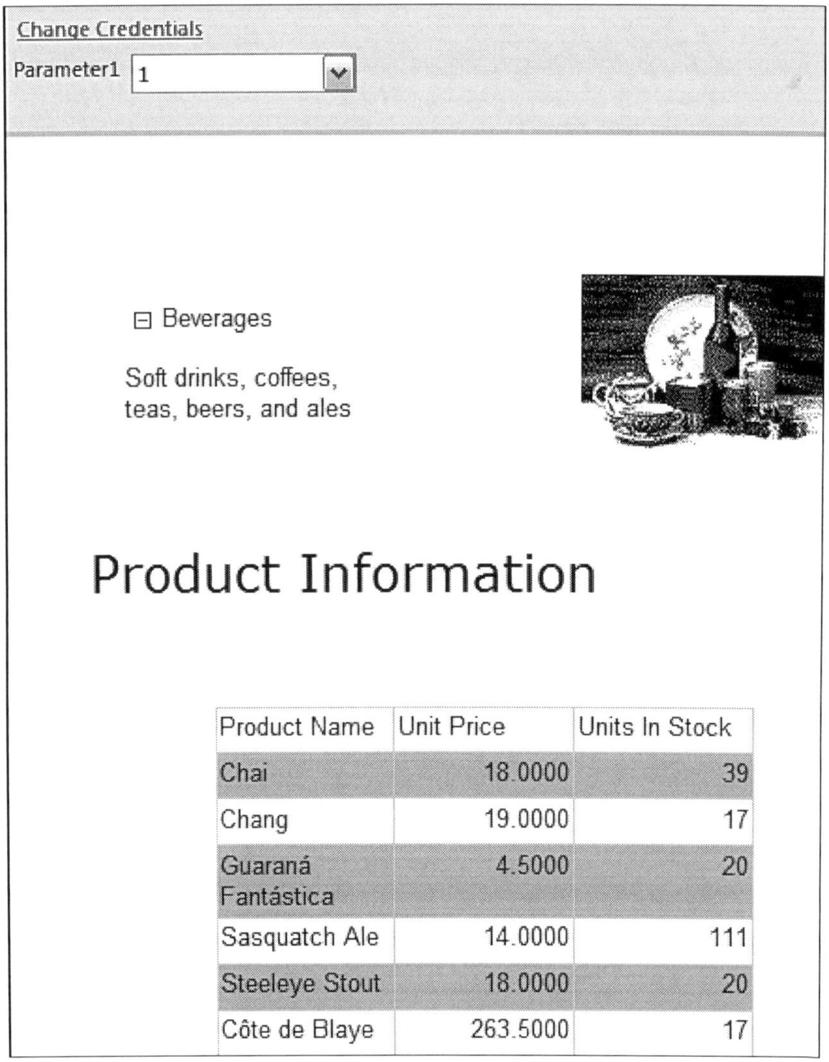

Depending on the size of the report the list items may repeat more than once in a report page. In this case place a Rectangle report item inside the List Data Region and move all the four items on the report to inside this rectangle.

Making the subreport a drill-down

This is a small report and it may not be of much importance. However, this section illustrates how you may set up the visibility of a subreport. The Subreport will be shown only when required. The drill-down feature may be implemented in other report types or data regions as well.

1. Right-click the subreport inside the **List**.
2. In the **Subreport Properties** window set the following:

   In the **Visibility** page:

   When the report is initially run: choose option **Hide**.

   Place a check mark for **Display can be toggled by this report item: Category-Name** (from the drop-down).
3. Click **OK** on the **Subreport Properties** window.
4. Click **Home** and click on **Run** to display the report.
5. Provide the login credentials (Just **admin** for login name) and click on the **View Report** button.

   The report gets displayed as shown (shown for a different parameter value):

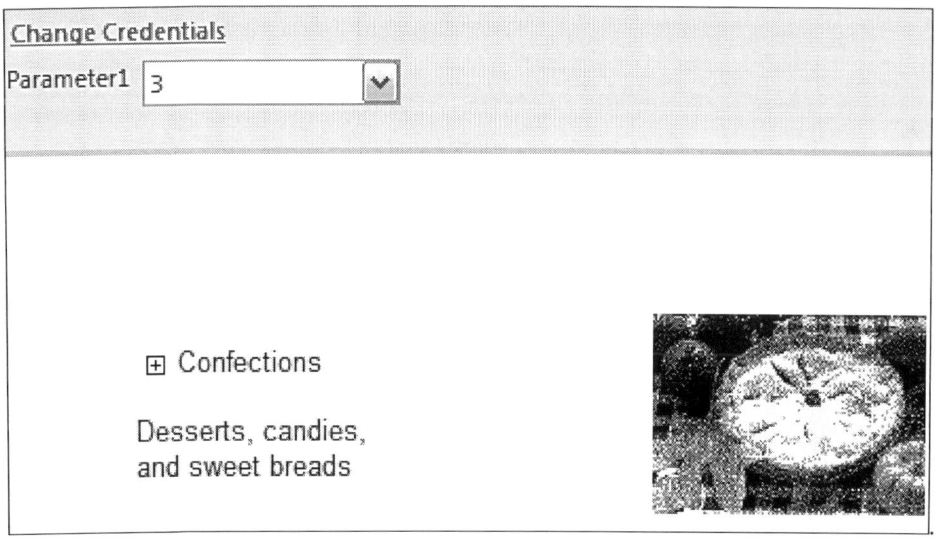

6. Click on **+** attached to the **CategoryName**.

   The subreport gets displayed and the **CategoryName** gets attached to a **–** sign.
7. Add other formatting properties and save the report as **MdbSub**.

Hands-on exercise 7.4: Creating a linked report

In this exercise, you will be using the Report Manager skills of Chapter 5 to create linked reports. You will start with the parameterized report created in *Hands-on 7.1*, the *QryReport*, deployed to the Report Server.

Follow on

You will be creating two folders (`London Office` and `Buenos Aires`) on the Report Manager into which you will be placing links (hyper) to this report from a shared folder (`International`) also on the Report Manager. You will also customize the reports as to what *London Office* and *Buenos Aires* can see in the report. Working with Report Manager has been described in great detail in Chapter 5 and only a few screenshots will be shown here.

Creating named folders for reports

You will be creating the three folders you will be using in this exercise. These are named folders you will be creating in Report Manager.

1. Create three folders in Report Manager. Herein, they are named `Buenos Aires`, `London Office`, and `International`.
2. Move **QryReport** into the folder named **International.**
3. Click **International** | **QryReport** | **Properties.**
4. Click on the button marked **Create Linked Report.**
5. Provide a **Name** and a **Description** to the linked report.
6 Click on **Change Location** button.
7. Choose **Buenos Aires.**

   Now the **Location:** displays **/Buenos Aires.**
8. Click on the **OK** button.
9. Click **OK** in the displayed page so that it gets saved to **Buenos Aires**.
10. Go to **Buenos Aires** folder and verify that the liked file is present.
11. Repeat the same steps and create a linked report and save it to the **London.**

Customizing the linked report for London Office

Here you want to configure the reports such that the linked report in the `Buenos Aires` folder displays only customers in Buenos Aires and the London Office can see only London Customers.

In the following, you will be customizing the report for the **London Office**. The steps can be repeated for the linked report in the **Buenos Aires** folder to customize the linked folder.

1. From the **Home** page click on **London Office** | **London Office Customers** | **Properties**.

   London Office Customers is the name of the Linked Report (`-->/International/QryReport`). The Properties page gets displayed as shown.

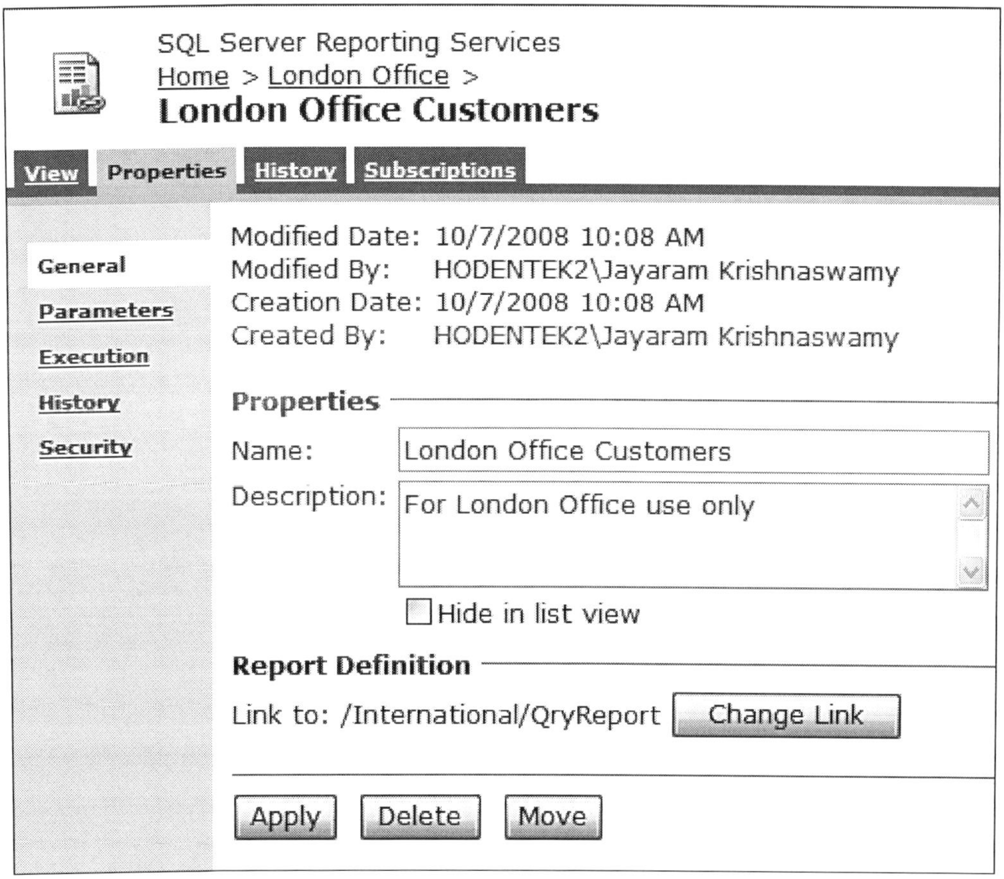

2. Click on the **Parameters** link.

   This opens the page where you can modify the parameters as shown:

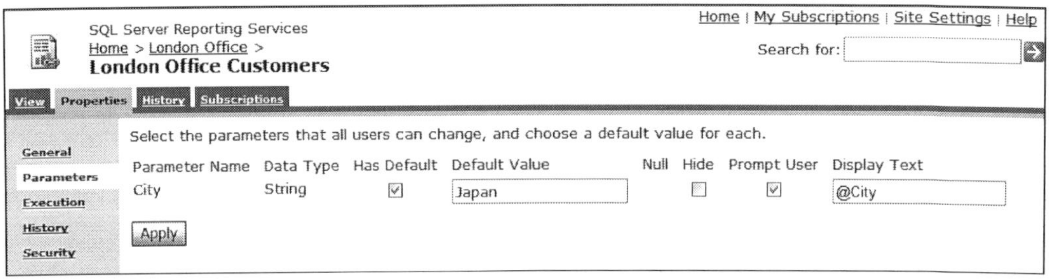

3. Change the default value to **London**. Place a check mark for **Hide**. The **Prompt User** gets disabled. Then click on the **Apply** button.

   The changes you made become effective immediately.

4. Now click on the **View** tab in **London Office Customers.**

   Now you will see the report displaying only **London Customers**.

Customizing the linked report for Buenos Aires

The procedure will be similar to that of the London office.

1. Follow the exact procedure for the Buenos Aires report.
2. Test and verify the linked report.

Hands-on exercise 7.5: Creating a drillthrough report

Let us say you have a contact list with just a name and email address, but you would like to know more details of the contact. Now, when you click on the contact's name, his detail will open in a separate report. This is different from a subreport. The subreport will open in the same report. The drillthrough reports are used normally to view unchanging or slowly changing data. You typically must have some kind of parameter that links the two reports.

For this exercise you need to create two reports, the target report and the report in which the link targets the report. This may become clear with the following figure and the hands-on steps that follow.

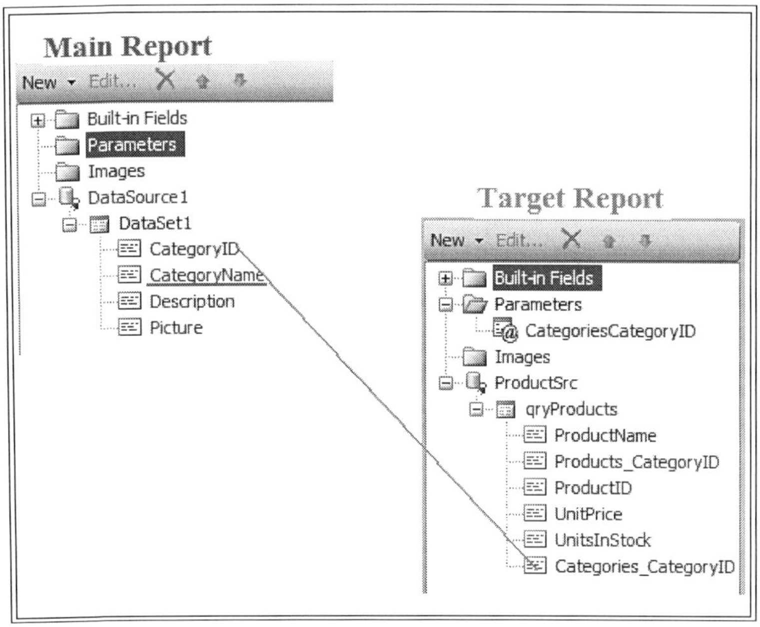

Follow on

You will create a target report (a parameterized report) and a main report. You will then use the **Action** property in the main report to call up the target report. You will be using the ODBC data source from the previous example.

1. Use the same ODBC used (DSN=rptDsn) in the previous hands-on and create a data source herein named `ProductSrc`.
2. Create a dataset using the following query against `ProductSrc`.

```
SELECT
  Products.ProductName
  , Products.CategoryID AS [Products CategoryID]
  , Products.ProductID
  ,Products.UnitPrice
  ,Products.UnitsInStock
  ,Categories.CategoryID AS [Categories CategoryID]
FROM
  Categories
```

```
    INNER JOIN Products
      ON Categories.CategoryID = Products.CategoryID
WHERE
    Categories.CategoryID = ?
```

3. Design a tabular report (use a Table) and drag-and-drop the fields **ProductName**, **UnitPrice** and **UnitsInStock** into the three columns of the table.
4. Make sure you see **Parameter Name=?** and **Parameter Value= [@CategoriesCategoryID]** in the dataset's **Parameters** page.
5. Verify that the report is working as designed (test for different parameter values) and save it on the Report Server as **ProductsSubreport.**

Create a main report

You will be using a simple query to get the data for the main report.

1. Create a datasource which is the same as `ProductSrc`.
2. Create a dataset using the following query against `ProductSrc`:

```
SELECT
  Categories.CategoryID
  ,Categories.CategoryName
  ,Categories.Description
  ,Categories.Picture
FROM
  Categories
```

3. Add a table data region to the report and populate its three columns by dragging and dropping the fields: **CategoryID**, **CategoryName**, and **Description**.
4. Right-click in the data cell for **CategoryName** to access its **Placeholder Properties...**.
5. In the **Placeholder Properties** page, click on the **Action** item to open its page.

6. Change the default so that the entries shown in the next figure are implemented. You may need to browse to the Report Server to pick the right report as well as work the drop-down handles to set the parameter correctly.

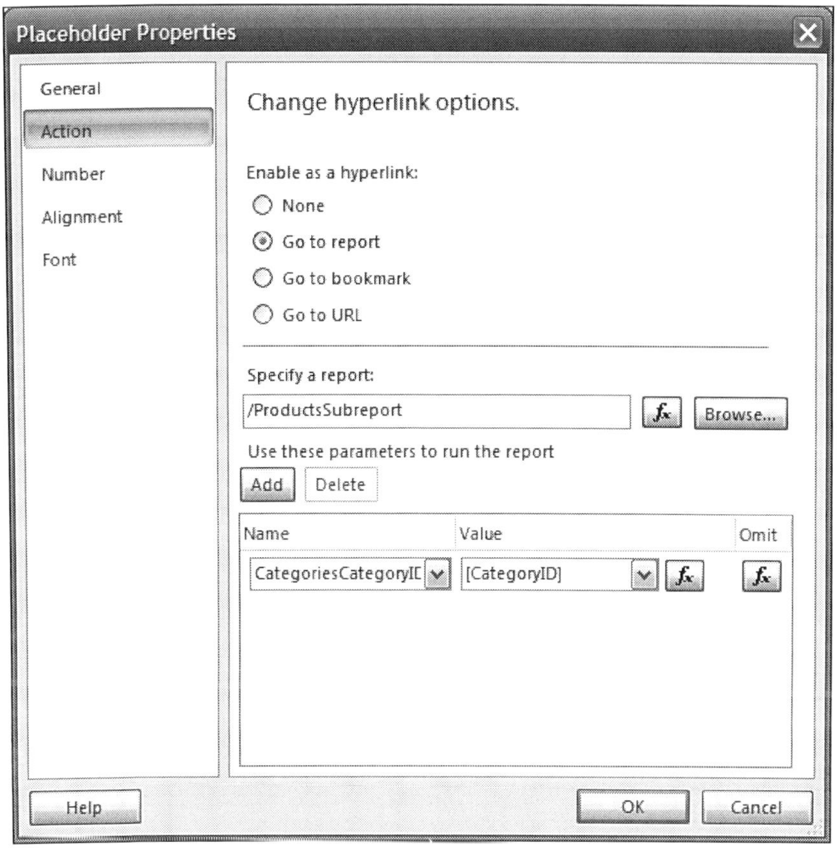

Verifying drillthrough action

After setting up the drillthrough action you must test to verify it works as intended.

1. Go to **Home** | **Run** to run the report. In the report that gets displayed, click on any **CategoryName** item and you will see product information gets displayed.

   This verifies that the drillthrough action was successful and the parameter was successfully passed. In general, it is not always needed to pass a parameter, except when you want to filter using a parameter.

2. In Report Manager, browse to the target report and hide its parameter by using the report's properties.

Hands-on exercise 7.6: Creating a report with XML data

XML data is being used extensively between businesses and there are times you may need to create report using XML formatted data. This hands-on exercise shows a simple example of creating a report based on data in an XML document. This can also be implemented using Visual Studio 2008 in both RDL and RDLC versions.

The XML data should be on your web server. Also, if you are using images, the image files must be easily accessible.

Although the example data `<wclass/>` is an XML document, the Query editor in Report Builder 2.0 needs extra tags like `<Query><wclass/></Query>` to process the query.

Follow on

The query tool in report builder works with SQL statements, Semantic Queries, or MDX queries. For XML, however, you can use the whole XML document in the query to run the query.

1. Copy the query you find in the following steps (the subsection, Create the Dataset for the Report) to `C:\inetpub\wwwroot` directory. Also save a couple of image files in JPG format. You will find their names in the query, but you can provide your own.
2. Create a **Data Source** with the following inputs:

   Name: XMLWebstudents (you may name it differently)

   Select Connection type: XML

   Connection String: http://localhost/webstudents.xml

   Credentials: Use Windows Authentication

Create the dataset for the report

The dataset for the XML document comes from a XMLDocument. You need to enclose the XMLDocument inside a `<query/>` root that the Report Builder expects.

1. Create a dataset with the following inputs:

   Name: WebStudentsQry

   Data source: XMLWebstudents

   Query type (Option): Text

Query:

```
<Query>
<wclass>
<!-- My students who attended my web programming class -->
<student id="1">
<name>Linda Jones</name>
<legacySkill>Access, VB5.0</legacySkill>
<photo>http://localhost/simple.jpg</photo>
</student>
<student id="2">
<name>Adam Davidson</name>
<legacySkill>Cobol, MainFrame</legacySkill>
<photo>http://localhost/simpleNet.jpg</photo>
</student>
<student id="3">
<name>Charles Boyer</name>
<legacySkill>HTML, Photoshop</legacySkill>
<photo>http://localhost/simplex.jpg</photo>
</student>
<student id="4">
<name>Charles Mann</name>
<legacySkill>Cobol, MainFrame</legacySkill>
<photo>http://localhost/simple.jpg</photo>
</student>
</wclass>
</Query>
```

If you test this file in the Query Designer, you should see result as shown.

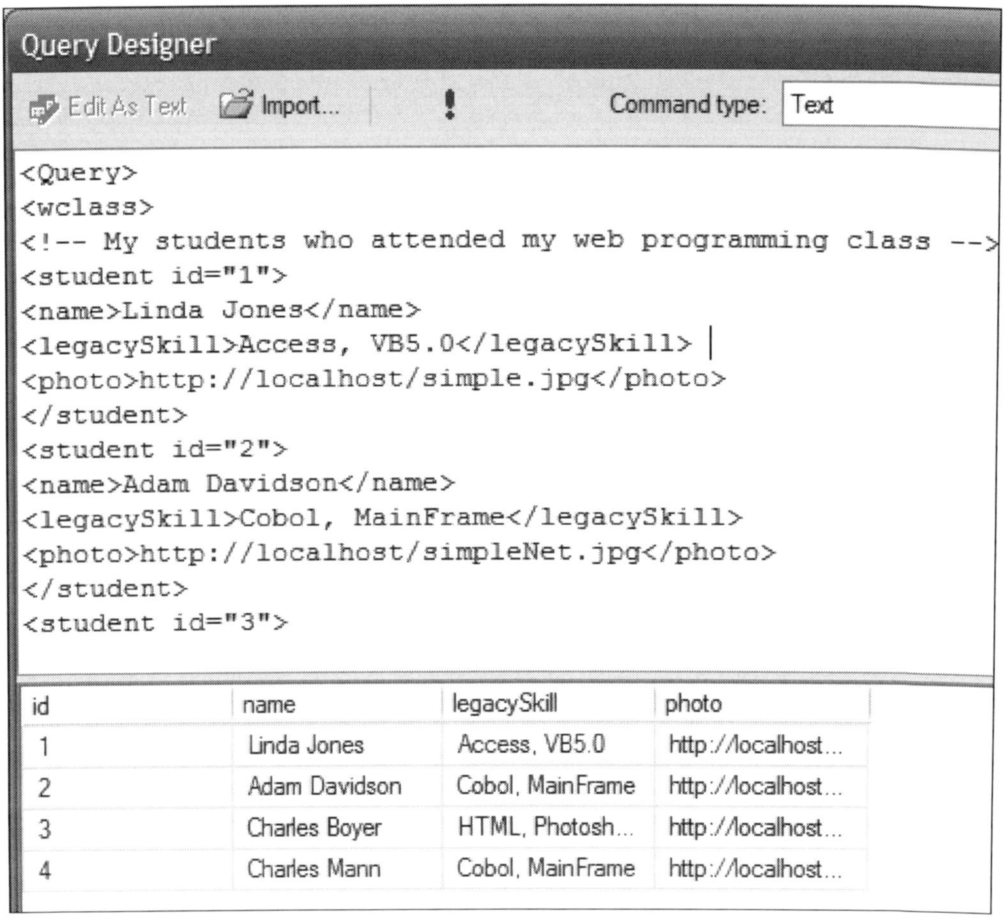

2. Create a tabular report.

Set image properties

As use can see that the image column is pointing to an URL in the column 'photo'. You need to remove the text control and insert a picture control followed by appropriately setting the image properties. This is what you will be doing here.

1. In the **Photo** column insert a **Image** from **Insert | Report Items.**

2. In the **Image**'s **Properties** page make the following entries:

   Name: Image1 (default is OK)

   Select the image source: External (from drop-down)

   Use this image: [photo]

3. Click **OK** to close the **Image Properties** window.
4. Test the report by running it and saving it to the Report Server.

Hands-on exercise 7.7: Ad hoc 1: Creating a tabular report with a Report Model

In this hands-on you will be creating a simple tabular report using the Report Model you created in Chapter 4. You will also meet some of the special features of the Query Designer interface.

Report Model, as described in Chapter 6, is a wizard driven model and there are not many changes you can make while it is being designed. The model may contain sometimes whimsical aggregates such as sum or average of CustomerID. Removal of such meaningless quantities should be the first priority. In the model created, no such "cleansing" has been implemented. While using a model, it is also necessary to change cryptic names to more meaningful ones. The model used in this exercise is "as is" generated from Visual Studio.

Follow on

This will follow the familiar steps except for some differences in the way each step is accomplished. The Query Designer tool is a major difference you will be seeing. The layout of the report is straight forward like the rest of the others. Based on your query design, the semantic query is generated by the tool. Once the dataset is created you can go back and forth and make changes: filter, group, and sort as much as you wish (the core idea behind ad hoc feature).

Create a data source

Reports are always based on data. Creating a report that obtains it data from a Report Model is no different.

1. Click on **New** | **Data Source...** under **Report Data** in Report Builder 2.0.
2. In the **Data Source Properties** page, change the default name to something different, herein **AdHocSrc1**.

   Use the option, **Use a shared connection or report model**.
3. Choose the **MyNorthwind** Model (`http://Hodentek2:8080/ResportServr_SANGAM/Models`) created in Chapter 4.
4. Click on the **OK** button.

   You will see a Shared Data Source **AdHocSrc1** added to your **Report Data window**.

As discussed in Chapter 4, the Report Model consists of entities, roles and fields. Entities are items which the Business users know about, such as category, order and so on. The roles define the interrelationship between entities. The next figure shows how the entity **Order** is related to the others such as **Order Details**, **Customer** and so on. Roles will help in consolidating related information in a single report (in SQL statement-based reporting, you would have been forced to make many joins between the tables to achieve the same result).

The fields list contains all the relevant information about an entity. The **Entities** in the left-hand corner shows all the entities for the **MyNorthwind** model. There were no perspectives (a subset of Entity) defined in the model and therefore, there are none in this list.

The Report gets filled up with data from the entity you choose to work with. You can use more than one entity for the report. It is a good idea to get used to the icons in the Fields: area shown in lower left. Actually they are quite obvious, Numeric items such as ID have a # sign, the date is represented by a calendar icon, the letter a represents a string quantity, and so on. The grouping of yellow squares represents an aggregate like avg, min or max. These aggregates are already in the model, but you can create a new one by clicking on the formula button.

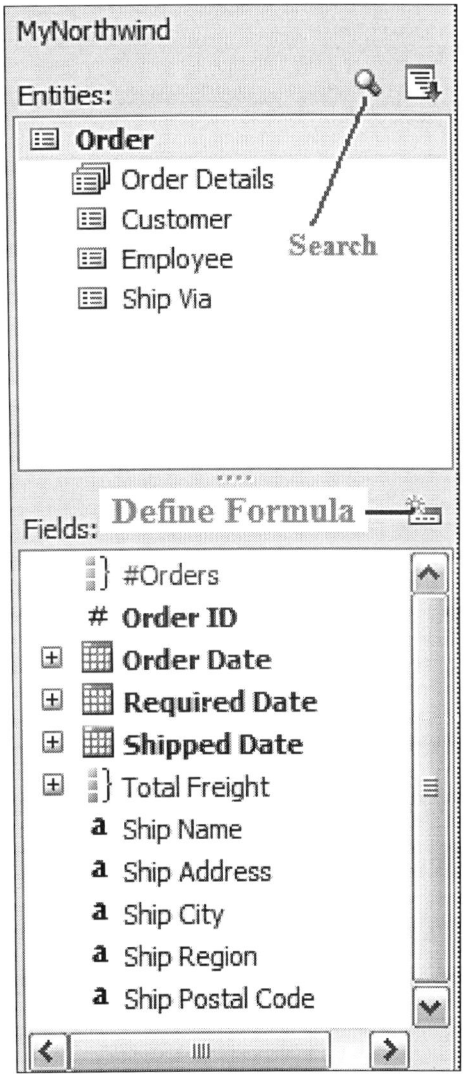

Creating a dataset

It is the dataset that gets into the report. From the data source you need to derive a dataset.

1. Right-click **AdHocSrc1 under Report Data** and choose **Add DataSet....**

   The **Dataset Properties** window gets displayed.

2. Change default **Dataset1** to a name of your own, herein **Adhoc2Qry**.

   The **Data source** comes up with the one you created in the previous step.

3. Click on the **Query Designer...** button.

   The **Query Designer** comes up as shown in the next figure:

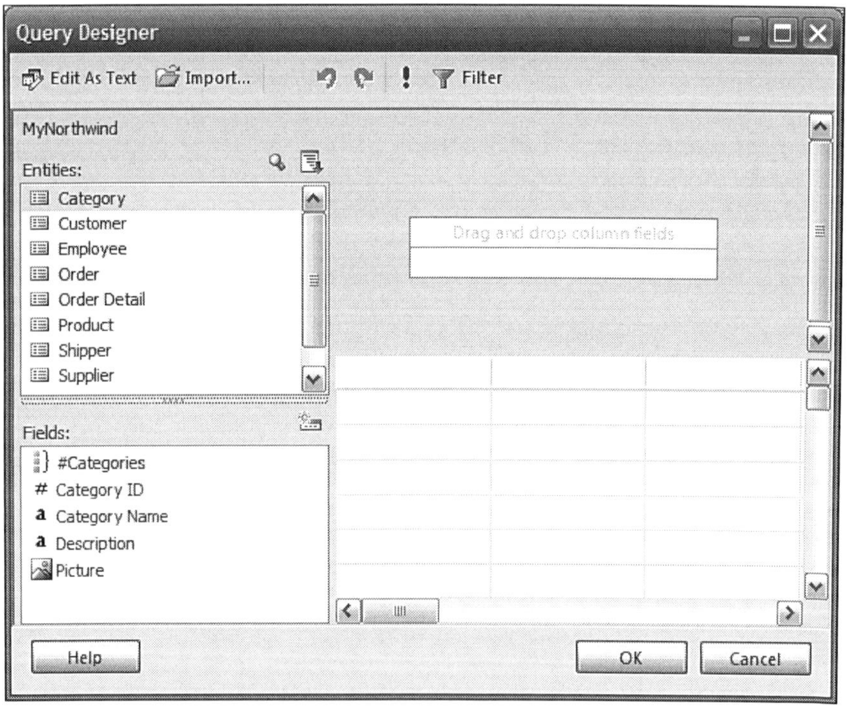

Fashioning a query

You will be using the visual guides (icons) in the UI to filter the data you would like to see. These icons are the familiar ones used in many reporting applications.

1. Double-click the entity **Order**.

   A table in the query design area gets populated as shown in the next figure:

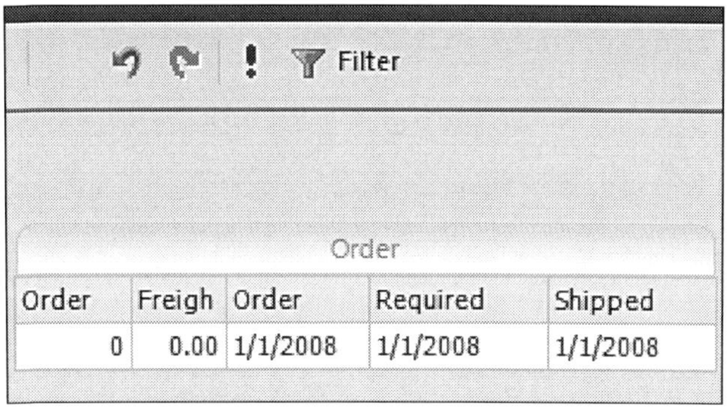

2. Click on the run (!) button at the top and verify that your query runs and the results of the query get displayed in the bottom of the window.

   Let us imagine that the business user does not want to see all of this and he wants to see some "*Filtered*" data.

3. Click on the filter (funnel icon) in the menu bar.

   It opens a window displaying **Orders with,** but otherwise empty.

   Let us say further the business user wants to see certain "Required Dates"

4. Now in the **Fields,** double-click **Required Date** (it gets highlighted in the fields list).

   This opens the **Filter Data** window as shown:

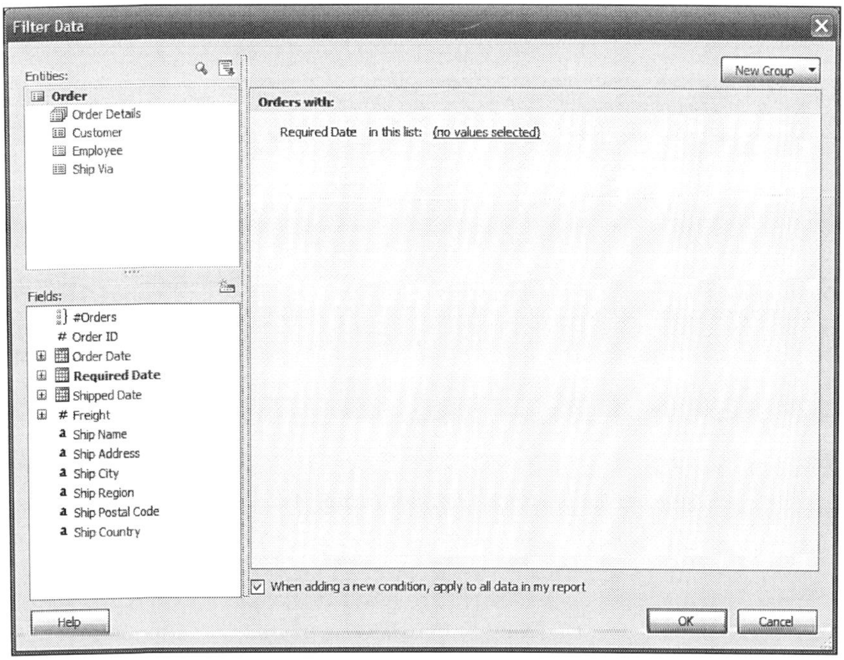

5. Click on **in this list.**

   The following drop-down is displayed:

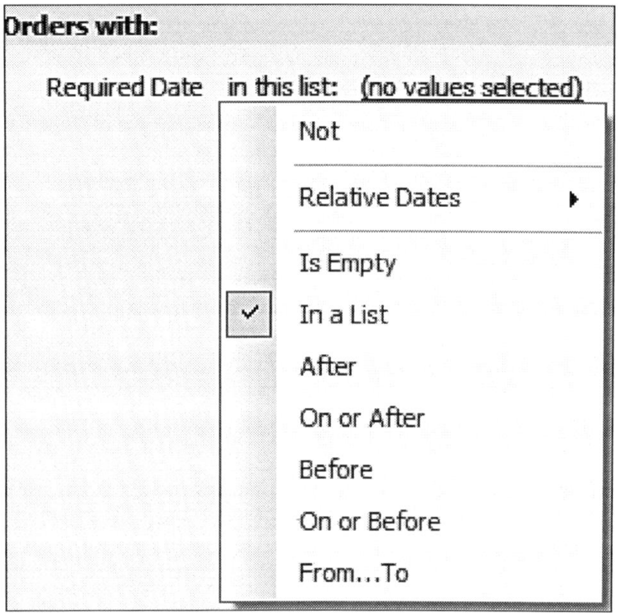

6. Skip this and click on **(no values selected)**.

   The **Filter List** window gets displayed. You can use this to select whatever from the available 454 choices for dates.

7. In the **Filter List** choose few arbitrary dates (use **>, >>,** and delete for rearranging or quitting the query.

8. Close **OK** on the **Filter List** window. Click **OK** on the **Filter Data** window.

9. Now run the query from the toolbar menu to see your filtered results.

   Now assume the user wants to see the total freight.

10. Click on the **Total Freight** in the **Fields** list.

    The total freight field gets added to the query as shown:

Order					
Order	Freigh	Order	Required	Shipped	Total
0	0.00	1/1/2008	1/1/2008	1/1/2008	0.0

11. Click on **Total** (column name or the data cell) and you will see the following (when you use data cell).

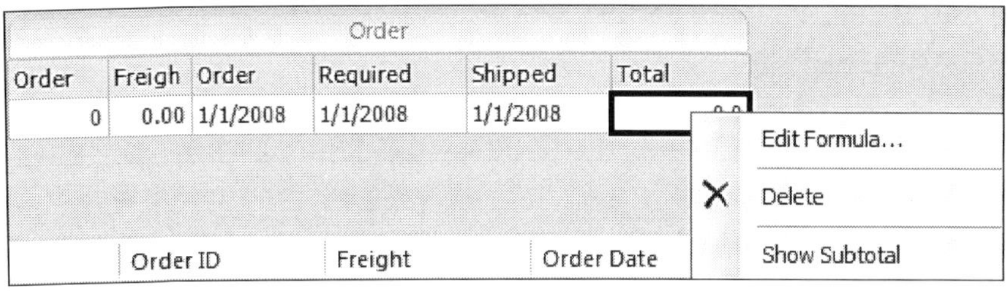

12. Choose **Show Subtotal.**

    A subtotal row will be added to the query as shown:

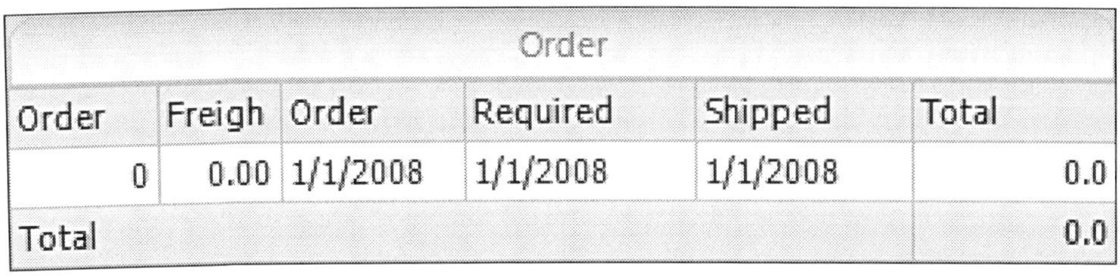

13. Run this query and verify that you get a total freight for all the orders.

    Presently there is no grouping defined and each order will also show a subtotal.

    The user notices that in the result there are orders that are not shipped in the list. Let us assume he wants to get rid of them from this list. All that he needs to do is to filter again.

14. Click on **Filter** and you go back to the window previously seen. Remove the dates with no shipped dates (5/20/1998 and 6/11/1998). Click **OK** on the **Filter List**. Click on the **Filter Data** window.
15. Run the query and verify that the rows for those dates have been removed.
16. Click on the **OK** button to the query designer.

    You will get back to the **Dataset Properties** window. Now you have generated a *semantic query* from the model based on the actions you took in the query designer as shown here.

Design and run the report

After getting the data you need to create a layout for your report. Herein you will use a table to display the data.

1. Click on the **OK** button in the query designer.
2. Click on the **New Table or Matrix wizard**.

   In the **New Table or Matrix** window the **Adhoc2Qry** is chosen by default.
3. Click on the **Next** button.
4. In the **Arrange fields** window drag all the fields from the **Available fields** to the **Values field** and click **Next**.
5. Click **OK** button on the **Choose the layout** page. **Choose a style** (herein **Slate**) in the following page and click the **Finish** button.
6. Now Run the report from **Home | Run**.
7. Verify that you have generated a tabular report which displays fields and filtering you chose in the query designer.
8. Save the report to the Report Server.

You can modify the report further based on principles discussed in the previous hands-on exercises.

Hands-on exercise 7.8: Ad hoc 2: Creating a matrix report with a Report Model

The Matrix data region was briefly introduced in Chapter 6. A matrix report is a report containing a matrix data region. A Matrix report also has rows and columns but what is of interest is in the intersection of column and row. This is where you find summarized information from your data. Report Builder 2.0 allows you to build comprehensive matrix reports with its very flexible Tablix data region. A simple explanation of matrix reports can be found at the following link: `http://aspalliance.com/1041_Creating_a_Crosstab_Report_in_Visual_Studio_2005_Using_Crystal_Reports.all`.

Follow on

In this hands-on, you will be using the MyNorthwind Report Model to create a matrix report from scratch and format some of its properties.

1. Create a new data source (herein named **Adhoc4**) by connecting to the MyNorthwind Report Model created in Chapter 6.
2. Right–click on **Adhoc4** and choose **Add Dataset....**
3. In the **Data Set Properties** window change the default dataset name (herein **Adhoc4Qry**) and click on the **Query Designer...**button.
4. Double-click the **Order** entity.

   The **Order** query with a number of fields gets added to the **Query Designer**.
5. Click the **Filter** icon.

   The **Filter Data** window comes up with the following text, "**Orders with:**".
6. Double-click **Required Date** in **Fields** which you find below the **Entities** list.

   The following gets added to the **Filter Data**'s design area:

   "**RequiredDate in this list: (no values selected)**.
7. Click on (**no values selected**).
8. In the **Filter List** select the following dates (click on a date in **Available Data** and click on the **>** button, or double-click on date):

   6/11/1998, 6/2/1998, 5/28/1998, 5/22/1998, 5/7/1998, 4/27/1998, 3/31/1998, 3/4/1998. You may also choose any of the available data.
9. Click on the **OK** button in the **Filter List** window.
10. In the **Filter Data** window click on the **OK** button.
11. In the **Query Designer** window, run the query to review the dataset returned by the query.

Add customer details and product information to the query

You will be adding customer details and product information by carefully going through the entities. You need to expand and look into the entities as you do in this section.

1. The **Order** entity is related to **Customer, Employee,** and **Ship Via** as well as **Order Details** (which in turn is related to Products) as shown in the **Entities** properties in the next figure.

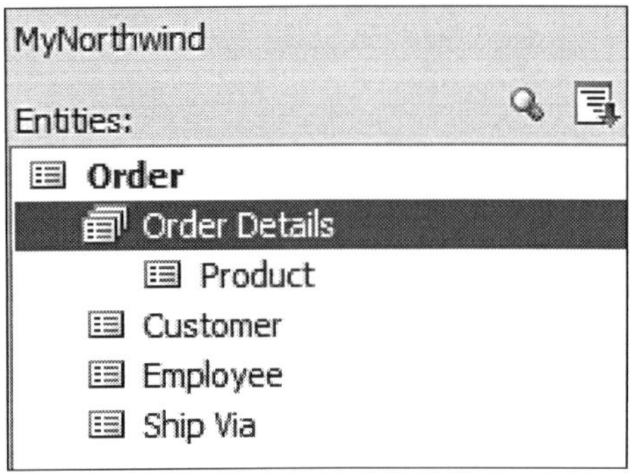

2. Click on **Customer** in **Entities** and double-click on **Company Name** and **City** in its fields.
3. Click on **ProductName** and click on **Total Unit Price**.

   Now you have fields from multiple entities.
4. Run (**!**) the query and verify that you have a dataset containing all the information you need.

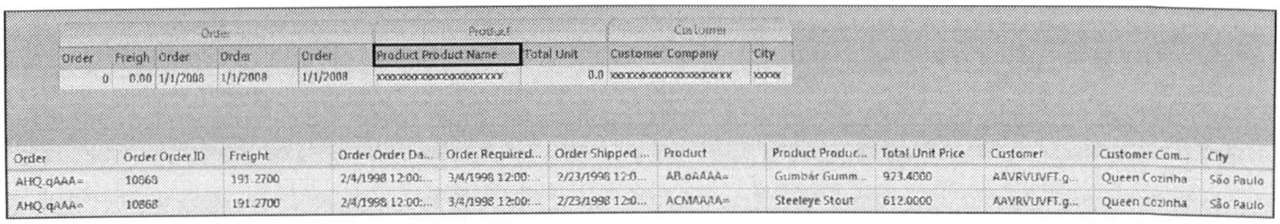

5. Click **OK** to the **Query Designer** and to the **Dataset Properties** window.

   The Dataset **Adhc4Qry** gets added to the **Report Data** window.
6. Go to **Insert | Insert Matrix** and click on the report body to add a matrix.
7. Drag-and-drop elements from the data set to the Matrix data region as follows:

   Product_Product_Name to **Rows Group**

   Order_Required_Date to **Columns Group**

   Freight to **Data** cell.

   Modify **Freight** using expression to display **SUM (Freight).**

8. Add a title to the report. The report design appears as shown below:

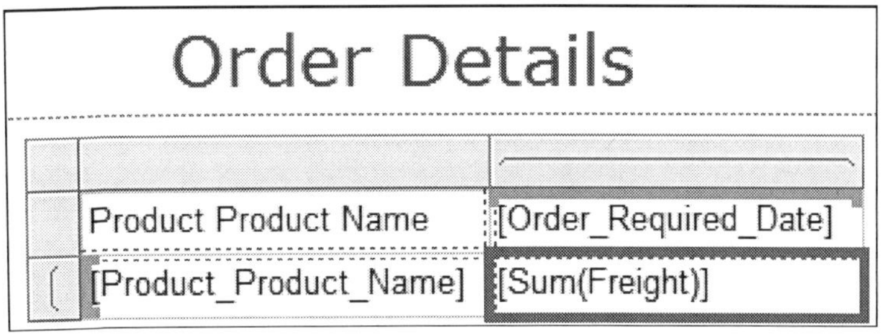

This is a simple matrix which shows the total freight for each of the products for the chosen required dates. But it is neither showing the total freight for all required dates for a single product nor the total for all products for a given required date.

9. Right-click on **Column Group Order_Required_Date** and from the drop-down choose **Insert Column | Outside Group-Right**.

   You will have added the third column to the matrix.

10. Right-click on the textbox for third Column, second row and set its value invoking the **Expression to: "=Sum (Fields! Freight.Value)".**

11. Run the report and verify that the last column gives the total freight for each product in the orders for all the required dates.

12. In a similar manner right-click the rows group and from the drop-down choose **Insert Row | Outside Group-below**.

    This adds the third row to the Matrix.

13. Right-click on the textbox in the third row, second column and set its value again to **"=Sum (Fields! Freight.Value)"** invoking the Expression.

14. Run the report and verify that you now have the total freight for all orders on a given required date.

    Now you want to get the grand total for all products on all required dates (which is the same as grand total for all required dates for all products).

15. In the textbox properties of the intersection of the last row with the last column set the value to `=Fields! Freight.Value` using the expression builder.

16. Run the report.

You should now see that the intersecting cell displays the grand total value.

You can apply filters to this matrix and get a more refined list depending on your requirement. You may also add parameters.

Apply filter to the report

In here you will be filtering the data further. These are set in the Tablix.

1. Click on the top left of the matrix and in its Tablix properties set the filters as shown in the next figure.

   The first filter in the **Tablix** properties filter page the following expression is evaluated:

   ```
   [Order_Required_Date] BETWEEN (=CDate ("May 5, 1998") (=CDate
   ("June 1, 1998") and for the next expression the value used
   is:[Freight] > (=CDEC(30.00))
   ```

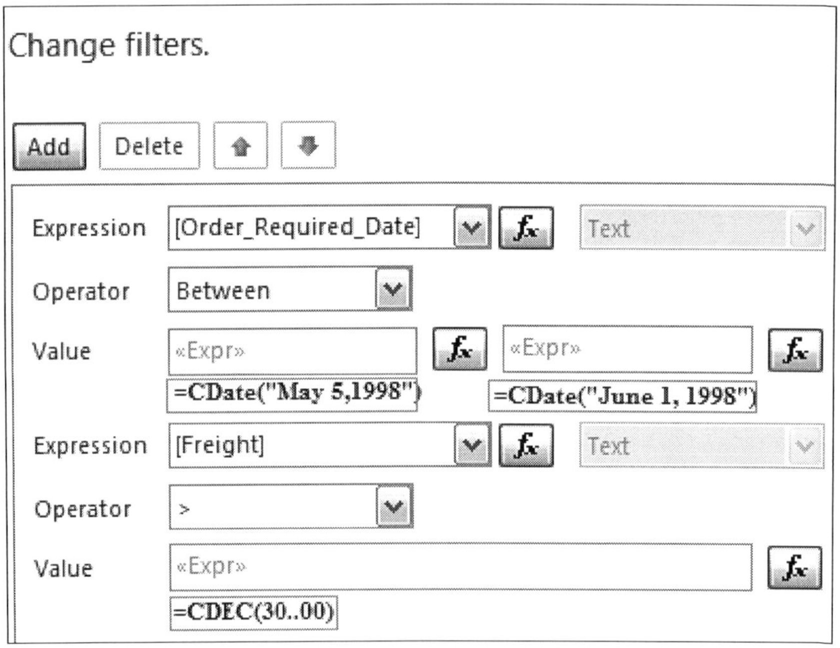

2. Use the **Home** menu item's formatting toolbar items or otherwise format the report to appear when run as shown:

Order Details

	Required Date			
Product Name	5/7/1998	5/22/1998	5/28/1998	**Total**
Boston Crab Meat			$81.73	$81.73
Chai		$46.62		$46.62
Chef Anton's Gumbo Mix		$46.62		$46.62
Jack's New England Clam Chowder			$81.73	$81.73
Røgede sild	$32.99			$32.99
Sasquatch Ale			$81.73	$81.73
Scottish Longbreads	$32.99			$32.99
Singaporean Hokkien Fried Mee	$32.99			$32.99
Tunnbröd	$32.99			$32.99
Total	$131.96	$93.24	$245.19	**$470.39**

10/13/2008 12:46:06 PM

Creating a report based on the Analysis Services cube

As previously mentioned, reports can be authored based on data in an Analysis Services cube using Report Builder 2.0. Some of the major steps involved in authoring are the following:

- Make sure the Analysis Services server is running.
- Connect to the source of the data in Analysis Services server.

For example, you can establish a connection to the Analysis Services database as shown in the following figure, which uses the Microsoft SQL Server Analysis Services (AdomdClient) to retrieve data from an Analysis Services database. You have to make sure you have provided the credentials information in the Report Builder interface.

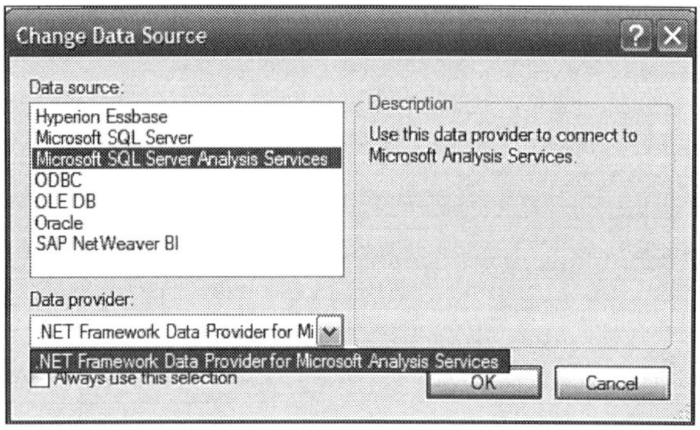

- Next you need to create a dataset based on this connection.

  When you try to create a dataset from Report Builder you will be immediately presented with the Query Designer tool after you provide authentication information to access the resource. When you choose the Query Builder option you will be presented with the interface shown.

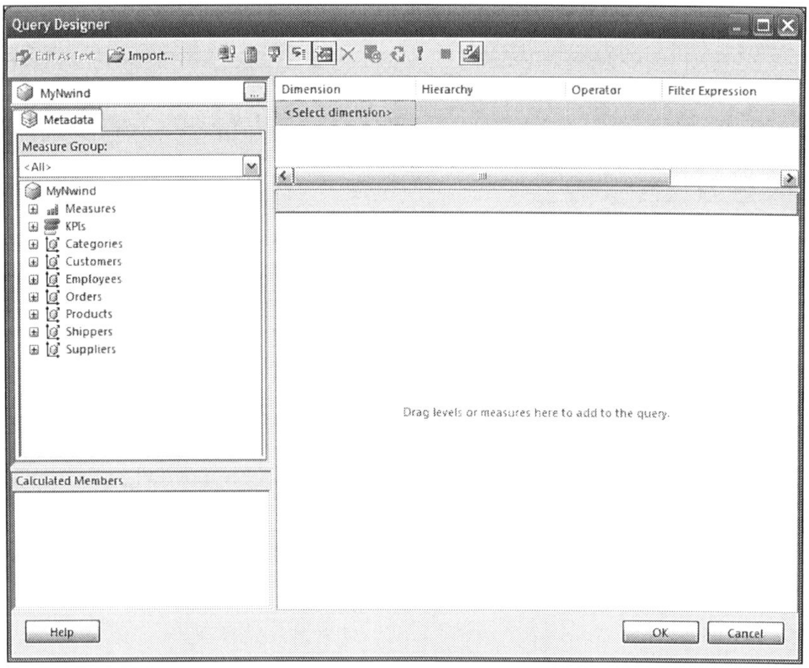

This designer is very much like the interface in the Analysis Server for browsing a CUBE on the Analysis Services. This is a highly interactive designer and you can set DIMENSIONS and look at MEASURES. The end result of this activity will be a dataset which represents the specific measures filtered from all the available data.

When you exit out of the Query Designer you will have created the dataset. The next step is the design of the layout. This is like any other layout you have designed in Report Builder.

After a report is designed you can of course modify both the Query and the layout.

Summary

This chapter describes the different kinds of reports you can author with Report Builder 2.0 such as parameterized reports, free form list reports, drill-down and drillthrough reports, subreports and so on. It also provides hands-on examples of getting data from SQL Server, Report Models and XML data documents. The steps to create a report based on an Analysis Services CUBE are also described. Many of the interactive features such as document maps, interactive sort and alternate row highlighting are also described and included in the exercises.

8

Programming Interfaces to Reporting Services

In this chapter, we will be looking at a number of programming interfaces available to work with the SQL Server Reporting Services. Using these interfaces, integration, maintenance of reports into Web and Windows application and configuring reporting services are facilitated.

Overview of programming interfaces

The programming interfaces include the following:

- URL access
- ReportViewer control
- The Reporting web services API
- Windows Management Instrumentation
- Reporting services utilities
- Miscellaneous

You will be working hands-on with most of them in this chapter and the rest are covered in the appendices.

URL access

The Reporting Services HTTP handler allows web clients to request a report from the Report Server using `GET` and `POST`. URL parameter prefixes are used in URL access (`http://msdn.microsoft.com/en-us/library/ms154042.aspx`). In the hands-on exercise you will be looking at one of the prefixes, namely `rs`. There are a couple of other prefixes that you can use, such as `rc`, `rv`, `dsu`, and `dsp`. The following table from Microsoft documentation provides a brief description of the action that is performed when the prefixes are used:

Prefix	**Action**
`rc`	Supplies a rendering extension with specific device information settings. For more information about device information settings and URL access, see *Specifying Device Information Settings in a URL*. This prefix is also used along with the commands that are targeted at the HTML Viewer.
`rs`	Targets the Report Server with specific parameters.
`rv`	Passes report parameters in a URL to a report that is stored in a SharePoint document library, for the Report Viewer Web Part Commands.
`dsu`	Specifies a user name in order to access a data source.
`dsp`	Specifies a password in order to access a data source.

The look and feel of a report can be customized using these prefixes. In addition to the URL parameters you can also pass the report parameters, if there are, to the URL following the syntax shown:

```
Protocol://server/virtualroot?[/pathinfo]&prefix:param=
  value[&prefix:param=value]...n]
```

ReportViewer control

There are two ReportViewer controls, one for Web applications and one for the Windows Form application. Also each of these has two processing modes, one remote and one local.

These controls can be added during design time or using code. Adding a control during design time involves dragging-and-dropping the control from the toolbox onto the design surface and pointing the control to use the report (using the control's smart task). In this way, the report gets embedded in the ReportViewer.

Using code for example, the following snippet in a Form's load event would instantiate a ReportViewer control and set it up for local processing:

```
    Private Sub Form1_Load(ByVal sender As Object, _
            ByVal e As System.EventArgs) Handles Me.Load
            Dim rv As New ReportViewer
            Me.Controls.Add(rv)
            rv.ProcessingMode = ProcessingMode.Local
        End Sub
```

In order to set the processing mode to "remote", substitute the following in the above code:

```
rv.ProcessingMode = ProcessingMode.Remote
```

In the remote mode, the report processing is done on the Report Server and the ReportViewer is conversing with the Report Server and obtains its data from the server. In the local mode, the Report Server is ignored and it need not even exist, however, it cannot process data. Data processing has to be carried out in the backend. The report is processed locally and you have to provide the data for the report. This data is provided in the form of a dataset.

ReportViewer processing in the remote mode has the full capability of rendering reports in a variety of formats, but in local mode rendering is limited to EXCEL and PDF.

In this section, you will work with both Windows Form and Web applications in the remote mode. This is a nice way to integrate your report on the Report Server with Web and Windows applications.

As soon as you instantiate a ReportViewer control to a web page or a Windows Form, a number of system-related assemblies get referenced in addition to referencing "*Microsoft.ReportViewer.Common*" and "*Microsoft.ReportViewer.WinForms (or WebForms)*" assemblies. These also get entered in the `web.config` file. Most of the methods and properties that will be used in the code are present in these. The best resources you should use are the *Object Browser* in Visual Studio 2008 and the Books Online (`http://msdn.microsoft.com/en-us/library/ms130214.aspx`).

The Reporting web services API

Simple Object Access Protocol (**SOAP**) that let applications exchange information over HTTP is the basis for the Reporting Services application programming interface. In Reporting Services there are two web service end points (SOAP end points are just URLs), one for report execution and one for management of a report on the Report Server.

The management service is exposed through ReportServer2005 for Report Server configured in the native mode, and ReportServer2006 for Report Server in the SharePoint mode. The report execution service for both modes of server is ReportExecution2005. In the hands-on examples, you will work with both the ReportExecution2005 and the ReportServer2005 Services. SharePoint mode is outside the scope of this book.

In Windows or Web applications, you begin to interact with these services by establishing a web proxy. This will give you access to the methods defined in these services. The best way to develop your understanding is to study the various methods the services provide. Remember that the *Object Browser* and intellisense give a great deal of support while writing the code. The hands-on will give you a flavor of what they are about and the plumbing details of working with them.

Windows Management Instrumentation

Windows Management Instrumentation (**WMI**) classes included in the Reporting Services allow the following:

- Local and remote control of Report Server and Report Manager
- Identifying the machines on the system running Reporting Services
- Administrators can make changes to the configurations of these, after the initial installation
- Local and remote administration tasks such as changing credentials, modifying the name of report server database and so on

The classes for working the above tasks are provided in the following:

- `MSReportServer_ConfigurationSetting` class
- `MSReportServer_ConfigurationSettingForSharePoint` class
- `MSReportManager_ConfigurationSetting` class

The hands-on exercise describes how you may provide access to a user as well as working with the WMI classes.

Reporting services utilities

In addition to reporting services application programming interfaces, there are a couple of command line utility programs that you can use with Reporting Services. You will be learning about them in *Appendix C*.

Miscellaneous

Some of the programming details that do not necessarily fall in the sections discussed above are addressed here:

- Using Microsoft SQL Server Integration Services

  In particular a method is described to leverage the SQL Server Integration Services (**SSIS**) to access a report on the Report Server and integrate it within the SSIS package. Although SSIS has a web service task which can access the Reporting web services, its methods are not accessible. They will be, however, available in the next major version of SQL Server 2008 (`http://hodentek.blogspot.com/2008/10/presently-this-is-not-working-in-sql.html`).

- Using custom code in expressions

  In addition to the *Expression* tool used in building value expressions, custom code can also be implemented to work with expression. You will be doing a hands-on exercise to understand the mechanics of building an expression with custom code.

Programming using URL access

In this section, you will be using URL access in both Web and Windows applications. You will also be using reports you created in earlier chapters.

Hands-on exercise 8.1: Displaying a report on the Report Server with an ASP.NET Web application using URL access

Reports on the Report Server are accessible using the URL. This is a good and easy way to enable viewing of a report on the Report Server from a Web application. There are two ways you can access reports from a Web application:

- Directly accessing the URL address of a specific Report Server from the Report Server site
- Passing query string parameters to a Report Server using a `POST` method

The first one we have seen already in the earlier chapters. Just type in the URL address of the report on the Report Server and you can view the report. In this exercise, you will use a link to the report, an IFRAME element to embed the report, and a FORM element's `POST` method to embed the report. You could also have a FRAMESET, and arrange for reports to display in the MAIN (parent) frame while clicking report link in the NAVIGATION (child) frame.

Follow on

While the hands-on uses the Report Server installed in Chapter 1, the reader must substitute the relevant references to his Report Server and pass applicable query parameters to his URL.

Launch VS2008 and create a web site. Herein a web site **UrlAccess** was created.

Using a link

1. In the **Default.aspx** page insert the following HTML content:

```
<a href="http://hodentek2:8080/ReportServer_SANGAM/
  Pages/ReportViewer.aspx?/MyWebStudents&rs:Command=Render">
  Display My Web Students</a>
```

   This will be displayed as a link in the display page of **Default.aspx.**

2. Browse using IE 6.0 (or above) to the **Default.aspx** page and click on the link **Display My Web Students**.

   The page is displayed as shown. You can see a full query string in the URL address:

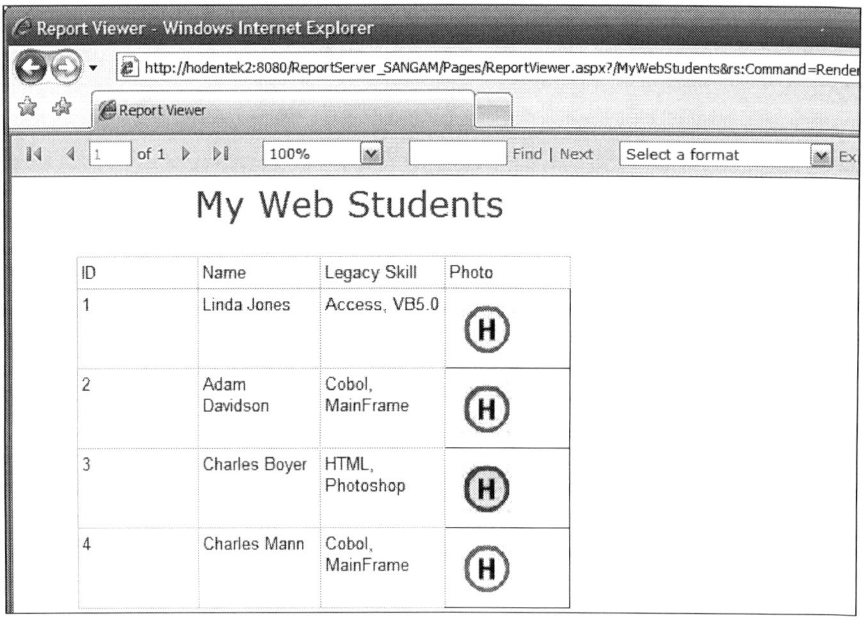

> You may have to provide the authentication information if you are using a browser other than IE 6.0 (Google Chrome 1.0, Safari 3.2.1 and so forth).

Passing the format to URL

The following syntax will now allow you to get the PDF formatted report:

```
http://hodentek2:8080/ReportServer_SANGAM/Pages/ReportViewer.
aspx?/ MyWebStudents&rs:Format=PDF&rs:Command=Render
```

To get the same result using the Reporting Services APIs will take lot more work, although, API can address more complex and custom scenarios.

Using an <iframe/>

Now back in the **Default.aspx** page type in the following after the link statement you entered earlier:

```
<h2>Order Information</h2>
<iframe id="Main" width="80%" height="600"
        src="http://hodentek2:8080/ReportServer_SANGAM?/RSPWiz08/
             OrderInformation&rs:Command=Render"></iframe>
```

Build the site and browse the **Default.aspx** page as before.The **Default.aspx** page gets displayed as shown (only part of it is shown here).

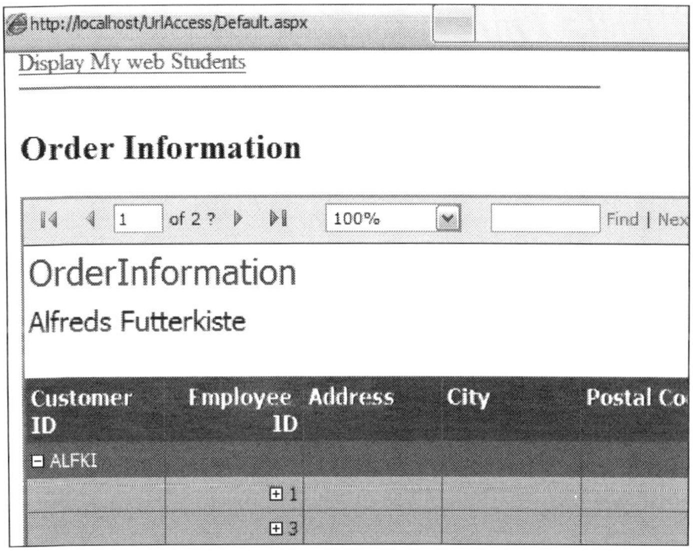

Using the POST method of a form

Post is one of the submission methods of HTML forms. It is specified as an attribute of a form. Herein the method "POST" looks up the action which is a link to the Reporting Services server.

1. Back in the **Default.aspx** design page, insert the following HTML fragment:

```
<form id="form1"
      action="http://hodentek2:8080/ReportServer_SANGAM?/
              MyWebStudents"
      method="post" target="_self">
```

```
<input type="hidden" name="rs:Command" value="Render"/>
<input type="hidden" name="rc:LinkTarget" value="main"/>
<input type="hidden" name="rs:Format" value="HTML4.0"/>
<input type="submit" value="Get My Web Students"/>
 </form>
 <hr />
```

2. Build the site and browse the **Default.aspx** page as before.

   Now the **Default.aspx** is displayed as shown. Make sure the form does not have the attribute `runat=server`.

3. Click on the button **Get My Web Students** and verify that the **MyWebStudents** report is displayed.

Hands-on exercise 8.2: Integrating a report on the Report Server with a Windows application using URL access

There are two ways you can display the report from a Windows application. They are:

- Using an embedded WebBrowser control
- Using the `Start()` method of the `Process` class to start an IE browser and pass the Report Server URL

We will program a Windows form for each of these methods.

Follow on

WebBrowser control is a very convenient tool when you want to bring in a web page to a Windows form. In this hands-on, you will use a web browser control placed on a Windows form to browse the URL of the report.

Using the WebBrowser control

In here, you will be rendering a report with URL access.

1. Create a **Windows Forms Application** in Visual Studio 2008.

   This creates a project with a **Form1.vb** file.

2. Drag-and-drop a **WebBrowser** control from **Common Controls** items in the **Toolbox** onto the form.
3. Code the **Form1**'s load event as follows:

```
Private Sub Form1_Load(ByVal sender As Object, _
    ByVal e As System.EventArgs) Handles Me.Load
        Dim url As String = _
        "http://hodentek2:8080/ReportServer_SANGAM?/" & _
    "ProductsSubreport &rs:Command=Render"
        WebBrowser1.Navigate(url)
    End Sub
```

When the page gets rendered the report will be displayed on the form.

Using Process.Start () method

In here, you will be using the `start()` method which takes two parameters, the IE browser and the URL.

1. Add a new form to the same **Windows Application** and drop a button control onto the form. Program the button's click event as follows:

```
Private Sub Button1_Click(ByVal sender As System.Object, _
        ByVal e As System.EventArgs) Handles Button1.Click
        Dim url As String = _
        "http://hodentek2:8080/ReportServer_SANGAM?/
        ProductsSubreport&" & _
                    " rs:Format=HTML4.0"
        Try
            System.Diagnostics.Process.Start("IExplore", url)
        Catch
```

```
                MessageBox.Show("Could not start the specified report
                using IE.", _
          "An error has occurred", MessageBoxButtons.OK,
           MessageBoxIcon.Error)
            End Try

    End Sub
```

2. Build the project and run. Click on **Button 1**. The report gets displayed.

Programming the ReportViewer control

In this section, you will be using the ReportViewer control to integrate your reports on the Report Server. You will work with programs for both Web and Windows applications.

Hands-on exercise 8.3: Integrating a report on the Report Server with an ASP.NET Web application

In this exercise, you will integrate a report on the Report Server into a web page hosted on your intranet web server. You will first instantiate a ReportViewer control, which you embed in the web page. You follow this up with getting the Report Viewer to display this report.

When you create a new web site project, the directory security is by default set for anonymous access. When you embed the ReportViewer control in a web page the `IUSR_<machine_name>`, the anonymous user should be able to access the report on the Report Server. In order to do this you will need to assign the `IUSR_<machine_name>` to one of the roles. This you should do in Report Manager as you did earlier in Chapter 5. In some cases you may need to assign the role of Content Manager of Report Builder role to the ASP.NET user.

Follow on

In here you will create an ASP.NET 2.0 web site project. You will then embed a Report Viewer Control that accesses a report on the report server by providing a relative path to the report.

1. Launch Visual Studio 2008 from its shortcut.
2. Click on **File** | **New** | **Web Site...**.

   The **New Web Site** window opens.

3. Provide a name for the web site by replacing the default, **Web Site**.

   Herein, it is named **RsRv**. The default will show up as http://localhost, which is the default for an ASP.NET web site. Port 80 is also the default port. You may also browse or use the drop-down to create this site on another site location or even a local file-based location. Herein, the default is accepted which creates the site, `http://localhost/RsRv` as shown:

4. Click **OK** on the **New Web Site**.

   The new web site will be created with the template folder items as shown:

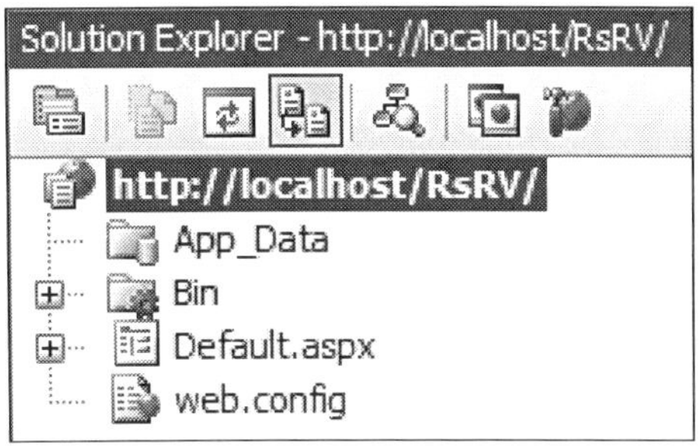

5. Drag-and-drop a **Microsoft ReportViewer** control from **Toolbox | Reporting** on to the **Default.aspx** page's design tabbed page.
6. In the **Default.aspx.vb** window, type in the code shown next. Make sure that you use the support provided by intellisense as you type in the code. The code you type in goes into `Page_Load()`. Make sure you add the `Imports` statement at the top of the page as shown:

```
Imports Microsoft.Reporting.WebForms

Partial Class _Default
    Inherits System.Web.UI.Page

    Protected Sub Page_Load(ByVal sender As Object, _
        ByVal e As System.EventArgs) Handles Me.Load
        If Not Page.IsPostBack Then
            Dim rv As New ReportViewer
            rv = ReportViewer1
            rv.ProcessingMode = ProcessingMode.Remote
            Dim srvRpt As ServerReport = rv.ServerReport
            srvRpt.ReportServerUrl = _
            New Uri("http://hodentek2:8080/ReportServer_SANGAM")
            srvRpt.ReportPath = ("/ProductsSubreport")
            rv.Visible = True
        End If
    End Sub
End Class
```

There are two processing modes, local mode and remote mode as discussed in Chapter 3. In this example, the remote processing mode (on the Report Server) is chosen. The **Server URL** is the URL of the Report Server as you have seen in all the past chapters. The **Report Path** is given relative to the Report Server. The **ProductsSubreport** is the one you created in Chapter 7, as shown here on the Report Server.

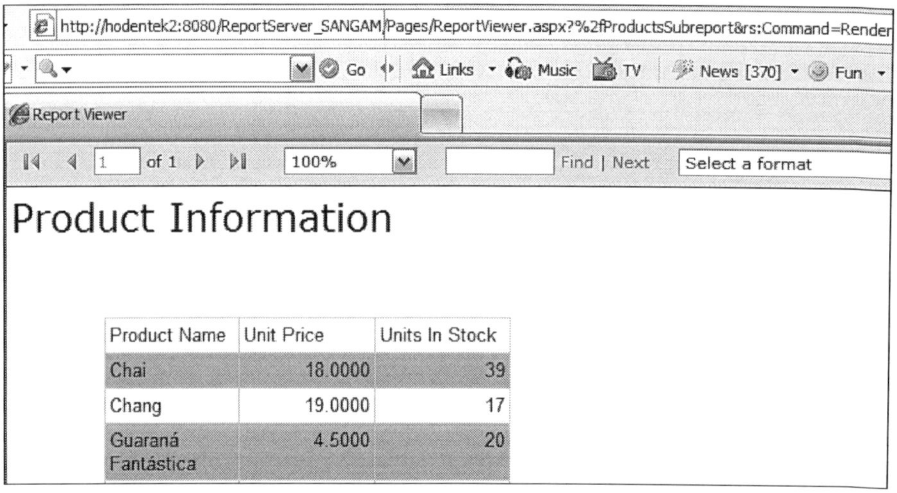

7. Now **Build** the project and browse the **Default.aspx** page on the IE.

   The **Default.aspx** is displayed as shown in the following screenshot:

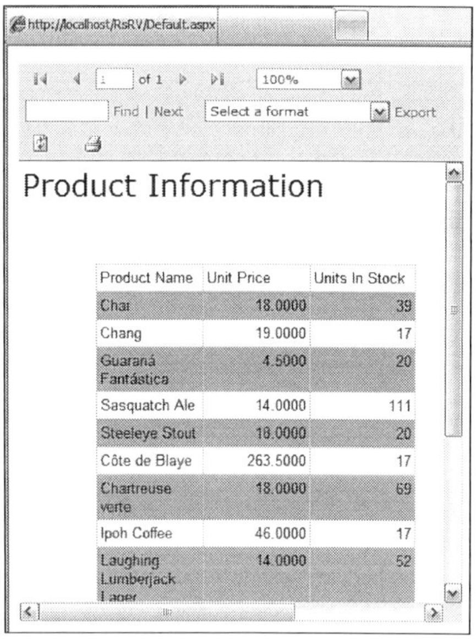

When the Microsoft ReportViewer is dropped on the **Default.aspx** page, all its properties and methods are accessible as in the intellisense drop-down, shown in the next figure. These can be used to customize some of the properties of the ReportViewer. The ReportViewer details get embedded in the `web.config` file of the site.

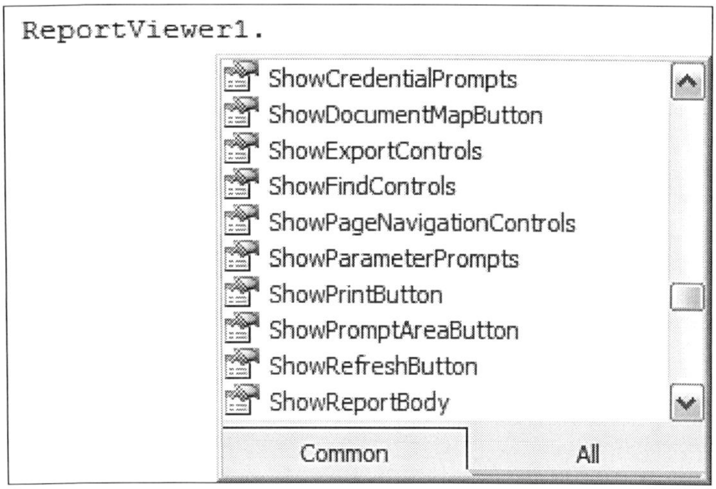

Hands-on exercise 8.4: Displaying a report on the Report Server in a Windows application

In Visual Studio 2008, you will create a Windows Forms application. You will then place a Microsoft ReportViewer control, like you did in the previous hands-on exercise. You will then write the code to access a report on the Report Server.

Follow on

In here you will embed a Report Viewer control in a Windows form to access a report on the report server. You will provide a path (relative) to the report on the report server.

1. Create a **Windows Forms Application** in Visual Studio 2008 from **File | New | Project...**.
2. In the **New Project** window, choose **Windows Forms Application** in **Visual Studio Installed templates** under **Visual Basic**. Provide a custom name for the form. Herein **WinWebSvc**.

3. Drag-and-drop the **MicrosoftReportViewer** (presently 9.0) control under **Reporting** in the **Toolbox** on to the form's design area.
4. Use the following to code the `Form1`'s `Load` event (complete code for **Form1.vb** is shown here).

```
Imports Microsoft.Reporting.WinForms
Public Class Form1

    Private Sub Form1_Load(ByVal sender As System.Object, _
        ByVal e As System.EventArgs) Handles MyBase.Load
        'Instantiate a report viewer
        Dim rv As ReportViewer
        rv = ReportViewer1
        ' Set the processing mode for the ReportViewer to Remote
        rv.ProcessingMode = ProcessingMode.Remote
        'set reference to a server report
        Dim srvRPt As Report
        srvRPt = rv.ServerReport
        'get a reference to default credentials
        Dim creds As System.Net.ICredentials
        creds = System.Net.CredentialCache.DefaultCredentials
        rv.ServerReport.ReportServerUrl = _
        New Uri("http://hodentek2:8080/ReportServer_SANGAM")
        rv.ServerReport.ReportPath = "/MdbSub"
        Me.ReportViewer1.RefreshReport()
    End Sub
End Class
```

In this example, the remote processing mode (on the Report Server) is chosen. The server URL is the URL of the Report Server as you have seen in all the previous chapters. The Report Path is given relative to the Report Server. The MdbSub report is the one you created in Chapter 7.

Publishing to the local web server

This application can be published to the local web server. When users access this application on the local web server, they will be asked to download.

1. Click on **Project | WinWebSvc...**.

   The **WinWebSvc** details will appear under this tab.

2. Click on the navigation item **Publish**.

   The **Publish** tabbed page of **WinWebSvc** appears as shown:

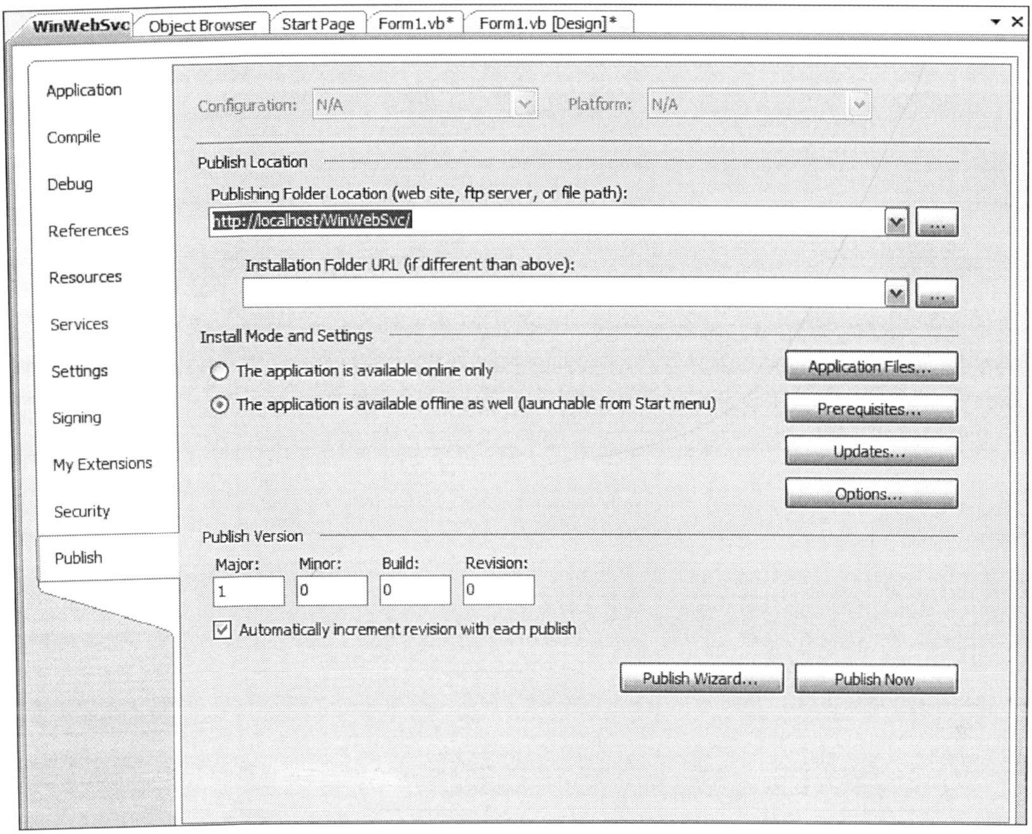

There are several options possible. You can choose a different installation folder. You can choose to send it as FTP or even persist to a file. Also, you can set it up for online or offline mode, and so forth. Here, the defaults will be used. Choosing the **Publish Wizard...** to publish will revisit all the options.

3. Click on **Publish Now** button.

   The report gets published and the following window is displayed:

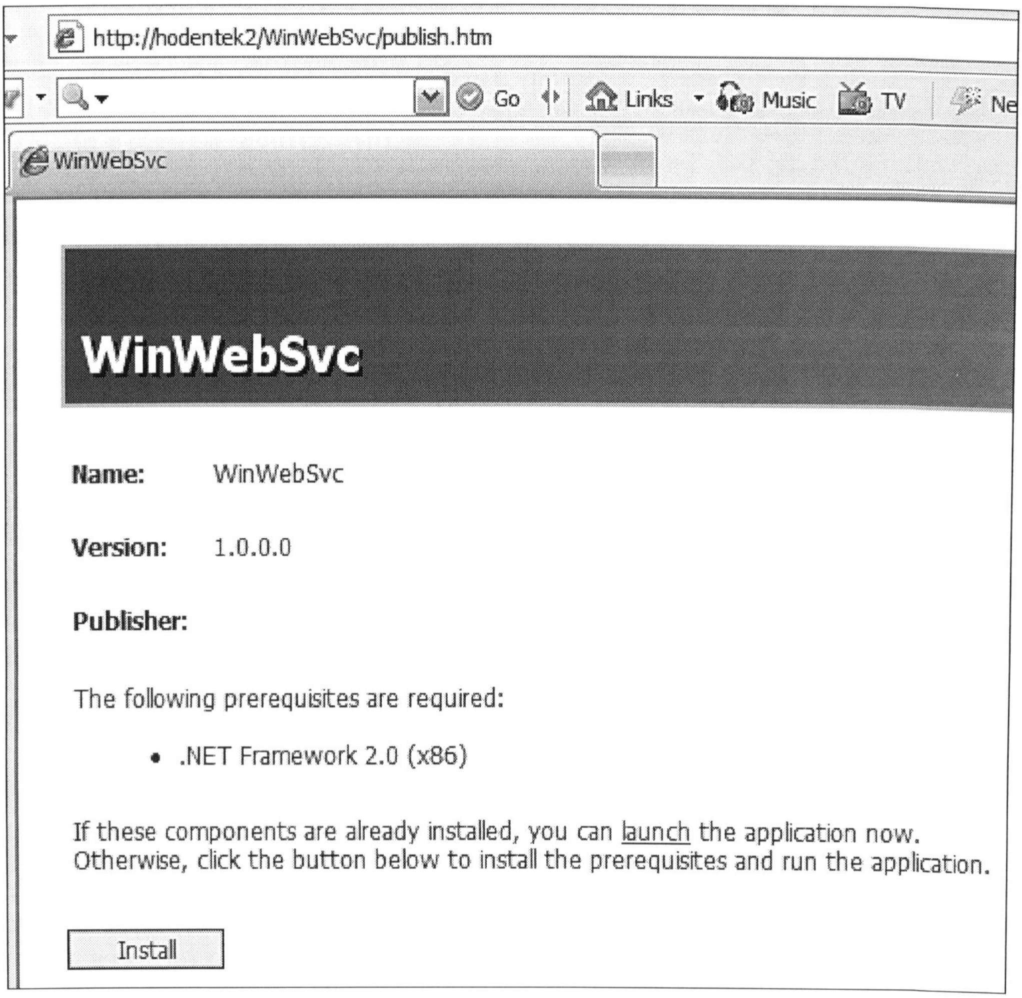

The **WinWebSvc** site in the localhost will have the following: `Application Files` folder and the files, `Publish.htm`, `setup.exe` and `WinWebSvc.application`. The application can be launched using the **Install** button.

> If you are using the latest IE browser, IE 8.0 RC1, the prerequisites information will not be displayed.

Programming with the Report Server web services API

In this section, you will be working with the Report Server API. In *Hands-on exercise 8.5*, you will work with ReportService2005 to interact with the Report Server to access items of the catalog on the server and create a DataSource on a named folder. In *Hands-on exercise 8.6*, you will work with the ReportExecution2005 end point to render a report on the Report Server into other formats. The APIs are extensive and the examples are really simple programs. However, they give you a handle on how to start using these APIs.

Hands-on exercise 8.5: Rendering a report on the Report Server with an ASP.NET Web application to other formats

In this hands-on, you will be accessing a report on the Report Server using the Reporting Services API. You will be creating a client which interacts with the Report Server and using the services provided by the server.

1. Create **TestRS2005** web site (ASP.NET3.5) in Visual Studio 2008. Use **HTTP**, **Visual Basic**.
2. Right-click the web site (**http://localhost/TestRS2005**) and from the drop-down choose **Add Web Reference...**.

3. In the **Add Web Reference** window shown, click on the drop-down list to access the following URL:

   ```
   http://hodentek2:8080/ReportServer_SANGAM/
   ReportService2005.asmx?wsdl
   ```

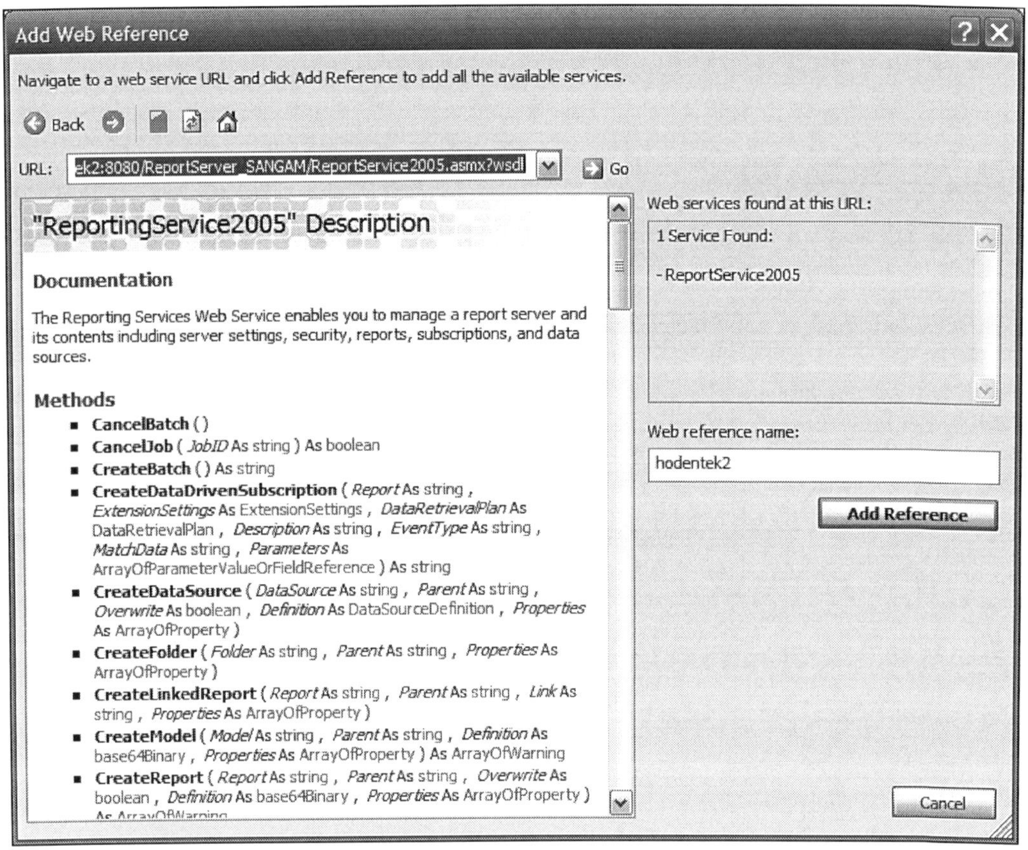

You will recognize that some of the methods you see in the **ReportingService** description are the same ones you used earlier in the Report Manager. The Report Manager is a client consuming this service. The ASP.NET coded here is also a client.

4. Click on the **Add Reference** button.

   This adds the service proxy to the web site folders by creating a new folder and adding the **Web Services Discovery Language** file.

5. Click on **View | Object Browser** and expand the web reference added as shown and review the various methods of this service.

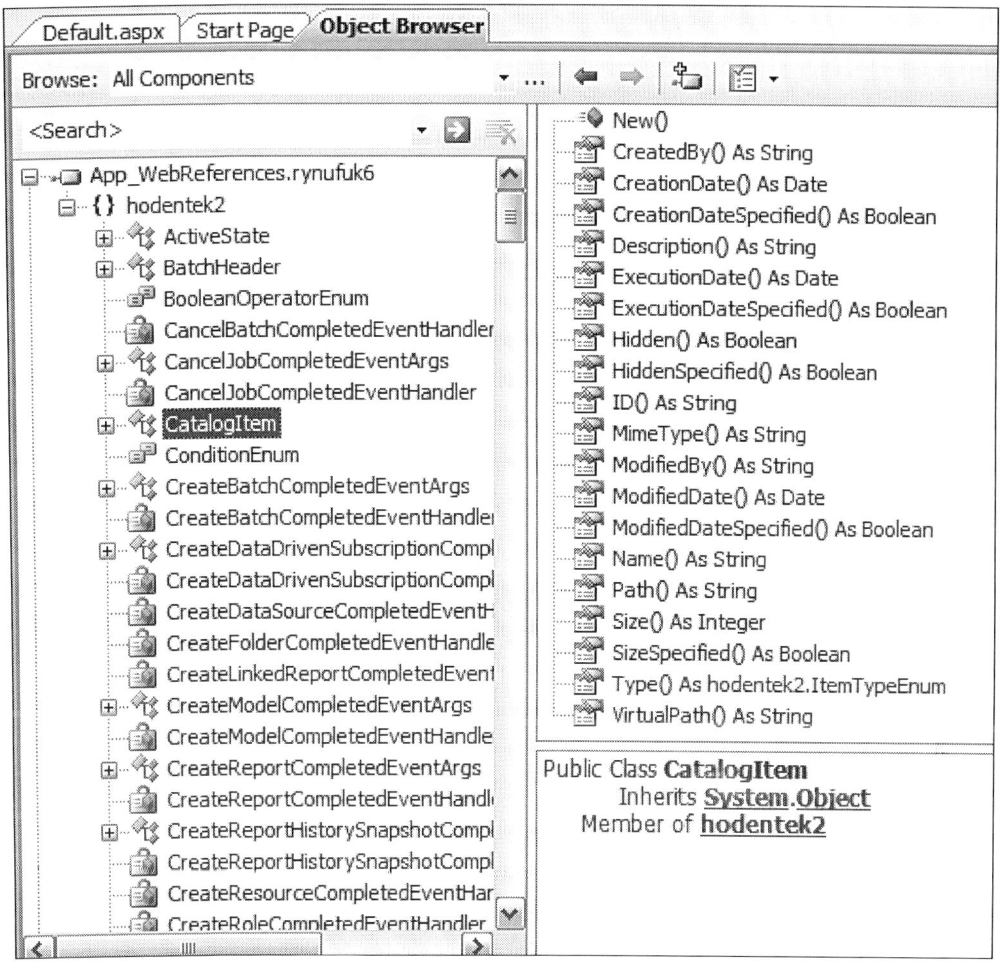

Finding reports and folders on the Report Server

In here you will be creating a simple user interface (a web page) to work with the Web Service API.

1. Add two button controls, three label controls, and two drop-down list controls to the **Default.aspx** page as shown:

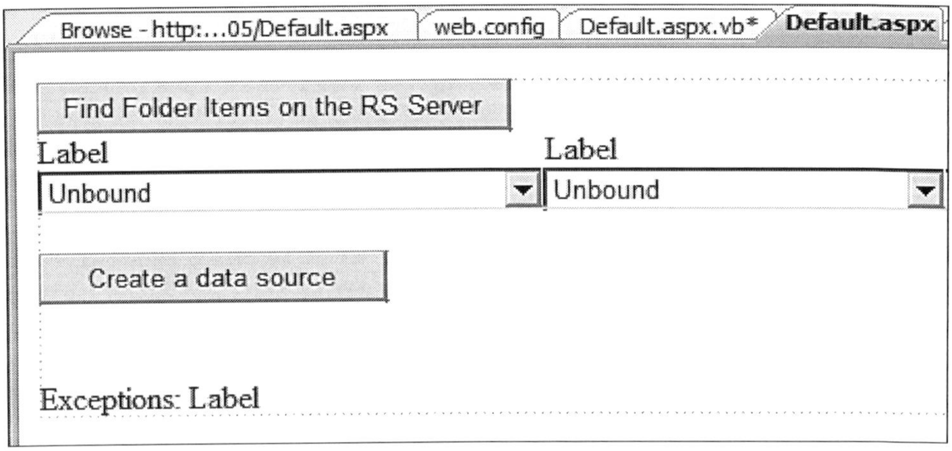

2. To the click event of the button with caption **Find Folder Items on the RS Server**, add code as shown (the code for the `Default.aspx.vb` is shown here and includes the button event)

```
Imports hodentek2.ReportingService2005
Imports System.Web.Services
Partial Class _Default
    Inherits System.Web.UI.Page

    Protected Sub FindItems_Click(ByVal sender As Object, _
        ByVal e As System.EventArgs) Handles FindItems.Click
        Label2.Text = "Reports"
        Label1.Text = "Folders"

        Dim myRS As New hodentek2.ReportingService2005
        myRS.Credentials = _
        System.Net.CredentialCache.DefaultCredentials

        Response.Write(myRS.Url.ToString() & vbCr)
        'Return the list of items in the Folder RSPWIz08 on the RS
        'Server
        Try
            Dim items As hodentek2.CatalogItem() = _
            myRS.ListChildren("/RSPWIz08", False)
            Dim catI As hodentek2.CatalogItem
            For Each catI In items
                'If the item is a report, add it to a combo box
                If catI.Type = hodentek2.ItemTypeEnum.Report Then
                    DropDownList1.Items.Add(catI.Name)
```

```
                End If
                If catI.Type = hodentek2.ItemTypeEnum.Folder Then
                    DropDownList2.Items.Add(catI.Name)
                End If
            Next catI
        Catch exception As System.Web.Services.Protocols.
          SoapException
            Label3.Text = exception.Message.ToString
        End Try
    End Sub
End Class
```

The code is pretty simple. The imports statement at the top provides the methods and properties in the web service. Observe that you can find the required arguments and their types from the *Object Browser* as shown here for **ListChildren ()** method.

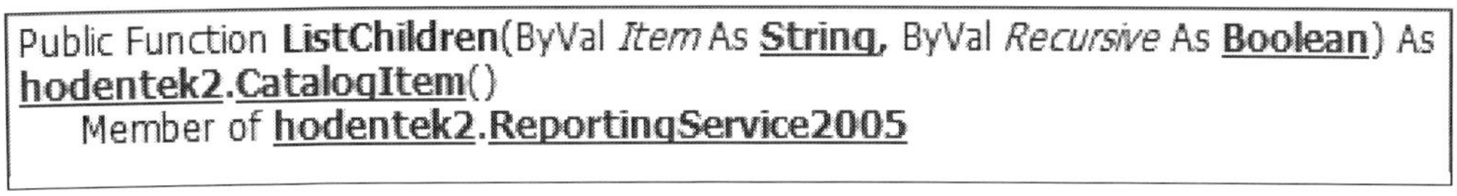

Also make sure you look for appropriate items in the *intellisense* drop-down as shown here:

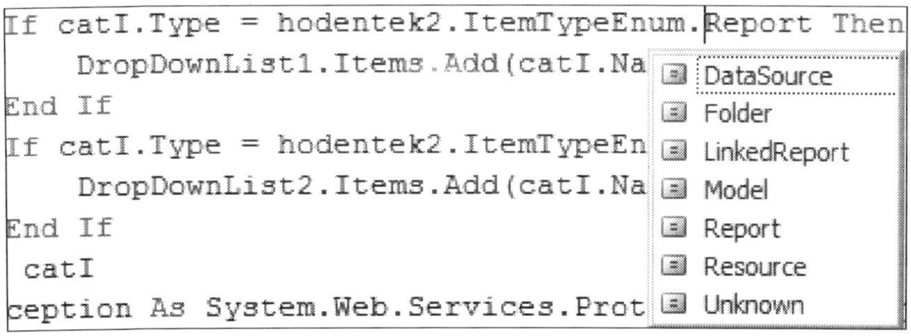

The "`If ...end if`" block will distinguish between a report and a folder and add it to the corresponding drop-down list box. The third label at the very bottom will display a message if there is a SOAP exception. For example, if you were to pass `//RSPWiz08` or `\RSPiz08` to the `ListChildren()` method, you would get an exception. You could add multiple ("`try..catch..end try`") blocks to troubleshoot if you need to.

One of the problems that you may encounter running this program is to do with the permissions on this folder. You will have to assign at least the *Browser* role to the ASP.NET user in the Reports Manager as shown. Failure to assign will result in the SOAP exception at run time (you will see this displayed in the label).

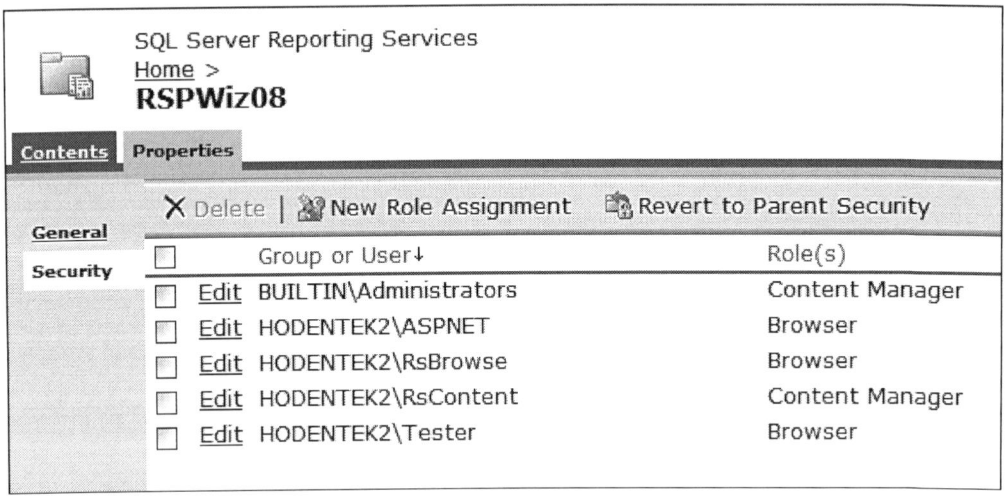

3. Build the project and browse the **Default.aspx** page and click on the button with the title "**Find the Folder items on the Report Server**".

Create DataSource () Method

In the previous example, you accessed an existing folder on the report server. In this section, you will create a new item on the Report Server. You will create a new DataSource in a named folder.

1. Type in the **CreateDataSource** in **Object Browser**'s find box as shown:

2. Review the arguments needed for the **CreateDataSource ()** method shown here from the **Object Browser**.

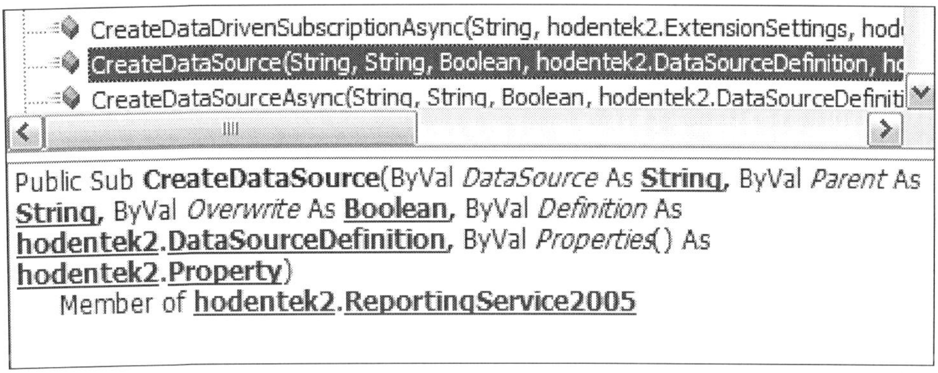

3. To the click event of the button with title **Create a Data Source,** add the following code:

```
Dim myRS As New hodentek2.ReportingService2005
        Try
            myRS.Credentials = System.Net.CredentialCache.
               DefaultCredentials
            Dim dsf As New hodentek2.DataSourceDefinition
            Dim conStr As String = ""
            Dim extension As String = ""
            dsf.ConnectString = conStr
            dsf.Extension = extension
            dsf.CredentialRetrieval = hodentek2. _
            CredentialRetrievalEnum.Integrated
            myRS.CreateDataSource("Test", "/RSPWiz08", True,
               dsf, Nothing)
        Catch exception As System.Web.Services.Protocols.
               SoapException
            Label3.Text = exception.Message.ToString
        End Try
```

You have already reviewed the arguments needed for the **CreateDataSource** method. Similarly, you can find the needed arguments for the **DataSource-Definition** as shown above from the *Object Browser*.

4. Build the project and browse to the web page.

The page comes up with an exception. Now if you bump the assignment to the ASP. NET user from *Browser Role* to *Content Manager Role* the exception goes away and a data source named **Test** will be created in the folder **RSPWIZ08**.

Hands-on exercise 8.6: Rendering a report on the Report Server with an ASP.NET Web application to other formats.

There are occasions where in you may want the report format to be something other than HTML such as PDF, Excel or Word. In this exercise, you will be accessing the Reporting Services to access a report on the Report Server and render it in other formats. You have seen the ease with which this can be accomplished with URL access.

In this exercise, you will be using the ReportExecutionService 2005, one of the two services provided by SSRS2008. In particular, you will be using the `Render()` method provided by this service to format a report on Report Server into other formats either for displaying or deploying on to another web site.

Follow on

Here you will be working with the Report Execution Service, the API that works with the reports. The Report Server API's execution endpoint is used here.

1. Launch Visual Studio 2008 and create a new web site. Herein, it is called **SrvRptToOthers**.
2. Right-click the project in **Solution Explorer** and from the drop-down choose the item, **Add Web Reference...**.

3. In the **Add Web Reference** Window type in the following:

   `http://hodentek2:8080/ReportServer_SANGAM/ReportExecution2005.asmx?wsdl`

   The program processes this information and if it exists or found, the **Report-ExecutionService** description is displayed as shown. The documentation lists all the methods that this service supports.

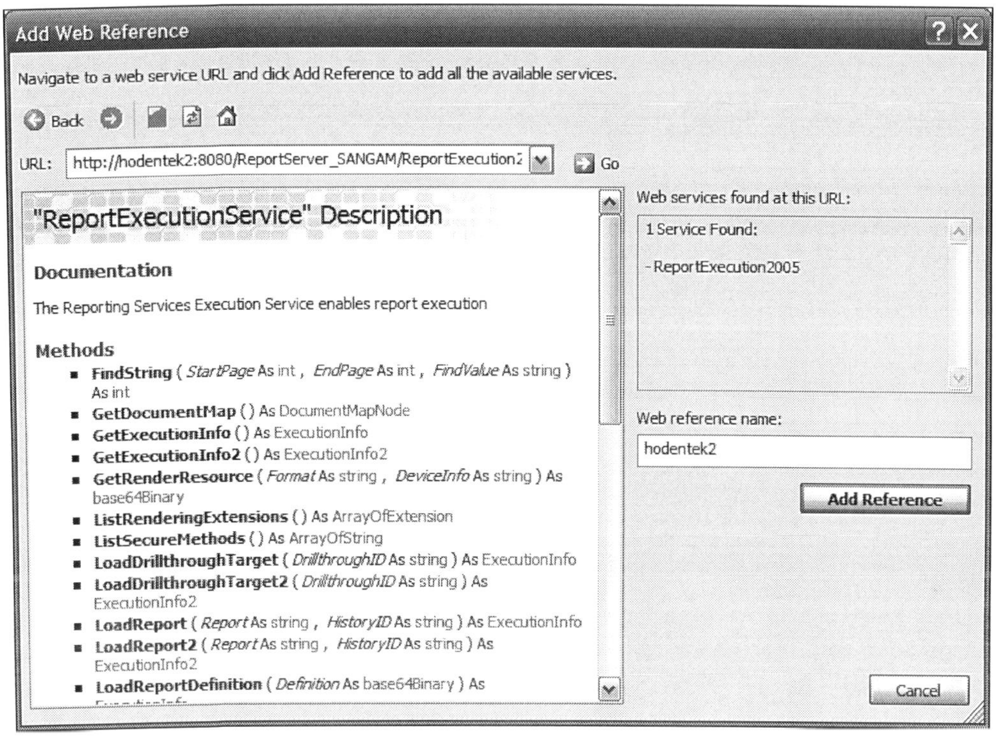

4. Click on the **Add Reference** button.

   This adds a web reference to the project as shown in the **Solution Explorer**. By adding this reference, you will be able to access all its methods. You should also look this up in the *Object Browser* which provides more details.

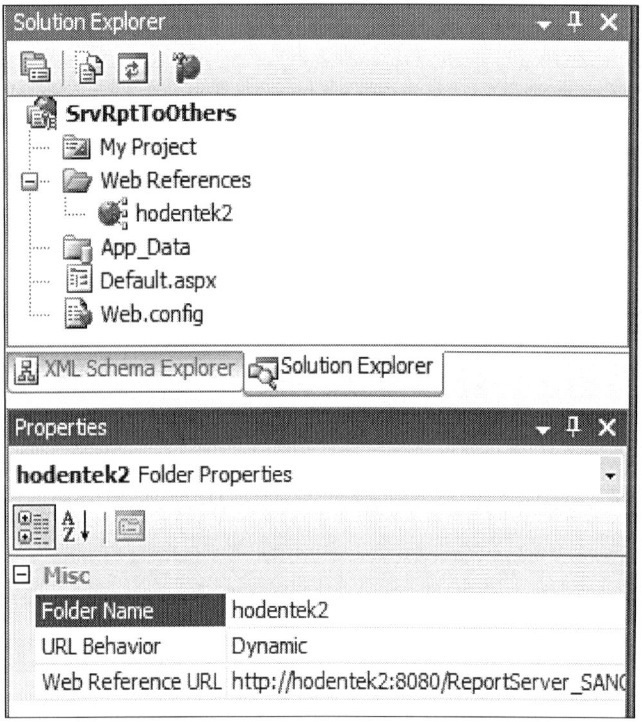

5. Drag-and-drop a button control on to the **Default.aspx** page and set up the code for the button click event as shown (the complete **Default.aspx.vb** is shown including the click event).

```
Imports SrvRptToPdf.hodentek2
Imports System.IO

Partial Public Class _Default
    Inherits System.Web.UI.Page

    Protected Sub Button1_Click(ByVal sender As Object, _
        ByVal e As EventArgs) Handles Button1.Click
        Dim rse As New ReportExecutionService
        'set up authorization
        rse.Credentials = System.Net.CredentialCache
                          .DefaultCredentials
        'arguments for the Render() method
```

```
        Dim reportPath As String = "/ProductsSubreport"
        Dim historyID As String = Nothing
        Dim extensio As String = ""
        Dim result As Byte() = Nothing
        Dim format As String = "PDF"
        Dim encoding As String = ""
        Dim mimeType As String = ""
        Dim warnings As Warning() = Nothing
        Dim streamIDs As String() = Nothing
        'declare ExecuteHeader and ExecuteInfo
        Dim executeInfo As New ExecutionInfo
        Dim executeHeader As New ExecutionHeader
        rse.ExecutionHeaderValue = executeHeader
        'Load report for execution
        executeInfo = rse.LoadReport(reportPath, historyID)
        Dim SessionID As String =rse.ExecutionHeaderValue.
                                 ExecutionID
        'code the Render() method
        result = rse.Render(format, Nothing, extensio, mimeType, _
        encoding, warnings, streamIDs)
        'clear the response
        Response.ClearContent()
        'add header
        Response.AppendHeader("content-length",
                               result.Length.ToString)
        'set up content type
        Response.ContentType = "application/pdf"
        Response.BinaryWrite(result)
        Response.Flush()
        Response.Close()
    End Sub
```

Basically the button click event accesses the `Render()` method on the Report Server by providing the authentication, execution and arguments needed for the `Render()` method.

6. Build the web site and browse the **Default.aspx** page. Click on the button for which the code was written.

   The report shown in the **ReportPath**, the **ProductsSubreport**, gets displayed in PDF format.

7. Make changes to the following lines in the above code as shown and build:

```
Dim format As String = "EXCEL"
Response.ContentType = "application/vnd.ms-excel"
```

8. Browse the **Default.aspx** page and verify that the report gets formatted into Excel format. Click on the **Open** button in the **File Download** window that is displayed as shown:

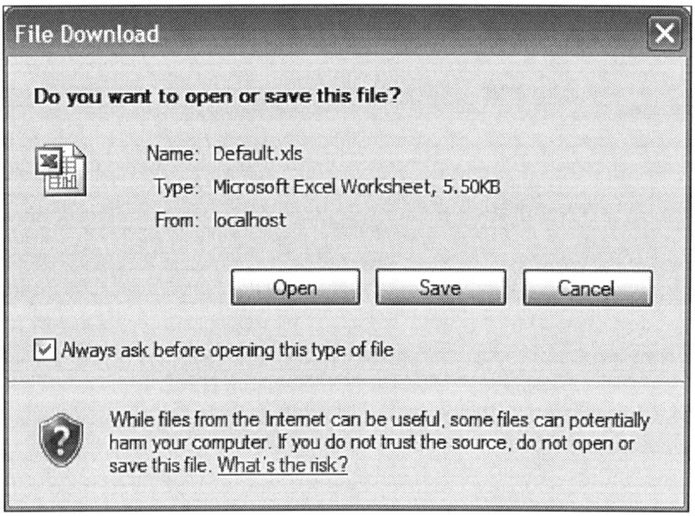

9. Make changes to the following lines in the previous code as shown and build:

```
Dim format As String = "WORD"
   Response.ContentType = "application/msword"
```

10. Verify that when you build and run the web site and browse to the **Default.aspx** page, you will see the report in the Word format.

Windows Management Instrumentation

WMI runs in a different process than the one in which it is used, as in this example. A connection to the WMI namespace is therefore required. Like any other process, this will also require permissions. As the owner of the computer, you may have this permission already but for a different user you may have to provide the permission. The second part of this hands-on show how to write code to obtain information regarding existing Report Server installations as well as describing how you may alter the configuration details using the methods available.

Hands-on exercise 8.7: Identifying the Report Server instance and modifying some of the properties

In this section, you will access the WMI class in the Report Server and look at all the attributes of the installation. You will also modify the Report Manager or the SMTP Server that sends out emails.

Setting up access permission to WMI namespace

As the owner of the machine who installed the service, the permission is already present. You need to give permissions to other users who may want to use the classes.

1. Click **Start** | **All Programs** |**Control Panel** | **Administrative Tools** | **Computer Management.**
2. Click on **Services** | **Applications** in the left-hand tree.
3. In the right-hand side, right-click WMI Control to access its properties.
4. In the Security tab expand the root node as shown to review the Report Server related security.

5. Click on **Admin** and click on **Security.**

   The folder security window "Security for `ROOT\Microsoft\Micros0ft\SqlServerReportServer\RS_SANGAM\Admin`" is displayed.

6. You provide permissions to the administrator or another Windows user who would be running the code. Close the open windows.

Accessing information about Report Server instances using WMI

As described in Chapter 1, there is only one Report Server installed on this machine. In general, there could be many Report Servers. The code would find the instances and provide their configuration information.

1. Create a Windows Forms application project in Visual Studio 2008.

   Herein it was named **WMI_RS.**

2. Drag-and-drop a label, a list box, and a button control onto the form.

3. Add the following code to the click event of the button after adding the imports statement to the code page as shown.

   Visual Basic is the language used for scripting WMI.

```
Imports System
Imports System.Management
Imports System.IO
Public Class Form1
    Private Sub Button2_Click(ByVal sender As System.Object, _
        ByVal e As System.EventArgs) Handles Button2.Click
        Dim WmiNamespace As String = _"\\Hodentek2\root\Microsoft\
               SqlServer\ReportServer\RS_SANGAM\v10\Admin"
        Dim WmiRSClass As String = _"\\Hodentek2\root\Microsoft\
               SqlServer\" & _"ReportServer\RS_SANGAM\v10\
                 admin:MSReportServer_ConfigurationSetting"
        Dim serverClass As New ManagementClass
        Dim scope As ManagementScope
        scope = New ManagementScope(WmiNamespace)
        'Connect to the Reporting Services namespace.
        scope.Connect()
        'Create the server class.
```

```
        serverClass = New ManagementClass(WmiRSClass)
        'Connect to the management object.
        serverClass.Get()
        If serverClass Is Nothing Then Throw New Exception
          ("No class found")
        Dim instances As ManagementObjectCollection =
             serverClass.GetInstances()
        Dim instance As New ManagementObject
        For Each instance In instances
            Label1.Text = ("Number of Instances detected:" &
                           instances.Count)
            Dim instProps As PropertyDataCollection =
                 instance.Properties
            '[The following code or similar code can be used for
            'modifying the instance properties:]
            'If instProps.Item("isReportManagerEnabled").Value =
                 False Then
            'instProps.Item("isReportManagerEnabled").Value = True
            'End If
            Dim prop As PropertyData
            For Each prop In instProps
                Dim name As String = prop.Name
                Dim val As Object = prop.Value
                ListBox2.Items.Add("Property Name: " + name & ":"
                & _"Property Value: " + val.ToString())
            Next
        Next
    End Sub
End Class
```

The WMI namespace is different from the default namespace for scripting.

4. Build the project and run the program.

5. Click on the button, Button 2, on Form 1.

   You should be able to see the properties of the identified instance as shown in the figure.

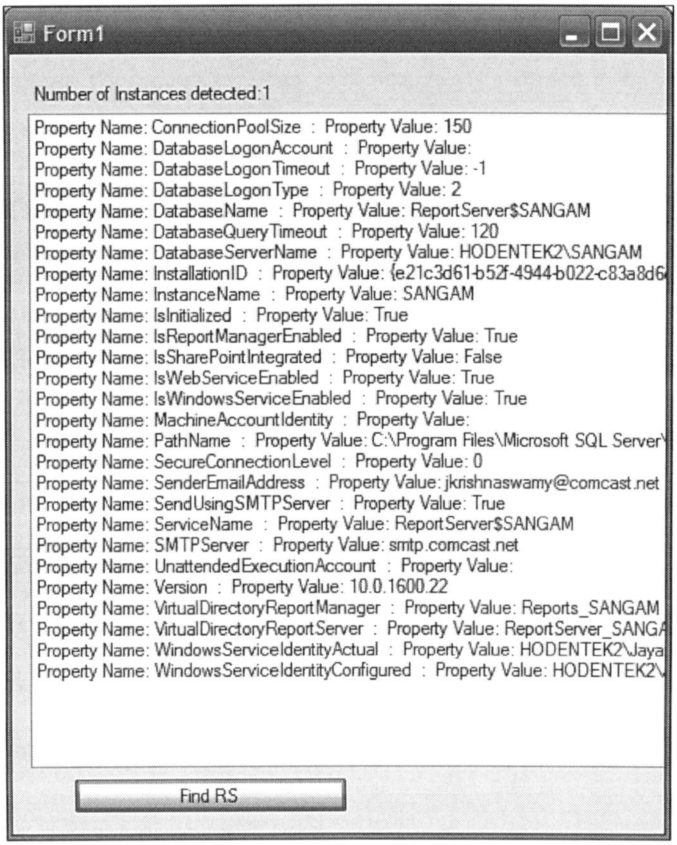

6. There are three lines of code commented out. Remove the comments and run the program again to verify that you can enable/disable Report Server or Report Manager (you have to use the property name as found in the above list).

   For example to enable/disable the Report Manager you need to use the following snippet:

```
If instProps.Item("isReportManagerEnabled").Value = False Then
          'instProps.Item("isReportManagerEnabled").Value = True
          'End If
```

Miscellaneous

There have been a lot of discussions about whether or not SQL Server Integration Services (SSIS) packages can be used to deliver multiple reports. Although you can establish a connection to the Reporting Services Web Service, the methods are not supported, yet. However, you can use an ActiveX task or a Script Task in SSIS to deliver a report in a package. In *Hands-on exercise 8.8,* you will create a Microsoft SQL Server Integration Services package in Visual Studio 2008 and use an ActiveX Script task to display a report on the Report Server. Since the method uses an URL, both Report Server as well as Web Server based reports can be used.

Although the Expression tool in Report Builder is very versatile, you may find attaching custom code will make it even more powerful. The example, although trivia, shows the plumbing needed to make custom code to work with Expression.

Hands-on exercise 8.8: Creating a SQL Server Integration Services Package to display a report from the Report Server

The scripting support in SQL Server Integration Services 2008 is well suited for many different kinds of applications. This hand-on exercise shows how you may display a report using a SSIS Package. Instead of the ActiveX Script Task used in this exercise you may also use the more powerful Script Task.

Before you start, you may note that VS 2008 / BIDS do not have the DTS 2000 run time installed. You need to run a program (`SQLServer2005_BC.msi`, X86) which you can download from Microsoft web site (`http://www.microsoft.com/downloads/details.aspx?FamilyID=228de03f-3b5a-428a-923f-58a033d316e1&DisplayLang=en`). After you run this installer you can go ahead with the rest of the exercise.

Follow on

You will be creating a package containing an ActiveX Script task and writing appropriate code to access the report.

1. Create an Integration Service project in VS 2008 or BIDS. Herein, **SsrsPack**.
2. Rename the package with a custom name. Herein, **SsrsRpt**.
3. Double-click **an ActiveX Script Task** under **Control Flow** items in the **Toolbox.**

4. Double-click the **ActiveX Script Task** in the **Control Flow** tab in the design area.
5. In the **General** page of the **ActiveX Script** task editor, add a description. Herein **Display a SSRS 2008 Report.**
6. In the **Script** page, type in **Main** for **the Entry Method.** In the text editor that is displayed for script (click in an empty area to bring up the text editor), type in the code as shown in the following screenshot:

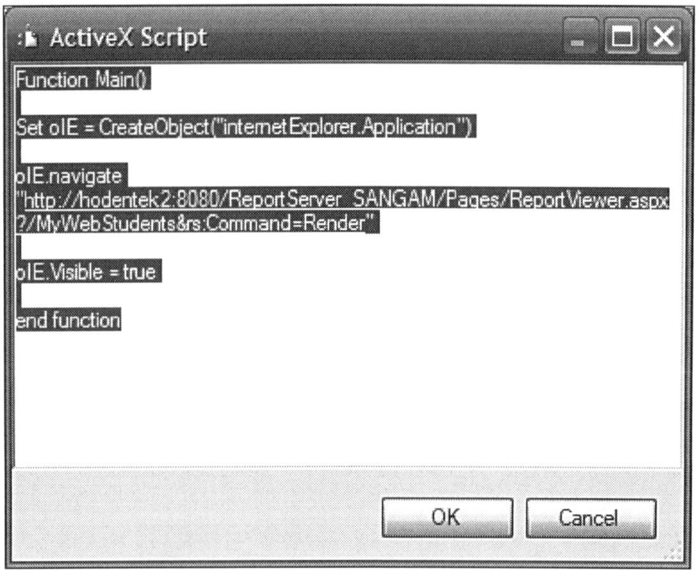

7. Close the above window as well as the **ActiveX Script** task editor.
8. Build the project and execute the package by right-clicking the highlighted ActiveX Script task and choosing **Execute** task.

After the processing is complete, the report is displayed.

Hands-on exercise 8.9: Using custom code in an expression

In the previous examples in the Report Builder, you have used the Expression support in various ways. In this section, you will be writing an expression that will look up a function and derive its value from the function in the custom code. The point of this exercise is to familiarize you with using this construct. The custom code can also leverage the built-in support in the Expression.

Follow on

Here you will be using a previously authored report and implementing custom code that will show a dollar amount in Yens.

1. Open the previously created report **ProductsSubreport** in design.

   The following design gets displayed as shown (however, you may open any report):

   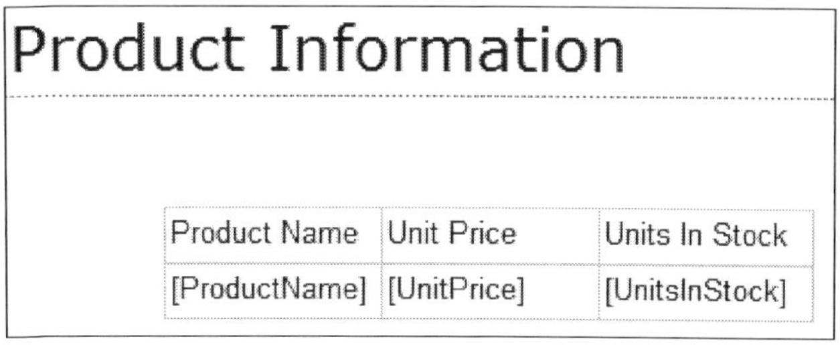

2. Add a column to the right of **UnitsInStock.**
3. Add a column heading **Price in Yen.**
4. Right-click on the report to open its properties.

   The **Report Properties** window opens.
5. Click on **Code** on the page navigation on the left.

   The **Write custom code for this report** page opens.
6. Type in the following code in the window:

   ```
   Public function InYen(x as double) as double
             return x*99.8'Present $/Yen
   end function
   ```
7. Now go back to the report design and type in an expression in the textbox below the **Price in Yen**:

   ```
   =FormatCurrency (Code.InYen(Fields!UnitPrice.Value))
   ```
8. Open the properties for the column that has the heading **Price in Yen** and for the **Language** property, type in **ja-JP** or use the drop-down pick list to select it.

9. Run the report from the ribbon menu **Home | Run.**

   The report gets displayed as shown:

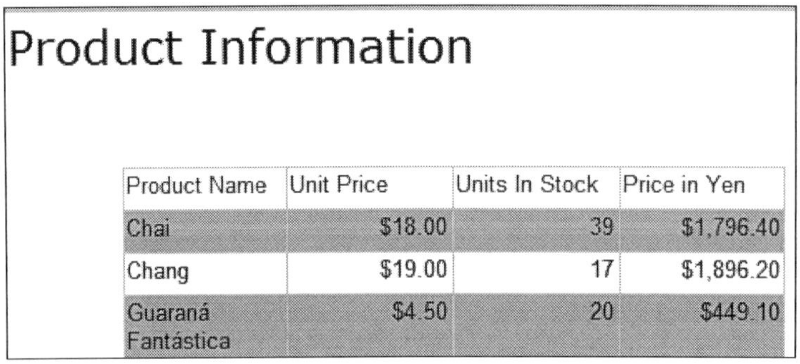

Product Information

Product Name	Unit Price	Units In Stock	Price in Yen
Chai	$18.00	39	$1,796.40
Chang	$19.00	17	$1,896.20
Guaraná Fantástica	$4.50	20	$449.10

Summary

The following programming interfaces that work with Reporting Services in SQL Server 2008 are described with hands-on examples: Reporting Services Application Programming Interfaces, Windows Management Instrumentation, Report Viewer Controls, URL Access, and custom code in an Expression. The Reporting Services utilities are described in the *Appendix C*.

9

Crystal Reports 2008 in Visual Studio 2008

In this chapter, we will be looking at Crystal Reports 2008 in Visual Studio 2008. You will be working with importing Crystal Report designed in reports 2008 as well as generating Crystal Reports in Visual Studio 2008's IDE.

Crystal Reports 2008

Crystal Reports has a long history of being bundled with Visual Basic and the Microsoft Visual Studio line of products as well as being the most popular reporting software with the lion's share of the market. The out of the box VS 2008 bundled version (version 12.0.0.0) has less functionality than the full version of Crystal Reports 2008. However, Crystal Reports Server (Business Objects Enterprise) provides the most complete reporting solution (manage, share and deliver). Since Visual Studio also has add-ins for other database vendor products such as IBM DB2, Oracle and SQL Anywhere, reports from these databases can also be created.

The new features in Crystal Reports .NET SDK are:

- Data transfer from a report to a Shockwave Flash
- Sort Controls
- Parameter panel and Group tree view
- Export in XML format
- Report processing indicator for larger reports.

The complete description of the new features of Crystal Reports may be found at: `http://www.businessobjects.com/pdf/product/catalog/crystalreports/cr_2008_whats_new.pdf`.

Hands-on exercise 9.1: Integrating a saved Crystal Report into an ASP.NET application in Visual Studio 2008

In this exercise you will be importing a Crystal Report into an ASP.NET application to make this report accessible from the intranet. In order to create this report, you will need a copy of Crystal Reports 2008. You may download an evaluation version from the following link:

```
http://www.businessobjects.com/product/catalog/crystalreports/
default.asp
```

You will create a Crystal Report using the same data as was used in the report you created earlier. The next figure shows a sample of the report created earlier in SSRS for purposes of comparing with the report created using Crystal Reports.

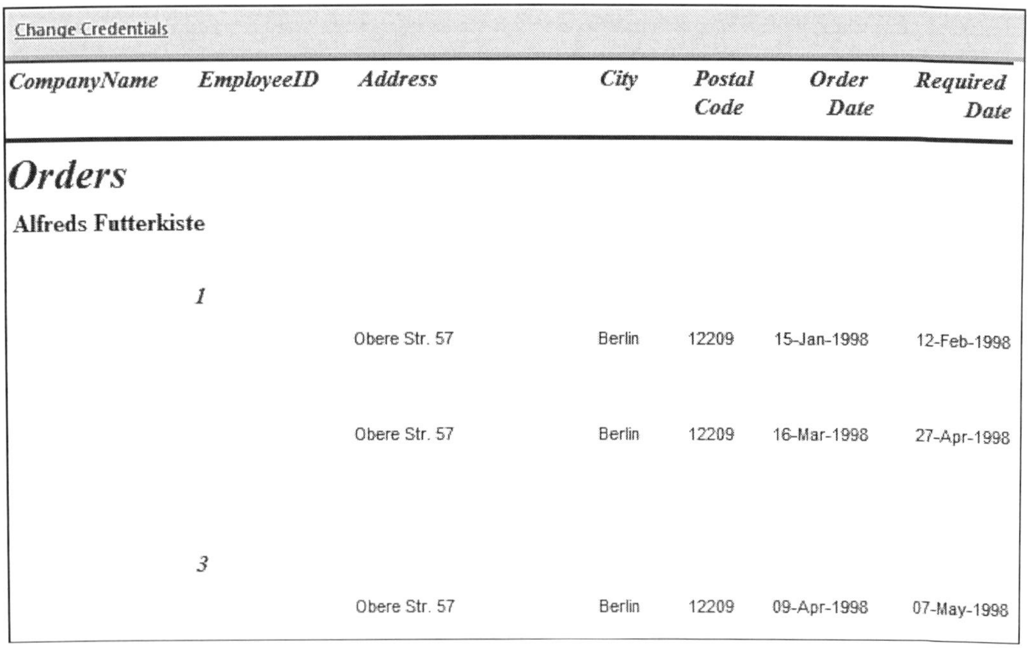

A preview of the report created in Crystal Reports 2008 is shown in the following figure:

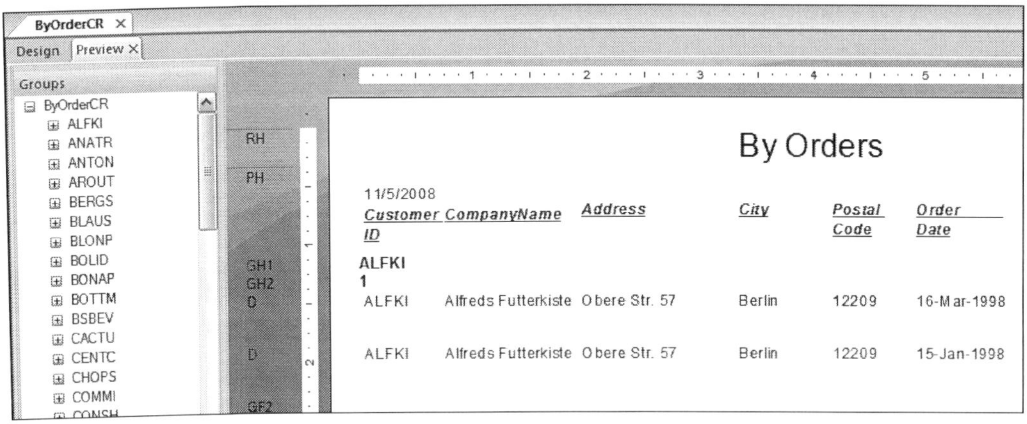

Follow on

CrystalReportViewer is an embeddable control which can display Crystal Reports. In this exercise we will be embedding the CrystalReportViewer in an ASP.NET web page.

1. Create a new ASP.NET website in Visual Studio 2008. Herein, it is named **CR2k8**. Add a web page with the name **ByOrders.aspx**.

   ByOrders.aspx opens in the designer.

2. Go to **Toolbox** | **Reporting**.

3. Drag-and-drop a **CrystalReportViewer** to the **ByOrders.aspx** page.

   CrystalReportViewer1 gets instantiated on the **ByOrders.aspx** page. The **CrystalReportViewer1** also has a *smart tasks* menu (only the smart tasks menu is shown) as shown:

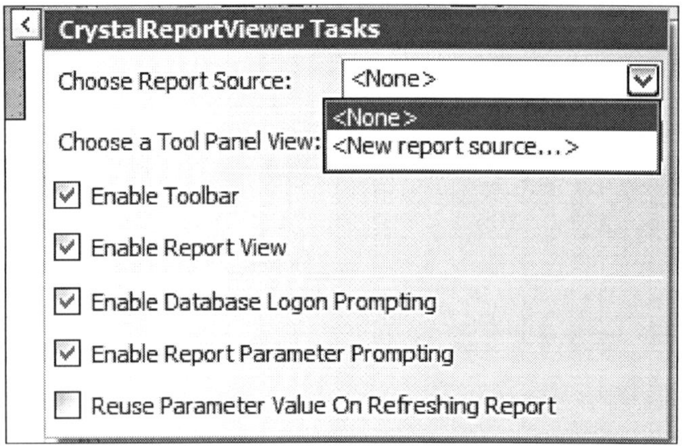

4. In the tasks drop-down, click on **<New report source...>**.

   This displays the **Crystal Report Source** window as shown. Specify a name for the **Crystal Report Source** control as shown:

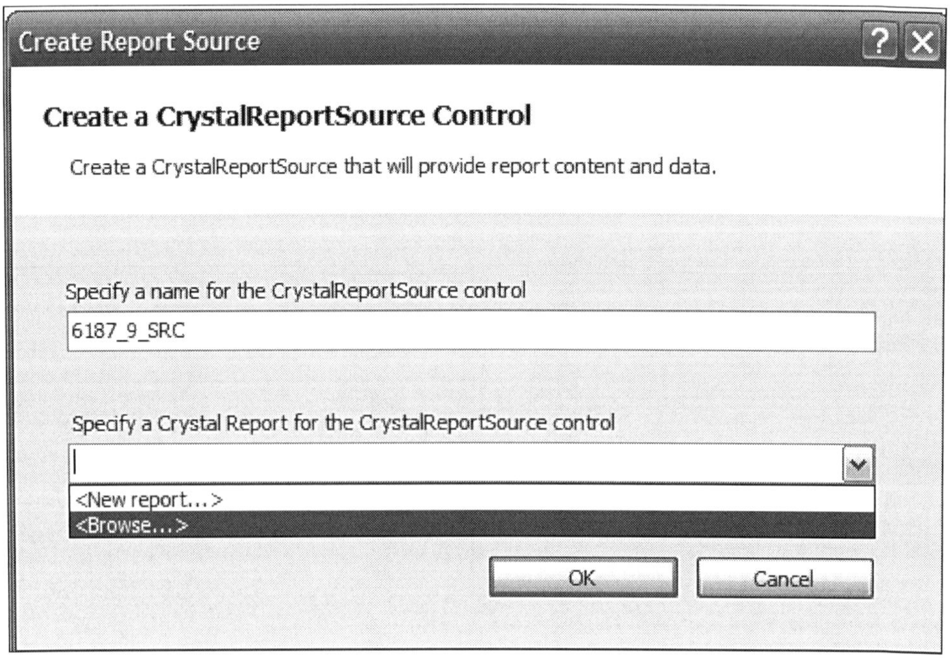

5. Click on the drop-down handle to **Specify a Crystal Report.....** and click to choose the **<Browse...>** option.
6. Browse to the saved location of the Crystal Report (whose preview you saw earlier) with the extension `.rpt` and choose the report.
7. Click **OK** on the **Create Report Source** window.

   The report gets added to the **ByOrders.aspx** page as shown:

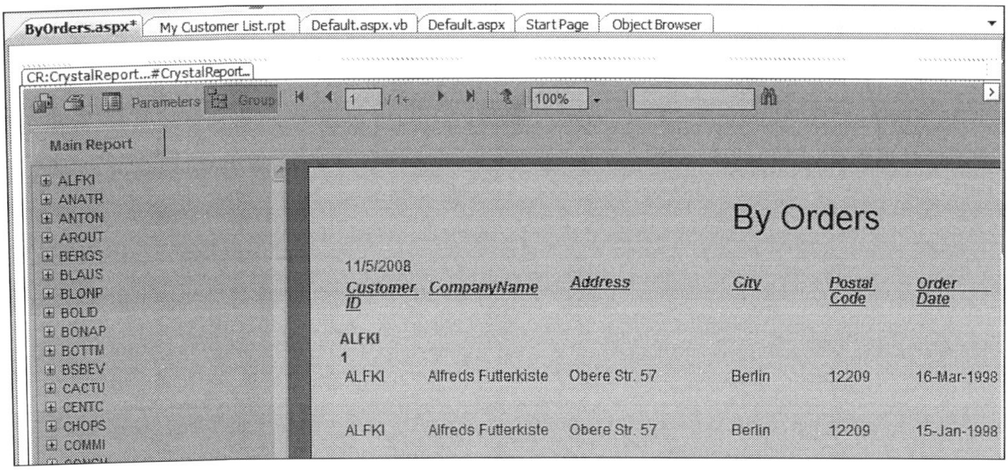

8. Click on the **Source** tab **ByOrders.aspx*** in the design view of the page

Review source and customize options

You can make changes to the design and customize the properties. You even get intellisense support for making changes.

When you place a Crystal Viewer control on a page from the toolbox, it gets placed inside the form element. This you should be able to see in the Source page as shown in this section.

1. Review the **Source** of this page.

   The relevant source code should appear as shown:

```
<form id="form1" runat="server">
    <div>
    </div>
    <CR:CrystalReportViewer ID="CrystalReportViewer1"
                            runat="server" AutoDataBind="True"
                            GroupTreeImagesFolderUrl=""
                            Height="1158px"
```

```
                                    ReportSourceID="ByOrdersCR"
                                    ToolbarImagesFolderUrl=""
                                    ToolPanelWidth="200px" Width="1059px"/>
<CR:CrystalReportSource ID="ByOrdersCR" runat="server">
    <Report FileName="C:\Documents and Settings\
                      Jayaram Krishnaswamy\Desktop\Crystal\
                      Crystal8\ByOrderCR.rpt">
    </Report>
</CR:CrystalReportSource>
</form>
```

The CrystalReportViewer can be customized using a large number of design time properties in the **Properties** window as shown in the following figure:

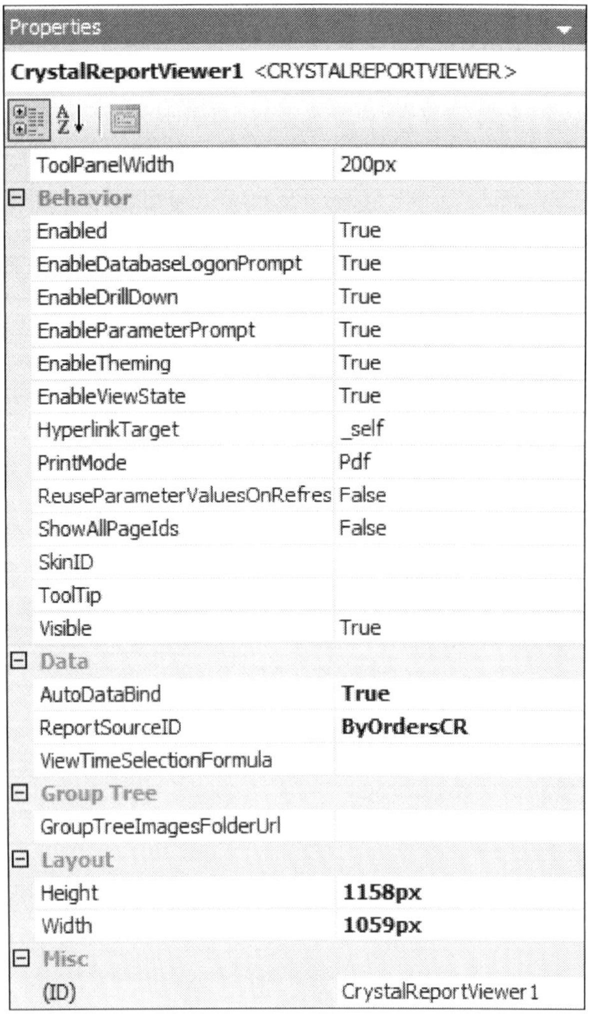

The design time properties can also be added to the page source as shown in the following figure:

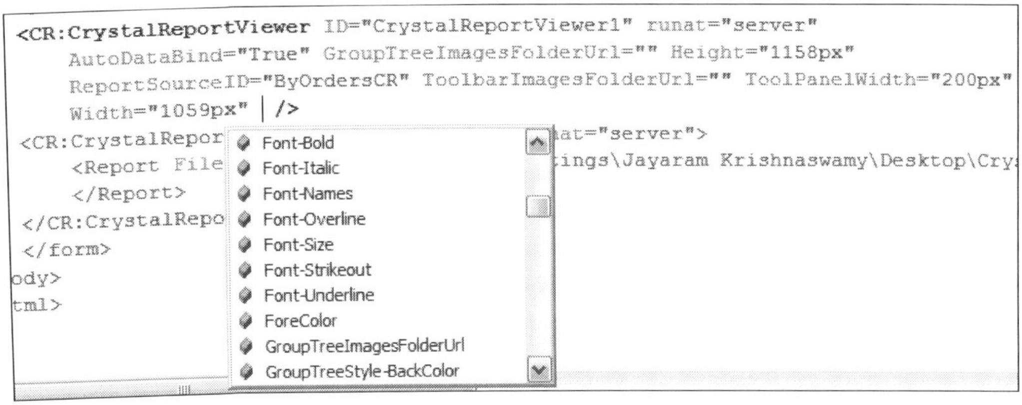

2. Build the project and browse the **ByOrders.aspx** page.

   The page gets displayed as shown with **Parameters** and **Group Tree** buttons at the top. The **Group Tree** page is tabbed in this default view. The **Group Tree** is displaying the **Document Map** you saw in your SSRS reports. You may observe that you can drill-down (by clicking on the plus sign) and bring to the top the details of any of the items in the navigation list. There is a nested group as well.

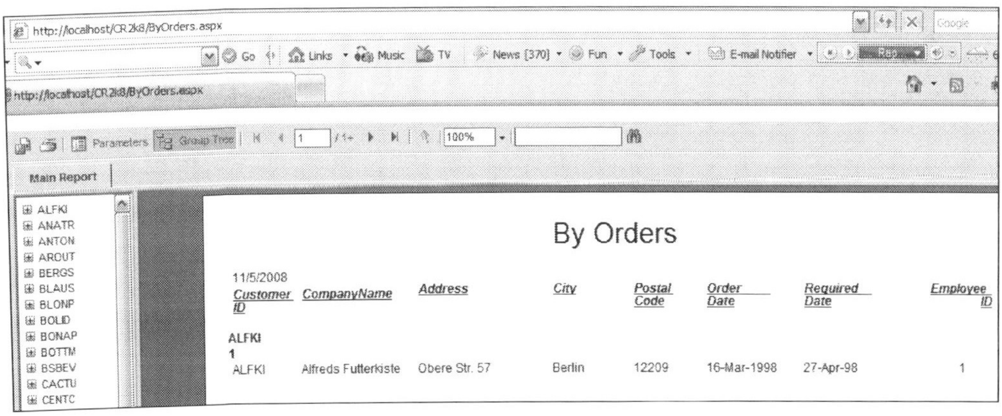

Filtering the displayed report

The report has brought with it a large number of rows. You may want to select only a couple of them to view. You can do this using the **Parameters** button.

1. With the refreshed page open in the browser, click on the **Parameters** button.

   The page gets displayed as shown:

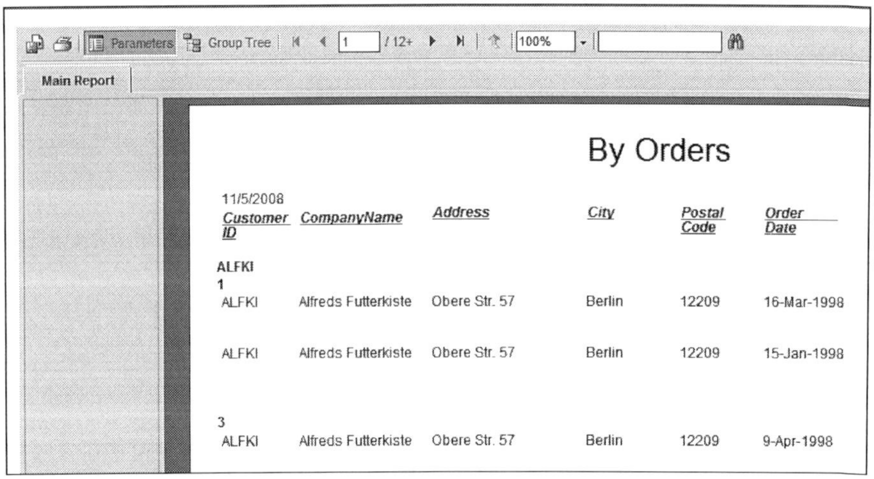

2. Now click on the numeral **1** (one of the nodes in the Group Tree) under **ALFKI.**

   The items for the chosen node only get into the report as shown. Notice the **1** to the right of **Main Report**. Now you can toggle between the **Main Report** and the parameterized report named **1.**

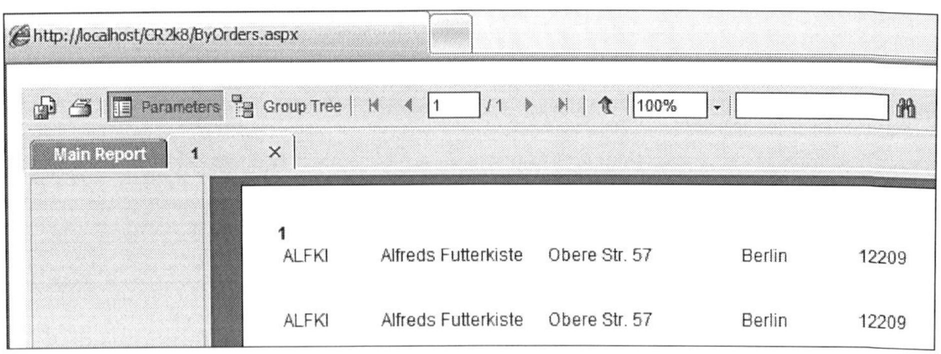

In this way you can add any number of special views of the report while it is in display. While you are working with the parameters the page is not refreshed.

Exporting the page using code

The Crystal Report that was added to the site was called **ByOrdersCR.rpt**. In the `Page_Load` event of the `ByOrders.aspx` page you can insert code to export this page to a specific location on your hard disk. Note that you need to give the ASP.NET user the permission to write to a file to succeed in this task. Since this is an ASP.NET web site project, the report is already available on the intranet.

1. Bring up the code page for the ByOrders.aspx page and insert the following code to export the page as an EXCEL page to a named location on the C:\ drive.

   In the intellisense drop-down, you can choose any of the several formats supported.

```
Partial Class ByOrders
    Inherits System.Web.UI.Page

    Protected Sub Page_Load (ByVal sender As Object, _
        ByVal e As System.EventArgs) Handles Me.Load
        ByOrdersCR.ReportDocument. _
        ExportToDisk(CrystalDecisions.Shared. _
            ExportFormatType.Excel, "C:\ByOrders.xls")
    End Sub
End Class
```

Hands-on exercise 9.2: Creating a Crystal Report and integrating it into a Windows forms application

Crystal Reports can be integrated into Windows forms applications as easily. The application can then be deployed on the client computers. Deploying the application from Visual Studio can be carried out in the following manner:

- ClickOnce deployment
- Windows Installer deployment
- Merge Modules deployment

The details are outside the scope of this book, but the following link can be accessed to learn the full details: `https://boc.sdn.sap.com/node/8012`.

Follow on

1. Create a new Visual Basic Windows Form Application project from **File | New | Project...** in Visual Studio 2008. Provide a name for the project. Herein, it is named **CR2008**.
2. Add a CrystalReportViewer to the default form, **Form1**, from **Toolbox | Reporting | CrystalReportViewer.**

   An instance of Crystal Report Viewer, **CrystalReportViewer1**, will be added to the form. The design time properties can be accessed from the **Property** window. By default it gets docked to the form at the top-left position and fills the form. You may change this by altering it in the **Properties** window.
3. Add a dataset to the project from **Project | Add New Item... | Dataset** from the **Common Items**. Provide a name. Herein, the default **DataSet1** is used. Click **OK** after providing the name.

   A schema file named **DataSet1.xsd** gets added to the project in the **Solution Explorer**.
4. Double-click the **DataSet1.xsd** file.

   The **Document Outline - DataSet1** window and the tabbed designer page for **DataSet1.xsd** gets opened. Read the instructions in the designer page.

Creating a typed dataset

Creating a dataset to retrieve data from the data source is the first step in designing any report including a Crystal Report. Visual Studio 2008 makes it very easy to create a dataset and provides support for many kinds of data sources.

1. Click on **View | Server Explorer**.

   The **Server Explorer** window gets displayed with all the existing connections as shown. The connections may be refreshed by clicking the **+** sign on any of the connections. If you do not see a connection you can make a new one. Follow this link to create a new **Data Connections** in **Server Explorer**: `http://hodentekhelp.blogspot.com/2008/11/how-do-i-set-up-data-connection-in.html`.

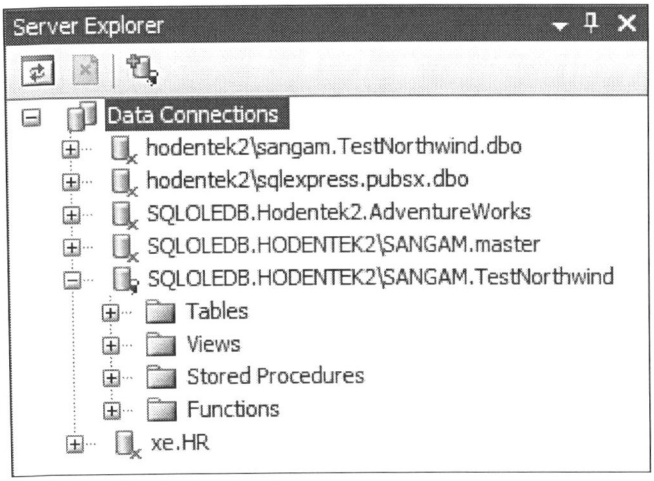

Here a connection to the SQL Server 2008 using OLE DB has been opened.

2. Expand the **Tables** node (by clicking on the **plus** sign) and drag-and-drop the **Employees** table on to the designer surface of **DataSet1.xsd**.

   The **Employees** table gets added to the designer surface as shown. Note that you may drag-and-drop a number of columns on to the designer (holding down *Ctrl* key) as well. In this case only those columns will be present in the schema.

Add a blank Crystal Report and add META data

After setting up the dataset you begin with a blank Crystal Report template and configure the report.

1. Add a Crystal Report to the project from **File | Add New Item...**or in the **Add New Item** window from **Common Items | Reporting**.

   A **CrystalReport1** gets added to the project and at the same time the **Crystal Reports Gallery Window** gets displayed.

2. Accept the default (**Using the Report Wizard**), choose **Standard,** and click **OK.**

   The **Standard Report Creation Wizard** gets displayed. Expand the **Project Data** node and the **ADO.NET DataSets** folder.

3. Expand the **CR2008.Dataset1.**

   The **Employees** object gets displayed. This is the dataset you created earlier.

4. Highlight the **Employees** object and transfer it to the **Selected Tables** area using the **>>** transfer button as shown:

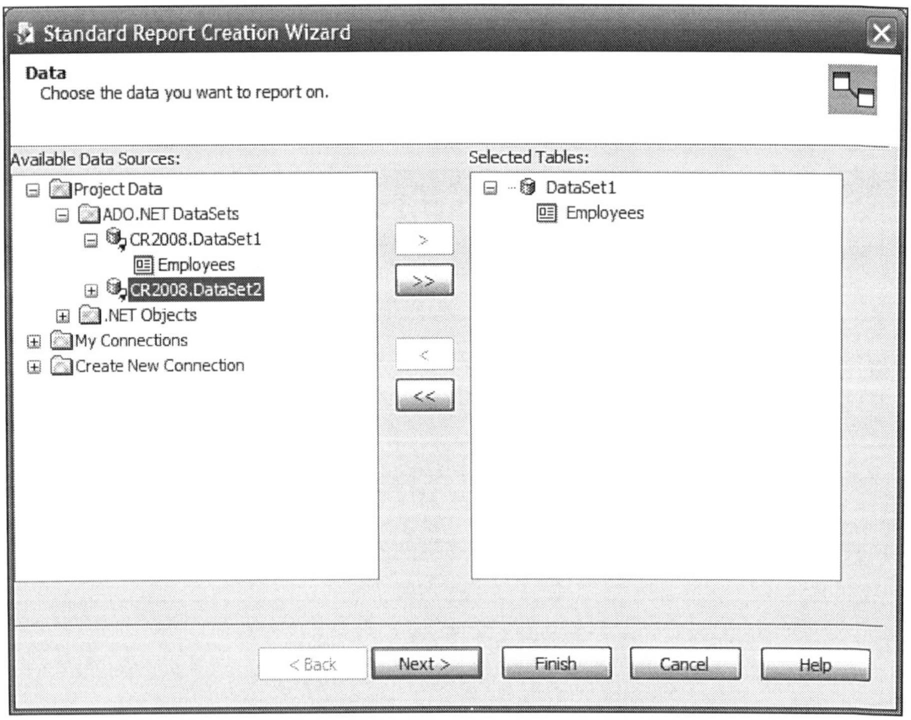

5. Click on the **Next** button.

   The **Fields** selection page of the wizard gets displayed.

6. Choose **EmployeeID, LastName, FirstName, BirthDate, HireDate, City** and **Country** and transfer them to the **Fields to display** area using the **>>** button. Click on the **OK** button.

   The **Groupings** page of the wizard gets displayed.

7. Add the **EmployeeID** to the **Group By** area using the **>>** button.

8. Click on the **Finish** button.

You could pursue this wizard till the end. For this exercise clicking the **Finish** button is ok.

The report gets populated with the fields selected as shown in the following figure. The **Field Explorer** also gets displayed. The report layout with the banded structure is now populated by the chosen fields. Here you can choose to make changes to the design as you would in Crystal Reports. You can drag items from the **Field Explorer** window and drop them into the report sections and use all the capabilities provided by the Crystal Reports add-in to Visual Studio 2008.

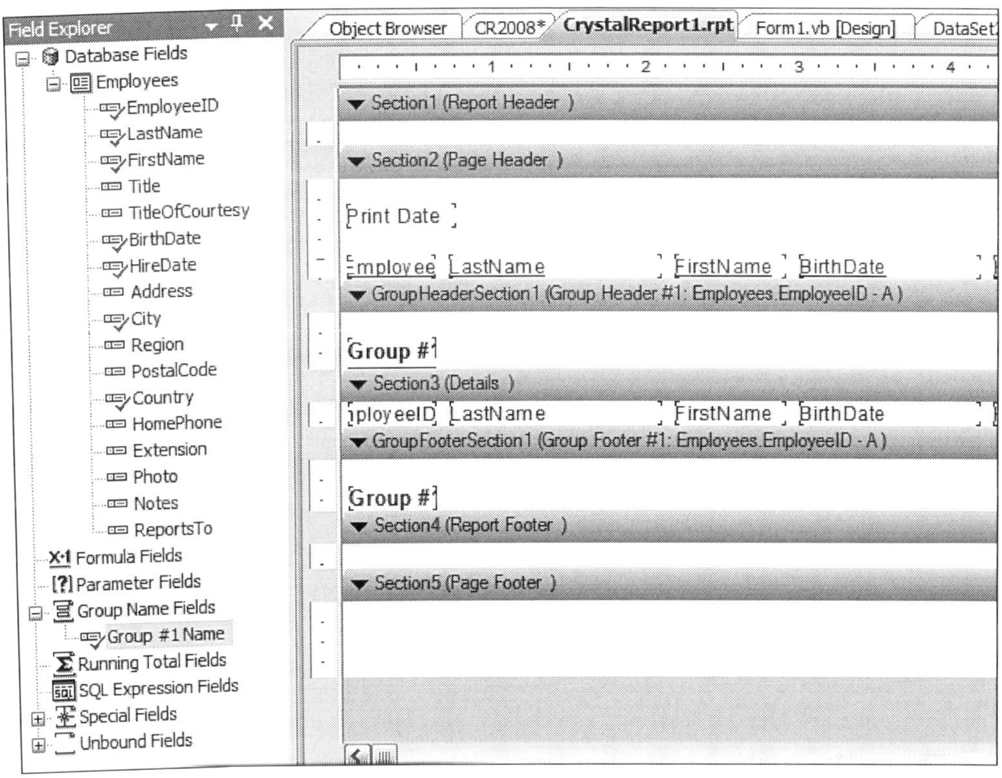

Add the report to the CrystalReportViewer

In the following, you will be enabling the report to be viewed using the CrystalReportViewer.

1. Click on **Form1,** which already has CrystalReportViewer and click on the **Smart Tasks**.
2. In the **CrystalReportViewer** tasks drop-down click on **Choose a Crystal Report....**
3. In the **Choose a Crystal Report -CrystalReportViewer1** window use the drop-down handle to choose **CrystalReport1**.

   The design view of the form with the CrystalReportViewer containing this report gets displayed as shown:

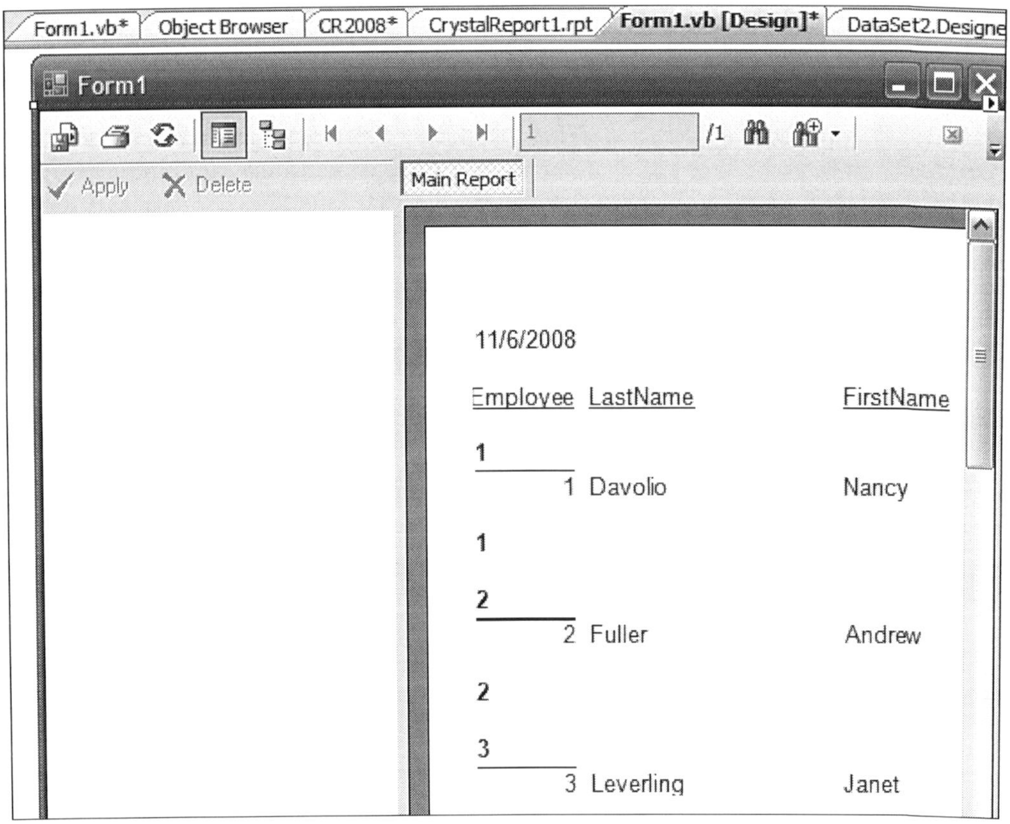

4. Build the project and verify that the report shows embedded in the form as designed.

   Similar to the previous hands-on you may add additional controls and code to change the run time look of the report and export the report to another format. In order to get a good handle on what is going on behind the wizard, make sure you open up and study the `Form1.Designer.vb` file.

Hands-on exercise 9.3: Creating a Crystal Report and populating it with data at runtime

In the previous example, we followed the graphic user interface wizard to set up the fields in the report and the **Server Explorer** to create a data connection. Sometimes you may want to have runtime control over your report so that you have more flexibility. In this section, you will supply the data to the report using data created by the ADO.NET objects at runtime. Also, create the fields' selection for the Crystal Report as in the previous hands-on.

Follow on

In this section, you will be creating a report using the Crystal Reports Engine code for interacting with the report. At first you need to add a reference to the library. You will follow it up by adding a report and hooking it up with the data source using code.

Create project and add references

This is an essential step before you can use the code from Crystal Reports. Since Crystal Reports is an add-in you have access to the dynamic link libraries. Make note of the versions you are adding.

1. Create a Windows forms application as in the previous hands-on. Provide a name for the project. Herein, it is named **CrDataSet**
2. Right click on the project and choose **Add Reference...**

3. The Add Reference window gets displayed as shown.

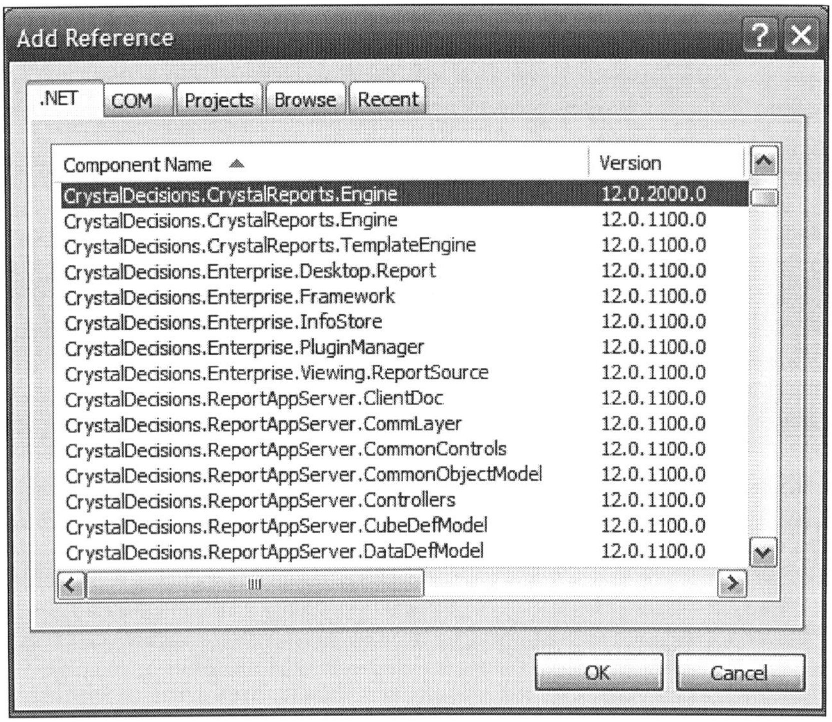

4. Add the following references and make sure you are using the same version for both: **CrystalDecisions.CrystalReports.Engine** and **CrystalDecisions.Shared** (scroll down the list to add this).

Add a Crystal Report and apply fields

1. Add a Crystal Report using the **Add New Item...** submenu item as in the previous case.

   CrystalReport1 gets added to the project.

2. Add a **Button** to the form as well as a **CrystalReportViewer** from the **Toolbox**.

3. Configure the Crystal Report as soon as it gets added by using the wizard to choose the fields shown in the following figure. These are the fields selected from the **Customers** table in the **TestNorthwind** database.

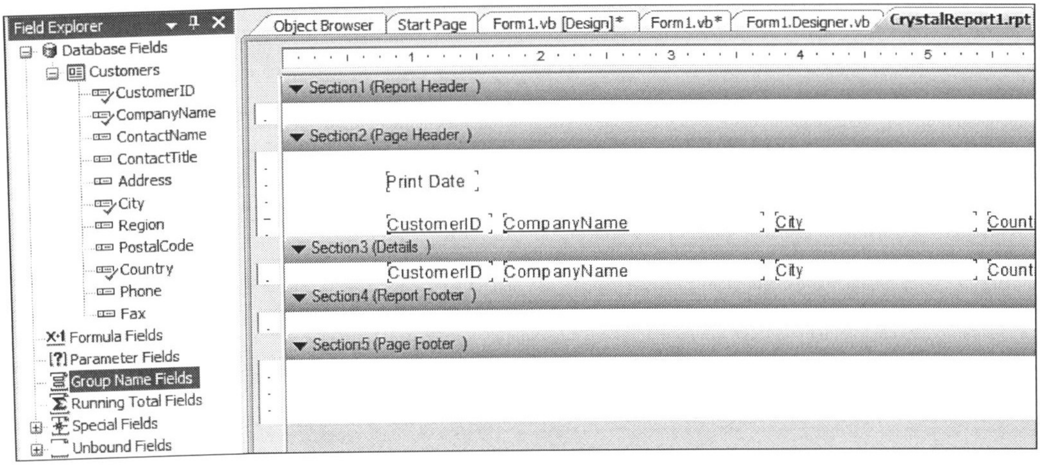

The design view of the form is as shown in the next figure. The fields are the ones you chose, but the data in this design view is dummy data as no datasource is connected yet.

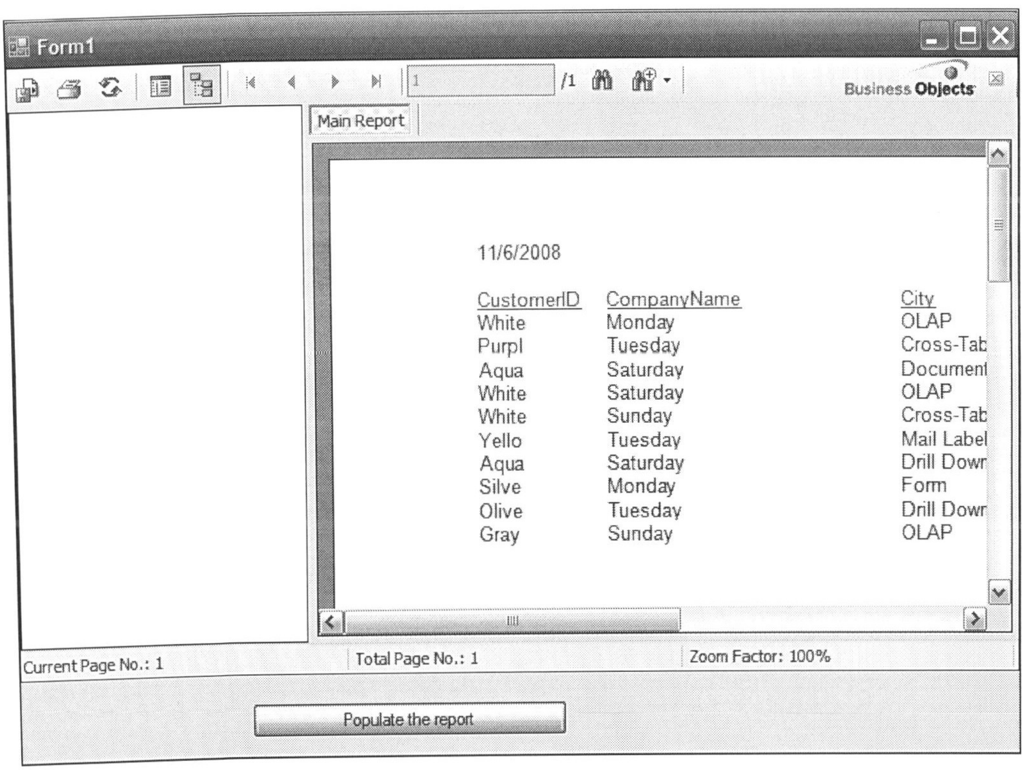

Add code, build, and run

The form that you have added to the project is to be associated with the events that take place on the form such as button clicks. The code shown next will provide the code for such an event. Again the name of the SQL Server Instance and the name of the database in your case will be different. You should make appropriate changes in the highlighted areas of the code. It is assumed the authentication is Windows authentication.

1. Add this code to the button's click event.

   The code includes the complete code for the form with annotations for each line.

   The `Imports` statements are necessary to access the methods/properties.

```
Imports CrystalDecisions.CrystalReports.Engine
Imports CrystalDecisions.Shared
Imports System.Data
Imports System.Data.OleDb
Public Class Form1

    Private Sub Button1_Click(ByVal sender As System.Object, _
        ByVal e As System.EventArgs) Handles Button1.Click
        'Instantiate a Crystal Report,crDocument
        Dim crDocument As New CrystalReport1
        'Instantiate a DataSet object, DataSet1
        Dim Dataset1 As New DataSet
        'Instantiate a new OLE DB Connection
        Dim oOleDbConn As New OleDbConnection
        'Instantiate a new OLEDB DataAdapter
        Dim oOleDbDataAdapter As New OleDbDataAdapter
       'Provide the connection information to your server
        databaase
        'You may need to provide data specific to your application
        Dim conStrg As String = "Provider=SQLOLEDB;" & _
        "Data Source=HODENTEK2\SANGAM;Integrated Security=SSPI;"& _
        "Initial Catalog=TestNorthwind"
        'Provide the Coonection string to the conneciton
        oOleDbConn.ConnectionString = conStrg
        'Define the Data Adapter with the SQL Statement and
          Connection Info
        oOleDbDataAdapter = _
        New OleDbDataAdapter("SELECT CustomerID, CompanyName," & _
        "City, Country FROM Customers GROUP BY CustomerID," & _
        "CompanyName, City, country order by Country", oOleDbConn)
        'Fill the Data Adaptr
        oOleDbDataAdapter.Fill(Dataset1, "Customers")
        'crDocument.SetDataSource(Dataset1)
```

```
            'Set the data source for the Report
            crDocument.Database.Tables(0).SetDataSource(Dataset1)
            'Set the Crystal Report as the
            'Report Source for the Report Viewer
            CrystalReportViewer1.ReportSource = crDocument
        End Sub

    End Class
```

2. Build the project and run the form. Click on Button1 and verify that the report gets populated by the records retrieved from the back-end server.

Hands-on exercise 9.4: Creating a Crystal Report and populating it with data from a stored procedure at run time

In the previous example, the data for the report came from a `SELECT` statement against a table in the database. In this exercise, you will be looking at a stored procedure that provides data for the report. At first you will create a stored procedure and test it in the SQL Server Management Studio. Next you will use this as a data source for the report by binding data to the report using code.

Follow on

In this hands-on you will create a stored procedure in the SQL Server 2008 Management Studio which you will later use as a data source for the Crystal Report. You will be using code to bind the data to the report.

Create a stored procedure and test it

In here we first create a stored procedure in the SQL Server Management Studio.

1. Create a stored procedure `Ord` in SQL Server Management Studio using the following statement:

```
USE [TestNorthwind]
GO

/****** Object: StoredProcedure [dbo].[Ord] Script Date:
11/04/2008 11:04:11 ******/
SET ANSI_NULLS ON
GO

SET QUOTED_IDENTIFIER ON
```

```
GO

Create Procedure [dbo].[Ord] @prd varchar(50)
as
SELECT     [Order Details].OrderID, [Order Details].UnitPrice,
[Order Details].Quantity, Products.ProductName
FROM          [Order Details] INNER JOIN
                      Products ON [Order Details].ProductID =
Products.ProductID

WHERE     (Products.ProductName = @prd)

GO
```

2. Verify that it returns data rows using the following statement:

   ```
   exec dbo.Ord 'Chai'
   ```

3. Add a second form to the `CrDataSet` project.
4. Add the following references and make sure you are using the same version for both.

   CrystalDecisions.CrystalReports.Engine and **CrystalDecisions.Shared** (scroll down the list to add this).

Add Crystal Report and configure the field source

In this section you will be configuring the graphic part of the report and link to the data source you are using.

1. Add a CrystalReportViewer control and a button to the form.
2. Add a Crystal Report to the project.

   Choose Standard in the Crystal Report Gallery using the Wizard.
3. In the Database Expert, choose OLEDB ADO and make a new Connection.
4. Use SQLClient provider and provide the name of the server and the name of the database. Use integrated security.
5. In the database expert expand the **TestNorthwind database** and choose the **Ord;1** stored procedure from the list as shown:

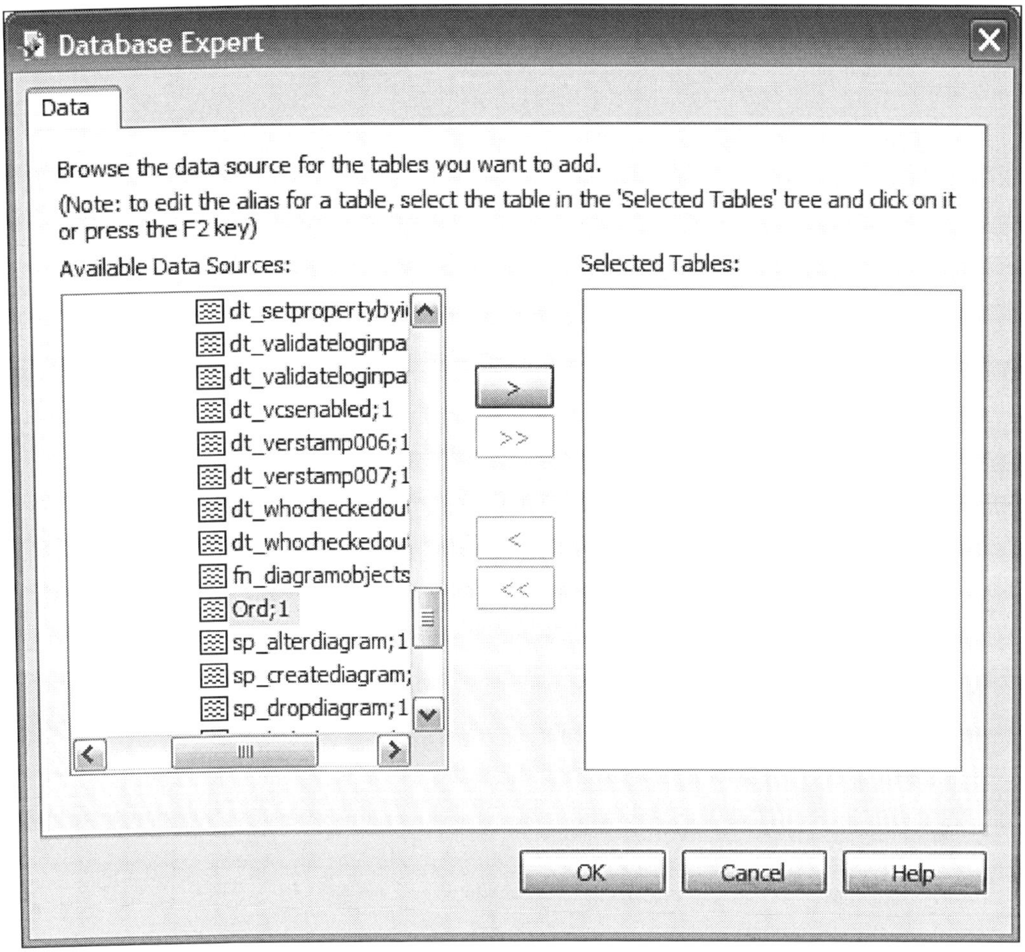

6. Add the stored procedure to the **Selected Tables** area using the **>>** button and click **OK.**

7. In the **Enter Values** window that gets displayed enter as shown after clearing **Set to Null** and click **OK.**

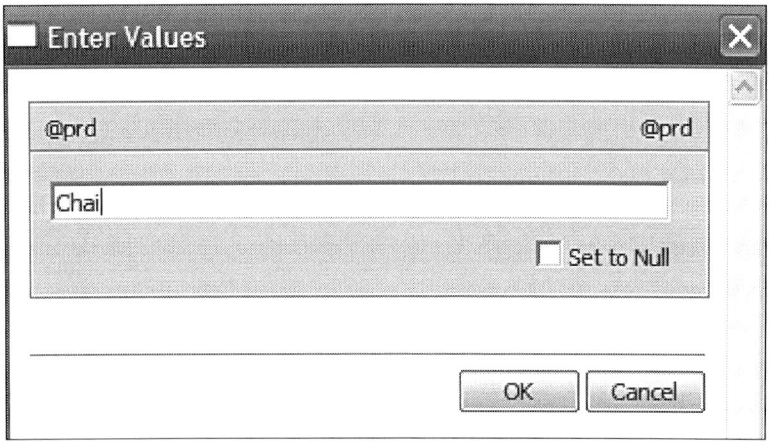

8. Click **OK** to the **Database Expert.**

Add fields to the Crystal Report

Drag-and-drop fields from the **Field Explorer** into the **Details** section of the **Crystal Report** as shown:

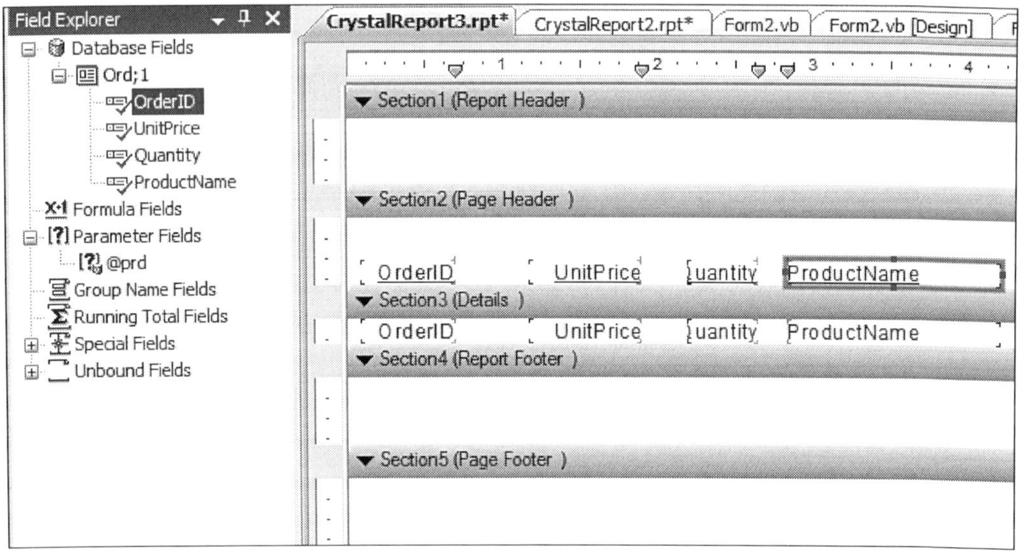

Add code for data binding

In here you will be associating the Crystal Report Viewer with the Crystal Report added to the project.

1. Add the following code to the `Button`'s click event. The code is for the entire form.

```
Imports CrystalDecisions.CrystalReports.Engine
Imports CrystalDecisions.Shared
Imports System.Data
Imports System.Data.OleDb
Public Class Form2
    Private Sub Button1_Click(ByVal sender As System.Object, _
        ByVal e As System.EventArgs) Handles Button1.Click
        'declare a crystal report
        Dim crDocument As New CrystalReport2
        'declare data related items in the next 4 lines
        Dim Dataset3 As New DataSet
        Dim oOleDbConnection As New OleDbConnection
        Dim oOleDbDataAdapter As New OleDbDataAdapter
        Dim conStrg As String = "Provider=SQLOLEDB;" & _
        "Data Source=HODENTEK2\SANGAM;Integrated Security=SSPI;" &
_
        "Initial Catalog=TestNorthwind"
        'Assign the connection string to the connection
        oOleDbConnection.ConnectionString = conStrg
        oOleDbConnection.Open()
        'declare a adoOleDbadapter
        oOleDbDataAdapter = New OleDbDataAdapter
        'declare a OleDBCommand
        Dim oCmd As New OleDbCommand
        'next 4 lines provide the attributes
        'use intellisense to advantage
        oCmd.CommandType = CommandType.StoredProcedure
        oCmd.CommandText = "ord"
        oCmd.Parameters.Add("prd", OleDbType.VarChar).Value =
          "chai"
        oCmd.Connection = oOleDbConnection
        'Data Adapter uses the SELECT Command
        oOleDbDataAdapter.SelectCommand = oCmd
        'Use the fill method of the Data Adpater(intellisense)
        oOleDbDataAdapter.Fill(Dataset3, "Ord;1")
        'Set up the data source for the report
        crDocument.Database.Tables(0).SetDataSource(Dataset3)
        'Set up the Report Source for the report viewer
        CrystalReportViewer1.ReportSource = crDocument
    End Sub
End Class
```

2. Build and run the form. Click on the button and verify that the report is populated by the designed data from the stored procedure.

> Note: You could provide a drop-down combo box with all **Product** names and feed this to the code. In this case you may have to create another dataset to bring in the product names to populate the combo box.

Hands-on exercise 9.5: Creating a Crystal Report and populating it with XML data.

Over the years XML has made enormous inroads into the IT arena. In this hands-on, you will query the SQL Server to return data in XML. You will have to slightly modify the returned data and use it for generating a report in Visual Studio using the Crystal Reports related report items. The following link gives you access to articles on how to work with TSQL enhancements in SQL Server that support XML:`http://hodentek.blogspot.com/2008/11/working-with-xml-in-sql-server-2000.html` but are not a pre-requisite for this hands-on.

Follow on

In order to see how you may generate report based on XML data, you will first create XML data by running a query against the TestNorthwind database.

1. Open SQL Server 2008 Management Studio. Connect to the **Data Engine** and run the following query:

```
Use TestNorthwind
Go
Select LastName, FirstName, City, Country
from Employees
for xml auto
Go
```

2. From the menu item **File,** save the result as XML and place it anywhere convenient. Herein the file is named, `Employees.xml`.

   If you look at the XML saved you will see that it is only a XML fragment. It is not well formed.

3. Place the contents of the XML file between the tags **<query> </query>** and save the file again (use a text editor).

   This process can be coded if necessary using File IO procedures.

4. Create an ASP.NET web site project in Visual Studio 2008. Herein the project is called **TestCrXml**.
5. From Solution **Explorer Project | Add New Item...** add a Crystal Report. Here it is called **Emp.rpt.**

   The **Crystal Reports Gallery** window gets displayed.
6. Choose **Standard** and use the default option: **Using the Report Wizard**. Click **OK.**
7. In the **Data** window of the **Standard Report Creation Wizard**, click on **Create New Connection**. Click on the **+** sign adjoining **ADO.NET (XML)**.
8. **In the ADO.NET (XML) connection window, browse to the saved XML file as shown:**

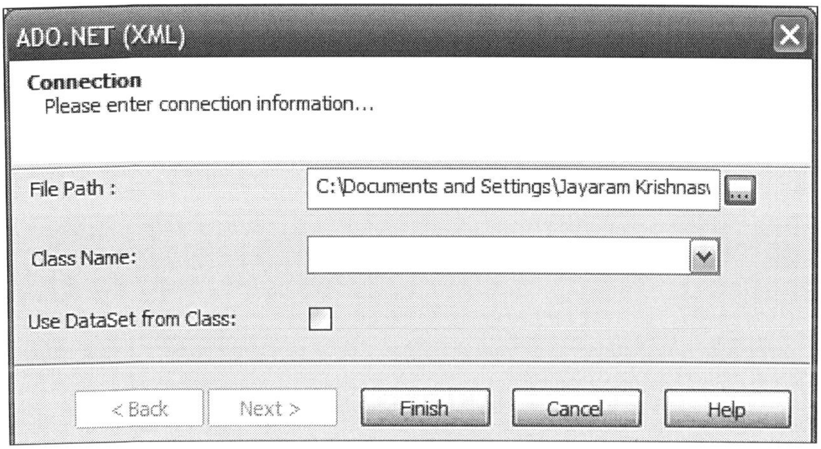

9. Click on **Finish**. Transfer the **Employees** table under **ADO.NET (XML) | query** to the **Selected Tables** area.
10. Click **Next**. In the **Fields** page of the wizard that shows up transfer all the fields on the left to the **Fields to Display** area with the **>>** button. Click **Finish**.
11. The `Emp.rpt` gets displayed with all the chosen fields inserted as well as the **Field Explorer** displaying the **Database Fields** chosen as shown.
12. Add a **Crystal Report Viewer** control to the **Default.aspx** page from the **Toolbox**. Click on the drop-down for smart tasks. In the smart tasks drop-down menu that get displayed, click on the handle for **Choose Report Source**.
13. Choose the **CrystalReportSource1**.

14. Build the web site and browse to the **Default.aspx** page on the IE and you will see the report on the IE browser as shown:

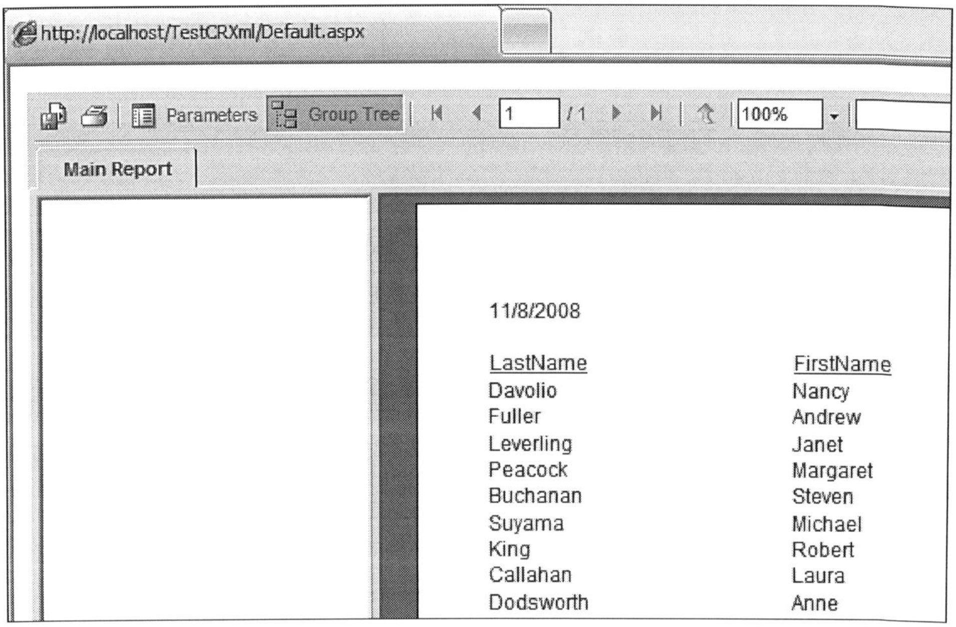

15. In the **Field Explorer** of the report, right-click **Group Name Fields** and in the pop-up choose Employees.Country as the group to be inserted.
16. Click **OK** on the **Insert Group** window where you made the above choice from the report fields.

    A **Group #1 Name** gets added to the **Field Explorer** as well as to the Crystal Report in the design view.
17. Build the project and browse to the **Default.aspx** page.
18. Verify that the grouping information you applied is effective in the display.

Summary

As Crystal Report for .NET is bundled with Visual Studio many readers would be interested in how the two programs work together in the Visual Studio 2008's IDE. The hands-on exercises show some of the different ways the features in the Visual Studio 2008 IDE can be leveraged to interact with Crystal Reports while designing the report as well as at runtime.

10

On Programmatically Creating an SSRS Report

In this chapter, the process of programmatically creating the SQL Server Reporting Services tabular report is described. You will be creating a very simple report using the provided code. The approach is to introduce the programming by creating the three parts of a report: connection, dataset, and layout.

Introduction

In order to design the MS SQL Server Reporting Services report programmatically you need to understand what goes into a report. We will start with a simple report shown in the next figure:

EmployeeID	LastName	FirstName	City	Country
	1Davolio	Nancy	Seattle	USA
	2Fuller	Andrew	Tacoma	USA

The above tabular report gets its data from the SQL Server database `TestNorthwind` using the query shown below:

```
Select EmployeeID, LastName, FirstName, City, Country from Employees.
```

As you have seen earlier, a report is based completely on a Report Definition file, a file in XML format. The file consists of information about the data connection, the datasource in which a dataset is defined, and the layout information together with the data bindings to the report.

In the following, we will be referring to the Report Server file called `RDLGenSimple.rdl`. This is a file written in Report Definition Language in XML Syntax. The next figure shows this file opened as an XML file with the significant nodes collapsed. Note the namespace references.

```
  <?xml version="1.0" encoding="utf-8" ?>
- <Report xmlns:rd="http://schemas.microsoft.com/SQLServer/reporting/reportdesigner"
    xmlns="http://schemas.microsoft.com/sqlserver/reporting/2008/01/reportdefinition">
  + <DataSources>
  + <DataSets>
  - <Body>
    + <ReportItems>
      <Height>1.5in</Height>
      <Style />
    </Body>
    <Width>8in</Width>
  - <Page>
      <Style />
    </Page>
    <ConsumeContainerWhitespace>true</ConsumeContainerWhitespace>
    <rd:ReportID>2fcb9c85-c354-489b-a367-e1cef8479c95</rd:ReportID>
    <rd:ReportUnitType>Inch</rd:ReportUnitType>
  </Report>
```

The significant items are the following:

- The XML Processing instructions
- The root element of the report collapsed and contained in the root element are:
    - The DataSources
    - Datasets
    - Contained in the `body` are the `ReportItems`
    - This is followed by the `Page` containing the `PageHeader` and `PageFooter` items

In order to generate a RDL file of the above type the XMLTextWriter class will be used in Visual Studio 2008. In some of the hands-on you have seen how to connect to the SQL Server programmatically as well as how to retrieve data using the ADO.NET objects. This is precisely what you will be doing in this hands-on exercise.

The XMLTextWriter Class

In order to review the properties of the `XMLTextWriter` you need to add a reference to the project (or web site) indicating this item. This is carried out by right-clicking the **Project (or Website) | Add Reference...** and then choosing **SYSTEM.XML** (`http://msdn.microsoft.com/en-us/library/system.xml (vs.71).aspx`) in the **Add Reference** window.

After adding the reference, the ObjectBrowser can be used to look at the details of this class as shown in the next figure. You can access this from **View | Object Browser**, or by clicking the *F2* key with your VS 2008 IDE open. A formal description of this can be found at the bottom of the next figure. The XMLTextWriter takes care of all the elements found in the XML DOM model (see for example, `http://www.devarticles.com/c/a/XML/Roaming-through-XMLDOM-An-AJAX-Prerequisite`).

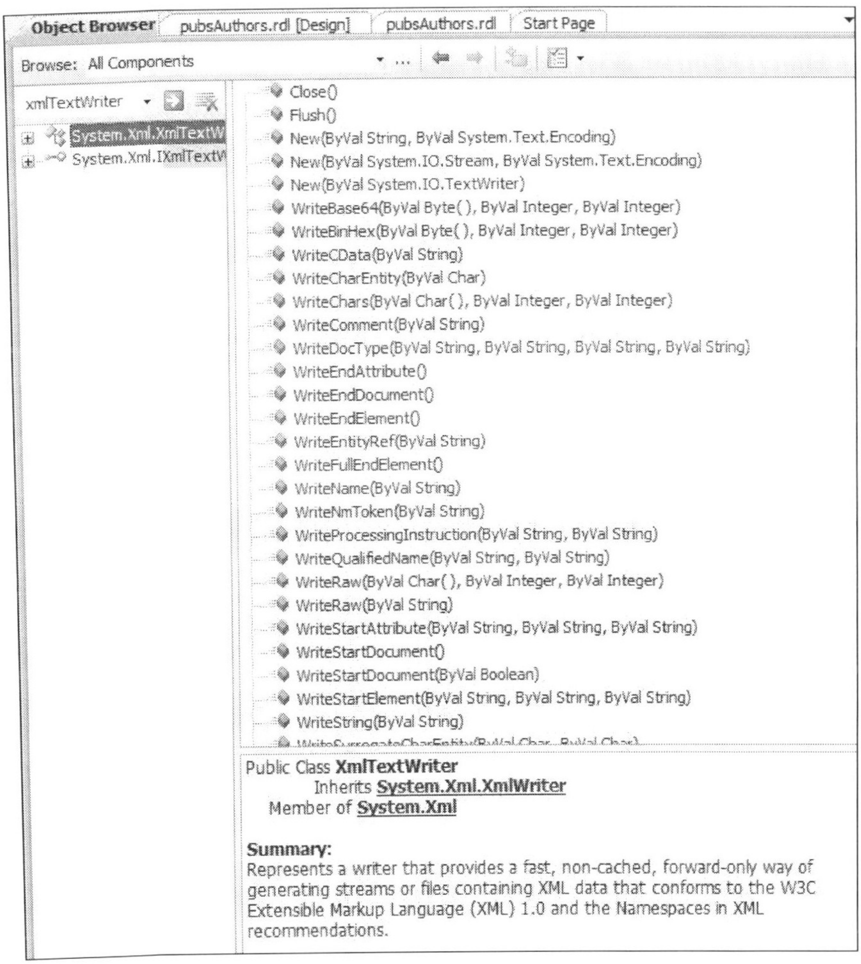

Hands-on exercise 10.1: Generating a Report Definition Language file using Visual Studio 2008

In this hands-on, you will be generating a server report that will display the report shown in the first figure. The coding you will be using is adopted from this article (`http://technet.microsoft.com/en-us/library/ms167274.aspx`) available at Microsoft TechNet (`http://technet.microsoft.com/en-us/sqlserver/default.aspx`).

Follow on

In this section, you will create a project and add a reference. You add code to the page that is executed by the button click events. The code is scripted and is not generated by any tool.

Create project and add reference

You will create a Visual Studio 2008 Windows Forms Application and add controls to create a simple user interface for testing the code.

1. Create a **Windows Forms Application** project in Visual Studio 2008 from **File | New | Project...** by providing a name. Herein, it is called **RDLGen2**.
2. Drag-and-drop two labels, three buttons and two textboxes onto the form as shown:

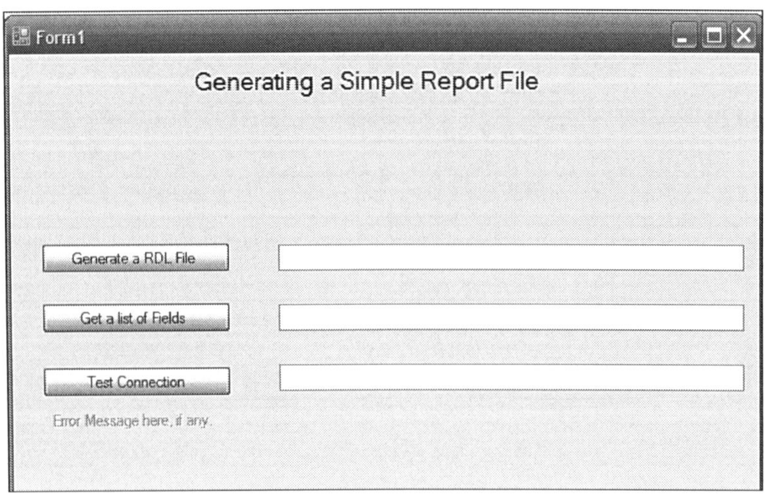

When the **Test Connection** button `Button1` in the code is clicked, a connection to the `TestNorthwind` database will be made. When the button is clicked, the code in the procedure `Connection ()` is executed. If there are any errors, they will show up in the label at the bottom. When the **Get list of Fields** button `Button2` in the code is clicked, the Query will be run against the database and the retrieved field list will be shown in the adjoining textbox. The **Generate a RDL file** button `Button 3` in the code, creates a report file at the location indicated in the code.

Copy and paste code

Remove the default code and replace it with the code shown.

Copy code the shown below and paste it to the `Form1`'s code page. The relevant statements are annotated in the code.

```
Imports System.Data
Imports System.Data.SqlClient
Imports System.IO.FileStream
Imports System.Xml.XmlWriter
Imports System.Text
Public Class Form1
    Private conn As New SqlConnection
    Private CmdText As String
    Private Flds As New ArrayList
    Private Const CONSTRG As String = _
    "Data Source=HODENTEK2\SANGAM;Initial Catalog=TestNorthwind;" & _
    "Integrated Security=True"

    Sub connection()
        If conn.State = ConnectionState.Open Then
            conn.Close()
        End If
        Try
            conn.ConnectionString = CONSTRG
            conn.Open()
        Catch e As System.Data.SqlClient.SqlException
            Label2.Text = e.Message.ToString
        End Try
    End Sub
    Sub GetFields()
        Dim command As SqlCommand
        Dim reader As SqlDataReader
        connection()
```

```
        ' Executing a query to retrieve a fields list for the report
        command = conn.CreateCommand()
        CmdText = "Select EmployeeID, LastName, " & _
        "FirstName, City, Country from Employees"
        command.CommandText = CmdText

        ' Execute and create a reader for the current command
        reader = command.ExecuteReader(CommandBehavior.SchemaOnly)


      'For each field in the resultset, add the name to an array list
        Flds = New ArrayList()
        Dim i As Integer
        For i = 0 To reader.FieldCount - 1
            Flds.Add(reader.GetName(i))
        Next i

    End Sub
    Sub Button1_Click(ByVal sender As System.Object, _
        ByVal e As System.EventArgs) Handles Button1.Click

        connection()
        TextBox2.Text = "Connection Open"
    End Sub

    Private Sub Button2_Click(ByVal sender As System.Object, _
        ByVal e As System.EventArgs) Handles Button2.Click

        GetFields()
        Dim txt = ""
        For I = 0 To Flds.Count - 1
            txt = txt + Flds.Item(I) + ","
        Next
        TextBox1.Text = txt
    End Sub
    Private Sub Button3_Click(ByVal sender As System.Object, _
            ByVal e As System.EventArgs) Handles Button3.Click

        connection()
        GetFields()
        GenerateRdl()
        TextBox3.Text = "File created at C:\RDLGen2.rdl"
    End Sub
    Public Sub GenerateRdl()
```

```
' Open a new RDL file stream for writing
Dim stream As IO.FileStream
stream = IO.File.OpenWrite("C:\RDLGen2.rdl")
'Dim Encoding As System.I
Dim writer As New Xml.XmlTextWriter(stream, Encoding.UTF8)
writer.Flush()
' Causes child elements to be indented
writer.Formatting = Xml.Formatting.Indented

' Report element
writer.WriteProcessingInstruction("xml", _
    "version=""1.0"" encoding=""utf-8""")
writer.WriteStartElement("Report")
writer.WriteAttributeString("xmlns", Nothing, _
  "http://schemas.microsoft.com/sqlserver/
    reporting/2003/10/reportdefinition")
writer.WriteElementString("Width", "6in")

' DataSource element
writer.WriteStartElement("DataSources")
writer.WriteStartElement("DataSource")
writer.WriteAttributeString("Name", Nothing, "DataSource1")
writer.WriteStartElement("ConnectionProperties")
writer.WriteElementString("DataProvider", "SQL")
writer.WriteElementString("ConnectString", CONSTRG)
writer.WriteElementString("IntegratedSecurity", "true")
writer.WriteEndElement() ' ConnectionProperties
writer.WriteEndElement() ' DataSource
writer.WriteEndElement() ' DataSources
'DataSet element
writer.WriteStartElement("DataSets")
writer.WriteStartElement("DataSet")
writer.WriteAttributeString("Name", Nothing, "DataSet1")

' Query element
writer.WriteStartElement("Query")
writer.WriteElementString("DataSourceName", "DataSource1")
writer.WriteElementString("CommandType", "Text")
writer.WriteElementString("CommandText", CmdText)
writer.WriteElementString("Timeout", "30")
writer.WriteEndElement() ' Query
' Fields elements
writer.WriteStartElement("Fields")
Dim fieldName As String
```

```
For Each fieldName In Flds
    writer.WriteStartElement("Field")
    writer.WriteAttributeString("Name", Nothing, fieldName)
    writer.WriteElementString("DataField", Nothing,
                              fieldName)
    writer.WriteEndElement() ' Field
Next fieldName

' End previous elements
writer.WriteEndElement() ' Fields
writer.WriteEndElement() ' DataSet
writer.WriteEndElement() ' DataSets
' Body element
writer.WriteStartElement("Body")
writer.WriteElementString("Height", "5in")

' ReportItems element
writer.WriteStartElement("ReportItems")

' Table element
writer.WriteStartElement("Table")
writer.WriteAttributeString("Name", Nothing, "Table1")
'start border width
writer.WriteStartElement("Style")
writer.WriteElementString("BorderWidth", "2pt")
writer.WriteEndElement() ' Style
'end Border width
writer.WriteElementString("DataSetName", "DataSet1")
writer.WriteElementString("Top", ".5in")
writer.WriteElementString("Left", ".5in")
writer.WriteElementString("Height", ".5in")

writer.WriteElementString("Width", _
(Flds.Count * 1.5).ToString() + "in")

' Table Columns
writer.WriteStartElement("TableColumns")
For Each fieldName In Flds
    writer.WriteStartElement("TableColumn")
    writer.WriteElementString("Width", "1.5in")
    writer.WriteEndElement() ' TableColumn
Next fieldName
writer.WriteEndElement() ' TableColumns
' Header Row
```

```
writer.WriteStartElement("Header")
writer.WriteStartElement("TableRows")
writer.WriteStartElement("TableRow")
writer.WriteElementString("Height", ".25in")
writer.WriteStartElement("TableCells")

For Each fieldName In Flds
    writer.WriteStartElement("TableCell")
    writer.WriteStartElement("ReportItems")

    ' Textbox
    writer.WriteStartElement("Textbox")
    writer.WriteAttributeString("Name", _
    Nothing, "Header" + fieldName)

    writer.WriteStartElement("Style")
    'add the next two lines to add style to header field
    writer.WriteElementString("TextDecoration", "Underline")
    writer.WriteElementString("FontWeight", "Bold")
    writer.WriteEndElement() ' Style
    writer.WriteElementString("Top", "0in")
    writer.WriteElementString("Left", "0in")
    writer.WriteElementString("Height", ".5in")
    writer.WriteElementString("Width", "1.5in")
    writer.WriteElementString("Value", fieldName)

    writer.WriteEndElement() ' Textbox
    writer.WriteEndElement() ' ReportItems
    writer.WriteEndElement() ' TableCell
Next fieldName

writer.WriteEndElement() ' TableCells
writer.WriteEndElement() ' TableRow
writer.WriteEndElement() ' TableRows
writer.WriteEndElement() ' Header
' Details Row
writer.WriteStartElement("Details")
writer.WriteStartElement("TableRows")
writer.WriteStartElement("TableRow")
writer.WriteElementString("Height", ".25in")
writer.WriteStartElement("TableCells")

For Each fieldName In Flds
    writer.WriteStartElement("TableCell")
    writer.WriteStartElement("ReportItems")
```

```
                ' Textbox
                writer.WriteStartElement("Textbox")
                writer.WriteAttributeString("Name", Nothing, fieldName)

                writer.WriteStartElement("Style")
                writer.WriteEndElement() ' Style
                writer.WriteElementString("Top", "0in")
                writer.WriteElementString("Left", "0in")
                writer.WriteElementString("Height", ".5in")
                writer.WriteElementString("Width", "1.5in")
                writer.WriteElementString("Value", _
                      "=Fields!" + fieldName + ".Value")
                'writer.WriteElementString("HideDuplicates", "DataSet1")
                writer.WriteEndElement() ' Textbox
                writer.WriteEndElement() ' ReportItems
                writer.WriteEndElement() ' TableCell
            Next fieldName

            ' End Details element and children
            writer.WriteEndElement() ' TableCells
            writer.WriteEndElement() ' TableRow
            writer.WriteEndElement() ' TableRows
            writer.WriteEndElement() ' Details
            ' End table element and end report definition file
            writer.WriteEndElement() ' Table
            writer.WriteEndElement() ' ReportItems
            writer.WriteEndElement() ' Body
            writer.WriteEndElement() ' Report
            ' Flush the writer and close the stream
            writer.Flush()
            stream.Close()
        End Sub 'GenerateRdl



    End Class
```

Build and execute

Before clicking on **Start Debugging**, build the project after you make any changes to the code.

Build the project and run the form.

The Report Definition file will be created at the location `C:\RDLGen2.rdl`. If the **Generate Report** button is clicked multiple times, backup copies of the report file will be created in the `C:\` drive.

Notes on adding style

You may alter the `<style/>` attributes in the code using the Report Definition API to test custom styling. Some styling was added to the column headers in the code. But the attributes that are listed in the API are the only ones admissible. For example, the styles that are allowed for a textbox are as in the following quoted error message when an attempt was made to use an invalid attribute.

> *Deserialization failed: The element 'Textbox' in namespace 'http://schemas.microsoft.com/sqlserver/reporting/2005/01/reportdefinition' has invalid child element 'FontWeight' in namespace 'http://schemas.microsoft.com/sqlserver/reporting/2005/01/reportdefinition'. List of possible elements expected: 'Style, Action, Top, Left, Height, Width, ZIndex, Visibility, ToolTip, Label, LinkToChild, Bookmark, RepeatWith, CustomProperties, Value, CanGrow, CanShrink, HideDuplicates, ToggleImage, UserSort, DataElementName, DataElementOutput, DataElementStyle' in namespace 'http://schemas.microsoft.com/sqlserver/reporting/2005/01/reportdefinition' as well as any element in namespace '##other'. Line 82, position 24.*

A similar kind of procedure can be used for generating Crystal Reports. Please refer to the Crystal Reports forum link in the *Appendix* on *Notes and References*.

Summary

A programmatic approach to authoring reports is sometimes required. Using an API enables developers to enhance features beyond what are available using built-in tools. SQL Server Reporting Services 2008 uses the strong support provided by the .NET Framework. Generating a very simple report file based on report definition language is described together with an introduction to the XMLTextWriter. A hands-on example is included for practicing with the code.

A
Queries and Datasets in SSRS 2008

In this Appendix, you will learn about the different sources of data that are used in the Reporting Services. You will also learn about the differences between the SQL queries, MDX and Semantic queries and how each of them is supported in the Query Designer.

Reporting Services data

Reporting Services obtains its data from data stores. The data is stored mostly in relational databases or in the form of XML. Data used in business intelligence will be mostly stored in OLAP (`http://www.olapreport.com/fasmi.htm`) databases. Reporting Services can access data in relational databases as well as OLAP data stores. It can also query data from semantic data models that are created by the Reporting Service's tools that lends itself to using more friendly syntax in easily recognizable business terms. You have already seen all of this in the various hands-on exercises. Here it is summarized.

Queries

Queries are questions posed to the data stores in order to extract some desired information. In doing so, the objective is to get a specific set of answers from the database that satisfies some limits or restraints.

SQL

Structured Query Language (http://en.wikipedia.org/wiki/SQL-92), SQL for short, is an ANSI (later by ISO) standard language used in accessing and manipulating relational databases. SQL is fully capable of CRUD (create, read, update and delete) operations. However, in Reporting Services the READ operation is mostly used. The Read operation is syntactily carried out by the `Select` statement in SQL. Transact-SQL (T-SQL) provides programmatic constructs to SQL to extend its capabilities. T-SQL is further enhanced by providing support to address widespread use of data in the form of XML. These extensions provide for a bidirectional data movement between XML and relational data. The SQL/T-SQL Enhancements can be executed in the SQL Server Management Studio. They can also be implemented within Visual Studio using .NET Framework's Common Language Runtime with a variety of programming languages.

SQL is set based. When you select some columns from a table, the returned data consists of row after row of the requested columns.

Here is a simple SQL Select statement:

```
Select * from Customers
```

This query returns all the rows of data in the `Customers` table for every column. This can be a huge amount of data if it is a huge table. The Select statement also allows you to get only a few chosen columns using a statement, such as this one:

```
Select CustomerLastName, CustomerPhone from Customers
```

SQL further allows you to further filter this data to give an even more reduced set using a statement such as this one.

```
Select LastName, Phone from Customers where City='Some City'
```

SQL also supports various additional clauses specific to the language, such as `WHERE`, `GROUP BY`, `ORDER BY`, `HAVING` and so on. If you are new to SQL, the best place to get some hands-on is the following site: http://www.w3schools.com/sql/default.asp.

Reporting Services data processing extensions can retrieve data from tables, stored procedures, views and other data structures defined on the underlying data. It does this using `Select` statement as you have seen in many of the hands-on exercises.

MDX

MDX , short for Multidimensional Expressions, is the language for querying multi dimensional data in OLAP (On-line Analytical Processing) databases. The widespread use of XML resulted in extending MDX with XML for Analysis. For an overview of MDX you may look up this Wikipedia link: `http://en.wikipedia.org/wiki/Multidimensional_Expressions`. Just as in SQL, the most frequently used MDX query is the MDX `SELECT` statement as in the following:

```
SELECT
{[Measures].[Order Details Count],[Measures].[Quantity]} on Columns
FROM MyNwind
Here the Analysis Services CUBE MyNwind is queried to return two
columns from its MEASURES
```

This very much resembles the earlier SQL syntax.

MDX is also a rich language capable of returning highly filtered data. For example, in a not so complicated example, the MDX can return a cross-section of data in its CUBE as in the following MDX.

```
SELECT
{[Measures].[Discount],[Quantity],[Order Details Count]} on Columns,
{[Categories].[Category ID].&[3],[Categories].[Category ID].&[8]} on
Rows
from MyNwind
```

The syntax becomes somewhat clearer if you associate the above query with the objects in the CUBE shown in the next figure. The **Measures** form the columns and the 'Dimension' (nodes except Categories from the DIMENSION group is shown just below the node KPIs) forms the rows. Specific items (IDs 3 and 8) from the 'Dimension' are returned from the CUBE, **MyNwind**.

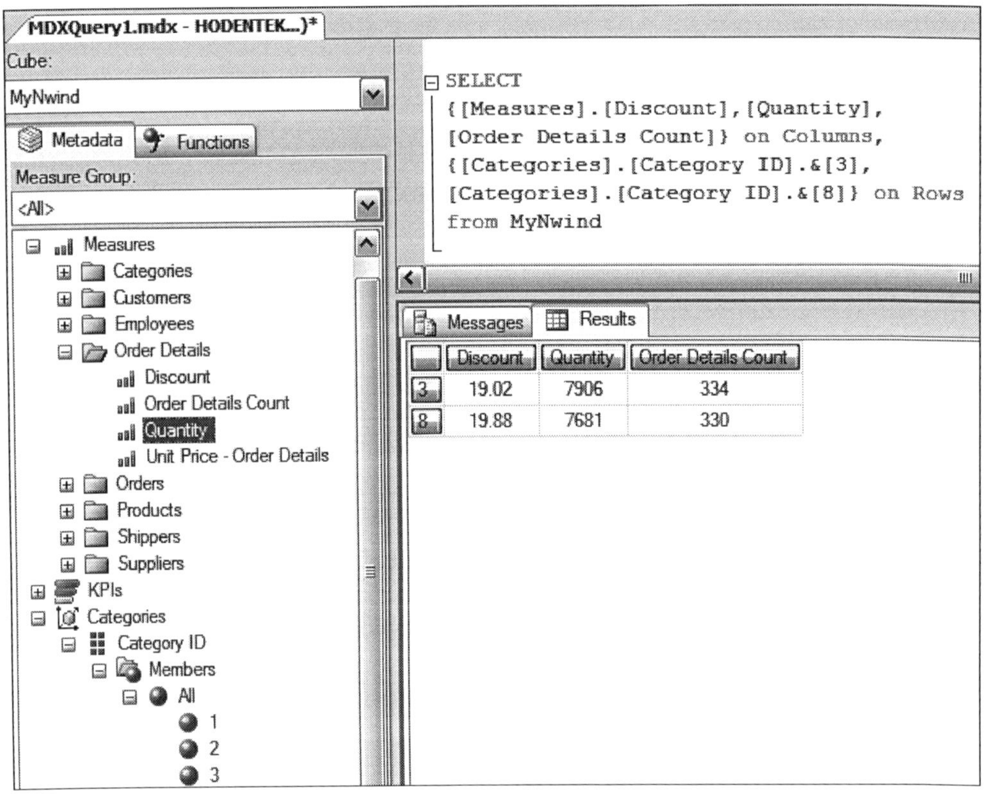

The links to the details regarding the CUBE are available in Chapter 5.

Semantic queries

For users who have no specialized knowledge of the database internals and for those who are not database savvy, the semantic queries provide a friendlier option. These users can query the database using business terms they are used to in their daily activities. The model consolidates this into a simple query that the unsophisticated user can use. The model is built upon the core data and provides a friendlier view of the underlying data.

Report Builder provides a user friendly interface to run semantic queries against report models built using Visual Studio 2008 and the Report Manager. The Hands-on exercise in Chapter 7, shows how to use the graphical interface to query the report model built in Chapter 4.

Query Designer

The Query Designer is available in Visual Studio's IDE as well as in the Report Builder. The graphic part of building a query is only available for SQL Servers, Analysis Servers and Report Models. Queries in Query Designer can only be run in text (such as directly typing in an SQL Statement) for other database products and XML as you have seen in the hands-on exercises. In the case of XML you can use an XML document as a source of the query. The query designer is indispensable for running MDX queries or queries against the Report models for those who are not comfortable in using these in text format.

Datasets

A prerequisite for creating a dataset is a connection to the data. Once the connection is established, the data can be retrieved in the form of dataset(s) using the various querying options discussed earlier. The dataset that you will come across in Report Builder or server report related projects is a refined view of data that would form report data. Whereas in the ASP.NET client reports as well as in Crystal Reports the dataset is the disconnected data that can interact with the database thorough the medium of data adapters which are objects in ADO.NET. In these reports the dataset (in the case of Windows Forms Application project) or the XSD schema (in the case of a Website or ASPNET project) is used. Similar objects are also used in Crystal Reports as you have seen in the hands-on exercises.

Summary

The various data sources that Reporting Services can draw its data from are discussed. Dataset as used in Reporting Services projects and the disconnected DataSet used in client applications are described.

B

Converting Reports between RDL and RDLC

In this Appendix, converting Reports with extensions RDL to RDLC and RDLC to RDL are discussed. In the hands-on you will convert an RDLC to an RDL.

Conversion of report files with extensions RDL and RDLC

RDL files (based on 2008 technology) created using either VS2008 / BIDS / ReportBuilder 2.0 cannot be converted into reports with RDLC extension This is because the structure of RDLC files in Visual Studio 2008 still adheres to the schema of 2005. For example, the RDLC schema is `http://schemas.microsoft.com/sqlserver/reporting/2005/01/reportdefinition`, which is still the definition of 2005.

Report files with the extension RDLC created using Visual Studio 2008 can however be converted into report files with extension RDL that can be hosted on the report server. This appendix and the hands-on describe this conversion. This makes the reusability of reports highly flexible. However, there are some restrictions for these conversions to be successful, as described later in the appendix.

The conversions can be best understood if the underlying differences are understood correctly. RDL files are for hosting reports on the report server. They can be authored using Visual Studio 2008 / BIDS or Report Builder 2.0. The RDLC files are reports built using Visual Studio as described in Chapter 3, which can be hosted on the local web server (or on the intranet). They do not even require SQL Server 2008 to be present.

Both kinds of files are defined by the Report Definition Language using what is called an XML schema. For both file types, the schema is the same file. However, in Visual Studio 2008, the schema definition for RDL files is 2008 technology (schema) whereas for the RDLC it has remained the 2005 technology (schema).

Both kinds of files use Datasets although they mean different things in the two file types as described in Appendix A. The similar name used for datasets is somewhat confusing as they do not mean exact the same thing.

Status of RDL to RDLC conversion

Presently the version of ReportViewer control shipped with Visual Studio 2008 (including SP1) does not permit this conversion. The RDL features such as **Tablix** are not supported and hence, RDL files created using 2008 technology cannot be converted to RDLC files (which have remained using the 2005 schema). Microsoft does not have a date for updating ReportViewer controls for use with Visual Studio 2008 with a corresponding RDLC 2008 definition.

RDLC to RDL conversion

Converting a RDLC file to a RDL file can be automatic or manual. For automatic conversion the following conditions have to be met:

- The RDLC files should have integrated security.
- Data for the report must have come from a data table and not a business object. Report server cannot process data from business objects.
- If the data source uses data from a SQL server database, the default data processing extension on the report server, namely the SQL server data processing extension, will be used.

The manual conversion is described in the hands-on.

Hands-on exercise B.1: RDLC to RDL conversion

The RDLC file created in Chapter 3 has been used, albeit with a different name. Follow the steps to convert it to a RDL file and view it on the Report Builder. The converted report may be deployed to the Report Server. The report definition file may also be brought into a report server project, and deployed to the report server after renaming the file extension. The schema of the file is then modified to adhere to the original file schema. This is then followed by building the project, and verifying the rendering of the report.

Follow on

You will be using an existing RDLC file and changing its file extension to RDL by renaming the extension. You will be importing this renamed file into Report Builder 2.0 and using the built-in Data Sources Wizard tool to provide the correct datasource to the report so that you have the same schema as in the original file.

1. Use a RDLC file (for example, a report created in Chapter 3). **TestRDLCFile.rdlc** is shown here:

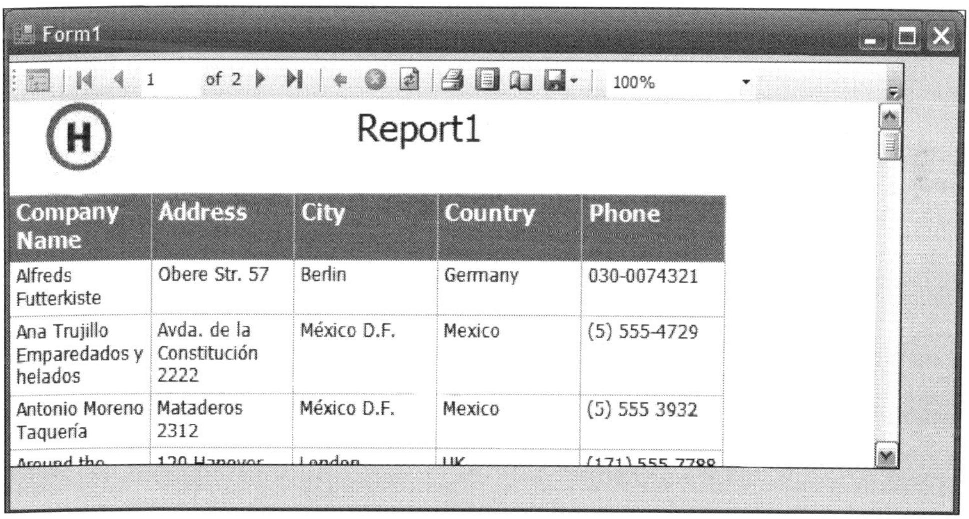

2. Open the file using an XML editor.

3. Copy this file and paste it to Notepad.
4. Rename this text file to **TestRLCfile.rdl** and save it to a known location.

   While renaming, you may get a warning that the file may become unusable. Ignore this warning.
5. Open Report Builder and from **Office Button | Open**, browse and get **TestRLCfile.rdl** into Report Builder as shown:

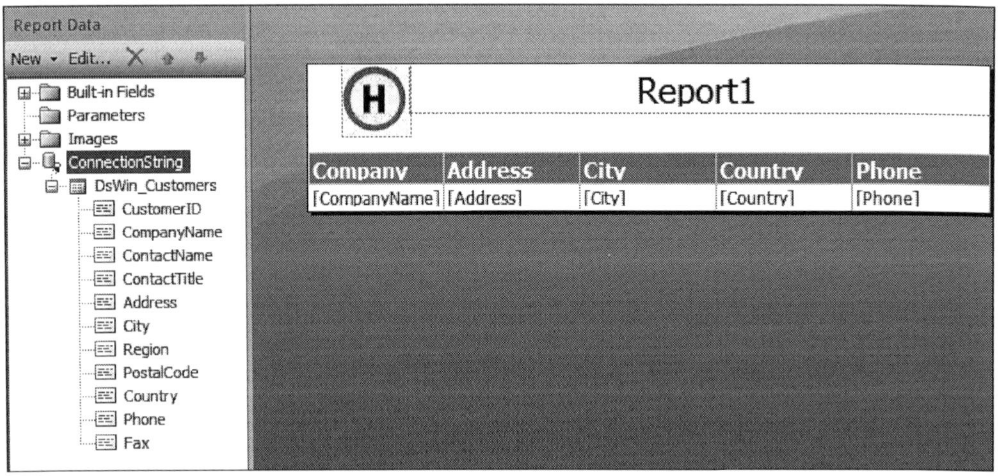

6. Run **TestRLCfile.rdl** from the icon on the "Ribbon".

   The report will not show up and indicates the following message: **One or more data sources is missing credentials.** The reason for this is that dataset has to be defined for the report with extension RDL.
7. Go back to design and double-click on **ConnectionString** under **Report Data.**

   The **Data Source Properties** window gets displayed. The **Use a connection embedded in my report** is displayed by default.
8. Click on the **Select connection type** drop-down handle.
9. Choose **Microsoft SQL Server** and click on the **Build** button.
10. In the window that pops up choose your SQL server. Here we have named it **Hodentek2\SANGAM**.
11. Stick with **Windows Authentication**, choose **TestNorthwind** and click **OK**. Click **OK** for the **Data Source Properties** window.

12. Run and confirm the report contents as shown:

Summary

Converting from a RDL file to a RDLC file is presently not supported in the shipped version of the Report Viewer in VS 2008 (see, `http://social.msdn.microsoft.com/forums/en-US/sqlreportingservices/thread/7fdb9e7e-f7f2-4b02-b494-9ee0474ae701/`). The manual conversion of RDLC to RDL is described. The Conversion from RDLC to RDL is easy and quick except some connection information may have to be provided.

C

Command line utilities

In this Appendix you will learn about the different command line utility programs available in SSRS 2008. You will also be working with a hands-on exercise showing how to create a datasource and deploy it to a folder on the Report Server.

Command line utilities

SQL Server Reporting Services 2008 provides the following built-in command line tools to support automating reporting services tasks.

- `rs`

  A wrapper for report services web service, this script processor tool can be used to automate deployment and administration.

- `rsconfig`

  When invoked, it stores encrypted values of account and connection information in `RSReportServer.config`.

- `rskeymgmt`

  You can extract, restore, create, and delete the symmetric key used to protect sensitive data (password) against intrusions. Also this command joins report server instances in a scaled-out deployment.

There are sample files to look at in the installation directory. These sample files may be found at `Samples\Reporting Services\Script Samples` and can be opened with Notepad for reviewing.

rs.exe

If you write a script file to be executed against SSRS 2008, the rs utility will process it. You can carry out most of the management and administration activities on the report server with this tool. You cannot use this with SharePoint server.

The Microsoft VB.NET code is supported (C# is not) and the script file is stored in a UTF-8 text file with an RSS (Reporting Services Script) extension. This extension is not unique in that it is used in contexts other than Reporting Services (see for example, `http://en.wikipedia.org/wiki/RSS_(disambiguation)`) including the most popular web feed format RSS (Really Simple Syndication). If you need to debug, you need to use VS 2008. Local admin rights are needed to run the scripts to access the Report Server.

The available samples that are part of the download are the following:

- `PublishSampleReports.rss`
- `ConfigureSystemProperties.rss`
- `AddItemSecurity.rss`
- `CancelRunningJobs.rss`

Syntax for using rs.exe

The help file provides complete information as to the usage of this tool from a DOS window, as shown here. In order to invoke this utility, no other program is needed and this utility can be invoked from any folder, as shown here. The help file lists the parameters (switches) that can be used with this utility.

```
C:\Documents and Settings\Jayaram Krishnaswamy>rs /?
Microsoft (R) Reporting Services RS
Version 10.0.1600.22 ((SQL_PreRelease).080709-1414 ) x86
Executes script file contents against the specified Report Server.
RS -i inputfile -s serverURL [-u username] [-p password]
   [-l timeout] [-b] [-e endpoint] [-v var=value] [-t]

        -i  inputfile   Script file to execute
        -s  serverURL   URL (including server and vroot) to execute
                        script against.
        -u  username    User name used to log in to the server.
        -p  password    Password used to log in to the server.
        -e  endpoint    Web service endpoint to use with the script.
                        Options are:
                        Exec2005 - The ReportExecution2005 endpoint
```

```
                    Mgmt2005 - The ReportService2005 endpoint
  -l   timeout      Number of seconds before the connection to the
                    server times out. Default is 60 seconds
                    and 0 is infinite time out.
  -b                Run as a batch and rollback if commands fail
  -v   var=value    Variables and values to pass to the script
  -t   trace        Include trace information in error message
```

Hands-on exercise C.1: Creating a data source and deploying to a folder on the server which uses the Pubsx database in SQL Express

In this exercise you will create a data source on the report server. In this hands-on a data source is created using the `rs.exe` utility that can be used to author a report based on the `Pubsx` database in the local SQLExpress 2005 Server. Pubsx is a copy of the Pubs database and may not be found in SQL Express. Any other database can be used in lieu of Pubsx as long as proper references to the server and database are made in the code. Also, in lieu of SQL Express you can use SQL Server 2008.

Follow on

You need to collect information about the connection to the database and the folder path on the report server into which you are placing this object. The script file is a text file and while you are saving it you need to provide the extensions `.rss`.

1. Use `Notepad.exe` or other text editor to create the following file.

```
'----------------------------------------
'------File name: CratePubsDB.rss------
'------Demo of rs.exe utility----------
'------the i switch requires an input file
'----- the s switch points to the Report 'Server url
'invocation as in C:\>rs -i 'CreatePubsDB.rss 'http://Hodentek2:8080/
ReportServer_SANGAM'----------------------------------------

Public Sub Main()
    rs.Credentials= System.Net.CredentialCache.DefaultCredentials
```

```
    CreateSampleDataSource( )
end sub

Public Sub CreateSampleDataSource( )
    'Define the data source definition.
        Dim definition As New DataSourceDefinition()

        Dim dsname as string
        dsname="PubsData"

dim parentPath as string
parentPath="/Data Sources"

dim extension as string="SQL"
    definition.CredentialRetrieval = CredentialRetrievalEnum.Integrated
    definition.ConnectString = "DataSource=HODENTEK2\SQLEXPRESS;
               Initial Catalog=pubsx;Integrated Security=True"
    definition.Enabled = True
    definition.EnabledSpecified = True
    definition.Extension = extension
    definition.ImpersonateUser = False
    definition.ImpersonateUserSpecified = True
    'Use the default prompt string.
    definition.Prompt = Nothing
    definition.WindowsCredentials =  False

Try
    rs.CreateDataSource(dsname,parentPath, False, definition, Nothing)
    Console.WriteLine("Data source {0} created successfully", dsname)

Catch e As Exception
    Console.WriteLine(e.Message)
End Try

End Sub
```

2. Save this file to a known location (here we are using `C:\` with the extension `.rss`.) Make sure that in the **Save** dialogue you have indicated **All files** and **UTF-8**.

3. Now type in and run the following at the command prompt:

```
C:\>rs -i CreatePubsDB.rss -s http://Hodentek2:8080/
  ReportServer_SANGAM
```

   If there are no compilation errors you should see the following:

```
C:\>rs -i CreatePubsDB.rss -s http://Hodentek2:8080/
  ReportServer_SANGAM

Data source PubsData created successfully

The command completed successfully
```

   In case a file by that name exists you may get an exception as shown here:

```
System.Web.Services.Protocols.SoapException: The item '/Data
Sources/PubsData' already exists. ---> Microsoft.ReportingServices.
Diagnostics.Utilities.ItemAlreadyExistsException: The item
 '/Data Sources/PubsData' already exists at
  Microsoft.ReportingServices.WebServer.
 ReportingService2005Impl.CreateDataSource(String DataSource,
                                            String Parent,
                                           Boolean Overwrite,
                                           DataSourceDefinition
                                            Definition,
                                           Property[] Properties)
at Microsoft.ReportingServices.WebServer.ReportingService2005.
CreateDataSource(String DataSource, String Parent,
                 Boolean Overwrite,
                 DataSourceDefinition Definition,
                 Property[] Properties)

The command completed successfully
```

4. Verify that the source was created in the specified folder on the Report Server using either the report server or the Report Manager.

Summary

Command line utility programs `rs`, `rsconfig`, and `rskeymgmt` are described. Details regarding the use of the `rs.exe` utility are described. The hands-on exercise shows how you may use the `rs.exe` to create and deploy a data source to a folder on the report server. This utility can be used for any of the activities to work with reporting services, as it is a wrapper for the reporting services web service.

D
Notes and References

In this Appendix, a number of notes, links, and references are provided. Most of these are direct references to Microsoft's web site, discussion thread links or blogs. These are in addition to those one may find in MSDN. Both Report Builder 2.0 and Report Manager have their own online references specific to their usage, which you may access from each of the tool's help menu.

Looking beyond Visual Studio 2008

Read Robert Bruckner's *Advanced Reporting Services* blog looking at the future of Reporting Services.

Better Report Viewing in Visual Studio 2010:

`http://blogs.msdn.com/robertbruckner/archive/2009/01/19/better-report-viewing-in-visual-studio-2010.aspx`

SQL Server bugs and remediation

No software is 100 percent free of bugs. Microsoft tracks bugs and you can access the bugs report in the Connect web site. Both active and closed bugs are displayed and you can search with keywords. You need registration to get the details.

`https://connect.microsoft.com/SQLServer/feedback/SearchResults.aspx?FeedbackOverviewType=6`

Best practices

- Best security practices before and after installing the SQL Server

  http://technet.microsoft.com/en-us/library/ms144228.aspx

- Building and Deploying Large Scale SQL Server Reporting Services Environments Technical Note Series describes scale out architecture and best practices, report catalog best practices, and performance optimization.

  http://sqlcat.com/technicalnotes/archive/2008/06/05/reporting-services-scale-out-architecture.aspx

Report definition and security

- Report Definition Language Reference:

  http://msdn.microsoft.com/en-us/library/ms155062.aspx

- RDL2005 November 2005 specifications download link:

  http://download.microsoft.com/download/c/2/0/c2091a26-d7bf-4464-8535-dbc31fb45d3c/rdlNov05.pdf

- RDL2008 specifications download link:

  http://download.microsoft.com/download/6/5/7/6575f1c8-4607-48d2-941d-c69622e11c32/RDL_spec_08.pdf

- Security Overview for Reporting Services in Native Mode. Discusses security needs end-to-end, taking into consideration the environment; types of reports; user access, distribution scenarios.

  http://msdn.microsoft.com/en-us/library/bb522781.aspx

Report authoring

- Using group variables in RS2008 for custom aggregation

  http://blogs.msdn.com/robertbruckner/archive/2008/07/20/Using-group-variables-in-reporting-services-2008-for-custom-aggregation.aspx

- Report Builder 2.0's online Help

  Installed when Report Builder 2.0 is installed, and provides screen-by-screen help reference.

- Bringing stored images into reports due to the OLE object header size as related to localization related issues

  http://forums.devarticles.com/microsoft-sql-server-5/displaying-image-fields-in-reporting-services-11844.html

Troubleshooting

- Detecting Version of RS related programs:

  `http://msdn.microsoft.com/en-us/library/bb630446.aspx`

- Windows Management Instrumentation (WMI)

  `http://msdn.microsoft.com/en-us/library/aa394572.aspx`

- Troubleshooting Concepts (Reporting Services): Covers the whole range from Installation and upgrade issues to report performance

  `http://msdn.microsoft.com/en-us/library/ms159135.aspx`

- Diagnose problems while running reports on the Report Server

  `http://blogs.msdn.com/lukaszp/archive/2007/01/31/how-to-diagnose-issues-when-running-reports-in-the-report-server.aspx`

- Errors and their sources. Cause and Resolution.

  `http://msdn.microsoft.com/en-us/library/ms165307.aspx`

ReportViewer control

- An excellent web resource to look up for ReportViewer covering a lot of ground including other links, faqs, licensing and so on

  `http://www.gotreportviewer.com/`

- You can read this to learn the differences between local mode and remote mode when using the ReportViewer control.

  `http://msdn.microsoft.com/en-us/library/aa964126.aspx#sqldocum_topic1`

- Discussion thread regarding RDLC with RDL 2008

  `http://social.msdn.microsoft.com/forums/en-US/sqlreportingservices/thread/01e0cc5a-023b-4367-94ef-3a1bbc745ef1/`

- Brian Hartman's Repot Viewer Blog: Only few entries and not updated recently

  `http://blogs.msdn.com/brianhartman/archive/2008/12/05/sql-server-2008-and-the-reportviewer-controls.aspx`

Moving and migrating

- Moving Reporting Services Databases to another computer

  `http://msdn.microsoft.com/en-us/library/ms156421.aspx`

- On copying SQL server databases, these two links should be useful in getting database samples from earlier SQL Server versions to SQL Server 2008
    - `http://www.packtpub.com/article/copying-database-sql-2008-copy-database-wizard`
    - `http://www.packtpub.com/article/moving-a-database-from-sql-server-2005-to-sql-server-2008-in-three-steps`

Free Microsoft software

- Microsoft ReportViewer add-on for Visual Web Developer 2008 Express Edition. VWD_RV_Addon_enu.exe(ver 9.0.0.0, 4.0 MB)

  `http://www.microsoft.com/downloads/thankyou.aspx?familyId=b67b9445-c206-4ff7-8716-a8129370fa1d&displayLang=en`

- Register and get a free copy of SQL Server 2008 Express. Get the SQL Server 2008 Express with advanced services that allows report authoring.

  `http://www.microsoft.com/express/sql/register/`

Source control

- It is a good practice to have source control in place. Microsoft Visual SourceSafe 2005 (This is the latest indicated for VS 2008)

  `http://msdn.microsoft.com/en-us/vs2005/aa718670.aspx`

- SourceGear Vault (SourceSafe KB compatible)

  `http://sourcegear.com/vault/index.html`

- Open Source plug-in for VS.NET

  `http://ankhsvn.open.collab.net/`

White papers

- Reporting Services 2005 White Papers:

  `http://www.microsoft.com/Sqlserver/2005/en/us/white-papers.aspx#RepServ`

- Reporting Services in SQL Server 2008:

  `http://www.microsoft.com/sqlserver/2008/en/us/wp-sql-2008-reporting-services.aspx`

Forums

- MSDN Forums:

  `http://forums.microsoft.com/msdn/default.aspx?siteid=1`

- Crystal Reports:

  `https://www.sdn.sap.com/irj/scn/forums`

Blogs

- `http://blogs.msdn.com/robertbruckner/default.aspx`
- `http://blogs.msdn.com/sqlrsteamblog/`
- `http://blogs.msdn.com/bimusings/`

Miscellaneous

Here are a few items noted while using SSRS 2008. It may be possible that these are specific to this installation. It is known however that IE behaves differently from other browsers even in IE 8.0 RC1.

Browser Response

Report Viewer works well with Google Chrome (Ver. 0.3 & 1.0), Firefox (Ver. 3.0.1) and Safari but Opera 9.0 cannot access the URLs. They all require service authentication.

The rendered Report Viewer in all browsers except IE seems much shorter (vertical dimension).

Customizing the look of Report Manager

The `ReportingServices.css` file in the Report Manager's folder can be used to customize Report Manager.

Regarding customizing the look of Report Manager, the next is quoted from the Books Online.

"There are default cascading stylesheets (`.css`) files that define styles for the report toolbar in HTML Viewer and for Report Manager. You can modify the default styles at your own risk to change the colors, fonts, and layout of the toolbar or Report Manager. Modifying the stylesheets incorrectly can result in errors when opening reports. Modifying stylesheets has no effect on the appearance of published reports that you run on a report server. In Reporting Services, reports do not reference stylesheets. Ad hoc reports that are auto-generated by the report server use style information that is stored as an embedded resource in the report server program files. Reports that you create in Report Designer use the fonts, colors, and layout that you specify in the report definition. Styles are created inline with the rest of the layout."

The author's experience in trying to change style was not completely successful. The style could be changed using the stylesheet as explained in Chapter 5 but could not revert it even after reverting the style information to its original state in the CSS file.

New Open Source Project's Report Designer

- fyiReporting Software RDL Project (Apache License Version 2.0) may be downloaded from:

  `http://www.fyireporting.com/`

- Some details and screenshots of reports authored using fyi Reporting software :

  `http://hodentek.blogspot.com/2008/11/new-open-source-projects-report.html`

Dundas Maps for RS and .NET

- These are available for evaluation downloads from the following link:

  `http://www.dundas.com/downloads/index.aspx`

- Windows Presentation Foundation and reports. This is not an integration of WPF and SSRS 2008 but a third party tool that can be used in Reporting:

  `http://www.componentone.com/SuperProducts/ReportsWPF/`

- Author's blog contains posts on SQL Server and report authoring tidbits:

  `http://hodentek.blogspot.com/2009/02/report-authoring-articles.html`

Index

Symbols

A

B

C

D

E

F

G

I

L

S

T

Thank you for buying
Learning SQL Server 2008 Reporting Services

About Packt Publishing

Packt, pronounced 'packed', published its first book "*Mastering phpMyAdmin for Effective MySQL Management*" in April 2004 and subsequently continued to specialize in publishing highly focused books on specific technologies and solutions.

Our books and publications share the experiences of your fellow IT professionals in adapting and customizing today's systems, applications, and frameworks. Our solution based books give you the knowledge and power to customize the software and technologies you're using to get the job done. Packt books are more specific and less general than the IT books you have seen in the past. Our unique business model allows us to bring you more focused information, giving you more of what you need to know, and less of what you don't.

Packt is a modern, yet unique publishing company, which focuses on producing quality, cutting-edge books for communities of developers, administrators, and newbies alike. For more information, please visit our website: `www.packtpub.com`.

Writing for Packt

We welcome all inquiries from people who are interested in authoring. Book proposals should be sent to `author@packtpub.com`. If your book idea is still at an early stage and you would like to discuss it first before writing a formal book proposal, contact us; one of our commissioning editors will get in touch with you.

We're not just looking for published authors; if you have strong technical skills but no writing experience, our experienced editors can help you develop a writing career, or simply get some additional reward for your expertise.

[PACKT] PUBLISHING

ASP.NET 3.5 Social Networking

ISBN: 978-1-847194-78-7 Paperback: 556 pages

An expert guide to building enterprise-ready social networking and community applications with ASP.NET 3.5

1. Create a full-featured, enterprise-grade social network using ASP.NET 3.5
2. Learn key new ASP.NET topics in a practical, hands-on way: LINQ, AJAX, C# 3.0, n-tier architectures, and MVC
3. Build friends lists, messaging systems, user profiles, blogs, message boards, groups, and more
4. Rich with example code, clear explanations, interesting examples, and practical advice – a truly hands-on book for ASP.NET developers

---

Windows Small Business Server SBS 2003: A Clear and Concise Administrator's Reference and How-To

ISBN: 978-1-904811-49-7 Paperback: 494 pages

Quickly find the information you need to install, configure and maintain all the features of SBS 2003 to get the job done

1. Comprehensive coverage
2. Structured for speed. Find it, do it, finish
3. Perfect companion to the MS Docs and KB

Please check **www.PacktPub.com** for information on our titles

8968412R0

Made in the USA
Lexington, KY
17 March 2011